CO-ALS-631

Desire
and
Imagination

CLASSIC ESSAYS IN SEXUALITY

EDITED BY REGINA BARRECA, PH.D.

A MERIDIAN BOOK

MERIDIAN

Published by the Penguin Group
Penguin Books USA Inc., 375 Hudson Street, New York, New York 10014, U.S.A.
Penguin Books Ltd, 27 Wrights Lane, London W8 5TZ, England
Penguin Books Australia Ltd, Ringwood, Victoria, Australia
Penguin Books Canada Ltd, 10 Alcorn Avenue, Toronto, Ontario, Canada M4V 3B2
Penguin Books (N.Z.) Ltd, 182–190 Wairau Road, Auckland 10, New Zealand

Penguin Books Ltd, Registered Offices:
Harmondsworth, Middlesex, England

First published by Meridian, an imprint of Dutton Signet,
a division of Penguin Books USA Inc.

First Printing, December, 1995
1 3 5 7 9 10 8 6 4 2

Introduction and author biographies copyright © Regina Barreca, 1995
All rights reserved

Excerpt from *Psychopathia Sexualis*, by Richard von Krafft-Ebing, reprinted by permission of the Putnam Publishing Group. Translation copyright © 1965 by G. P. Putnam's Sons.

"Femininity" by Sigmund Freud, reprinted from *New Introductory Lectures on Psycho-Analysis* by Sigmund Freud, translated from the German by James Strachey, with the permission of W. W. Norton & Company, Inc. Copyright 1933 by Sigmund Freud, renewed © 1961 by W.J.H. Sprott. English translation copyright © 1964, 1965 by James Strachey. Permission to reprint "Femininity" from *The Standard Edition of the Complete Psychological Works of Sigmund Freud* in the United Kingdom was granted by The Institute of Psychoanalysis and the Hogarth Press.

 REGISTERED TRADEMARK—MARCA REGISTRADA

LIBRARY OF CONGRESS CATALOGING IN PUBLICATION DATA
Desire and imagination : Victorian essays in sexuality / edited by
Regina Barreca.
    p.   cm.
    ISBN 0–452–01150–7
    1. Sex customs—History—Sources.   I. Barreca, Regina.
    HQ16.D47   1995
    306.7—dc20   95–9654
                                                CIP

Printed in the United States of America
Set in Janson Text
Designed by Jesse Cohen

Without limiting the rights under copyright reserved above, no part of this publication may be reproduced, stored in or introduced into a retrieval system, or transmitted, in any form, or by any means (electronic, mechanical, photocopying, recording, or otherwise), without the prior written permission of both the copyright owner and the above publisher of this book.

BOOKS ARE AVAILABLE AT QUANTITY DISCOUNTS WHEN USED TO PROMOTE PRODUCTS OR SERVICES. FOR INFORMATION PLEASE WRITE TO PREMIUM MARKETING DIVISION, PENGUIN BOOKS USA INC., 375 HUDSON STREET, NEW YORK, NEW YORK 10014.

ESSAYS THAT EXAMINE THE
FOUNDATION OF OUR IDEAS ABOUT SEXUAL BEHAVIOR

"Society in America" by Harriet Martineau (1837)
A wonderfully reasoned look at women's "place" in nineteenth-century America.

"Psychopathia Sexualis" by Dr. Richard von Krafft-Ebing (1871)
Arguing that "sexual feeling is really the root of all ethics, and no doubt of aestheticism and religion," Krafft-Ebing warns against "unbridled love" and ends with a discussion of fetishism, including the preference of men for blondes and the weakness of females for military uniforms!

"The Functions and Disorders of the Reproductive Organs"
by William Acton (1875)
This Victorian surgeon considered himself an expert on male and female sexuality and became the most famous proponent of the Victorian notion of female passionlessness.

"Married Love" by Marie Stopes (1918)
Unlike Sanger, who argued that birth control was needed to alleviate poverty, Stopes saw it as a means of increasing women's sexual pleasure by removing the fear of conception. A radical document, this piece is a milestone in feminist history written by the woman who opened the first birth control clinic in England, the Mother's Clinic, which still operates today.

DESIRE AND IMAGINATION

REGINA BARRECA, Ph.D., is Professor of English at the University of Connecticut, and a founding editor of *LIT: Literature, Interpretation, and Theory*. She is the author of *Perfect Husbands and Other Fairy Tales, They Used to Call Me Snow White, But I Drifted,* and *Sex and Death in Victorian Literature,* and the editor of *The Penguin Book of Women's Humor*. She lives with her husband in Connecticut.

This book is dedicated with affection and respect to Dr. Rose Quiello, whose research on medicine and sexuality made this book possible.

Acknowledgments

My sincere and boundless thanks to the colleagues and friends who helped make this book possible, especially friend and researcher Rose Quiello, assistant Julie Nash, editor Julia Moskin, and agent Diane Cleaver. I also want to thank the staff of the Homer Babbidge Library, especially at interlibrary loan. I am grateful to the Research Foundation at the University of Connecticut for their support.

Contents

INTRODUCTION:
DESIRE AND IMAGINATION

The language of authority is a powerful weapon. Ponderous phrases and grave pronouncements, even if empty, can be weighty enough to compress theories, assumptions, or possibilities into facts. Perhaps the very word "authority" should always be embraced by quotation marks, signaling the responsible reader's skepticism about the very notion of authority itself, especially when coupled with matters of sex, gender, power, and morality.

Collected here are twenty early "authorities" on matters of sexuality, men and women who in their own day were considered to be at the forefront of scientific research. Their early contributions to the scientific analysis of eroticism, gender, and sexuality continue to inform our culture's responses to these issues.

This volume provides a window to the world of early medical and psychological research into sexuality, deviance, and sexual preferences and practices. *Desire and Imagination* brings together twenty works that, anachronistic as they may seem, nevertheless remain important because they laid the foundation for many of our belief systems today. Placing these documents side by side, examining them in terms of what we do and do not believe now, will illuminate the ways we define what is valid in terms of sexuality and what is regarded with suspicion. In retrieving and re-forming our definitions of and ideas about sexuality and gender, we return to the past in order to illuminate our present and orient our future.

Like aged, eccentric relatives who haunt the corners of a family gathering, the figures here are ignored by those who would wish for more sophisticated predecessors; but they cannot be dismissed in any search for authentic origins. Our understanding of sexuality in the present is rooted in the belief systems constructed by their past. Richard von Krafft-Ebing, one of the most significant researchers of his day, writes in *Psychopathia Sexualis: A Medico-Forensic Study* that "sexual feeling is really the root of all ethics, and no doubt of aestheticism and religion." And these essays continue to point to the root of the continuing contemporary debate about what is normal and right in terms of sexual life.

"WHERE IS IT WRITTEN?"

"Where is it written . . ." we ask, when confronted with conflicts between sexual practice and preference and cultural, social, religious, and intellectual norms. "Where is it written that sex is dirty? That homosexuality is deviant and destructive? That women cannot have both a maternal and intellectual life? That masturbation weakens the body? That women are dehumanized by cyclical hormonal changes? That men are plagued by incessant lust that must be curtailed at all costs? That having too much sex—or enjoying sex too much—leads to every misery, from a sallow complexion to insanity, impotence, and death?"

These essays are, in fact, where these ideas were written. Perhaps they do not record the first instance anyone ever thought, spoke, or wrote about these issues, but they nevertheless constitute a range of characteristic opinions and visions held by important figures from 1837 to 1929.

Written, for the most part, by hand and with pen and ink, these words were then set in type to be available to the medical and scholarly community until, finally, it seems, they were set in stone by social forces eager to support or refute a narrow and confining view of sexuality. Vigorously argued, plausible, and even seductive, these essays demand examination not only as historical documents but as vital pieces of rhetoric; even when exciting trepidation or revulsion, it is clear that the authors wrote with the full force of their belief behind them. It is reductive but not misrepresentative to argue that the works collected here helped not only to foster certain doctrines but to institutionalize them, so effectively that in some cases they remained essentially unchallenged for over a century.

THE IMPACT OF THE HISTORICAL MOMENT

The backdrop for these works spans a century that saw itself as wrestling equally with the forces of nature and technology, with theories of natural selection and unnatural acts, with the drive to triumph over the evils of passion while passionately arguing for the triumph of fecundity and creation. Serious about wanting to improve the condition of life for individuals both "lesser" and "greater" than themselves, these researchers and writers made it their business to classify and comment upon the sexual and physiological phenomena available for their observation.

Some of the arguments appear shocking in the circularity of their reasoning, but we should not be surprised by the internal logic informing much of the writing presented here. Any society's attempt to unravel unresolvable conflicts must lead to a rhetoric of speculation characterized more by verbal machinations than by truly enlightened analysis. In part this is true because the enlightened analysis of one age is often regarded as the self-serving manipulations of ideology by another. If the reader recalls that the writers were grappling with something completely new to them, the rationales behind encouraging or discouraging certain specific behaviors can emerge more clearly. That we do not agree with the causes, treatments, or effects of the behaviors described by these writers does not mean we should dismiss them out of hand. The essays themselves affirm the freedom of the nineteenth-century and early-twentieth-century thinker to analyze human nature even as they reveal the restrictions of the intellectual and social environment of the day.

Like Adam naming the animals, these writers launched themselves into a sexual wilderness where everything cried out for a label and where nothing had been classified systematically before. That their idea of "system" was far from the disinterested scientific method it purported to be is clear to any reader, and is, in part, what makes these essays particularly compelling.

Yet there is no easy summary for the historical period because every assertion about its character can find its opposition all too easily: To say that this period of time was ruled by repressive misogynists is to ignore the many men and women who were speaking out not only for women's rights but for the rights of all human beings to be fully integrated into the social order regardless of gender, sexual preference, or political opinion. Speaking for perhaps one of the first times about activities that had previously been invoked only by silence, the writers collected here resemble those poor souls who found themselves at the Tower of Babel: Attempting to unravel the mysteries of sexuality, they nevertheless remained unable or unwilling to agree on the terms of discourse.

THE GOOD NEWS AND THE BAD NEWS

Taken as a group, these essays graphically demonstrate that in the nineteenth and early twentieth centuries accepted medical and scientific discourse blurred its way into the discourse of morality and social manipulation. The good news was that sexuality was being discussed openly; the bad news was that it was apparently being discussed most influentially by those who appear to have had a less than scientifically constructed agenda. But when has science ever fully freed itself from the dictates of the culture? The loudest voices will most likely seem to the contemporary reader to be emerging from the narrowest band of speakers; this was something of a closed circle. Those dictating the script, it appears, didn't want additional dialogue.

But this is not quite the case, and in that interesting margin lie some fascinating exchanges. The remarkable number of cross-references and the authentic sense of dialogue among many of the writers is telling. True, they formed a community, but it was a community complete with dissenters. Work by Ellis dovetailed with work done by Krafft-Ebing, and Tarnowsky's work also fit right in; Sanger met both Stopes and Ellis; Freud collaborated on work concerning hysteria; Browne knew and was influenced by Freud; Maudsley was horrified by what he read in Mill but encouraged by what he read in Clarke. It seems as if an exponential number of other connections could also be traced among the essays, which, like individual dots, form a picture otherwise undiscernible once a line is drawn through them and the pattern is made clear.

CONVENIENCE AND CONVENTION IN CONTEXT

What are some of the most striking patterns? Conveniently for a society that emphasized work and the danger of idle hands, nearly anything that went on in bed for more than fifteen minutes was a sign of disease. William Acton went so far as to claim that "it is, indeed, a wise provision that in some human beings the act should last but a short time—some few minutes." Otherwise, Acton implies, serious damage could be done to a range of bodily functions. It was no longer necessary to rely on the argument that a sensual or passionate nature was an insult to God, who contrived human life for duty, not pleasure. Science had "proved" how dangerous sex was.

Viewing the private act of sexual intimacy through the public lens of medicine or philosophical science was revolutionary. This revolutionary practice, however, often led to remarkably conservative conclusions. Much was challenged but little was overthrown. Dominant creeds usually remained intact, culling support from the scientific methods now supporting their beliefs. Diagnosis was used to uphold dogma; religion found a home in the laboratory whether or not it was welcomed there. Science was gender-specific, and no detail was too small to mention.

Exercise was good, claimed William Acton, because it kept the hands and mind away from the attractions of the genital organs. But exercise was not good for women, warned Weir Mitchell, since it led to overstimulation and either a decrease or increase of blood to the reproductive system in the female body. In other words, exercise happily kept men from thinking about reproduction but unhappily kept women from performing it as well. What was good for the goose was distinctly unmanning for the gander, and heaven knew that the gander could be granted liberties that would confine the goose to an asylum for the rest of her days.

HOT FLASHES AND POWER SURGES

Women are bound by the cycles of their bodies, according to Clarke, who asserted that if a woman "put her will into the education of her brain," she necessarily withdraws it from her reproductive organs (presumably where it is in constant demand, even for an unmarried virgin). Intellectual activity poses a threat to the woman in particular as well as society in general since "the system does not do two things well at the same time. One or the other suffers from neglect, when the attempt is made," leading Weir Mitchell's readers to the conclusion that a woman can choose to use her brain or her uterus, but that she will short-circuit emotionally and physically should she dare to employ both at the same time—as if she were some sort of electrical appliance. It can be argued that these writers offered their own versions of "surge protectors" for women who might otherwise overload their systems and shut down the physical plant. (Indeed, considering the rising current of incipient feminism among the women of the day, perhaps what were regarded as merely hot flashes were actually power surges.)

Although the positive nature of sex within marriage was often underscored by these authors, sex outside the marital bed (or too often within it) was flagged as everything from unnerving to unnatural. Even though it could safely be argued that a woman who hated to sleep with her husband was insane, it could also be argued that a man who wanted to sleep too often with his wife was suffering from a mania. It could even be argued that death was preferable to certain sexually eccentric practices; in one classic Havelock Ellis moment we are presented with the case history of a man who, although attracted to other men, was married to a woman. Ellis's position indicated that, while he saw homosexuality ("inversion") as tragic, he also considered women astonishingly fragile (and expendable). "A divorce was in contemplation," Ellis stated, "when, fortunately for all parties concerned, the wife suddenly died."

While we might not agree with Ellis that the wife got off easily in this arrangement, we nevertheless should recognize and respect the fact that Ellis was concerned with sexual and social realignments. With such a caveat in place, however, we should also feel uncomfortable with the fact that Ellis regarded death as preferable to divorce, especially if it was the wife who had the grace to pass away in order to avoid scandal. We should also feel free to disagree with a few of Ellis's other generalizations.

We might find ourselves disagreeing, for example, with Ellis's discussion of the scientific premise that male homosexuals cannot whistle—but that female homosexuals can. "The frequent inability of male inverts to whistle was first pointed out by Ultrich, and Hirschfeld has found it in 23 per cent. Many of my cases confess to this inability, while some of the women inverts can whistle admirably." Making his argument in the manner of his day, Ellis cited unnamed sources as evidence or even proof of his position. "One of my correspondents, M.N., writes to me," declared Ellis, " 'with regard to the general inability of inverts to whistle (I am not able to do so myself), their fondness for green (my favorite color), their feminine calligraphy, skill at female occupations, etc., these all seem to me but indications of the one principle. To go still farther and include trivial things, few inverts even smoke in the same manner and with the same enjoyment as a man; they have seldom the male facility at games, cannot throw a mark with precision, or even spit!' " Pushing the implications of such a belief system to its logical ends, it becomes clear that if faced with a suitor who can't whistle or spit, a woman should look for a more masculine partner.

WHATEVER IS, IS RIGHT

When we learn from Henry Maudsley, a physician who specialized in studying psychological affliction in the mid-nineteenth century, that "if it were not that woman's organization and functions found their fitting home in a position different from, if not subordinate to, that of men, she would not so long have kept that position," we are not hearing a doctor as much as an inflexible man who does not approve of the changes he senses in the social atmosphere. Maudsley does not argue, primarily, from the point of view presumably awarded him by his position on the scientific faculty at University College, London. Instead he argues here as a philosopher might, citing a first cause that does not depend solely on biological or physiological observation. When Maudsley declared that if women deserved equality under the law or in access to education they would have already achieved these goals, he had left the hospital and entered the legislature. He had moved from medicine into the courts of law, the halls of education, and, for all intents and purposes, the pulpit.

It matters a great deal, however, that Maudsley grounded his assertions of "fact" in discussions of physiology because that was where he could bring the weight of his particular authority to bear on the argument. He could speak to the way that women were destined, by biology, for one function alone: "In the first place, a proper regard to the physical nature of women means attention given, in their training, to their peculiar functions and to their foreordained work as mothers and nurses of children. Whatever aspirations of an intellectual kind they may have, they cannot be relieved from the performance of those offices so long as it is thought necessary that mankind should continue on earth." By extension, then, an educated woman posed a threat to the very future of the species. "For it would be an ill thing, if it should so happen, that we got the advantages of a quantity of female intellectual work at the price of a puny, enfeebled, and sickly race. In this relation, it must be allowed that women do not and cannot stand on the same level as men."

A blueprint for establishing the nineteenth-century conviction of the spiritual, intellectual, and moral inferiority of women can also be found in a work by Edward Clarke, *Sex in Education*, which carries the quite remarkable subtitle "A Fair Chance for the Girls." The remarkable nature of this subtitle lies in the fact that Clarke believed that women would suffer horribly if they received an intellectually invigorating education. To be fair to women, Clarke wanted to keep them away from the books. A Harvard University professor, much admired by Maudsley (who quoted him in support of his own position), Clarke presented a number of "case histories" to prove his point. Referring to a young woman from a "good family" who refused to listen to his advice concerning the dangers of receiving an education, he drew attention to the fact that, faced with "constant, sustained work, recitation and study for all days alike," the "brilliant scholar" would experience "a hemorrhage once a month that would make the stroke oar of the University crew falter," presumably as a direct result of learning Latin.

Clarke's tone deepened as he explained that "before the expiration of the second year, Nature began to assert her authority. The paleness of Miss A's complexion increased. An unaccountable and uncontrollable twitching of a rhythmical sort got into the muscles of her face, and made her hands go and feet jump. She was sent home, and her physician called, who at once diagnosticated chorea (St. Vitus' dance) and said she studied too hard."

It would be as difficult for a student in a contemporary university classroom to assert that the threat of St. Vitus' dance hung over her, thereby rendering her unable to study for an exam, as it would be to convince Clarke that higher education for women seems to produce educated women and not invalids, hysterics, or maniacs. In the cosmology established, accepted, and exacerbated by his "research," women were in a fixed relationship to men. The scientific principle informing Clarke's theory rested on the following: "The physiological motto is, educate a man for manhood, a woman for womanhood, both for humanity." Surely it is difficult to ignore the point that any number of words could and perhaps should be substituted for *physiological*, (*dominant*, *oppressive*, and *tyrannical* leap to mind) but it is important to stress that it was precisely this "physiological" model that convinced Clarke's followers of the inextricable link between appropriate biological function and suppressed intellectual activity.

Even more disturbing than these nascent psychologists was a surgeon, Isaac Baker Brown, whose practice of removing the clitoris in his patients caused him, finally, to be thrown out of the Obstetrical Society in London for failing to tell his patients the specific physiological details of what he considered his nearly infallible treatment for hysteria. Brown's rhetoric indicates that he was as certain of the operation's social benefits to his patients as he was of its medical function. "Objections have been advanced against the morality of the operation," intoned the surgeon, "and I am here at a loss how to give an answer, for I can hardly conceive how such a question can be raised against a method of treatment which has for its object the cure of the disease, that is rapidly tending to lower the moral tone, and which treatment is dictated by the loftiest and most moral considerations." He went on to note, in his defense, that "I never operate or sanction an operation on any patient under ten years of age, which is the earliest date of puberty." That his treatment was either idiosyncratic or potentially damaging was not addressed by the doctor except in the most cursory terms.

The operation, as described by Brown, involved the stuff of nightmares: "The patient having been placed completely under the influence of chloroform, the clitoris is freely exised either by scissors or knife—I always prefer the scissors. The wound is then firmly plugged with graduated compresses of lint, and a pad, well secured by a T-bandage." The operation didn't stop with the scissors and bandage, however; an emotional element is factored in to ensure that the effects of Brown's treatment were fully incorporated. "The strictest quiet must be enjoined," Brown warned, "and attention of relatives, if possible, avoided, so that the moral influence of medical attendant and nurse may be uninterruptedly maintained."

Case after case offers, almost uncannily, the same story: an unhappy woman comes to his office (sometimes showing signs of having masturbated—"irritating" herself, in Brown's terms), undergoes the operation, and becomes almost magically a good wife and mother. "Mrs. O came under my care in 1862. She had been ill ever since marriage, five years previously; having distaste for the society of her husband, always laid upon the sofa, and under medical treatment. Evidence of peripheral excitement being manifest, I performed my usual operation. She rapidly lost all the hysterical symptoms which had previously existed. . . . A young lady, at age 20, came under my care in 1863, having for two years past suffered . . . great irritability of temper, been disobedient to her mother's wishes, and had sleepless nights, restless desire for society, and was constantly seeking admiration; all these symptoms culminating in a monomania that every gentleman she admired was in love with her, and she insisted on always sending her *carte de visite* to her favoured one for the time being. In her quieter moments she would spend much time in serious reading. On being consulted, I quickly discovered that all these symptoms arose from peripheral excitement. . . . The usual plan of treatment was followed with the most rapid and marked success. . . . All her delusions disappeared, and after three or four months of careful watching, with change of air, she was perfectly well in every respect. A year afterwards she married, and ten months later gave birth to a healthy son." There is no question in Brown's writings to indicate that he did not consider himself as offering sufficient clinical observation to validate his theory and practice. That his patients were forever deprived of sexual feeling was apparently considered a small price to pay to secure her peace of mind—not only for the woman but for her husband and family.

It is difficult to avoid the connection between Brown's methods of securing appropriate feminine submissiveness and the operations performed well into the 1950s—lobotomies—which were designed to have the same general effect. While the medical practitioners were not themselves monsters, it is hard not to see their handiwork as monstrous. Informed by and fully believing in the rightness of their own scientific method, the practitioners apparently ignored the psychological underpinnings of their theories, not seeing any misogyny or tyranny in what they regarded as their offerings of salvation to women otherwise lost to self-importance or emotional discomfort.

That either self-importance or emotional discomfort was simply a response to the world in which these women lived was apparently dismissed as a sign of illness. The doctors saw themselves as offering a cure.

DISSENTING VOICES

The declarations in the following pages did not pass into common currency without being noted and discredited as bankrupt by other notable thinkers of the day. Harriet Martineau's *Society in America* made a case for comparing the position of the woman in society to the position of the slave. "In short, indulgence is given her as a substitute for justice," argued Martineau. "Her case differs from that of the slave, as to the principle, just so far as this; that the indulgence is large and universal, instead of petty and capricious." Perhaps even more disconcerting to her contemporaries was her disgust at marriages of convenience, those arrangements whereby girls are encouraged to wed "men old enough to be their fathers." Martineau bridled at these brides because they—or, more accurately, the social system in which they came of age—bartered their humanity and integrity for the pleasures of a financially secure future. They sold themselves, perhaps, but Martineau argued against the notion that there could be such a thing as a willing slave.

The time-honored custom of marrying off pretty young women to the highest bidders, regarded by many as a form of social engineering that translated the dynamics of Darwin's "survival of the fittest" to a form of "survival for the richest," is censured by Martineau without apology. "I have no sympathy for those who, under any pressure of circumstances, sacrifice their heart's-love for legal prostitution; and no environment of beauty or sentiment can deprive the fact of its coarseness. . . . The unavoidable consequence of such a mode of marrying is that the sanctity of marriage is impaired, and that vice succeeds. Any one must see at a glance that if men and women marry those whom they do not love, they must love those whom they do not marry." The brilliant economy of the final sentence in no way undermined its nearly revolutionary message: If women (as well as men) do not find passion with their spouses, they will seek it elsewhere.

Echoing Martineau and elegantly turning the antiwoman language of the day's "great thinkers" on its head is Eliza Burt Gamble, who addressed in her work *The Sexes in Science and History* the argument that women were naturally unable to assume positions of power within society because they were emotionally unstable, erratic, and prone to hysteria. Gamble contradicted Darwin and made a case for the "unnatural" process of selection imposed on women who must marry in order to survive. "Since women as economic and sexual slaves have become dependent upon men for their support, no male biped has been too stupid, too ugly, or too vicious to take to himself a mate and perpetuate his imperfections." She went on to address the fact that women had traditionally been regarded as the sexual predator, even in an environment where their sexuality had to be masked: "Woman's ankles and throat seem to be the most formidable foes against which innocent man has to contend, so the concealment of these offending members is deemed absolutely necessary for his protection and safety." In her hands, we see very clearly that in such matters, the very phrase "conventional wisdom" becomes virtually oxymoronic.

In no less effective terms, Marie Jenney Howe also delighted in casting aspersions on thinkers who espoused the belief that a woman's place was either in the home or the hospital. In her parody "An Anti-Suffrage Monologue," the speaker declared that women will be made sick by the responsibilities of voting: "I don't want to be misunderstood in my reference to woman's inability to vote," argues the anti-suffragette speaker who mimics perfectly the "scientific" discourse of women's inferiority. "Of course she could get herself to the polls and lift a piece of paper. I don't doubt that. What I refer to is the pressure on the brain, the effect of this mental strain on woman's delicate nervous organization and on her highly wrought sensitive nature. Have you ever pictured to yourself Election Day with women voting? Can you imagine how women, having undergone this terrible ordeal, with their delicate systems all upset, will come out of the voting booths and be led away by policemen, and put into ambulances, while they are fainting and weeping, half laughing, half crying, and having fits upon the public highway? Don't you think that if a woman is going to have a fit, it is far better for her to have it in the privacy of her own home?"

In respecting the physical needs of women as fully developed sexual beings and not just as potential mothers out seeking reliable mates, Martineau, Gamble, and Howe constructed a version of femininity that eclipsed those before and after who believed that all female sexual response derived from and depended on their need to reproduce inside a socially structured union. Martineau's position wove together the need for political and sexual freedom and began a cry for women's emancipation that has carried on well into our own century.

CONTROVERSIES, CONUNDRUMS, AND CONCLUSIONS

The writers collected here embody the paradox of publicly analyzing what people try to keep secret. The business of discussing matters of sexuality and power has become less treacherous in the years between the initial publication of these essays and their reprinting in this volume, but the intimate lives of women and men have become no less dangerous, no less worrying, and perhaps no less constricted by social and cultural forces than they were when Martineau published her groundbreaking essay. Imagining the sexual self is still troubling and puzzling, and to be effective still involves a deep examination of personal assumptions even as a reader approaches the supposedly solid ground of intellectual, psychological, and scientific discourse. These writers were responding to a need in their world to examine and provide documentation of what had been considered darkly and permanently buried.

Their essays are as necessarily rooted in their world as our analysis is rooted in our own, and the dramatically different angle of vision we bring to their material may well distort our perceptions even as we point out the distortions we find in their works. They all valued sexuality, even if they valued it differently. And on those occasions when their values might have harmed the usually all too willing victims, we might not want to forgive what we see as their ignorance and brutality, but perhaps we can better place them within a context that at least makes clear why their methodologies held the appeal that they did. Above all, these essays illustrate the way that authority itself is based on shifting social, historical, and cultural needs. This is a lesson best kept current and made use of when faced with any declaration of another word that should always appear in quotation marks—and that word is "fact."

HARRIET MARTINEAU

FROM

SOCIETY IN AMERICA

Harriet Martineau (1802–1876): Considered a radical during her own lifetime, Harriet Martineau was one of the best-known women of the nineteenth century. She was born in Norwich, England, the daughter of Unitarian parents who educated all of their eight children to earn their own livings. Between her strict parents, rough siblings, and ill health, Martineau's childhood was unhappy.

In her twenties she became an independent writer after the deaths of her father, brother, and fiancé. In her autobiography, published in 1877, Martineau describes her near-marriage as a potential disaster, fortunately avoided by her fiancé's death: "It was happiest for us both that our union was prevented by any means. I am, in truth, thankful for not having married at all. . . . My strong will, combined with an anxiety of conscience, makes me fit only to live alone."

Martineau credited this independence with her success as a writer. Influenced by John Stuart Mill, she published a series of stories entitled Illustrations of Political Economy *from 1832 to 1834, which was well received and established her as an important journalist. Despite four years of invalidism in the 1840s, she was a prolific author and journalist until her death. She was devoted to women's issues and supported the Married Woman's Property Bill in 1857. Her writings range from children's stories to novels to articles for the* London Daily News.

CHAPTER II.

WOMAN.

The vale best discovereth the hill. There is little friendship in the world, and least of all between equals, which was wont to be magnified. That that is, is between superior and inferior, whose fortunes may comprehend the one the other.

Bacon.

If a test of civilization be sought, none can be so sure as the condition of that half of society over which the other half has power, —from the exercise of the right of the strongest. Tried by this test, the American civilization appears to be of a lower order than might have been expected from some other symptoms of its social state. The Americans have, in the treatment of women, fallen below, not only their own democratic principles, but the practice of some parts of the Old World.

The unconsciousness of both parties as to the injuries suffered by women at the hands of those who hold the power is a sufficient proof of the low degree of civilization in this important particular at which they rest. While woman's intellect is confined, her morals crushed, her health ruined, her weaknesses encouraged, and her strength punished, she is told that her lot is cast in the paradise of women: and there is no country in the world where there is so much boasting of the "chivalrous" treatment she enjoys. That is to say,—she has the best place in stagecoaches: when there are not chairs enough for everybody, the gentlemen stand: she hears oratorical flourishes on public occasions about wives and home, and apostrophes to woman: her husband's hair stands on end at the idea of her working, and he toils to indulge her with money: she has liberty to get her brain turned by religious excitements, that her attention may be diverted from morals, politics, and philosophy; and, especially, her morals are guarded by the strictest observance of propriety in her presence. In short, indulgence is given her as a substitute for justice. Her case differs from that of the slave, as to the principle, just so far as this; that the indulgence is large and universal, instead of petty and capricious. In both cases, justice is denied on no better plea than the right of the strongest. In both cases, the acquiescence of the many, and the burning discontent of the few, of the oppressed testify, the one to the actual degradation of the class, and the other to its fitness for the enjoyment of human rights.

The intellect of woman is confined. I met with immediate proof of this. Within ten days of my landing, I encountered three outrageous pedants, among the ladies; and in my progress through the country I met with a greater variety and extent of female pedantry than the experience of a lifetime in Europe would afford. I could fill the remainder of my volume with sketches: but I forbear, through respect even for this very pedantry. Where intellect has a fair chance, there is no pedantry, among men or women. It is the result of an intellect which cannot be wholly passive, but must demonstrate some force, and does so through the medium of narrow morals. Pedantry indicates the first struggle of intellect with its restraints; and it is therefore a hopeful symptom.

The intellect of woman is confined by an unjustifiable restriction of both methods of education,—by express teaching, and by the discipline of circumstance. The former, though prior in the chronology of each individual, is a direct consequence of the latter, as regards the whole of the sex. As women have none of the objects in life for which an enlarged education is considered requisite, the education is not given. Female education in America is much what it is in England. There is a profession of some things being taught which are supposed necessary because everybody learns them. They serve to fill up time, to occupy attention harmlessly, to improve conversation, and to make women something like companions to their husbands, and able to teach their children somewhat. But what is given is, for the most part, passively received; and what is obtained is, chiefly, by means of the memory. There is rarely or never a careful ordering of influences for the promotion of clear intellectual activity. Such activity, when it exceeds that which is necessary to make the work of the teacher easy, is feared and repressed. This is natural enough, as long as women are excluded from the objects for which men are trained. While there are natural rights which women may not use, just claims which are not to be listened to, large objects which may not be approached, even in imagination, intellectual activity is dangerous: or, as the phrase is, unfit. Accordingly, marriage is the only object left open to woman.

Philosophy she may pursue only fancifully, and under pain of ridicule: science only as a pastime, and under a similar penalty. Art is declared to be left open: but the necessary learning, and, yet more, the indispensable experience of reality, are denied to her. Literature is also said to be permitted: but under what penalties and restrictions? I need only refer to the last three pages of the review of Miss Sedgwick's last novel in the *North American Review*, to support all that can be said of the insolence to which the intellect of women is exposed in America. I am aware that many blush for that article, and disclaim all sympathy with it: but the bare fact that any man in the country could write it, that any editor could sanction it, that such an intolerable scoff should be allowed to find its way to the light, is a sufficient proof of the degradation of the sex. Nothing is thus left for women but marriage.—Yes; Religion, is the reply.—Religion is a temper, not a pursuit. It is the moral atmosphere in which human beings are to live and move. Men do not live to breathe: they breathe to live. A German lady of extraordinary powers and endowments remarked to me with amazement on all the knowledge of the American women being based on theology. She observed that in her own country theology had its turn with other sciences, as a pursuit: but nowhere, but with the American women, had she known it make the foundation of all other knowledge. Even while thus complaining, this lady stated the case too favorably. American women have not the requisites for the study of theology. The difference between theology and religion, the science and the temper, is yet scarcely known among them. It is religion which they pursue as an occupation; and hence its small results upon the conduct, as well as upon the intellect. We are driven back upon marriage as the only appointed object in life: and upon the conviction that the sum and substance of female education in America, as in England, is training women to consider marriage as the sole object in life, and to pretend that they do not think so.

The morals of women are crushed. If there be any human power and business and privilege which is absolutely universal, it is the discovery and adoption of the principle and laws of duty. As every individual, whether man or woman, has a reason and a conscience, this is a work which each is thereby authorized to do for him or herself. But it is not only virtually prohibited to beings who, like the American women, have scarcely any objects in life proposed to them; but the whole apparatus of opinion is brought to bear offensively upon individuals among women who exercise freedom of mind in deciding upon what duty is, and the methods by which it is to be pursued. There is nothing extraordinary to the disinterested observer in women being so grieved at the case of slaves,—slave wives and mothers, as well as spirit-broken men,—as to wish to do what they could for their relief: there is nothing but what is natural in their being ashamed of the cowardice of such white slaves of the north as are deterred by intimidation from using their rights of speech and of the press, in behalf of the suffering race, and in their resolving not to do likewise: there is nothing but what is justifiable in their using their moral freedom, each for herself, in neglect of the threats of punishment: yet there were no bounds to the efforts made to crush the actions of women who thus used their human powers in the abolition question, and the convictions of those who looked on, and who might possibly be warmed into free action by the beauty of what they saw. It will be remembered that they were women who asserted the right of meeting and of discussion, on the day when Garrison was mobbed in Boston. Bills were posted about the city on this occasion, denouncing these women as casting off the refinement and delicacy of their sex: the newspapers, which laud the exertions of ladies in all other charities for the prosecution of which they are wont to meet and speak, teemed with the most disgusting reproaches and insinuations: and the pamphlets which related to the question all presumed to censure the act of duty which the women had performed in deciding upon their duty for themselves.—One lady, of high talents and character, whose books were very popular before she did a deed greater than that of writing any book, in acting upon an unusual conviction of duty, and becoming an abolitionist, has been almost excommunicated since. A family of ladies, whose talents and conscientiousness had placed them high in the estimation of society as teachers, have lost all their pupils since they declared their anti-slavery opinions. The reproach in all the many similar cases that I know is, not that the ladies hold anti-slavery opinions, but that they act upon them. The incessant outcry about the retiring modesty of the sex proves the opinion of the censors to be that fidelity to conscience is inconsistent with retiring modesty. If it be so, let the modesty succumb. It can be only a false modesty which can be thus endangered. No doubt, there were people in Rome who were scandalized at the unseemly boldness of Christian women who stood in the amphitheater to be torn in pieces for their religion. No doubt there were many gentlemen in the British army who thought it unsuitable to the retiring delicacy of the sex that the wives and daughters of the revolutionary heroes should be revolutionary heroines. But the event has a marvelous efficacy in modifying the ultimate sentence. The bold Christian women, the brave American wives and daughters of half a century ago are honored, while the intrepid moralists of the present day, worthy of their grandmothers, are made the confessors and martyrs of their age.

I could cite many conversations and incidents to show how the morals of women are crushed: but I can make room for only one. Let it be the following. A lady, who is considered unusually clearheaded and sound-hearted where trying questions are not concerned, one day praised very highly Dr. Channing's work on Slavery. "But," said she, "do not you think it a pity that so much is said on slavery just now?"

"No. I think it necessary and natural."

"But people who hold Dr. Channing's belief about a future life cannot well make out the case of the slaves to be so very bad. If the present life is but a moment in comparison with the eternity to come, can it matter so very much how it is spent?"

"How does it strike you about your own children? Would it reconcile you to their being made slaves, that they could be so only for three-score years and ten?"

"Oh no. But yet it seems as if life would so soon be over."

"And what do you think of their condition at the end of it? How much will the purposes of human life have been fulfilled?"

"The slaves will not be punished, you know, for the state they may be in; for it will be no fault of their own. Their masters will have the responsibility; not they."

"Place the responsibility where you will. Speaking according to your own belief, do you think it of no consequence whether a human being enters upon a future life utterly ignorant and sensualized, or in the likeness of Dr. Channing, as you described him just now?"

"Of great consequence, certainly. But then it is no business of ours; of us women, at all events."

"I thought you considered yourself a Christian."

"So I do. You will say that Christians should help sufferers, whoever and wherever they may be. But not women, in all cases, surely."

"Where, in your Christianity, do you find the distinction made?"

She could only reply that she thought women should confine themselves to doing what could be done at home. I asked her what her Christian charity would bid her do, if she saw a great boy beating a little one in the street.

"Oh, I parted two such the other day in the street. It would have been very wrong to have passed them by."

"Well: if there are a thousand strong men in the south beating ten thousand weak slaves, and you can possibly help to stop the beating by a declaration of your opinion upon it, does not your Christian duty oblige you to make such a declaration, whether you are man or woman? What in the world has your womanhood to do with it?"

How fearfully the morals of woman are crushed appears from the prevalent persuasion that there are virtues which are peculiarly masculine, and others which are peculiarly feminine. It is amazing that a society which makes a most emphatic profession of its Christianity, should almost universally entertain such a fallacy: and not see that, in the case they suppose, instead of the character of Christ being the meeting point of all virtues, there would have been a separate gospel for women, and a second company of agents for its diffusion. It is not only that masculine and feminine employments are supposed to be properly different. No one in the world, I believe, questions this. But it is actually supposed that what are called the hardy virtues are more appropriate to men, and the gentler to women. As all virtues nourish each other, and can not otherwise be nourished, the consequence of the admitted fallacy is that men are, after all, not nearly so brave as they ought to be; nor women so gentle. But what is the manly character till it be gentle? The very word magnanimity cannot be thought of in relation to it till it becomes mild—Christ-like. Again, what can a woman be, or do, without bravery? Has she not to struggle with the toils and difficulties which follow upon the mere possession of a mind? Must she not face physical and moral pain— physical and moral danger? Is there a day of her life in which there are not conflicts wherein no one can help her—perilous work to be done, in which she can have neither sympathy nor aid? Let her lean upon man as much as he will, how much is it that he can do for her?—from how much can he protect her? From a few physical perils, and from a very few social evils. This is all. Over the moral world he has no control, except on his own account; and it is the moral life of human beings which is all in all. He can neither secure any woman from pain and grief, nor rescue her from the strife of emotions, nor prevent the film of life from cracking under her feet with every step she treads, nor hide from her the abyss which is beneath, nor save her from sinking into it at last alone. While it is so, while woman is human, men should beware how they deprive her of any of the strength which is all needed for the strife and burden of humanity. Let them beware how they put her off her watch and defense, by promises which they cannot fulfill;—promises of a guardianship which can arise only from within; of support which can be derived only from the freest moral action,—from the self-reliance which can be generated by no other means.

But, it may be asked, how does society get on,—what does it do? for it acts on the supposition of there being masculine and feminine virtues,—upon the fallacy just exposed.

It does so; and the consequences are what might be looked for. Men are ungentle, tyrannical. They abuse the right of the strongest, however they may veil the abuse with indulgence. They want the magnanimity to discern woman's human rights; and they crush her morals rather than allow them. Women are, as might be anticipated, weak, ignorant, and subservient, in as far as they exchange self-reliance for reliance on anything out of themselves. Those who will not submit to such a suspension of their moral functions, (for the work of self-perfection remains to be done, sooner or later,) have to suffer for their allegiance to duty. They have all the need of bravery that the few heroic men who assert the highest rights of women have of gentleness, to guard them from the encroachment to which power, custom, and education, incessantly conduce.

Such brave women and such just men there are in the United States, scattered among the multitude, whose false apprehension of rights leads to an enormous failure of duties. There are enough of such to commend the true understanding and practice to the simplest minds and most faithful hearts of the community, under whose testimony the right principle will spread and flourish. If it were not for the external prosperity of the country, the injured half of its society would probably obtain justice sooner than in any country of Europe. But the prosperity of America is a circumstance unfavorable to its women. It will be long before they are put to the proof as to what they are capable of thinking and doing: a proof to which hundreds, perhaps thousands, of Englishwomen have been put by adversity, and the result of which is a remarkable improvement in their social condition, even within the space of ten years. Persecution for opinion, punishment for all manifestations of intellectual and moral strength, are still as common as women who have opinions and who manifest strength: but some things are easy, and many are possible of achievement, to women of ordinary powers, which it would have required genius to accomplish but a few years ago.

SECTION I.

MARRIAGE.

If there is any country on earth where the course of true love may be expected to run smooth, it is America. It is a country where all can marry early, where there need be no anxiety about a worldly provision, and where the troubles arising from conventional considerations of rank and connection ought to be entirely absent. It is difficult for a stranger to imagine beforehand why all should not love and marry naturally and freely, to the prevention of vice out of the marriage state, and of the common causes of unhappiness within it. The anticipations of the stranger are not, however, fulfilled: and they never can be while the one sex overbears the other. Marriage is in America more nearly universal, more safe, more tranquil, more fortunate than in England: but it is still subject to the troubles which arise from the inequality of the parties in mind and in occupation. It is more nearly universal, from the entire prosperity of the country: it is safer, from the greater freedom of divorce, and consequent discouragement of swindling, and other vicious marriages: it is more tranquil and fortunate from the marriage vows being made absolutely reciprocal; from the arrangements about property being generally far more favorable to the wife than in England; and from her not being made, as in England, to all intents and purposes the property of her husband. The outward requisites to happiness are nearly complete, and the institution is purified from the grossest of the scandals which degrade it in the Old World: but it is still the imperfect institution which it must remain while women continue to be ill-educated, passive, and subservient: or well-educated, vigorous, and free only upon sufferance.

The institution presents a different aspect in the various parts of the country. I have spoken of the early marriages of silly children in the south and west, where, owing to the disproportion of numbers, every woman is married before she well knows how serious a matter human life is. She has an advantage which very few women elsewhere are allowed: she has her own property to manage. It would be a rare sight elsewhere to see a woman of twenty-one in her second widowhood, managing her own farm or plantation; and managing it well, because it had been in her own hands during her marriage. In Louisiana, and also in Missouri, (and probably in other States,) a woman not only has half her husband's property by right at his death, but may always be considered as possessed of half his gains during his life; having at all times power to bequeath that amount. The husband interferes much less with his wife's property in the south, even through her voluntary relinquishment of it, than is at all usual where the cases of women having property during their marriage are rare. In the southern newspapers, advertisements may at any time be seen, running thus:—"Mrs. A, wife of Mr. A, will dispose of &c. &c." When Madame Lalaurie was mobbed in New Orleans, no one meddled with her husband or his possessions; as he was no more responsible for her management of her human property than anybody else. On the whole, the practice seems to be that the weakest and most ignorant women give up their property to their husbands; the husbands of such women being precisely the men most disposed to accept it: and that the strongest-minded and most conscientious women keep their property, and use their rights; the husbands of such women being precisely those who would refuse to deprive their wives of their social duties and privileges.

If this condition of the marriage law should strike any English persons as a peculiarity, it is well that they should know that it is the English law which is peculiar, and not that of Louisiana. The English alone vary from the old Saxon law, that a wife shall possess half, or a large part, of her husband's earnings or makings. It is so in Spanish, French, and Italian law; and probably in German, as the others are derived thence. Massachusetts has copied the faults of the English law, in this particular; and I never met with any lawyer, or other citizen with whom I conversed on the subject, who was not ashamed of the barbarism of the law under which a woman's property goes into her husband's hands with herself. A liberal-minded lawyer of

Boston told me that his advice to testators always is to leave the largest possible amount to the widow, subject to the condition of her leaving it to the children: but that it is with shame that he reflects that any woman should owe that to his professional advice which the law should have secured to her as a right. I heard a frequent expression of indignation that the wife, the friend and helper of many years, should be portioned off with a legacy, like a salaried domestic, instead of having her husband's affairs come legally, as they would naturally, into her hands. In Rhode Island, a widow is entitled to one-third of her husband's property: and, on the sale of any estate of his during his life, she is examined, in the absence of the husband, as to her will with regard to her own proportion of it. There is some of the apparatus of female independence in the country. It will be most interesting to observe to what uses it is put, whenever the restraints of education and opinion to which women are subject, shall be so far relaxed as to leave them morally free.

I have mentioned that divorce is more easily obtained in the United States than in England. In no country, I believe, are the marriage laws so iniquitous as in England, and the conjugal relation, in consequence, so impaired. Whatever may be thought of the principles which are to enter into laws of divorce, whether it be held that pleas for divorce should be one, (as narrow interpreters of the New Testament would have it;) or two, (as the law of England has it;) or several, (as the Continental and United States' laws in many instances allow,) nobody, I believe, defends the arrangement by which, in England, divorce is obtainable only by the very rich. The barbarism of granting that as a privilege to the extremely wealthy, to which money bears no relation whatever, and in which all married persons whatever have an equal interest, needs no exposure beyond the mere statement of the fact. It will be seen at a glance how such an arrangement tends to vitiate marriage: how it offers impunity to adventurers, and encouragement to every kind of mercenary marriages: how absolute is its oppression of the injured party: and how, by vitiating marriage, it originates and aggravates licentiousness to an incalculable extent. To England alone belongs the disgrace of such a method of legislation. I believe that, while there is little to be said for the legislation of any part of the world on this head, it is nowhere so vicious as in England.

Of the American States, I believe New York approaches nearest to England in its laws of divorce. It is less rigid, in as far as that more is comprehended under the term "cruelty." The husband is supposed to be liable to cruelty from the wife, as well as the wife from the husband. There is no practical distinction made between rich and poor by the process being rendered expensive: and the cause is more easily resumable after a reconciliation of the parties. In Massachusetts, the term "cruelty" is made so comprehensive, and the mode of sustaining the plea is so considerately devised, that divorces are obtainable with peculiar ease. The natural consequence follows: such a thing is never heard of. A long-established and very eminent lawyer of Boston told me that he had known of only one in all his experience. Thus it is wherever the law is relaxed, and, *caeteris paribus*, in proportion to its relaxation: for the obvious reason, that the protection offered by law to the injured party causes marriages to be entered into with fewer risks, and the conjugal relation carried on with more equality. Retribution is known to impend over violations of conjugal duty. When I was in North Carolina, the wife of a gamester there obtained a divorce without the slightest difficulty. When she had brought evidence of the danger to herself and her children,—danger pecuniary and moral,—from her husband's gambling habits, the bill passed both Houses without a dissenting voice.

It is clear that the sole business which legislation has with marriage is with the arrangement of property; to guard the reciprocal rights of the children of the marriage and the community. There is no further pretense for the interference of the law, in any way. An advance towards the recognition of the true principle of legislative interference in marriage has been made in England, in the new law in which the agreement of marriage is made a civil contract, leaving the religious obligation to the conscience and taste of the parties. It will be probably next perceived that if the civil obligation is fulfilled, if the children of the marriage are legally and satisfactorily provided for by the parties, without the assistance of the legislature, the legislature has, in principle, nothing more to do with the matter. This principle has been acted upon in the marriage arrangements of Zurich, with the best effects upon the morals of the conjugal relation. The parties there are married by a form; and have liberty to divorce themselves without any appeal to law, on showing that they have legally provided for the children of the marriage. There was some previous alarm about the effect upon morals of the removal of such important legal restrictions: but the event justified the confidence of those who proceeded on the conviction that the laws of human affection, when not tampered with, are more sacred and binding than those of any legislature that ever sat in council. There was some levity at first, chiefly on the part of those who were suffering under the old system: but the morals of the society soon became, and have since remained, peculiarly pure.

It is assumed in America, particularly in New England, that the morals of society there are peculiarly pure. I am grieved to doubt the fact: but I do doubt it. Nothing like a comparison between one country and another in different circumstances can be instituted: nor would any one desire to enter upon such a comparison. The bottomless vice, the all-pervading corruption of European society, cannot, by possibility, be yet paralleled in America: but neither is it true that any outward prosperity, any arrangement of circumstances, can keep a society pure while there is corruption in its social methods, and among its principles of individual action. Even in America, where every young man may, if he chooses, marry at twenty-one, and appropriate all the best comforts of domestic life,—even here there is vice. Men do not choose to marry early, because they have learned to think other things of more importance than the best comforts of domestic life. A gentleman of Massachusetts, who knows life and the value of most things in it, spoke to me with deep concern of the alteration in manners which is going on: of the increase of bachelors, and of mercenary marriages; and of the fearful consequences. It is too soon for America to be following the Old World in its ways. In the Old World, the necessity of thinking of a maintenance before thinking of a wife has led to requiring a certain style of living before taking a wife; and then, alas! to taking a wife for the sake of securing a certain style of living. That this species of corruption is already spreading in the New World is beyond a doubt;—in the cities, where the people who live for wealth and for opinion congregate.

I was struck with the great number of New England women whom I saw married to men old enough to be their fathers. One instance which perplexed me exceedingly, on my entrance into the country, was explained very little to my satisfaction. The girl had been engaged to a young man whom she was attached to: her mother broke off the engagement, and married her to a rich old man. This story was a real shock to me; so persuaded had I been that in America, at least, one might escape from the disgusting spectacle of mercenary

marriages. But I saw only too many instances afterwards. The practice
was ascribed to the often-mentioned fact of the young men migrating
westwards in large numbers, leaving those who should be their wives
to marry widowers of double their age. The Auld Robin Gray story
is a frequently enacted tragedy here: and one of the worst symptoms
that struck me was, that there was usually a demand upon my sympathy in such cases. I have no sympathy for those who, under any
pressure of circumstances, sacrifice their heart's-love for legal prostitution; and no environment of beauty or sentiment can deprive the
fact of its coarseness: and least of all could I sympathize with women
who set the example of marrying for an establishment in a new country, where, if anywhere, the conjugal relation should be found in its
purity.

The unavoidable consequence of such a mode of marrying is that
the sanctity of marriage is impaired, and that vice succeeds. Any one
must see at a glance that if men and women marry those whom they
do not love, they must love those whom they do not marry. There
are sad tales in country villages, here and there, which attest to this;
and yet more in towns, in a rank of society where such things are
seldom or never heard of in England. I rather think that married life
is immeasurably purer in America than in England: but that there is
not otherwise much superiority to boast of. I can only say that I
unavoidably knew of more cases of lapse in highly respectable families
in one State than ever came to my knowledge at home; and that they
were got over with a disgrace far more temporary and superficial than
they could have been visited with in England. I am aware that in
Europe the victims are chosen, with deliberate selfishness, from
classes which cannot make known their perils and their injuries; while
in America, happily, no such class exists. I am aware that this destroys
all possibility of a comparison: but the fact remains that the morals
of American society are less pure than they assume to be. If the common boast be meant to apply to the rural population, at least let it
not be made, either in pious gratitude, or patriotic conceit, by the
aristocratic city classes, who, by introducing the practice of mercenary
marriages, have rendered themselves responsible for whatever dreadful consequences may ensue.

The ultimate and very strong impression on the mind of a
stranger, pondering the morals of society in America, is that human
nature is much the same everywhere, whatever may be its environ-

ment of riches or poverty; and that it is justice to the human nature, and not improvement in fortunes, which must be looked to as the promise of a better time. Laws and customs may be creative of vice; and should be therefore perpetually under process of observation and correction: but laws and customs cannot be creative of virtue: they may encourage and help to preserve it; but they cannot originate it. In the present case, the course to be pursued is to exalt the aims, and strengthen the self-discipline of the whole of society, by each one being as good as he can make himself, and relying on his own efforts after self-perfection rather than on any fortunate arrangements of outward social circumstances. Women, especially, should be allowed the use and benefit of whatever native strength their Maker has seen fit to give them. It is essential to the virtue of society that they should be allowed the freest moral action, unfettered by ignorance, and un-intimidated by authority: for it is unquestioned and unquestionable that if women were not weak, men could not be wicked: that if women were bravely pure, there must be an end to the dastardly tyranny of licentiousness.

ALEXANDER WALKER

FROM

INTERMARRIAGE

Alexander Walker (ca. 1783–1853): British anthropologist Alexander Walker studied humans and animals in an effort to explain the way "Beauty, Health, and Intellect" as well as "Deformity, Disease, and Insanity" were passed on from one generation to the next. He dedicated Intermarriage *to Thomas Knight, president of the Horticultural Society, in which he was active.*

His theories were influential in Victorian society, as they addressed a concern, articulated by Sir A. Carlisle, that "our aristocracy, by exclusive intermarriages among ancient families, proceed blindly to breed in contempt of deformities, of feeble intellect, or of hereditary madness . . . until their race becomes extinct." Many believed that Walker's observations could be put to good use in "selecting the fit progenitors of our race."

PART II.

SEXUAL RELATIONS ARISING FROM THESE CONDITIONS, AND CONNECTED WITH, OR LEADING TO INTERMARRIAGE.

SECTION I.

USEFUL GUIDANCE AND DANGEROUS RESTRAINT.

It has now been seen that, at puberty, life is superabundant; that that superabundance is employed in the reproduction of itself; and that, in doing so, the passions and the will are vehemently engaged. Accordingly, the habits contracted at this age are very powerful, and are intimately connected with future health or disease. Hence, at this age, the importance of

Useful Guidance.

Every effort ought, of course, to be made so to direct young persons, that they may be least exposed to the evils that now beset them.

Those who are too robust should be occasionally confined to a more meager diet; and all the exciting substances which accelerate precocity should be carefully shunned, such as chocolate, ragouts, meat suppers, and vinous or spirituous drinks. For the same reason should be avoided retention of urine and constipation, which attract the blood towards the parts whence it is desirable to withhold it.

The habit of cleanliness, practiced from the earliest youth, becomes a valuable corrective at puberty.

An important subject of observation is clothing, and the necessity of habituating young people to cold, particularly with regard to the reproductive organs. "Trousers," it is observed, "either very warm, or lined with woolen stuff, are highly improper, both on account of uncleanliness, and consequences which it is desirable to prevent. Those worn by girls at an early age have been known to produce fatal irritation."

Young persons should not be permitted to lie on down beds; nor, if long sedentary, to sit on soft chairs, to which rush or wooden bottomed ones are greatly preferable. Neither should they be allowed to remain in bed longer than requisite, or to lie down needlessly on couches.

While the languishings of love spring up in soft repose, strong exercise extinguishes tender sentiments, and at the same time produces a revulsion to the other organs. The history of the goddess of hunting is a philosophical allegory, which expresses the great truth, that bodily exercise extinguishes all violent disposition to the pleasures of love. "Otia si tollas, periere cupidinis arcus," is a sentiment that ought never to be forgotten.

Care should even be taken to prevent young persons habitually leaning against anything, so as not to have all their muscles in action.

In lads, activity, so necessary to an equal distribution of the nutritive juices, must be fostered by all the means described by Donald

Walker, in the most accurate and perfect work on the subject, entitled MANLY EXERCISES, in which are described, and illustrated by plates, walking, running, leaping, vaulting, balancing, skating, climbing, swimming, rowing, sailing, riding, driving, &c.

To young women, exercise will be frequently necessary to prevent attachment to fanciful objects, as well as the tendency to dwell on those subjects which it is desirable to avoid. With this view, and eminently to improve personal beauty, the work of the same author, entitled LADIES' EXERCISES, illustrated by numerous plates, is absolutely indispensable. The work is not merely the only thing of the kind worthy of being named, but it is highly original, founded altogether on physiological principles, and strongly approved by the most distinguished members of the medical profession.

The directing of the habits is an important branch of education.

Ignorant mothers know not how frightful those habits are which they first teach by tickling. It is a modification of this, leading only to degrading sensuality, which the effeminate Indians practice under the name of shampooing—a kind of pressing and kneading of the naked body when they come from the bath, which is performed by the delicate hands of females instructed in the operation, and which leaves those subjected to it in a state of voluptuous debility, inconsistent with all manly faculties. This was practiced by the degenerate Romans, among whom women, on quitting the bath, were shampooed by handsome and vigorous slaves, for the almost avowed purpose, that by means of the sympathy between the skin and the reproductive organs, sexual influences might be excited. And it is the beginning of this art that senseless mothers and servants practice when they tickle children.

It is the duty of such persons, on the contrary, even to prevent children from rubbing one thigh against the other, from sitting with their knees crossed, a circumstance particularly injurious to girls, and from playing at such games as riding upon sticks, see-sawing, striding across the edge of a chair, or over the knees.

The back, also, and spinal marrow should never be directly exposed to the fire, as that has a powerful influence on the reproductive system. The best means of warmth is exercise; and even additional clothing, which may be thrown aside when no longer requisite, is preferable to fires.

As to flowers, their odor causes a shock to the sense of smell, which infuses throughout the body a voluptuous feeling.

In regard to particular pursuits, the guide should choose those best adapted to the young person's taste. Sedentary professions requiring more skill than strength, should be left to women, who would perfectly succeed in them, while a vast number of vigorous men must then be employed in labors more worthy of them.

Cold ablutions diminish the sensibility which must otherwise do mischief; and swimming and exercise in cold water are remarkably useful.

If a young person gives unequivocal signs of excessive sensibility, all books depicting exaggerated sentiments must be withheld. The reading of fashionable novels is sure to falsify the judgment of the young by the most absurd exaggerations, to render their duties distasteful, and even to predispose to disease.

"The classics, and even the Bible," observes Friedlander, "can be given them only in extracts, if we are desirous that they should meet with nothing that we deem obscene." If, very unfortunately, such a thing should occur, it must pass unnoticed. Montaigne, speaking of a young girl, says, "She was reading a French book in my presence, and the word *fouteau*, which is the name of a tree, occurred. The lady who acted as governess stopped her short rather sharply, and made her pass over this supposed naughty word. I did not interfere, because I would not derange their rules, for I do not interfere with this mode of government: the female police is very mysterious, but it must be left to them. But, if I mistake not, the conversation of twenty footmen would not, in six months, have impressed upon the fancy the meaning, application, and all the consequences of the sound of these naughty syllables, as strongly as this good lady did by her reprimand and interdiction."

Even the study of the fine arts may render the imagination too active. Of these, drawing is the least objectionable; and music, being the language of passion, is the most dangerous, especially music of the more impassioned and voluptuous nature.

A better means of discouraging the passions is the cultivation of the intellectual faculties. Great advantage would result, to a young girl at puberty, from the study of history, geography, and the various branches of natural history, pursuits which at once dissipate the passions, and are useful to rural economy, and many of the arts of industry.

For the sake, indeed, of the powerful influence which maternal education has on progeny, all the faculties with which reasoning, calculation, the mechanical and various positive sciences are associated, should be in some degree employed; and, on such subjects, habitual exercise of the memory would usefully engage much valuable time and prevent all injurious use of it.

In fine, every occupation of the mind likely to produce or foster emotions ought to be proscribed.—There is danger, as an able writer observes, even in austere religion, for daily experience shows but too well, that, in the exclusive worship and love of a superior being, the young girl looks for nothing, and finds nothing, but food for tender emotions—with her, love of God is still love.

On the important subject of example, it need scarcely be said, that young persons are sure to observe and interpret any loose joke, or indecent language that coarse-minded people utter before them.

Not less carefully ought the example of improper conduct to be guarded against. Several young persons should never be suffered to sleep together in one bed, nor even in the close vicinity of married persons or domestics.

For similar reasons, education in boarding-schools is highly dangerous, especially at this period. Intimacies spring up between pupils nearly of the same age; they repose confidence in each other as to their most secret thoughts; and they endeavor to verify the conjectures they have formed respecting sexual affairs. Meanwhile, some other friend in the confidence of this *tugendbund*, who had returned home and seen the world, visits the unfortunates still remaining at school, when a speedy disclosure takes place of all her discoveries made as to the subjects they have so often discussed; and to show that her generosity is commensurate with her new importance, she occasionally supplies those works whose amorous pages have been kindly made known to them by the most positive interdiction of the teachers. Hence, the barriers raised up by modesty are surmounted, and depraved habits are contracted.

But, though a boarding-school is a hot-bed of vice to all who have reached puberty, that is far from being the time for introduction to the world and to the other sex; and retirement among elder female relatives is then the wisest mode of life. Theaters should be carefully avoided, particularly representations in which the softer passions are excited, or seductive music is the principal portion: comedy, as a mere picture of manners and characters, is less objectionable.

When, in spite of the best management, a young girl exhibits change or irregularity of character, becomes subject to sighs and tears, of which no cause is apparent, and betakes herself to solitude, then, muscular exercise sufficient to produce slight fatigue, agreeable society, and powerful diversions, are means that must be adopted.

It is equally foolish and dangerous, in parents and others charged with the education of girls, to try to conceal from them all knowledge as to the results of the position in which they are placed by the circumstance of nubility; for girls, in spite of watchful vigilance and every obstacle, are soon enabled, by natural instinct and by unremitting observation, to instruct themselves in all that pertains to love, and to substitute, for true and invaluable instruction, those false notions which are most likely to be followed by fatal results.

Love assuredly, such as it is described in the mischievous trash called fashionable novels, or even as artificial society often presents it, is at utter variance with the plan of nature. It is denaturalized and factitiously exalted by the obstacles which it encounters from prejudices relative to birth, rank, and fortune, and by the want of employment and of objects of real interest among the easy classes. Without such obstacles, love might produce happiness, instead of delirium, might be the embellisher, not the occupier, the consoler, not the arbiter of life.

To the youth, the argument may well be employed, that it is in his interest to restrain his desires, even though he may be capable of reproduction; that he must learn to earn the means of living before he increase the number of those requiring it; and that moreover his sole object in the world is not to find food and procreate his species, without leaving any trace of honorable advancement behind him. Finally, other sentiments may be awakened; ambition, dignity, and the universal respect of his fellow men.

So, also, it is the duty of her guide, when the maiden has recovered from the tumult of puberty, to explain to her the general nature of the sexual relations to which she is destined, to put her upon her guard against the disguises which love assumes and the stratagems it employs, to place it, on the contrary, before her in the character it must assume in marriage, to make her aware of the modifications that possession produces in the ardor of mankind, and the certainty of its being eventually calm and moderate, and to teach her to control her affections till they are in accordance with those proprieties upon which the conduct of life is made to depend.

Unluckily, experience too often presents obstacles to unions passionately desired. In such a case, if the maiden cannot be united to the object of her attachment, the nervous system must be weakened, and the muscular system strengthened, by a more active mode of life, by long walks, and as much bodily exercise as possible, beginning always by gentle tasks, and gradually imposing upon herself others that in a greater degree exercise the organs.

There are, however, youths and maidens whose temperaments are, on the contrary, lively, fickle, and incapable of attachment, and with whom, consequently, means of a directly opposite tendency must be employed—all those, in short, which were deprecated in the former case.

Dangerous Restraint.

To prevent the increase of population, mechanical means, such as infibulation, have been employed.

Infibulation consisted in passing a ring through the prepuce, which was drawn down over the glans. The comedians and tragedians of Greece employed this method to preserve their voice; and Winkelman, in the "Monumenti Inediti," has given us a drawing of a bronze antique representing that condition. Similar was the fibula worn at Rome by the singers, to preserve their voices. The precaution, however, was laughed at; and Martial speaks of singers who sometimes broke their rings, and had to be again taken to the smith. When, indeed, we recollect how very relaxed and elastic the prepuce is, and how insensible to pain, it is evident that little effect could be produced by such means.

Infibulation seems to have been in use in many parts of Asia and Africa. Women also were subjected to it, and, in that case, the operation was performed by sewing together parts that nature has separated, and leaving only sufficient space for natural evacuations. Such also is the practice at present. Amongst some people, however, a ring is deemed sufficient; that for girls being immovable, whilst that for women is not so.

Browne found infibulation practiced in Darfour, the operation being performed at the age of eleven or twelve years. Burkhardt also says that the daughters of the Arabs, Ababde, and Dajafeere, who inhabit the western banks of the Nile, from Thebes as high as the cataracts, and generally those of all the people to the south of Kenne and Esne, as far as Sennaar, undergo excision of the clitoris between three and six years of age; that the healing of the wound is contrived to close the parts except at one place, for the natural evacuations; and that the adhesions are not broken until the day before marriage, and in the presence of the intended bridegroom. Some, however, have these parts sewn up, and, like eunuchs, become more valuable on account of their unfitness for sexual purposes.

Among the civilized nations of modern times, the same object is kept in view, though means so rude are not adopted. Laws and injunctions, more or less severe, answer the same purpose. While laws, to prevent too early unions, impose on the maiden the duty of chastity before legal marriage, mothers frame the most austere injunctions, which, for a while, dominate over youthful timidity. She dare not advance a step, utter a word, or cast a look, but at the hazard of severe reproof or of malignant comment. Struggling to guard against herself, she must learn to stifle nature; and, at the age of gaiety and happiness, must pass life "in a state of exhibition, in vestments constricting the chest, compressing respiration, impeding the circulation and the movement of the limbs," and producing the frightful diseases already described.

While the condition of a young woman is thus a state of violence against nature, and our manners demand so vigilant a surveillance, it is not very wisely complained that girls are dissembling, nor very wonderful that they escape from this struggle between the development of the organs of reproduction and that inactivity of them which society demands. The most fatal consequences, indeed, accrue from this, both to the physical and moral state of woman: escape is frequent; ruin inevitable.

Grimm, therefore, is not far wrong when he says, "The morals of women are founded altogether on arbitrary principles; their honor is not true honor; their decency is a false decency; and their merit, all the becomingness of their state, consists in dissembling and disguising the natural sentiments, which a chimerical duty requires them to conquer, and which with all their efforts they cannot annihilate."

The most ungenerous portion of all this is that, when the worst consequences ensue from these regulations, their victims alone are blamed; and that even philosophers have endeavored to show that, in such cases, woman alone is criminal, because, as they assert, woman has no motive to err. This unjust conclusion renders the discussion of this delicate subject indispensable.

"As people dispute about everything," says Rousel (blind to the bearing and importance of the question), "it has been inquired if the pleasure which woman experiences in reproduction is greater than that experienced by man—an idle question, worthy of the school, and as useless as it is impossible of solution. It is essential, without doubt, and even the duty of a sensible and intelligent being, not to consent to be happy alone, and without being assured that others are so; but it is a vain subtlety to seek to determine the precise measure of happiness which occurs to each."

Now, the question is neither "vain" nor "impossible of solution." I have already shown that woman has a vital system larger than that of man. I may now add that she has a larger reproductive system. It follows that their functions are corresponding. It is with these vital and reproductive organs and functions that the whole life of woman is associated. To know, indeed, the precise degree of their importance to her, and the necessity of their frequent or enduring employment, it is only necessary to observe their relatively greater development. On this ground alone, then, all that is connected with love is far more essential to woman than to man.

But, to advance in this argument—I have also shown that, in reproduction and progeny, the organs of sense and the anterior part of the brain go always along with the vital system; and anatomy shows that these parts are relatively larger in woman than in man. It follows that, in her, sensibility and its perceptions are greater; and consequently that she must derive, from the employment of these vital and reproductive organs, far higher pleasure than man.

This anatomical and physiological fact is similarly the sole foundation of such empirical observations as the following:—"When we consider that their nervous system is more sensible and active than man's, that their skin is more soft and delicate, that their sensations are more intimate and internal, that their breasts are exquisitely sensible, and that they yield more easily to the seduction of fond caresses, we may conclude with De Lignac that their enjoyments are more extended and more connected with the whole of their economy than man's. Impregnation seems to take place in them by the concurrence of every portion of the body agitated by sensations of pleasure. They throw more of abandonment into it than man, since for the pleasures of love they sacrifice the timidity natural to their sex, and the idea, which is always painful, of the pangs of childbearing, and the anxieties of maternity."

But I have also shown that the cerebel, or organ of the will, is small in woman; and therefore, though the pleasures of love are more essential to her organization, more easily yielded to on every opportunity, and more exquisitely enjoyed, yet they are less determined, and more easily suffer suspense or renunciation. Neglect of anatomy and physiology has made all writers mistake on this subject, as is done in a following statement, not understood by the writer, and explicable only by the anatomical and physiological fact expressed in the first sentence of this paragraph. "Women constantly retard enjoyment, or prevent it altogether, solely by the influence of the will, acted upon by the most trifling motive. They even do more: they sometimes renounce it without a murmur."

The statement of these truths, and exposition of the common errors on the subject, render it unnecessary to reply further to the false representations that have been made as to the absence of necessity and the diminished degree of these pleasures in woman.

In the following passage, "It has always appeared to me unreasonable to suppose that nature has bestowed *the most powerful desires* upon that sex which is prevented by its own weakness from seeking to satisfy them according to inclination; that *the most imperious inclination* should be joined to the necessity of waiting and to the pretense of refusal; that the individual in whom a passive state predominates almost constantly should be of *a warmer constitution* than the male who carries in himself a cause of permanent activity,"—in this passage, the error, indicated by the words in italics, is in not seeing that, though in conformity with the larger vital and reproductive system of woman, is the necessity for its frequent or enduring employment, and in conformity with her larger organs of sense and anterior part of the brain (parts, as will be seen, always accompanying the vital and reproductive system), is the possession of greater sensibility and capacity for pleasure,—yet her smaller cerebel or organ of will renders her less determined in pleasure, and enables her to yield to suspense or renunciation,—in fact, that there is greater necessity for and greater capacity of pleasure, but greater power of yielding to momentary circumstances affecting these,—a fact which is in perfect analogy with the whole of the female character. But, to yield is one thing; to forego is another. The necessity and the capacity of pleasure, are as clearly established as is the power of yielding to circumstances.

All, however, that has been said on this subject is interesting chiefly because it exposes the injustice and wickedness of the following conclusion, founded solely on the statements which have just been refuted,—"That man is not so unjust as he is accounted, in requiring from woman that strict fidelity which, in particular circumstances (such as absence), he is unable to exercise himself."

I have just said, with respect to woman, that, "to yield is one thing; to forego is another: the necessity and the capacity of pleasure, are as clearly established as is the power of yielding to circumstances." It is gratifying that here pathology comes in aid of physiology. Cabanis says, "In general, women, in this respect, support excesses more easily, and privations more difficultly: at least, these privations, when they are not absolutely voluntary, have ordinarily for women, especially in a state of solitude and indolence, inconveniences which they have but rarely for men."

SECTION II.

Unnatural Indulgence and Absolute Continence.

As soon as puberty is accomplished, instinct leads the youth to satisfy desire, and if no object of the other sex is cast in the way, and he is unchecked by timidity or other considerations, he falls into

Unnatural Indulgence.

Of this, it is necessary to trace rapidly the origin and effects as described by the best observers, for those whose duty it is to protect youth from its fatal consequences.

"Surprising artfulness and obstinacy are employed by young people in maintaining secrecy respecting crimes of this description. But a youth may be suspected, when, at the period of puberty, he seeks to remain in solitary places generally alone, more rarely with a particular comrade.

"This vice soon renders him careless of his parents and the persons who have the care of him, as well as indifferent to the sports of his equals; he falls into a distaste for everything except the opportunity of indulgence; all his thoughts are directed to the parts at this period subject to irritation; sensibility, imagination and passion are inflamed; and the secretion of the reproductive liquid augmenting, withdraws a very precious portion from the blood.

"The muscles of the youth consequently become soft; he is idle; his body becomes bent; his gait is sluggish; and he is scarcely able to support himself.—The digestion becomes enfeebled; the breath, fetid; the intestines, inactive; the excrements, hardened in the rectum and producing additional irritation of the seminal conduits in its vicinity. The circulation, being no longer free, the youth sighs often; the complexion is livid; and the skin, on the forehead especially, is studded with pimples.—The corners of the mouth are lengthened; the nose becomes sharp; the sunken eyes, deprived of brilliance and enclosed in blue circles, are cast down; no look remains of gaiety; the very aspect is criminal. General sensibility becomes excessive, producing tears without cause; perception is weakened, and memory almost destroyed; distraction or absence of mind renders the judgment unfit for any operation; the imagination gives birth only to fantasies and fears without grounds; the slightest allusion to the dominating passion produces motion of the muscles of the face, the flush of shame, or a state of despair; the desires become capricious, and envy rankles in the mind, or there ensues a total disgust. The wretched being finishes by shunning the face of men, and dreading the observation of women; his character is entirely corrupted, or his mind is totally stupefied. Involuntary loss of the reproductive liquid at last takes place during the daily motions; and there ensues a total exhaustion, bringing on heaviness of the head, singing in the ears, and frequent faintings, or a sensation as if ants were running from the head down the back, together with pains, convulsive tremblings, and partial paralysis."

Long previous to these severe effects, the losses which have been described arrest the increase of stature, and stop the growth of all the organs, and the development of all the functions. It is an earlier puberty which renders the southern people shorter than the northern. And a sense of this seems to have prevailed from the remotest times. Amongst the Germans, according to Julius Caesar, the act of reproduction was not permitted to adolescents before twenty without incurring infamy; and to this he attributes the stature and strength of that simple people.

An incapability of ever giving life to strong and robust children is another effect of these losses, which precedes the total ruin of the individual.

Intelligent instructors will know both how to divine the bad habits of their pupils, and how to avoid all excitement of them.

Much attention has recently been paid to the nature of punishments. There are few of them that should not be avoided; but to punish a child by shutting him up alone in a room is a sad error, if there be any reason to suspect him of bad habits.

Medicinal remedies, astringents, sudorifics, &c., are weakening and injurious in other respects; and mechanical means directly applied to the organs, are likely to draw the attention, and determine the blood, to the part whence it should be diverted.

Moral means consist of good habits previous to puberty, the influence of fear and respect, and that of the nobler feelings predominating over the baser passions.

This assuredly will be more easily accomplished in well-directed private education than in public schools.

When conviction of the existence of bad habits is acquired, it becomes necessary to speak to the subject of them mildly and rationally respecting his injurious practice.—It is feared that the works on the subject, if they have cured some, have made others acquainted with vice of this kind. But there can be no danger in placing such works in the hands of children whose conduct has given rise to suspicion.

In such cases, exciting and superabundant food is highly injurious. The diet should be chiefly or altogether vegetable; and no vinous or spirituous drinks should be permitted. The latter are indeed, of themselves, quite sufficient to produce, at any time, the worst habits; and the parent who has suffered their use, has no right to complain either of precocious puberty, or of unnatural indulgences.

As it is well known, that the almost unremitting employment of his muscles diverts the laborer from this vice, whilst shepherds, who watch their flocks in sequestered places, have been generally accused of it, it is evident that if, in youths, the superabundance of nervous power were carried off by exercise, they would be rendered more tranquil and more attentive to instruction, and would consequently make greater progress in knowledge.

When boys suffer nocturnal affections of this kind, involuntarily produced, similar care and treatment are required. All that heats the imagination and is likely to recur in dreams must then be avoided, as should every physical circumstance tending to assist it—suppers, down beds, hot bed-clothing, &c.

Such affections, when awake, are the results of confirmed disease, requiring the union of medical treatment with physical and moral education.

The vice, which has now been described in boys, appears to be still more common among girls, and produces similar symptoms.

In general, the victims of this depravity are announced by their aspect. "The roses fade from the cheeks; the face assumes an appearance of faintness and weakness; the skin becomes rough; the eyes lose their brightness, and a livid circle surrounds them; the lips become colorless; and all the features sink down, and become disordered."

If the depravity be not arrested, general disease and local affections of the organs of reproduction ensue—acrid leucorrhoea, ulcerations of the vulvo-uterine canal, falling and various diseases of the matrix, abortions, and sometimes nymphomania and furor uterinus, terminate life amidst delirium and convulsions.

Sapphic tastes form another aberration of love, of which Sappho and the lovers of their own sex were accused by Seneca, St. Augustine, &c. "Her ode, breathing the languor, abandonment, delirium, ecstasy, and convulsions of love, was addressed, not to a lover, but to one of her female companions; and, amongst the fragments of her poetry, are some voluptuous verses addressed to two Grecian girls, her pupils and lovers." As there were many women at Lesbos who adopted the habits of Sappho, the term Lesbian habits was used to express these.—The women of Lesbos also fell into other errors, which gained them the epithet of Fellatrix.

These turpitudes, as if they were natural but unfortunate compensations to women subject to polygamy, are said to be still well known to the Turkish and Syrian women at their baths. And it is not improbable, that this occasioned, in southern countries, the excision of the clitoris.

It is evident that the victims of this depravity demand the most active vigilance of mothers, if they desire to preserve either the morals or the health of their daughters. It is evident, also, that the same practices are scarcely less injurious at a more advanced age.

Absolute Continence.

This consists in abstaining, owing generally to religious notions, from the indulgences of love, although the individual feels the strongest desire for them; and, in general, it is attended with the most deplorable results.

In such cases, the effects vary, but they generally are continual priapism, frequent itching, inordinate desires, taciturnity, moroseness, or ferocity, determination of blood to the head, lassitude and disgust at everything abstracting the mind from the prevailing passion, incapability of averting attention from voluptuous images, and partial madness, succeeded by general insanity and terminated by death.

An ecclesiastic, mentioned by Buffon, forwarded him a memoir describing the torments of his celibacy, and the various sensations and ideas experienced by him during an erotic delirium of six months' duration.

"This ecclesiastic, Monsieur M——, presented all the attributes of a sanguine temperament, the premature development of which commenced at the age of eleven. Paternal despotism, the direction of his studies and affections, superstitious habits, Pythagorean regimen, fastings and macerations, were all employed to change, to stifle, or rather to mutilate nature.

"At the age of thirty-two, being then bound by a vow of eternal celibacy, he began to feel the action of the reproductive organs in a more lively manner, and his health was injured.

"At this period, he says, in his own account, 'my forced continence produced through all my senses a sensibility, or rather an irritation, I had never before felt.—I fixed my looks on two females, who made so strong an impression on my eyes, and through them on my imagination, that they appeared to me to be illuminated, and glittering with a fire like electric sparks: I retired speedily, thinking it was an illusion of the devil.

" 'Some days afterwards, I suddenly felt a contraction and a violent tension in all my limbs, accompanied by a frightful convulsive movement, similar to that which follows an attack of epilepsy. This state was succeeded by delirium.—My imagination was next assailed with a host of obscene images, suggested by the desires of nature.—These chimeras were soon followed by warlike ardors, in which I seized the four bed-posts, made them into a bundle, and hurled them against my bedroom-door, with such force as to drive it off the hinges.*

" 'In the course of my delirium, I drew plans and compartments on the floor of my room; and so exact was my eye, and so steady my hand, that, without any instrument, I traced them with perfect accuracy.

" 'I was again seized with martial fury, and imagined myself successively Achilles, Caesar, and Henry the Fourth.—A short time afterwards, I declared I would marry, and I thought I saw before me women of every nation and of every color.

" 'I at first selected a certain number, corresponding with the number of the different nations I had conquered; and it appeared to me, that I should marry each of these women according to the rites and customs of her nation. There was one whom I regarded as queen over the rest. This was a young lady I had seen some days before the commencement of my disease.—I was, at this moment, desperately amorous; I expressed my desires aloud in the most energetic manner; yet I had never, in all my life, read any romance or tale of love; I had never embraced, never even saluted, a woman; I spoke, however, very indecently of my desire to every one, without reflecting upon my sacred character; and I was quite surprised that my relations found fault with my proposals, and condemned my conduct.

" 'This state of amorous crisis was followed by a tolerably tranquil sleep, during which I experienced nothing but pleasure.—Returning reason brought all my woes. I reflected upon their cause; I recognized it; and, without daring to combat it, I exclaimed with Job, "Cur data lux misero?" ' "

The state of woman, under similar circumstances, is not less severe. If love acquire a determined character in one whose nervous system is at all excitable, the state of virginity, at variance as after puberty it is with the impulses and intentions of nature, becomes one of great suffering.

---

* This alternate direction of nervous influence to the brain itself and to the muscles is very remarkable; and it forms an excellent illustration of the value of exercise in all cases of this kind.

A strong feeling of duty, and the emotion of fear, may lead her for a time to withstand the powerful impulse of nature. But that power is unceasingly operating; imagination is constantly filled with pictures of the happiness for which she longs; desire at last bursts through the restraints of reason. If she then redouble her efforts, and, by unceasing attention and unrelaxing resolve, stifle the voice of nature, this struggle speedily immerses her in languor and melancholy.

Such a state must finally become morbid.

Dr. M. Good quotes, from Professor Frank, of Vienna, the case of a lady of his acquaintance, of a warm and amorous constitution, who was unfortunately married to a very debilitated and impotent man, and who, although she often betrayed unawares, by her looks and gestures, the secret fire that consumed her, yet, from a strong moral principle, resisted all criminal gratification: after a long struggle, her health at last gave way, and a slow fever released her from her sufferings.

Chlorosis is frequently the first malady that makes its appearance. The catamenia, too, are frequently suppressed, occur at irregular periods, or are complicated by painful symptoms—the consequence of the irritability of the reproductive organs, produced by privation and inactivity. It is asserted, indeed, that, in this respect, excess is less injurious than privation, and that the most voluptuous women menstruate most easily.

The stomach frequently becomes unable to retain any substance, however light. The nervous susceptibility often affects the heart; its movements, either by fits or permanently, becoming quick, irregular, and strong, and constituting palpitation. Frequently also this nervous predominance is felt throughout the organization; and syncopes form the prelude to what are called vapors. Sometimes, likewise, girls fall into profound melancholy, and abandon themselves to despair.

If marriage be not permitted to terminate this state, injury fatal to life may be its consequence.

In the extravagance of passion, suicide may be perpetrated. More frequently occur a general perversion of sensibility, and all the degrees of hysterism, especially if the maiden has a strong tendency to love, nurtured by good living, an easy sedentary life, the reading of fashionable novels, or exciting conversations with the other sex, while she is still kept under the eyes of a vigilant superintendent.

An attack of hysteria is generally characterized by yawning, stretching, *a variable state of mind*, or extravagant caprices, tears, and laughter without cause, fluttering and palpitation with urgent flatulence, rumbling in the belly, *a flow of limpid urine*, a feeling as if a ball *(the globus hystericus)* were rolling about in the abdomen, ascending to the stomach and fauces, and there causing a sense of strangulation, as well as of oppression about the chest and difficulty of respiration, fainting, loss of sensation, motion and speech, death-like coldness of the extremities or of the body generally; also muscular rigidity, and convulsive movements, the patient twisting the body, striking herself, and tearing the breast; and this followed by *a degree of coma*, stupor, and apparent sleep; but consciousness by degrees returning, amidst sobs, sighs and tears.

Hysterical epilepsy may take place, the paroxysms of which are sometimes preceded by dimness of sight, vertiginous confusion, pain of the head, ringing in the ears, flatulence of the stomach and bowels, palpitation of the heart, and occasionally of the aura epileptica, or feeling as if cold air, commencing in some part of the extremities, directed its course up to the head. During the fit, the patient falls upon the ground, and rolls thereon; the muscles of the face are distorted; the tongue is thrust out of the mouth, and often bitten; the eyes turn in their orbits; she cries or shrieks, emitting a foaming saliva; and she struggles with such violence that several persons are required to hold her. The belly is tense and grumbling; there are frequent eructations; and the excretions, particularly the urinary, are passed involuntarily. After a time more or less considerable, the patient gradually recovers, with yawning and sense of lassitude, scarcely answers, and is ignorant of what has occurred to her.

These effects, we are told, have been observed in Canary birds, which if, when separated from their females, they can see them without being able to reach them, sing continually, and never cease till their distress is terminated by an attack of epilepsy.

Other affections, as catalepsies, ecstasies, &c., frequently depend upon the reproductive organs: and in Roman Catholic countries, in former times, half-insane devotees were found among old maids thus affected, and became, in consequence, the fitting instruments of the artful propagators of ridiculous creeds.

In some cases, the dominant passion interferes with the other operations of intellect, and produces insanity. It has been already observed, that no one becomes insane before puberty; and that the period of the greatest reproductive ardor is that of the highest mental excitement.

Accordingly, many young women become insane either from erotic or religious excitement (physiologically regarded they are the same), from the love even of the beings of their own imagination;— for it is justly observed, "Such are the wants of the heart in women, that they are caught by and attach themselves to chimeras, when the reality is wanting to their sensibility."

The worst disease resulting from this cause is nymphomania, or furor uterinus. The women whom celibacy renders most liable to it, have been observed to be of small stature, and to have somewhat bold features, the skin dark, the complexion ruddy, the mammae quickly developed, the sensibility great, and the catamenia considerable.

The very commencement of puberty is generally the time when the disease of which furor uterinus is the aggravated form, begins to arise out of the temperament just described and from various accidental causes, as loose reading or conversation, obscene paintings or engravings, and bad example arising from close intercourse with dissolute persons.

In persons suffering under this disease, says Dr. M. Good, "there is often, at first, some degree of melancholy, with frequent sighings; but the eyes roll in wanton glances, the cheeks are flushed, the bosom heaves, and every gesture exhibits the lurking desire, and is enkindled by the distressing flame that burns within. . . . The disease is strikingly marked by the movements of the body, and the salacious appearance of the countenance, and even the language that proceeds from the lips." They, indeed, use the most lascivious language and gestures, even invite men without distinction, and abuse them if they repel their advances.

The diseases also of the matrix and mammae occur chiefly amongst unmarried females. Old maids are especially liable to these diseases, because their organs have not fulfilled their functions. Schirrous indurations and cancers often form in these parts, especially at the final cessation of the catamenia. Hydatids also form in the matrix or ovaries, so as to resemble pregnancy.

ISAAC BAKER BROWN

FROM

ON THE CURABILITY OF CERTAIN FORMS OF INSANITY, EPILEPSY, CATALEPSY, AND HYSTERIA IN FEMALES

Isaac Baker Brown (1812–1873): A general practitioner and later a surgeon, Isaac Baker Brown knew Sigmund Freud personally and was influenced by his ideas on female sexuality. As a surgeon at St. Mary's Hospital, he began practicing gynecology and performing clitoridectomies. Brown's writings contradicted William Acton's belief that most women experience no sexual feelings at all. In contrast, Brown believed that women were controlled by their reproductive systems and that sexual arousal in women led to a number of illnesses from epilepsy to insanity. His career ended in disgrace in 1867 when he was expelled from the Obstetrical Society for failing to tell his patients the nature of the operations he was performing.

PREFACE.

In offering this little book to my professional brethren, I do not for one moment wish it to be understood that I claim any originality in the surgical treatment herein described.

Having read with great interest the Lectures on the "Physiology and Pathology of the Central Nervous System," delivered by Dr. Brown-Séquard before the Royal College of Surgeons of England, in

1858, and published in *The Lancet*, I was struck with a fact much insisted upon by the learned physiologist, namely, the great mischief which might be caused in the system generally, and in the nervous centers especially, by peripheral excitement.

CHAPTER I.

INTRODUCTORY.

As the title of this book implies, I do not intend to occupy the attention of my readers with all the numerous varieties of insanity and other nervous disorders to which females are liable, but only those which I believe to be curable by surgical means; nor is it my intention in this category to include slight cases, but to confine myself to such as cause more or less severe functional derangement, or which lead to serious organic lesions.

The class of diseases on which I shall dwell are those depending on (or arising from) a loss of nerve tone, caused by continual abnormal irritation of a nerve center.

This is no very new theory; but it has been for Dr. Handfield Jones, by a large number of cases and experiments, as collated in his admirable work on "Functional Nervous Disorders," to make it "abundantly clear that the great majority of disorders we have to treat at the present time show more or less marked indications of failure of nervous power." Dr. Jones confines himself "to such disorders as are termed functional;" and I agree with him that "it seems a vain dispute, whether in strict accuracy there are, or are not, any such disorders; . . . for it is perfectly certain that there are very grave disorders in which the most careful scrutiny fails to detect any actual change, in which complete recovery is perfectly possible, and in which the 'juvantia' are such as to operate more in modifying the power of the organs than the texture." Dr. Jones then gives two typical cases of functional and organic disease, between which, as he justly observes, "there intervene numerous instances of more or less mixed character;" and adds that "disease which commences essentially as functional may end as organic."

I am so pleased to be supported by my old friend and colleague in views that I myself have long entertained, that I intend, without further preface, to make his researches the whole substratum of my work; and hope to show how, on the basis of Dr. Jones's experiments, it is possible to prove the philosophy of my own practice.

Whichever of the terms, "inhibitory influence" (Handfield Jones and Lister), "reflex relaxation" (Brinton), or "reflex paralysis" (Brown-Séquard) be used, the fact is ceded by all, that "the energetic operation of an afferent nerve" (Lister), or some impression acting injuriously on an afferent nerve (Handfield Jones), or, again, "an actually existing irritation" (Brown-Séquard), exerts an injurious effect on its nerve center, this state being, as Dr. Brown-Séquard thinks, increased or diminished according to the activity of the irritation, and ceasing with its entire removal, or, more probably, as Dr. Handfield Jones affirms, persisting after the cessation of the cause which has morbidly affected it. This latter view appears to me the more generally correct one, because it can hardly be expected that a gradual disease will be suddenly removed, there having been no time for recovery of nerve power.

In Dr. Handfield Jones's Lumleian Lectures, delivered last year before the College of Physicians, he thus sums up his views on this subject:—"The essential idea of the inhibitory theory is, that an impression conveyed to a nervous center by afferent nerves may weaken or paralyze, instead of exciting, its action, either from the congenital or acquired debility and sensitiveness of the nerve itself, or because the impression is unduly intense or absolutely injurious. Both these things have in every case to be considered—viz., the state of the nerve force, and the kind and amount of impression, as the resulting phenomena will vary with the variation of either."

Dr. Jones next takes it as a matter of certainty, "that a nervous center may be more or less completely paralyzed without having undergone organic change, in consequence of some enfeebling morbid influence;" and quotes from Dr. Gull "a most interesting instance of complete paraplegia induced by sexual excess, in which nothing abnormal could be detected in the cord, even by careful microscopy. This was paralysis from simple exhaustion."

Still continuing, Dr. Jones draws attention to the anatomical fact of the remarkably close manner in which "the different nerve centers, or parts of a nerve center, are connected by commissural fibers," and how, "from a pathological point of view, the same connection is often very manifest. The general exhaustion induced by excess of venery" and other cases "are examples which show how excessive consumption of nerve force in one part weakens it also in others; and this can only be adequately explained by the intricate commissural connection between the various centers."

The truth of all these views is well exemplified, as Dr. Kidd has stated, in cases of epilepsy, which "may originate only in irritation of bad teeth acting on the brain, or worms irritating the nerves of the stomach, and so on as to other peripheral irritations; the chief skill being to find out the spot from which the irritation radiates."

A case is also quoted by Dr. Jones, in the Lumleian Lectures, as having occurred in the practice of Mr. Castle, of New York, where diseased teeth produced paraplegia, which soon ceased after their removal.

Long and frequent observation convinced me that a large number of affections peculiar to females depended on loss of nerve power, and that this was produced by peripheral irritation, arising originally in some branches of the pudic nerve, more particularly the incident nerve supplying the clitoris, and sometimes the small branches which supply the vagina, perinaeum, and anus.

Closer observation satisfied me that the greater or less severity of the functional affections observed, depended on the amount and length of irritation, and the consequent amount of loss of nerve power.

Nor are functional disorders the only consequence, but in some cases, severe organic lesions.

The progress of the disease may be divided into eight distinct stages—No. 8 being arrived at, by gradations more or less distinct, directly from No. 1.

1. HYSTERIA (including dyspepsia and menstrual irregularities).
2. SPINAL IRRITATION, with reflex action on uterus, ovaries, &c., and giving rise to uterine displacements, amaurosis, hemiplegia, paraplegia, &c.
3. EPILEPTOID FITS, or HYSTERICAL EPILEPSY.
4. CATALEPTIC FITS.
5. EPILEPTIC FITS.
6. IDIOTCY.
7. MANIA.
8. DEATH.

My statement, that death is indeed the direct climax of the series, might be proved by several cases which have occurred in my own practice, one only of which I shall relate. Before doing so, I may mention that Dr. James Russell, of Birmingham, has recorded a case in the *Medical Times and Gazette*, Oct. 31, 1863, in which a male patient, age 32, died under his care in the Birmingham General Hospital. Complete paralysis both of sensation and motion in the lower part of the body and lower extremities attacked him after an unusually excessive venereal indulgence. There had been gradual exhaustion for the last twelve or fourteen years, from this cause. There was no attempt at recovery, and he died in four months from the date of the attack.

The case that occurred in my own practice was as follows: ————, age 19, has been gradually becoming ill since the age of nine; does not look older than the latter age, though the sexual organs are as highly developed as they should be. Has been for many months in a metropolitan hospital suffering from acute headache, but has received no benefit. For two years has been perfectly blind.

She was found dead, and with every evidence of having expired during a paroxysm of abnormal excitement.

These cases will illustrate how important it is to arrest the disease *ab initio*, and the treatment must be the same whether we wish to cure functional disturbance, arrest organic disease, or, finally, if we have only a chance, of averting death itself.

The time required for recovery must depend, not only, as has been already hinted, on the duration of illness, but also on the peculiar temperament of the patient, and judicious after-treatment; this latter requiring long perseverance on the part of both practitioner and the friends of his patient; and it is as we meet a favorable or unfavorable case that the opinions of Brown-Séquard, as to instant cure on removal of irritation, or of Handfield Jones, as to cure after a long interval, are verified.

I have pleasure in stating that, with reference to the origin of most nervous affections of females, I have, in frequent conversation with Brown-Séquard, found that the views of this distinguished physiologist entirely coincide with my own, and he often expressed himself as satisfied that destruction of the nerve causing irritation was the only effective cure; the best mode of carrying out this destruction was, in his opinion, yet to be determined. He used actual cautery.

I hope to be able to show that a far more humane and effectual method is that which I constantly practice, and for the last six or seven years have openly and consistently advocated. Of course, from the very novelty of these views, I have been met with many objections, such as unsexing the female, preventing the normal excitement consequent on marital intercourse, or actually, as some most absurdly and unphilosophically assert, causing sterility: whereas my cases will show fact to be directly converse to all these theories; and it is curious that a physician for many years connected with one of our largest metropolitan hospitals, and recognized as a standard writer on female diseases, has in writing condemned my practice in not very measured terms, but is himself constantly in the habit of trying to subdue this peripheral irritation by continual application of the strongest caustics to the seat of the irritation; thereby showing that he recognizes the source of evil, but is not yet able to see that a superficial sore will not destroy deep-seated nerve irritation. It wants, I imagine, little argument to prove that so far from this practice being beneficial, it is likely, by causing increased irritation, to be positively injurious.

Other practitioners follow Dr. Brown-Séquard's plan of applying actual cautery to the irritant nerve; and many more have advanced as far as the operation—which I was formerly in the habit of practicing—subcutaneous division of the nerve. I have long abandoned this method as being no more certain in its effect than kindred operations on various branches of the fifth nerve for tic douloureux.

Another objection has been made that several of my cases have not been permanently cured, but have had relapses in a few weeks or months. This must necessarily be so with all new methods of treatment; but each such case is of incalculable importance, as teaching me to exclude any but temporary hope of relief to some, while to others I can speak all the more positively as to their ultimate permanent recovery.

Experience seems to teach that in those patients whose brains have been so weakened by long continued peripheral excitement, causing frequent and increasing losses of nerve force, there is not sufficient mental power to enable them to control any less powerful irritation of smaller branches of the pudic nerve than that removed by operation.

This lesser excitement acts chiefly, I imagine, by preventing restoration, in the same manner as a drunkard whose brain is weakened by long indulgence in his baneful habit cannot resist temptation, but is, however, affected by much smaller quantities of stimuli, than when strong, he was able to take.

A striking instance of this kind occurred to me last year.

One of our most distinguished obstetric physicians requested me to operate on a lady who had been for some twenty years under very many eminent practitioners without any but temporary benefit. The result of the operation was most marked; the irritation subsided, the patient improved in health, and we confidently expected permanent relief. Yet in a few weeks after she left our hands and that of the nurse, irritation, resembling pruritus, gradually returned, and with it the other old symptoms.

In all cases of a similar nature which have come under my care, I have insisted on the importance of the patient being kept for a long time under careful medical watching and good nursing, and from the results already obtained from cases in which these precautions have been exercised, I feel confident of success for the future.

Lastly, objections have been advanced against the morality of the operation, and I am here at a loss how to give an answer, for I can hardly conceive how such a question can be raised against a method of treatment which has for its object the cure of a disease, that is rapidly tending to lower the moral tone, and which treatment is dictated by the loftiest and most moral considerations. I may here observe that before commencing treatment, I have always made a point of having my diagnosis confirmed by the patient or her friends.

To the philosophical and charitable mind, indeed, the whole subject is one of the greatest interest, and will lead us to ask the question, may not this "inhibitory influence," originating in early life, act so powerfully on the mind as to unhinge it from that steadiness which is essential to enable it to keep the passions under control of the will; to enable, indeed, the moral tone to overcome abnormal excitement? And if this be true, does not common charity lead us to think that cases treated by friends and spiritual advisers, as controllable at the will of the individual, may be in reality simply cases of physical illness amenable to medical and surgical treatment? Is it not better to look the matter steadily in the face, and instead of banishing the unhappy sufferers from their home and from society, endeavor to check their otherwise hopeless career towards some of the latter stages of this disease, to restore their mental power, and make them happy and useful members of the community?

On this consideration I shall not now dwell further. Every one must feel it to be a vast and important one, affecting the well-being of the whole human race.

All I am now aiming at is to show that many, if not all, such cases may be cured. If this is done, I shall indeed be able to say that I am amply repaid.

I have the gratification of being able to name the following gentlemen who have been led to adopt my views and treatment in proper cases:—Sir James Simpson; Dr. Beattie, of Dublin; Sir John Fife and Dr. Dawson, of Newcastle-on-Tyne; Dr. Duke, late of Chichester; Dr. Shettle, of Shaftesbury; John Harrison, Esq., of Chester; Drs. Savage, Routh, and Rogers, in London; my eldest son, Mr. Boyer Brown, now practicing in New South Wales; with my colleagues in the "London Surgical Home," Dr. Barratt, and Messrs. Harper, Chambers, I. B. Brown, Junior, and Bantock, and very many others.

CHAPTER II.

SYMPTOMS AND PROGRESS OF DISEASE—AGE AND CLASS OF PATIENTS TO BE TREATED—OPERATION —AFTER-TREATMENT, ETC.

Every medical practitioner must have met with a certain class of cases which has set at defiance every effort at diagnosis, baffled every treatment, and belied every prognosis. He has experienced great anxiety and annoyance, and felt how unsatisfactory was his treatment to the friends of his patient: and this, not so much because he was ignorant of the cause, as that he was unable to offer any hope of relief.

The period when such illness attacks the patient is about the age of puberty, and from that time up to almost every age the following train of symptoms may be observed, some being more or less marked than others in the various cases.

The patient becomes restless and excited, or melancholy and retiring; listless and indifferent to the social influences of domestic life. She will be fanciful in her food, sometimes express even a distaste for it, and apparently (as her friends will say) live upon nothing. She will

always be ailing, and complaining of different affections. At first, perhaps, dyspepsia and sickness will be observed; then pain in the head
and down the spine; pain, more or less constant, in the lower part of
the back, or on either side in the lumbar region. There will be wasting
of the face and muscles generally; the skin sometimes dry and harsh,
at other times cold and clammy. The pupil will be sometimes firmly
contracted, but generally much dilated. This latter symptom together
with a hard cord-like pulse and a constantly moist palm are, my son
informs me, considered by Mr. Moore, Colonial Surgeon of South
Australia, pathognomonic of this condition. There will be quivering
of the eyelids, and an inability to look one straight in the face. On
inquiring further, there is found to be disturbance or irregularity in
the uterine functions, there being either complete cessation of the
catamenia, or too frequent periods, generally attended with pain; constant leucorrhoea also frequently existing. Often a great disposition
for novelties is exhibited, the patient desiring to escape from home,
fond of becoming a nurse in hospitals, "soeur de charité," or other
pursuits of the like nature, according to station and opportunities.

To these symptoms in the single female will be added, in the
married, distaste for marital intercourse, and very frequently either
sterility or a tendency to abort in the early months of pregnancy.

These physical evidences of derangement, if left unchecked,
gradually lead to more serious consequences. The patient either becomes a confirmed invalid, always ailing, and confined to bed or sofa,
or, on the other hand, will become subject to catalepsy, epilepsy,
idiotcy, or insanity. In any case, and more especially when the disease
progresses as far as these latter stages, it will almost universally be
found that there are serious exacerbations at each menstrual period.

On personal examination, the peculiar straight and coarse hirsute
growth; the depression in the center of the perinaeum; the peculiar
follicular secretion; the alteration of structure of the parts, mucous
membrane taking on the character of skin; and muscle having become
hypertrophied and generally tending towards a fibrous or cartilagi-
nous degeneration will all be recognized by the practitioner who has
once had his attention drawn to these subjects.

Having ascertained the cause and nature of the disease, there are
one or two points to be considered before operative measures are
decided on.

First, as to age. Although there is no doubt that patients may suffer from peripheral irritation of the pudic nerve from the earliest childhood, I never operate or sanction an operation on any patient under ten years of age, which is the earliest date of puberty. In children younger than this, milder treatment with careful watching will be found sufficient if it be thoroughly persevered in.

There are again, after puberty, cases which give rise to but slight disturbance, but in which the sufferers are they who love to enlist sympathy from the charitable, and will be ill, or affect to be ill, in spite of any and every treatment.

When I have decided that my patient is a fit subject for surgical treatment, I at once proceed to operate, after the ordinary preliminary measures of a warm bath and clearance of the portal circulation.

The patient having been placed *completely* under the influence of chloroform, the clitoris is freely excised either by scissors or knife— I always prefer the scissors. The wound is then firmly plugged with graduated compresses of lint, and a pad, well secured by a T bandage.

A grain of opium is introduced per rectum, the patient placed in bed, and most carefully watched by a nurse, to prevent haemorrhage by any disturbance of the dressing. The neglect of this precaution will be frequently followed by alarming haemorrhage, and consequent injurious results.

The diet must be unstimulating, and consist of milk, farinaceous food, fish, and occasionally chicken; all alcoholic or fermented liquors being strictly prohibited. The strictest quiet must be enjoined, and the attention of relatives, if possible, avoided, so that the moral influence of medical attendant and nurse may be uninterruptedly maintained.

A month is generally required for perfect healing of the wound, at the end of which time it is difficult for the uninformed, or non-medical, to discover any trace of an operation.

The rapid improvement of the patient immediately after removal of the source of irritation is most marked; first in the countenance, and soon afterwards by improved digestion and other evidences of healthy assimilation.

It cannot be too often repeated that this improvement can only be made permanent, in many cases, by careful watching and moral training, on the part of both patient and friends.

In the large majority of cases, I have administered no medicines, trusting entirely to recovery, after the removal of the source of irritation. Sometimes, however, we may be materially aided by the use of such medicines as the bromides of potassium and ammonium, belladonna, &c.

CHAPTER III.

HYSTERIA, WITH CASES.

It may, perhaps, be necessary before relating cases which I have treated, suffering from hysteria, to state briefly what I understand by this term. The word Hysteria was doubtless originally used in the belief that it depended on excessive reflex action of the nerves of the uterus and ovaries, when these organs were excited by disease or other causes; but this view is a very limited one, for, as Dr. Handfield Jones says, "it does not appear that females suffering with irritable uterus are more hysterical, often not so much so, as those who have no such disorder." There is, however, as I have already mentioned, in almost all hysterical patients, an exacerbation at the menstrual periods.

Dr. Copland's opinion, that "increased reflex excitability of the nerves of the female generative organs is one principal causative condition of hysterical affections," appears to me the correct one. Romberg also says, "From the time when hysteria has taken root, the reflex action preponderates throughout the organism, and renders the individual more dependent upon external stimuli."

I have alluded in the last chapter to those patients who have no desire to get well. Such I am not considering; and although I believe that all the complaints of an hysterical patient are more or less exaggerated, my experience differs from that of Dr. Handfield Jones, who believes that such patients are not "*bonâ fide* anxious to get well." In his view he is supported by Dr. Prout, who considers that "the whole energies of the patient's mind are bent on deception;" and by Dr. Watson, who says that "the deceptive appearances displayed in the bodily functions and feelings find their counterpart in the mental." I am confident that I have met with many instances in which the nerve power has become so weakened that the patient, without having organic disease, really feels all the symptoms she describes, and is only too anxious to be cured. The cases I shall now narrate are a few of a large number that have come under my care, and I am not without hope that their relation may show that hysteria, instead of being a term of reproach, does truly represent a curable disease.

The following was the first case that came under my notice, after I had satisfied myself of the correctness of my views on the subject:—

CASE I. HYSTERIA—FIVE YEARS' ILLNESS— OPERATION—CURE IN TWO MONTHS.

D. E., aet. 26, single; admitted into the London Surgical Home Oct. 12, 1859.

History.—She had been a dressmaker in Yorkshire to all the best families around, but for the last five years had been so ill as to render her unable to do any work, and had been entirely supported by her former customers. When in that neighborhood, on a professional visit to a lady, I was requested to see, amongst others, this poor *ci-devant* dressmaker. Her physiognomy at once told me the nature of the case; she was much attenuated, having for a long time been unable to retain any food, always being sick, with great pain, immediately after meals. She had constant acid eructations; was so weak as to be at times unable to cross the room; complained of a burning, aching pain, with great weakness at the lower part of the back. Her catamenia were irregular, with much leucorrhoea; bowels generally costive. She was very melancholy, and expressed a most earnest desire to be cured. I advised her admission to the Home, and on October 15, I divided the clitoris subcutaneously. This being my first operation, I did not know the consequences of performing the operation in this manner. For two days the haemorrhage was profuse and uncontrollable. Sleep was procured by opiates. I ordered ℥ij of olive oil to be rubbed into her chest every night, with a view to nutrition of her attenuated frame. A moderately generous diet was given, *but no stimulants*. She was quite well in two months, and has never since had a day's illness. She resumed her occupation as a dressmaker, and recovered nearly all her former customers. 1865.—I have heard almost yearly of this patient, and lately had a letter from the lady to whom I previously referred, saying that my patient is perfectly well and in robust health.

CASE II. TWO YEARS' ILLNESS—OPERATION—CURES.

P. F., aet. 21, single; admitted into the London Surgical Home Jan. 7, 1861.

History.—Attributes her illness to having strained herself two years ago, when lifting a heavy saucepan from the fire. Has ever since that time suffered great pain in the back and side, much worse when she walks, but tolerably easy in the prone position. Catamenia very irregular, both as to time and quantity. Great pain in defecation. Bowels very constipated. Has been eleven weeks in a metropolitan general hospital, and thirteen weeks in a special hospital for women, from both of which she was discharged as having nothing the matter, because she had no evident disease. She had, however, been treated for uterine disease.

On examination, the uterus was found to be quite healthy; there was, however, evidence of excitation of the pudic nerve.

Jan. 10. The clitoris completely excised.

Jan. 16. Is much better.

Jan. 31. Discharged from the Home, cured. Is quite well in her health, having lost all aches and pains, and being able to defecate without the slightest uneasiness.

CASE III. HYSTERIA—THIRTEEN YEARS' ILLNESS—
STERILITY—OPERATION—CURE, AND
SUBSEQUENTLY THREE PREGNANCIES.

S. S., aet. 33, married; admitted into the London Surgical Home February 23, 1861.

History.—Although married several years, has had no children. About a year ago suffered from pain in the right side, which, however, being treated was cured. In April last the pain returned in the back, and at short intervals has recurred. At times the pain is so severe that she is unable to walk. Has for thirteen years suffered from leucorrhoea, globus hystericus, &c.; and has always had distaste for marital intercourse.

Examination confirming me in the diagnosis I had formed of this case, I, on February 28, operated in the usual manner. Her recovery was retarded by an attack of jaundice, but in May she was discharged cured.

In July, 1862, this patient was seen quite well and ruddy, and had long lost all her old symptoms. She had been once pregnant, but miscarried at three months.

In July, 1865, she came to town with her youngest child. She was quite well, and had never been ill since the operation.

Remarks.—This was the first case of this nature under my care, in which the patient, formerly sterile, became pregnant after removal of the cause of her illness.

CASE IV. HYSTERIA, WITH SLEEPLESSNESS— SIX YEARS' ILLNESS—OPERATION—CURE.

H. R., aet. 55, single; admitted into the London Surgical Home Nov. 18, 1861.

History.—For six years has suffered from a feeling of fullness, weight, and heat at the lower part of abdomen, with pain in the back, and "bearing down." At this time her menses had just ceased. Has not slept well for three or four years. Wakes every hour. Is always restless and fidgety. Frequent desire to micturate, with pain on doing so, and often desire without power to void it. Bowels costive; digestion indifferent.

She is a nervous, restless woman, with glistening and constantly wandering eye—pupils dilated. Has suffered from peripheral irritation for many years.

Nov. 21, 1861. Usual operation performed. A week later, slept well for four hours, the first time for many years.

Dec. 1. Has lost the irritability of the bladder, and passes water every four hours only; lost also the bearing-down pain; restless excitement gone.

Dec. 7. Eats and sleeps well; is cheerful and grateful; leaves the Home cured, having been in only three weeks.

In 1863 was perfectly well.

CASE V. FISSURE OF THE RECTUM, WITH HYSTERIA— OPERATION FOR THE FORMER—RELIEF— SUBSEQUENT OPERATION FOR HYSTERIA—CURE.

Mrs. L., aet. 55; admitted into the London Surgical Home Dec. 9, 1861.

History.—Is a widow. Has for many years suffered from all the inconveniences of a fissure of the rectum, combined with bad digestion, undue nervous excitability, and sleepless nights. Is very anxious to be cured. It being thought that all these symptoms might be due to a painful fissure of the rectum, the ordinary operation for this affection was performed on December 12. The bowels were opened in a few days without pain, and the fissure was healing well. Being, however, still sleepless, excitable, and irritable, questions were asked which showed that a further operation for removal of another source of irritation was advisable; therefore, on December 24, I performed my usual operation. The next night she slept well. She became quiet and cheerful, and on January 6, 1862, she was discharged quite well.

Remarks.—This case is very interesting, as it shows that there may exist at the same time more than one irritation exerting inhibitory influence.

CASE VI. HYSTERIA, WITH EPILEPTIFORM ATTACKS IN CHILDHOOD—VARIOUS AILMENTS FOR THIRTEEN YEARS—OPERATION—NO BENEFIT.

H. D., aet. 23 single; admitted into the London Surgical Home April, 1862.

History.—When very young, until ten years of age, had frequent fits. Improved in health till she was fourteen years of age, when she began to suffer from abdominal enlargement. First menstruated at nineteen. Is constantly sick after meals. Has been in nearly every hospital in London. The patient is very hysterical, and is always *talking* religion.

On examination the abdomen was found very tympanitic. Under chloroform this state quite subsided. Walls of abdomen fat and muscular. Body generally well nourished. Evidence of continual irritation of the pudic nerve.

April 3. Operation as usual.

For some time after the operation this patient was much better of the sickness, and great interest was manifested by several visitors in her case; she never, however, received permanent benefit, being a regular impostor, and discovered on several occasions tying handkerchiefs, &c., tightly round her waist to make her abdomen swell. She was discharged as incurable.

Remarks.—This case I have inserted as a warning. It is no fault of the operation if it fail in such cases.

CASE VII. HYSTERIA—SEVERAL YEARS' ILLNESS—
OPERATION—CURE.

Miss M., aet. 42; admitted into the London Surgical Home April 13, 1862.

History.—Has felt ailing for many years, but for the last two has suffered pain in the uterine region, and, on pressure, over the ovaries. This pain is accompanied by bearing down, and a sense of distension. Suffers from considerable leucorrhoea. Menstruation regular, and during the period the pain is absent. Bowels regular. Sleep disturbed. Feels depressed, and is inclined to melancholia.

On examination there was no congestion of uterus or enlargement of ovaries, but there was evidence of peripheral irritation of the pudic nerve.

April 17. Usual operation performed.

She rapidly improved; sleep and cheerfulness returned, and all pain left her. She expressed herself as not having been so well for many years.

May 13. Left the Home, having gained flesh and strength, and being quite cured of all her bad symptoms.

Remarks.—Interest attaches to this case, as instead of exacerbation, there was diminution of the symptoms during menstruation.

CASE VIII. HYSTERIA—MANY YEARS' ILLNESS—
PHANTOM TUMOR—OPERATION—CURE.

A. B., aet. 24; admitted into the London Surgical Home July 16, 1862.

History.—Is a single woman, and procures a living by dressmaking. When younger, was a nurse-maid. Catamenia commenced before she was thirteen, but she was not regular until she was nineteen, since which the function has proceeded normally both in time and quantity. Has for many years been ailing, and always had something the matter. Has suffered from intense irritation in the genital region, especially in the bladder, and she has constant pain in the back. For two years has been treated at a dispensary for an abdominal tumor; during this period she has taken much medicine, but without benefit.

On examination the abdomen was found increased in size and universally tympanitic. Under the influence of chloroform the swelling entirely subsided.

July 17. Usual operation performed under the influence of chloroform.

Sept. 2. She was discharged quite cured, all her hysterical symptoms having left her, and the tumor never having been seen since the day of operation.

CASE IX. HYSTERIA—FIVE YEARS' ILLNESS—STERILITY— OPERATION—CURE—PREGNANCY—TWO CHILDREN.

Mrs. O. came under my care in 1862. She had been ill ever since marriage, five years previously; having distaste for the society of her husband, always laid upon the sofa, and under medical treatment. Evidence of peripheral excitement being manifest, I performed my usual operation. She rapidly lost all the hysterical symptoms which had previously existed; and in about a year came up to town to consult me concerning a tumor, which greatly frightened her, as she feared it was ovarian. I discovered that she was six months pregnant. She was delivered at full time of a healthy child. In 1865 she again called on me to show herself, not only in robust health, but pregnant for the second time.

CASE X. HYSTERIA—IRRITATION OF RIGHT OVARY— MENORRHAGIA—NINE YEARS' ILLNESS— OPERATION—CURE.

C. M. A., aet. 28, single; admitted into the London Surgical Home June 22, 1863.

History.—Since the age of 19 has been more or less subject to uterine flooding; for the first three years lost blood every day. Has been five times in a metropolitan hospital; always better while there, but as bad as ever as soon as she left. The bleeding is much worse at each menstrual period. She passes large coagula; has constant pain in the back, headache, and palpitation of the heart, and cannot sleep; is dreadfully pale and anaemic.

Examination showed great irritation over right ovary, and there was evidence of long-continued peripheral irritation.

July 2. Usual operation.

July 7. Menstruation came on in a moderate flow.

July 10. Menstruation ceased; is much better, and there is sign of returning color in the face.

July 31. Has improved considerably, and had no return of the bleeding. To be discharged cured.

CASE XI. HYSTERIA—MANY YEARS' ILLNESS— OPERATION—CURE—MARRIAGE AND PROGENY.

Emma K., aet. 22, single; admitted September 16, 1863, into the London Surgical Home.

History.—Commenced menstruating at 15 years of age, but owing to the use of cold water during a period, the secretion was arrested for six months; the function was then restored, and has ever since continued normal. At 16 she suffered from piles, which occasioned very much irritation and pain after each evacuation, aggravated by constipation and by walking. Though regular as to time, there is always excessive catamenial flow, and it lasts for eight days. Has been under long and varied medical treatment, without benefit.

Examination showed peripheral irritation, as evinced by the abnormal condition of the external genitals.

Sept. 17, 1863. The usual operation performed.

Oct. 1. Progressing most favorably.

Oct. 22. Leaves quite cured.

1866. This lady married, and was delivered August, 1865, of a living child. She is still quite well.

It will have been observed that one very prominent symptom in many of the foregoing cases is sleeplessness, or, perhaps more properly, frequent wakefulness at nights, and constant restless movements in the day. These are the cases which, if left to go on, are very liable to terminate in insanity. The three following are instances in which the hysteria was verging on this state, and as they can hardly be classed under the head of insanity, I prefer narrating them here.

CASE XII. HYSTERIA—MENTAL ABERRATION, AND TENDENCY TO MELANCHOLIA—EIGHT YEARS' ILLNESS—OPERATION—CURE.

In December, 1861, a single lady consulted me, giving the following history of her illness:—

Has not been well for seven or eight years; has felt languid, and not so lively as formerly. For the last two years has menstruated every three weeks, and the flow has lasted four or five days. There is considerable white discharge from the vagina after each period, lasting for a week. Great irritation about vulva, perinaeum, and anus before and during each menstrual period. For the last five or six years had had occasional irresistible and unaccountable fits of depression; thinks that it is her mind—if her mind were as strong as her body she would be pretty well: her memory is good, but mind weak. Has suffered from great pain at lower part of the back; says she cannot rise from a chair without great difficulty, on account of a feeling of stiffness in hips and trembling of the legs (this is probably owing to a swelling of the hip-joint, as all the joints of her fingers and ankles are swollen). Says she can sit quietly to crochet or needlework, but cannot sit quietly to think, or compose her mind to write a letter: has not written a letter properly for three years. Has been subject to attacks of melancholy and weeping, without any tangible cause, but which she cannot resist. Suffers from want of sleep, and at night frequently lies awake four or five hours together. Appetite good; bowels costive.

In appearance is fresh-colored and plump, but she says she is thinner than formerly; dark eyes; large dilated pupils.

On examination there was evidence of great irritation about the vulva, and constriction of the anus, with a very small fissure.

Dec. 21. I divided the fissure, and performed my usual operation.

Dec. 31. Very much improved; swelling of the joints much less.

Jan. 1. She sat up, and feels much better. Her spirits are improved; has no pain in the joints; sleeps well. In another month she returned home quite well, and has continued so to the present time.

CASE XIII. EXTREME HYSTERIA, VERGING ON INSANITY— FIVE YEARS' ILLNESS—OPERATION—CURE.

Mrs.———, aet. 32, married; admitted into the London Surgical Home August 5, 1862.

History.—Has been married twelve years, but has had no children nor miscarriages. Has always enjoyed pretty good health until about five years ago, when she began to suffer from leucorrhoea and great pain during menstruation. Catamenia regular in time and quantity. Her bladder is so irritable that sometimes she has to pass her water every half-hour; the urine sometimes very much loaded. Suffers from headache and giddiness in the morning. Says that for the last three years the act of coition has been accomplished without the least pleasure, but with pain. Bowels are opened regularly and without pain.

August 7. Having diagnosed the cause of the disease, the usual operation was performed.

August 9. A severe attack of erysipelas came on, and she was very ill for some days, but she made a good recovery.

A few days after the operation this patient was observed to be occasionally very violent and unmanageable, and to have at these times a wild maniacal look. On questioning her husband, it appeared that for several years she had been subject to fits of violent excitement, especially during the menstrual period, and that at such times "she would fly at him and rend his skin, like a tigress."

This patient made a good recovery; she remained quite well, and became in every respect a good wife.

CASE XIV. EXTREME HYSTERIA— INCIPIENT INSANITY—OPERATION—CURE.

Mrs. R., aet. 42; admitted into the London Surgical Home Aug. 5, 1862.

History.—Has been married, but has been a widow for twelve years. Is companion to a lady. Never had any family. Has been ailing for some years, but has not suffered severely until the last six months. Suffers most from pain in the lower part of the abdomen, and from constant burning and irritation about the vulva. During the last few months has become very nervous and fidgety; never can remain quiet, and says that lately she "has had a sort of lost feeling, particularly when writing; being unable to compose her thoughts, or concentrate her mental energies." Has suffered from considerable irritability of the bladder; and her urine is often full of thick deposit. Catamenia regular in time and quantity. Cannot sleep.

On examination, is a very nervous woman, her eyes restless and never quiet; constant twitchings of the limbs, and occasionally an appearance almost of insanity about her expression. There is every evidence of a long-continued inhibitory influence.

August 7. The usual operation performed.

August 8. Feels very comfortable. Slept better last night than for some years.

August 9. Is improving wonderfully: the expression of countenance completely changed.

Sept. 9. Left quite well. Has got fat, and has now a cheerful face and manner. Says she feels a different being, and is quite astonished at her own improvement. Has lost all her nervous twitchings and other uncomfortable symptoms, and has now a comfortable night's rest.

CHAPTER IV.

SPINAL IRRITATION, WITH CASES.

There are perhaps few terms so difficult to define as spinal irritation, for the gradations from hysteria to this state are extremely easy; and, indeed, it will have been seen that in the foregoing chapter most of the patients complained of pain in the spine, and that there was more or less functional disturbance in all of them. The term is also used so freely and vaguely that great caution is necessary in attempting to explain its meaning. Dr. Handfield Jones's term, "Spinal Paresis," seems to me an excellent one; by it he means "a state in which, without demonstrable organic change, there is greater or less enfeeblement of the functional power" of the spinal cord. The sensory or motor power may be affected, but rarely both together.

The cause of spinal irritation, or paresis, may be defined in one word—"debility;" this debility always, or almost always, being due to inhibitory irritation.

This state of things may give rise to wide and varied disorders, all the symptoms of which are asthenic in their character, and all of which are marked by extreme nervous prostration.

Without doubt,—for all authors agree on this point, one of the most prominent causes is peripheral irritation of the pudic nerve, producing undue exhaustion.

It is difficult to say how this is produced, but most probably it is that, "owing to the intimate commissural connections between the lumbar enlargement of the cord, where the pudic nerves are implanted (they themselves being small and remote in their origin from the brain); and the superior and nobler nervous centers, the intense excitation of even a small and remote center is communicated to the others, which, as this subsides, fall as much below, as they have previously been stimulated above par. The depression is proportional to the previous excitement."

The cases I shall have to relate which may fairly be called cases of spinal irritation are few in number, for the reason I have stated, that they are but a continuation of hysteria, and, indeed, but a state of things of which epileptiform and epileptic fits are the direct sequence.

It is, however, well to draw attention to the fact that it is in cases of spinal irritation that we observe functional derangements, which are very likely to pass into actual organic diseases; and it is in this class of cases, which are essentially of a chronic character, that very long and persistent perseverance must be pursued. I would, therefore, advise all who meet with them to warn their patients beforehand that they must not be weary and faint-hearted if recovery does not come as soon as hoped for.

CASE XV. SPINAL IRRITATION, AND SUPPOSED UTERINE DISPLACEMENT—SIX YEARS' ILLNESS— OPERATION—CURE.

In 1860, I was requested to see a young lady, aet. 20, of whom I had the following history:—For six years she had been confined to a spinal couch, and had also been supposed to suffer from retroversion of the uterus. She had worn a spinal apparatus, attached to which was a steel spring, pressing on sacrum and pubis, and intended "to support the perinaeum, and keep the uterus in position." Had been treated with caustics and other therapeutic agents for uterine disease. I found the uterus normal in position and healthy in appearance; but on further questioning and examination, I diagnosed peripheral irritation of the pudic nerve. My opinion was strongly contested, as I was told that the young lady was very religious; but, as I explained, her illness was to be attributed solely to a physical condition, and was not at all necessarily immoral; I was then met with the objection that, in the event of marriage, my operation might interfere with marital happiness and prevent procreation. I explained how, physiologically, these objections were untenable, but was then unable to adduce actual cases in contradiction of them.

Ultimately I performed my operation in the usual manner. For want of proper attention on the part of the nurse, the dressing was three times displaced; but, nevertheless, at the end of a month this lady was well enough to walk three miles.

Up to this date she has remained quite well.

CASE XVI. DYSMENORRHOEA—FIVE YEARS' ILLNESS—OPERATION—CURE.

D. A., aet. 23; admitted into the London Surgical Home Aug. 4, 1863.

History.—Has never been very strong; but five years ago had an attack of gastric fever. Since then has suffered constantly from great pain during the menstrual period. Occasionally loses a great deal, and passes large clots of blood. During this time has suffered almost constantly from leucorrhoea. Suffers severely from pain over region of left ovary and in the spine. Is hardly ever free from headaches. Is very restless; never sleeps well; frequently faints; and has little or no appetite. All her ills are exaggerated at the menstrual epoch.

August 7. Usual operation performed.

Sept. 1. Is menstruating without pain.

Sept. 30. Again menstruating without pain, and in normal quantity. Is to be discharged cured.

CASE XVII. SPINAL IRRITATION AND LOSS OF USE OF RIGHT LEG—FIVE YEARS' ILLNESS— OPERATION—CURE.

M. B., aet. 30, single; admitted into the London Surgical Home Nov. 15, 1861.

History.—Five years ago first began to suffer pain in the right leg, which was ascribed to sciatica. Fourteen months since this pain became so bad that she could not walk, and she lost all use of her right leg, at the same time felt great weakness and pain in the back, preventing her sitting. For eight months has been confined to a spinal couch. Is a spare anaemic woman; dark hair and eyes; dilated pupils; very restless and nervous in her movements, and of a very irritable temper. Has suffered from peripheral irritation since an early age.

Nov. 26, 1861. Usual operation performed.

Dec. 27. She has gradually improved in health and temper since the operation, and is now quite able to walk about her room without help.

She was a long time before her nerve tone was thoroughly restored, but she ultimately got quite strong and continues well.

CASE XVIII. HYSTERIA AND SPINAL IRRITATION TWELVE YEARS—FISSURE OF RECTUM, RECENT DURATION—OPERATION—CURE.

R. C. R., aet. 35 years, single; admitted into the London Surgical Home April 15, 1861.

History.—Has been suffering for nearly twelve years, at intervals of from six months to six weeks, with pain in the womb and right side, sudden spasms of the limbs, coming on at frequent and irregular intervals. Great pain down the spine and lower part of the back and loins. Has often attacks of severe sickness. Is usually costive. Has lately suffered great pain in defecation. Catamenia regular. Great want of sleep and appetite. Says she is always low-spirited, moping, and listless. Has had much medical treatment.

On examination there was found evidence of peripheral excitement of the pudic nerve, and there also existed a fissure of the rectum.

April 18. The usual operation performed, and the fissure of the rectum incised.

After this time defecation was performed without pain. Sleep, appetite, and cheerful spirits returned. She had no more spasmodic twitchings, but she still complained of intense pain in the back on sitting and walking. She was discharged in June much relieved, but not well.

Nov. 9, 1861. I received a letter from this lady, stating that she now suffered no pain and was perfectly well. She was stout, and better in every respect than she had been for the last twelve years.

CASE XIX. MENORRHAGIA—MENTAL DELUSION— TWO YEARS' ILLNESS—OPERATION—CURE— SUBSEQUENT MARRIAGE AND PROGENY.

A young lady, aet. 20, came under my care in 1863, having for two years past suffered from almost constant menorrhagia, during which time she had suffered great irritability of temper, been disobedient to her mother's wishes, and had sleepless nights, restless desire for society, and was constantly seeking admiration; all these symptoms culminating in a monomania that every gentleman she admired was in love with her, and she insisted on always sending her *carte de visite* to her favored one for the time being. In her quieter moments she would spend much time in serious reading. On being consulted, I quickly discovered that all these symptoms arose from peripheral excitement, and that there existed no organic disease to cause the menorrhagia. The usual plan of treatment was followed with the most rapid and marked success. She went the full interval between the ensuing menstrual periods, and the secretion was normal in quantity. All her delusions disappeared, and after three or four months of careful watching, with change of air, she was perfectly well in every respect. A year afterwards she married, and ten months later gave birth to a healthy son. She is now again pregnant.

CASE XX. SPINAL IRRITATION, GIVING RISE TO MENORRHAGIA AND AMAUROSIS— OPERATION—CURE.

A single lady, aet. 35, came under my care in 1863. Had been out of health for some years, suffering from continuous menorrhagia, seldom being free more than ten days or a fortnight in the month. Was thin and spare in appearance; often complaining of headache, especially over the brow and orbits; and, in fact, nearly a confirmed invalid. Latterly she had become almost blind from amaurosis; she could only read the largest type, and not at all by candlelight. Had come to London from the country, and placed herself under the care of one of the most eminent ophthalmic surgeons, who had treated her for three months without the slightest benefit. When I saw her I immediately discovered that long-continued peripheral excitement had caused all her disorders. Quickly after the operation, menstruation became regular; in ten days she was able to read in bed; in a month she was quite well. I frequently hear of her now, as in robust health.

Remarks.—Beyond a grain of opium after the operation, this patient never had any medicine. I have had other cases exactly similar, with like result.

CASE XXI. SPINAL IRRITATION—LOSS OF POWER IN LOWER EXTREMITIES—OPERATION— RAPID IMPROVEMENT.

Last year I was requested to see a lady, aet. 46, who had been married to a second husband seventeen years without issue, but had two children by her first marriage. Had not menstruated for two years. Has been in ill health for many years, and undergone a variety of medical treatment without benefit. In May, 1863, first began to lose the power of her legs, and to suffer from attacks of pain in the back, shooting up to the spine. She was at this time in Paris, where she consulted several men of eminence, and was treated for uterine disease, but still without benefit. She returned to London in June, 1863, and placed herself under the care of her usual medical attendant. Relief, after some time, not being afforded, she consulted several eminent surgeons in the metropolis. She was told that she had paralysis of the lower extremities, and that nothing could be done with a hope of effecting cure. From January, 1865, she was for six months under the care of an eminent general practitioner, who exhausted the resources of his art, but in vain. She was, in fact, "given up."

As a last resource, I was applied to. I saw her in August at her own house. Her countenance had a worn and haggard expression; her body was emaciated; skin harsh, dry, and scaly; the lower extremities hung as if paralyzed, but sensibility and voluntary motion—the latter, however, very weak—were not entirely absent. She complained of severe spasmodic attacks of agonizing pain shooting up the spine, like tetanic shocks. Her appetite was very defective, digestion was impaired, the bowels disordered, and sleep was hardly ever procured. There was also partial ptosis of the left upper eyelid. On examination, I found a deep and acutely painful fissure, with large piles and loose skin around the anus, and all the well-marked signs of peripheral irritation of the clitoris.

August, 1865. I operated, Dr. Kidd administering chloroform. I divided the fissure, tied the piles with three ligatures, cut off the loose skin around the anus, and removed the clitoris and elongated labia in my usual manner.

It was gratifying to observe the early relief of her more severe symptoms; by the third day the spasmodic attacks ceased, little or no pain was complained of, and the improvement of the digestive system was most marked, the patient enjoying chops, game, &c., within ten days, and no longer "a martyr to flatulence and dyspepsia." The digestion was, however, easily deranged, and great care was necessary. At the end of seven weeks, having already on several occasions been driven out in a carriage, she was removed to the country, where she remained for three weeks. It may be here stated that the patient suffered much from the very sultry weather of September, and that improvement was much more rapid when colder weather set in. On her return, she was able to stand for a few minutes with her hands resting on the shoulders of another. Remaining in town for some weeks, she again left for the sea-side, where she stayed about three weeks, and returned to town in the beginning of this year. Her condition is now as follows:—

She looks remarkably well in the face, which has entirely lost its expression of suffering. She is free from pain. Sensibility in the lower extremities is perfect; their muscular power is greatly improved. She can raise herself from a chair so as to rest on her hands and feet, and is able to walk across her room, holding the hands of her maid, who retreats before her. She sleeps well every night, and her digestion is in very fair order. She is now able to sit up to all her meals, and to sit in an upright chair for hours together, whereas formerly she was constantly in the recumbent position.

CHAPTER V.

EPILEPTOID CONVULSIONS, OR HYSTERICAL EPILEPSY, WITH CASES.

In the chapter on hysteria, cases have been recorded of frequent faintings, without spasms, and of spasmodic twitchings of limbs without fainting, *i.e.*, without loss of consciousness. We now come to cases more marked and chronic, and having many of the characters of epilepsy. They may be brought to us by the friends of the patient as genuine epileptics. The diagnosis is in some cases difficult, but for the most part easy. Dr. Russell Reynolds has summed up the distinctive features so ably that I cannot do better than quote his final remarks on this subject:—

"The paroxysm resembles epilepsy, and sometimes closely, but it differs in essential particulars. The difference is not one only of degree, neither is it to be determined by the relation of hysterical convulsion to pain, nor solely by the nature of the spasm. The diagnosis is to be based upon a combination of features. The paroxysms follow hysteric prodomata. At their onset there is constriction of the throat and epigastrium; there are plaintive cries, sobbings, or laughings, which reappear at the close; *sensibility, perception, and volition are rarely, if ever, completely lost;* the face undergoes little change; there is a twinkling movement of the eyelids; there is no marked dilatation of the pupil; *there is rarely foaming or bitten tongue;* the attacks are of long duration; respiratory movements are disorderly, but there are no evidences of marked asphyxia; the pulse is small; there is no stupor, but only general exhaustion after the attack; and although the paroxysms may recur for many years, and be followed by a peculiar kind of mania, they are rarely followed by dementia."

I fully agree with Dr. Reynolds that what are called the "diagnostic signs of hysteria," as frequent micturition of clear pale urine, tympanitis, nausea, &c., have no value in aiding our inquiry as to the nature of these fits: they may be witnessed, and with as great frequency, after epileptic seizures.

One practical point exists; namely, that in hysterical epilepsy the patient seldom, I believe never, in falling hurts herself, whereas true epileptics frequently suffer considerable bodily injuries.

CASE XXII. NINE YEARS' ILLNESS—EPILEPTIFORM ATTACKS—THREE YEARS' DURATION— OPERATION—CURE.

G. M., single; admitted into the London Surgical Home December 18, 1860.

History.—For the last nine years has suffered greatly and regularly during the menstrual periods. Has been much worse for the last three years, during which time has, at each menstrual period, been frequently taken in a fit, dropping down suddenly and fainting right off; this state lasting for two or three hours. Being in service, this has caused her much trouble, as none of her employers would keep her. For the last six months has suffered severe pain over right ovary, increased by exercise or pressure, and at the menstrual period. Believing that the dysmenorrhoea and fits both arose from the same cause, on January 3, clitoris was cut down to the base. After this operation she never had a fit, and all untoward symptoms left her except the dysmenorrhoea; she was therefore re-admitted May 27, 1861, and there being some narrowing of the cervix, it was incised with the hysterotome. June 21, catamenia came on without pain, and continued to do so regularly. In July she was well enough to return to service.

April, 1865. Her mother called at my house to say that this patient had been married some months, and was shortly expecting her confinement. She had remained quite well since the operation.

CASE XXIII. EPILEPTOID FITS—FIFTEEN YEARS— ILLNESS FOR TWENTY-SIX YEARS— OPERATION—CURE.

F. A. C., aet. 41, single; admitted into the London Surgical Home Nov. 6, 1863.

History.—Says she had congestion of the brain fifteen years ago; since that period cannot remember being well, but from the age of fifteen has been of delicate health. Has suffered from fits for the last fourteen or fifteen years; is never long free from them. During an attack she is not entirely unconscious, but possesses no power to control them nor to speak. Has pain at lower part of spine of a gnawing character. She is a miserable, nervous creature, with pinched features and a wandering restless expression of the eye. There is evidence of injurious peripheral irritation since a very early age.

Nov. 12. Operation as usual under chloroform.

Nov. 19. Is wonderfully better. The expression of her face is much happier, and the face itself has filled out considerably. No pain in the back since the operation.

Dec. 24. Discharged perfectly cured.

CASE XXIV. HYSTERICAL EPILEPSY—LONG DURATION— OPERATION—CURE.

G. C., aet. 25; admitted into the London Surgical Home Jan. 28, 1864.

History.—Has been delicate from childhood. For some months has suffered from a peculiar dragging pain in the lower part of the abdomen. Menstruates regularly. Suffers from "burning" and irritability of bladder. Has constant and severe headache. Has for a long time suffered from "epileptic fits" (on careful observation they were found not to be genuine epileptic), occurring twice or thrice a week. Is a melancholy object, with "woe-begone" expression; listless and indifferent to conversation and surrounding objects; when spoken to, does not answer rationally, and frequently only in monosyllables. Is very reserved and taciturn.

Feb. 4. Patient being under chloroform, the clitoris was excised.

Feb. 13. Progressing favorably; much improved in appearance; more cheerful; converses freely and rationally; expresses herself as grateful for her restoration to health.

March 1. Having had no return of the fits, and lost all her hysterical symptoms, she was discharged cured.

CASE XXV. HYSTERIA AND EPILEPTIFORM ATTACK— MANY YEARS' ILLNESS—OPERATION—CURE.

R. D., aet. 31; admitted into the London Surgical Home Feb. 17, 1864.

History.—Married eight years, with one child. Her husband is in the navy, and often absent from home. Previous to her marriage had a severe illness, in which she was delirious, and again in 1860, when she lost her reason for six weeks. "Was very feverish and could retain no food on the stomach." The menstrual periods are most irregular, six or eight months sometimes elapsing between each appearance. Has not menstruated since June last. Has great difficulty in passing her urine. For many years has suffered from fits of an epileptiform character, having, in an attack, convulsions and rigidity, but never hurting herself in falling, foaming at the mouth, nor biting her tongue.

Feb. 18. Clitoris excised.

Feb. 24. Much improved, free from pain or difficulty in micturition. Is quite cheerful, and has had no attack since the operation.

March 26. Still gaining strength, looks much better, and says she now feels well.

March 28. Discharged cured.

CASE XXVI. EPILEPTIFORM FITS AND GENERAL HYSTERIA—FOUR YEARS' DURATION— OPERATION—CURE.

Mrs. F., aet. 44; admitted into the London Surgical Home April 23, 1864.

History.—Married sixteen years, but her husband has been abroad for the past seven years. Had inflammation of the womb four years ago, and since that time has continually suffered from bearing-down pains. Frequent desire to micturate. Pain in the loins and spine, sleepless nights, loss of appetite, and other hysterical symptoms. Has slight "epileptic fits" two or three times a week, more frequently at catamenial periods, which are regular in appearance and not profuse. Has no premonition of fits; is but partially conscious; at first struggles, then becomes rather rigid, and on recovery is always exhausted. Patient is most anxious to be cured of her attacks, of the cause of which she is fully conscious.

April 25. Clitoris excised, under chloroform.

April 26. Had a good night, better than for years.

April 30. Progressing most favorably. Patient expresses great gratitude for the relief she has obtained. She left the Home a month later looking and feeling quite well; the last note in the case-book being "a very grateful patient."

CASE XXVII. EPILEPTIFORM FITS— SIX YEARS' DURATION— OPERATION—CURE.

F. W., aet. 33, single; admitted into the London Surgical Home May 23, 1864.

History.—Has suffered from fits for more than six years, much more frequently the last six months; having now as many as four or five during the day—always one or two. The fits vary in length from one to three hours' duration. Is conscious during the attacks, but unable to speak, or in any way to control them. Is invariably worse during the menstrual periods. Suffers from palpitation of the heart.

Examination showed a highly inflamed and sensitive condition of the external generative organs; the patient herself confirmed my opinion of the cause of her attacks.

May 28. Clitoris excised—free haemorrhage allowed before the dressings were applied.

June 12. Left her bed today; has had no fit since the operation, and says she feels well.

June 20. Takes daily exercise, is free from pain, the wound is healed, and her health daily improving. Action of the heart much more moderate.

July 19. Discharged cured, not having had one hysterical attack since the operation.

CASE XXVIII. HYSTERICAL EPILEPSY—
THREE YEARS AND A HALF DURATION—
OPERATION—CURE.

C. E. S., aet. 24, single; admitted into the London Surgical Home Oct. 17, 1864.

History.—Has been ill for about three years and a half, suffering frequently from an aggravated form of hysterical attacks, with many of the characters of epilepsy, but with only partial insensibility, and without foaming. Is often sick, and suffers from severe pain on the right side, with a feeling of pressure on the lower bowel, with a dragging and bearing-down pain around the loins. Catamenia regular; more subject to the fits at these periods. No difficulty in micturition, but a rather frequent desire to micturate; and urine often loaded.

Oct. 20. The clitoris was excised.

This patient improved very rapidly; passed upwards of a month and a menstrual period in the Home without any return of the fits. All pain over the ovarian regions, and in the loins, &c., left her, and she was discharged Nov. 26, perfectly cured.

CHAPTER VI.

CATALEPSY, WITH CASES.

This affection is extremely rare, and I consider myself favored in having witnessed three well-marked cases. "It occurs chiefly," says Dr. Jones, "in those who have weakly and excitable nervous systems, feeble health, and ill-governed minds, and who may be said to possess neither a 'mens sana,' nor a 'corpus sanum.' " That this is true there is not the least doubt, and the first case—one of semi-catalepsy, or hysterical catalepsy—shows how completely it is a nervous affection, and depending, at any rate at the commencement of the disease, very much on mental control.

There are also, it is true, one or two rare cases on record which were caused by growths on the brain; and it is sometimes "encountered in tubercular meningitis, or chronic softening of the brain." —*Reynolds.*

That the cause in the three cases in my own practice was excitation of the pudic nerve may, I think, most fairly be concluded from the fact that after the operation neither patient had a single fit.

To those who have not seen a patient suffering from this disease, a few words from Dr. Reynolds may be necessary:—

"The pathognomonic symptom is the persistence of the limbs in a state of balanced muscular contraction, so that they retain the position in which they were placed at the commencement of the attack. The limbs may be readily moved by the observer, but they retain the attitudes in which they are left, and these sometimes for hours, sometimes for days.

"Perception and volition are lost; the condition resembles that of 'brown study;' the circulation and respiration are uninterrupted."

Catalepsy seems to rank between tetanus and epilepsy, and, according to Dr. Jones, depends on the simultaneous morbid affection of various nerve centers which, when separately affected, produce but one disorder,—hysteria, tetanus, or epilepsy.

CASE XXIX. HYSTERICAL CATALEPSY—MANY YEARS' DURATION—OPERATION—RELIEF—REMARKS.

Mrs. ———, aet. 33, widow; admitted into the London Surgical Home May 5, 1865.

History.—Never had any children, and but one miscarriage. Menstruation began when she was fourteen, and she was then first attacked with fits. From the patient's description, they would seem to have then been of a cataleptic character; there was no loss of consciousness. From the age of 21 up to the present time, besides slight convulsive attacks in the daytime, she has been subject to fits at night, occurring irregularly, but averaging one a week, and always after each menstrual period. They commence with a strong convulsion, which lasts for a few minutes, and is succeeded by perfect rigidity of the body and unconsciousness for half an hour or more. Are preceded by headache during the day. Catamenia appear regularly, but are scanty. Acknowledges constant peripheral excitation, and says that, during marriage, she never had pleasure *in coitu*. The dilated pupil, hot skin, moist palm, and other unmistakable symptoms, plainly pointed to the cause of her disorder.

May 6. Excision of clitoris and the very elongated nymphae. Free haemorrhage was allowed before the wound was dressed.

The operation was, in this instance, only successful in diminishing the frequency and intensity of the fits. The following is the description given by the house-surgeon of an attack some days after the operation:—

"While conversing with the house-surgeon this morning, she had a slight convulsive attack, not lasting more than thirty seconds, and characterized by the following phenomena:—No loss of consciousness, rigidity of limbs, with tonic contraction of the flexor muscles, and strong contraction of the orbicularis palpebrarum."

Whenever visited, and frequently when the wound was dressed, these fits recurred; but towards the end of the month the number considerably diminished.

She was discharged on June 15th, very much improved in health, and decidedly relieved by the operation.

CASE XXX. HYSTERICAL CATALEPTIC FITS OF LONG DURATION—OPERATION—CURE.

H. L., aet. 25, single; admitted into the London Surgical Home January 27, 1864.

History.—This patient was sent to me by Dr. Pennefather, of Tottenham, with the following letter:—

"Dear Sir,—The girl———was some time since suffering from religious monomania; she is of hysterical habit and weak constitution, ever complaining of abdominal pain or uneasiness."

She also gave the following additional account of herself:—

"Began to feel unwell about twelve months since. Had a very bad fever about five months ago, which left her perfectly prostrated. Always felt weak, and more or less subject to fits. Menstruation regular and never profuse. Great pain in the back and bearing-down feeling in the lower part of the body. Complains of great pain in defecation. Sea-bathing has benefited her temporarily. Is incessantly crying without cause or power to prevent herself."

The day following admission she had a fit of a cataleptic nature, and lasting twenty-five minutes. After the fit the patient was left very prostrated.

In addition to symptoms of pudic irritation, there was a small fissure of the rectum.

January 24. Clitoris excised, and fissure divided. There was considerable secondary haemorrhage in the excising, which, however, seemed to have a beneficial effect, as after it the patient expressed herself as more comfortable, and slept quietly.

Feb. 14. Much more cheerful; has had no cataleptic attack or symptom of hysteria since the operation.

Feb. 28. Has improved daily, and leaves the Home this day cured.

CASE XXXI. CATALEPTIC FITS—TWO YEARS' ILLNESS— OPERATION—CURE.

M. N., aet. 17; admitted into the London Surgical Home September 4, 1861.

History.—Was perfectly well up to the age of fifteen, when she went to a boarding-school in the West of England. In the course of three or four months she became subject to all symptoms of hysteria, and from that time gradually got worse, having fits, at first mild in character and of rare occurrence, but gradually more severe and frequent, till she became a confirmed cataleptic. For several months before admission, she had been attacked with as many as four or five fits a day, and during the whole journey from the North of England to London she was unconscious and rigidly cataleptic. She was seen immediately on arrival, and there was no doubt that it was a genuine case of this disease. So sensitive was she, that if any one merely touched her bed, or walked across the room, she would immediately be thrown into the cataleptic state.

Before making any personal examination, Mr. Brown ascertained both from her mother and herself, that she had long indulged in self-excitation of the clitoris, having first been taught by a school-fellow. The commencement of her illness corresponded exactly with the origin of its cause; in fact, cause and effect were here so perfectly manifested that it hardly wanted anything more than the history to enable one to form a correct diagnosis. All the other symptoms attending these cases were, however, well marked.

The next day after admission she was operated upon, and from that date she never had a fit. She remained in the Home for several weeks. Five weeks after operation, she walked all over Westminster Abbey, whereas for quite a year and a half before treatment, she had been incapable of the slightest exertion.

CASE XXXII. CATALEPTIC FITS—MANY YEARS' DURATION—OPERATION—CURE.

In 1861 I saw a lady, aet. 50, single—a patient of Dr. Dawson, of Newcastle-on-Tyne.

She had been suffering from cataleptic attacks for several years, gradually increasing in severity. As in the previous case, the mere touching or shaking of her bed would induce an attack—indeed, the simple brushing of her dress by any one passing her when she walked out of doors, would immediately be followed by a fit. History and examination plainly confirming me in my opinion as to the cause of her attacks, the usual treatment was adopted, and from that time to this she has never had an attack.

CASE XXXIII. CATALEPTIC FITS—SIX YEARS' DURATION—OPERATION—CURE.

Miss———, aet. 38, single; admitted into the London Surgical Home August 10, 1865.

History.—Was tolerably well until two years and a half ago, but since that time has suffered more or less from menorrhagia, with severe pain in back. Has also severe smarting pain in the bowels, and has frequently lost a considerable quantity of blood *per anum.* Has always been subject to hysterical attacks, but for the last six years has had fits of a much more serious character. They have increased in severity, duration, and frequency, and it is on account of them that she seeks relief. Almost immediately after admission, this patient had a fit, and she was kept a fortnight under observation, that the nature of the attacks might be thoroughly investigated.

She would have a fit sometimes twice a day; but on an average about every other day—either early in the morning or late in the evening. She was most generally attacked when walking about the room—sometimes when sitting—but she was never observed to have one when asleep. She would at the commencement of an attack cease walking, or doing whatever she was employed in; her face would become very pale and set; the eyelids, at first quivering, would be fixed; the eyes wide open and looking upwards, the pupils very dilated. Her mouth would be rigidly shut, and during the attack it was impossible by any means to open it. Her arms would fall straight by her side, and be immovable; the hands unclenched, and fingers extended. If standing, she would be quite upright, and require no support. If sitting, she would always stand up when a fit was coming on. If lying, she would be extended straight on her back. The fit would last for two or three hours, and on a few occasions for as many as six hours. The experiment was frequently made of moving her arms when in the cataleptic state, and on such occasions the limb would remain in the position in which it was placed, till the end of the attack. She was always perfectly unconscious, and no kind of stimulant was of the slightest use in restoring her during the paroxysm—time alone was of avail. The attack was sudden, but the recovery to consciousness was but gradual; she would appear as if awoke from a deep sleep, and would be very exhausted, but express no desire for food, wine, or other stimulants. As soon as she recovered, she would sleep for many hours, and awake quite well, but still weak.

Aug. 24. The clitoris was excised, and a painful fissure of the rectum divided. She never had a fit after the operation. Menstruation came on on the 28th, in moderate flow.

Oct. 5. This patient has improved wonderfully since operation, and now looks extremely well. The wound is quite healed. She takes walks daily, and has had no fits, and is to be discharged as cured.

In November she called at the Home, to say that she was quite well, and had never had the slightest return of her former illness; she menstruates regularly and normally.

Feb., 1866. She remains well.

CHAPTER VII.

EPILEPSY, WITH CASES.

Referring my readers for full information on the pathology and history of epilepsy to Dr. Russell Reynolds's exhaustive treatise on the subject already referred to, I would mention, as shortly as possible, a few facts which are necessary to be borne in mind, with especial reference to the class of cases which I am now considering.

Dr. J. C. Prichard, in writing of diseases of the nervous system, has well said that "few diseases are better characterized by their symptoms than epilepsy; yet in this instance there is such a variety in the phenomena as renders it difficult to contrive a definition in a few words which may comprehend every form of the complaint."

I have said that when convulsions become chronic they are considered to take on an epileptiform character. Now, although we know that in a few cases involuntary spasm may take place in sleep, *i.e.*, with loss of consciousness, I think we may, for all general purposes, take as a definition of epilepsy a chronic convulsive disease, each convulsive attack being accompanied with "sudden and complete loss of consciousness," this latter symptom being considered by the late Dr. Todd as "the pathognomonic symptom of the disease," but only, as Dr. Reynolds has shown, "when it occurs as a paroxysmal or occasional event."

The causes of epilepsy are various—"partly physical, partly immaterial." Of the former are injuries and tumors of the brain or meninges, intestinal worms, renal and biliary calculi, &c. &c. These are termed by Dr. Handfield Jones "eccentric causes." As "centric causes," he names "poisoning of the blood from retention of excrementitious matter; this, by deranging the nutrition of the nervous tissue, generates the abnormal excitability, which then manifests itself without any special irritant. Various causes of exhaustion, such as haemorrhage and excessive discharges, venereal excesses, prolonged want of sleep, unremitting pain," &c., are all "centric" causes of epilepsy.

Dr. Reynolds is right in considering epilepsy an idiopathic disease, inasmuch as it occurs, without discoverable organic lesion with which it can be associated, and because there is no structural lesion of the brain, or spinal cord, to be found constantly associated with it; but when he says that it is idiopathic because, "in many cases, eccentric irritation cannot be shown to be the cause of the attacks," I cannot go with him. Epilepsy is a name signifying a disease, which may be idiopathic, or may arise from a variety of causes; but that eccentric irritation is a powerful and very frequent cause, there is not the slightest doubt. Dr. Reynolds classes it as second of six in a table given in his book, physical conditions being mentioned as first; and finding, in a hundred cases, that 24-63 have no assignable cause, and 18-84 are doubtful, he gives 13-04 as due to eccentric irritation.

In considering peripheral irritation of the pudic nerve as a cause of this disease, we must, I think, consider mental emotion, which occupies the highest rank in causes of epilepsy, in conjunction with that second in the list,—eccentric irritation. I would, therefore, classify the cause of epilepsy depending on such irritation as both eccentric and centric. The former, inasmuch as it produces exhaustion, and, by deranging the nutrition of the nervous tissue, generates abnormal excitability; the latter, for that it is a physical excitant which is not only "a mere provocative of the paroxysms, the convulsions being supposed to ensue as the reflex results of irritation, but that it actually *sets up* in the nervous centers that state of excitability which is the essence of the disorder." Further still, looking on epilepsy as a direct sequel of hysteria, when it is produced by excitation of the pudic nerve, the patients are, in an eminent degree, predisposed to the disease.

Women are also more naturally prone to epilepsy from mental emotion than men; "Emotional disturbance being assigned," says Dr. Reynolds, "as the cause of their attacks in so many as 36 percent, whereas in the male sex there were only 13 per cent who referred their diseases to that cause."

It would be out of place in a work of this nature to detail at length the symptoms of these attacks. Whether they are truly epileptic will be seen as the cases are related. I have been very careful to separate those which seemed to be of an hysterical or epileptoid nature; and have had the advantage of being able to show the greater number of them to many eminent members of the medical profession, who have witnessed my practice in the London Surgical Home.

CASE XXXIV. EPILEPTIC FITS—TWELVE YEARS' DURATION—OPERATION—CURE.

S. F., aet. 41, single; admitted into the London Surgical Home Dec. 16, 1861.

History.—Was always ailing, and hysterical for many years. Catamenia appeared early, and always rather profuse. For the last twelve years has suffered from epileptic fits; recurring frequently every week or fortnight, and lately as often as every day. Has constant headaches; is losing memory and all power of concentrating her ideas. Has no premonition of seizure; falls down; is unconscious; has frequently bitten her tongue; and "froths" at the mouth. Says she has had several attacks of haematemesis. She was a dressmaker, and had so frequently, on her way to or from business, fallen in the streets, that she had been carried into almost every hospital in London, and a large number of open surgeries.

On examination there was found every indication of irritation about the vulva, and also a small polypus of the os uteri, which latter was large and patulous.

Dec. 19. Usual operation of excision; polypus uteri also removed.

The recovery of this patient was rapid and uninterrupted. After the operation, she never had a fit, and hardly a headache. She was discharged Jan. 20, 1862, perfectly well, and with greatly increased mental power. When heard of at commencement of 1864, she remained well, and had had no recurrence of any of her old symptoms.

CASE XXXV. EPILEPTIC FITS—FIVE YEARS' DURATION—
PRECEDED BY CATALEPTIC FITS, DURING
THE TEN PREVIOUS YEARS—OPERATION—CURE.

In the beginning of April, 1862, a single lady, aet. 28, came under my notice, giving the following account of herself.—When about ten years old had a fit, whilst she was sitting at needlework; she fell down suddenly as if dead, and remained insensible for two hours; was very ill for three weeks after the attack. Was quite well until the age of fourteen, when she began to have them every three months. When about twenty-two had an interval of eleven months without a fit, but frequently fainted during that period. During the time she was in the fits she would be perfectly unconscious. She was told that her limbs were quite rigid, and always remained in the exact position in which they were when the fit commenced. In 1857 the fits changed in their nature—the patient at first falling down quietly, but subsequently becoming very convulsed, and trying to hurt herself. The first of this nature lasted two hours and three-quarters. Has lately had them much oftener, but not always of the severe form. Has had eight severe fits in the last two years and a half, besides the milder, which come sometimes a dozen in a fortnight. Is unconscious, but always knows when she has had one. Foams at the mouth, but makes no noise. Has frequently fallen down suddenly in church and other public places. Has been under many physicians, all of whom have been of opinion that she is suffering from genuine epilepsy.

April 2. Clitoris excised.

April 6. Has had no attack, but complains of occasional pain in the top of her head.

She never had an attack after the operation. Returned home in a month, and shortly afterwards she was thrown out of a pony chaise; she had no fit, but wrote that, prior to treatment, a very much slighter accident would have immediately produced one.

I heard of this lady later in the year; she was still quite well. Not having heard since from her, as was agreed when she left me, I am satisfied that she has had no relapse.

CASE XXXVI. EPILEPTIC FITS—MANY YEARS' DURATION—OPERATION—CURE.

N. L. M., aet. 21; admitted into the London Surgical Home May 9, 1863.

History.—Married four years and had two children; the labors have been bad, and followed by severe haemorrhage. Had aborted at six weeks, a fortnight previous to admission, and had lost a large quantity of blood. First suffered from epileptic fits at puberty; had several before marriage, and has had four or five since marriage; but has never had a fit when pregnant. Not very regular in menstruation, which is accompanied with severe pain. Has constant pain on right side of head, in back, loins, &c. Great pain in micturating and on defecation. She is always totally unconscious during the fits, and they are followed by extreme prostration. Is of melancholy aspect, excessively anaemic, and somewhat chlorotic; even the mucous membranes (of mouth especially) are blanched. The cause of her fits being diagnosed, the usual *operation* was performed May 14.

May 18. Progressing excellently.

May 20. There was great irritability of the bladder, which, however, was immediately relieved by an alkaline and henbane mixture.

May 31. Has not had any return of her bad symptoms until today, when, on being removed to a strange ward, she had a fit, not of violent character, and followed by a heavy drowsiness.

June 2. Is quite herself again.

July 4. Has left quite well in every respect, and when heard of many months later remained well.

Remarks.—The fit following on change of this patient from one ward to another where there were strangers, shows how important it is for a permanent cure, that visitors and relatives should not be allowed to excite and agitate a patient suffering from these attacks after an operation is performed, and when the mind is hardly restored to its natural balance.

CASE XXXVII. EPILEPTIC FITS—TWO YEARS' DURATION—OPERATION—CURE.

H. C., aet. 20, single; admitted into the London Surgical Home Feb. 24, 1864.

History.—About three years since, first commenced ailing. Menstruation ceased for four months, when it appeared for two days. Fifteen months then elapsed before the function was restored. Epileptic fits have been developed for about two years. The patient at the commencement of an attack is strongly convulsed, has no premonition, and is perfectly unconscious. Frequently falls when walking in the streets. Has often hurt herself in her falls, and also bitten her tongue. Has the usual symptoms of bearing-down of the womb, and pain in the loins. No pain in defecation. Bowels costive. Pain in micturition, and sometimes retention of urine, occasionally not passing any for two days.

March 3. Clitoris excised in the usual manner under chloroform. Was restless and hysterical for the first six days, when she improved daily, became cheerful, and much more intelligent. She never had another fit, and on April 13, being quite cured, was, at her own request, retained in the Home as a servant. She remained there under observation for six months, during which time she had not only no return of her former attacks, but progressively improved in health, and her menstruation became quite regular.

Since that time she has been living as cook in a family which I frequently visit, and it is therefore certain that she remains perfectly well.

CASE XXXVIII. SEVERE AND FREQUENT EPILEPTIC
FITS FOR THREE YEARS AND A HALF—
OPERATION—CURE.

C. T., aet. 21; admitted into the London Surgical Home June 23,
1864.

History.—Health always good till three years ago, when, after a
severe fright, she became very excited and had a fit. Since that time
has been continually subject to them. She never passes a day without
two or three, and frequently has as many as six, or even eight, in the
twenty-four hours. Is most subject to them at night when sleeping.
Is always suffering from headache. Her mental powers are somewhat
impaired, as she has very slight recollection of persons, or of events,
from day to day. Catamenia very irregular. Has not menstruated since
March last. Bowels costive; pulse regular and firm. Is of a sallow
complexion, with vacant and weak expression of countenance. Acknowledges great and constant irritation of pudic nerve.

During the day previous to operation, special notice was taken
of the nature of the fits. They are epileptic; for although she does
not foam at the mouth, she has, on more than one occasion, *bitten
her tongue*, and is *perfectly unconscious*. There is no rigidity, but a constant struggling, and, unless restrained, the hands always, during an
attack, are carried to the seat of irritation.

June 23. The usual operation of excision was performed under
chloroform. As soon as she recovered, she managed to remove the
dressings. Haemorrhage for two hours was the result. When arrested,
two grains of opium were administered, which produced sleep. On
awaking, she again endeavored to remove the dressings; but, her
hands being confined, she was unable to do so. She had no more fits,
and but a few hysterical attacks. On July 17th she was discharged, as
her parents were anxious for her return. She had not then had a fit
of any kind for sixteen days.

August 15. I received the following letter from her father:—

"Dear Sir,—It would be very unkind in me, and much out of
place, to hide from you and the world at large what have been my
feelings during the past three weeks. My daughter, C. T., came to
your Home, Stanley Terrace, Notting Hill, on the 23rd of June last,
to be treated by you for epilepsy, or epileptic fits, having been af-

flicted for three years and a half. The class of fit you may better judge of than myself; sufficient to say, they were very bad and very frequent. I am happy to say, and acquaint you, that since her return she has not had a single symptom of fit or hysteria of any kind. Her general health is also very good, and fast improving, and I do hope, by the blessing of God, she may continue so. If you have any desire to see her, I shall feel in duty bound to let her wait upon you, with her mother, at any time you may think fit to appoint, as your opinion just at this time might have a still more happy effect for the future. You are quite at liberty to use this for the benefit of the Institution in whatever way you may like or seem good."

A twelvemonth later, this patient was still free from any return of the fits.

CASE XXXIX. EPILEPSY, WITH DEMENTIA—ONE YEAR'S DURATION—OPERATION—CURE.

A. H., aet. 17; admitted into the London Surgical Home June 28, 1864.

History.—Catamenia first appeared three years ago. They have continued regular to the present time. About twelve months since was observed, whenever sent on an errand from home, that she would wander about in an absent manner, and return home having forgotten all about any message which had been given her. About this time fits were first developed; they increased in frequency and intensity, and she now has them daily, and one or more of less violent character nearly every night in her sleep. When seized, she falls, struggles violently, foams at the mouth, often bites her tongue, and is totally unconscious to all around her. After a fit, she sinks into a deep sleep, which lasts for two hours. Has no recollection on awaking of what has taken place. Acknowledges to frequent injurious habits, but is unconscious of their being the cause of her illness. Is vague in all her ideas and conversation, and has almost entirely lost her memory.

Both history and personal examination plainly showed what was the cause of her attacks.

On July 7 the clitoris was completely excised. She had no return of the fits; and on the 23rd the following report appears in the case book:—"Left her bed today. Is greatly changed; quite rational in all her movements; converses freely and quietly, remembers passing events from day to day, and it is indeed almost impossible to recognize in her the half-idiotic, almost demented girl who entered the Home less than a month ago."

She remained in the Home some time longer for observation. Fits never returned; her mind improved daily, and she was discharged as perfectly cured.

CASE XL. EPILEPTIC FITS—TWO YEARS AND A HALF DURATION—OPERATION—RELIEF.

S. Z., aet. 16, single; admitted into the London Surgical Home October 20, 1865.

History.—Was strong and well until two and a half years ago, when she had an epileptic fit in the middle of the night. Can assign no cause for the attack. For a long time had a fit once a month, but lately once a week. The catamenia appeared six months before the first fit, and have always been regular. There is no exacerbation at menstrual epoch. Complains of great irritation of pudendals for three years.

Nov. 2. Since admission this patient has been watched: she has had two fits, both of a genuine epileptic character.

Mr. Brown this day performed his usual operation. She went on well till the 10th, when she had a slight fit; there being irresistible irritation, the hands were restrained. A lotion of bromide of ammonium was ordered to be applied to the wound, and 20 grains of the bromide to be given in water three times daily.

She convalesced well, and had no more attacks till the 29th, when, her hands having been released only a few minutes previously, she had a fit, and the nurse found one hand on the wound. She was conscious during the attack, which was not so violent as before treatment.

Dec. 2. Discharged relieved. If this patient could be under control for a few months, she would probably be cured.

CASE XLI. EPILEPTIC FITS, WITH DEMENTIA— THIRTY YEARS' DURATION— OPERATION—CURE.

M. F., aet. 44, single; admitted into the London Surgical Home December 8, 1865.

History.—Epileptic fits first attacked her when she was about 14, at which age she menstruated. For the first few years there was a long interval between each, but they gradually became more frequent and violent. Latterly she has had several during the week of each menstrual period, and as a rule none in the interval. Catamenia have been tolerably regular in appearance, but rather profuse. Is tall, pale, and thin; has a dull and somewhat vacant expression; is very eccentric in her manners and conversation; is frequently observed, both day and night, by the nurses to practice injurious habits, to which she acknowledges for the last thirty years. The fits are genuine epileptic.

On examination, there is evidence of very long-continued peripheral irritation, and also a fissure of rectum.

Dec. 12. The usual operation on clitoris and rectum.

Dec. 13. In the absence of nurse, removed the dressing, and immediately had a fit. To have opium 1 grain, with ¼ grain of extract of belladonna, every six hours.

Under this treatment the patient improved daily, became cheerful, rational, tractable, and much more sensible in her conversation.

She passed two menstrual epochs, but without a fit, and she was discharged perfectly cured.

I have a much larger number of cases occurring in private practice, but, for that reason, am obliged to omit them. I shall, however, when a longer time has elapsed, publish them.

CHAPTER VIII.

IDIOTCY AND INSANITY, WITH CASES.

It will be recollected how, at the end of the chapter on Hysteria, I gave three cases of extreme nervous irritability, with sleeplessness, and tendency to an unhinging of the mental equilibrium. We now come to insanity itself. It would be vain to talk of the varieties of forms in which this state may be seen, when produced by abnormal peripheral irritation of the pudic nerve. It is, however, worthy of notice how each history seems to tell its own explanation of the cause; and after the first few days of treatment, when excitement, caused by irritation from the wound and a natural repugnance to restraint, has passed off, how rapid is the improvement, and how permanent is the result. I have no hesitation in saying that in no case am I so certain of a permanent cure as in acute nympho-mania; for I have never after my treatment seen a recurrence of the disease, whereas, under medical treatment, of how short duration is but too frequently the benefit.

CASE XLIII. INCIPIENT SUICIDAL MANIA— MANY YEARS' GRADUAL ILLNESS— OPERATION—CURE.

R. T., aet. 39, single; admitted into the London Surgical Home Oct. 22, 1861.

History.—Has been ailing for many years, and given great trouble and anxiety to her friends. For some time past she has been very strange in her manner, very restless, never quiet, constantly wakeful, threatening suicide, talking to people, even perfect strangers, of her ailments and their causes, of which she is fully conscious. Was formerly modest and quiet.

On examination, she is a fine woman, of restless appearance and manner; eye wandering and unsteady; pupil dilated. The cause of her mental derangement being obvious, on

Oct. 24 the usual operation was performed.

The improvement in her mental and bodily health was wonderful: she gained flesh, and became cheerful and modest. She was discharged six weeks after admission.

When heard of in February, 1863, this patient continued quite well.

The first case of actual insanity that came under my care was a patient of Dr. Warren Diamond, then resident in his private asylum. I cannot do better than transcribe the account which he sent me with the following note:—

"Effra Hall, Brixton, S.

"DEAR SIR,—A month having elapsed since you gave up your patient, I forward some particulars of the case, and shall be glad to answer more fully any special time or state you would like to know more about. You will, perhaps, be able to pick

something out of this rambling account that may be interesting to you. Hoping you will excuse omissions, &c.

"Believe me, yours faithfully,

"Warren H. Diamond."

"I. Baker Brown, Esq."

CASE XLIV. SEVERAL YEARS' ILLNESS—TWO MONTHS' INSANITY—OPERATION—CURE.

"Miss E. R., aet. 34, single; no occupation, living with her friends;
hair light reddish-brown; face set and vacant, with an occasional
pained expression; eyes fixed and dull; extremities damp and cold;
stature moderate and well formed. Has for several years past been
looked on by her friends as different from others—strange and eccentric. Would go out and walk away into the country alone for miles,
and come back exhausted. When friends called, would start up and
run round the garden, or to the top of the house and back again,
giving no reason for it but that she must do it. Always exceedingly
irritable and passionate. Unless some excitement was going on, was
listless and unable to rouse herself. When at parties, was so forward
and open in her manners, that she was generally avoided by gentlemen. *Never had an offer of marriage.* Her mother died about a year
and a half ago, but she took no notice of the occurrence, and was
consequently remarked on by her friends. Since then she has been
getting more strange and peculiar. About February last, a sister told
her, in joke, that if she did not take care she would soon become a
fit subject for Dr. Diamond, little thinking how soon it would happen.
She recently made enemies of old friends, so that her brothers could
not make out why they fell off. Would sit or stand without noticing
them when they called; and asked them what they wanted that they
came to her house (she was the eldest of the family).

"I was consulted about her in the end of March, but had then none
of her previous history. She was vacant and dreamy; talked of flowers
which she called her friends; said 'people's faces were masks; that she
was quite unable to rouse or employ herself, as she was changed;' very
uncertain in appetite, going a day without her food; not sleeping at
night, and for the last few nights showing such great excitement and
passion, that her sisters were required to sit up with her.

"I recommended change along the south coast, with sea-bathing, &c. She did not improve; and the attendant informing me of a constant irritation of the vulva, lotions were used, but without benefit. Her general health and appetite improved; but not the mind. She could not sleep, and would not bear narcotics; *stimulants acted as narcotics*, but soon lost their effect.

"Bowels regular; pulse small and slow; action of heart being irritable, and not corresponding at all times to the power or quantity of the pulse. She sits up in bed, nursing the pillow, and talking to it as if it were a baby; says 'that she died last Sunday'—'is lost'—'is buried.'

"When out of doors, great difficulty is experienced in getting her in again; she wishes to wander away, without aim or purpose. Having given my opinion to her friends, I was authorized to admit her April 18, 1861. Before she left home, she continued calling out, 'Take me to a mad-house! take me quick, or I shall never get well!' She persisted in saying 'she was dead,' and 'she felt buried.' Answers in monosyllables. Her pupil is contracted and fixed. At night she does not sleep, and is in such a continual state of excitement that the attendant cannot sleep with her. Has lost all natural modesty in manner and speech. Is not blasphemous. Before me is perfectly reserved and correct in her manner. When I ask questions, she will, after a pause, answer in monosyllables, or repeat the question over and over again, as if trying to grasp the meaning and ally her thoughts. Unless walked about, will stand for hours in one place, gaping, yawning, and throwing her arms about listlessly. She was in this state when you saw her, and from what you told me of your experience of the operation and its results, I was led to infer relief from it in this case, as the delusion of having died on a certain day was movable and could be reasoned away; but the heavy oppressed feeling still made her say, 'But if I am not dead, I am lost, or changed,' and naturally led back to the idea. I ascribed the state of her mind to weakening of the body, and general nervous irritation caused by long-continued reflex excitation; and I believed that if the source of irritation could be removed, her mental health would follow as her blood became healthy, and fit to make reparation.

"I was led to think more of her uterine state from her expression of pain when she was walked about, and she was reported by the nurse as always complaining of her back, at the lower part, and of great tenderness on pressure over the ovaries.

"May 27, 1861. You operated on her, she being under the influence of chloroform. She was naturally restless afterwards, not understanding why she was kept in bed. Profuse menstruation came on in the evening, which had not happened for four months previously, and then always very scanty and with much pain. Half an ounce of laudanum, with oil, was rubbed into her chest during four hours; she did not, however, sleep, but continued moaning all night.

"May 28. Easier, and more herself—takes her food.

"May 29. Slept well last night, without opiates; says she shall now get well and be able to go home; answers questions more readily, and makes longer replies. *Pupil dilated and acts slowly.* Her nurse says she is quite altered in every way, and compares the change in her mind since the operation to 'dividing the tightened strings of a fiddle, and letting them all loose.'

"June 2. Left her bed; is still menstruating; appears cheerful; asks questions now, and converses for short periods; has done a few stitches of needlework; says nothing about 'being lost or dead' since the operation. Surface of body and extremities warm. Freaky, anxious look about her eyes and nose gone. Laughs and jokes. Says 'she has been in a dream' 'that things now seem light,' and 'that she means to get well.'

"July 3. She has gradually improved and become more natural in her habits and ideas; sleeps soundly every night; takes her meals well; walks about without compulsion; takes a pride in making herself neat, and has washed and dressed herself ever since she left her bed; is perfectly modest in manner and conversation. Her friends remark on the great improvement in her mind, she having had no delusions. Her mental state is, however, weak—what might better be called foolish, with some amount of willful obstinacy. The family medical attendant, and, in fact, every one who has been in her company, notice the extraordinary change that has taken place in her since your operation. I think the present state of her mind results from the long-continued exhaustion, and to restore it will be a matter of time. Her pupils act naturally."

I have often since heard of this lady as perfectly well, and as never having had recurrence of illness. In 1865 I was consulted on the propriety of marriage, to which I gave my full consent.

CASE XLV. ACUTE INSANITY—TWO MONTHS—
OPERATION—CURE.

Miss————, aet. 17, moderate height, and well formed, hair light golden, grey eyes and fair complexion, came under my care June 19, 1861.

History (taken from her mother).—When ten years old, had inflammation of the womb, and after she recovered began to menstruate. The function continued regularly until about eight months ago, since when the catamenia have appeared every ten days, and, in fact, have been hardly ever absent. In the latter part of last April she left home for change of air, and returned May 15th, when her mother noticed that she was thinner than before her departure, and, on inquiry, it appeared that during the latter part of her stay she had been very excited, at other times very low, sometimes laughing and singing, and requiring port wine and brandy at all times of the day, though generally abstemious, and never taking wine or other stimuli. The first night after her return home she went to one of her sisters' rooms and began to talk of being married; did not sleep all that night.

May 17th. Was found to be rather wild in the morning; was taken out for a drive during the day; did not sleep that night, from constant excitement of the genitals. Had been seen by her ordinary medical attendant, who ordered opiates, but without the effect of giving her sleep. On the 21st, another physician saw her, and ordered opiates, but without effect, as she did not have an hour's sleep night or day.

May 22nd. An eminent authority in female diseases was called in, and also, among other remedies, ordered opiates at night-time, but with no effect. She continued raving and rambling till June 8th, when a physician, who devotes himself to mental diseases, saw her; he said that her mind was not affected, but that her behavior was caused simply by debility, and ordered wine, eggs, &c., and a *strong opiate*, but without the desired effect.

June 17. Was much worse. The last physician again saw her; said that she was quite mad, must be taken from home, and could never recover. She called her mother "Monsieur le Diable," and her father "God." She was constantly irritating her clitoris, and indulged in most immodest behavior. Was ordered ext. cannabis indicæ, and slept three hours. 19th. No better, and on this day I first saw her; she was then wild in expression of countenance, and on entering the room she addressed me as "Your Majesty," and said "I was the Queen." She also asked, "Why has your Majesty condescended to visit me?"

June 21. Before operating, the patient being under chloroform, I made an examination, and found my diagnosis verified by the existence of all the ordinary local symptoms. The hymen was quite absent. (In one of her paroxysms she had stuffed a pocket handkerchief into the vagina.) I performed my usual operation, and immediately administered two grains of opium. She passed a tolerable night, not being noisy, but not sleeping.

June 22. Tolerably quiet. Not aware of what is passing around her, but apparently comfortable. To have broth and milk diet—*no stimulants*.

June 23. Passed a quiet night; but did not sleep much, though she had a grain of opium. Dressing removed. Wound looking well.

June 24. Has not passed quite such a good night—rather noisy.

June 25. Menses came on. Has had a very bad night, and been very troublesome. Chloroform administered to insensibility several times in the course of the day. A liniment, containing seven drachms of soap liniment and one drachm of laudanum, to be rubbed in to the chest constantly. This seemed to quiet her.

June 27. Has passed a rather better night, sleeping a little; but towards morning she became very noisy, and chloroform was again administered. To have the liniment rubbed in at night.

June 28. A much better night.

June 29. Has had a very fair night; and from this time she gradually improved, sleeping well and being generally quite rational; her appetite also improved.

July 7. Menstruation occurred, and she was not so well for a day or two, as she attempted to irritate the wound; but, being carefully watched, was prevented.

July 10. Catamenia ceased. Is quiet again.

July 11. Went out in a bath chair, and said she enjoyed the airing. From this time she gradually got better, and on the 28th she went into the country for change. Her menses came on five weeks from the last appearance; she was quite quiet all the time. Since then she has menstruated regularly every three weeks, and in normal quantity.

A year after operation she had a slight relapse of melancholy, and fears were entertained that she was again going to be ill; but a brisk purgation of calomel completely dispersed all symptoms.

1866. I have frequently heard of this young lady. She is now in good health, moving in high society, and universally admired.

CASE XLVI. HYSTERICAL HOMICIDAL MANIA—
ONE YEAR'S DURATION—OPERATION—CURE.

In December, 1861, Mrs.——came under my care, by the recommendation of Dr. Forbes Winslow. She gave me the following history of herself:—

History.—She was 57, and had had four children and two premature labors. The last child was born twenty-three years ago. Twenty months since had an attack of erysipelas in the face, with eruptions on different parts of the body. Has never been well since, and last August had another attack of erysipelas. Is constantly suffering with shiverings, followed by burning heat and sweating, with prickling heat of the skin. For the last year has never slept for more than an hour; always waking with a *start*; feeling frantic, and very hot and flushed. Has a constant feeling that she will be lost eternally, and of this she is constantly speaking.

From her husband I learnt the following:—

After her last confinement, twenty-three years ago, she had puerperal mania, from which she did not completely recover for six months. About a year ago she began to show symptoms of mental derangement, first exhibited in religious subjects, she constantly declaring that her soul was irrevocably lost. About eight months ago she first tried to destroy herself, by endeavoring to jump out of the window, &c., and it was at this time thought advisable to place her in an asylum, where she was kept four months, and when she left she was for a time much better. While an inmate of the asylum, was made to take much exercise, for which her husband says she is always better.

She gradually got worse, and came under the care of Dr. Forbes Winslow, to whom I am indebted for the case. Her husband says that for the last two or three months she has slept pretty well from 10 P.M. till 2 A.M., when she would suddenly wake, and warn him that a "frenzy" was coming on. This frenzy consisted in her rising up, fighting out with her arms, and scratching or tearing any one near her; in the paroxysm the desire was always to destroy her husband. After a few minutes the mania would subside, and be succeeded, first by a kind of stupor, and then very profuse perspirations. One peculiarity about her is, that when in this state she does or says anything foolish, she knows it, and is afterwards very annoyed and ashamed of her conduct. She has a great fear that she will be permanently mad.

The appetite has always been good, though she has said lately that she cannot bear food, and that it always causes a horrid taste in her mouth. She has, in a desultory manner, read many medical works, and fancies that every one of her organs is in some way or other diseased.

On examination, she had the appearance of a woman about 60. Her eyes, of a dark grey, were never quiet, and could not look you straight in the face; the pupil was much and constantly dilated. The tongue quite clean, and pulse good. Heart, lungs, and other organs seemed to be healthy. She owned with great shame to long-continued pernicious habits.

Dec. 14. I performed my usual operation.

Dec. 21. Has very much improved, and had no "frenzies" since the operation; sleeps well, and for many hours, but will not own to being better. Complains of her skin being dry, and "burning hot." It is, however, moist and cool; at times she perspires freely.

Dec. 26. Both husband and nurse consider her much improved. She has been up both yesterday and today; sleeps and eats well. She is, however, sulky; says she is very bad, and shall soon die.

A fortnight later she was quite well, being entirely free since the operation from maniacal attacks; but she complained to my son, Mr. Boyer Brown, that I had unsexed her. He answered that nothing of the sort had been done, but that the operation had prevented her from making herself ill. From this time she steadily improved, and walked out with her husband every day, who called on me many weeks later to express his gratitude for the complete restoration of his wife to health; for whereas before his nights were passed in constant fear, rendering his life most wretched, his home was now one of comfort and happiness both night and day.

CASE XLVII. ACUTE HYSTERICAL MANIA— FOUR MONTHS' DURATION—OPERATION—CURE.

Miss ———, aet. 23, was sent to me by Mr. Radcliffe, stating that she had been brought over from Ireland as an insane patient, and that everything had been settled for her admission to some asylum, when he was induced to consult me on the last day before her entering one.

He stated that the paroxysms always came on at half-past five or six every evening: I replied, if the attacks depended on peripheral irritation, that an operation would at once prevent recurrence of the attacks. She was accordingly admitted into the London Surgical Home Feb. 6, 1864.

When admitted, said she had taken no food for three days, and asked for a cup of tea, which was given her. Enema was also administered.

3:45 P.M. Was seized with a fit, throwing her arms up over her head, and then appearing as if comatose. In about twenty minutes revived: the lips began to quiver, and she gradually became conscious, saying, "I want a knife—I want blood!" She asked for the matron's hand, that she might bite it off.

[The fit coming on earlier on this day was doubtless due to excitement consequent on her removal.]

5 P.M. Mr. Baker Brown saw her; as soon as he came near her, she seized his shoulder with great violence; was wild, and would not answer questions; but gradually became soothed, and allowed an examination.

Externally, the abdomen showed signs of a child having been born, and the mammae had certainly contained milk. The *clitoris* was enlarged and hard; the *nymphoe* long and flabby; the mucous membrane roughened and discolored.

Per vaginam, the *uterus* was found to be retroverted; there was also a fissure of the *rectum*.

Operation, 5:30 P.M. Was very violent under the first attempts to administer chloroform. She was long in being brought under its influence, but when once thoroughly anesthetized, bore it exceedingly well.

The clitoris was excised, the elongated nymphae removed, and the fissure of the rectum divided. The wounds were dressed in the usual manner, and the patient having had two grains of opium administered, was ordered to be constantly watched.

In twenty minutes awoke from the chloroform. Was calm, and slept at intervals during the night.

Feb. 7, 10 A.M. Visited by Mr. B. Brown. Present—Mr. I. B. Brown, Junior, House-Surgeon, and Matron. Pulse quick but steady; tongue brown and furred; breath offensive; gums spongy; pupil natural; countenance rather flushed; skin moist and warm.

The following answers were given to questions asked of her by Mr. Brown, seventeen hours after operation, and are in her own words; much, however, of the information was volunteered without questions:—

"Last March, instead of sliding down a slope, I jumped. This caused displacement of my womb. I suffered great agonies. I was fomented with hot water. I thought it was my back that was hurt. Since then I have been subject to fainting and weakness. I suffer great irritation about my private parts—cannot keep my hands away. The irritation is worse at night. I am obliged to relieve the irritation by rubbing—sometimes for two or three minutes at a time. There is always a discharge. I feel very depressed afterwards. At times I have lost my brain, and felt as if I did not care for living. I would like to have my hands untied; I will be very quiet. Have been separated from my relatives for three years. I shan't tell you how long I have been married—(a pause). I am very rude—I beg your pardon. I have been married three years. I had a baby two years ago: it was not born at the full time—I think five months. I don't know whether it was alive. I left home with my friend when I was sixteen (?). It is two years since I left him. I am now twenty-three.

"After the accident, suffered great pain." Mr. Brown here looked at her gums, and she immediately said, "Oh, yes; I had mercury given me by Surgeon ———, in Dublin: he said it was my spine. He did not examine my womb. Dr. ———examined it, and said there was great displacement. I have been better for treatment at times. My brain has been affected. I have fought very much. I have wanted a child's blood. I have had it sometimes by sucking the wounds of a child. When in a fit, I don't know what is going on around, or what is being said, but I recognize people's voices. I am not regular. Was kept in bed last September for six weeks for flooding; was so for ten days after I was put in bed. Was the same in Paris last year. I was studying in Paris to fit myself for a governess."

The following are extracts from a letter voluntarily sent to Mr. Brown by a lady with whom the patient lived for many months, and left only three weeks previous to admission. Having stated that for some time she was hysterical, and becoming daily more excitable, the letter says—

"On the 13th of September last, she for the first time seemed delirious when going to bed. This was mentioned next morning to

Surgeon ———, who declared it to be nervous irritability of the
spine. . . . On the 27th, Dr. ——— was called in, and at once gave
his opinion that there was ailment of the womb. He then ordered
small blisters on the lower part of the stomach, which in less than
ten hours relieved her, and removed the mania. She had not any
reason for *many* days previous, and was sinking. . . . On the 3rd of
October, Dr. ——— fixed an instrument to support the womb; and,
except during the time when the intensity of pain caused it, there was
no delirium; for a few days she got claret, which seemed to excite her
greatly, so it was discontinued; but on the 13th of October I was
desired to give her port wine in abundance. She was excessively weak,
and mania so dreadful, that she made several attempts to injure herself
and me. She got as many as eight large glasses of best port on some
days; strong beef-tea, chicken soup, and all the nourishment possible.
It was not only suggested, but it was advised to remove her to a
lunatic asylum; however, feeling that certainly nine-tenths of her time
she was perfectly sane, and could know well where she was and with
whom, I did not like the idea of placing so young a creature in an
asylum. I kept her here, and watched her day and night; she never
was left alone for one moment for three months. . . . I ought to
mention that the order for abundance of wine, &c., was from the
opinion that 'want of blood to the brain' caused the mania; and that
the intense inflammation of all internal organs was relieved by blisters
on the lower part of the stomach and by mercury."

Feb. 8. Lint removed from rectum, and wounds dressed. Is calm
and rational; passed a quiet day.

Feb. 10. Very restless; obliged to restrain hands and legs.

Feb. 11. Better; says her head feels heavy; countenance cheerful;
manner quiet and rational.

Feb. 12. Very excited and irritable; constantly managing to free
her hands; will allow no one near her.—2 P.M.: Is quite maniacal; has
managed to irritate the wounds, and also the mammæ. To have one
grain of opium in pill, and ten grains of bromide of ammonium three
times a day.

Feb. 13, 6 A.M. Hands again free; repeat opium. Slept afterwards
till 4 P.M., when she awoke calm and rational.—9 P.M. Slept again.

Feb. 14. Very restless, and at times violent. Bandages removed
and jacket substituted.

Feb. 15. Much better; rational, and conversing cheerfully.

Feb. 16. Improving.

Feb. 17. At her urgent request, hands were freed, but shortly after she became excited.

Feb. 19. More sensible; had today symptoms of a severe bilious attack, which upset her for some days.

Feb. 24. Much better; allowed to see her sister—the first time since the operation.

March 1. Much improved; has written to her sister, and amused herself knitting and reading during the day.

March 2. Allowed to dress; seemed to enjoy the change, and is very cheerful.

March 4. Visited by her sister; has been quietly cheerful all day. Is certainly improving wonderfully.

March 20. Took a walk, and enjoyed it.

March 25. Spent the day away from the Home with her sister; returned looking quite well, and all the better for the change.

April 2. Discharged quite cured.

This patient remained perfectly well, and I hear has since been legally married.

CASE XLVIII. INCIPIENT MANIA—ONE YEAR'S DURATION—OPERATION—CURE— SUBSEQUENT PREGNANCY.

In 1863, Mrs. S. M., married, mother of three children, aet. 30, came under my care, because she had been suffering for more than a year from menorrhagia, which had gradually affected her mind, causing her to have a great distaste for her husband; so much so, that he and his friends were induced seriously to contemplate a separation. On the first examination, her face indicated mental disturbance, eyes restless, pupils dilated, and manner generally excitable. She told me that she could not sleep at night, complained of constant weary uneasiness in her womb, pain in her back, great pain on defecation, constant desire to micturate. She said she was glad to be away from home, as she made every one around her unhappy. Believed that she would be a permanently insane patient, and never expected to return to her family again.

On more minute examination, I found irritable clitoris and labia, a painful fissure of the rectum, with great relaxation of the sphincter ani, which, on inquiry, was found to be caused by the frequent introduction of her finger, with a view to peripheral irritation. At her own request, she had long been separated *à mensâ* from her husband, on account of her great distaste for him and cohabitation with him.

I pursued the usual surgical treatment, which was followed by uninterrupted success; and after two months' treatment, she returned to her husband, resumed cohabitation, and stated that all her distaste had disappeared; soon became pregnant, resumed her place at the head of her table, and became a happy and healthy wife and mother. She was in due time safely delivered, and has ever since remained in perfect health.

Remarks.—From observations of this case, one feels compelled to say, may not it be typical of many others where there is a judicial separation of husband and wife, with all the attendant domestic miseries, and where, if medical and surgical treatment were brought to bear, all such unhappy measures would be obviated?

A careful perusal of the cases related in the foregoing pages will show that all the theoretical objections mentioned in the introductory chapter, as having been raised against my treatment, have been fully contradicted by facts. Of the permanency of the result, I myself am fully satisfied; and I hope at a future time, by a much larger number of cases, to confirm others in the same opinion.

JOHN STUART MILL

FROM

THE SUBJECTION OF WOMEN

John Stuart Mill (1806–1873): John Stuart Mill was born in London and received a distinguished education from his father, James Mill, a disciple of Jeremy Bentham. The younger Mill later questioned his father's Benthamite views, having been influenced by Romantic and Victorian writers such as Wordsworth, Coleridge, and Carlisle. He valued feelings, the growth of personality, and poetry and developed a number of influential political, economic, and social theories.

Mill married Harriet Taylor in 1851 after a long friendship. Though critics have questioned Mill's high regard for his wife's abilities and contributions to his work, it seems certain that she induced in him a sympathy for the working class and the aims of socialism. His early major works, A System of Logic *(1843) and* Principles of Political Economy *(1848), and* On Liberty *(1859), a collaboration with Harriet Taylor Mill, established him as a major writer of Victorian social criticism.*

Mill feared what he saw as the increasing conformity of British society and believed that individuals had to be free to develop their own personalities without social restrictions except where such control was necessary to prevent intrusions on the liberties of others. Claiming in On Liberty *that society had no rights over "conduct which merely concerns itself," Mill argued that private morality was not a matter of public concern. Apparently, family planning did not fall under the category of "private morality." In* Principles of Political Economy *Mill discusses population control. Like Darwin, he was influenced by Malthus's work on population. Placing concerns about culture over productivity, Mill argued that sexual "restraint" was necessary to prevent the decline of "intellectual and moral culture."*

Following his wife's death in 1858, Mill spent a good deal of time in France and continued to write. The Subjection of Women *appeared in 1869. Mill died in Avignon in 1873. His autobiography, edited by his stepdaughter, Helen Taylor, was published that same year.*

CHAPTER I.

The object of this Essay is to explain, as clearly as I am able, the grounds of an opinion which I have held from the very earliest period when I had formed any opinions at all on social or political matters, and which, instead of being weakened or modified, has been constantly growing stronger by the progress of reflection and the experience of life: That the principle which regulates the existing social relations between the two sexes—the legal subordination of one sex to the other—is wrong in itself, and now one of the chief hindrances to human improvement; and that it ought to be replaced by a principle of perfect equality, admitting no power or privilege on the one side, nor disability on the other.

The very words necessary to express the task I have undertaken show how arduous it is. But it would be a mistake to suppose that the difficulty of the case must lie in the insufficiency or obscurity of the grounds of reason on which my conviction rests. The difficulty is that which exists in all cases in which there is a mass of feeling to be contended against. So long as an opinion is strongly rooted in the feelings, it gains rather than loses in stability by having a preponderating weight of argument against it. For if it were accepted as a result of argument, the refutation of the argument might shake the solidity of the conviction; but when it rests solely on feeling, the worse it fares in argumentative contest, the more persuaded its adherents are that their feeling must have some deeper ground, which the arguments do not reach; and while the feeling remains, it is always throwing up fresh intrenchments of argument to repair any breach made in the old. And there are so many causes tending to make the feelings connected with this subject the most intense and most deeply rooted of all those which gather round and protect old institutions and customs, that we need not wonder to find them as yet less undermined and loosened than any of the rest by the progress of the great modern spiritual and social transition; nor suppose that the barbarisms to which men cling longest must be less barbarisms than those which they earlier shake off.

In every respect the burden is hard on those who attack an almost universal opinion. They must be very fortunate, as well as unusually capable, if they obtain a hearing at all. They have more difficulty in obtaining a trial than any other litigants have in getting a verdict. If they do extort a hearing, they are subjected to a set of logical requirements totally different from those exacted from other people. In all other cases, the burden of proof is supposed to lie with the affirmative. If a person is charged with a murder, it rests with those who accuse him to give proof of his guilt, not with himself to prove his innocence. If there is a difference of opinion about the reality of any alleged historical event, in which the feelings of men in general are not much interested, as the Siege of Troy, for example, those who maintain that the event took place are expected to produce their proofs, before those who take the other side can be required to say anything; and at no time are these required to do more than show that the evidence produced by the others is of no value. Again, in practical matters, the burden of proof is supposed to be with those who are against liberty; who contend for any restriction or prohibition; either any limitation of the general freedom of human action, or any disqualification or disparity of privilege affecting one person or kind of persons, as compared with others. The *à priori* presumption is in favor of freedom and impartiality. It is held that there should be no restraint not required by the general good, and that the law should be no respecter of persons, but should treat all alike, save where dissimilarity of treatment is required by positive reasons, either of justice or of policy. But of none of these rules of evidence will the benefit be allowed to those who maintain the opinion I profess. It is useless for me to say that those who maintain the doctrine that men have a right to command and women are under an obligation to obey, or that men are fit for government and women unfit, are on the affirmative side of the question, and that they are bound to show positive evidence for the assertions, or submit to their rejection. It is equally unavailing for me to say that those who deny to women any freedom or privilege rightly allowed to men, having the double presumption against them that they are opposing freedom and recommending partiality, must be held to the strictest proof of their case, and unless their success be such as to exclude all doubt, the judgment ought to go against them. These would be thought good pleas in any common case; but they will not be thought so in this instance. Before I could hope to make any impression, I should be expected not only to answer all that has ever been said by those who take the other side of the question, but to imagine all that could be said by them—to find them in reasons, as well as answer all I find: and besides refuting all arguments for the affirmative, I shall be called upon for invincible positive arguments to prove a negative. And even if I could do all this, and leave the opposite party with a host of unanswered arguments against them, and not a single unrefuted one on their side, I should be thought to have done little; for a cause supported on the one hand by universal usage, and on the other by so great a preponderance of popular sentiment, is supposed to have a presumption in its favor, superior to any conviction which an appeal to reason has power to produce in any intellects but those of a high class.

I do not mention these difficulties to complain of them: first, because it would be useless; they are inseparable from having to contend through people's understandings against the hostility of their feelings and practical tendencies: and truly the understandings of the majority of mankind would need to be much better cultivated than has ever yet been the case, before they can be asked to place such reliance in their own power of estimating arguments, as to give up practical principles in which they have been born and bred and which are the basis of much of the existing order of the world, at the first argumentative attack which they are not capable of logically resisting. I do not therefore quarrel with them for having too little faith in argument, but for having too much faith in custom and the general feeling. It is one of the characteristic prejudices of the reaction of the nineteenth century against the eighteenth, to accord to the unreasoning elements in human nature the infallibility which the eighteenth century is supposed to have ascribed to the reasoning elements. For the apotheosis of Reason we have substituted that of Instinct; and we call everything instinct which we find in ourselves and for which we cannot trace any rational foundation. This idolatry, infinitely more degrading than the other, and the most pernicious of the false worships of the present day, of all of which it is now the main support, will probably hold its ground until it gives way before a sound psychology, laying bare the real root of much that is bowed down to as the intention of Nature and the ordinance of God. As regards the present question, I am willing to accept the unfavorable conditions which the prejudice assigns to me. I consent that established custom, and the general feeling, should be deemed conclusive against me, unless that custom and feeling from age to age can be

shown to have owed their existence to other causes than their sound-
ness, and to have derived their power from the worse rather than the
better parts of human nature. I am willing that judgment should go
against me, unless I can show that my judge has been tampered with.
The concession is not so great as it might appear; for to prove this
is by far the easiest portion of my task.

The generality of a practice is in some cases a strong presumption
that it is, or at all events once was, conducive to laudable ends. This
is the case, when the practice was first adopted, or afterward kept up,
as a means to such ends, and was grounded on experience of the mode
in which they could be most effectually attained. If the authority of
men over women, when first established, had been the result of a
conscientious comparison between different modes of constituting
the government of society; if, after trying various other modes of
social organization—the government of women over men, equality
between the two, and such mixed and divided modes of government
as might be invented—it had been decided, on the testimony of experience, that the mode in which women are wholly under the rule
of men, having no share at all in public concerns, and each in private
being under the legal obligation of obedience to the man with whom
she has associated her destiny, was the arrangement most conducive
to the happiness and well-being of both; its general adoption might
then be fairly thought to be some evidence that, at the time when it
was adopted, it was the best: though even then the considerations
which recommended it may, like so many other primeval social facts
of the greatest importance, have subsequently, in the course of ages,
ceased to exist. But the state of the case is in every respect the reverse
of this. In the first place, the opinion in favor of the present system,
which entirely subordinates the weaker sex to the stronger, rests upon
theory only; for there never has been trial made of any other: so that
experience, in the sense in which it is vulgarly opposed to theory,
cannot be pretended to have pronounced any verdict. And in the
second place, the adoption of this system of inequality never was
the result of deliberation, or forethought, or any social ideas, or
any notion whatever of what conduced to the benefit of humanity or
the good order of society. It arose simply from the fact that from the
very earliest twilight of human society, every woman (owing to the
value attached to her by men, combined with her inferiority in muscular strength) was found in a state of bondage to some man. Laws

and systems of polity always begin by recognizing the relations they find already existing between individuals. They convert what was a mere physical fact into a legal right, give it the sanction of society, and principally aim at the substitution of public and organized means of asserting and protecting these rights, instead of the irregular and lawless conflict of physical strength. Those who had already been compelled to obedience became in this manner legally bound to it. Slavery, from being a mere affair of force between the master and the slave, became regularized and a matter of compact among the masters, who, binding themselves to one another for common protection, guaranteed by their collective strength the private possessions of each, including his slaves. In early times, the great majority of the male sex were slaves, as well as the whole of the female. And many ages elapsed, some of them ages of high cultivation, before any thinker was bold enough to question the rightfulness, and the absolute social necessity, either of the one slavery or of the other. By degrees such thinkers did arise: and (the general progress of society assisting) the slavery of the male sex has, in all the countries of Christian Europe at least (though, in one of them, only within the last few years), been at length abolished, and that of the female sex has been gradually changed into a milder form of dependence. But this dependence, as it exists at present, is not an original institution, taking a fresh start from considerations of justice and social expediency—it is the primitive state of slavery lasting on, through successive mitigations and modifications occasioned by the same causes which have softened the general manners, and brought all human relations more under the control of justice and the influence of humanity. It has not lost the taint of its brutal origin. No presumption in its favor, therefore, can be drawn from the fact of its existence. The only such presumption which it could be supposed to have must be grounded on its having lasted till now, when so many other things which came down from the same odious source have been done away with. And this, indeed, is what makes it strange to ordinary ears, to hear it asserted that the inequality of rights between men and women has no other source than the law of the strongest.

That this statement should have the effect of a paradox, is in some respects creditable to the progress of civilization, and the improvement of the moral sentiments of mankind. We now live—that is to say, one or two of the most advanced nations of the world now live—in a state in which the law of the strongest seems to be entirely abandoned as the regulating principle of the world's affairs: nobody professes it, and, as regards most of the relations between human beings, nobody is permitted to practice it. When any one succeeds in doing so, it is under cover of some pretext which gives him the semblance of having some general social interest on his side. This being the ostensible state of things, people flatter themselves that the rule of mere force is ended; that the law of the strongest cannot be the reason of existence of anything which has remained in full operation down to the present time. However any of our present institutions may have begun, it can only, they think, have been preserved to this period of advanced civilization by a well-grounded feeling of its adaptation to human nature, and conduciveness to the general good. They do not understand the great vitality and durability of institutions which place right on the side of might; how intensely they are clung to; how the good as well as the bad propensities and sentiments of those who have power in their hands, become identified with retaining it; how slowly these bad institutions give way, one at a time, the weakest first, beginning with those which are least interwoven with the daily habits of life; and how very rarely those who have obtained legal power because they first had physical, have ever lost their hold of it until the physical power had passed over to the other side. Such shifting of the physical force not having taken place in the case of women; this fact, combined with all the peculiar and characteristic features of the particular case, made it certain from the first that this branch of the system of right founded on might, though softened in its most atrocious features at an earlier period than several of the others, would be the very last to disappear. It was inevitable that this one case of a social relation grounded on force, would survive through generations of institutions grounded on equal justice, an almost solitary exception to the general character of their laws and customs; but which, so long as it does not proclaim its own origin, and as discussion has not brought out its true character, is not felt to jar with modern civilization, any more than domestic slavery among the Greeks jarred with their notion of themselves as a free people.

The truth is, that people of the present and the last two or three generations have lost all practical sense of the primitive condition of humanity; and only the few who have studied history accurately, or have much frequented the parts of the world occupied by the living representatives of ages long past, are able to form any mental picture of what society then was. People are not aware how entirely, in former ages, the law of superior strength was the rule of life; how publicly and openly it was avowed, I do not say cynically or shamelessly—for these words imply a feeling that there was something in it to be ashamed of, and no such notion could find a place in the faculties of any person in those ages, except a philosopher or a saint. History gives a cruel experience of human nature, in showing how exactly the regard due to the life, possessions, and entire earthly happiness of any class of persons, was measured by what they had the power of enforcing; how all who made any resistance to authorities that had arms in their hands, however dreadful might be the provocation, had not only the law of force but all other laws, and all the notions of social obligation against them; and in the eyes of those whom they resisted, were not only guilty of crime, but of the worst of all crimes, deserving the most cruel chastisement which human beings could inflict. The first small vestige of a feeling of obligation in a superior to acknowledge any right in inferiors, began when he had been induced, for convenience, to make some promise to them. Though these promises, even when sanctioned by the most solemn oaths, were for many ages revoked or violated on the most trifling provocation or temptation, it is probable that this, except by persons of still worse than the average morality, was seldom done without some twinges of conscience. The ancient republics, being mostly grounded from the first upon some kind of mutual compact, or at any rate formed by an union of persons not very unequal in strength, afforded, in consequence, the first instance of a portion of human relations fenced round, and placed under the dominion of another law than that of force. And though the original law of force remained in full operation between them and their slaves, and also (except so far as limited by express compact) between a commonwealth and its subjects, or other independent commonwealths; the banishment of that primitive law, even from so narrow a field, commenced the regeneration of human nature, by giving birth to sentiments of which experience soon demonstrated the immense value even for material interests, and which thenceforward only required to be enlarged, not created. Though slaves were no part of the commonwealth, it was in the free states that slaves were first felt to have rights as human beings. The Stoics were, I believe, the first (except so far as the Jewish law constitutes an exception) who taught as a part of morality that men were bound by moral obligations to their slaves. No one, after Christianity became ascendent, could ever again have been a stranger to this belief, in theory; nor, after the rise of the Catholic Church, was it ever without persons to stand up for it. Yet to enforce it was the most arduous task which Christianity ever had to perform. For more than a thousand years the Church kept up the contest, with hardly any perceptible success. It was not for want of power over men's minds. Its power was prodigious. It could make kings and nobles resign their most valued possessions to enrich the Church. It could make thousands, in the prime of life and the height of worldly advantages, shut themselves up in convents to work out their salvation by poverty, fasting, and prayer. It could send hundreds of thousands across land and sea, Europe and Asia, to give their lives for the deliverance of the Holy Sepulcher. It could make kings relinquish wives who were the object of their passionate attachment, because the Church declared that they were within the seventh (by our calculation the fourteenth) degree of relationship. All this it did; but it could not make men fight less with one another, nor tyrannize less cruelly over the serfs, and when they were able, over burgesses. It could not make them renounce either of the applications of force; force militant, or force triumphant. This they could never be induced to do until they were themselves in their turn compelled by superior force. Only by the growing power of kings was an end put to fighting except between kings, or competitors for kingship; only by the growth of a wealthy and warlike bourgeoisie in the fortified towns, and of a plebeian infantry which proved more powerful in the field than the undisciplined chivalry, was the insolent tyranny of the nobles over the bourgeoisie and peasantry brought within some bounds. It was persisted in not only until, but long after, the oppressed had obtained a power enabling them often to take conspicuous vengeance; and on the Continent much of it continued to the time of the French Revolution, though in England the earlier and better organization of the democratic classes put an end to it sooner, by establishing equal laws and free national institutions.

If people are mostly so little aware how completely, during the greater part of the duration of our species, the law of force was the avowed rule of general conduct, any other being only a special and exceptional consequence of peculiar ties—and from how very recent a date it is that the affairs of society in general have been even pretended to be regulated according to any moral; as little do people remember or consider how institutions and customs which never had any ground but the law of force, last on into ages and states of general opinion which never would have permitted their first establishment. Less than forty years ago, Englishmen might still by law hold human beings in bondage as salable property: within the present century they might kidnap them and carry them off, and work them literally to death. This absolutely extreme case of the law of force, condemned by those who can tolerate almost every other form of arbitrary power, and which, of all others, presents features the most revolting to the feelings of all who look at it from an impartial position, was the law of civilized and Christian England within the memory of persons now living: and in one-half of Anglo-Saxon America three or four years ago, not only did slavery exist, but the slave-trade, and the breeding of slaves expressly for it, was a general practice between slave states. Yet not only was there a greater strength of sentiment against it, but, in England at least, a less amount either of feeling or of interest in favor of it than of any other of the customary abuses of force: for its motive was the love of gain, unmixed and undisguised; and those who profited by it were a very small numerical fraction of the country, while the natural feeling of all who were not personally interested in it, was unmitigated abhorrence. So extreme an instance makes it almost superfluous to refer to any other: but consider the long duration of absolute monarchy. In England at present it is the almost universal conviction that military despotism is a case of the law of force, having no other origin or justification. Yet in all the great nations of Europe except England it either still exists, or has only just ceased to exist, and has even now a strong party favorable to it in all ranks of the people, especially among persons of station and consequence. Such is the power of an established system, even when far from universal; when not only in almost every period of history there have been great and well-known examples of the contrary system, but these have almost invariably been afforded by the most illustrious and most prosperous communities. In this case, too, the possessor of the undue power, the person directly interested in it, is only one person, while those who are subject to it and suffer from it are literally all the rest. The yoke is naturally and necessarily humiliating to all persons, except the one who is on the throne, together with, at most, the one who expects to succeed to it. How different are these cases from that of the power of men over women! I am not now prejudging the question of its justifiableness. I am showing how vastly more permanent it could not but be, even if not justifiable, than these other dominations which have nevertheless lasted down to our own time. Whatever gratification of pride there is in the possession of power, and whatever personal interest in its exercise, is in this case not confined to a limited class, but common to the whole male sex. Instead of being, to most of its supporters, a thing desirable chiefly in the abstract, or, like the political ends usually contended for by factions, of little private importance to any but the leaders; it comes home to the person and hearth of every male head of a family, and of every one who looks forward to being so. The clodhopper exercises, or is to exercise, his share of the power equally with the highest nobleman. And the case is that in which the desire of power is the strongest: for every one who desires power, desires it most over those who are nearest to him, with whom his life is passed, with whom he has most concerns in common, and in whom any independence of his authority is oftenest likely to interfere with his individual preferences. If, in the other cases specified, powers manifestly grounded only on force, and having so much less to support them, are so slowly and with so much difficulty got rid of, much more must it be so with this, even if it rests on no better foundation than those. We must consider, too, that the possessors of the power have facilities in this case, greater than in any other, to prevent any uprising against it. Every one of the subjects lives under the very eye, and almost, it may be said, in the hands, of one of the masters—in closer intimacy with him than with any of her fellow-subjects; with no means of combining against him, no power of even locally overmastering him, and, on the other hand, with the strongest motives for seeking his favor and avoiding to give him offense. In struggles for political emancipation, everybody knows how often its champions are bought off by bribes, or daunted by terrors. In the case of women, each individual of the subject-class is in a chronic state of bribery and intimidation combined. In setting up the standard of resistance, a large number of the leaders, and still more of the followers, must make an almost complete sacrifice of the pleasures or the alleviations of their own individual lot. If ever any system of privilege and enforced subjection had its yoke tightly riveted on the necks of those who are kept down by it, this has. I have not yet shown that it is a wrong system; but every one who is capable of thinking on the subject must see that even if it is, it was certain to outlast all other forms of unjust authority. And when some of the grossest of the other forms still exist in many civilized countries, and have only recently been got rid of in others, it would be strange if that which is so much the deepest rooted had yet been perceptibly shaken anywhere. There is more reason to wonder that the protests and testimonies against it should have been so numerous and so weighty as they are.

Some will object that a comparison cannot fairly be made between the government of the male sex and the forms of unjust power which I have adduced in illustration of it, since these are arbitrary, and the effect of mere usurpation, while it on the contrary is natural. But was there ever any domination which did not appear natural to those who possessed it? There was a time when the division of mankind into two classes, a small one of masters and a numerous one of slaves, appeared, even to the most cultivated minds, to be a natural, and the only natural, condition of the human race. No less an intellect, and one which contributed no less to the progress of human thought, than Aristotle, held this opinion without doubt or misgiving; and rested it on the same premises on which the same assertion in regard to the dominion of men over women is usually based, namely, that there are different natures among mankind, free natures and slave natures; that the Greeks were of a free nature, the barbarian races of Thracians and Asiatics of a slave nature. But why need I go back to Aristotle? Did not the slave-owners of the Southern United States maintain the same doctrine, with all the fanaticism with which men cling to the theories that justify their passions and legitimate their personal interests? Did they not call heaven and earth to witness that the dominion of the white man over the black is natural, that the black race is by nature incapable of freedom, and marked out for slavery?—some even going so far as to say that the freedom of manual laborers is an unnatural order of things anywhere. Again, the theorists of absolute monarchy have always affirmed it to be the only natural form of government; issuing from the patriarchal, which was the primitive and spontaneous form of society, framed on the model of the paternal, which is anterior to society itself, and, as they contend, the most natural authority of all. Nay, for that matter, the law of force itself, to those who could not plead any other, has always seemed the most natural of all grounds for the exercise of authority. Conquering races hold it to be Nature's own dictate that the conquered should obey the conquerors, or, as they euphoniously paraphrase it, that the feebler and more unwarlike races should submit to the braver and manlier. The smallest acquaintance with human life in the Middle Ages, shows how supremely natural the dominion of the feudal nobility over men of low condition appeared to the nobility themselves, and how unnatural the conception seemed, of a person of the inferior class claiming equality with them, or exercising authority over them. It hardly seemed less so to the class held in subjection. The emancipated serfs and burgesses, even in their most vigorous struggles, never made any pretension to a share of authority; they only demanded more or less limitation to the power of tyrannizing over them. So true is it that unnatural generally means only uncustomary, and that everything which is usual appears natural. The subjection of women to men being a universal custom, any departure from it quite naturally appears unnatural. But how entirely, even in this case, the feeling is dependent on custom appears by ample experience. Nothing so much astonishes the people of distant parts of the world, when they first learn anything about England, as to be told that it is under a queen: the thing seems to them so unnatural as to be almost incredible. To Englishmen this does not seem in the least degree unnatural, because they are used to it; but they do feel it unnatural that women should be soldiers or members of Parliament. In the feudal ages, on the contrary, war and politics were not thought unnatural to women, because not unusual; it seemed natural that women of the privileged classes should be of manly character, inferior in nothing but bodily strength to their husbands and fathers. The independence of women seemed rather less unnatural to the Greeks than to other ancients, on account of the fabulous Amazons (whom they believed to be historical), and the partial example afforded by the Spartan women; who, though no less subordinate by law than in other Greek states, were more free in fact; and being trained to bodily exercises in the same manner with men, gave ample proof that they were not naturally disqualified for them. There can be little doubt that Spartan experience suggested to Plato, among many other of his doctrines, that of the social and political equality of the two sexes.

But, it will be said, the rule of men over women differs from all these others in not being a rule of force: it is accepted voluntarily; women make no complaint, and are consenting parties to it. In the first place, a great number of women do not accept it. Ever since there have been women able to make their sentiments known by their writings (the only mode of publicity which society permits to them), an increasing number of them have recorded protests against their present social condition: and recently many thousands of them, headed by the most eminent women known to the public, have petitioned Parliament for their admission to the Parliamentary Suffrage. The claim of women to be educated as solidly, and in the same branches of knowledge, as men, is urged with growing intensity, and with a great prospect of success; while the demand for their admission into professions and occupations hitherto closed against them, becomes every year more urgent. Though there are not in this country, as there are in the United States, periodical Conventions and an organized party to agitate for the Rights of Women, there is a numerous and active Society organized and managed by women, for the more limited object of obtaining the political franchise. Nor is it only in our own country and in America that women are beginning to protest, more or less collectively, against the disabilities under which they labor. France, and Italy, and Switzerland, and Russia now afford examples of the same thing. How many more women there are who silently cherish similar aspirations, no one can possibly know; but there are abundant tokens how many *would* cherish them, were they not so strenuously taught to repress them as contrary to the proprieties of their sex. It must be remembered, also, that no enslaved class ever asked for complete liberty at once. When Simon de Montfort called the deputies of the commons to sit for the first time in Parliament, did any of them dream of demanding that an assembly, elected by their constituents, should make and destroy ministries, and dictate to the king in affairs of state? No such thought entered into the imagination of the most ambitious of them. The nobility had already these pretensions; the commons pretended to nothing but to be exempt from arbitrary taxation, and from the gross individual oppression of the king's officers. It is a political law of nature that those who are under any power of ancient origin never begin by complaining of the power itself, but only of its oppressive exercise. There is never any want of women who complain of ill usage by their husbands. There would be infinitely more, if complaint were not the greatest of all provocatives to a repetition and increase of the ill usage. It is this which frustrates all attempts to maintain the power but protect the woman against its abuses. In no other case (except that of a child) is the person who has been proved judicially to have suffered an injury, replaced under the physical power of the culprit who inflicted it. Accordingly, wives, even in the most extreme and protracted cases of bodily ill usage, hardly ever dare avail themselves of the laws made for their protection; and if, in a moment of irrepressible indignation, or by the interference of neighbors, they are induced to do so, their whole effort afterward is to disclose as little as they can, and to beg off their tyrant from his merited chastisement.

All causes, social and natural, combine to make it unlikely that women should be collectively rebellious to the power of men. They are so far in a position different from all other subject classes, that their masters require something more from them than actual service. Men do not want solely the obedience of women, they want their sentiments. All men, except the most brutish, desire to have, in the woman most nearly connected with them, not a forced slave but a willing one, not a slave merely, but a favorite. They have therefore put everything in practice to enslave their minds. The masters of all other slaves rely, for maintaining obedience, on fear,—either fear of themselves or religious fears. The masters of women wanted more than simple obedience, and they turned the whole force of education to effect their purpose. All women are brought up from the very earliest years in the belief that their ideal of character is the very opposite to that of men; not self-will and government by self-control, but submission and yielding to the control of others. All the moralities tell them that it is the duty of women, and all the current sentimentalities that it is their nature, to live for others, to make complete abnegation of themselves, and to have no life but in their affections. And by their affections are meant the only ones they are allowed to have—those to the men with whom they are connected, or to the children who constitute an additional and indefeasible tie between them and a man. When we put together three things—first, the natural attraction between opposite sexes; secondly, the wife's entire dependence on the husband, every privilege or pleasure she has being either his gift, or depending entirely on his will; and lastly, that the principal object of human pursuit, consideration, and all objects of social ambition, can in general be sought or obtained by her only through him, it would be a miracle if the object of being attractive to men had not become the polar star of feminine education and formation of character. And this great means of influence over the minds of women having been acquired, an instinct of selfishness made men avail themselves of it to the utmost as a means of holding women in subjection, by representing to them meekness, submissiveness, and resignation of all individual will into the hands of a man, as an essential part of sexual attractiveness. Can it be doubted that any of the other yokes which mankind have succeeded in breaking, would have subsisted till now if the same means had existed, and had been as sedulously used, to bow down their minds to it? If it had been made the object of the life of every young plebeian to find personal favor in the eyes of some patrician, of every young serf with some seigneur; if domestication with him, and a share of his personal affections, had been held out as the prize which they all should look out for, the most gifted and aspiring being able to reckon on the most desirable prizes; and if, when this prize had been obtained, they had been shut out by a wall of brass from all interests not centering in him, all feelings and desires but those which he shared or inculcated; would not serfs and seigneurs, plebeians and patricians, have been as broadly distinguished at this day as men and women are? And would not all but a thinker here and there have believed the distinction to be a fundamental and unalterable fact in human nature?

The preceding considerations are amply sufficient to show that custom, however universal it may be, affords in this case no presumption, and ought not to create any prejudice, in favor of the arrangements which place women in social and political subjection to men. But I may go further, and maintain that the course of history, and the tendencies of progressive human society, afford not only no presumption in favor of this system of inequality of rights, but a strong one against it; and that, so far as the whole course of human improvement up to this time, the whole stream of modern tendencies, warrants any inference on the subject, it is that this relic of the past is discordant with the future, and must necessarily disappear.

For what is the peculiar character of the modern world—the difference which chiefly distinguishes modern institutions, modern social ideas, modern life itself, from those of times long past? It is, that human beings are no longer born to their place in life, and chained down by an inexorable bond to the place they are born to, but are free to employ their faculties, and such favorable chances as offer, to achieve the lot which may appear to them most desirable. Human society of old was constituted on a very different principle. All were born to a fixed social position, and were mostly kept in it by law, or interdicted from any means by which they could emerge from it. As some men are born white and others black, so some were born slaves and others freemen and citizens; some were born patricians, others plebeians; some were born feudal nobles, others commoners and *roturiers*. A slave or serf could never make himself free, nor, except by the will of his master, become so. In most European countries it was not till toward the close of the Middle Ages, and as a consequence of the growth of regal power, that commoners could be ennobled. Even among nobles, the eldest son was born the exclusive heir to the paternal possessions, and a long time elapsed before it was fully established that the father could disinherit him. Among the industrious classes, only those who were born members of a guild, or were admitted into it by its members, could lawfully practice their calling within its local limits; and nobody could practice any calling deemed important, in any but the legal manner—by processes authoritatively prescribed. Manufacturers have stood in the pillory for presuming to carry on their business by new and improved methods. In modern Europe, and most in those parts of it which have participated most largely in all other modern improvements, diametrically opposite doctrines now prevail. Law and government do not undertake to prescribe by whom any social or industrial operation shall or shall not be conducted, or what modes of conducting them shall be lawful. These things are left to the unfettered choice of individuals. Even the laws which required that workmen should serve an apprenticeship, have in this country been repealed: there being ample assurance that in all cases in which an apprenticeship is necessary, its necessity will suffice to enforce it. The old theory was that the least possible should be left to the choice of the individual agent; that all he had to do should, as far as practicable, be laid down for him by superior wisdom. Left to himself he was sure to go wrong. The modern conviction, the fruit of a thousand years of experience, is that things in which the individual is the person directly interested, never go right but as they are left to his own discretion; and that any regulation of them by authority, except to protect the rights of others, is sure to be mischievous. This conclusion, slowly arrived at, and not adopted until almost every possible application of the contrary theory had been made with disastrous result, now (in the industrial department) prevails universally in the most advanced countries, almost universally in all that have pretensions to any sort of advancement. It is not that all processes are supposed to be equally good, or all persons to be equally qualified for everything; but that freedom of individual choice is now known to be the only thing which procures the adoption of the best processes, and throws each operation into the hands of those who are best qualified for it. Nobody thinks it necessary to make a law that only a strong-armed man shall be a blacksmith. Freedom and competition suffice to make blacksmiths strong-armed men, because the weak-armed can earn more by engaging in occupations for which they are more fit. In consonance with this doctrine, it is felt to be an overstepping of the proper bounds of authority to fix beforehand, on some general presumption, that certain persons are not fit to do certain things. It is now thoroughly known and admitted that if some such presumptions exist, no such presumption is infallible. Even if it be well grounded in a majority of cases, which it is very likely not to be, there will be a minority of exceptional cases in which it does not hold: and in those it is both an injustice to the individuals, and a detriment to society, to place barriers in the way of their using their faculties for their own benefit and for that of others. In the cases, on the other hand, in which the unfitness is real, the ordinary motives of human conduct will on the whole suffice to prevent the incompetent person from making, or from persisting in, the attempt.

If this general principle of social and economical science is not true; if individuals, with such help as they can derive from the opinion of those who know them, are not better judges than the law and the government, of their own capacities and vocation; the world cannot too soon abandon this principle, and return to the old system of regulations and disabilities. But if the principle is true, we ought to act as if we believed it, and not to ordain that to be born a girl instead of a boy, any more than to be born black instead of white, or a commoner instead of a nobleman, shall decide the person's position through all life—shall interdict people from all the more elevated social positions, and from all, except a few, respectable occupations. Even were we to admit the utmost that is ever pretended as to the superior fitness of men for all the functions now reserved to them, the same argument applies which forbids a legal qualification for members of Parliament. If only once in a dozen years the conditions of eligibility exclude a fit person, there is a real loss, while the exclusion of thousands of unfit persons is no gain; for if the constitution of the electoral body disposes them to choose unfit persons, there are always plenty of such persons to choose from. In all things of any difficulty and importance, those who can do them well are fewer than the need, even with the most unrestricted latitude of choice; and any limitation of the field of selection deprives society of some chances of being served by the competent, without ever saving it from the incompetent.

At present, in the more improved countries, the disabilities of women are the only case, save one, in which laws and institutions take persons at their birth, and ordain that they shall never in all their lives be allowed to compete for certain things. The one exception is that of royalty. Persons still are born to the throne; no one, not of the reigning family, can ever occupy it, and no one even of that family can, by any means but the course of hereditary succession, attain it. All other dignities and social advantages are open to the whole male sex; many indeed are only attainable by wealth, but wealth may be striven for by any one, and is actually obtained by many men of the very humblest origin. The difficulties, to the majority, are indeed insuperable without the aid of fortunate accidents; but no male human being is under any legal ban; neither law nor opinion superadd artificial obstacles to the natural ones. Royalty, as I have said, is excepted; but in this case every one feels it to be an exception—an anomaly in the modern world, in marked opposition to its customs and principles, and to be justified only by extraordinary special expediencies, which, though individuals and nations differ in estimating their weight, unquestionably do in fact exist. But in this exceptional case, in which a high social function is, for important reasons, bestowed on birth instead of being put up to competition, all free nations contrive to adhere in substance to the principle from which they nominally derogate; for they circumscribe this high function by conditions avowedly intended to prevent the person to whom it ostensibly belongs from really performing it; while the person by whom it is performed, the responsible minister, does obtain the post by a competition from which no full-grown citizen of the male sex is legally excluded. The disabilities, therefore, to which women are sub-

ject from the mere fact of their birth, are the solitary examples of the
kind in modern legislation. In no instance except this, which comprehends half the human race, are the higher social functions closed
against any one by a fatality of birth which no exertions, and no
change of circumstances can overcome; for even religious disabilities
(besides that in England and in Europe they have practically almost
ceased to exist) do not close any career to the disqualified person in
case of conversion.

The social subordination of women thus stands out an isolated
fact in modern social institutions; a solitary breach of what has become their fundamental law; a single relic of an old world of thought
and practice exploded in everything else, but retained in the one thing
of most universal interest; as if a gigantic dolmen, or a vast temple
of Jupiter Olympius, occupied the site of St. Paul's and received daily
worship, while the surrounding Christian churches were only resorted
to on fasts and festivals. This entire discrepancy between one social
fact and all those which accompany it, and the radical opposition
between its nature and the progressive movement which is the boast
of the modern world, and which has successively swept away everything else of an analogous character, surely affords, to a conscientious
observer of human tendencies, serious matter for reflection. It raises
a prima facie presumption on the unfavorable side, far outweighing
any which custom and usage could in such circumstances create on
the favorable; and should at least suffice to make this, like the choice
between republicanism and royalty, a balanced question.

The least that can be demanded is that the question should not
be considered as prejudged by existing fact and existing opinion, but
open to discussion on its merits, as a question of justice and expediency; the decision on this, as on any of the other social arrangements
of mankind, depending on what an enlightened estimate of tendencies
and consequences may show to be most advantageous to humanity in
general, without distinction of sex. And the discussion must be a real
discussion, descending to foundations, and not resting satisfied with
vague and general assertions. It will not do, for instance, to assert in
general terms that the experience of mankind has pronounced in favor
of the existing system. Experience cannot possibly have decided between two courses, so long as there has only been experience of one.
If it be said that the doctrine of the equality of the sexes rests only
on theory, it must be remembered that the contrary doctrine also has

only theory to rest upon. All that is proved in its favor by direct experience, is that mankind have been able to exist under it, and to attain the degree of improvement and prosperity which we now see; but whether that prosperity has been attained sooner, or is now greater, than it would have been under the other system, experience does not say. On the other hand, experience does say that every step in improvement has been so invariably accompanied by a step made in raising the social position of women that historians and philosophers have been led to adopt their elevation or debasement as on the whole the surest test and most correct measure of the civilization of a people or an age. Through all the progressive period of human history, the condition of women has been approaching nearer to equality with men. This does not of itself prove that the assimilation must go on to complete equality; but it assuredly affords some presumption that such is the case.

Neither does it avail anything to say that the *nature* of the two sexes adapts them to their present functions and position, and renders these appropriate to them. Standing on the ground of common sense and the constitution of the human mind, I deny that any one knows, or can know, the nature of the two sexes, as long as they have only been seen in their present relation to one another. If men had ever been found in society without women, or women without men, or if there had been a society of men and women in which the women were not under the control of the men, something might have been positively known about the mental and moral differences which may be inherent in the nature of each. What is now called the nature of women is an eminently artificial thing—the result of forced repression in some directions, unnatural stimulation in others. It may be asserted without scruple that no other class of dependents have had their character so entirely distorted from its natural proportions by their relation with their masters; for, if conquered and slave races have been, in some respects, more forcibly repressed, whatever in them has not been crushed down by an iron heel has generally been let alone, and if left with any liberty of development, it has developed itself according to its own laws; but in the case of women, a hothouse and stove cultivation has always been carried on of some of the capabilities of their nature, for the benefit and pleasure of their masters. Then, because certain products of the general vital force sprout luxuriantly and reach a great development in this heated atmosphere and under this active nurture and watering, while other shoots from the same root, which are left outside in the wintry air, with ice purposely heaped all round them, have a stunted growth, and some are burnt off with fire and disappear; men, with that inability to recognize their own work which distinguishes the unanalytic mind, indolently believe that the tree grows of itself in the way they have made it grow, and that it would die if one-half of it were not kept in a vapor-bath and the other half in the snow.

Of all difficulties which impede the progress of thought, and the formation of well-grounded opinions on life and social arrangements, the greatest is now the unspeakable ignorance and inattention of mankind in respect to the influences which form human character. Whatever any portion of the human species now are, or seem to be, such, it is supposed, they have a natural tendency to be: even when the most elementary knowledge of the circumstances in which they have been placed clearly points out the causes that made them what they are. Because a cottier deeply in arrears to his landlord is not industrious, there are people who think that the Irish are naturally idle. Because constitutions can be overthrown when the authorities appointed to execute them turn their arms against them, there are people who think the French incapable of free government. Because the Greeks cheated the Turks, and the Turks only plundered the Greeks, there are persons who think that the Turks are naturally more sincere: and because women, as is often said, care nothing about politics except their personalities, it is supposed that the general good is naturally less interesting to women than to men. History, which is now so much better understood than formerly, teaches another lesson: if only by showing the extraordinary susceptibility of human nature to external influences, and the extreme variableness of those of its manifestations which are supposed to be most universal and uniform. But in history, as in traveling, men usually see only what they already had in their own minds; and few learn much from history, who do not bring much with them to its study.

Hence, in regard to that most difficult question, what are the natural differences between the two sexes—a subject on which it is impossible in the present state of society to obtain complete and correct knowledge—while almost everybody dogmatizes upon it, almost all neglect and make light of the only means by which any partial insight can be obtained into it. This is an analytic study of the most important department of psychology, the laws of the influence of circumstances on character. For, however great and apparently ineradicable the moral and intellectual differences between men and women might be, the evidence of their being natural differences could only be negative. Those only could be inferred to be natural which could not possibly be artificial—the residuum, after deducting every characteristic of either sex which can admit of being explained from education or external circumstances. The profoundest knowledge of the laws of the formation of character is indispensable to entitle any one to affirm even that there is any difference, much more what the difference is, between the two sexes considered as moral and rational beings; and since no one, as yet, has that knowledge (for there is hardly any subject which, in proportion to its importance, has been so little studied), no one is thus far entitled to any positive opinion on the subject. Conjectures are all that can at present be made; conjectures more or less probable, according as more or less authorized by such knowledge as we yet have of the laws of psychology, as applied to the formation of character.

Even the preliminary knowledge, what the differences between the sexes now are, apart from all question as to how they are made what they are, is still in the crudest and most incomplete state. Medical practitioners and physiologists have ascertained, to some extent, the differences in bodily constitution; and this is an important element to the psychologist; but hardly any medical practitioner is a psychologist. Respecting the mental characteristics of women, their observations are of no more worth than those of common men. It is a subject on which nothing final can be known, so long as those who alone can really know it, women themselves, have given but little testimony, and that little, mostly suborned. It is easy to know stupid women. Stupidity is much the same all the world over. A stupid person's notions and feelings may confidently be inferred from those which prevail in the circle by which the person is surrounded. Not so with those whose opinions and feelings are an emanation from their own nature and faculties. It is only a man here and there who has any tolerable knowledge of the character even of the women of his own family. I do not mean of their capabilities; these nobody knows, not even themselves, because most of them have never been called out. I mean their actually existing thoughts and feelings. Many a man thinks he perfectly understands women, because he has had amatory relations with several, perhaps with many of them. If he is a good observer, and his experience extends to quality as well as quantity, he may have learnt something of one narrow department of their nature—an important department, no doubt. But of all the rest of it, few persons are generally more ignorant, because there are few from whom it is so carefully hidden. The most favorable case which a man can generally have for studying the character of a woman, is that of his own wife: for the opportunities are greater, and the cases of complete sympathy not so unspeakably rare. And, in fact, this is the source from which any knowledge worth having on the subject has, I believe, generally come. But most men have not had the opportunity of studying in this way more than a single case; accordingly one can, to an almost laughable degree, infer what a man's wife is like from his opinions about women in general. To make even this one case yield any result, the woman must be worth knowing, and the man not only a competent judge, but of a character so sympathetic in itself, and so well adapted to hers, that he can either read her mind by sympathetic intuition, or has nothing in himself which makes her shy of disclosing it. Hardly anything, I believe, can be more rare than this conjunction. It often happens that there is the most complete unity of feeling and community of interests as to all external things, yet the one has as little admission into the internal life of the other as if they were common acquaintance. Even with true affection, authority on the one side and subordination on the other prevent perfect confidence. Though nothing may be intentionally withheld, much is not shown. In the analogous relation of parent and child, the corresponding phenomenon must have been in the observation of every one. As between father and son, how many are the cases in which the father, in spite of real affection on both sides, obviously to all the world does not know, nor suspect, parts of the son's character familiar to his companions and equals. The truth is that the position of looking up to another is extremely unpropitious to complete sincerity and openness with him. The fear of losing ground in his opinion or in his feelings is so strong that even in an upright character, there is an unconscious tendency to show only the best side, or the side which, though not the best, is that which he most likes to see; and it may be confidently said that thorough knowledge of one another hardly exists, but between persons who, besides being intimates, are equals. How much more true, then, must all this be, when the one is not only under the authority of the other, but has it inculcated on her as a duty to reckon everything else subordinate to his comfort and pleasure, and to let him neither see nor feel anything coming from her, except what is agreeable to him. All these difficulties stand in the way of a man's obtaining any thorough knowledge even of the one woman whom alone, in general, he has sufficient opportunity of studying. When we further consider that to understand one woman is not necessarily to understand any other woman; that even if he could study many women of one rank, or of one country, he would not thereby understand women of other ranks or countries; and even if he did, they are still only the women of a single period of history; we may safely assert that the knowledge which men can acquire of women, even as they have been and are, without reference to what they might be, is wretchedly imperfect and superficial, and always will be so, until women themselves have told all that they have to tell.

And this time has not come; nor will it come otherwise than gradually. It is but of yesterday that women have either been qualified by literary accomplishments, or permitted by society, to tell anything to the general public. As yet very few of them dare tell anything, which men, on whom their literary success depends, are unwilling to bear. Let us remember in what manner, up to a very recent time, the expression, even by a male author, of uncustomary opinions, or what are deemed eccentric feelings, usually was, and in some degree still is, received; and we may form some faint conception under what impediments a woman, who is brought up to think custom and opinion her sovereign rule, attempts to express in books anything drawn from the depths of her own nature. The greatest woman who has left writings behind her sufficient to give her an eminent rank in the literature of her country, thought it necessary to prefix as a motto to her boldest work, "Un homme peut braver l'opinion; une femme doit s'y soumettre."* The greater part of what women write about women is mere sycophancy to men. In the case of unmarried women, much of it seems only intended to increase their chance of a husband. Many, both married and unmarried, overstep the mark, and inculcate a servility beyond what is desired or relished by any man, except the very vulgarest. But this is not so often the case as, even at a quite late period, it still was. Literary women are becoming more free-spoken,

* Title page of Mme. de Stael's *Delphine*.

and more willing to express their real sentiments. Unfortunately, in this country especially, they are themselves such artificial products that their sentiments are compounded of a small element of individual observation and consciousness, and a very large one of acquired associations. This will be less and less the case, but it will remain true to a great extent, as long as social institutions do not admit the same free development of originality in women which is possible to men. When that time comes, and not before, we shall see, and not merely hear, as much as it is necessary to know of the nature of women, and the adaptation of other things to it.

I have dwelt so much on the difficulties which at present obstruct any real knowledge by men of the true nature of women, because in this as in so many other things "opinio copiae inter maximas causas inopiae est;" and there is little chance of reasonable thinking on the matter, while people flatter themselves that they perfectly understand a subject of which most men know absolutely nothing, and of which it is at present impossible that any man, or all men taken together, should have knowledge which can qualify them to lay down the law to women as to what is, or is not, their vocation. Happily, no such knowledge is necessary for any practical purpose connected with the position of women in relation to society and life. For, according to all the principles involved in modern society, the question rests with women themselves,—to be decided by their own experience, and by the use of their own faculties. There are no means of finding what either one person or many can do, but by trying,—and no means by which any one else can discover for them what it is for their happiness to do or leave undone.

One thing we may be certain of,—that what is contrary to women's nature to do, they never will be made to do by simply giving their nature free play. The anxiety of mankind to interfere in behalf of nature, for fear lest nature should not succeed in effecting its purpose, is an altogether unnecessary solicitude. What women by nature cannot do, it is quite superfluous to forbid them from doing. What they can do, but not so well as the men who are their competitors, competition suffices to exclude them from; since nobody asks for protective duties and bounties in favor of women; it is only asked that the present bounties and protective duties in favor of men should be recalled. If women have a greater natural inclination for some things than for others, there is no need of laws or social inculcation to make

the majority of them do the former in preference to the latter. Whatever women's services are most wanted for, the free play of competition will hold out the strongest inducements to them to undertake.
And, as the words imply, they are most wanted for the things for
which they are most fit; by the apportionment of which to them, the
collective faculties of the two sexes can be applied on the whole with
the greatest sum of valuable result.

The general opinion of men is supposed to be that the natural
vocation of a woman is that of a wife and mother. I say, is supposed
to be, because, judging from acts—from the whole of the present
constitution of society—one might infer that their opinion was the
direct contrary. They might be supposed to think that the alleged
natural vocation of women was of all things the most repugnant to
their nature; insomuch that if they are free to do anything else—if
any other means of living, or occupation of their time and faculties,
is open, which has any chance of appearing desirable to them—there
will not be enough of them who will be willing to accept the condition said to be natural to them. If this is the real opinion of men
in general, it would be well that it should be spoken out. I should
like to hear somebody openly enunciating the doctrine (it is already
implied in much that is written on the subject)—"It is necessary to
society that women should marry and produce children. They will
not do so unless they are compelled. Therefore it is necessary to
compel them." The merits of the case would then be clearly defined.
It would be exactly that of the slave-holders of South Carolina and
Louisiana. "It is necessary that cotton and sugar should be grown.
White men cannot produce them. Negroes will not, for any wages
which we choose to give. *Ergo* they must be compelled." An illustration still closer to the point is that of impressment. Sailors must absolutely be had to defend the country. It often happens that they will
not voluntarily enlist. Therefore there must be the power of forcing
them. How often has this logic been used! and, but for one flaw in
it, without doubt it would have been successful up to this day. But it
is open to the retort—First pay the sailors the honest value of their
labor. When you have made it as well worth their while to serve you,
as to work for other employers, you will have no more difficulty than
others have in obtaining their services. To this there is no logical
answer except "I will not:" and as people are now not only ashamed,
but are not desirous, to rob the laborer of his hire, impressment is

no longer advocated. Those who attempt to force women into marriage by closing all other doors against them, lay themselves open to a similar retort. If they mean what they say, their opinion must evidently be that men do not render the married condition so desirable to women, as to induce them to accept it for its own recommendations. It is not a sign of one's thinking the boon one offers very attractive, when one allows only Hobson's choice, "That or none." And here, I believe, is the clew to the feelings of those men who have a real antipathy to the equal freedom of women. I believe they are afraid, not lest women should be unwilling to marry, for I do not think that any one in reality has that apprehension; but lest they should insist that marriage should be on equal conditions; lest all women of spirit and capacity should prefer doing almost anything else, not in their own eyes degrading, rather than marry, when marrying is giving themselves a master, and a master too of all their earthly possessions. And truly, if this consequence were necessarily incident to marriage, I think that the apprehension would be very well founded. I agree in thinking it probable that few women, capable of anything else, would, unless under an irresistible *entrainement*, rendering them for the time insensible to anything but itself, choose such a lot, when any other means were open to them of filling a conventionally honorable place in life: and if men are determined that the law of marriage shall be a law of despotism, they are quite right, in point of mere policy, in leaving to women only Hobson's choice. But, in that case, all that has been done in the modern world to relax the chain on the minds of women, has been a mistake. They never should have been allowed to receive a literary education. Women who read, much more women who write, are, in the existing constitution of things, a contradiction and a disturbing element: and it was wrong to bring women up with any acquirements but those of an odalisque, or of a domestic servant.

DR. RICHARD VON KRAFFT-EBING

FROM

PSYCHOPATHIA SEXUALIS

A MEDICO-FORENSIC STUDY

Richard von Krafft-Ebing (1840–1902): Richard von Krafft-Ebing was a German neurologist and professor in Strassburg, Grazm, and Vienna. His classic textbook on psychiatry, Psychopathia Sexualis, *was enormously influential and impacted on Adler, Jung, and Ellis among others, though Ellis, particularly, objected to many of his ideas. Krafft-Ebing detailed case histories of various sexual dysfunctions, and was actively involved in the debate as to whether male homosexuality was an innate or acquired "pathology." He equated love with sexual desire and affirmed that it "can only exist between persons of different sex capable of sexual intercourse." He was familiar with Freud's work on hypnosis and respected him, though he claimed that the Breuer-Freud method was ineffective on his own patients.*

The propagation of the human race is not left to mere accident or the caprices of the individual, but is guaranteed by the hidden laws of nature which are enforced by a mighty, irresistible impulse. Sensual enjoyment and physical fitness are not the only conditions for the enforcement of these laws, but higher motives and aims, such as the desire to continue the species or the individuality of mental and physical qualities beyond time and space, exert a considerable influence. Man puts himself at once on a level with the beast if he seeks to gratify lust alone, but he elevates his superior position when by curbing the animal desire he combines with the sexual functions ideas of morality, of the sublime, and the beautiful.

Placed upon this lofty pedestal he stands far above nature and draws from inexhaustible sources material for nobler enjoyments, for serious work and for the realization of ideal aims. Maudsley justly claims that sexual feeling is the basis upon which social advancement is developed.

If man were deprived of sexual distinction and the nobler enjoyments arising therefrom, all poetry and probably all moral tendency would be eliminated from his life.

Sexual life no doubt is the one mighty factor in the individual and social relations of man which discloses his powers of activity, of acquiring property, of establishing a home, of awakening altruistic sentiments toward a person of the opposite sex, and toward his own issue as well as toward the whole human race.

Sexual feeling is really the root of all ethics, and no doubt of aestheticism and religion.

The sublimest virtues, even the sacrifice of self, may spring from sexual life, which, however, on account of its sensual power, may easily degenerate into the lowest passion and basest vice.

Love unbridled is a volcano that burns down and lays waste all around it; it is an abyss that devours all—honor, substance and health.

It is of great psychological interest to follow up the gradual development of civilization and the influence exerted by sexual life upon habits and morality. The gratification of the sexual instinct seems to be the primary motive in man as well as in beast. Sexual intercourse is done openly, and man and woman are not ashamed of their nakedness. The savage races, *e.g.*, Australasians, Polynesians, Malays of the Philippines are still in this stage. Woman is the common property of man, the spoil of the strongest and mightiest, who chooses the most winsome for his own, a sort of instinctive sexual selection of the fittest.

Woman is a "chattel," an article of commerce, exchange or gift, a vessel for sensual gratification, an implement for toil. The presence of shame in the manifestations and exercise of the sexual functions, and of modesty in the mutual relations between the sexes, are the foundations of morality. Thence arises the desire to cover the nakedness ("and they saw that they were naked") and to perform the act in private.

The development of this grade of civilization is furthered by the conditions of frigid climes which necessitate the protection of the whole body against the cold. It is an anthropological fact that modesty can be traced to much earlier periods among northern races.[1]

Another element which tends to promote the refined development of sexual life is the fact that woman ceases to be a "chattel." She becomes an individual being, and, although socially still far below man, she gradually acquires rights, independence of action, and the privilege to bestow her favors where she inclines. She is wooed by man. Traces of ethical sentiments pervade the rude sensual appetite, idealization begins and community of woman ceases. The sexes are drawn to each other by mental and physical merits and exchange favors of preference. In this stage woman is conscious of the fact that her charms belong only to the man of her choice. She seeks to hide them from others. This forms the foundation of modesty, chastity and sexual fidelity so long as love endures.

This development is hastened wherever nomadic habits yield to the spirit of colonization, where man establishes a household. He feels the necessity for a companion in life, a housewife in a settled home.

The Egyptians, the Israelites and the Greeks reached this level at early periods; so did the Teutonic races. Its principal characteristics are high appreciation of virginity, chastity, modesty and sexual fidelity in strong contrast to the habits of other peoples where the host places the personal charms of the wife at the disposal of the guest.

The history of Japan furnishes a striking proof that this high grade of civilization is often the last stage of moral development, for in that country to within twenty years ago prostitution was not considered to impair in any way the social status of the future wife.

Christianity raised the union of the sexes to a sublime position by making woman socially the equal of man and by elevating the bond of love to a moral and religious institution.[2] Thence emanates the

[1] According to *Westermarck, op. cit.*, it was "not the feeling of shame which suggested the garment, but the garment engendered shame. The desire to make themselves more attractive originated the habit among men and women to cover their nakedness."

[2] This assertion may be modified insofar that the symbolical and sacramental character of matrimony was clearly defined only by the Council of Trent, although the spirit of Christianity always tended to raise woman from the inferior position which she occupied in previous centuries and in the Old Testament.

The tradition that woman was created from the rib of the sleeping man (see Genesis) is one of the causes of delay in this direction, for after the fall she is told "thy will shall be subject to man." According to the Old Testament, woman is responsible for the fall of man, and this became the cornerstone of Christian teaching. Thus the social position of woman had to be neglected, as it were, until the spirit of Christianity had conquered tradition and scholastic tenets.

fact that the love of man, if considered from the standpoint of advanced civilization, can only be of a monogamic nature and must rest upon a staple basis. Even though nature should claim merely the law of propagation, a community (family or state) cannot subsist without the guarantee that the offspring thrive physically, morally and intellectually. From the moment when woman was recognized the peer of man, when monogamy became a law and was consolidated by legal, religious and moral conditions, the Christian nations obtained a mental and material superiority over the polygamic races, and especially over Islam.

Mohammed strove to raise woman from the position of the slave, and mere handmaid of enjoyment, to a higher social and matrimonial grade; yet she remained still far below man, who alone could obtain divorce, and that on the easiest terms.

Above all things Islamism excludes woman from public life and enterprise, and stifles her intellectual and moral advancement. The Mohammedan woman is simply a means for sensual gratification and the propagation of the species; while in the sunny balm of Christian doctrine, blossom forth her divine virtues and her qualities of housewife, companion and mother. What a contrast!

It is a remarkable fact that the Gospels (barring divorce, Matt. xix, 9) contain not a word in favor of woman. The clemency shown toward the adulteress and the penitent Magdalen do not affect the position of woman in general. The Epistles of St. Paul definitely insist that no change can be permitted in the position of woman (2 Cor. xi, 3–12; Eph. v, 22, "woman shall be subject to man," and 23, "woman shall fear man").

How much the fathers of the Church are prejudiced against woman on account of Eve's part in the temptation may be easily learned from *Tertullian*: "Woman, thou shouldst ever go in mourning and sackcloth, thy eyes filled with tears. Thou has brought about the ruin of mankind." *St. Jerome* has aught but good to say about woman. "Woman is the gate of the devil, the road of evil, the sting of the scorpion" ("De Cultu Feminarum," i. 1).

Canon law declares: "Man only is created to the image of God, not woman; therefore woman shall serve him and be his handmaid."

The Provincial Council of Macon (sixth century) seriously discussed the question whether woman had a soul at all.

These opinions of the Church had a sympathetic influence upon the peoples who embraced Christianity. Among the converted Germanic races the *dower value* of woman fell considerably (J. *Falke*, "Die ritterliche Gesellschaft," Berlin, 1862, p. 49. *Re* the valuation of the two sexes among the Jews, *cf.* 3 Moses, xxvii, 3–4).

Even polygamy, which is distinctly recognized in the Old Testament (Deut. xxi, 15) is nowhere in the New Testament definitely prohibited. In fact, many Christian princes (*e.g.*, the Merovingian kings: Chlotar I, Charibert I, Pippin I and other Frankish nobles) indulged in polygamy without a protest being raised by the Church at the time (*Weinhold*, "Die deutschen Frauen im Mittelalter," ii, p. 15; *cf. Unger*, "Marriage," etc., and *Louis Bridel*, "La Femme et le Droit" Paris, 1884).

Compare the two religions and their standard of future happiness. The Christian expects a heaven of spiritual bliss absolutely free from carnal pleasure; the Mohammedan an eternal harem, a paradise among lovely houris. Yet, in spite of the aid which religion, law, education and the moral code offer him, the Christian (to subdue his sensual inclination) often drags pure and chaste love from its sublime pedestal and wallows in the quagmire of sensual enjoyment and lust.

Life is a never-ceasing duel between the animal instinct and morality. Only willpower and a strong character can emancipate man from the meanness of his corrupt nature, and teach him how to enjoy the pure pleasures of love and pluck the noble fruits of earthly existence.

It is an open question whether the moral status of mankind has undergone an improvement in our times. No doubt society at large shows a greater veneer of modesty and virtue, and vice is not as flagrantly practiced as of yore.

The reader of Scherr will gain the impression that our moral code is not so gross as was that of the Middle Ages, even if only more refined manners have taken the place of former coarseness.

In comparing the various stages of civilization it becomes evident that, despite periodical relapses, public morality has made steady progress, and that Christianity is the chief factor in this advance.

We are certainly far beyond sodomitic idolatry, the public life, legislation and religious exercises of ancient Greece, not to speak of the worship of Phallus and Priapus in vogue among the Athenians and Babylonians, or the Bacchanalian feasts of the Romans and the privileged position held by the courtesans of those days.

There are stagnant and fluctuating periods in this slow progress, but they are only like the ebb- and flood-tide of sexual life in the individual.

The episodes of moral decay always coincide with the progression of effeminacy, lewdness and luxuriance of the nations. These phenomena can only be ascribed to the higher and more stringent demands which circumstances make upon the nervous system. Exaggerated tension of the nervous system stimulates sensuality, leads the individual as well as the masses to excesses, and undermines the very foundations of society, and the morality and purity of family life. The material and moral ruin of the community is readily brought about by debauchery, adultery and luxury. Greece, the Roman

Empire, and France under Louis XIV and XV are striking examples of this assertion. In such periods of civic and moral decline the most monstrous excesses of sexual life may be observed, which, however, can always be traced to psychopathological or neuropathological conditions of the nation involved.

Large cities are hotbeds in which neuroses and low morality are bred, *vide* the history of Babylon, Nineveh, Rome and the mysteries of modern metropolitan life. It is a remarkable fact that among savages and half-civilized races sexual intemperance is not observed (except among the Aleutians and the Oriental and Nama-Hottentot women who practice masturbation).[1]

The study of sexual life in the individual naturally deals with its various phases, beginning with the stage of puberty to the extinction of sexual feeling.

Mantegazza draws a beautiful picture of the bodings and yearnings of awakening love, of the mysterious sensations, foretastes and impulses that fill the heart, long before the period of puberty has arrived. Psychologically speaking, this is, perhaps, the most momentous epoch of life, for the wealth of ideas and sentiments engendered through it forms the standard by which psychic activity may be measured.

The advance of puberty develops the impulses of youth, hitherto vague and undefined, into conscious realization of the sexual power. The psychological reactions of animal passion manifest themselves in the irresistible desires of intimacy, and the longing to bestow the strange affections of nature upon others.

Religion and poetry frequently become the temporary haven of rest, even after the period of storm and stress is passed. Religious enthusiasm is more commonly met with in the young than the old. The lives of the saints[2] are replete with remarkable records of temp-

---

[1] *Friedreich* ("Hdb. der gerichtlichärztlich, Praxis," 1843, i, p. 271) is of a different opinion, for according to him the Red Indians of America are addicted to the practice of pederasty. *Cf.* also *Lombroso*, p. 42, and *Bloch*, Beiträge zur Etiologie der Psychopathia Sexualis, 2, Theil, 1903.

[2] *Cf. Friedreich* ("Gerichtl. Psychologie," p. 389) who quotes numerous examples. For instance, *Blankebin*, the nun, was constantly tormented by the thought of what could have become of that part of Christ which was removed in circumcision.

Veronica Juliani, beatified by Pope Pius II in memory of the divine lamb, took a real lamb to bed with her, kissed it and suckled it on her breasts.

St. Catharine of Genoa often burned with such intense inward fire that in order to cool herself she would throw herself upon the ground crying, "Love, love, I can endure it no longer." At the

tations. The religious feasts of the ancients often degenerated into orgies, or into mystic cults of a voluptuous character. Even the meetings of certain modern sects dissolve themselves simply into obscene practices.

On the contrary we find that the sexual instinct, when disappointed and unappeased, frequently seeks and finds a substitute in religion.

Even where psychopathological conditions are diagnosed beyond dispute, this relation between religious and sexual feelings can easily be established. The cause of religious insanity is often to be found in sexual aberration. In psychosis a motley mixture of religious and sexual delusions is observable, *viz.*, in female lunatics who imagine that they are or will be the mother of God, and especially in persons slaves to masturbation. The cruel, sensual acts of chastisement, violation, emasculation and even crucifixion, perpetrated upon self by religious maniacs, bear out this assertion.

Any attempt to explain the psychological relations between religion and love must needs meet with difficulties, for analogous instances are met with in great numbers.

Sexual inclinations and religious leanings (if considered as psychological factors) are composed of two elements.

Schleiermacher recognized the primary feeling of dependence as the paramount element in religion, long before modern anthropological and ethnographic research in the domain of primitive causes arrived at the same conclusions.

The secondary and truly ethical element, *i.e.*, the love of God, enters the religious sentiment only when a higher stage of culture is attained. At first, the double-faced, now benevolent, now angry, chimeras of complicated mythologies take the place of the evil spirits, until they in turn are dislodged by the benign form of the deity, the giver of perpetual happiness, whether it be in the shape of Jehovah as the author of all earthly blessings, or Allah who bestows physical

---

same time she felt a peculiar inclination to her confessor. One day lifting his hand to her nose she noticed a peculiar odor which penetrated to her heart "a heavenly perfume that would awaken the dead."

St. *Armelle* and St. *Elizabeth* were troubled with a similar longing for the Infant Jesus. The temptations of St. *Anthony, of Padua,* are known to the world. Of significance is an old Protestant prayer: "Oh! that I had found thee, bless'd Emanuel; that thou wert with me in my bed, to bring delight to body and soul. Come and be mine. My heart shall be thy resting place."

delight in Paradise, or Christ who is gone before to prepare mansions of eternal light and bliss, or Nirvana who reigns in the heaven of the Buddhist.

The primary element of *sexual preference* is love, *i.e.*, the expectation of unsurpassed pleasure. The secondary element is the feeling of dependence, although it is in reality the root from which spring both alike, as the former may be entirely absent. It certainly exists in a stronger measure in woman, on account of her social position, and the passive part which she takes in the act of procreation; but at times it is also found in men who are of a feminine type.

Religion as well as sexual love is mystical and transcendental. In sexual love the real object of the instinct, *i.e.*, propagation of the species, is not always present to the mind during the act, and the impulse is much stronger than could be justified by the gratification that can possibly be derived from it. Religious love strives for the possession of an object that is absolutely ideal, and cannot be defined by experimental knowledge. Both are metaphysical processes which give unlimited scope to imagination.

They converge, however, in a similar *indefinite* focus; for the gratification of the sensual appetite promises a boon which far surpasses all other conceivable pleasures, and faith has in store a bliss that endures forever.

In either condition the mind is conscious of the enormous importance of the object to be obtained; thus impulses often become irresistible and overcome all opposing motives. But because neither of them can at times grasp the real object of their existence they easily degenerate into fanaticism in which intensity of emotion overbalances clearness and stability of reason. Expectation of unfathomed bliss is now coupled with reckless resignation and unconditional submission.

Owing to this conformity it happens that under high tension one dislodges the other, or that both make their appearance together; for every violent upheaval in the soul must necessarily sweep along its surroundings. Nature, always the same, draws alike upon these two spheres of conception, now forcing one, then the other, into stronger activity which degenerates even into acts of cruelty either actively exercised or passively endured.

In religious life this may assume the shape of self-sacrifice or self-destruction, prompted by the idea that the victim is necessary for the material sustenance of the deity. The sacrifice is brought as a sign of reverence or submission, as a tribute, as an atonement for sins committed, or as a price wherewith to purchase happiness.

If, however, the offering consists in self-punishment—and that occurs in all religions!—it serves not only as a symbol of submission, or an equivalent in the exchange of present pain for future bliss, but everything that is thought to come from the deity, all that is done in obedience to divine mandates or to the honor of the Godhead, is felt directly as pleasure. Thus religious exuberance leads to ecstasy, a condition in which consciousness is so preoccupied with feelings of mental pleasure that distress is stripped of its painful quality.

Exaggerated religious enthusiasm also finds pleasure in the sacrifice of another person, when rapture combines with sympathy.

Similar manifestations may be observed in sexual life, as will be shown later on under the headings of Sadism and Masochism.

Thus the relations existing between religion, lust, and cruelty[1] may be condensed into the formula: Religious and sexual hyperesthesia at the acme of development show the same volume of intensity and the same quality of excitement, and may therefore under given circumstances interchange. Both will in certain pathological states degenerate into cruelty.

Sexual influence is just as potent in the awakening of aesthetic sentiments. What other foundation is there for the plastic art or poetry? From (sensual) love arises that warmth of fancy which alone can inspire the creative mind, and the fire of sensual feeling kindles and preserves the glow and fervor of art.

This explains the sensual natures of great poets and artists.

The world of fancy keeps pace with the development of sexual power. Whoever during that period cannot be animated by the ideals of all that is great, noble and beautiful remains a "Philistine" all his life. Even the dolt tries his hand at poetry when in love.

On the borders of physiological reaction may be observed those mysterious processes of maturing puberty which give origin to obscure yearnings and moods of despondency and *Weltschmerz*, rendering life tedious, and coupled with the impulse to inflict pain and

---

[1] This may be observed in the actual life as well as in the fiction and the plastic arts of degenerate eras. For instance, *Bernini's* carving, which represents St. Teresa "sinking in an hysterical faint upon a marble cloud, whilst an amorous angel plunges the arrow (of divine love) into her heart."—*Lübke.*

sorrow upon others (weak analogies of a psychological connection between lust and cruelty).

First love forever trends in a romantic idealizing direction. It wraps the beloved object in the halo of perfection. In its incipient stages it is of a platonic character, and turns rather to forms of poetry and history. With the approach of puberty it runs the risk of transferring the idealizing powers upon persons of the opposite sex, even though mentally, physically and socially they be of an inferior station. To this may easily be traced many cases of misalliance, abduction, elopement and errors of early youth, and those sad tragedies of passionate love that are in conflict with the principles of morality or social standing, and often terminate in murder, self-destruction and double suicide.

Purely sensual love is never true and lasting, for which reason first love is, as a rule, but a passing infatuation, a fleeting passion.

True love is rooted in the recognition of the moral and mental qualities of the beloved person, and is equally ready to share pleasures and sorrows and even to make sacrifices. True love shrinks from no dangers or obstacles in the struggle for the undisputed possession of the beloved.

Deeds of daring and heroism lie in its wake. But unless the moral foundation be solid it will lead to crime, and jealousy often mars its beauty.

The love of the feeble-minded is based upon sentimentality, and when unrequited results in suicide.

Sentimental love is likely to degenerate into a burlesque, especially when the sensual element lacks force (*e.g.*, the Knight of Joggenburg, Don Quixote and many of the minstrels and troubadours of the Middle Ages).

This kind of love is nauseating and has a repulsive or ludicrous effect on others, while true love and its manifestations command sympathy, respect and even fear.

Love when weak is frequently turned away from its real object into different channels, such as voluptuous poetry, bizarre aesthetics or religion. In the latter case it readily falls a prey to mysticism, fanaticism, sectarianism or religious mania. A smattering of all this can always be found in the immature love of early puberty. The poetical effusions of that period of life are only then worthy of perusal when emanating from the pen of the truly endowed genius.

Ethical surroundings are necessary in order to elevate love to its true and pure form, but, notwithstanding, sensuality will ever remain its principal basis.

Platonic love is a platitude, a misnomer for "kindred spirits."

Since love implies the presence of sexual desire it can only exist between persons of different sex capable of sexual intercourse. When these conditions are wanting or destroyed, it is replaced by friendship.

The sexual functions of man exercise a very marked influence upon the development and preservation of character. Manliness and self-reliance are not the qualities which adorn the impotent onanist.

Gyurkovechky is correct in his observation that virility establishes the ratio of difference between old men and young, and that impotence impairs health, mental freshness, activity, self-confidence and imagination. The damage stands in proportion to the age of the subject and the extent of his debauchery.

The sudden loss of the virile powers often produces melancholia, or is the cause of suicide when life without love is a mere blank.

In cases where the reaction is less pronounced, the victim is morose, peevish, egotistical, jealous, narrow-minded, cowardly, devoid of energy, self-respect and honor.

The *skopzes*, for instance, after castration rapidly degenerate.

This matter will be further elucidated under the heading "Effeminatio."

In the sedate matron this condition is of minor psychological importance, though it is noticeable. The biological change affects her but little if her sexual career has been successful, and loving children gladden the maternal heart. The situation is different, however, where sterility has denied that happiness, or where enforced celibacy prevented the performance of the natural functions.

These facts characterize strongly the differences that prevail in the psychology of sexual life in man and woman, and the dissimilarity of sexual feeling and desire in both.

Man has beyond doubt the stronger sexual appetite of the two. From the period of pubescence he is instinctively drawn toward woman. His love is sensual, and his choice is strongly prejudiced in favor of physical attractions. A mighty impulse of nature makes him aggressive and impetuous in his courtship. Yet the law of nature does not wholly fill his psychic being. Having won the prize, his love is temporarily eclipsed by other vital and social interests.

Woman, however, if physically and mentally normal, and properly educated, has but little sensual desire. If it were otherwise, marriage and family life would be empty words. As yet the man who avoids women, and the woman who seeks men, are sheer anomalies.

Woman is wooed for her favor. She remains passive. Her sexual organization demands it, and the dictates of good breeding come to her aid.

Nevertheless, sexual consciousness is stronger in woman than in man. Her need of love is greater, it is continual not periodical, but her love is more spiritual than sensual. Man primarily loves woman as his wife, and then as the mother of his children; the first place in woman's heart belongs to the father of her child, the second to him as husband. Woman is influenced in her choice more by mental than by physical qualities. As mother she divides her love between offspring and husband. Sensuality is merged in the mother's love. Thereafter the wife accepts marital intercourse not so much as a sensual gratification than as a proof of her husband's affection.

Woman loves with her whole soul. To woman love is life, to man it is the joy of life. Misfortune in love bruises the heart of man; but it ruins the life of woman and wrecks her happiness. It is really a psychological question worthy of consideration whether woman can truly love twice in her life. Woman's mind certainly inclines more to monogamy than that of man.

In the sexual demands of man's nature will be found the motives of his weakness toward woman. He is enslaved by her, and becomes more and more dependent upon her as he grows weaker, and the more he yields to sensuality. This accounts for the fact that in the periods of decline and luxury, sensuousness was the predominant factor. Whence arises the social danger when courtesans and their dependents rule the State and finally encompass its ruin.

History shows that great (states) men have often been the slaves of women in consequence of the neuropathic conditions of their constitution.

It shows a masterly psychological knowledge of human nature that the Roman Catholic Church enjoins celibacy upon its priests in order to emancipate them from sensuality, and to concentrate their entire activity in the pursuit of their calling. Nevertheless it is a pity that the celibate state deprives the priest of the ennobling influence exercised by love and marital life upon the character.

From the fact that by nature man plays the aggressive role in sexual life, he is exposed to the danger of overstepping the limits set by law and morality.

The unfaithfulness of the wife, as compared with that of the husband, is morally of much wider bearing, and should always meet with severer punishment at the hands of the law. The unfaithful wife not only dishonors herself, but also her husband and her family, not to speak of the possible uncertainty of paternity.

Natural instincts and social position are frequent causes of disloyalty in man (the husband), while the wife is surrounded by many protecting influences.

Sexual intercourse is of different import to the spinster and to the bachelor. Society claims of the latter modesty, but exacts of the former chastity as well. Modern civilization concedes only to the wife that exalted position in which woman sexually furthers the moral interests of society.

The ultimate aim, the ideal, of woman, even when she is dragged in the mire of vice, ever is and will be marriage. Woman, as Mantegazza properly observes, seeks not only gratification of sensual desires, but also protection and support for herself and her offspring. No matter how sensual man may be, unless also thoroughly depraved, he seeks for a consort only that woman whose chastity he cannot doubt.

The emblem and ornament of woman aspiring to this state, truly worthy of herself, is modesty, so beautifully defined by Mantegazza as "one of the forms of physical self-esteem."

To discuss here the evolution of this, the most graceful of virtues in woman, is out of place, but most likely it is an outgrowth of the gradual rise of civilization.

A remarkable contrast may be found in the occasional exposure of physical charms, conventionally sanctioned by the world of fashion, in which even the most discreet maiden will indulge when robed for the ballroom, theater, or similar social function. Although the reasons for such a display are obvious, the modest woman is fortunately no more conscious of them than of the motives which underlie periodical fashions that bring certain forms of the body into undue prominence, to say nothing of corsets, etc.

In all times, and among all races, the women are fond of toilet and finery. In the animal kingdom nature has distinguished the male with the greater beauty. Men designate women as the beautiful sex, a gallantry which clearly arises from their sensual requirements. So long as woman seeks only self-gratification in personal adornment, and so long as she remains unconscious of the psychological reasons for thus making herself attractive, no objection can be raised against it, but when done with the fixed purpose to please men it degenerates into coquetry.

Under analogous circumstances man would make himself ridiculous.

Woman far surpasses man in the natural psychology of love, partly because evolution and training have made love her proper element, and partly because she is animated by more refined feelings (Mantegazza).

Even the best of breeding concedes to man that he look upon woman mainly as a means by which to satisfy the cravings of his natural instinct, though it confines him only to the woman of his choice. Thus civilization establishes a binding social contract which is called marriage, and grants by legal statutes protection and support to the wife and her issue.

It is important, and on account of certain pathological manifestations (to be referred to later on), indispensable, to examine into those psychological events which draw man and woman into that close union which concentrates the fullness of affection upon the beloved one only to the exclusion of all other persons of the same sex.

If one could demonstrate design in the processes of nature—adaptation cannot be denied them—then the fact of fascination by one person of the opposite sex with indifference toward all others, as it occurs between true and happy lovers, would appear as a wonderful provision to ensure monogamy for the promotion of its object.

The scientific observer finds in this loving bond of hearts by no means simply a mystery of souls, but he can refer it nearly always to certain physical or mental peculiarities by which the attracting power is qualified.

Hence the words *fetish* and *fetishism*. The word *fetish* signifies an object, or parts or attributes of objects, which by virtue of association to sentiment, personality, or absorbing ideas, exert a charm (the Portuguese "fetisso") or at least produce a peculiar individual impression which is in no wise connected with the external appearance of the sign, symbol or fetish.[1]

The individual valuation of the fetish extending even to unreasoning enthusiasm is called *fetishism*. This interesting psychological phenomenon may be explained by an empirical law of association, *i.e.*, the relation existing between the notion itself and the parts thereof which are essentially active in the production of pleasurable emotions. It is most commonly found in *religious* and *erotic* spheres. *Religious* fetishism finds its original motive in the delusion that its object, *i.e.*, the idol, is not a mere symbol, but possesses divine attributes, and ascribes to it peculiar wonder-working (relics) or protective (amulets) virtues.

Erotic fetishism makes an idol of physical or mental qualities of a person or even merely of objects used by that person, etc., because they awaken mighty associations with the beloved person, thus originating strong emotions of sexual pleasure. Analogies with religious fetishism are always discernible; for, in the latter, the most insignificant objects (hair, nails, bones, etc.) become at times fetishes which produce feelings of delight and even ecstasy.

The germ of sexual love is probably to be found in the individual charm (fetish) with which persons of opposite sex sway each other.

The case is simple enough when the sight of a person of the opposite sex occurs simultaneously with sexual excitement, whereby the latter is intensified.

Emotional and optical impressions combine and are so deeply imbedded in the mind that a recurring sensation awakens the visual memory and causes renewed sexual excitement, even orgasm and pollution (often only in dreams), in which case the physical appearance acts as a fetish.

Binet, while discussing other questions, contends that mere peculiarities, whether physical or mental, may have the effect of the fetish if their perception coincides with sexual emotion.

Experience shows that chance controls in a large measure this mental association, that the nature of the fetish varies with the personality of the individual, thus arousing the oddest sympathies or antipathies.

---

[1] *Cf. Max Müller* who derives the word fetish etymologically from *factitius, i.e.,* artificial, insignificant.

These physiological facts of fetishism often account for the affections that suddenly arise between man and woman, the preference of a certain person to all others of the same sex. Since the fetish assumes the form of a distinctive mark it is clear that its effect can only be of an individual character. Being accentuated by the strongest feelings of pleasure, it follows that existing faults in the beloved are overlooked ("Love is blind") and an infatuation is produced which appears incomprehensible or silly to others. Thus it happens that the devoted lover who worships and invests his love with qualities which in reality do not exist is looked upon by others simply as mad. Thus love exhibits itself now as a mere passion, now as a pronounced psychical anomaly which attains what seemed impossible, renders the ugly beautiful, the profane sublime, and obliterates all consciousness of existing duties toward others.

Tarde argues that the type of this fetish (ism) varies with persons as well as with nations, but that the ideal of beauty remains the same among civilized peoples of the same era.

Binet has more thoroughly analyzed and studied this *fetishism of love*.

From it springs the particular choice for slender or plump forms, for blondes or brunettes, for particular form or color of the eyes, tone of the voice, odor of the hair or body (even artificial perfume), shape of the hand, foot or ear, etc., which constitute the individual charm, the first link in a complicated chain of mental processes, all converging in that one focus, love, *i.e.*, the physical and mental possession of the beloved.

This fact establishes the existence of *physiological* fetishism.

Without showing a pathological condition, the fetish may exercise its power so long as its leading qualities represent the integral parts, and so long as the love engendered by it comprises the entire mental and physical personality.

"Normal love appears to us as a symphony of tones," Max Dessoir (pseudonym Ludwig Brunn) in an article "The Fetishism of Love" cleverly says:

"Normal love appears to us as a symphony of tones of all kinds. It is roused by the most varied agencies. It is, so to speak, polytheistic. Fetishism recognizes only the tone-color of a single instrument; it issues forth from a single motive; it is monotheistic."

Even moderate thought will carry the conviction that the term real love (so often misused) can only apply where the entire person of the beloved becomes the physical and mental object of veneration.

Of course, there is always a sensual element in love, *i.e.*, the desire to enjoy the full possession of the beloved object, and, in union with it, to fulfill the laws of nature.

But where the body of the beloved person is made the sole object of love, or if sexual pleasure only is sought without regard to the communion of soul and mind, true love does not exist. Neither is it found among the disciples of Plato, who love the soul only and despise sexual enjoyment. In the one case the body is the fetish, in the other the soul, and love is fetishism.

Instances such as these represent simply transitions to pathological fetishism.

This assumption is enhanced by another criterion of true love, *viz.*, the mental satisfaction derived from the sexual act.[1]

A striking phenomenon in fetishism is that among the many things which may serve as fetishes there are some which gain that significance more commonly than others; for instance, the HAIR, the HAND, the FOOT of women, or the expression of the EYE. This is important in the pathology of fetishism.

Woman certainly seems to be more or less conscious of these facts. For she devotes great attention to her hair and often spends an unreasonable amount of time and money upon its cultivation. How carefully the mother looks after her little daughter's hair! What an important part the hairdresser plays! The falling out of the hair causes despair to many a young lady. The author remembers the case of a

---

[1] *Magnan's* "spinal cérébral postérieur," who finds gratification with any sort of woman, is only animated by lust. Meretricious love that is purchased cannot be genuine *(Mantegazza)*. Whoever coined the adage: "When the light is removed, there is no difference between women," was a cynic, indeed. The power to perform love's act is by no means a guarantee of the noblest enjoyment of love.

There are urnings who are potent for women—men who do not love their wives, but are nevertheless able to perform the marital "duty." In the majority of these cases even lustful pleasure is absent; for it is simply an onanistic act rendered possible by the aid of imagination which substitutes another beloved being. This deception may, indeed, superinduce sexual pleasure, but, rudimentary gratification as it is, it can only arise from a psychic trick, just as in solitary onanism voluptuous satisfaction is obtained chiefly with the assistance of fancy. As a matter of fact that degree of orgasm which completes the lustful act is entirely dependent upon the intervention of fancy.

Where psychic impediments exist (such as indifference, disgust, aversion, fear of contagion or impregnation, etc.) the feeling of sexual gratification seems to be wanting altogether.

vain woman who fell into melancholia on account of this trouble, and finally committed suicide. A favorite subject of conversation among ladies is coiffures. They are envious of each other's luxuriant tresses.

Beautiful hair is a mighty fetish with many men. In the legend of the Lorelei, who lured men to destruction, the "golden hair" which she combs with a golden comb appears as a fetish. Frequently the *hand* or the *foot* possesses an attractiveness no less powerful; but in these instances masochistic and sadistic feelings often—though not always—assist in determining the peculiar kind of fetish.

By a transference through association of ideas, *gloves* or *shoes* obtain the significance of a fetish.

Max Dessoir points out that among the customs of the Middle Ages drinking from the shoe of a beautiful woman (still to be found in Poland) played a remarkable part in gallantry and homage. The shoe also plays an important role in the legend of Aschenbrödel.

The *expression of the eye* is particularly important as a means of kindling the spark of love. A neuropathic eye frequently affects persons of either sex as a fetish. "Madame, your beautiful eyes make me die of love" (Molière).

There are many examples showing that *odors* of the body become fetishes.

This fact is taken advantage of in the "Ars amandi" by woman either consciously or unconsciously. Ruth sought to attract Boaz by perfuming herself. The demimonde of ancient and modern times is noted for its lavish use of strong scents. Jäger, in his *Discovery of the Soul*, calls attention to many olfactory sympathies.

Cases are known where men have married ugly women solely because their personal odors were exceedingly pleasing.

Binet makes it probable that the voice also may act as a fetish.

Belot in his novel *Les baigneuses de Trouville* makes the same assertion. Binet thinks that many marriages with singers are due to the fetish of their voices. He also observes that among the singing birds the voice has the same sexual significance as odors among the quadrupeds. The birds allure by their song, and the male that sings most beautifully is joined at night by the charmed mate.

The pathological facts of masochism and sadism show that mental peculiarities may also act as fetishes but in a wider sense.

Thus the fact of idiosyncrasies is explained, and the old proverb "There is no use in disputing about taste" retains its force.

With regard to fetishism in woman, science must at least for the present time be content with mere conjectures. This much seems to be certain, that being a physiological factor, its effects are analogous to those in men, *i.e.*, producing sexual sympathies toward persons of the same sex.

Details will come to our knowledge only when medical women enter into the study of this subject.

We may take it for granted that the physical as well as the mental qualities of man assume the form of the female fetish. In most cases, no doubt, physical attributes in the male exercise this power without regard to the existence of conscious sensuality. On the other hand it will be found that the mental superiority of man constitutes the attractive power where physical beauty is wanting. In the upper "strata" of society this is more apparent, even if we disregard the enormous influence exercised by "blue blood" and high breeding. The possibility that superior intellectual development favors advancement in social position, and opens the way to a brilliant career, does not seem to weigh heavily in the balance of judgment.

The fetishism of body and mind is of importance in progeneration; it favors the selection of the fittest and the transmission of physical and mental virtues.

Generally speaking the following masculine qualities impose on woman, *viz.*, physical strength, courage, nobility of mind, chivalry, self-confidence, even self-assertion, insolence, bravado and a conscious show of mastery over the weaker sex.

A "Don Juan" impresses many women and elicits admiration, for he establishes the proof of his virile powers, although the inexperienced maiden can in no wise suspect the many risks of lues and chronic urethritis she runs from a marital union with this otherwise interesting rake.

The successful actor, musician or vocal artist, the circus rider, the athlete and even the criminal often fascinate the bread-and-butter miss as well as the maturer woman. At any rate, women rave over them and inundate them with love letters.

It is a well-known fact that the female heart has predominant weakness for military uniforms, that of the cavalryman ever having the preference.

The hair of man, especially the beard, the emblem of virility, the secondary symbol of generative power—is a predominant fetish with woman. In the measure in which women bestow special care upon the cultivation of their hair, men who seek to attract and please women cultivate the elegant growth of the beard, and especially that of the mustache.

The eye as well as the voice exert the same charm. Singers of renown easily touch woman's heart. They are overwhelmed with love letters and offers of marriage. Tenors have a decided advantage.

Binet refers to an observation of this character made by Dumas in his novel *La maison du vent*. A woman who falls in love with a tenor voice loses her virtue.

The author has thus far not succeeded in obtaining facts with regard to pathological fetishism in woman.

MASOCHISM IN WOMEN

In women, voluntary subjection to the opposite sex is a physiological phenomenon. Owing to her passive role in procreation and long-existent social conditions, ideas of subjection are, in women, normally connected with the idea of sexual relations. They form, so to speak, the harmonics which determine the tone-quality of feminine feeling.

Anyone conversant with the history of civilization knows in what a state of absolute subjection woman was always kept until a relatively high degree of civilization was reached;[1] and an attentive observer of life may still easily recognize how the custom of unnumbered generations, in connection with the passive role with which woman has been endowed by nature, has given her an instinctive inclination to voluntary subordination to man; he will notice that exaggeration of customary gallantry is very distasteful to women, and that a deviation from it in the direction of masterful behavior, though loudly reprehended, is often accepted with secret satisfaction.[2] Under the veneer of polite society the instinct of feminine servitude is everywhere discernible.

[1] The laws of the early Middle Ages gave the husband the right to kill the wife; those of the later Middle Ages, the right to beat her. The latter right was used freely, even by those of high standing (*cf. Schultze*, "Das höfische Leben zur Zeit des Minnesangs," Bd. i, p. 163 *et seq.*). Yet, by the side of this, the paradoxical chivalry of the Middle Ages stands unexplained.

[2] *Cf.* Lady Milford's words in *Schiller's* "Kabale und Liebe": "We women can only choose between ruling and serving; but the highest pleasure power affords is but a miserable substitute, if the greater joy of being the slaves of a man we love is denied us!" (Act II, Scene I).

Thus it is easy to regard masochism in general as a pathological growth of specific feminine mental elements—as an abnormal intensification of certain features of the psychosexual character of women—and to seek its primary origin in that sex. It may, however, be held to be established that, in women, an inclination to subordination to men (which may be regarded as an acquired, purposeful arrangement, a phenomenon of adaptation to social requirements) is to a certain extent a normal manifestation.

The reason that, under such circumstances, the "poetry" of the symbolic act of subjection is not reached lies partly in the fact that man has not the vanity of that weakling who would improve the opportunity by the display of his power (as the ladies of the Middle Ages did toward the love-serving knights), but prefers to realize solid advantages. The barbarian has his wife plow for him, and the civilized lover speculates about her dowry; she willingly endures both.

Cases of pathological increase of this instinct of subjection, in the sense of feminine masochism, are probably frequent enough, but custom represses their manifestation. Many young women like nothing better than to kneel before their husbands or lovers. Among the lower classes of Slavs it is said that the wives feel hurt if they are not beaten by their husbands. A Hungarian official informs me that the peasant women of the Somogyer Comitate do not think they are loved by their husbands until they have received the first box on the ear as a sign of love.

It would probably be difficult for the physician to find cases of feminine masochism.[1] Intrinsic and extraneous restraints—modesty and custom—naturally constitute in women insurmountable obstacles to the expression of perverse sexual instinct. Thus it happens that, up to the present time, but two cases of masochism in women have been scientifically established.

CASE 84.

Miss X., twenty-one years of age; her mother was a morphia maniac and died some years ago from nervous disorders. Her uncle (mother's side) was also a morphia-eater. One brother of the girl was neuras-

---

[1] Seydel, "Vierteljahresschr. f. ger. Med.," 1893, vol. ii, quotes as an instance of masochism the patient of Dieffenbach, who repeatedly and purposely dislocated her arm in order to experience lustful sensations when it was being set, anesthetics not being known then.

thenic, another a masochist (wished to be beaten with a cane by proud, noble ladies). Miss X. had never had a severe illness, but at times suffered from headaches. She considered herself to be physically sound, but periodically insane, *viz.*, when she was haunted by the fancies which she thus described:

Since her earliest youth she fancied herself being whipped. She simply reveled in these ideas, and had the most intense desire to be severely punished with a rattan cane.

This desire, she claimed, originated from the fact that at the age of five a friend of her father's took her for fun across his knees, pretending to whip her. Since then she had longed for the opportunity of being caned, but to her great regret her wish was never realized. At these periods she imagined herself as absolutely helpless and fettered. The mere mention of the words "rattan cane" and "to whip" caused her intense excitement. Only for the last two years had she associated these ideas with the male sex. Previously she only thought of a severe schoolmistress or simply a hand.

Now she wished to be the slave of a man whom she loved; she would kiss his feet if he would only whip her.

She did not understand that these manifestations were of a sexual nature.

A few quotations from her letters are characteristic as bearing upon the masochistic character of this case:

In former years I seriously contemplated going into a lunatic asylum whenever these ideas worried me. I fell upon this idea while reading how the director of an insane asylum pulled a lady by the hair from her bed and beat her with a cane and a riding-whip. I longed to be treated in a similar manner at such an institute, and have therefore unconsciously associated my ideas with the male sex. I liked, however, best to think of brutal, uneducated female warders beating me mercilessly.

Lying (in fancy) before him, he puts one foot on my neck while I kiss the other. I revel in the idea of being whipped by him; but this changes often, and I fancy quite different scenes in which he beats me. At times I take the blows as so many tokens of love—he is at first extremely kind and tender, and then, in the excess of his love, he beats me. I fancy that to beat me for love's sake gives him the highest pleasure. Often I have dreamed that I was his slave—but, mind you, not his female slave! For instance, I have imagined that he was Robinson and I the savage that served him. I often look at the pictures in which Robinson puts his foot on the neck of the savage. I now find an explanation of these strange fancies: I look upon woman in general as low, far below man; but I am otherwise extremely proud and quite indomitable, whence it arises that I think as a man (who is by nature proud and superior). This renders my humiliation before the man I love the more intense. I have also fancied myself to be his female slave; but this does not suffice, for after all every woman can be the slave of her husband.

CASE 85.

Miss v. X., aged thirty-five; of greatly predisposed family. For some years she had been in the initial stages of delusion of persecution. This sprang from cerebro-spinal neurasthenia, the origin of which was found to be sexual hyperexcitation. At twenty-four she was given to masturbation. As a result of disappointment in an engagement, she began to practice masturbation and psychical onanism. *Inclination toward persons of her own sex never occurred.* The patient says: "At the age of six or eight I conceived a desire to be whipped. Since I had never been whipped, and had never been present when others were thus punished, I cannot understand how I came to have this strange desire. I can only think that it is congenital. With these ideas of being whipped I had a feeling of actual delight, and pictured in my fancy how fine it would be to be whipped by one of my female friends. I never had any thought of being whipped by a man. I reveled in the idea, and never attempted any actual realization of my fancies, which disappeared after my tenth year. Only when I read Rousseau's *Confessions*, at the age of thirty-four, did I understand what my longing for whippings meant, and that my abnormal ideas were like those of Rousseau."

On account of its original character and the reference to Rousseau, this case may with certainty be called a case of masochism. The fact that it is a female friend who is conceived in imagination as whipping her is explained by the circumstance that the masochistic desire was here present in the mind of a child before the psychical *vita sexualis* had developed and the instinct for the male had been awakened. Antipathic sexual instinct is here expressly excluded.

CASE 86.

A physician in the General Hospital of Vienna had his attention drawn to a girl who used to call on the medical assistants of the institution. When meeting one of them she would express great delight at meeting a medical man and ask him to at once undertake a gynecological examination on her. She said she would make resistance, but he must take no notice of that, on the contrary ask her to be calm and proceed with the examination. If X. consented, the scene would be enacted as she desired. She would resist, and thus work herself up into a high state of sexual excitement. If the medical man refused to proceed any further, she would beg him not to desist. It was quite evident that the examination was only requested for the purpose of inducing the highest possible degree of orgasm. When the medical man refused coitus she felt deeply offended, but begged him to let her come again. Money she never accepted.

It is apparent that orgasm was not induced by the mere palpation of the genitals, but the exciting cause undoubtedly lay in the act of force, which was always demanded and which became the equivalent of coitus. It is evidently a manifestation belonging in the province of masochism in woman.

AN ATTEMPT TO EXPLAIN MASOCHISM

The facts of masochism are certainly among the most interesting in the domain of psychopathology. An attempt at explanation must first seek to distinguish in them the essential from the unessential. The distinguishing characteristic in masochism is certainly the unlimited subjection to the will of a person of the opposite sex (in sadism, on the contrary, the unlimited mastery of this person), with the awakening and accompaniment of lustful sexual feelings to the degree of orgasm. From the foregoing it is clear that the particular manner in which this relation of subjection or domination is expressed, whether merely in symbolic acts or whether there is also a desire to suffer pain at the hands of a person of the opposite sex, is a subordinate matter.

While sadism may be looked upon as a pathological intensification of the masculine sexual character in its psychical peculiarities, masochism rather represents a pathological degeneration of the distinctive psychical peculiarities of woman. But masculine masochism is undoubtedly frequent; and it is this that comes most frequently under observation and almost exclusively makes up the series of observed cases. The reason for this has been previously stated.

Two sources of masochism can be distinguished in the sphere of normal phenomena. The first is, that in the state of lustful excitement every impression made by the person giving rise to the sexual stimulus, independently of the nature of its action, is pleasing to the individual excited.

It is entirely physiological that playful taps and light blows should be taken for caresses,[1]

> Like the lover's pinch, which hurts and is desired.
> —*Antony and Cleopatra*, v, 2

From here the step is not long to a state where the wish to experience a very intense impression at the hands of the consort leads to a desire for blows, etc., in cases of pathological intensification of lust; for pain is ever a ready means for producing intense bodily impressions. Just as in sadism the sexual emotion leads to a state of exaltation in which the excessive motor excitement implicates neighboring nervous tracts, so in masochism an ecstatic state arises, in which the rising flood of a single emotion ravenously devours and covers with lust every impression coming from the beloved person.

The second and, indeed, the most important source of maso-

---

[1] Analogous facts are found in the animal kingdom. *Pulmonata Cuv.*, for instance, possess a small calcareous staff which lies hidden in a special pouch of the body, but is at the time of mating projected and used as a means of sexual excitement, producing, beyond doubt, pain.

chism is to be sought in a widespread phenomenon, which, though it is extraordinary and abnormal, yet by no means lies within the domain of sexual perversion.

I here refer to the very prevalent fact that in innumerable instances, which occur in all varieties, one individual becomes dependent on another of the opposite sex, in a very extraordinary and remarkable manner—even to the loss of all independent willpower; a dependence which forces the party in subjection to acts and suffering which greatly prejudice personal interest, and often enough lead to offenses against both morality and law.

This dependence, however, differs from the manifestations of normal life only in the intensity of the sexual feeling that here comes in play, and in the slight degree of willpower necessary for the maintenance of its equilibrium. The difference is one of intensity, not of quality, as in masochistic manifestations.

This dependence of one person upon another of the opposite sex—abnormal but not perverse, a phenomenon possessing great interest when regarded from a forensic standpoint—I designate *"sexual bondage,"*[1] for the relations and circumstances attending it have in all respects the character of bondage. The will of the ruling[2] individual dominates that of the person in subjection, just as the master's does that of bondsmen.

This "sexual bondage," as has been said, is certainly an abnormal phenomenon. It begins with the first deviation from the normal. The degree of dependence of one person upon another, or of two upon each other, resulting from individual peculiarity in the intensity of motives that in themselves are normal, constitutes the normal standard established by law and custom. Sexual bondage is not a perverse manifestation, however; the instinctive activities at work here are the

---

[1] *Cf.* the author's article, "Über geschlechtliche Hörigkeit und Masochismus," in the "Psychiatrische Jahrbücher," Bd. x, p. 169 *et seq.*, where this subject is treated in detail, and particularly from the forensic standpoint.

[2] The expressions "slave" and "slavery," though often used metaphorically under such circumstances, are avoided here because they are the favorite expressions of masochism, from which this "bondage" must be strictly differentiated.

The expression "bondage" is not to be construed to mean *J. S. Mill's* "Bondage of Woman." What *Mill* designates with this expression are laws and customs, social and historical facts. Here, however, we always speak of facts having peculiar individual motives that even conflict with prevalent customs and laws. Besides, it has reference to either sex.

same as those that set in motion—even though it be with less violence—the psychical *vita sexualis* which moves entirely within normal limits.

Fear of losing the companion and the desire to keep him always content, amiable, and inclined to sexual intercourse are here the motives of the individual in subjection. An extraordinary degree of love —which, particularly in women, does not always indicate an unusual degree of sensuality—and a weak character are the simple elements of this extraordinary process.[1]

The motive of the dominant individual is egotism which finds unlimited room for action.

The manifestations of sexual bondage are various in form, and the cases are very numerous.[2] At every step in life we find men that have fallen into sexual bondage. Among married men, henpecked husbands belong to this category, particularly elderly men who marry young wives and try to overcome the disparity of years and physical defects by unconditional submission to the wife's every whim; and unmarried men of ripe maturity, who seek to better their last chance of love by unlimited sacrifice, are also to be enumerated here. Here belong, also, men of any age, who, seized by hot passion for a woman, meet coldness and calculation, and have to capitulate on hard conditions; men of loving natures who allow themselves to be persuaded to marriage by notorious prostitutes; men who, to run after adventuresses, leave everything and jeopardize their future; husbands and fathers who leave wife and child, to lay the income of a family at the feet of a harlot.

But, numerous as the examples of masculine "bondage" are, every observer of life who is at all unprejudiced must allow that they are far from equaling in number and importance the cases of feminine

[1] Perhaps the most important element is, that by the habit of submission a kind of mechanical obedience, without consciousness of its motives, which operates with automatic certainty, may be established, having no opposing motives to contend with, because it lies beyond the threshold of consciousness; and it may be used by the dominant individual like an inanimate instrument.

[2] Sexual bondage, of course, plays a role in all literature. Indeed, for the poet, the extraordinary manifestations of the sexual life that are not perverse form a rich and open field. The most celebrated description of masculine "bondage" is that by *Abbé Prévost*, "Manon Lescault." An excellent description of feminine "bondage" is that of "Leone Leoni," by *George Sand*. But first of all comes *Kleist's* "Käthchen von Heilbronn," who himself called it the counterpart of (sadistic) "Penthesilea." *Halm's* "Griseldis" and many other similar poems also belong here.

"bondage." This is easily explained. For a man, love is almost always only an episode, and he has many other and important interests; for a woman, on the other hand, love is the principal thing in life, and, until the birth of children, always her first interest. After this it is still oftener her first thought, but always takes at least the second place. But what is still more important, a man ruled by this impulse easily satisfies it in embraces for which he finds unlimited opportunities. A woman in the upper classes of society, if she has a husband, is bound to him alone; and even in the lower classes there are still great obstacles to polyandry. Therefore, *a woman's husband means for her the whole sex*, and his importance to her becomes very great. It must also be considered that the normal relation established by law and custom between husband and wife is far from being one of equality. In itself it expresses a sufficient predominance of woman's dependence. The concessions she makes to her lover, to retain the love which it would be almost impossible for her to replace, only plunge her deeper in bondage; and this increases the insatiable demands of husbands resolved to use their advantage and traffic in women's readiness to sacrifice themselves.

Here may be placed the fortune-hunter, who for money allows himself to be enveloped in the easily created illusions of a maiden; the seducer, and the man who compromises wives, calculating on blackmail; the gilded army officer and the musician with the lion's mane, who know so well how to stammer "Thee or death!" as a means to pay debts and provide a life of ease. Here, too, belong the kitchen-soldier, whose love the cook returns with love *plus* means to satisfy a different appetite; the drinker, who consumes the savings of the mistress he marries; and the man who with blows compels the prostitute on whom he lives to earn a certain sum for him daily. These are only a few of the innumerable forms of bondage into which woman is forced by her greater need of love and the difficulties of her position.

It was necessary to give the subject of "sexual bondage" here brief consideration, for in it may be clearly discerned the soil from which the main root of masochism springs. The relationship of these two phenomena of psychical sexual life is immediately apparent. Bondage and masochism both consist of the unconditional subjection of the individual affected with this abnormality to a person of the opposite

sex, and of domination of the former by the latter.[1] The two phenomena, however, must be strictly differentiated; they are not different in degree, but in quality.

Sexual bondage is not a perversion and not pathological; the
elements from which it arises—love and weakness of will—are not
perverse; it is only their simultaneous activity that produces the abnormal result which is so opposed to self-interest, and often to custom and law. The motive, in obedience to which the subordinated
individual acts and endures tyranny, is the normal instinct toward
women (or men), the satisfaction of which is the price of bondage.
The acts of the person in subjection, by means of which the bondage
is expressed, are performed at the command of the ruling individual,
to satisfy selfishness, etc. For the subordinated individual they have
no independent purpose; they are only the means to an end—to obtain or retain possession of the ruling individual. Finally, bondage is
a result of love for a particular person; it first appears when this love
is awakened.

In masochism, which is decidedly abnormal and a perversion, this
is all very different. The motive underlying the acts and suffering of
the person in subjection is here the charm afforded by the tyranny
in itself. There may, at the same time, be a desire for coitus with the
dominant person, but the impulse is directed to the acts which serve
to express the tyranny, as the immediate objects of gratification.
These acts in which masochism is expressed are, for the individual in
subjection, not means to an end, as in bondage, but the end in themselves. Finally, in masochism the longing for subjection occurs a
priori before the occurrence of an inclination to any particular object
of love.

The connection between bondage and masochism may be assumed by reason of the correspondence of the two phenomena in the
objective condition of dependence, notwithstanding the difference in
their motives; and the transformation of the abnormality into the
perversion probably takes place in the following manner: Anyone living for a long time in sexual bondage becomes disposed to acquire a
slight degree of masochism. Love that willingly bears the tyranny of

---

[1] Cases may occur in which the sexual bondage is expressed in the same acts that are common in
masochism. When rough men beat their wives, and the latter suffer for love, without, however,
having a desire for blows, we have a pseudo form of bondage that may simulate masochism.

the loved one then becomes an immediate love of tyranny. *When the idea of being tyrannized is for a long time closely associated with the lustful thought of the beloved person, the lustful emotion is finally transferred to the tyranny itself, and the transformation to perversion is completed.* This is the manner in which masochism may be acquired by cultivation.[1]

Thus a mild degree of masochism may arise from "bondage"— become acquired; but genuine, complete, deep-rooted masochism, with its feverish longing for subjection from the time of earliest youth, is congenital.

The explanation of the origin of the perversion—infrequent though it be—of fully developed masochism is most probably to be found in the assumption that it arises from the more frequent abnormality of "sexual bondage," through which, now and then, *this abnormality is hereditarily transferred to a psychopathic individual in such a manner that it becomes transformed into a perversion.* It has been previously shown how a slight displacement of the psychical elements under consideration may effect this transition. Whatever effects associating habits may have on possible cases of acquired masochism, the same effects are produced by the varying tricks of heredity upon

---

[1] It is highly interesting, and dependent upon the nature of bondage and masochism, which essentially correspond in external effects, that to illustrate the former certain playful, metaphorical expressions are in general use; such as "slavery," "to bear chains," "bound," "to hold the whip over," "to harness to the triumphal car," "to lie at the feet," "henpecked," etc.—all things which, literally carried out, form the objects of the masochist's desire. Such similes are frequently used in daily life and have become trite. They are derived from the language of poetry. Poetry has always recognized, within the general idea of the passion of love, the element of dependence in the lover who practices self-sacrifice spontaneously or of necessity. The facts of "bondage" have also always presented themselves to the poetical imagination. When the poet chooses such expressions as those mentioned to picture the dependence of the lover in striking similes, *he proceeds exactly on the same lines as does the masochist, viz.*, to intensify the idea of his dependence (his ultimate aim), he creates such situations in reality. In ancient poetry, the expression "domina" is used to signify the loved one, with a preference for the simile of "casting in chains" (*e.g., Horace,* Od. iv, 11). From antiquity through all the centuries to our own times (*cf. Grillparzer,* "Ottokar," Act v: "To rule is sweet, almost as sweet as to obey") the poetry of love is filled with similar phrases and similes. The history of the word "mistress" is also interesting. But poetry reacts on life. It is probable that the courtly chivalry of the Middle Ages arose in this way. In its reverence for women as "mistresses" in society and in individual love-relations; its transference of the relations of feudalism and vassalage to the relation between the knight and his lady; its submission to all feminine whims; its love-tests and vows; its duty of obedience to every command of the lady—in all this, chivalry appears as a systematic, poetical development of the "bondage" of love. Certain extreme manifestations, like the deeds and sufferings of *Ulrich von Lichtenstein* or *Pierre Vidal* in the service of their ladies; or the practice of the fraternity of the "Galois" in France, whose members sought martyrdom in love and subjected themselves to all kinds of suffering—these clearly have a masochistic character, and demonstrate the natural transformation of one phenomenon into the other.

original masochism. No new element is thereby added to "bondage," but on the contrary the very element is deleted which cements love and dependence, and thereby distinguishes "bondage" from masochism and abnormality from perversion. It is quite natural that only the instinctive element is transmitted.

This transition from abnormality into perversion, through hereditary transference, takes place very easily where the psychopathic constitution of the descendant presents the other factor of masochism—*i.e.*, what has been previously called its main root—the tendency of sexually hyperesthetic natures to assimilate all impressions coming from the beloved person with the sexual impression.

From these two elements—from "sexual bondage" on the one hand and from the above-mentioned disposition to sexual ecstasy, which apperceives even maltreatment with lustful emotion, on the other—the roots of which may be traced back to the field of physiological facts, masochism arises from the basis of psychopathic predisposition, insofar as its sexual hyperesthesia intensifies first all the physiological accessories of the *vita sexualis* and, finally, only its abnormal accompaniments, to the pathological degree of perversion.[1]

At any rate, masochism, as a congenital sexual perversion, constitutes a functional sign of degeneration in (almost exclusively) hereditary taint; and this clinical deduction is confirmed in my cases of masochism and sadism. It is easy to demonstrate that the peculiar, psychically anomalous direction of the sexual life represented in masochism is an original abnormality, and not, so to speak, cultivated in a predisposed individual by passive flagellation, through association of ideas, as Rousseau and Binet contend. This is shown by the numerous cases of masochism—in fact, the majority—in which flagellation never appears, in which the perverse impulse is directed exclusively to purely symbolic acts expressing subjection without any

[1] If it be considered that, as shown above, "sexual bondage" is a phenomenon observed much more frequently and in a more pronounced degree in the female sex than in the male, the thought arises that masochism (if not always, at least as a rule) is an inheritance of the "bondage" of feminine ancestry. Thus it comes into a relation—though distant—with antipathic sexual instinct, as a transference to the male of a perversion really belonging to the female.

It must, however, be emphasized that "bondage" also plays no unimportant role in the masculine *vita sexualis*, and that masochism in man may also be explained without any such transference of feminine elements. It must also be remembered here that masochism, as well as its counterpart, sadism, occurs in irregular combination with antipathic sexual instinct.

actual infliction of pain. This is demonstrated by the whole series of observations, from Case 50, given here.

The same result—namely, that passive flagellation is not the nucleus around which all the rest is gathered—is reached when closer study is given to the cases in which passive flagellation plays a role, as in Cases 50 and 52. Case 58 is particularly instructive in relation to this; for in this instance there can be no thought of a sexually stimulating effect by punishment received in youth. Moreover, in this case, connection with an early experience is not possible; for the situation constituting the object of principal sexual interest is absolutely incapable of being carried out by a child.

Finally, the origin of masochism from purely psychical elements, on confronting it with sadism, is convincingly demonstrated. That passive flagellation occurs so frequently in masochism is explained simply by the fact that it is the most extreme means of expressing the relation of subjection.

I repeat that the decisive points in the differentiation of simple passive flagellation from flagellation dependent upon masochistic desire are, that in the former the act is a means to render coitus, or at least ejaculation, possible; and that in the latter it is a means of gratification of masochistic desires.

As we have already seen, masochists subject themselves to all other kinds of maltreatment and suffering in which there can be no question of reflex excitation of lust. Since such cases are numerous, we must in these acts (as well as in flagellation in masochists, having like significance) seek to ascertain the relation in which pain and lust stand to each other. From the statement of a masochist it is as follows:

The relation is not of such a nature that what causes physical pain is here simply perceived as physical pleasure; for the person in a state of masochistic ecstasy feels no pain, either because, by reason of his emotional state (like that of the soldier in battle), the physical effect on his cutaneous nerves is not apperceived, or because (as with religious martyrs and enthusiasts), in the preoccupation of consciousness with lustful emotion, the idea of maltreatment remains merely a symbol, without its quality of pain.

To a certain extent there is overcompensation of physical pain in the psychical pleasure, and only the excess remains in consciousness as psychical lust. This also undergoes an increase, since, either through reflex spinal influence or through a peculiar coloring in the sensorium of sensory impressions, a kind of hallucination of bodily pleasure takes place, with a vague localization of the objectively projected sensation.

In the self-torture of religious enthusiasts (fakirs, howling dervishes, religious flagellants) there is an analogous state, only with a difference in the quality of pleasurable feeling. Here the conception of martyrdom is also apperceived without its pain; for consciousness is filled with the pleasurably colored idea of serving God, atoning for sins, deserving heaven, etc., through martyrdom.

In order to give masochism its proper place in the sphere of sexual perversion, we must proceed from the fact that it is a manifestation of psychical characteristics of the feminine type transcending into pathological conditions, insofar as its determining marks are suffering, subjection to the will of others, and to force. Among people of a lower class of culture the subjection of women is extended even to brutality. This flagrant proof of dependence is felt by women even with sensual pleasure and accepted as a token of love. It is probable that the woman of high civilization looks upon the role of being overshadowed by the male consort as an acceptable situation which forms a portion of the lustful feeling developed in the sexual act. The daring and self-confident demeanor of men undoubtedly exercises a sexual charm over women. It cannot be doubted that the masochist considers himself in a passive, feminine role toward his mistress and that his sexual gratification is governed by the success his illusion experiences in the complete subjection to the will of the consort. The pleasurable feeling, call it lust, resulting from this act differs per se in no wise from the feeling which women derive from the sexual act.

The masochistically inclined individual seeks and finds an equivalent for his purpose in the fact that he endows in his imagination the consort with certain masculine psychical sexual characteristics— i.e., in a perverse manner, insofar as the sadistic female partner constitutes his ideal.

From this emanates the deduction that masochism is, properly speaking, only a rudimentary form of antipathic sexual instinct. It is a partial *effemination* which has only apperceived the secondary sexual characteristics of the psychical sexual life.

This assumption is supported by the fact that heterosexual masochists consider themselves merely as individuals endowed with feminine feelings.[1] Observation shows that they really possess feminine traits of character. This renders it intelligible that the masochistic element is so frequently found in homosexual men.[2]

In the woman masochist also these relations to antipathic sexual instinct are to be found. *Cf.*, Case 84. Moll quotes a typical case of homosexuality in a woman afflicted with passive flagellantism and koprolagnia:

CASE 87.

Miss X., aged twenty-six. At the age of six mutual cunnilingus; then up to seventeen for lack of opportunity, solitary masturbation. Since then cunnilingus with various female friends, at times playing the passive, at others the active role, always producing ejaculation in herself. For years koprolagnia. She experienced the greatest pleasure in licking the anus of her beloved women friends, and licked the menstrual blood of her friend. The same effect was gained by flagellation on her buttocks by a naked and strong female friend. The thought of performing koprolagnia in a male person was repulsive to her. Satisfaction in cunnilingus by a male she only obtained when she imagined that the act was performed by a woman, not by a man. Coitus with a man she disdained. Erotic dreams were always of a homosexual nature and were confined to active or passive cunnilingus. During the mutual kissing, the greatest pleasure was the biting by her companion, by preference in the lobe of the ear, causing pain and subsequent swelling.

X. always had a leaning to male occupations, loved to be among men as one of their own. From her tenth to her fifteenth year she

---

[1] *Cf.* Cases 57 and 58.

[2] *Cf.* Case 67 in *Schrenck-Notzing; Moll*, Contr. Sexualempfindung, 3rd edition, p. 265 (gentleman who pestered an officer with letters in which he begged him to be allowed to clean his boots); *ibidem*, p. 281 (gentleman who was agitated by two wishes, *viz.*: (1) to be a woman that he might have coitus with the man he loved, (2) to be maltreated by the same); *ibidem*, Case 17; *ditto*, p. 283 (man who finds satisfaction in the act with another man only when the latter rubs his back with a hard brush till the blood flows); p. 284 (koprolagnia); p. 317; *v. Krafft*, Psycop. sexual., 6th edit., Case 43; 8th edit., Cases 46, 114, 115; *item*, Jahrb. f. Psychiatrie, xii, pp. 339 and 351; *item*, "Arbeiten," iv, p. 134.

worked in the brewery of a relative, if possible clad in trousers and a leather apron. She was bright, intelligent and good-natured, and felt quite happy in her perverse, homosexual existence. She smoked and drank beer. Female larynx (Dr. Flatau), small, badly developed breasts, large hands and feet.

EDWARD H. CLARKE

FROM

SEX IN EDUCATION: A FAIR CHANCE FOR THE GIRLS

Edward Clarke (1820–1877): A Harvard University professor, Edward Clarke wrote Sex in Education: A Fair Chance for the Girls, *which was published in 1873. It asserted that university education for women resulted in a number of reproductive diseases and disorders, ultimately rendering them unfit to bear children. Henry Maudsley responded favorably to this work a year later in* Sex in Mind and in Education.

PART I.

INTRODUCTORY.

"Is there any thing better in a State than that both women and men be rendered the very best? There is not."—Plato.

It is idle to say that what is right for man is wrong for woman. Pure reason, abstract right and wrong, have nothing to do with sex: they neither recognize nor know it. They teach that what is right or wrong for man is equally right and wrong for woman. Both sexes are bound by the same code of morals; both are amenable to the same divine law. Both have a right to do the best they can; or, to speak more justly, both should feel the duty, and have the opportunity, to do their best. Each must justify its existence by becoming a complete development of manhood and womanhood; and each should refuse whatever limits or dwarfs that development.

The problem of woman's sphere, to use the modern phrase, is not to be solved by applying to it abstract principles of right and wrong. Its solution must be obtained from physiology, not from ethics or metaphysics. The question must be submitted to Agassiz and Huxley, not to Kant or Calvin, to Church or Pope. Without denying the self-evident proposition, that whatever a woman can do, she has a right to do, the question at once arises, What can she do? And this includes the further question, What can she best do? A girl can hold a plow, and ply a needle, after a fashion. If she can do both better than a man, she ought to be both farmer and seamstress; but if, on the whole, her husband can hold best the plow, and she ply best the needle, they should divide the labor. He should be master of the plow, and she mistress of the loom. The *quaestio vexata* of woman's sphere will be decided by her organization. This limits her power, and reveals her divinely-appointed tasks, just as man's organization limits his power, and reveals his work. In the development of the organization is to be found the way of strength and power for both sexes. Limitation or abortion of development leads both to weakness and failure.

Neither is there any such thing as inferiority or superiority in this matter. Man is not superior to woman, nor woman to man. The relation of the sexes is one of equality, not of better and worse, or of higher and lower. By this it is not intended to say that the sexes are the same. They are different, widely different from each other, and so different that each can do, in certain directions, what the other cannot; and in other directions, where both can do the same things, one sex, as a rule, can do them better than the other; and in still other matters they seem to be so nearly alike, that they can interchange labor without perceptible difference. All this is so well known, that it would be useless to refer to it, were it not that much of the discussion of the irrepressible woman-question, and many of the efforts for bettering her education and widening her sphere, seem to ignore any difference of the sexes; seem to treat her as if she were identical with man, and to be trained in precisely the same way; as if her organization, and consequently her function, were masculine, not feminine. There are those who write and act as if their object were to assimilate

woman as much as possible to man, by dropping all that is distinc-
tively feminine out of her, and putting into her as large an amount
of masculineness as possible. These persons tacitly admit the error
just alluded to, that woman is inferior to man, and strive to get rid
of the inferiority by making her a man. There may be some subtle
physiological basis for such views—some strange quality of brain; for
some who hold and advocate them are of those, who, having missed
the symmetry and organic balance that harmonious development
yields, have drifted into an hermaphroditic condition. One of this
class, who was glad to have escaped the chains of matrimony, but
knew the value and lamented the loss of maternity, wished she had
been born a widow with two children. These misconceptions arise
from mistaking difference of organization and function for difference
of position in the scale of being, which is equivalent to saying that
man is rated higher in the divine order because he has more muscle,
and woman lower because she has more fat. The loftiest ideal of
humanity, rejecting all comparisons of inferiority and superiority between the sexes, demands that each shall be perfect in its kind, and
not be hindered in its best work. The lily is not inferior to the rose,
nor the oak superior to the clover: yet the glory of the lily is one,
and the glory of the oak is another; and the use of the oak is not the
use of the clover. That is poor horticulture which would train them
all alike.

When Col. Higginson asked, not long ago, in one of his charming essays, that almost persuade the reader, "Ought women to learn
the alphabet?" and added, "Give woman, if you dare, the alphabet,
then summon her to the career," his physiology was not equal to his
wit. Women will learn the alphabet at any rate; and man will be
powerless to prevent them, should he undertake so ungracious a task.
The real question is not, *Shall* women learn the alphabet? but *How*
shall they learn it? In this case, how is more important than ought
or shall. The principle and duty are not denied. The method is not
so plain.

The fact that women have often equalled and sometimes excelled
men in physical labor, intellectual effort, and lofty heroism, is sufficient proof that women have muscle, mind, and soul, as well as men;
but it is no proof that they have had, or should have, the same kind
of training; nor is it any proof that they are destined for the same
career as men. The presumption is, that if woman, subjected to a

masculine training, arranged for the development of a masculine organization, can equal man, she ought to excel him if educated by a feminine training, arranged to develop a feminine organization. Indeed, I have somewhere encountered an author who boldly affirms the superiority of women to all existences on this planet, because of the complexity of their organization. Without undertaking to endorse such an opinion, it may be affirmed, that an appropriate method of education for girls—one that should not ignore the mechanism of their bodies or blight any of their vital organs—would yield a better result than the world has yet seen.

Gail Hamilton's statement is true, that, "a girl can go to school, pursue all the studies which Dr. Todd enumerates, except *ad infinitum*; know them, not as well as a chemist knows chemistry or a botanist botany, but as well as they are known by boys of her age and training, as well, indeed, as they are known by many college-taught men, enough, at least, to be a solace and a resource to her; then graduate before she is eighteen, and come out of school as healthy, as fresh, as eager, as she went in." But it is not true that she can do all this, and retain uninjured health and a future secure from neuralgia, uterine disease, hysteria, and other derangements of the nervous system, if she follows the same method that boys are trained in. Boys must study and work in a boy's way, and girls in a girl's way. They may study the same books, and attain an equal result, but should not follow the same method. Mary can master Virgil and Euclid as well as George; but both will be dwarfed,—defrauded of their rightful attainment,—if both are confined to the same methods. It is said that Elena Cornaro, the accomplished professor of six languages, whose statue adorns and honors Padua, was educated like a boy. This means that she was initiated into, and mastered, the studies that were considered to be the peculiar dower of men. It does not mean that her life was a man's life, her way of study a man's way of study, or that, in acquiring six languages, she ignored her own organization. Women who choose to do so can master the humanities and the mathematics, encounter the labor of the law and the pulpit, endure the hardness of physic and the conflicts of politics; but they must do it all in woman's way, not in man's way. In all their work they must respect their own organization, and remain women, not strive to be men, or they will ignominiously fail. For both sexes, there is no exception to the law, that their greatest power and largest attainment lie in the perfect development of their organization. "Woman," says a late writer, "must be regarded as woman, not as a nondescript animal, with greater or less capacity for assimilation to man." If we would give our girls a fair chance, and see them become and do their best by reaching after and attaining an ideal beauty and power, which shall be a crown of glory and a tower of strength to the republic, we must look after their complete development as women. Wherein they are men, they should be educated as men; wherein they are women, they should be educated as women. The physiological motto is, Educate a man for manhood, a woman for womanhood, both for humanity. In this lies the hope of the race.

Perhaps it should be mentioned in this connection, that, throughout this paper, education is not used in the limited and technical sense of intellectual or mental training alone. By saying there is a boy's way of study and a girl's way of study, it is not asserted that the intellectual process which masters Juvenal, German, or chemistry, is different for the two sexes. Education is here intended to include what its etymology indicates, the drawing out and development of every part of the system; and this necessarily includes the whole manner of life, physical and psychical, during the educational period. "Education," says Worcester, "comprehends all that series of instruction and discipline which is intended to enlighten the understanding, correct the temper, and form the manners and habits, of youth, and fit them for usefulness in their future stations." It has been and is the misfortune of this country, and particularly of New England, that education, stripped of this, its proper signification, has popularly stood for studying, without regard to the physical training or no training that the schools afford. The cerebral processes by which the acquisition of knowledge is made are the same for each sex; but the mode of life which gives the finest nurture to the brain, and so enables those processes to yield their best result, is not the same for each sex. The best educational training for a boy is not the best for a girl, nor that for a girl best for a boy.

The delicate bloom, early but rapidly fading beauty, and singular pallor of American girls and women have almost passed into a proverb. The first observation of a European that lands upon our shores is, that our women are a feeble race; and, if he is a physiological observer, he is sure to add, They will give birth to a feeble race, not of women only, but of men as well. "I never saw before so many

pretty girls together," said Lady Amberley to the writer, after a visit
to the public schools of Boston; and then added, "They all looked
sick." Circumstances have repeatedly carried me to Europe, where I
am always surprised by the red blood that fills and colors the faces
of ladies and peasant girls, reminding one of the canvas of Rubens
and Murillo; and am always equally surprised on my return, by
crowds of pale, bloodless female faces, that suggest consumption,
scrofula, anemia, and neuralgia. To a large extent, our present system
of educating girls is the cause of this pallor and weakness. How our
schools, through their methods of education, contribute to this unfortunate result, and how our colleges that have undertaken to educate girls like boys, that is, in the same way, have succeeded in
intensifying the evils of the schools, will be pointed out in another
place.

It has just been said that the educational methods of our schools
and colleges for girls are, to a large extent, the cause of "the thousand
ills" that beset American women. Let it be remembered that this is
not asserting that such methods of education are the sole cause of
female weaknesses, but only that they are one cause, and one of the
most important causes of it. An immense loss of female power may
be fairly charged to irrational cooking and indigestible diet. We live
in the zone of perpetual pie and doughnut; and our girls revel in
those unassimilable abominations. Much also may be credited to artificial deformities strapped to the spine, or piled on the head, much
to corsets and skirts, and as much to the omission of clothing where
it is needed as to excess where the body does not require it; but, after
the amplest allowance for these as causes of weakness, there remains
a large margin of disease unaccounted for. Those grievous maladies
which torture a woman's earthly existence, called leucorrhoea, amenorrhoea, dysmenorrhoea, chronic and acute ovaritis, prolapsus uteri,
hysteria, neuralgia, and the like, are indirectly affected by food, clothing, and exercise; they are directly and largely affected by the causes
that will be presently pointed out, and which arise from a neglect of
the peculiarities of a woman's organization. The regimen of our
schools fosters this neglect. The regimen of a college arranged for
boys, if imposed on girls, would foster it still more.

The scope of this paper does not permit the discussion of these
other causes of female weaknesses. Its object is to call attention to
the errors of physical training that have crept into, and twined them-

selves about, our ways of educating girls, both in public and private schools, and which now threaten to attain a larger development, and inflict a consequently greater injury, by their introduction into colleges and large seminaries of learning, that have adopted, or are preparing to adopt, the co-education of the sexes. Even if there were space to do so, it would not be necessary to discuss here the other causes alluded to. They are receiving the amplest attention elsewhere. The gifted authoress of "The Gates Ajar" has blown her trumpet with no uncertain sound, in explanation and advocacy of a new-clothes philosophy, which her sisters will do well to heed rather than to ridicule. It would be a blessing to the race, if some inspired prophet of clothes would appear, who should teach the coming woman how, in pharmaceutical phrase, to fit, put on, wear, and take off her dress,—

"Cito, Tuto, et Jucunde."

Corsets that embrace the waist with a tighter and steadier grip than any lover's arm, and skirts that weight the hips with heavier than maternal burdens, have often caused grievous maladies, and imposed a needless invalidism. Yet, recognizing all this, it must not be forgotten that breeches do not make a man, nor the want of them unmake a woman.

Let the statement be emphasized and reiterated until it is heeded, that woman's neglect of her own organization, though not the sole explanation and cause of her many weaknesses, more than any single cause, adds to their number, and intensifies their power. It limits and lowers her action very much, as man is limited and degraded by dissipation. The saddest part of it all is, that this neglect of herself in girlhood, when her organization is ductile and impressible, breeds the germs of diseases that in later life yield torturing or fatal maladies. Every physician's notebook affords copious illustrations of these statements. The number of them which the writer has seen prompted this imperfect essay upon a subject in which the public has a most vital interest, and with regard to which it acts with the courage of ignorance.

Two considerations deserve to be mentioned in this connection. One is, that no organ or function in plant, animal, or human kind can be properly regarded as a disability or source of weakness. Through ignorance or misdirection, it may limit or enfeeble the animal or being that misguides it; but, rightly guided and developed, it is either in itself a source of power and grace to its parent stock, or a necessary stage in the development of larger grace and power. The female organization is no exception to this law; nor are the particular set of organs and their functions with which this essay has to deal an exception to it. The periodical movements which characterize and influence woman's structure for more than half her terrestrial life, and which, in their ebb and flow, sway every fiber and thrill every nerve of her body a dozen times a year, and the occasional pregnancies which test her material resources, and cradle the race, are, or are evidently intended to be, fountains of power, not hindrances, to her. They are not infrequently spoken of by women themselves with half-smothered anathemas; often endured only as a necessary evil and sign of inferiority; and commonly ignored, till some steadily-advancing malady whips the recalcitrant sufferer into acknowledgment of their power, and respect for their function. All this is a sad mistake. It is a foolish and criminal delicacy that has persuaded woman to be so ashamed of the temple God built for her as to neglect one of its most important services. On account of this neglect, each succeeding generation, obedient to the law of hereditary transmission, has become feebler than its predecessor. Our great-grandmothers are pointed at as types of female physical excellence; their great-granddaughters as illustrations of female physical degeneracy. There is consolation, however, in the hope, based on substantial physiological data, that our great-granddaughters may recapture their ancestors' bloom and force. "Three generations of wholesome life," says Mr. Greg, "might suffice to eliminate the ancestral poison, for the *vis medicatrix naturae* has wonderful efficacy when allowed free play; and perhaps the time may come when the worst cases shall deem it a plain duty to curse no future generations with the *damnosa hereditas*, which has caused such bitter wretchedness to themselves."

The second consideration is the acknowledged influence of beauty. "When one sees a god-like countenance," said Socrates to Phaedrus, "or some bodily form that represents beauty, he reverences it as a god, and would sacrifice to it." From the days of Plato till now, all have felt the power of woman's beauty, and been more than willing to sacrifice to it. The proper, not exclusive search for it is a legitimate inspiration. The way for a girl to obtain her portion of this radiant halo is by the symmetrical development of every part of her organization, muscle, ovary, stomach and nerve, and by a physiological management of every function that correlates every organ; not by neglecting or trying to stifle or abort any of the vital and integral parts of her structure, and supplying the deficiency by invoking the aid of the milliner's stuffing, the colorist's pencil, the druggist's compounds, the doctor's pelvic supporter, and the surgeon's spinal brace.

When travelling in the East, some years ago, it was my fortune to be summoned as a physician into a harem. With curious and not unwilling step I obeyed the summons. While examining the patient, nearly a dozen Syrian girls—a grave Turk's wifely crowd, his matrimonial bouquet and armful of connubial bliss—pressed around the divan with eyes and ears intent to see and hear a Western Hakim's medical examination. As I looked upon their well-developed forms, their brown skins, rich with the blood and sun of the East, and their unintelligent, sensuous faces, I thought that if it were possible to marry the Oriental care of woman's organization to the Western liberty and culture of her brain, there would be a new birth and loftier type of womanly grace and force.

PART III.

CHIEFLY CLINICAL.

"Et l'on nous persuadera difficilement que lorsque les hommes ont tant de peine à être hommes, les femmes puissent, tout en restant femmes, devenir hommes aussi, mettant ainsi la main sur les deux rôles, exerçant la double mission, résumant le double caractère de l'humanité! Nous perdrons la femme, et nous n'aurons pas l'homme. Voila ce qui nous arrivera. On nous donnera ce quelque chose de monstreux, cet être répugnant, qui déjà parait à notre horizon." ——LE COMTE A. DE GASPARIN.

"Facts given in evidence are premises from which a conclusion is to be drawn. The first step in the exercise of this duty is to acquire a belief of the truth of the facts." ——RAM, *on Facts.*

Clinical observation confirms the teachings of physiology. The sick chamber, not the schoolroom; the physician's private consultation, not the committee's public examination; the hospital, not the college, the workshop, or the parlor,—disclose the sad results which modern social customs, modern education, and modern ways of labor, have entailed on women. Examples of them may be found in every walk of life. On the luxurious couches of Beacon Street; in the palaces of Fifth Avenue; among the classes of our private, common, and normal schools; among the female graduates of our colleges; behind the counters of Washington Street and Broadway; in our factories, workshops, and homes,—may be found numberless pale, weak, neuralgic, dyspeptic, hysterical, menorraghic, dysmenorrhoeic girls and women, that are living illustrations of the truth of this brief monograph. It is not asserted here that improper methods of study, and a disregard of the reproductive apparatus and its functions, during the educational life of girls, are the sole causes of female diseases; neither is it asserted that all the female graduates of our schools and colleges are pathological specimens. But it is asserted that the number of these graduates who have been permanently disabled to a greater or less degree by these causes is so great, as to excite the gravest alarm, and to demand the serious attention of the community. If these causes should continue for the next half-century, and increase in the same ratio as they have for the last fifty years, it requires no prophet to foretell that the wives who are to be mothers in our republic must be drawn from trans-atlantic homes. The sons of the New World will have to re-act, on a magnificent scale, the old story of unwived Rome and the Sabines.

We have previously seen that the blood is the life, and that the loss of it is the loss of so much life. Deluded by strange theories, and groping in physiological darkness, our fathers' physicians were too often Sangrados. Nourishing food, pure air, and haematized blood were stigmatized as the friends of disease and the enemies of convalescence. Oxygen was shut out from and carbonic acid shut into the chambers of phthisis and fever; and veins were opened, that the currents of blood and disease might flow out together. Happily, those days of ignorance, which God winked at, and which the race survived, have passed by. Air and food and blood are recognized as Nature's restoratives. No physician would dare, nowadays, to bleed either man or woman once a month, year in and year out, for a quarter of a century continuously. But girls often have the courage, or the ignorance, to do this to themselves. And the worst of it is, that the organization of our schools and workshops, and the demands of social life and polite society, encourage them in this slow suicide. It has already been stated that the excretory organs, by constantly eliminating from the system its effete and used material, the measure and source of its force, keep the machine in clean, healthy, and working order, and that the reproductive apparatus of woman uses the blood as one of its agents of elimination. Kept within natural limits, this elimination is a source of strength, a perpetual fountain of health, a constant renewal of life. Beyond these limits it is a hemorrhage, that, by draining away the life, becomes a source of weakness and a perpetual fountain of disease.

The following case illustrates one of the ways in which our present school methods of teaching girls generate a menorrhagia and its consequent evils. Miss A——, a healthy, bright, intelligent girl, entered a female school, an institution that is commonly but oddly called a *seminary* for girls, in the State of New York, at the age of fifteen. She was then sufficiently well developed, and had a good color; all the functions appeared to act normally, and the catamenia were fairly established. She was ambitious as well as capable, and aimed to be among the first in the school. Her temperament was what physiologists call nervous,—an expression that does not denote a fidgety make, but refers to a relative activity of the nervous system. She was always anxious about her recitations. No matter how carefully she prepared for them, she was ever fearful lest she should trip a little, and appear to less advantage than she hoped. She went to school regularly every week, and every day of the school year, just as boys do. She paid no more attention to the periodical tides of her organization than her companions; and that was none at all. She recited standing at all times, or at least whenever a standing recitation was the order of the hour. She soon found, and this history is taken from her own lips, that for a few days during every fourth week, the effort of reciting produced an extraordinary physical result. The attendant anxiety and excitement relaxed the sluices of the system that were already physiologically open, and determined a hemorrhage as the concomitant of a recitation. Subjected to the inflexible rules of the school, unwilling to seek advice from any one, almost ashamed of her own physique, she ingeniously protected herself against exposure, and went on intellectually leading her companions, and physically defying nature. At the end of a year, she went home with a gratifying report from her teachers, and pale cheeks and a variety of aches. Her parents were pleased, and perhaps a little anxious. She is a good scholar, said her father; somewhat overworked possibly; and so he gave her a trip among the mountains, and a week or two at the seashore. After her vacation she returned to school, and repeated the previous year's experience,—constant, sustained work, recitation and study for all days alike, a hemorrhage once a month that would make the stroke oar of the University crew falter, and a brilliant scholar. Before the expiration of the second year, Nature began to assert her authority. The paleness of Miss A's complexion increased. An unaccountable and uncontrollable twitching of a rhythmical sort got into the muscles of her face, and made her hands go and feet jump. She was sent home, and her physician called, who at once diagnosticated chorea (St. Vitus' dance), and said she had studied too hard, and wisely prescribed no study and a long vacation. Her parents took her to Europe. A year of the sea and the Alps, of England and the Continent, the Rhine and Italy, worked like a charm. The sluiceways were controlled, the blood saved, and color and health returned. She came back seemingly well, and at the age of eighteen went to her old school once more. During all this time not a word had been said to her by her parents, her physician, or her teachers, about any periodical care of herself; and the rules of the school did not acknowledge the catamenia. The labor and regimen of the school soon brought on the old menorrhagic trouble in the old way, with the addition of occasional faintings to emphasize Nature's warnings. She persisted in getting her education, however, and graduated at nineteen, the first scholar, and an invalid. Again her parents were gratified and anxious. She is overworked, said they, and wondered why girls break down so. To insure her recovery, a second and longer travel was undertaken. Egypt and Asia were added to Europe, and nearly two years were allotted to the cure. With change of air and scene her health improved, but not so rapidly as with the previous journey. She returned to America better than she went away, and married at the age of twenty-two. Soon after that time she consulted the writer on account of prolonged dyspepsia, neuralgia, and dysmenorrhoea, which had replaced menorrhagia. Then I learned the long history of her education, and of her efforts to study just as boys do. Her attention had never been called before to the danger she had incurred while at school. She is now what is called getting better, but has the delicacy and weaknesses of American women, and, so far, is without children.

It is not difficult, in this case, either to discern the cause of the trouble, or to trace its influence, through the varying phases of disease, from Miss A——'s school-days, to her matronly life. She was well, and would have been called robust, up to her first critical period. She then had two tasks imposed upon her at once, both of which required for their perfect accomplishment a few years of time and a large share of vital force: one was the education of the brain, the other of the reproductive system. The schoolmaster superintended the first, and Nature the second. The school, with puritanic inflexibility, demanded every day of the month; Nature, kinder than the school, demanded less than a fourth of the time,—a seventh or an eighth of it would have probably answered. The schoolmaster might have yielded somewhat, but would not; Nature could not. The pupil, therefore, was compelled to undertake both tasks at the same time. Ambitious, earnest, and conscientious, she obeyed the visible power and authority of the school, and disobeyed, or rather ignorantly sought to evade, the invisible power and authority of her organization. She put her will into the education of her brain, and withdrew it from elsewhere. The system does not do two things well at the same time. One or the other suffers from neglect, when the attempt is made. Miss A—— made her brain and muscles work actively, and diverted blood and force to them when her organization demanded active work, with blood and force for evolution in another region. At first the schoolmaster seemed to be successful. He not only made his pupil's brain manipulate Latin, chemistry, philosophy, geography, grammar, arithmetic, music, French, German, and the whole extraordinary catalogue of an American young lady's school curriculum, with acrobatic skill; but he made her do this irrespective of the periodical tides of her organism, and made her perform her intellectual and muscular calisthenics, obliging her to stand, walk, and recite, at the seasons of highest tide. For a while she got on nicely. Presently, however, the strength of the loins, that even Solomon put in as a part of his ideal woman, changed to weakness. Periodical hemorrhages were the first warning of this. As soon as loss of blood occurred regularly and largely, the way to imperfect development and invalidism was open, and the progress easy and rapid. The nerves and their centers lacked nourishment. There was more waste than repair,—no margin for growth. St. Vitus' dance was a warning not to be neglected, and the schoolmaster resigned to the doctor. A long vacation enabled the system to retrace its steps, and recover force for evolution. Then the school resumed its sway, and physiological laws were again defied. Fortunately graduation soon occurred, and unintermitted, sustained labor was no longer enforced. The menorrhagia ceased, but persistent dysmenorrhea now indicates the neuralgic friction of an imperfectly developed reproductive apparatus. Doubtless the evil of her education will infect her whole life.

The next case is drawn from different social surroundings. Early associations and natural aptitude inclined Miss B—— to the stage; and the need of bread and butter sent her upon it as a child, at what age I do not know. At fifteen she was an actress, determined to do her best, and ambitious of success. She strenuously taxed muscle and brain at all times in her calling. She worked in a man's sustained way, ignoring all demands for special development, and essaying first to dis-establish, and then to bridle, the catamenia. At twenty she was eminent. The excitement and effort of acting periodically produced the same result with her that a recitation did under similar conditions with Miss A——. If she had been a physiologist, she would have known how this course of action would end. As she was an actress, and not a physiologist, she persisted in the slow suicide of frequent hemorrhages, and encouraged them by her method of professional education, and later by her method of practicing her profession. She tried to ward off disease, and repair the loss of force, by consulting various doctors, taking drugs, and resorting to all sorts of expedients; but the hemorrhages continued, and were repeated at irregular and abnormally frequent intervals. A careful local examination disclosed no local disturbance. There was neither ulceration, hypertrophy, or congestion of the os or cervix uteri; no displacement of any moment, or ovarian tenderness. In spite of all her difficulties, however, she worked on courageously and steadily in a man's way and with a woman's will. After a long and discouraging experience of doctors, work, and weaknesses, when rather over thirty years old, she came to Boston to consult the writer, who learned at that time the details just recited. She was then pale and weak. A murmur in the veins, which a French savant, by way of dedication to the Devil, christened *bruit de diable*, a baptismal name that science has retained, was audible over her jugulars, and a similar murmur over her heart. Palpitation and labored respiration accompanied and impeded effort. She complained most of her head, which felt "queer," would not go to sleep as formerly, and often gave her turns, in which there was a mingling of dizziness, semi-consciousness, and fear. Her education and work, or rather method of work, had wrought out for her anemia and epileptiform attacks. She got two or three physiological lectures, was ordered to take iron, and other nourishing food, allow time for sleep, and, above all, to arrange her professional work in harmony with the rhythmical or periodical action of woman's constitution. She made the effort to do this, and, in six months, reported herself in better health—though far from well—than she had been for six years before.

This case scarcely requires analysis in order to see how it bears on the question of a girl's education and woman's work. A gifted and healthy girl, obliged to get her education and earn her bread at the same time, labored upon the two tasks zealously, perhaps over-much, and did this at the epoch when the female organization is busy with the development of its reproductive apparatus. Nor is this all. She labored continuously, yielding nothing to Nature's periodical demand for force. She worked her engine up to highest pressure, just as much at flood-tide as at other times. Naturally there was not nervous power enough developed in the uterine and associated ganglia to restrain the laboring orifices of the circulation, to close the gates; and the flood of blood gushed through. With the frequent repetition of the flooding, came inevitably the evils she suffered from,—Nature's penalties. She now reports herself better; but whether convalescence will continue will depend upon her method of work for the future.

Let us take the next illustration from a walk in life different from either of the foregoing. Miss C—— was a bookkeeper in a mercantile house. The length of time she remained in the employ of the house, and its character, are a sufficient guaranty that she did her work well. Like the other clerks, she was at her post, *standing*, during business hours, from Monday morning till Saturday night. The female pelvis being wider than that of the male, the weight of the body, in the upright posture, tends to press the upper extremities of the thighs out laterally in females more than in males. Hence the former can stand less long with comfort than the latter. Miss C——, however, believed in doing her work in a man's way, infected by the not uncommon notion that womanliness means manliness. Moreover, she would not, or could not, make any more allowance for the periodicity of her organization than for the shape of her skeleton. When about twenty years of age, perhaps a year or so older, she applied to me for advice in consequence of neuralgia, backache, menorrhagia, leucor-rhoea, and general debility. She was anemic, and looked pale, care-worn, and anxious. There was no evidence of any local organic affection of the pelvic organs. "Get a woman's periodical remission from labor, if intermission is impossible, and do your work in a wom-an's way, not copying a man's fashion, and you will need very little apothecary's stuff," was the advice she received. "I *must* go on as I am doing," was her answer. She tried iron, sitz-baths, and the like: of course they were of no avail. Latterly I have lost sight of her, and, from her appearance at her last visit to me, presume she has gone to a world where backache and male and female skeletons are unknown.

Illustrations of this sort might be multiplied; but these three are sufficient to show how an abnormal method of study and work may and does open the flood-gates of the system, and, by letting blood out, lets all sorts of evil in. Let us now look at another phase; for menorrhagia and its consequences are not the only punishments that girls receive for being educated and worked just like boys. Nature's methods of punishing men and women are as numerous as their or-gans and functions, and her penalties as infinite in number and gra-dation as her blessings.

Amenorrhoea is perhaps more common than menorrhagia. It of-ten happens, however, during the first critical epoch, which is iso-chronal with the technical educational period of a girl, that after a few occasions of catamenial hemorrhage, moderate perhaps but still hemorrhage, which are not heeded, the conservative force of Nature steps in, and saves the blood by arresting the function. In such in-stances, amenorrhoea is a result of menorrhagia. In this way, and in others that we need not stop to inquire into, the regimen of our schools, colleges, and social life, that requires girls to walk, work, stand, study, recite, and dance at all times as boys can and should, may shut the uterine portals of the blood up, and keep poison in, as well as open them, and let life out. Which of these two evils is worse in itself, and which leaves the largest legacy of ills behind, it is difficult to say. Let us examine some illustrations of this sort of arrest.

Miss D—— entered Vassar College at the age of fourteen. Up to that age, she had been a healthy girl, judged by the standard of American girls. Her parents were apparently strong enough to yield her a fair dower of force. The catamenial function first showed signs of activity in her Sophomore Year, when she was fifteen years old.

Its appearance at this age[1] is confirmatory evidence of the normal state of her health at that period of her college career. Its commencement was normal, without pain or excess. She performed all her college duties regularly and steadily. She studied, recited, stood at the blackboard, walked, and went through her gymnastic exercises, from the beginning to the end of the term, just as boys do. Her account of her regimen there was so nearly that of a boy's regimen, that it would puzzle a physiologist to determine, from the account alone, whether the subject of it was male or female. She was an average scholar, who maintained a fair position in her class, not one of the anxious sort, that are ambitious of leading all the rest. Her first warning was fainting away, while exercising in the gymnasium, at a time when she should have been comparatively quiet, both mentally and physically. This warning was repeated several times, under the same circumstances. Finally she was compelled to renounce gymnastic exercises altogether. In her Junior Year, the organism's periodical function began to be performed with pain, moderate at first, but more and more severe with each returning month. When between seventeen and eighteen years old, dysmenorrhoea was established as the order of that function. Coincident with the appearance of pain, there was a diminution of excretion; and, as the former increased, the latter became more marked. In other respects she was well; and, in all respects, she appeared to be well to her companions and to the faculty of the college. She graduated before nineteen, with fair honors and a poor physique. The year succeeding her graduation was one of steadily-advancing invalidism. She was tortured for two or three days out of every month; and, for two or three days after each season of torture, was weak and miserable, so that about one sixth or fifth of her time was consumed in this way. The excretion from the blood, which had been gradually lessening, after a time substantially stopped, though a periodical effort to keep it up was made. She now suffered from what is called amenorrhoea. At the same time she became pale, hysterical, nervous in the ordinary sense, and almost constantly complained of headache. Physicians were applied to for aid: drugs were administered; travelling, with consequent change of air and scene, was

[1] It appears, from the researches of Mr. Whitehead on this point, that an examination of four thousand cases gave fifteen years six and three-quarter months as the average age in England for the appearance of the catamenia.—Whitehead, *on Abortion, &c.*

undertaken; and all with little apparent avail. After this experience, she was brought to Boston for advice, when the writer first saw her, and learned all these details. She presented no evidence of local uterine congestion, inflammation, ulceration, or displacement. The evidence was altogether in favor of an arrest of the development of the reproductive apparatus, at a stage when the development was nearly complete. Confirmatory proof of such an arrest was found in examining her breast, where the milliner had supplied the organs Nature should have grown. It is unnecessary for our present purpose to detail what treatment was advised. It is sufficient to say, that she probably never will become physically what she would have been had her education been physiologically guided.

This case needs very little comment: its teachings are obvious. Miss D—— went to college in good physical condition. During the four years of her college life, her parents and the college faculty required her to get what is popularly called an education. Nature required her, during the same period, to build and put in working-order a large and complicated reproductive mechanism, a matter that is popularly ignored,—shoved out of sight like a disgrace. She naturally obeyed the requirements of the faculty, which she could see, rather than the requirements of the mechanism within her, that she could not see. Subjected to the college regimen, she worked four years in getting a liberal education. Her way of work was sustained and continuous, and out of harmony with the rhythmical periodicity of the female organization. The stream of vital and constructive force evolved within her was turned steadily to the brain, and away from the ovaries and their accessories. The result of this sort of education was, that these last-mentioned organs, deprived of sufficient opportunity and nutriment, first began to perform their functions with pain, a warning of error that was unheeded; then, to cease to grow;[1] next, to set up once a month a grumbling torture that made life miserable; and, lastly, the brain and the whole nervous system, disturbed, in

---

[1] The arrest of development of the uterus, in connection with amenorrhoea, is sometimes very marked. In the New York Medical Journal for June, 1873, three such cases are recorded, that came under the eye of those excellent observers, Dr. E. R. Peaslee and Dr. T. G. Thomas. In one of these cases, the uterine cavity measured one and a half inches; in another, one and seven-eighths inches; and, in a third, one and a quarter inches. Recollecting that the normal measurement is from two and a half to three inches, it appears that the arrest of development in these cases occurred when the uterus was half or less than half grown. Liberal education should avoid such errors.

obedience to the law, that, if one member suffers, all the members suffer, became neuralgic and hysterical. And so Miss D—— spent the few years next succeeding her graduation in conflict with dysmenorrhoea, headache, neuralgia, and hysteria. Her parents marvelled at her ill-health; and she furnished another text for the often-repeated sermon on the delicacy of American girls.

It may not be unprofitable to give the history of one more case of this sort. Miss E—— had an hereditary right to a good brain and to the best cultivation of it. Her father was one of our ripest and broadest American scholars, and her mother one of our most accomplished American women. They both enjoyed excellent health. Their daughter had a literary training,—an intellectual, moral, and aesthetic half of education, such as their supervision would be likely to give, and one that few young men of her age receive. Her health did not seem to suffer at first. She studied, recited, walked, worked, stood, and the like, in the steady and sustained way that is normal to the male organization. She *seemed* to evolve force enough to acquire a number of languages, to become familiar with the natural sciences, to take hold of philosophy and mathematics, and to keep in good physical case while doing all this. At the age of twenty-one she might have been presented to the public, on Commencement Day, by the president of Vassar College or of Antioch College or of Michigan University, as the wished-for result of American liberal female culture. Just at this time, however, the catamenial function began to show signs of failure of power. No severe or even moderate illness overtook her. She was subjected to no unusual strain. She was only following the regimen of continued and sustained work, regardless of Nature's periodical demands for a portion of her time and force, when, without any apparent cause, the failure of power was manifested by moderate dysmenorrhoea and diminished excretion. Soon after this the function ceased altogether; and up to this present writing, a period of six or eight years, it has shown no more signs of activity than an amputated arm. In the course of a year or so after the cessation of the function, her head began to trouble her. First there was headache, then a frequent congested condition, which she described as a "rush of blood" to her head; and, by and by, vagaries and forebodings and despondent feelings began to crop out. Coincident with this mental state, her skin became rough and coarse, and an inveterate acne covered her face. She retained her appetite, ability to exercise and sleep. A careful local examination of the pelvic organs, by an expert, disclosed no lesion or displacement there, no ovaritis or other inflammation. Appropriate treatment faithfully persevered in was unsuccessful in recovering the lost function. I was finally obliged to consign her to an asylum.

The arrest of development of the reproductive system is most obvious to the superficial observer in that part of it which the milliner is called upon to cover up with pads, and which was alluded to in the case of Miss D——. This, however, is too important a matter to be dismissed with a bare allusion. A recent writer has pointed out the fact and its significance with great clearness. "There is another marked charge," says Dr. Nathan Allen, "going on in the female organization at the present day, which is very significant of something wrong. In the normal state, Nature has made ample provision in the structure of the female for nursing her offspring. In order to furnish this nourishment, pure in quality and abundant in quantity, she must possess a good development of the sanguine and lymphatic temperament, together with vigorous and healthy digestive organs. Formerly such an organization was very generally possessed by American women, and they found but little difficulty in nursing their infants. It was only occasionally, in case of some defect in the organization, or where sickness of some kind had overtaken the mother, that it became necessary to resort to the wet-nurse or to feeding by hand. And the English, the Scotch, the German, the Canadian, the French, and the Irish women now living in this country generally nurse their children: the exceptions are rare. But how is it with our American women who become mothers? To those who have never considered this subject, and even to medical men who have never carefully looked into it, the facts, when correctly and fully presented, will be surprising. It has been supposed by some that all, or nearly all, our American women could nurse their offspring just as well as not; that the disposition only was wanting, and that they did not care about having the trouble or confinement necessarily attending it. But this is a great mistake. This very indifference or aversion shows something wrong in the organization as well as in the disposition: if the physical system were all right, the mind and natural instincts would generally be right also. While there may be here and there cases of this kind, such an indisposition is not always found. It is a fact that large numbers of our women are anxious to nurse their offspring, and make the attempt: they persevere for a while,—perhaps for weeks or months,—and then fail. . . . There is still another class that cannot nurse at all, *having neither the organs nor nourishment* requisite even to make a beginning. . . . Why should there be such a difference between the women of our times and their mothers or grandmothers? Why should there be such a difference between our American women and those of foreign origin residing in the same locality, and surrounded by the same external influences? The explanation is simple: they have not the right kind of organization; there is a want of proper development of the lymphatic and sanguine temperaments,—a marked deficiency in the organs of nutrition and secretion. You cannot draw water without good, flowing springs. *The brain and nervous system have, for a long time, made relatively too large a demand upon* the organs of digestion and assimilation, while the exercise and *development of certain other tissues in the body have been sadly neglected.* . . . In consequence of the great neglect of physical exercise, and the *continuous application to study*, together with various other influences, large numbers of our American women have altogether an undue predominance of the nervous temperament. If only here and there an individual were found with such an organization, not much harm comparatively would result; but, when a majority or nearly all have it, the evil becomes one of no small magnitude." And the evil, it should be added, is not simply the inability to nurse; for, if one member suffers, all the members suffer. A woman, whether married or unmarried, whether called to the offices of maternity or relieved from them, who has been defrauded by her education or otherwise of such an essential part of her development, is not so much of a woman, intellectually and morally as well as physically, in consequence of this defect. Her nervous system and brain, her instincts and character, are on a lower plane, and incapable of their harmonious and best development, if she is possessed, on reaching adult age, of only a portion of a breast and an ovary, or none at all.

When arrested development of the reproductive system is nearly or quite complete, it produces a change in the character, and a loss of power, which it is easy to recognize, but difficult to describe. As this change is an occasional attendant or result of amenorrhoea, when the latter, brought about at an early age, is part of an early arrest, it should not be passed by without an allusion. In these cases, which are not of frequent occurrence at present, but which may be evolved by our methods of education more numerously in the future, the system tolerates the absence of the catamenia, and the consequent non-elimination of impurities from the blood. Acute or chronic disease, the ordinary result of this condition, is not set up, but, instead, there is a change in the character and development of the brain and nervous system. There are in individuals of this class less adipose and more muscular tissue than is commonly seen, a coarser skin, and, generally, a tougher and more angular make-up. There is a corresponding change in the intellectual and psychical condition,—a dropping out of maternal instincts, and an appearance of Amazonian coarseness and force. Such persons are analogous to the sexless class of termites. Naturalists tell us that these insects are divided into males and females, and a third class called workers and soldiers, who have no reproductive apparatus, and who, in their structure and instincts, are unlike the fertile individuals.

A closer analogy than this, however, exists between these human individuals and the eunuchs of Oriental civilization. Except the secretary of the treasury, in the cabinet of Candace, queen of Ethiopia, who was baptized by Philip and Narses, Justinian's general, none of that class have made any impression on the world's life, that history has recorded. It may be reasonably doubted if arrested development of the female reproductive system, producing a class of agenes,[1] not epicenes, will yield a better result of intellectual and moral power in the nineteenth century, than the analogous class of Orientals exhibited. Clinical illustrations of this type of arrested growth might be given, but my pen refuses the ungracious task.

Another result of the present methods of educating girls, and one different from any of the preceding, remains to be noticed. Schools and colleges, as we have seen, require girls to work their brains with full force and sustained power, at the time when their organization periodically requires a portion of their force for the performance of a periodical function, and a portion of their power for the building

---

[1] According to the biblical account, woman was formed by subtracting a rib from man. If, in the evolution of the future, a third division of the human race is to be formed by subtracting sex from woman,—a retrograde development,—I venture to propose the term agene (α without, $\gamma\epsilon\nu o\varsigma$ sex) as an appropriate designation for the new development. Count Gasparin prophesies it thus: "Quelque chose de monstreux, cet être répugnant, qui déjà parait à notre horizon," a free translation of Virgil's earlier description:—

"Monstrum horrendum, informe, ingens, cui lumen ademtum."

3d, 658 *line.*

up of a peculiar, complicated, and important mechanism,—the engine within an engine. They are required to do two things equally well at the same time. They are urged to meditate a lesson and drive a machine simultaneously, and to do them both with all their force. Their organizations are expected to make good sound brains and nerves by working over the humanities, the sciences, and the arts, and, at the same time, to make good sound reproductive apparatuses, not only without any especial attention to the latter, but while all available force is withdrawn from the latter and sent to the former. It is not materialism to say, that, as the brain is, so will thought be. Without discussing the French physiologist's dictum, that the brain secretes thought as the liver does bile, we may be sure, that without brain there will be no thought. The quality of the latter depends on the quality of the former. The metamorphoses of brain manifest, measure, limit, enrich, and color thought. Brain tissue, including both quantity and quality, correlates mental power. The brain is manufactured from the blood; its quantity and quality are determined by the quantity and quality of its blood supply. Blood is made from food; but it may be lost by careless hemorrhage, or poisoned by deficient elimination. When frequently and largely lost or poisoned, as I have too frequent occasion to know it often is, it becomes impoverished, —anemic. Then the brain suffers, and mental power is lost. The steps are few and direct, from frequent loss of blood, impoverished blood, and abnormal brain and nerve metamorphosis, to loss of mental force and nerve disease. Ignorance or carelessness leads to anemic blood, and that to an anemic mind. As the blood, so the brain; as the brain, so the mind.

The cases which have hitherto been presented illustrate some of the evils which the reproductive system is apt to receive in consequence of obvious derangement of its growth and functions. But it may, and often does, happen that the catamenia are normally performed, and that the reproductive system is fairly made up during the educational period. Then force is withdrawn from the brain and nerves and ganglia. These are dwarfed or checked or arrested in their development. In the process of waste and repair, of destructive and constructive metamorphosis, by which brains as well as bones are built up and consolidated, education often leaves insufficient margin for growth. Income derived from air, food, and sleep, which should largely, may only moderately exceed expenditure upon study and work, and so leave but little surplus for growth in any direction; or, what more commonly occurs, the income which the brain receives is all spent upon study, and little or none upon its development, while that which the nutritive and reproductive systems receive is retained by them, and devoted to their own growth. When the school makes the same steady demand for force from girls who are approaching puberty, ignoring Nature's periodical demands, that it does from boys, who are not called upon for an equal effort, there must be failure somewhere. Generally either the reproductive system or the nervous system suffers. We have looked at several instances of the former sort of failure; let us now examine some of the latter.

Miss F—— was about twenty years old when she completed her technical education. She inherited a nervous diathesis as well as a large dower of intellectual and aesthetic graces. She was a good student, and conscientiously devoted all her time, with the exception of ordinary vacations, to the labor of her education. She made herself mistress of several languages, and accomplished in many ways. The catamenial function appeared normally, and, with the exception of occasional slight attacks of menorrhagia, was normally performed during the whole period of her education. She got on without any sort of serious illness. There were few belonging to my clientele who required less professional advice for the same period than she. With the ending of her school life, when she should have been in good trim and well equipped, physically as well as intellectually, for life's work, there commenced, without obvious cause, a long period of invalidism. It would be tedious to the reader, and useless for our present purpose, to detail the history and describe the protean shapes of her sufferings. With the exception of small breasts, the reproductive system was well developed. Repeated and careful examinations failed to detect any derangement of the uterine mechanism. Her symptoms all pointed to the nervous system as the *fons et origo mali*. First general debility, that concealed but ubiquitous leader of innumerable armies of weakness and ill, laid siege to her, and captured her. Then came insomnia, that worried her nights for month after month, and made her beg for opium, alcohol, chloral, bromides, any thing that would bring sleep. Neuralgia in every conceivable form tormented her, most frequently in her back, but often, also, in her head, sometimes in her sciatic nerves, sometimes setting up a tic douloureux, sometimes causing a fearful dysmenorrhoea and frequently making her head ache for days together. At other times hysteria got hold of her, and made her fancy herself the victim of strange diseases. Mental effort of the slightest character distressed her, and she could not bear physical exercise of any amount. This condition, or rather these varying conditions, continued for some years. She followed a careful and systematic regimen, and was rewarded by a slow and gradual return of health and strength, when a sudden accident killed her, and terminated her struggle with weakness and pain.

Words fail to convey the lesson of this case to others with any thing like the force that the observation of it conveyed its moral to those about Miss F——, and especially to the physician who watched her career through her educational life, and saw it lead to its logical conclusion of invalidism and thence towards recovery, till life ended. When she finished school, as the phrase goes, she was considered to be well. The principal of any seminary or head of any college, judging by her looks alone, would not have hesitated to call her rosy and strong. At that time the symptoms of failure which began to appear were called signs of previous overwork. This was true, but not so much in the sense of overwork as of erroneously-arranged work. While a student, she wrought continuously,—just as much during each catamenial week as at other times. As a consequence, in her metamorphosis of tissue, repair did little more than make up waste. There were constant demands of force for constant growth of the system generally, equally constant demands of force for the labor of education, and periodical demands of force for a periodical function. The regimen she followed did not permit all these demands to be satisfied, and the failure fell on the nervous system. She accomplished intellectually a good deal, but not more than she might have done, and retained her health, had the order of her education been a physiological one. It was not Latin, French, German, mathematics, or philosophy that undermined her nerves; nor was it because of any natural inferiority to boys that she failed; nor because she undertook to master what women have no right to learn: she lost her health simply because she undertook to do her work in a boy's way and not in a girl's way.

Let us learn the lesson of one more case. These details may be tedious; but the justification of their presence here are the importance of the subject they illustrate and elucidate, and the necessity of acquiring a belief of the truth of the facts of female education.

Miss G—— worked her way through New England primary, grammar, and high schools to a Western college, which she entered with credit to herself, and from which she graduated, confessedly its first scholar, leading the male and female youth alike. All that need be told of her career is that she worked as a student, continuously and perseveringly, through the years of her first critical epoch, and for a few years after it, without any sort of regard to the periodical type of her organization. It never appeared that she studied excessively in other respects, or that her system was weakened while in college by fevers or other sickness. Not a great while after graduation, she began to show signs of failure, and some years later died under the writer's care. A post-mortem examination was made, which disclosed no disease in any part of the body, except in the brain, where the microscope revealed commencing degeneration.

This was called an instance of death from over-work. Like the preceding case, it was not so much the result of over-work as of unphysiological work. She was unable to make a good brain that could stand the wear and tear of life, and a good reproductive system that should serve the race, at the same time that she was continuously spending her force in intellectual labor. Nature asked for a periodical remission, and did not get it. And so Miss G—— died, not because she had mastered the wasps of Aristophanes and the Mécanique Céleste, not because she had made the acquaintance of Kant and Kölliker, and ventured to explore the anatomy of flowers and the secrets of chemistry, but because, while pursuing these studies, while doing all this work, she steadily ignored her woman's make. Believing that woman can do what man can, for she held that faith, she strove with noble but ignorant bravery to compass man's intellectual attainment in a man's way, and died in the effort. If she had aimed at the same goal, disregarding masculine and following feminine methods, she would be alive now, a grand example of female culture, attainment, and power.

These seven clinical observations are sufficient to illustrate the fact that our modern methods of education do not give the female organization a fair chance, but that they check development, and invite weakness. It would be easy to multiply such observations, from the writer's own notes alone, and, by doing so, to swell this essay into a portly volume; but the reader is spared the needless infliction.

Other observers have noticed similar facts, and have urgently called attention to them.

Dr. Fisher, in a recent excellent monograph on insanity, says, "A few examples of injury from *continued* study will show how mental strain affects the health of young girls particularly. Every physician could, no doubt, furnish many similar ones."

"Miss A—— graduated with honor at the normal school after several years of close study, much of the time out of school; never attended balls or parties; sank into a low state of health at once with depression. Was very absurdly allowed to marry while in this state, and soon after became violently insane, and is likely to remain so."

"Miss A—— graduated at the grammar school, not only first, but *perfect*, and at once entered the normal school; was very ambitious to sustain her reputation, and studied hard out of school; was slow to learn, but had a retentive memory; could seldom be induced to go to parties, and, when she did go, studied while dressing, and on the way; was assigned extra tasks at school, because she performed them so well; was a *fine healthy girl in appearance*, but broke down permanently at end of second year, and is now a victim of hysteria and depression."

"Miss C——, of a nervous organization, and quick to learn; her health suffered in normal school, so that her physician predicted insanity if her studies were not discontinued. She persevered, however, and is now an inmate of a hospital, with hysteria and depression."

"A certain proportion of girls are predisposed to mental or nervous derangement. The same girls are apt to be quick, brilliant, ambitious, and persistent at study, and need not stimulation, but repression. For the sake of a temporary reputation for scholarship, they risk their health at the *most susceptible period* of their lives, and break down *after the excitement of school-life has passed away*. For *sexual reasons* they cannot compete with boys, whose outdoor habits still further increase the difference in their favor. If it was a question of schoolteachers instead of schoolgirls, the list would be long of young women whose health of mind has become bankrupt by a *continuation* of the mental strain commenced at school. Any method of relief in our school-system to these over-susceptible minds should be welcomed, even at the cost of the intellectual supremacy of woman in the next generation."

The fact which Dr. Fisher alludes to, that many girls break down not during but *after* the excitement of school or college life, is an important one, and is apt to be overlooked. The process by which the development of the reproductive system is arrested, or degeneration of brain and nerve-tissue set a going, is an insidious one. At its beginning, and for a long time after it is well on in its progress, it would not be recognized by the superficial observer. A class of girls might, and often do, graduate from our schools, higher seminaries, and colleges, that appear to be well and strong at the time of their graduation, but whose development has already been checked, and whose health is on the verge of giving way. Their teachers have known nothing of the amenorrhoea, menorrhagia, dysmenorrhoea, or leucorrhoea which the pupils have sedulously concealed and disregarded; and the cunning devices of dress have covered up all external evidences of defect; and so, on graduation day, they are pointed out by their instructors to admiring committees as rosy specimens of both physical and intellectual education. A closer inspection by competent experts would reveal the secret weakness which the labor of life that they are about to enter upon too late discloses.

The testimony of Dr. Anstie of London, as to the gravity of the evils incurred by the sort of erroneous education we are considering, is decided and valuable. He says, "For, be it remembered, the epoch of sexual development is one in which an enormous addition is being made to the expenditure of vital energy; besides the continuous processes of growth of the tissues and organs generally, the sexual apparatus, with its nervous supply, is making *by its development heavy demands* upon the nutritive powers of the organism; and it is scarcely possible but that portions of the nervous centers, not directly connected with it, should proportionally suffer in their nutrition, probably through defective blood supply. When we add to this the abnormal strain that is being put on the brain, in many cases, by a forcing plan of mental education, we shall perceive a source not merely of exhaustive expenditure of nervous power, but of secondary irritation of centers like the medulla oblongata that are probably already somewhat lowered in power of vital resistance, and proportionably *irritable.*" A little farther on, Dr. Anstie adds, "But I confess, that, with me, the result of close attention given to the pathology of neuralgia has been the evergrowing conviction, that, next to the influence of neurotic inheritance, there is no such frequently powerful factor in the construction of the neuralgic habit as mental warp of a certain kind, the product of an unwise education." In another place, speaking of the liability of the brain to suffer from an unwise education, and referring to the sexual development that we are discussing in these pages, he makes the following statement, which no intelligent physician will deny, and which it would be well for all teachers who care for the best education of the girls intrusted to their charge to ponder seriously. "I would also go farther, and express the opinion, that peripheral influences of an extremely powerful and *continuous* kind, where they concur with one of those critical periods of life at which the central nervous system is relatively weak and unstable, can occasionally set going a non-inflammatory centric atrophy, which may localize itself in those nerves upon whose centers the morbific peripheral influence is perpetually pouring in. Even such influences as the psychical and emotional, be it remembered, must be considered peripheral." The brain of Miss G——, whose case was related a few pages back, is a clinical illustration of the accuracy of this opinion.

Dr. Weir Mitchell, one of our most eminent American physiologists, has recently borne most emphatic testimony to the evils we have pointed out: "Worst of all," he says, "to my mind, most destructive in every way, is the American view of female education. The time taken for the more serious instruction of girls extends to the age of eighteen, and rarely over this. During these years, they are undergoing such organic development as renders them remarkably sensitive." . . . "To show more precisely how the growing girl is injured by the causes just mentioned" (forced and continued study at the sexual epoch) "would carry me upon subjects unfit for full discussion in these pages; but no thoughtful reader can be much at a loss as to my meaning." . . . "Today the American woman is, to speak plainly, physically unfit for her duties as woman, and is, perhaps, of all civilized females, the least qualified to undertake those weightier tasks which tax so heavily the nervous system of man. She is not fairly up to what Nature asks from her as wife and mother. How will she sustain herself under the pressure of those yet more exacting duties which now-a-days she is eager to share with the man?"

In our schools it is the ambitious and conscientious girls, those who have in them the stuff of which the noblest women are made, that suffer, not the romping or lazy sort; and thus our modern ways of education provide for the "non-survival of the fittest." A speaker told an audience of women at Wesleyan Hall not long ago that he once attended the examination of a Western college, where a girl beat the boys in unravelling the intracacies of Juvenal. He did not report the consumption of blood and wear of brain tissue that in her college way of study correlated her Latin, or hint at the possibility of arrested development. Girls of bloodless skins and intellectual faces may be seen any day, by those who desire the spectacle, among the scholars of our high and normal schools,—faces that crown, and skins that cover, curving spines, which should be straight, and neuralgic nerves that should know no pain. Later on, when marriage and maternity overtake these girls, and they "live laborious days" in a sense not intended by Milton's line, they bend and break beneath the labor, like loaded grain before a storm, and bear little fruit again. A training that yields this result is neither fair to the girls nor to the race.

Let us quote the authority of such an acute and sagacious observer as Dr. Maudsley, in support of the physiological and pathological views that have been here presented. Referring to the physiological condition and phenomena of the first critical epoch, he says, "In the great mental revolution caused by the development of the sexual system at puberty, we have the most striking example of the intimate and essential sympathy between the brain, as a mental organ, and other organs of the body. The change of character at this period is not by any means *limited to the appearance of the sexual feelings*, and their sympathetic ideas, but, when traced to its ultimate reach, will be found to extend to the highest feelings of mankind, social, moral, and even religious." He points out the fact that it is very easy by improper training and forced work, during this susceptible period, to turn a physiological into a pathological state. "The great mental revolution which occurs at puberty may go beyond its physiological limits in some instances, and become pathological." "The time of this mental revolution is at best a trying period for youth." "The monthly activity of the ovaries, which marks the advent of puberty in women, has a notable effect upon the mind and body; wherefore it may become an important cause of mental and physical derangement." With regard to the physiological effects of arrested development of the reproductive apparatus in women, Dr. Maudsley uses the following plain and emphatic language: "The forms and habits of mutilated men approach those of women; and women, whose ovaries and uterus remain for some cause in a state of complete inaction, approach the forms and habits of men. It is said, too, that, in hermaphrodites, the mental character, like the physical, participates equally in that of both sexes. While woman preserves her sex, she will necessarily be feebler than man, and, having her special bodily and mental characters, will have, to a certain extent, her own sphere of activity; where she has become thoroughly masculine in nature, or hermaphrodite in mind,—when, in fact, she has pretty well divested herself of her sex,—then she may take his ground, and do his work; but she will have lost her feminine attractions, and probably also her chief feminine functions." It has been reserved for our age and country, by its methods of female education, to demonstrate that it is possible in some cases to divest a woman of her chief feminine functions; in others, to produce grave and even fatal disease of the brain and nervous system; in others, to engender torturing derangements and imperfections of the reproductive apparatus that imbitter a lifetime. Such, we know, is not the object of a liberal female education. Such is not the consummation which the progress of the age demands. Fortunately, it is only necessary to point out and prove the existence of such erroneous methods and evil results to have them avoided. That they can be avoided, and that woman can have a liberal education that shall develop all her powers, without mutilation or disease, up to the loftiest ideal of womanhood, is alike the teaching of physiology and the hope of the race.

In concluding this part of our subject, it is well to remember the statement made at the beginning of our discussion, to the following effect, viz., that it is not asserted here, that improper methods of study and a disregard of the reproductive apparatus and its functions, during the educational life of girls, are the *sole* causes of female diseases; neither is it asserted that *all* the female graduates of our schools and colleges are pathological specimens. But it is asserted that the number of these graduates who have been permanently disabled to a greater or less degree, or fatally injured, by these causes, is such as to excite the *gravest alarm*, and to demand the serious attention of the community.

The preceding physiological and pathological data naturally open the way to a consideration of the co-education of the sexes.

HENRY MAUDSLEY

"Sex in Mind and in Education"

Henry Maudsley (1835–1918): At the age of twenty-two Henry Maudsley received his medical degree in London. He worked in a number of mental hospitals from 1857 to 1862 but eventually began his private practice as a physician in West London Hospital and was also a professor at University College, London.

Maudsley is considered to be among the second generation of "mad doctors" who moved the study and treatment of psychological afflictions out of the asylums and into the more profitable private practices. Like others of his generation, he began treating nervous and hysterical disorders, particularly those of women. Unlike William Acton, he believed that women had sexual desires, albeit minor ones. Joining the hypnosis debate made popular by Freud and Breuer, Maudsley published The Pathology of Mind *(1879), which argued against the frequent use of hypnosis on susceptible patients "for there is danger of [the patient's] mind being weakened temporarily or permanently."*

Those who view without prejudice, or with some sympathy, the movements for improving the higher education of women, and for throwing open to them fields of activity from which they are now excluded, have a hard matter of it sometimes to prevent a feeling of reaction being aroused in their minds by the arguments of the most eager of those who advocate the reform. Carried away by their zeal into an enthusiasm which borders on or reaches fanaticism, they seem positively to ignore the fact that there are significant differences between the sexes, arguing in effect as if it were nothing more than an affair of clothes, and to be resolved, in their indignation at woman's wrongs, to refuse her the simple rights of her sex. They would do better in the end if they would begin by realizing the fact that the male organization is one, and the female organization another, and that, let come what come may in the way of assimilation of female and male education and labor, it will not be possible to transform a woman into a man. To the end of the chapter she will retain her special functions, and must have a special sphere of development and activity determined by the performance of those functions.

It is quite evident that many of those who are foremost in their zeal for raising the education and social status of woman have not given proper consideration to the nature of her organization, and to the demands which its special functions make upon its strength. These are matters which it is not easy to discuss out of a medical journal; but, in view of the importance of the subject at the present stage of the question of female education, it becomes a duty to use plainer language than would otherwise be fitting in a literary journal. The gravity of the subject can hardly be exaggerated. Before sanctioning the proposal to subject woman to a system of mental training which has been framed and adapted for men, and under which they have become what they are, it is needful to consider whether this can be done without serious injury to her health and strength. It is not enough to point to exceptional instances of women who have undergone such a training, and have proved their capacities when tried by the same standard as men; without doubt there are women who can, and will, so distinguish themselves, if stimulus be applied and opportunity given; the question is, whether they may not do it at a cost which is too large a demand upon the resources of their nature. Is it well for them to contend on equal terms with men for the goal of man's ambition?

Let it be considered that the period of the real educational strain will commence about the time when, by the development of the sexual system, a great revolution takes place in the body and mind, and an extraordinary expenditure of vital energy is made, and will continue through those years after puberty when, by the establishment of periodical functions, a regularly recurring demand is made upon the resources of a constitution that is going through the final stages of its growth and development. The energy of a human body being a definite and not inexhaustible quantity, can it bear, without injury, an excessive mental drain as well as the natural physical strain which is so great at that time? Or, will the profit of the one be to the detriment of the other? It is a familiar experience that a day of hard physical work renders a man incapable of hard mental work; his available energy having been exhausted. Nor does it matter greatly by what channel the energy be expended; if it be used in one way it is not available for use in another. When Nature spends in one direction, she must economize in another direction. That the development of puberty does draw heavily upon the vital resources of the female constitution, needs not to be pointed out to those who know the nature of the important physiological changes which then take place. In persons of delicate constitution who have inherited a tendency to disease, and who have little vitality to spare, the disease is apt to break out at that time; the new drain established having deprived the constitution of the vital energy necessary to withstand the enemy that was lurking in it. The time of puberty and the years following it are therefore acknowledged to be a critical time for the female organization. The real meaning of the physiological changes which constitute puberty is that the woman is thereby fitted to conceive and bear children, and undergoes the bodily and mental changes that are connected with the development of the reproductive system. At each recurring period there are all the preparations for conception, and nothing is more necessary to the preservation of female health than that these changes should take place regularly and completely. It is true that many of them are destined to be fruitless so far as their essential purpose is concerned, but it would be a great mistake to suppose that on that account they might be omitted or accomplished incompletely, without harm to the general health. They are the expressions of the full physiological activity of the organism. Hence it is that the outbreak of disease is so often heralded, or accompanied, or followed by suppression or irregularity of these functions. In all cases they make a great demand upon the physiological energy of the body; they are sensitive to its sufferings, however these be caused; and, when disordered, they aggravate the mischief that is going on.

When we thus look the matter honestly in the face, it would seem plain that women are marked out by nature for very different offices in life from those of men, and that the healthy performance of her special functions renders it improbable she will succeed, and unwise for her to persevere, in running over the same course at the same pace with him. For such a race she is certainly weighted unfairly. Nor is it a sufficient reply to this argument to allege, as is sometimes done, that there are many women who have not the opportunity of getting married, or who do not aspire to bear children; for whether they care to be mothers or not, they cannot dispense with those physiological functions of their nature that have reference to that aim, however much they might wish it, and they cannot disregard them in the labor of life without injury to their health. They cannot choose but to be women; cannot rebel successfully against the tyranny of their organization, the complete development and function whereof must take place after its kind. This is not the expression of prejudice nor of false sentiment; it is the plain statement of a physiological fact. Surely, then, it is unwise to pass it by; first or last it must have its due weight in the determination of the problem of woman's education and mission; it is best to recognize it plainly, however we may conclude finally to deal with it.

It is sometimes said, however, that sexual difference ought not to have any place in the culture of mind, and one hears it affirmed with an air of triumphant satisfaction that there is no sex in mental culture. This is a rash statement, which argues want of thought or insincerity of thought in those who make it. There is sex in mind as distinctly as there is sex in body; and if the mind is to receive the best culture of which its nature is capable, regard must be had to the mental qualities which correlate differences of sex. To aim, by means of education and pursuits in life, to assimilate the female to the male mind, might well be pronounced as unwise and fruitless a labor as it would be to strive to assimilate the female to the male body by means of the same kind of physical training and by the adoption of the same pursuits. Without doubt there have been some striking instances of extraordinary women who have shown great mental power, and these may fairly be quoted as evidence in support of the right of women to the best mental culture; but it is another matter when they are adduced in support of the assertion that there is no sex in mind, and that a system of female education should be laid down on the same lines, follow the same method, and have the same ends in view, as a system of education for men.

Let me pause here to reflect briefly upon the influence of sex upon mind. In its physiological sense, with which we are concerned here, mind is the sum of those functions of the brain which are commonly known as thought, feeling, and will. Now the brain is one among a number of organs in the commonwealth of the body; with these organs it is in the closest physiological sympathy by definite paths of nervous communication, has special correspondence with them by internuncial nerve-fibers; so that its functions habitually feel and declare the influence of the different organs. There is an intimate consensus of functions. Though it is the highest organ of the body, the coordinating center to which impressions go and from which responses are sent, the nature and functions of the inferior organs with which it lives in unity, affect essentially its nature as the organ of mental functions. It is not merely that disorder of a particular organ hinders or oppresses these functions, but it affects them in a particular way; and we have good reason to believe that this special pathological effect is a consequence of the specific physiological effect which each organ exerts naturally upon the constitution and function of mind. A disordered liver gives rise to gloomy feelings; a diseased heart to feelings of fear and apprehension; morbid irritation of the reproductive organs, to feelings of a still more special kind—these are familiar facts; but what we have to realize is, that each particular organ has, when not disordered, its specific and essential influence in the production of certain passions or feelings. From of old the influence has been recognized, as we see in the doctrine by which the different passions were located in particular organs of the body, the heart, for example, being made the seat of courage, the liver the seat of jealousy, the bowels the seat of compassion; and although we do not now hold that a passion is aroused anywhere else than in the brain, we believe nevertheless that the organs are represented in the primitive passions, and that when the passion is aroused into violent action by some outward cause, it will discharge itself upon the organ and throw its functions into commotion. In fact, as the uniformity of thought among men is due to the uniform operation of the external senses, as they think alike because they have the same number and kind of senses, so the uniformity of their fundamental passions is due probably to the uniform operation of the internal organs of the body upon the brain; they feel alike because they have the same number and kind of internal organs. If this be so, these organs come to be essential constituents of our mental life.

The most striking illustration of the kind of organic action which

I am endeavoring to indicate is yielded by the influence of the reproductive organs upon the mind; a complete mental revolution being made when they come into activity. As great a change takes place in the feelings and ideas, the desires and will, as it is possible to imagine, and takes place in virtue of the development of their functions. Let it be noted then that this great and important mental change is different in the two sexes, and reflects the difference of their respective organs and functions. Before experience has opened their eyes, the dreams of a young man and maiden differ. If we give attention to the physiology of the matter, we see that it cannot be otherwise, and if we look to the facts of pathology, which would not fitly be in place here, they are found to furnish the fullest confirmation of what might have been predicted. To attribute to the influence of education the mental differences of sex which declare themselves so distinctly at puberty, would be hardly less absurd than to attribute to education the bodily differences which then declare themselves. The comb of a cock, the antlers of a stag, the mane of a lion, the beard of a man, are growths in relation to the reproductive organs which correlate mental differences of sex as marked almost as these physical differences. In the first years of life, girls and boys are much alike in mental and bodily character, the differences which are developed afterwards being hardly more than intimated, although some have thought the girl's passion for her doll evinces even at that time a forefeeling of her future functions; during the period of reproductive activity, the mental and bodily differences are declared most distinctly; and when that period is past, and man and woman decline into second childhood, they come to resemble one another more again. Furthermore, the bodily form, the voice, and the mental qualities of mutilated men approach those of women; while women whose reproductive organs remain from some cause in a state of arrested development, approach the mental and bodily habits of men.

No psychologist has yet devoted himself to make, or has succeeded in making, a complete analysis of the emotions, by resolving the complex feelings into their simple elements and tracing them back from their complex evolutions to the primitive passions in which they are rooted; this is a promising and much-needed work which remains to be done; but when it is done, it will be shown probably that they have proceeded originally from two fundamental instincts, or—if we add consciousness of nature and aim—passions, namely, that of self-

preservation, with the ways and means of self-defense which it in-
spires and stimulates, and that of propagation, with the love of
offspring and other primitive feelings that are connected with it.
Could we in imagination trace mankind backwards along the path
stretching through the ages, on which it has gone forward to its present height and complexity of emotion, and suppose each new emotional element to be given off at the spot where it was acquired, we
should view a road along which the fragments of our high, special
and complex feelings were scattered, and should reach a starting-point
of the primitive instincts of self-preservation and propagation. Considering, then, the different functions of the sexes in the operation of
the latter instinct, and how a different emotional nature has necessarily been grafted on the original differences in the course of ages,[1]
does it not appear that in order to assimilate the female to the male
mind it would be necessary to undo the life-history of mankind from
its earliest commencement? Nay, would it not be necessary to go still
farther back to that earliest period of animal life upon earth before
there was any distinction of sex?

If the foregoing reflections be well grounded, it is plain we ought
to recognize sex in education, and to provide that the method and
aim of mental culture should have regard to the specialties of woman's physical and mental nature. Each sex must develop after its kind;
and if education in its fundamental meaning be the external cause to
which evolution is the internal answer, if it be the drawing out of the
internal qualities of the individual into their highest perfection by the
influence of fitting external conditions, there must be a difference in
the method of education of the two sexes answering to differences in
their physical and mental natures. Whether it be only the statement
of a partial truth, that "for valor he" is formed, and "for beauty she
and sweet attractive grace," or not, it cannot be denied that they are
formed for different functions, and that the influence of those functions pervades and affects essentially their entire beings. There is sex
in mind and there should be sex in education.

Let us consider, then, what an adapted education must have regard to. In the first place, a proper regard to the physical nature of

---

[1] The instinct of propagation is what we are concerned with here, but it should not be overlooked,
that, in like manner, a difference of character would grow out of the instinct of self-preservation
and the means of self-defense prompted by it.

women means attention given, in their training, to their peculiar functions and to their foreordained work as mothers and nurses of children. Whatever aspirations of an intellectual kind they may have, they cannot be relieved from the performance of those offices so long as it is thought necessary that mankind should continue on earth. Even if these be looked upon as somewhat mean and unworthy offices in comparison with the nobler functions of giving birth to and developing ideas; if, agreeing with Goethe, we are disposed to hold— Es wäre doch immer hübscher wenn man die Kinder von den Baumen schüttelte; it must still be confessed that for the great majority of women they must remain the most important offices of the best period of their lives. Moreover they are work which, like all work, may be well or ill done, and which, in order to be done well, cannot be done in a perfunctory manner, as a thing by the way. It will have to be considered whether women can scorn delights, and live laborious days of intellectual exercise and production, without injury to their functions as the conceivers, mothers, and nurses of children. For it would be an ill thing, if it should so happen, that we got the advantages of a quantity of female intellectual work at the price of a puny, enfeebled, and sickly race. In this relation, it must be allowed that women do not and cannot stand on the same level as men.

In the second place, a proper regard to the mental nature of women means attention given to those qualities of mind which correlate the physical differences of her sex. Men are manifestly not so fitted mentally as women to be the educators of children during the early years of their infancy and childhood; they would be almost as much out of place in going systematically to work to nurse babies as they would be in attempting to suckle them. On the other hand, women are manifestly endowed with qualities of mind which specially fit them to stimulate and foster the first growths of intelligence in children, while the lifebond and special sympathies which a mother has with her child as a being which, though individually separate, is still almost a part of her nature, give her an influence and responsibilities which are specially her own. The earliest dawn of an infant's intelligence is its recognition of its mother as the supplier of its wants, as the person whose near presence is associated with the relief of sensations of discomfort, and with the production of feelings of comfort; while the relief and pleasure which she herself feels in yielding it warmth and nourishment strengthens, if it was not originally the foundation of, that strong love of offspring which, with unwearied patience, surrounds its wayward youth with a thousand ministering attentions. It can hardly be doubted that if the nursing of babies were given over to men for a generation or two, they would abandon the task in despair or in disgust, and conclude it to be not worth while that mankind should continue on earth. But "can a woman forget her sucking child, that she should not have compassion on the son of her womb?" Those can hardly be in earnest who question that woman's sex is represented in mind, and that the mental qualities which spring from it qualify her specially to be the successful nurse and educator of infants and young children.

Furthermore, the female qualities of mind which correlate her sexual character adapt her, as her sex does, to be the helpmate and companion of man. It was an Eastern idea, which Plato has expressed allegorically, that a complete being had in primeval times been divided into two halves, which have ever since been seeking to unite together and to reconstitute the divided unity. It will hardly be denied that there is a great measure of truth in the fable. Man and woman do complement one another's being. This is no less true of mind than it is of body; is true of mind indeed as a consequence of its being true of body. Some may be disposed to argue that the qualities of mind which characterize women now, and have characterized them hitherto, in their relations with men, are in great measure, mainly if not entirely, the artificial results of the position of subjection and dependence which she has always occupied; but those who take this view do not appear to have considered the matter as deeply as they should; they have attributed to circumstances much of what unquestionably lies deeper than circumstances, being inherent in the fundamental character of sex. It would be a delusive hope to expect, and a mistaken labor to attempt, to eradicate by change of circumstances the qualities which distinguish the female character, and fit woman to be the helpmate and companion of man in mental and bodily union.

So much may be fairly said on general physiological grounds. We may now go on to inquire whether external effects have been observed from subjecting women to the same kind of training as men. The facts of experience in this country are not such as warrant a full and definite answer to the inquiry, the movement for revolutionizing the education of women being of a recent date. But in America the same method of training for the sexes in mixed classes has been largely applied; girls have gone with boys through the same curriculum of study, from primary to grammar schools, from schools to graduation in colleges, working eagerly under the stimulus of competition, and disdaining any privilege of sex. With what results? With one result certainly—that while those who are advocates of the mixed system bear favorable witness to the results upon both sexes, American physicians are beginning to raise their voices in earnest warnings and protests. It is not that girls have no ambition, nor that they fail generally to run the intellectual race which is set before them, but it is asserted that they do it at a cost to their strength and health which entails lifelong suffering, and even incapacitates them for the adequate performance of the natural functions of their sex. Without pretending to endorse these assertions, which it would be wrong to do in the absence of sufficient experience, it is right to call attention to them, and to claim serious consideration for them; they proceed from physicians of high professional standing, who speak from their own experience, and they agree moreover with what perhaps might have been feared or predicted on physiological grounds. It may fairly be presumed that the stimulus of competition will act more powerfully on girls than on boys; not only because they are more susceptible by nature, but because it will produce more effect upon their constitutions when it is at all in excess. Their nerve-centers being in a state of greater instability, by reason of the development of their reproductive functions, they will be the more easily and the more seriously deranged. A great argument used in favor of a mixed education is that it affords adequate stimulants to girls for thorough and sustained work, which have hitherto been a want in girls' schools; that it makes them less desirous to fit themselves only for society, and content to remain longer and work harder at school. Thus it is desired that emulation should be used in order to stimulate them to compete with boys in mental exercises and aims, while it is not pretended they can or should compete with them in those outdoor exercises and pursuits which are of such great benefit in ministering to bodily health, and to success in which boys, not unwisely perhaps, attach scarcely less honor than to intellectual success. It is plain then that the stimulus of competition in studies will act more powerfully upon them, not only because of their greater constitutional susceptibility, but because it is left free to act without the compensating balance of emulation in other fields of activity. Is it right, may well be asked, that it should be so applied? Can woman rise high in spiritual development of any kind unless she take a holy care of the temple of her body?[1]

A small volume, entitled "Sex in Education," which has been published recently by Dr. Edward Clarke of Boston, formerly a Professor in Harvard College, contains a somewhat startling description of the baneful effects upon female health which have been produced by an excessive educational strain. It is asserted that the number of female graduates of schools and colleges who have been permanently disabled to a greater or less degree by improper methods of study, and by a disregard of the reproductive apparatus and its functions, is so great as to excite the gravest alarm, and to demand the serious attention of the community. "If these causes should continue for the next half-century, and increase in the same ratio as they have for the last fifty years, it requires no prophet to foretell that the wives who are to be the mothers in our republic must be drawn from Transatlantic homes. The sons of the New World will have to re-act, on a magnificent scale, the old story of unwived Rome and the Sabines." Dr. Clarke relates the clinical histories of several cases of tedious illness, in which he traced the cause unhesitatingly to a disregard of the function of the female organization. Irregularity, imperfection, arrest, or excess occurs in consequence of the demand made upon the vital powers at times when there should rightly be an intermission or remission of labor, and is followed first by pallor, lassitude, debility, sleeplessness, headache, neuralgia, and then by worse ills. The course of events is something in this wise. The girl enters upon the hard work of school or college at the age of fifteen years or thereabouts, when the function of her sex has perhaps been fairly established; ambitious to stand high in class, she pursues her studies with diligence, perseverance, constancy, allowing herself no days of relaxation or rest out of the schooldays, paying no attention to the periodical tides of her organization, unheeding a drain "that would make the stroke oar of the University crew falter." For a time all seems to

---

[1] Of all the intellectual errors of which men have been guilty, perhaps none is more false and has been more mischievous in its consequences than the theologico-metaphysical doctrine which inculcated contempt of the body as the temple of Satan, the prison-house of the spirit, from which the highest aspiration of mind was to get free. It is a foolish and fruitless labor to attempt to divorce or put asunder mind and body, which nature has joined together in essential unity; and the right culture of the body is not less a duty than, is indeed essential to, the right culture of the mind.

go well with her studies; she triumphs over male and female competitors, gains the front rank, and is stimulated to continued exertions in order to hold it. But in the long run nature, which cannot be ignored or defied with impunity, asserts its power: excessive losses occur; health fails; she becomes the victim of aches and pains, is unable to go on with her work, and compelled to seek medical advice. Restored to health by rest from work, a holiday at the sea-side, and suitable treatment, she goes back to her studies, to begin again the same course of unheeding work, until she has completed the curriculum, and leaves college a good scholar but a delicate and ailing woman, whose future life is one of more or less suffering. For she does not easily regain the vital energy which was recklessly sacrificed in the acquirement of learning; the special functions which have relation to her future offices as woman, and the full and perfect accomplishment of which is essential to sexual completeness, have been deranged at a critical time; if she is subsequently married, she is unfit for the best discharge of maternal functions, and is apt to suffer from a variety of troublesome and serious disorders in connection with them. In some cases the brain and the nervous system testify to the exhaustive effects of undue labor, nervous and even mental disorders declaring themselves.

Such is a picture, painted by an experienced physician, of the effects of subjecting young women to the method of education which has been framed for young men. Startling as it is, there is nothing in it which may not well be true to nature. If it be an effect of excessive and ill-regulated study to produce derangement of the functions of the female organization, of which so far from there being an antecedent improbability there is a great probability, then there can be no question that all the subsequent ills mentioned are likely to follow. The important physiological change which takes place at puberty, accompanied, as it is, by so great a revolution in mind and body, and by so large an expenditure of vital energy, may easily and quickly overstep its healthy limits and pass into a pathological change, under conditions of excessive stimulation, or in persons who are constitutionally feeble and whose nerve-centers are more unstable than natural; and it is a familiar medical observation that many nervous disorders of a minor kind, and even such serious disorders as chorea, epilepsy, insanity, are often connected with irregularities or suppression of these important functions.

In addition to the ill effects upon the bodily health which are produced directly by an excessive mental application, and a consequent development of the nervous system at the expense of the nutritive functions, it is alleged that remoter effects of an injurious character are produced upon the entire nature, mental and bodily. The arrest of development of the reproductive system discovers itself in the physical form and in the mental character. There is an imperfect development of the structure which Nature has provided in the female for nursing her offspring.

> "Formerly," writes another American physician, Dr. N. Allen, "such an organization was generally possessed by American women, and they found but little difficulty in nursing their infants. It was only occasionally, in case of some defect in the organization, or where sickness of some kind had overtaken the mother, that it became necessary to resort to the wet-nurse, or to feeding by hand. And the English, the Scotch, the German, the Canadian, the French, and the Irish women who are living in this country, generally nurse their children: the exceptions are rare. But how is it with our American women who become mothers? It has been supposed by some that all, or nearly all of them, could nurse their offspring just as well as not; that the disposition only was wanting, and that they did not care about having the trouble or confinement necessarily attending it. But this is a great mistake. This very indifference or aversion shows something wrong in the organization, as well as in the disposition: if the physical system were all right, the mind and natural instincts would generally be right also. While there may be here and there cases of this kind, such an indisposition is not always found. It is a fact that large numbers of our women are anxious to nurse their offspring, and make the attempt: they persevere for a while—perhaps for weeks or months—and then fail. . . . There is still another class that cannot nurse at all, having neither the organs nor nourishment necessary to make a beginning."

Why should there be such a difference between American women and those of foreign origin residing in the same locality, or between them and their grandmothers? Dr. Allen goes on to ask. The answer he finds in the undue demands made upon the brain and nervous system to the detriment of the organs of nutrition and secretion.

> In consequence of the great neglect of physical exercise, and the continuous application to study, together with various other influences, large numbers of our American women have altogether an undue predominance of the nervous temperament. If only here and there an individual were found with such an organization, not much harm comparatively would result; but when a majority, or nearly a majority have it, the evil becomes one of no small magnitude.

To the same effect writes Dr. Weir Mitchell, an eminent American physiologist.

> Worst of all, to my mind, most destructive in every way, is the American view of female education. The time taken for the more serious instruction of girls extends to the age of eighteen, and rarely over this. During these years they are undergoing such organic development as renders them remarkably sensitive. . . . Today the American woman is, to speak plainly, physically unfit for her duties as woman, and is, perhaps, of all civilized females, the least qualified to undertake those weightier tasks which tax so heavily the nervous system of man. She is not fairly up to what Nature asks from her as wife and mother. How will she sustain herself under the pressure of those yet more exacting duties which nowadays she is eager to share with man?

Here then is no uncertain testimony as to the effects of the American system of female education: some women who are without the instinct or desire to nurse their offspring, some who have the desire but not the capacity, and others who have neither the instinct nor the capacity. The facts will hardly be disputed, whatever may finally be the accepted interpretation of them. It will not probably be argued that an absence of the capacity and the instinct to nurse is a result of higher development, and that it should be the aim of woman, as she advances to a higher level, to allow the organs which minister to this function to waste and finally to become by disuse as rudimentary in her sex as they are in the male sex. Their development is notably in close sympathy with that of the organs of reproduction, an arrest thereof being often associated with some defect of the latter; so that it might perhaps fairly be questioned whether it was right and proper, for the race's sake, that a woman who has not the wish and power to nurse should indulge in the functions of maternity. We may take note, by the way, that those in whom the organs are wasted invoke the dressmaker's aid in order to gain the appearance of them; they are not satisfied unless they wear the show of perfect womanhood. However, it may be in the plan of evolution to produce at some future period a race of sexless beings who, undistracted and unharassed by the ignoble troubles of reproduction, shall carry on the intellectual work of the world, not otherwise than as the sexless ants do the work and the fighting of the community.

Meanwhile, the consequences of an imperfectly developed reproductive system are not sexual only; they are also mental. Intellectually and morally there is a deficiency, or at any rate a modification answering to the physical deficiency; in mind, as in body, the individual fails to reach the ideal of a complete and perfect womanhood. If the aim of a true education be to make her reach *that*, it cannot certainly be a true education which operates in any degree to unsex her; for sex is fundamental, lies deeper than culture, cannot be ignored or defied with impunity. You may hide nature, but you cannot extinguish it. Consequently it does not seem impossible that if the attempt to do so be seriously and persistently made, the result may be a monstrosity—something which having ceased to be woman is yet not man—"ce quelque chose de monstrueux," which the Comte A. de Gasparin forebodes, "cet être répugnant, qui déjà paraît à notre horizon."

The foregoing considerations go to show that the main reason of woman's position lies in her nature. That she has not competed with men in the active work of life was probably because not having had the power she had not the desire to do so, and because having the capacity of functions which man has not she has found her pleasure in performing them. It is not simply that man being stronger in body than she is has held her in subjection, and debarred her from careers of action which he was resolved to keep for himself; her maternal functions must always have rendered, and must continue to render, most of her activity domestic. There have been times enough in the history of the world when the freedom which she has had, and the position which she has held in the estimation of men, would have enabled her to assert her claims to other functions, had she so willed it. The most earnest advocate of her rights to be something else than what she has hitherto been would hardly argue that she has always been in the position of a slave kept in forcible subjection by the superior physical force of men. Assuredly, if she has been a slave, she has been a slave content with her bondage. But it may perhaps be said that in that lies the very pith of the matter—that she is not free, and does not care to be free; that she is a slave, and does not know or feel it. It may be alleged that she has lived for so many ages in the position of dependence to which she was originally reduced by the superior muscular strength of man, has been so thoroughly imbued with inherited habits of submission and overawed by the influence of customs never questioned, that she has not the desire for emancipation; that thus a moral bondage has been established more effectual than an actual physical bondage. That she has now exhibited a disposition to emancipate herself, and has initiated a movement to that end, may be owing partly to the easy means of intellectual intercommunication in this age, whereby a few women scattered through the world, who felt the impulses of a higher inspiration, have been enabled to co-operate in a way that would have been impossible in former times, and partly to the awakened moral sense and to the more enlightened views of men which have led to the encouragement and assistance, instead of the suppression, of their efforts.

It would be rash to assert that there is not some measure of truth in these arguments. Let any one who thinks otherwise reflect upon the degraded condition of women in Turkey, where habit is so ingrained in their nature, and custom so powerful over the mind, that they have neither thought nor desire to attain to a higher state, and "nought feel their foul disgrace:" a striking illustration how women may be demoralized and yet not know nor feel it, and an instructive lesson for those who are anxious to form a sound judgment upon the merits of the movement for promoting their higher education and the removal of the legal disabilities under which they labor. It is hardly possible to exaggerate the effects of the laws and usages of a country upon the habits of thought of those who, generation after generation, have been born, and bred, and have lived under them. Were the law which ordains that when a father dies intestate, all the

real property of which he is possessed shall be inherited by his eldest
son, his other children being sent empty away, enacted for the first
time, there is no one, probably, who would not be shocked by its
singular injustice; yet the majority of persons in this country are far
from thinking it extraordinary or unjust, and a great many of them
would deem it a dangerous and wicked doctrine to question its justice.
Only a few weeks ago, a statesman who has held high offices in a
Conservative ministry, in an address to electors, conjured them not
to part with the principle of primogeniture, and declared that there
was no change in the law which he would so vehemently oppose as
this: "let them but follow the example of a neighboring nation in this
respect, and there was an end of their personal freedom and liberty!"
So much do the laws and usages of a country affect the feelings and
judgments of those who dwell therein. If we clearly apprehend the
fact, and allow it the weight which it deserves, it will be apparent that
we must hesitate to accept the subordinate position which women
have always had as a valid argument for the justice of it, and a sufficient reason why they should continue for ever in it.

But may we not fairly assert that it would be no less a mistake
in an opposite direction to allow no weight to such an argument?
Setting physiological considerations aside, it is not possible to suppose
that the whole explanation of woman's position and character is that
man, having in the beginning found her pleasing in his eyes and
necessary to his enjoyment, took forcible possession of her, and has
ever since kept her in bondage, without any other justification than
the right of the strongest? Superiority of muscular strength, without
superiority of any other kind, would not have done that, any more
than superiority of muscular strength has availed to give the lion or
the elephant possession of the earth. If it were not that woman's
organization and functions found their fitting home in a position different from, if not subordinate to, that of men, she would not so long
have kept that position. If she is to be judged by the same standard
as men, and to make their aims her aims, we are certainly bound to
say that she labors under an inferiority of constitution by a dispen-
sation which there is no gainsaying. This is a matter of physiology,
not a matter of sentiment; it is not a mere question of larger or
smaller muscles, but of the energy and power of endurance of the
nerve-force which drives the intellectual and muscular machinery; not
a question of two bodies and minds that are in equal physical con-

ditions, but of one body and mind capable of sustained and regular hard labor, and of another body and mind which for one quarter of each month during the best years of life is more or less sick and unfit for hard work. It is in these considerations that we find the true explanation of what has been from the beginning until now, and what must doubtless continue to be, though it be in a modified form. It may be a pity for woman that she has been created woman, but, being such, it is as ridiculous to consider herself inferior to man because she is not man, as it would be for man to consider himself inferior to her because he cannot perform her functions. There is one glory of the man, another glory of the woman, and the glory of the one differeth from that of the other.

Taking into adequate account the physiology of the female organization, some of the statements made by the late Mr. Mill in his book on the subjection of women strike one with positive amazement. He calls upon us to own that what is now called the nature of women is an eminently artificial thing, the result of forced repression in some directions, of unnatural stimulation in others; that their character has been entirely distorted and disguised by their relations with their masters, who have kept them in so unnatural a state; that if it were not for this there would not be any material difference, nor perhaps any difference at all, in the character and capacities which would unfold themselves; that they would do the same things as men fully as well on the whole, if education and cultivation were adapted to correcting, instead of aggravating, the infirmities incident to their temperament; and that they have been robbed of their natural development, and brought into their present unnatural state, by the brutal right of the strongest which man has used. If these allegations contain no exaggeration, if they be strictly true, then is this article an entire mistake.

Mr. Mill argues as if when he has shown it to be probable that the inequality of rights between the sexes has no other source than the law of the strongest, he had demonstrated its monstrous injustice. But is that entirely so? After all there is a right in might—the right of the strong to be strong. Men have the right to make the most of their powers, to develop them to the utmost, and to strive for, and if possible gain and hold, the position in which they shall have the freest play. It would be a wrong to the stronger if it were required to limit its exertions to the capacities of the weaker. And if it be not so limited, the result will be that the weaker must take a different position. Men will not fail to take the advantage of their strength over women: are no laws then to be made which, owning the inferiority of women's strength, shall ordain accordingly, and so protect them really from the mere brutal tyranny of might? Seeing that the greater power cannot be ignored, but in the long run must tell in individual competition, it is a fair question whether it ought not to be recognized in social adjustments and enactments, even for the necessary protection of women. Suppose that all legal distinctions were abolished, and that women were allowed free play to do what they could, as it may be right they should—to fail or succeed in every career upon which men enter; that all were conceded to them which their extremest advocates might claim for them; do they imagine that if they, being in a majority, combined to pass laws which were unwelcome to men, the latter would quietly submit? Is it proposed that men should fight for them in war, and that they, counting a majority of votes, should determine upon war? Or would they no longer claim a privilege of sex in regard to the defense of the country by arms? If all barriers of distinction of sex raised by human agency were thrown down, as not being warranted by the distinctions of sex which Nature has so plainly marked, it may be presumed that the great majority of women would continue to discharge the functions of maternity, and to have the mental qualities which correlate these functions; and if laws were made by them, and their male supporters of a feminine habit of mind, in the interests of babies, as might happen, can it be supposed that, as the world goes, there would not soon be a revolution in the State by men, which would end in taking all power from women and reducing them to a stern subjection? Legislation would not be of much value unless there were power behind to make it respected, and in such case laws might be made without the power to enforce them, or for the very purpose of coercing the power which could alone enforce them.

So long as the differences of physical power and organization between men and women are what they are, it does not seem possible that they should have the same type of mental development. But while we see great reason to dissent from the opinions, and to distrust the enthusiasm, of those who would set before women the same aims as men, to be pursued by the same methods, it must be admitted that they are entitled to have all the mental culture and all the freedom necessary to the fullest development of their natures. The aim of female education should manifestly be the perfect development, not of manhood but of womanhood, by the methods most conducive thereto: so may women reach as high a grade of development as men, though it be of a different type. A system of education which is framed to fit them to be nothing more than the superintendents of a household and the ornaments of a drawingroom, is one which does not do justice to their nature, and cannot be seriously defended. Assuredly those of them who have not the opportunity of getting married suffer not a little, in mind and body, from a method of education which tends to develop the emotional at the expense of the intellectual nature, and by their exclusion from appropriate fields of practical activity. It by no means follows, however, that it would be right to model an improved system exactly upon that which has commended itself as the best for men. Inasmuch as the majority of women will continue to get married and to discharge the functions of mothers, the education of girls certainly ought not to be such as would in any way clash with their organization, injure their health, and unfit them for these functions. In this matter the small minority of women who have other aims and pant for other careers, cannot be accepted as the spokeswomen of their sex. Experience may be left to teach them, as it will not fail to do, whether they are right or wrong in the ends which they pursue and in the means by which they pursue them: if they are right, they will have deserved well the success which will reward their faith and works; if they are wrong, the error will avenge itself upon them and upon their children, if they should ever have any. In the worst event they will not have been without their use as failures; for they will have furnished experiments to aid us in arriving at correct judgments concerning the capacities of women and their right functions in the universe. Meanwhile, so far as our present lights reach, it would seem that a system of education adapted to women should have regard to the peculiarities of their constitution, to the special functions in life for which they are destined, and to the range and kind of practical activity, mental and bodily, to which they would seem to be foreordained by their sexual organization of body and mind.

HENRY MAUDSLEY.

Note.—It is fair to say that other reasons for the alleged degeneracy of American women are given. For example, a correspondent writes from America:—"The medical mind of the United States is arrayed in a very ill-tempered opposition, on assumed physiological grounds, to the higher education of women in a continuous curriculum, and especially to that co-education which some colleges in the Western States, Oberlin, Antioch, inaugurated twenty years ago, and which latterly Cornell University has adopted. The experience of Cornell is too recent to prove anything; but the Quaker college of Swarthmore claims a steady improvement on the health of its girl-graduates, dating from the commencement of their college course; and the Western colleges report successful results, mentally, morally, and physically, from their co-education experiment. Ignoring these facts, the doctors base their war-cry on the not-to-be-disputed fact that American women are growing into more and more of invalidism with every year. Something of this is perhaps due to climate. I will not say to food; for the American *menu*, in the cities at least, has improved since Mr. Dickens's early days, and has learned to combine French daintiness, very happily, with the substantial requirements of an English table.

"American men, as a rule, 'break down' between forty and fifty, when an Englishman is but beginning to live his public and useful life. The mad excitement of business you have, as well as we; so it must be the unrest of the climate, and their unphilosophical refusal of open-air pleasures and exercise, which are to blame in the case of the men.

"There are other reasons which go to make up the languid young-ladyhood of the American girl. Her childhood is denied the happy out-door sports of her brothers. There is a resolute shutting out of everything like a noisy romp; the active games and all happy, boisterous plays, by field or roadside, are not *proper* to her! She is cased in a cramping dress, so heavy and inconvenient that no boy could wear it for a day without falling into gloomy views of life. All this martyrdom to propriety and fashion tells upon strength and symmetry, and the girl reaches womanhood a wreck. That she reaches it at all, under these suffering and bleached-out conditions, is due to her superior elasticity to resist a method of education which would have killed off all the boys years before. * * * There are abundant statistics to prove that hard study is the discipline and tonic most girls need to supplant the too great sentimentality and useless day-dreams fostered by fashionable idleness, and provocative of 'nerves,' melancholy, and inanition generally, and, so far as statistics can, that the women-graduates of these colleges make as healthy and happy wives and mothers as though they had never solved a mathematical problem, nor translated Aristotle."

CHARLES DARWIN

FROM

THE DESCENT OF MAN AND SELECTION IN RELATION TO SEX

Charles Darwin (1809–1882): While studying medicine at the University of Edinburgh and later theology at Cambridge, Charles Darwin found himself more interested in his hobby, natural history, than in either of his intended careers. In 1831 he set out on a five-year voyage around the world to study geographical information. His biographer, Sir Gavin de Beer, credited this voyage with making Darwin a scientist while at the same time destroying his health. As a result of a bug bite, Darwin suffered from a bacterial infestation of the heart and intestines for the rest of his life.

Following his return to England in 1836, Darwin concluded that his findings challenged the accepted beliefs that species are fixed in nature and that like produces like. Influenced by Malthus's work on population and Sir Charles Lytell's Principles of Geology, *as well as by his own observations of farmers selecting stock for breeding, he began writing* On the Origin of Species, *a project that took twenty years. Published in 1859, it set out Darwin's theories of evolution, discussing sexual preference and choice as a product of natural selection.*

Darwin revised Origin *several times, adding the phrase "Survival of the Fittest," which would become influential to social Darwinism, a movement in which Darwin himself had no part. His book polarized the scientific community and was successful in England, America, and particularly Germany. In the nonscientific community,*

On the Origin of Species caused a great deal of shock and distress and was viewed by many as an affront to Christian teachings.

Darwin continued to write and defend his theory of evolution throughout his life, studying plants and animals for further evidence. He was one of the first scientists to move studies of biology into traditionally moral arenas.

PART III.

SEXUAL SELECTION IN RELATION TO MAN,
AND CONCLUSION.

Differences between man and woman—Causes of such differences and of certain characters common to both sexes—Law of battle—Differences in mental powers, and voice—On the influence of beauty in determining the marriages of mankind —Attention paid by savages to ornaments—Their ideas of beauty in woman—The tendency to exaggerate each natural peculiarity.

With mankind the differences between the sexes are greater than in most of the Quadrumana, but not so great as in some, for instance, the mandrill. Man on an average is considerably taller, heavier, and stronger than woman, with squarer shoulders and more plainly-pronounced muscles. Owing to the relation which exists between muscular development and the projection of the brows, the superciliary ridge is generally more marked in man than in woman. His body, and especially his face, is more hairy, and his voice has a different and more powerful tone. In certain races the women are said to differ slightly in tint from the men. For instance, Schweinfurth, in speaking of a negress belonging to the Monbuttoos, who inhabit the interior of Africa a few degrees north of the Equator, says, "Like all her race, she had a skin several shades lighter than her husband's, being something of the color of half-roasted coffee." As the women labor in the fields and are quite unclothed, it is not likely that they differ in color from the men owing to less exposure to the weather. European women are perhaps the brighter colored of the two sexes, as may be seen when both have been equally exposed.

Man is more courageous, pugnacious and energetic than woman, and has a more inventive genius. His brain is absolutely larger, but whether or not proportionately to his larger body, has not, I believe, been fully ascertained. In woman the face is rounder; the jaws and the base of the skull smaller; the outlines of the body rounder, in parts more prominent; and her pelvis is broader than in man;[1] but this latter character may perhaps be considered rather as a primary than a secondary sexual character. She comes to maturity at an earlier age than man.

As with animals of all classes, so with man, the distinctive characters of the male sex are not fully developed until he is nearly mature; and if emasculated they never appear. The beard, for instance, is a secondary sexual character, and male children are beardless, though at an early age they have abundant hair on the head. It is probably due to the rather late appearance in life of the successive variations whereby man has acquired his masculine characters, that they are transmitted to the male sex alone. Male and female children resemble each other closely, like the young of so many other animals in which the adult sexes differ widely; they likewise resemble the mature female much more closely than the mature male. The female, however, ultimately assumes certain distinctive characters, and in the formation of her skull, is said to be intermediate between the child and the man. Again, as the young of closely allied though distinct species do not differ nearly so much from each other as do the adults, so it is with the children of the different races of man. Some have even maintained that race-differences cannot be detected in the infantile skull. In regard to color, the newborn negro child is reddish nut-brown, which soon becomes slaty-gray; the black color being fully developed within a year in the Soudan, but not until three years in Egypt. The eyes of the negro are at first blue, and the hair chestnut-brown rather than black, being curled only at the ends. The children of the Australians immediately after birth are yellowish-brown, and become dark at a later age. Those of the Guaranys of Paraguay are whitish-yellow, but they acquire in the course of a few

[1] Ecker, translation in "Anthropological Review," Oct. 1868, pp. 351–356. The comparison of the form of the skull in men and women has been followed out with much care by Welcker.

weeks the yellowish-brown tint of their parents. Similar observations have been made in other parts of America.

I have specified the foregoing differences between the male and female sex in mankind, because they are curiously like those of the Quadrumana. With these animals the female is mature at an earlier age than the male; at least this is certainly the case in the Cebus azarae. The males of most species are larger and stronger than the females, of which fact the gorilla affords a well-known instance. Even in so trifling a character as the greater prominence of the superciliary ridge, the males of certain monkeys differ from the females, and agree in this respect with mankind. In the gorilla and certain other monkeys, the cranium of the adult male presents a strongly-marked sagittal crest, which is absent in the female; and Ecker found a trace of a similar difference between the two sexes in the Australians. With monkeys when there is any difference in the voice, that of the male is the more powerful. We have seen that certain male monkeys have a well-developed beard, which is quite deficient, or much less developed in the female. No instance is known of the beard, whiskers, or mustache being larger in the female than in the male monkey. Even in the color of the beard there is a curious parallelism between man and the Quadrumana, for with man when the beard differs in color from the hair of the head, as is commonly the case, it is, I believe, almost always of a lighter tint, being often reddish. I have repeatedly observed this fact in England; but two gentlemen have lately written to me, saying that they form an exception to the rule. One of these gentlemen accounts for the fact by the wide difference in color of the hair on the paternal and maternal sides of his family. Both had been long aware of this peculiarity (one of them having often been accused of dyeing his beard), and had been thus led to observe other men, and were convinced that the exceptions were very rare. Dr. Hooker attended to this little point for me in Russia, and found no exception to the rule. In Calcutta, Mr. J. Scott, of the Botanic Gardens, was so kind as to observe the many races of men to be seen there, as well as in some other parts of India, namely two races in Sikhim, the Bhoteas, Hindoos, Burmese, and Chinese, most of which races have very little hair on the face; and he always found that when there was any difference in color between the hair of the head and the beard, the latter was invariably lighter. Now with monkeys, as has already been stated, the beard frequently differs strikingly in color from the hair of the head, and in such cases it is always of a lighter hue, being often pure white, sometimes yellow or reddish.[1]

In regard to the general hairiness of the body, the women in all races are less hairy than the men; and in some few Quadrumana the under side of the body of the female is less hairy than that of the male.[2] Lastly, male monkeys, like men, are bolder and fiercer than the females. They lead the troop, and when there is danger, come to the front. We thus see how close is the parallelism between the sexual differences of man and the Quadrumana. With some few species, however, as with certain baboons, the orang and the gorilla, there is a considerably greater difference between the sexes, as in the size of the canine teeth, in the development and color of the hair, and especially in the color of the naked parts of the skin, than in mankind.

All the secondary sexual characters of man are highly variable, even within the limits of the same race; and they differ much in the several races. These two rules hold good generally throughout the animal kingdom. In the excellent observations made on board the Novara,[3] the male Australians were found to exceed the females by only 65 millim. in height, whilst with the Javans the average excess was 218 millim.; so that in this latter race the difference in height between the sexes is more than thrice as great as with the Australians. Numerous measurements were carefully made of the stature, the circumference of the neck and chest, the length of the back-bone and of the arms, in various races; and nearly all these measurements show that the males differ much more from one another than do the females. This fact indicates that, as far as these characters are concerned, it is the male which has been chiefly modified, since the several races diverged from their common stock.

The development of the beard and the hairiness of the body

[1] Mr. Blyth informs me that he has only seen one instance of the beard, whiskers, &c., in a monkey becoming white with old age, as is so commonly the case with us. This, however, occurred in an aged Macacus cynomolgus, kept in confinement, whose mustaches were "remarkably long and human-like." Altogether this old monkey presented a ludicrous resemblance to one of the reigning monarchs of Europe, after whom he was universally nick-named. In certain races of man the hair on the head hardly ever becomes gray; thus Mr. D. Forbes has never, as he informs me, seen an instance with the Aymaras and Quichuas of S. America.

[2] This is the case with the females of several species of Hylobates, see Geoffrey St.-Hilaire and F. Cuvier, "Hist. Nat. des Mamm." tom. i. See, also, on H. lar. "Penny Cyclopedia," vol. ii. pp. 149, 150.

[3] The results were deduced by Dr. Weisbach from the measurements made by Drs. K. Scherzer and Schwarz, see "Reise der Novara: Anthropolog. Theil," 1867, ss. 216, 231, 234, 236, 239, 269.

differ remarkably in the men of distinct races, and even in different tribes or families of the same race. We Europeans see this amongst ourselves. In the Island of St. Kilda, according to Martin, the men do not acquire beards until the age of thirty or upwards, and even then the beards are very thin. On the Europaeo-Asiatic continent, beards prevail until we pass beyond India; though with the natives of Ceylon they are often absent, as was noticed in ancient times by Diodorus. Eastward of India beards disappear, as with the Siamese, Malays, Kalmucks, Chinese, and Japanese; nevertheless the Ainos, who inhabit the northernmost islands of the Japan Archipelago, are the hairiest men in the world. With negroes the beard is scanty or wanting, and they rarely have whiskers; in both sexes the body is frequently almost destitute of fine down.[1] On the other hand, the Papuans of the Malay Archipelago, who are nearly as black as negroes, possess well-developed beards. In the Pacific Ocean the inhabitants of the Fiji Archipelago have large bushy beards, whilst those of the not distant archipelagoes of Tonga and Samoa are beardless; but these men belong to distinct races. In the Ellice group all the inhabitants belong to the same race; yet on one island alone, namely Nunemaya, "the men have splendid beards"; whilst on the other islands "they have, as a rule, a dozen straggling hairs for a 'beard.' "

Throughout the great American continent the men may be said to be beardless; but in almost all the tribes a few short hairs are apt to appear on the face, especially in old age. With the tribes of North America, Catlin estimates that eighteen out of twenty men are completely destitute by nature of a beard; but occasionally there may be seen a man, who has neglected to pluck out the hairs at puberty, with a soft beard an inch or two in length. The Guaranys of Paraguay differ from all the surrounding tribes in having a small beard, and even some hair on the body, but no whiskers. I am informed by Mr. D. Forbes, who particularly attended to this point, that the Aymaras and Quichuas of the Cordillera are remarkably hairless, yet in old age a few straggling hairs occasionally appear on the chin. The men of these two tribes have very little hair on the various parts of the body where hair grows abundantly in Europeans, and the women have

---

[1] On the beards of negroes, Vogt, "Lectures," &c. p. 127; Waltz, "Introduct. to Anthropology," Engl. translat. 1863, vol. i. p. 96. It is remarkable that in the United States ("Investigations in Military and Anthropological Statistics of American Soldiers," 1869, p. 569) the pure negroes and their crossed offspring seem to have bodies almost as hairy as Europeans.

none on the corresponding parts. The hair on the head, however, attains an extraordinary length in both sexes, often reaching almost to the ground; and this is likewise the case with some of the N. American tribes. In the amount of hair, and in the general shape of the body, the sexes of the American aborigines do not differ so much from each other, as in most other races.[1] This fact is analogous with what occurs with some closely allied monkeys; thus the sexes of the chimpanzee are not as different as those of the orang or gorilla.

In the previous chapters we have seen that with mammals, birds, fishes, insects, etc., many characters, which there is every reason to believe were primarily gained through sexual selection by one sex, have been transferred to the other. As this same form of transmission has apparently prevailed much with mankind, it will save useless repetition if we discuss the origin of characters peculiar to the male sex together with certain other characters common to both sexes.

Law of Battle.—With savages, for instance the Australians, the women are the constant cause of war both between members of the same tribe and between distinct tribes. So no doubt it was in ancient times; "nam fuit ante Helenam mulier teterrima belli causa." With some of the North American Indians, the contest is reduced to a system. That excellent observer, Hearne, says:—"It has ever been the custom among these people for the men to wrestle for any woman to whom they are attached; and, of course, the strongest party always carries off the prize. A weak man, unless he be a good hunter, and wellbeloved, is seldom permitted to keep a wife that a stronger man thinks worth his notice. This custom prevails throughout all the tribes, and causes a great spirit of emulation among their youth, who are upon all occasions, from their childhood, trying their strength and skill in wrestling." With the Guanas of South America, Azara states that the men rarely marry till twenty years old or more, as before that age they cannot conquer their rivals.

Other similar facts could be given; but even if we had no evidence on this head, we might feel almost sure, from the analogy of the higher Quadrumana, that the law of battle had prevailed with man

---

[1] Prof. and Mrs. Agassiz ("Journey in Brazil," p. 530) remark that the sexes of the American Indians differ less than those of the negroes and of the higher races. See, also, Rengger, ibid. p. 3, on the Guaranys.

during the early stages of his development. The occasional appearance at the present day of canine teeth which project above the others, with traces of a diastema or open space for the reception of the opposite canines, is in all probability a case of reversion to a former state, when the progenitors of man were provided with these weapons, like so many existing male Quadrumana. It was remarked in a former chapter that as man gradually became erect, and continually used his hands and arms for fighting with sticks and stones, as well as for the other purposes of life, he would have used his jaws and teeth less and less. The jaws together with their muscles would then have been reduced through disuse, as would the teeth through the not well understood principles of correlation and economy of growth; for we everywhere see that parts, which are no longer of service, are reduced in size. By such steps the original inequality between the jaws and teeth in the two sexes of mankind would ultimately have been obliterated. The case is almost parallel with that of many male Ruminants, in which the canine teeth have been reduced to mere rudiments, or have disappeared, apparently in consequence of the development of horns. As the prodigious difference between the skulls of the two sexes in the orang and gorilla stands in close relation with the development of the immense canine teeth in the males, we may infer that the reduction of the jaws and teeth in the early male progenitors of man must have led to a most striking and favorable change in his appearance.

There can be little doubt that the greater size and strength of man, in comparison with woman, together with his broader shoulders, more developed muscles, rugged outline of body, his greater courage and pugnacity, are all due in chief part to inheritance from his half-human male ancestors. These characters would, however, have been preserved or even augmented during the long ages of man's savagery, by the success of the strongest and boldest men, both in the general struggle for life and in their contests for wives; a success which would have ensured their leaving a more numerous progeny than their less favored brethren. It is not probable that the greater strength of man was primarily acquired through the inherited effects of his having worked harder than woman for his own subsistence and that of his family; for the women in all barbarous nations are compelled to work at least as hard as the men. With civilized people the arbitrament of battle for the possession of the women has long ceased;

on the other hand, the men, as a general rule, have to work harder than the women for their joint subsistence, and thus their greater strength will have been kept up.

Difference in the Mental Powers of the Two Sexes.—With respect to differences of this nature between man and woman, it is probable that sexual selection has played a highly important part. I am aware that some writers doubt whether there is any such inherent difference; but this is at least probable from the analogy of the lower animals which present other secondary sexual characters. No one disputes that the bull differs in disposition from the cow, the wild-boar from the sow, the stallion from the mare, and, as is well known to the keepers of menageries, the males of the larger apes from the females. Woman seems to differ from man in mental disposition, chiefly in her greater tenderness and less selfishness; and this holds good even with savages, as shown by a well-known passage in Mungo Park's Travels, and by statements made by many other travelers. Woman, owing to her maternal instincts, displays these qualities towards her infants in an eminent degree; therefore it is likely that she would often extend them towards her fellow-creatures. Man is the rival of other men; he delights in competition, and this leads to ambition which passes too easily into selfishness. These latter qualities seem to be his natural and unfortunate birthright. It is generally admitted that with woman the powers of intuition, of rapid perception, and perhaps of imitation, are more strongly marked than in man; but some, at least, of these faculties are characteristic of the lower races, and therefore of a past and lower state of civilization.

The chief distinction in the intellectual powers of the two sexes is shown by man's attaining to a higher eminence, in whatever he takes up, than can woman—whether requiring deep thought, reason, or imagination, or merely the use of the senses and hands. If two lists were made of the most eminent men and women in poetry, painting, sculpture, music (inclusive both of composition and performance), history, science, and philosophy, with half-a-dozen names under each subject, the two lists would not bear comparison. We may also infer, from the law of the deviation from averages, so well illustrated by Mr. Galton, in his work on "Hereditary genius," that if men are capable of a decided pre-eminence over women in many subjects, the average of mental power in man must be above that of woman.

Amongst the half-human progenitors of man, and amongst savages, there have been struggles between the males during many generations for the possession of the females. But mere bodily strength and size would do little for victory, unless associated with courage, perseverance, and determined energy. With social animals, the young males have to pass through many a contest before they win a female, and the older males have to retain their females by renewed battles. They have, also, in the case of mankind, to defend their females, as well as their young, from enemies of all kinds, and to hunt for their joint subsistence. But to avoid enemies or to attack them with success, to capture wild animals, and to fashion weapons, requires the aid of the higher mental faculties, namely, observation, reason, invention, or imagination. These various faculties will thus have been continually put to the test and selected during manhood; they will, moreover, have been strengthened by use during this same period of life. Consequently, in accordance with the principle often alluded to, we might expect that they would at least tend to be transmitted chiefly to the male offspring at the corresponding period of manhood.

Now, when two men are put into competition, or a man with a woman, both possessed of every mental quality in equal perfection, save that one has higher energy, perseverance, and courage, the latter will generally become more eminent in every pursuit, and will gain the ascendancy.[1] He may be said to possess genius—for genius has been declared by a great authority to be patience; and patience, in this sense, means unflinching, undaunted perseverance. But this view of genius is perhaps deficient; for without the higher powers of the imagination and reason, no eminent success can be gained in many subjects. These latter faculties, as well as the former, will have been developed in man, partly through sexual selection,—that is, through the contest of rival males, and partly through natural selection,—that is, from success in the general struggle for life; and as in both cases the struggle will have been during maturity, the characters gained will have been transmitted more fully to the male than to the female offspring. It accords in a striking manner with this view of the modification and reinforcement of many of our mental faculties by sexual

[1] J. Stuart Mill remarks ("The Subjection of Women," 1869, p. 122), "The things in which man most excels woman are those which require most plodding, and long hammering at single thoughts." What is this but energy and perseverance?

selection, that, firstly, they notoriously undergo a considerable change at puberty, and, secondly, that eunuchs remain throughout life inferior in these same qualities. Thus man has ultimately become superior to woman. It is, indeed, fortunate that the law of the equal transmission of characters to both sexes prevails with mammals; otherwise it is probable that man would have become as superior in mental endowment to woman, as the peacock is in ornamental plumage to the peahen.

It must be borne in mind that the tendency in characters acquired by either sex late in life, to be transmitted to the same sex at the same age, and of early acquired characters to be transmitted to both sexes, are rules which, though general, do not always hold. If they always held good, we might conclude (but I here exceed my proper bounds) that the inherited effects of the early education of boys and girls would be transmitted equally to both sexes; so that the present inequality in mental power between the sexes would not be effaced by a similar course of early training; nor can it have been caused by their dissimilar early training. In order that woman should reach the same standard as man, she ought, when nearly adult, to be trained to energy and perseverance, and to have her reason and imagination exercised to the highest point; and then she would probably transmit these qualities chiefly to her adult daughters. All women, however, could not be thus raised, unless during many generations those who excelled in the above robust virtues were married, and produced offspring in larger numbers than other women. As before remarked of bodily strength, although men do not now fight for their wives, and this form of selection has passed away, yet during manhood, they generally undergo a severe struggle in order to maintain themselves and their families; and this will tend to keep up or even increase their mental powers, and, as a consequence, the present inequality between the sexes.[1]

Voice and Musical Powers.—In some species of Quadrumana there is a great difference between the adult sexes, in the power of their voices

---

[1] An observation by Vogt bears on this subject: he says, "It is a remarkable circumstance, that the difference between the sexes, as regards the cranial cavity, increases with the development of the race, so that the male European excels much more the female, than the negro the negress. Welcker confirms this statement of Huschke from his measurements of negro and German skulls." But Vogt admits ("Lectures on Man," Eng. translat. 1864, p. 81) that more observations are requisite on this point.

and in the development of the vocal organs; and man appears to have inherited this difference from his early progenitors. His vocal cords are about one-third longer than in woman, or than in boys; and emasculation produces the same effect on him as on the lower animals, for it "arrests that prominent growth of the thyroid, etc., which accompanies the elongation of the cords." With respect to the cause of this difference between the sexes, I have nothing to add to the remarks in the last chapter on the probable effects of the long-continued use of the vocal organs by the male under the excitement of love, rage and jealousy. According to Sir Duncan Gibb, the voice and the form of the larynx differ in the different races of mankind; but with the Tartars, Chinese, etc., the voice of the male is said not to differ so much from that of the female, as in most other races.

The capacity and love for singing or music, though not a sexual character in man, must not here be passed over. Although the sounds emitted by animals of all kinds serve many purposes, a strong case can be made out, that the vocal organs were primarily used and perfected in relation to the propagation of the species. Insects and some few spiders are the lowest animals which voluntarily produce any sound; and this is generally effected by the aid of beautifully constructed stridulating organs, which are often confined to the males. The sounds thus produced consist, I believe in all cases, of the same note, repeated rhythmically; and this is sometimes pleasing even to the ears of man. The chief and, in some cases, exclusive purpose appears to be either to call or charm the opposite sex.

The sounds produced by fishes are said in some cases to be made only by the males during the breeding-season. All the air-breathing Vertebrata necessarily possess an apparatus for inhaling and expelling air, with a pipe capable of being closed at one end. Hence when the primeval members of this class were strongly excited and their muscles violently contracted, purposeless sounds would almost certainly have been produced; and these, if they proved in any way serviceable, might readily have been modified or intensified by the preservation of properly adapted variations. The lowest Vertebrates which breathe air are Amphibians; and of these, frogs and toads possess vocal organs, which are incessantly used during the breeding-season, and which are often more highly developed in the male than in the female. The male alone of the tortoise utters a noise, and this only during the season of love. Male alligators roar or bellow during the same season.

Every one knows how much birds use their vocal organs as a means of courtship; and some species likewise perform what may be called instrumental music.

In the class of Mammals, with which we are here more particularly concerned, the males of almost all the species use their voices during the breeding-season much more than at any other time; and some are absolutely mute excepting at this season. With other species both sexes, or only the females, use their voices as a love-call. Considering these facts, and that the vocal organs of some quadrupeds are much more largely developed in the male than in the female, either permanently or temporarily during the breeding-season; and considering that in most of the lower classes the sounds produced by the males, serve not only to call but to excite or allure the female, it is a surprising fact that we have not as yet any good evidence that these organs are used by male mammals to charm the females. The American Mycetes caraya perhaps forms an exception, as does the Hylobates agilis, an ape allied to man. This gibbon has an extremely loud but musical voice. Mr. Waterhouse states, "It appeared to me that in ascending and descending the scale, the intervals were always exactly half-tones; and I am sure that the highest note was the exact octave to the lowest. The quality of the notes is very musical; and I do not doubt that a good violinist would be able to give a correct idea of the gibbon's composition, excepting as regards its loudness." Mr. Waterhouse then gives the notes. Professor Owen, who is a musician, confirms the foregoing statement, and remarks, though erroneously, that this gibbon "alone of brute mammals may be said to sing." It appears to be much excited after its performance. Unfortunately, its habits have never been closely observed in a state of nature; but from the analogy of other animals, it is probable that it uses its musical powers more especially during the season of courtship.

This gibbon is not the only species in the genus which sings, for my son, Francis Darwin, attentively listened in the Zoological Gardens to H. leuciscus whilst singing a cadence of three notes, in true musical intervals and with a clear musical tone. It is a more surprising fact that certain rodents utter musical sounds. Singing mice have often been mentioned and exhibited, but imposture has commonly been suspected. We have, however, at last a clear account by a well-known observer, the Rev. S. Lockwood, of the musical powers of an American species, the Hesperomys cognatus, belonging to a genus distinct from that of the English mouse. This little animal was kept in confinement, and the performance was repeatedly heard. In one of the two chief songs, "the last bar would frequently be prolonged to two or three; and she would sometimes change from C sharp and D, to C natural and D, then warble on these two notes awhile, and wind up with a quick chirp on C sharp and D. The distinctness between the semitones was very marked, and easily appreciable to a good ear." Mr. Lockwood gives both songs in musical notation; and adds that though this little mouse "had no ear for time, yet she would keep to the key of B (two flats) and strictly in a major key. . . . Her soft clear voice falls an octave with all the precision possible; then at the wind up, it rises again into a very quick trill on C sharp and D."

A critic has asked how the ears of man, and he ought to have added of other animals, could have been adapted by selection so as to distinguish musical notes. But this question shows some confusion on the subject; a noise is the sensation resulting from the co-existence of several aërial "simple vibrations" of various periods, each of which intermits so frequently that its separate existence cannot be perceived. It is only in the want of continuity of such vibrations, and in their want of harmony inter se, that a noise differs from a musical note. Thus an ear to be capable of discriminating noises—and the high importance of this power to all animals is admitted by every one— must be sensitive to musical notes. We have evidence of this capacity even low down in the animal scale: thus Crustaceans are provided with auditory hairs of different lengths, which have been seen to vibrate when the proper musical notes are struck. As stated in a previous chapter, similar observations have been made on the hairs of the antennae of gnats. It has been positively asserted by good observers that spiders are attracted by music. It is also well known that some dogs howl when hearing particular tones.[1] Seals apparently appreciate music, and their fondness for it "was well known to the ancients, and is often taken advantage of by the hunters at the present day."

Therefore, as far as the mere perception of musical notes is concerned, there seems no special difficulty in the case of man or of any

---

[1] Several accounts have been published to this effect. Mr. Peach writes to me that he has repeatedly found that an old dog of his howls when B flat is sounded on the flute, and to no other note. I may add another instance of a dog always whining, when one note on a concertina, which was out of tune, was played.

other animal. Helmholtz has explained on physiological principles why concords are agreeable, and discords disagreeable to the human ear; but we are little concerned with these, as music in harmony is a late invention. We are more concerned with melody, and here again, according to Helmholtz, it is intelligible why the notes of our musical scale are used. The ear analyzes all sounds into their component "simple vibrations," although we are not conscious of this analysis. In a musical note the lowest in pitch of these is generally predominant, and the others which are less marked are the octave, the twelfth, the second octave, etc., all harmonies of the fundamental predominant note; any two notes of our scale have many of these harmonic over-tones in common. It seems pretty clear then, that if an animal always wished to sing precisely the same song, he would guide himself by sounding those notes in succession, which possess many over-tones in common—that is, he would choose for his song, notes which belong to our musical scale.

But if it be further asked why musical tones in a certain order and rhythm give man and other animals pleasure, we can no more give the reason than for the pleasantness of certain tastes and smells. That they do give pleasure of some kind to animals, we may infer from their being produced during the season of courtship by many insects, spiders, fishes, amphibians, and birds; for unless the females were able to appreciate such sounds and were excited or charmed by them, the persevering efforts of the males, and the complex structures often possessed by them alone, would be useless; and this it is impossible to believe.

Human song is generally admitted to be the basis or origin of instrumental music. As neither the enjoyment nor the capacity of producing musical notes are faculties of the least use to man in reference to his daily habits of life, they must be ranked amongst the most mysterious with which he is endowed. They are present, though in a very rude condition, in men of all races, even the most savage; but so different is the taste of the several races, that our music gives no pleasure to savages, and their music is to us in most cases hideous and unmeaning. Dr. Seemann, in some interesting remarks on this subject, "doubts whether even amongst the nations of Western Europe, intimately connected as they are by close and frequent intercourse, the music of the one is interpreted in the same sense by the others. By traveling eastwards we find that there is certainly a different language of music. Songs of joy and dance-accompaniments are no longer, as with us, in the major keys, but always in the minor." Whether or not the half-human progenitors of man possessed, like the singing gibbons, the capacity of producing, and therefore no doubt of appreciating musical notes, we know that man possessed these faculties at a very remote period. M. Lartet has described two flutes, made out of the bones and horns of the reindeer, found in caves together with flint tools and the remains of extinct animals. The arts of singing and of dancing are also very ancient, and are now practiced by all or nearly all the lowest races of man. Poetry, which may be considered as the offspring of song, is likewise so ancient, that many persons have felt astonished that it should have arisen during the earliest ages of which we have any record.

We see that the musical faculties, which are not wholly deficient in any race, are capable of prompt and high development, for Hottentots and Negroes have become excellent musicians, although in their native countries they rarely practice anything that we should consider music. Schweinfurth, however, was pleased with some of the simple melodies which he heard in the interior of Africa. But there is nothing anomalous in the musical faculties lying dormant in man: some species of birds which never naturally sing, can without much difficulty be taught to do so; thus a house-sparrow has learnt the song of a linnet. As these two species are closely allied, and belong to the order of Insessores, which includes nearly all the singing-birds in the world, it is possible that a progenitor of the sparrow may have been a songster. It is more remarkable that parrots, belonging to a group distinct from the Insessores, and having differently constructed vocal organs, can be taught not only to speak, but to pipe or whistle tunes invented by man, so that they must have some musical capacity. Nevertheless it would be very rash to assume that parrots are descended from some ancient form which was a songster. Many cases could be advanced of organs and instincts originally adapted for one purpose, having been utilized for some distinct purpose.* Hence the capacity

---

* Since this chapter was printed, I have seen a valuable article by Mr. Chauncey Wright ("North Amer. Review," Oct. 1870, page 293), who, in discussing the above subject, remarks, "There are many consequences of the ultimate laws or uniformities of nature, through which the acquisition of one useful power will bring with it many resulting advantages as well as limiting disadvantages, actual or possible, which the principle of utility may not have comprehended in its action." As I have attempted to show in an early chapter of this work, this principle has an important bearing on the acquisition by man of some of his mental characteristics.

for high musical development, which the savage races of man possess, may be due either to the practice by our semi-human progenitors of some rude form of music, or simply to their having acquired the proper vocal organs for a different purpose. But in this latter case we must assume, as in the above instance of parrots, and as seems to occur with many animals, that they already possessed some sense of melody.

Music arouses in us various emotions, but not the more terrible ones of horror, fear, rage, etc. It awakens the gentler feelings of tenderness and love, which readily pass into devotion. In the Chinese annals it is said, "Music hath the power of making heaven descend upon earth." It likewise stirs up in us the sense of triumph and the glorious ardor for war. These powerful and mingled feelings may well give rise to the sense of sublimity. We can concentrate, as Dr. Seemann observes, greater intensity of feeling in a single musical note than in pages of writing. It is probable that nearly the same emotions, but much weaker and far less complex, are felt by birds when the male pours forth his full volume of song, in rivalry with other males, to captivate the female. Love is still the commonest theme of our songs. As Herbert Spencer remarks, "Music arouses dormant sentiments of which we had not conceived the possibility, and do not know the meaning; or, as Richter says, tells us of things we have not seen and shall not see." Conversely, when vivid emotions are felt and expressed by the orator, or even in common speech, musical cadences and rhythm are instinctively used. The negro in Africa when excited often bursts forth in song; "another will reply in song, while the company, as if touched by a musical wave, murmur a chorus in perfect unison." Even monkeys express strong feelings in different tones— anger and impatience by low,—fear and pain by high notes. The sensations and ideas thus excited in us by music, or expressed by the cadences of oratory, appear from their vagueness, yet depth, like mental reversions to the emotions and thoughts of a long-past age.

All these facts with respect to music and impassioned speech become intelligible to a certain extent, if we may assume that musical tones and rhythm were used by our half-human ancestors during the season of courtship, when animals of all kinds are excited not only by love, but by the strong passions of jealousy, rivalry, and triumph. From the deeply-laid principle of inherited associations, musical tones in this case would be likely to call up vaguely and indefinitely the strong emotions of a long-past age. As we have every reason to suppose that articulate speech is one of the latest, as it certainly is the highest, of the arts acquired by man, and as the instinctive power of producing musical notes and rhythms is developed low down in the animal series, it would be altogether opposed to the principle of evolution, if we were to admit that man's musical capacity has been developed from the tones used in impassioned speech. We must suppose that the rhythms and cadences of oratory are derived from previously developed musical powers.[1] We can thus understand how it is that music, dancing, song, and poetry are such very ancient arts. We may go even further than this, and, as remarked in a former chapter, believe that musical sounds afforded one of the bases for the development of the language.[2]

As the males of several quadrumanous animals have their vocal organs much more developed than in the females, and as a gibbon, one of the anthropomorphous apes, pours forth a whole octave of musical notes and may be said to sing, it appears probable that the progenitors of man, either the males or females or both sexes, before acquiring the power of expressing their mutual love in articulate language, endeavored to charm each other with musical notes and rhythm. So little is known about the use of the voice by the Quadrumana during the season of love, that we have no means of judging whether the habit of singing was first acquired by our male or female ancestors. Women are generally thought to possess sweeter voices than men, and as far as this serves as any guide, we may infer that they first acquired musical powers in order to attract the other sex.

[1] See the very interesting discussion on the "Origin and Function of Music," by Mr. Herbert Spencer, in his collected "Essays," 1858, p. 359. Mr. Spencer comes to an exactly opposite conclusion to that at which I have arrived. He concludes, as did Diderot formerly, that the cadences used in emotional speech afford the foundation from which music has been developed; whilst I conclude that musical notes and rhythm were first acquired by the male or female progenitors of mankind for the sake of charming the opposite sex. Thus musical tones became firmly associated with some of the strongest passions an animal is capable of feeling, and are consequently used instinctively, or through association, when strong emotions are expressed in speech. Mr. Spencer does not offer any satisfactory explanation, nor can I, why high or deep notes should be expressive, both with man and the lower animals, of certain emotions. Mr. Spencer gives also an interesting discussion on the relations between poetry, recitative, and song.

[2] I find in Lord Monboddo's "Origin of Language," vol. i. (1774), p. 469, that Dr. Blacklock likewise thought "that the first language among men was music, and that before our ideas were expressed by articulate sounds, they were communicated by tones, varied according to different degrees of gravity and acuteness."

But if so, this must have occurred long ago, before our ancestors had become sufficiently human to treat and value their women merely as useful slaves. The impassioned orator, bard, or musician, when with his varied tones and cadences he excites the strongest emotions in his hearers, little suspects that he uses the same means by which his half-human ancestors long ago aroused each other's ardent passions, during their courtship and rivalry.

The Influence of Beauty in Determining the Marriages of Mankind.—In civilized life man is largely, but by no means exclusively, influenced in the choice of his wife by external appearance; but we are chiefly concerned with primeval times, and our only means of forming a judgment on this subject is to study the habits of existing semi-civilized and savage nations. If it can be shown that the men of different races prefer women having various characteristics, or conversely with the women, we have then to inquire whether such choice, continued during many generations, would produce any sensible effect on the race, either on one sex or both according to the form of inheritance which has prevailed.

It will be well first to show in some detail that savages pay the greatest attention to their personal appearance.[1] That they have a passion for ornament is notorious; and an English philosopher goes so far as to maintain, that clothes were first made for ornament and not for warmth. As Professor Waitz remarks, "However poor and miserable man is, he finds a pleasure in adorning himself." The extravagance of the naked Indians of South America in decorating themselves is shown "by a man of large stature gaining with difficulty enough by the labor of a fortnight to procure in exchange the chica necessary to paint himself red." The ancient barbarians of Europe during the Reindeer period brought to their caves any brilliant or singular objects which they happened to find. Savages at the present day everywhere deck themselves with plumes, necklaces, armlets, ear-

[1] A full and excellent account of the manner in which savages in all parts of the world ornament themselves, is given by the Italian traveler, Prof. Mantegazza, "Rio de la Plata, Viaggi e Studi," 1867, pp. 525–545: all the following statements, when other references are not given, are taken from this work. See, also, Waltz, "Introduct. to Anthropolog." Eng. transl. vol. i. 1863, p. 275, et passim. Lawrence also gives very full details in his "Lectures on Physiology," 1822. Since this chapter was written Sir J. Lubbock has published his "Origin of Civilization," 1870, in which there is an interesting chapter on the present subject, and from which (pp. 42, 48) I have taken some facts about savages dyeing their teeth and hair, and piercing their teeth.

rings, etc. They paint themselves in the most diversified manner. "If painted nations," as Humboldt observes, "had been examined with the same attention as clothed nations, it would have been perceived that the most fertile imagination and the most mutable caprice have created the fashions of painting, as well as those of garments."

In one part of Africa the eyelids are colored black; in another the nails are colored yellow or purple. In many places the hair is dyed of various tints. In different countries the teeth are stained black, red, blue, etc., and in the Malay Archipelago it is thought shameful to have white teeth "like those of a dog." Not one great country can be named, from the Polar regions in the north to New Zealand in the south, in which the aborigines do not tattoo themselves. This practice was followed by the Jews of old, and by the ancient Britons. In Africa some of the natives tattoo themselves, but it is a much more common practice to raise protuberances by rubbing salt into incisions made in various parts of the body; and these are considered by the inhabitants of Kordofan and Darfur "to be great personal attractions." In the Arab countries no beauty can be perfect until the cheeks "or temples have been gashed." In South America, as Humboldt remarks, "a mother would be accused of culpable indifference towards her children, if she did not employ artificial means to shape the calf of the leg after the fashion of the country." In the Old and New Worlds the shape of the skull was formerly modified during infancy in the most extraordinary manner, as is still the case in many places, and such deformities are considered ornamental. For instance, the savages of Colombia deem a much flattened head "an essential point of beauty."

The hair is treated with especial care in various countries; it is allowed to grow to full length, so as to reach to the ground, or is combed into "a compact frizzled mop, which is the Papuan's pride and glory." In Northern Africa "a man requires a period of from eight to ten years to perfect his coiffure." With other nations the head is shaved, and in parts of South America and Africa even the eyebrows and eyelashes are eradicated. The natives of the Upper Nile knock out the four front teeth, saying that they do not wish to resemble brutes. Further south, the Batokas knock out only the two upper incisors, which, as Livingstone remarks, gives the face a hideous appearance, owing to the prominence of the lower jaw; but these people think the presence of the incisors most unsightly, and on beholding some Europeans cried out, "Look at the great teeth!" The chief Sebituani tried in vain to alter this fashion. In various parts of Africa and in the Malay Archipelago the natives file the incisors into points like those of a saw, or pierce them with holes, into which they insert studs.

As the face with us is chiefly admired for its beauty, so with savages it is the chief seat of mutilation. In all quarters of the world the septum and more rarely the wings of the nose are pierced; rings, sticks, feathers, and other ornaments being inserted into the holes. The ears are everywhere pierced and similarly ornamented, and with the Botocudos and Lenguas of South America the hole is gradually so much enlarged that the lower edge touches the shoulder. In North and South America and in Africa either the upper or lower lip is pierced; and with the Botocudos the hole in the lower lip is so large that a disc of wood, four inches in diameter, is placed in it. Mante-gazza gives a curious account of the shame felt by a South American native and of the ridicule which he excited, when he sold his tembeta,—the large colored piece of wood which is passed through the hole. In Central Africa the women perforate the lower lip and wear a crystal, which, from the movement of the tongue, has "a wriggling motion, indescribably ludicrous during conversation." The wife of the chief of Latooka told Sir S. Baker that Lady Baker "would be much improved if she would extract her four front teeth from the lower jaw, and wear the long pointed polished crystal in her under lip." Further south with the Makalolo, the upper lip is perforated, and a large metal and bamboo ring, called a pelelé, is worn in the hole. "This caused the lip in one case to project two inches beyond the tip of the nose; and when the lady smiled the contraction of the muscles elevated it over the eyes. 'Why do the women wear these things?' the venerable chief, Chinsurdi, was asked. Evidently surprised at such a stupid question, he replied, 'For beauty! They are the only beautiful things women have; men have beards, women have none. What kind of a person would she be without the pelelé? She would not be a woman at all with a mouth like a man, but no beard.' "

Hardly any part of the body, which can be unnaturally modified, has escaped. The amount of suffering thus caused must have been extreme, for many of the operations require several years for their completion, so that the idea of their necessity must be imperative.

The motives are various; the men paint their bodies to make themselves appear terrible in battle; certain mutilations are connected with religious rites, or they mark the age of puberty, or the rank of the man, or they serve to distinguish the tribes. Amongst savages the same fashions prevail for long periods,[1] and thus mutilations, from whatever cause first made, soon come to be valued as distinctive marks. But self-adornment, vanity, and the admiration of others seem to be the commonest motives. In regard to tattooing, I was told by the missionaries in New Zealand that when they tried to persuade some girls to give up the practice, they answered, "We must just have a few lines on our lips; else when we grow old we shall be so very ugly." With the men of New Zealand, a most capable judge says, "to have fine tattooed faces was the great ambition of the young, both to render themselves attractive to the ladies, and conspicuous in war." A star tattooed on the forehead and a spot on the chin are thought by the women in one part of Africa to be irresistible attractions. In most, but not all parts of the world, the men are more ornamented than the women, and often in a different manner; sometimes, though rarely, the women are hardly at all ornamented. As the women are made by savages to perform the greatest share of the work, and as they are not allowed to eat the best kinds of food, so it accords with the characteristic selfishness of man that they should not be allowed to obtain, or use the finest ornaments. Lastly, it is a remarkable fact, as proved by the foregoing quotations, that the same fashions in modifying the shape of the head, in ornamenting the hair, in painting, tattooing, in perforating the nose, lips, or ears, in removing or filing the teeth, etc., now prevail, and have long prevailed, in the most distant quarters of the world. It is extremely improbable that these practices, followed by so many distinct nations, should be due to tradition from any common source. They indicate the close similarity of the mind of man, to whatever race he may belong, just as do the almost universal habits of dancing, masquerading, and making rude pictures.

Having made these preliminary remarks on the admiration felt by savages for various ornaments, and for deformities most unsightly in

[1] Sir S. Baker (ibid. vol. i. p. 210) speaking of the natives of Central Africa says, "every tribe has a distinct and unchanging fashion for dressing the hair." See Agassiz ("Journey in Brazil," 1868, p. 318) on the invariability of the tattooing of the Amazonian Indians.

our eyes, let us see how far the men are attracted by the appearance of their women, and what are their ideas of beauty. I have heard it maintained that savages are quite indifferent about the beauty of their women, valuing them solely as slaves; it may therefore be well to observe that this conclusion does not at all agree with the care which the women take in ornamenting themselves, or with their vanity. Burchell gives an amusing account of a Bush-woman who used as much grease, red ochre, and shining powder "as would have ruined any but a very rich husband." She displayed also "much vanity and too evident a consciousness of her superiority." Mr. Winwood Reade informs me that the negroes of the West Coast often discuss the beauty of their women. Some competent observers have attributed the fearfully common practice of infanticide partly to the desire felt by the women to retain their good looks. In several regions the women wear charms and use love-philters to gain the affections of the men; and Mr. Brown enumerates four plants used for this purpose by the women of North-Western America.

Hearne, an excellent observer, who lived many years with the American Indians, says, in speaking of the women, "Ask a Northern Indian what is beauty, and he will answer, a broad flat face, small eyes, high cheekbones, three or four broad black lines across each cheek, a low forehead, a large broad chin, a clumsy hook nose, a tawny hide, and breasts hanging down to the belt." Pallas, who visited the northern parts of the Chinese empire, says "those women are preferred who have the Mandschú form; that is to say, a broad face, high cheekbones, very broad noses, and enormous ears;" and Vogt remarks that the obliquity of the eye, which is proper to the Chinese and Japanese, is exaggerated in their pictures for the purpose, as it "seems, of exhibiting its beauty, as contrasted with the eye of the red-haired barbarians." It is well known, as Huc repeatedly remarks, that the Chinese of the interior think Europeans hideous, with their white skins and prominent noses. The nose is far from being too prominent, according to our ideas, in the natives of Ceylon; yet "the Chinese in the seventh century, accustomed to the flat features of the Mongol races, were surprised at the prominent noses of the Cingalese; and Thsang described them as having 'the beak of a bird, with the body of a man.' "

Finlayson, after minutely describing the people of Cochin China, says that their rounded heads and faces are the chief characteristics;

and, he adds, "the roundness of the whole countenance is more striking in the women, who are reckoned beautiful in proportion as they
display this form of face." The Siamese have small noses with divergent nostrils, a wide mouth, rather thick lips, a remarkably large face,
with very high and broad cheekbones. It is, therefore, not wonderful
that "beauty, according to our notion is a stranger to them. Yet they
consider their own females to be much more beautiful than those of
Europe."

It is well known that with many Hottentot women the posterior
part of the body projects in a wonderful manner; they are steatopy-
gous; and Sir Andrew Smith is certain that this peculiarity is greatly
admired by the men. He once saw a woman who was considered a
beauty, and she was so immensely developed behind that when seated
on level ground she could not rise, and had to push herself along
until she came to a slope. Some of the women in various negro tribes
have the same peculiarity; and, according to Burton, the Somal men
"are said to choose their wives by ranging them in a line, and by
picking her out who projects farthest a tergo. Nothing can be more
hateful to a negro than the opposite form."

With respect to color, the negroes railed Mungo Park on the
whiteness of his skin and the prominence of his nose, both of which
they considered as "unsightly and unnatural conformations." He in
return praised the glossy jet of their skins and the lovely depression
of their noses; this they said was, "honey-mouth," nevertheless they
gave him food. The African Moors, also, "knitted their brows and
seemed to shudder" at the whiteness of his skin. On the eastern coast,
the negro boys when they saw Burton, cried out, "Look at the white
man; does he not look like a white ape?" On the western coast, as
Mr. Winwood Reade informs me, the negroes admire a very black
skin more than one of a lighter tint. But their horror of whiteness
may be attributed, according to this same traveler, partly to the belief
held by most negroes that demons and spirits are white, and partly
to their thinking it a sign of ill-health.

The Banyai of the more southern part of the continent are negroes, but "a great many of them are of a light coffee-and-milk color,
and, indeed, this color is considered handsome throughout the whole
country;" so that here we have a different standard of taste. With the
Kafirs, who differ much from negroes, "the skin, except among the
tribes near Delagoa Bay, is not usually black, the prevailing color

being a mixture of black and red, the most common shade being chocolate. Dark complexions, as being most common are naturally held in the highest esteem. To be told that he is light-colored, or like a white man, would be deemed a very poor compliment by a Kafir. I have heard of one unfortunate man who was so very fair that no girl would marry him." One of the titles of the Zulu king is "You who are black." Mr. Galton, in speaking to me about the natives of S. Africa, remarked that their ideas of beauty seem very different from ours; for in one tribe two slim, slight, and pretty girls were not admired by the natives.

Turning to other quarters of the world: in Java, a yellow, not a white girl, is considered, according to Madame Pfeiffer, a beauty. A man of Cochin China "spoke with contempt of the wife of the English Ambassador, that she had white teeth like a dog, and a rosy color like that of potato-flowers." We have seen that the Chinese dislike our white skin, and that the N. Americans admire "a tawny hide." In S. America, the Yuracaras, who inhabit the wooded, damp slopes of the eastern Cordillera, are remarkably pale-colored, as their name in their own language expresses; nevertheless they consider European women as very inferior to their own.

In several of the tribes of North America the hair on the head grows to a wonderful length; and Catlin gives a curious proof how much this is esteemed, for the chief of the Crows was elected to this office from having the longest hair of any man in the tribe, namely ten feet and seven inches. The Aymaras and Quichuas of S. America likewise have very long hair; and this, as Mr. D. Forbes informs me, is so much valued as a beauty that cutting it off was the severest punishment which he could inflict on them. In both the Northern and Southern halves of the continent the natives sometimes increase the apparent length of their hair by weaving into it fibrous substances. Although the hair on the head is thus cherished, that on the face is considered by the North American Indians "as very vulgar," and every hair is carefully eradicated. This practice prevails throughout the American continent from Vancouver's Island in the north to Tierra del Fuego in the south. When York Minster, a Fuegian on board the "Beagle," was taken back to his country, the natives told him he ought to pull out the few short hairs on his face. They also threatened a young missionary, who was left for a time with them, to strip him naked, and pluck the hairs from his face and body, yet he was far from being a hairy man. This fashion is carried so far that the Indians of Paraguay eradicate their eyebrows and eyelashes, saying that they do not wish to be like horses.

It is remarkable that throughout the world the races which are almost completely destitute of a beard dislike hairs on the face and body, and take pains to eradicate them. The Kalmucks are beardless, and they are well known, like the Americans, to pluck out all straggling hairs; and so it is with the Polynesians, some of the Malays, and the Siamese. Mr. Veitch states that the Japanese ladies "all objected to our whiskers, considering them very ugly, and told us to cut them off, and be like Japanese men." The New Zealanders have short, curled beards; yet they formerly plucked out the hairs on the face. They had a saying that "there is no woman for a hairy man;" but it would appear that the fashion has changed in New Zealand, perhaps owing to the presence of Europeans, and I am assured that beards are now admired by the Maories.

On the other hand, bearded races admire and greatly value their beards; among the Anglo-Saxons every part of the body had a recognized value; "the loss of the beard being estimated at twenty shillings, while the breaking of a thigh was fixed at only twelve." In the East men swear solemnly by their beards. We have seen that Chinsurdi, the chief of the Makalolo in Africa, thought that beards were a great ornament. In the Pacific the Fijian's beard is "profuse and bushy, and is his greatest pride;" whilst the inhabitants of the adjacent archipelagoes of Tonga and Samoa are "beardless, and abhor a rough chin." In one island alone of the Ellice group "the men are heavily bearded, and not a little proud thereof."

We thus see how widely the different races of man differ in their taste for the beautiful. In every nation sufficiently advanced to have made effigies of their gods or of their deified rulers, the sculptors no doubt have endeavored to express their highest ideal of beauty and grandeur. Under this point of view it is well to compare in our mind the Jupiter or Apollo of the Greeks with the Egyptian or Assyrian statues; and these with the hideous bas-reliefs on the ruined buildings of Central America.

I have met with very few statements opposed to this conclusion. Mr. Winwood Reade, however, who has had ample opportunities for observation, not only with the negroes of the West Coast of Africa, but with those of the interior who have never associated with Europeans, is convinced that their ideas of beauty are on the whole the same as ours; and Dr. Rohlfs writes to me to the same effect with respect to Bornu and the countries inhabited by the Pullo tribes. Mr. Reade found that he agreed with the negroes in their estimation of the beauty of the native girls; and that their appreciation of the beauty of European women corresponded with ours. They admire long hair, and use artificial means to make it appear abundant; they admire also a beard, though themselves very scantily provided. Mr. Reade feels doubtful what kind of nose is most appreciated: a girl has been heard to say, "I do not want to marry him, he has got no nose;" and this shows that a very flat nose is not admired. We should, however, bear in mind that the depressed, broad noses and projecting jaws of the negroes of the West Coast are exceptional types with the inhabitants of Africa. Notwithstanding the foregoing statements, Mr. Reade admits that negroes "do not like the color of our skin; they look on blue eyes with aversion, and they think our noses too long and our lips too thin." He does not think it probable that negroes would ever prefer the most beautiful European woman, on the mere grounds of physical admiration, to a good-looking negress.[1]

The general truth of the principle, long ago insisted on by Humboldt, that man admires and often tries to exaggerate whatever characters nature may have given him, is shown in many ways. The practice of beardless races extirpating every trace of a beard, and often all the hairs on the body, affords one illustration. The skull has been greatly modified during ancient and modern times by many nations; and there can be little doubt that this has been practiced, especially in N. and S. America, in order to exaggerate some natural and admired peculiarity. Many American Indians are known to admire a head so extremely flattened as to appear to us idiotic. The natives on the northwestern coast compress the head into a pointed cone; and it is their constant practice to gather the hair into a knot on the top of the head, for the sake, as Dr. Wilson remarks, "of increasing the

[1] The "African Sketch Book," vol. ii. 1873, pp. 253, 394, 521. The Fuegians, as I have been informed by a missionary who long resided with them, consider European women as extremely beautiful; but from what we have seen of the judgment of the other aborigines of America, I cannot but think that this must be a mistake, unless indeed the statement refers to the few Fuegians who have lived for some time with Europeans, and who must consider us as superior beings. I should add that a most experienced observer, Capt. Burton, believes that a woman whom we consider beautiful is admired throughout the world, "Anthropological Review," March, 1864, p. 245.

apparent elevation of the favorite conoid form." The inhabitants of Arakhan "admire a broad, smooth forehead, and in order to produce it, they fasten a plate of lead on the heads of the newborn children." On the other hand, "a broad, well-rounded occiput is considered a great beauty" by the natives of the Fiji islands.

As with the skull, so with the nose; the ancient Huns during the age of Attila were accustomed to flatten the noses of their infants with bandages, "for the sake of exaggerating a natural conformation." With the Tahitians, to be called long-nose is considered an insult, and they compress the noses and foreheads of their children for the sake of beauty. The same holds with the Malays of Sumatra, the Hottentots, certain Negroes, and the natives of Brazil. The Chinese have by nature unusually small feet; and it is well known that the women of the upper classes distort their feet to make them still smaller. Lastly, Humboldt thinks that the American Indians prefer coloring their bodies with red paint in order to exaggerate their natural tint; and until recently European women added to their naturally bright colors by rouge and white cosmetics; but it may be doubted whether barbarous nations have generally had any such intention in painting themselves.

In the fashions of our own dress we see exactly the same principle and the same desire to carry every point to an extreme; we exhibit, also, the same spirit of emulation. But the fashions of savages are far more permanent than ours; and whenever their bodies are artificially modified, this is necessarily the case. The Arab women of the Upper Nile occupy about three days in dressing their hair; they never imitate other tribes, "but simply vie with each other in the superlativeness of their own style." Dr. Wilson, in speaking of the compressed skulls of various American races, adds, "such usages are among the least eradicable, and long survive the shock of revolutions that change dynasties and efface more important national peculiarities." The same principle comes into play in the art of breeding; and we can thus understand, as I have elsewhere explained, the wonderful development of the many races of animals and plants, which have been kept merely for ornament. Fanciers always wish each character to be somewhat increased; they do not admire a medium standard; they certainly do not desire any great and abrupt change in the character of their breeds; they admire solely what they are accustomed to, but they ardently desire to see each characteristic feature a little more developed.

The senses of man and of the lower animals seem to be so constituted that brilliant colors and certain forms, as well as harmonious and rhythmical sounds, give pleasure and are called beautiful; but why this should be so, we know not. It is certainly not true that there is in the mind of man any universal standard of beauty with respect to the human body. It is, however, possible that certain tastes may in the course of time become inherited, though there is no evidence in favor of this belief; and if so, each race would possess its own innate ideal standard of beauty. It has been argued that ugliness consists in an approach to the structure of the lower animals, and no doubt this is partly true with the more civilized nations, in which intellect is highly appreciated; but this explanation will hardly apply to all forms of ugliness. The men of each race prefer what they are accustomed to; they cannot endure any great change; but they like variety, and admire each characteristic carried to a moderate extreme.[1] Men accustomed to a nearly oval face, to straight and regular features, and to bright colors admire, as we Europeans know, these points when strongly developed. On the other hand, men accustomed to a broad face, with high cheekbones, a depressed nose, and a black skin admire these peculiarities when strongly marked. No doubt characters of all kinds may be too much developed for beauty. Hence a perfect beauty, which implies many characters modified in a particular manner, will be in every race a prodigy. As the great anatomist Bichat long ago said, if every one were cast in the same mold, there would be no such thing as beauty. If all our women were to become as beautiful as the Venus de Medici, we should for a time be charmed; but we should soon wish for variety; and as soon as we had obtained variety, we should wish to see certain characters a little exaggerated beyond the then existing common standard.

On the effects of the continued selection of women according to a different standard of beauty in each race—On the causes which interfere with sexual selection in civilized and savage nations—Conditions favorable to sexual selection during primeval times—On the manner of action of sexual selection with

---

[1] Mr. Bain has collected ("Mental and Moral Science," 1868, pp. 304–314) about a dozen more or less different theories of the idea of beauty; but none are quite the same as that here given.

mankind—On the women in savage tribes having some power
to choose their husbands—Absence of hair on the body, and
development of the beard—Color of the skin—Summary.

We have seen in the last chapter that with all barbarous races
ornaments, dress, and external appearance are highly valued; and that
the men judge of the beauty of their women by widely different standards. We must next inquire whether this preference and the consequent selection during many generations of those women, which
appear to the men of each race the most attractive, has altered the
character either of the females alone, or of both sexes. With mammals
the general rule appears to be that characters of all kinds are inherited
equally by the males and females; we might therefore expect that with
mankind any characters gained by the females or by the males
through sexual selection, would commonly be transferred to the offspring of both sexes. If any change has thus been effected, it is almost
certain that the different races would be differently modified, as each
has its own standard of beauty.

With mankind, especially with savages, many causes interfere
with the action of sexual selection as far as the bodily frame is concerned. Civilized men are largely attracted by the mental charms of
women, by their wealth, and especially by their social position; for
men rarely marry into a much lower rank. The men who succeed in
obtaining the more beautiful women will not have a better chance of
leaving a long line of descendants than other men with plainer wives,
save the few who bequeath their fortunes according to primogeniture.
With respect to the opposite form of selection, namely of the more
attractive men by the women, although in civilized nations women
have free or almost free choice, which is not the case with barbarous
races, yet their choice is largely influenced by the social position and
wealth of the men; and the success of the latter in life depends much
on their intellectual powers and energy, or on the fruits of these same
powers in their forefathers. No excuse is needed for treating this
subject in some detail; for, as the German philosopher Schopenhauer
remarks, "the final aim of all love intrigues, be they comic or tragic,
is really of more importance than all other ends in human life. What
it all turns upon is nothing less than the composition of the next
generation. . . . It is not the weal or woe of any one individual, but
that of the human race to come, which is here at stake."

There is, however, reason to believe that in certain civilized and semi-civilized nations sexual selection has effected something in modifying the bodily frame of some of the members. Many persons are convinced, as it appears to me with justice, that our aristocracy, including under this term all wealthy families in which primogeniture has long prevailed, from having chosen during many generations from all classes the more beautiful women as their wives, have become handsomer, according to the European standard, than the middle classes; yet the middle classes are placed under equally favorable conditions of life for the perfect development of the body. Cook remarks that the superiority in personal appearance "which is observable in the erees or nobles in all the other islands (of the Pacific) is found in the Sandwich islands;" but this may be chiefly due to their better food and manner of life.

The old traveler Chardin, in describing the Persians, says their "blood is now highly refined by frequent intermixtures with the Georgians and Circassians, two nations which surpass all the world in personal beauty. There is hardly a man of rank in Persia who is not born of a Georgian or Circassian mother." He adds that they inherit their beauty, "not from their ancestors, for without the above mixture, the men of rank in Persia, who are descendants of the Tartars, would be extremely ugly."[1] Here is a more curious case; the priestesses who attended the temple of Venus Erycina at San-Giuliano in Sicily were selected for their beauty out of the whole of Greece; they were not vestal virgins, and Quatrefages, who states the foregoing fact, says that the women of San-Giuliano are now famous as the most beautiful in the island, and are sought by artists as models. But it is obvious that the evidence in all the above cases is doubtful.

The following case, though relating to savages, is well worth giving from its curiosity. Mr. Winwood Reade informs me that the Jollofs, a tribe of negroes on the west coast of Africa, "are remarkable for their uniformly fine appearance." A friend of his asked one of these men, "How is it that every one whom I meet is so fine-looking, not only your men, but your women?" The Jollof answered, "It is very easily explained: it has always been our custom to pick out our worst-looking slaves and to sell them." It need hardly be added that

[1] These quotations are taken from Lawrence ("Lectures on Physiology," etc. 1822, p. 393), who attributes the beauty of the upper classes in England to the men having long selected the more beautiful women.

with all savages, female slaves serve as concubines. That this negro should have attributed, whether rightly or wrongly, the fine appearance of his tribe to the long-continued elimination of the ugly women is not so surprising as it may at first appear; for I have elsewhere shown that negroes fully appreciate the importance of selection in the breeding of their domestic animals, and I could give from Mr. Reade additional evidence on this head.

The Causes Which Prevent or Check the Action of Sexual Selection with Savages.—The chief causes are, first, so-called communal marriages or promiscuous intercourse; secondly, the consequences of female infanticide; thirdly, early betrothals; and lastly, the low estimation in which women are held, as mere slaves. These four points must be considered in some detail.

It is obvious that as long as the pairing of man, or of any other animal, is left to mere chance, with no choice exerted by either sex, there can be no sexual selection; and no effect will be produced on the offspring by certain individuals having had an advantage over others in their courtship. Now it is asserted that there exist at the present day tribes which practice what Sir J. Lubbock by courtesy calls communal marriages; that is, all the men and women in the tribe are husbands and wives to one another. The licentiousness of many savages is no doubt astonishing, but it seems to me that more evidence is requisite, before we fully admit that their intercourse is in any case promiscuous. Nevertheless all those who have most closely studied the subject,[1] and whose judgment is worth much more than mine, believe that communal marriage (this expression being variously guarded) was the original and universal form throughout the world, including therein the intermarriage of brothers and sisters. The late Sir A. Smith, who had traveled widely in S. Africa, and knew much about the habits of savages there and elsewhere, expressed to

---

[1] Sir J. Lubbock, "The Origin of Civilization," 1870, chap. iii. especially pp. 60–67. Mr. M'Lennan, in his extremely valuable work on "Primitive Marriage," 1865, p. 163, speaks of the union of the sexes "in the earliest times as loose, transitory, and in some degree promiscuous." Mr. M'Lennan and Sir J. Lubbock have collected much evidence on the extreme licentiousness of savages at the present time. Mr. L. H. Morgan, in his interesting memoir on the classificatory system of relationship ("Proc. American Acad. of Sciences," vol. vii. Feb. 1868, p. 475), concludes that polygamy and all forms of marriage during primeval times were essentially unknown. It appears also, from Sir J. Lubbock's work, that Bachofen likewise believes that communal intercourse originally prevailed.

me the strongest opinion that no race exists in which woman is considered as the property of the community. I believe that his judgment
was largely determined by what is implied by the term marriage.
Throughout the following discussion I use the term in the same sense
as when naturalists speak of animals as monogamous, meaning
thereby that the male is accepted by or chooses a single female, and
lives with her either during the breeding-season or for the whole year,
keeping possession of her by the law of might; or, as when they speak
of a polygamous species, meaning that the male lives with several
females. This kind of marriage is all that concerns us here, as it suffices for the work of sexual selection. But I know that some of the
writers above referred to, imply by the term marriage, a recognized
right, protected by the tribe.

The indirect evidence in favor of the belief of the former prevalence of communal marriages is strong, and rests chiefly on the terms
of relationship which are employed between the members of the same
tribe, implying a connection with the tribe, and not with either parent. But the subject is too large and complex for even an abstract to
be here given, and I will confine myself to a few remarks. It is evident
in the case of such marriages, or where the marriage tie is very loose,
that the relationship of the child to its father cannot be known. But
it seems almost incredible that the relationship of the child to its
mother should ever be completely ignored, especially as the women
in most savage tribes nurse their infants for a long time. Accordingly,
in many cases the lines of descent are traced through the mother
alone, to the exclusion of the father. But in other cases the terms
employed express a connection with the tribe alone, to the exclusion
even of the mother. It seems possible that the connection between
the related members of the same barbarous tribe, exposed to all sorts
of danger, might be so much more important, owing to the need of
mutual protection and aid, than that between the mother and her
child, as to lead to the sole use of terms expressive of the former
relationships; but Mr. Morgan is convinced that this view is by no
means sufficient.

The terms of relationship used in different parts of the world
may be divided, according to the author just quoted, into two great
classes, the classificatory and descriptive,—the latter being employed
by us. It is the classificatory system which so strongly leads to the
belief, that communal and other extremely loose forms of marriage

were originally universal. But as far as I can see, there is no necessity on this ground for believing in absolutely promiscuous intercourse; and I am glad to find that this is Sir J. Lubbock's view. Men and women, like many of the lower animals, might formerly have entered into strict though temporary unions for each birth, and in this case nearly as much confusion would have arisen in the terms of relationship, as in the case of promiscuous intercourse. As far as sexual selection is concerned, all that is required is that choice should be exerted before the parents unite, and it signifies little whether the unions last for life or only for a season.

Besides the evidence derived from the terms of relationship, other lines of reasoning indicate the former wide prevalence of communal marriage. Sir J. Lubbock accounts for the strange and widely-extended habit of exogamy—that is, the men of one tribe taking wives from a distinct tribe,—by communism having been the original form of intercourse; so that a man never obtained a wife for himself unless he captured her from a neighboring and hostile tribe, and then she would naturally have become his sole and valuable property. Thus the practice of capturing wives might have arisen; and from the honor so gained it might ultimately have become the universal habit. According to Sir J. Lubbock, we can also thus understand "the necessity of expiation for marriage as an infringement of tribal rites, since, according to old ideas, a man had no right to appropriate to himself that which belonged to the whole tribe." Sir J. Lubbock further gives a curious body of facts showing that in old times high honor was bestowed on women who were utterly licentious; and this, as he explains, is intelligible, if we admit that promiscuous intercourse was the aboriginal, and therefore long revered custom of the tribe.[1]

Although the manner of development of the marriage-tie is an obscure subject, as we may infer from the divergent opinions on several points between the three authors who have studied it most closely, namely, Mr. Morgan, Mr. M'Lennan, and Sir J. Lubbock, yet from the foregoing and several other lines of evidence it seems probable[2] that the habit of marriage, in any strict sense of the word, has

[1] "Origin of Civilization," 1870, p. 86. In the several works above quoted, there will be found copious evidence on relationship through the females alone, or with the tribe alone.

[2] Mr. C. Staniland Wake argues strongly ("Anthropologia," March, 1874, p. 197) against the views held by these three writers on the former prevalence of almost promiscuous intercourse; and he thinks that the classificatory system of relationship can be otherwise explained.

been gradually developed; and that almost promiscuous or very loose intercourse was once extremely common throughout the world. Nevertheless from the strength of the feeling of jealousy all through the animal kingdom, as well as from the analogy of the lower animals, more particularly of those which come nearest to man, I cannot believe that absolutely promiscuous intercourse prevailed in times past, shortly before man attained to his present rank in the zoological scale. Man, as I have attempted to show, is certainly descended from some ape-like creature. With the existing Quadrumana, as far as their habits are known, the males of some species are monogamous, but live during only a part of the year with the females; of this the orang seems to afford an instance. Several kinds, for example some of the Indian and American monkeys, are strictly monogamous, and associate all the year round with their wives. Others are polygamous, for example the gorilla and several American species, and each family lives separate. Even when this occurs, the families inhabiting the same district are probably somewhat social: the chimpanzee, for instance, is occasionally met with in large bands. Again, other species are polygamous, but several males, each with his own females, live associated in a body, as with several species of baboons.[1] We may indeed conclude from what we know of the jealousy of all male quadrupeds, armed, as many of them are, with special weapons for battling with their rivals, that promiscuous intercourse in a state of nature is extremely improbable. The pairing may not last for life, but only for each birth; yet if the males which are the strongest and best able to defend or otherwise assist their females and young were to select the more attractive females, this would suffice for sexual selection.

Therefore, looking far enough back in the stream of time, and judging from the social habits of man as he now exists, the most probable view is that he aboriginally lived in small communities, each with a single wife, or if powerful with several, whom he jealously guarded against all other men. Or he may not have been a social animal, and yet have lived with several wives, like the gorilla; for all the natives "agree that but one adult male is seen in a band; when the young male grows up, a contest takes place for mastery, and the

---

[1] Brehm ("Illust. Theirleben," B. i. p. 77) says Cynocephalus hamadryas lives in great troops containing twice as many adult females as adult males. See Rengger on American polygamous species, and Owen ("Anat. of Vertebrates," vol. iii. p. 746) on American monogamous species. Other references might be added.

strongest, by killing and driving out the others, establishes himself as the head of the community." The younger males, being thus expelled and wandering about, would, when at last successful in finding a partner, prevent too close interbreeding within the limits of the same family.

Although savages are now extremely licentious, and although communal marriages may formerly have largely prevailed, yet many tribes practice some form of marriage, but of a far more lax nature than that of civilized nations. Polygamy, as just stated, is almost universally followed by the leading men in every tribe. Nevertheless there are tribes, standing almost at the bottom of the scale, which are strictly monogamous. This is the case with the Veddahs of Ceylon: they have a saying, according to Sir J. Lubbock, "that death alone can separate husband and wife." An intelligent Kandyan chief, of course a polygamist, "was perfectly scandalized at the utter barbarism of living with only one wife, and never parting until separated by death." It was, he said, "Just like the Wanderoo monkeys." Whether savages who now enter into some form of marriage, either polygamous or monogamous, have retained this habit from primeval times, or whether they have returned to some form of marriage, after passing through a stage of promiscuous intercourse, I will not pretend to conjecture.

Infanticide.—This practice is now very common throughout the world, and there is reason to believe that it prevailed much more extensively during former times. Barbarians find it difficult to support themselves and their children, and it is a simple plan to kill their infants. In South America some tribes, according to Azara, formerly destroyed so many infants of both sexes, that they were on the point of extinction. In the Polynesian Islands women have been known to kill from four or five to even ten of their children; and Ellis could not find a single woman who had not killed at least one. Wherever infanticide prevails the struggle for existence will be in so far less severe, and all the members of the tribe will have an almost equally good chance of rearing their few surviving children. In most cases a larger number of female than of male infants are destroyed, for it is obvious that the latter are of more value to the tribe, as they will, when grown up, aid in defending it, and can support themselves. But the trouble experienced by the women in rearing children, their consequent loss of beauty, the higher estimation set on them when few and their happier fate, are assigned by the women themselves, and by various observers, as additional motives for infanticide. In Australia, where female infanticide is still common, Sir G. Grey estimated the proportion of native women to men as one to three; but others say as two to three. In a village on the eastern frontier of India, Colonel MacCulloch found not a single female child.

When, owing to female infanticide, the women of a tribe were few, the habit of capturing wives from neighboring tribes would naturally arise. Sir J. Lubbock, however, as we have seen, attributes the practice in chief part to the former existence of communal marriage, and to the men having consequently captured women from other tribes to hold as their sole property. Additional causes might be assigned, such as the communities being very small, in which case marriageable women would often be deficient. That the habit was most extensively practiced during former times, even by the ancestors of civilized nations, is clearly shown by the preservation of many curious customs and ceremonies, of which Mr. M'Lennan has given an interesting account. In our own marriages the "best man" seems originally to have been the chief abettor of the bridegroom in the act of capture. Now as long as men habitually procured their wives through violence and craft, they would have been glad to seize on any woman, and would not have selected the more attractive ones. But as soon as the practice of procuring wives from a distant tribe was effected through barter, as now occurs in many places, the more attractive women would generally have been purchased. The incessant crossing, however, between tribe and tribe, which necessarily follows from any form of this habit, would tend to keep all the people inhabiting the same country nearly uniform in character; and this would interfere with the power of sexual selection in differentiating the tribes.

The scarcity of women, consequent on female infanticide, leads, also, to another practice, that of polyandry, still common in several parts of the world, and which formerly, as Mr. M'Lennan believes, prevailed almost universally; but this latter conclusion is doubted by Mr. Morgan and Sir J. Lubbock. Whenever two or more men are compelled to marry one woman, it is certain that all the women of the tribe will get married, and there will be no selection by the men of the more attractive women. But under these circumstances the women no doubt will have the power of choice, and will prefer the more attractive men. Azara, for instance, describes how carefully a Guana woman bargains for all sorts of privileges, before accepting some one or more husbands; and the men in consequence take unusual care of their personal appearance. So amongst the Todas of India, who practice polyandry, the girls can accept or refuse any man. A very ugly man in these cases would perhaps altogether fail in getting a wife, or get one later in life; but the handsomer men, although more successful in obtaining wives, would not, as far as we can see, leave more offspring to inherit their beauty than the less handsomer husbands of the same women.

Early Betrothals and Slavery of Women.—With many savages it is the custom to betroth the females whilst mere infants; and this would effectually prevent preference being exerted on either side according to personal appearance. But it would not prevent the more attractive women from being afterwards stolen or taken by force from their husbands by the more powerful men; and this often happens in Australia, America, and elsewhere. The same consequences with reference to sexual selection would to a certain extent follow, when women are valued almost solely as slaves or beasts of burden, as is the case with many savages. The men, however, at all times would prefer the handsomest slaves according to their standard of beauty.

We thus see that several customs prevail with savages which must greatly interfere with, or completely stop, the action of sexual selection. On the other hand, the conditions of life to which savages are exposed, and some of their habits, are favorable to natural selection; and this comes into play at the same time with sexual selection. Savages are known to suffer severely from recurrent famines; they do not increase their food by artificial means; they rarely refrain from marriage,[1] and generally marry whilst young. Consequently they must be subjected to occasional hard struggles for existence, and the favored individuals will alone survive.

At a very early period, before man attained to his present rank in the scale, many of his conditions would be different from what now obtains amongst savages. Judging from the analogy of the lower

[1] Burchell says ("Travels in S. Africa," vol. ii. 1824, p. 58), that among the wild nations of Southern Africa, neither men nor women ever pass their lives in a state of celibacy. Azara ("Voyages dans l'Amerique Merid." tom. ii. 1809, p. 21) makes precisely the same remark in regard to the wild Indians of South America.

animals he would then either live with a single female, or be a polygamist. The most powerful and able males would succeed best in
obtaining attractive females. They would also succeed best in the general struggle for life, and in defending their females, as well as their
offspring, from enemies of all kinds. At this early period the ancestors
of man would not be sufficiently advanced in intellect to look forward
to distant contingencies; they would not foresee that the rearing of
all their children, especially their female children, would make the
struggle for life severer for the tribe. They would be governed more
by their instincts and less by their reason, than are savages at the
present day. They would not at that period have partially lost one of
the strongest of all instincts, common to all the lower animals, namely
the love of their young offspring; and consequently they would not
have practiced female infanticide. Women would not have been thus
rendered scarce, and polyandry would not have been practiced; for
hardly any other cause, except the scarcity of women seems sufficient
to break down the natural and widely prevalent feeling of jealousy,
and the desire of each male to possess a female for himself. Polyandry
would be a natural stepping-stone to communal marriages or almost
promiscuous intercourse; though the best authorities believe that this
latter habit preceded polyandry. During primordial times there would
be no early betrothals, for this implies foresight. Nor would women
be valued merely as useful slaves or beasts of burthen. Both sexes, if
the females as well as the males were permitted to exert any choice,
would choose their partners not for mental charms, or property, or
social position, but almost solely from external appearance. All the
adults would marry or pair, and all the offspring, as far as that was
possible, would be reared; so that the struggle for existence would be
periodically excessively severe. Thus during these times all the conditions for sexual selection would have been more favorable than at
a later period, when man had advanced in his intellectual powers but
had retrograded in his instincts. Therefore, whatever influence sexual
selection may have had in producing the differences between the races
of man, and between man and the higher Quadrumana, this influence
would have been more powerful at a remote period than at the present day, though probably not yet wholly lost.

The Manner of Action of Sexual Selection with Mankind.—With primeval men under the favorable conditions just stated, and with those

savages who at the present time enter into any marriage tie, sexual selection has probably acted in the following manner, subject to greater or less interference from female infanticide, early betrothals, etc. The strongest and most vigorous men,—those who could best defend and hunt for their families, who were provided with the best weapons and possessed the most property, such as a large number of dogs or other animals,—would succeed in rearing a greater average number of offspring than the weaker and poorer members of the same tribes. There can, also, be no doubt that such men would generally be able to select the more attractive women. At present the chiefs of nearly every tribe throughout the world succeed in obtaining more than one wife. I hear from Mr. Mantell, that, until recently, almost every girl in New Zealand, who was pretty, or promised to be pretty, was tapu to some chief. With the Kafirs, as Mr. C. Hamilton states, "the chiefs generally have the pick of the women for many miles round, and are most persevering in establishing or confirming their privilege." We have seen that each race has its own style of beauty, and we know that it is natural to man to admire each characteristic point in his domestic animals, dress, ornaments, and personal appearance, when carried a little beyond the average. If then the several foregoing propositions be admitted, and I cannot see that they are doubtful, it would be an inexplicable circumstance, if the selection of the more attractive women by the more powerful men of each tribe, who would rear on an average a greater number of children, did not after the lapse of many generations somewhat modify the character of the tribe.

When a foreign breed of our domestic animals is introduced into a new country, or when a native breed is long and carefully attended to, either for use or ornament, it is found after several generations to have undergone a greater or less amount of change, whenever the means of comparison exist. This follows from unconscious selection during a long series of generations—that is, the preservation of the most approved individuals—without any wish or expectation of such a result on the part of the breeder. So again, if during many years two careful breeders rear animals of the same family, and do not compare them together or with a common standard, the animals are found to have become, to the surprise of their owners, slightly different. Each breeder has impressed, as Von Nathusius well expresses it, the character of his own mind—his own taste and judgment—on his animals. What reason, then, can be assigned why similar results should not follow from the long-continued selection of the most admired women by those men of each tribe, who were able to rear the greatest number of children? This would be unconscious selection, for an effect would be produced, independently of any wish or expectation on the part of the men who preferred certain women to others.

Let us suppose the members of a tribe, practicing some form of marriage, to spread over an unoccupied continent; they would soon split up into distinct hordes, separated from each other by various barriers, and still more effectually by the incessant wars between all barbarous nations. The hordes would thus be exposed to slightly different conditions and habits of life, and would sooner or later come to differ in some small degree. As soon as this occurred, each isolated tribe would form for itself a slightly different standard of beauty;[1] and then unconscious selection would come into action through the more powerful and leading men preferring certain women to others. Thus the differences between the tribes, at first very slight, would gradually and inevitably be more or less increased.

With animals in a state of nature, many characters proper to the males, such as size, strength, special weapons, courage and pugnacity, have been acquired through the law of battle. The semi-human progenitors of man, like their allies the Quadrumana, will almost certainly have been thus modified; and, as savages still fight for the possession of their women, a similar process of selection has probably gone on in a greater or less degree to the present day. Other characters proper to the males of the lower animals, such as bright colors and various ornaments, have been acquired by the more attractive males having been preferred by the females. There are, however, exceptional cases in which the males are the selecters, instead of having been the selected. We recognize such cases by the females being more highly ornamented than the males—their ornamental characters having been transmitted exclusively or chiefly to their female offspring. One such case has been described in the order to which man belongs, that of the Rhesus monkey.

[1] An ingenious writer argues, from a comparison of the pictures of Raphael, Rubens, and modern French artists, that the idea of beauty is not absolutely the same even throughout Europe: see the "Lives of Haydn and Mozart," by Bombet (otherwise M. Beyle), English translat. p. 278.

Man is more powerful in body and mind than woman, and in the savage state he keeps her in a far more abject state of bondage, than does the male of any other animal; therefore it is not surprising that he should have gained the power of selection. Women are everywhere conscious of the value of their own beauty; and when they have the means, they take more delight in decorating themselves with all sorts of ornaments than do men. They borrow the plumes of male birds, with which nature has decked this sex in order to charm the females. As women have long been selected for beauty, it is not surprising that some of their successive variations should have been transmitted exclusively to the same sex; consequently that they should have transmitted beauty in a somewhat higher degree to their female than to their male offspring, and thus have become more beautiful, according to general opinion, than men. Women, however, certainly transmit most of their characters, including some beauty, to their offspring of both sexes; so that the continued preference by the men of each race for the more attractive women, according to their standard of taste, will have tended to modify in the same manner all the individuals of both sexes belonging to the race.

With respect to the other form of sexual selection (which with the lower animals is much the more common), namely, when the females are the selecters, and accept only those males which excite or charm them most, we have reason to believe that it formerly acted on our progenitors. Man in all probability owes his beard, and perhaps some other characters, to inheritance from an ancient progenitor who thus gained his ornaments. But this form of selection may have occasionally acted during later times; for in utterly barbarous tribes the women have more power in choosing, rejecting, and tempting their lovers, or of afterwards changing their husbands, than might have been expected. As this is a point of some importance, I will give in detail such evidence as I have been able to collect.

Hearne describes how a woman in one of the tribes of Arctic America repeatedly ran away from her husband and joined her lover; and with the Charruas of S. America, according to Azara, divorce is quite optional. Amongst the Abipones, a man on choosing a wife bargains with the parents about the price. But "it frequently happens that the girl rescinds what has been agreed upon between the parents and the bridegroom, obstinately rejecting the very mention of marriage." She often runs away, hides herself, and thus eludes the bridegroom. Captain Musters, who lived with the Patagonians, says that their marriages are always settled by inclination; "if the parents make a match contrary to the daughter's will, she refuses and is never compelled to comply." In Tierra del Fuego a young man first obtains the consent of the parents by doing them some service, and then he attempts to carry off the girl; "but if she is unwilling, she hides herself in the woods until her admirer is heartily tired of looking for her, and gives up the pursuit; but this seldom happens." In the Fiji Islands the man seizes on the woman whom he wishes for his wife by actual or pretended force; but "on reaching the home of her abductor, should she not approve of the match, she runs to some one who can protect her; if, however, she is satisfied, the matter is settled forthwith." With the Kalmucks there is a regular race between the bride and bridegroom, the former having a fair start; and Clarke "was assured that no instance occurs of a girl being caught, unless she has a partiality to the pursuer." Amongst the wild tribes of the Malay Archipelago there is also a racing match; and it appears from M. Bourien's account, as Sir J. Lubbock remarks, that "the race 'is not to the swift, nor the battle to the strong,' but to the young man who has the good fortune to please his intended bride." A similar custom, with the same result, prevails with the Koraks of North-Eastern Asia.

Turning to Africa: The Kafirs buy their wives, and girls are severely beaten by their fathers if they will not accept a chosen husband; but it is manifest from many facts given by the Rev. Mr. Shooter that they have considerable power of choice. Thus very ugly, though rich men, have been known to fail in getting wives. The girls, before consenting to be betrothed, compel the men to show themselves off first in front and then behind, and "exhibit their paces." They have been known to propose to a man, and they not rarely run away with a favored lover. So again, Mr. Leslie, who was intimately acquainted with the Kafirs, says, "it is a mistake to imagine that a girl is sold by her father in the same manner, and with the same authority, with which he would dispose of a cow." Amongst the degraded Bushmen of S. Africa, "when a girl has grown up to womanhood without having been betrothed, which, however, does not often happen, her lover must gain her approbation, as well as that of the parents." Mr. Winwood Reade made inquiries for me with respect to the negroes of Western Africa, and he informs me that "the women, at least among the more intelligent Pagan tribes, have no difficulty in getting the husbands whom they may desire, although it is considered unwomanly to ask a man to marry them. They are quite capable of falling in love, and of forming tender, passionate, and faithful attachments." Additional cases could be given.

We thus see that with savages the women are not in quite so abject a state in relation to marriage, as has often been supposed. They can tempt the men whom they prefer, and can sometimes reject those whom they dislike, either before or after marriage. Preference on the part of the women, steadily acting in any one direction, would ultimately affect the character of the tribe; for the women would generally choose not merely the handsomest men, according to their standard of taste, but those who were at the same time best able to defend and support them. Such well-endowed pairs would commonly rear a larger number of offspring than the less favored. The same result would obviously follow in a still more marked manner, if there was selection on both sides; that is, if the more attractive, and at the same time more powerful men were to prefer, and were preferred by, the more attractive women. And this double form of selection seems actually to have occurred, especially during the earlier periods of our long history.

We will now examine a little more closely some of the characters which distinguish the several races of man from one another and from the lower animals, namely, the greater or less deficiency of hair on the body, and the color of the skin. We need say nothing about the great diversity in the shape of the features and of the skull between the different races, as we have seen in the last chapter how different is the standard of beauty in these respects. These characters will therefore probably have been acted on through sexual selection; but we have no means of judging whether they have been acted on chiefly from the male or female side. The musical faculties of man have likewise been already discussed.

Absence of Hair on the Body, and Its Development on the Face and Head. —From the presence of the woolly hair or lanugo on the human foetus, and of rudimentary hairs scattered over the body during maturity, we may infer that man is descended from some animal which was born hairy and remained so during life. The loss of hair is an inconvenience and probably an injury to man, even in a hot climate, for he is thus exposed to the scorching of the sun, and to sudden chills, especially during wet weather. As Mr. Wallace remarks, the natives in all countries are glad to protect their naked backs and shoulders with some slight covering. No one supposes that the nakedness of the skin is any direct advantage to man; his body therefore cannot have been divested of hair through natural selection.[1] Nor, as shown in a former chapter, have we any evidence that this can be due to the direct action of climate, or that it is the result of correlated development.

The absence of hair on the body is to a certain extent a secondary sexual character; for in all parts of the world women are less hairy than men. Therefore we may reasonably suspect that this character has been gained through sexual selection. We know that the faces of several species of monkeys, and large surfaces at the posterior end of the body of other species, have been denuded of hair; and this we may safely attribute to sexual selection, for these surfaces are not only vividly colored, but sometimes, as with the male mandrill and female rhesus, much more vividly in the one sex than in the other, especially during the breeding-season. I am informed by Mr. Bartlett that, as these animals gradually reach maturity, the naked surfaces grow larger compared with the size of their bodies. The hair, however, appears to have been removed, not for the sake of nudity, but that the color of the skin may be more fully displayed. So again with many birds, it appears as if the head and neck had been divested of feathers through sexual selection, to exhibit the brightly-colored skin.

As the body in woman is less hairy than in man, and as this character is common to all races, we may conclude that it was our female semi-human ancestors who were first divested of hair, and that this occurred at an extremely remote period before the several races had diverged from a common stock. Whilst our female ancestors were gradually acquiring this new character of nudity, they must have transmitted it almost equally to their offspring of both sexes whilst young; so that its transmission, as with the ornaments of many mam-

[1] "Contributions to the Theory of Natural Selection," 1870, p. 346. Mr. Wallace believes (p. 350) "that some intelligent power has guided or determined the development of man;" and he considers the hairless condition of the skin as coming under this head. The Rev. T. R. Stebbing, in commenting on this view ("Transactions of Devonshire Assoc. for Science," 1870) remarks, that had Mr. Wallace "employed his usual ingenuity on the question of man's hairless skin, he might have seen the possibility of its selection through its superior beauty or the health attaching to superior cleanliness."

mals and birds, has not been limited either by sex or age. There is nothing surprising in a partial loss of hair having been esteemed as an ornament by our ape-like progenitors, for we have seen that innumerable strange characters have been thus esteemed by animals of all kinds, and have consequently been gained through sexual selection. Nor is it surprising that a slightly injurious character should have been thus acquired; for we know that this is the case with the plumes of certain birds, and with the horns of certain stags.

The females of some of the anthropoid apes, as stated in a former chapter, are somewhat less hairy on the under surface than the males; and here we have what might have afforded a commencement for the process of denudation. With respect to the completion of the process through sexual selection, it is well to bear in mind the New Zealand proverb, "There is no woman for a hairy man." All who have seen photographs of the Siamese hairy family will admit how ludicrously hideous is the opposite extreme of excessive hairiness. And the king of Siam had to bribe a man to marry the first hairy woman in the family; and she transmitted this character to her young offspring of both sexes.

Some races are much more hairy than others, especially the males; but it must not be assumed that the more hairy races, such as the European, have retained their primordial condition more completely than the naked races, such as the Kalmucks or Americans. It is more probable that the hairiness of the former is due to partial reversion; for characters which have been at some former period long inherited are always apt to return. We have seen that idiots are often very hairy, and they are apt to revert in other characters to a lower animal type. It does not appear that a cold climate has been influential in leading to this kind of reversion; excepting perhaps with the negroes, who have been reared during several generations in the United States,[1] and possibly with the Ainos, who inhabit the northern islands

[1] "Investigations into Military and Anthropological Statistics of American Soldiers," by B. A. Gould, 1869; p. 568:—Observations were carefully made on the hairiness of 2129 black and colored soldiers, whilst they were bathing; and by looking to the published table, "it is manifest at a glance that there is but little, if any, difference between the white and the black races in this respect." It is, however, certain that negroes in their native and much hotter land of Africa, have remarkably smooth bodies. It should be particularly observed, that both pure blacks and mulattoes were included in the above enumeration; and this is an unfortunate circumstance, as in accordance with a principle, the truth of which I have elsewhere proved, crossed races of man would be eminently liable to revert to the primordial hairy character of their early ape-like progenitors.

of the Japan Archipelago. But the laws of inheritance are so complex that we can seldom understand their action. If the greater hairiness of certain races be the result of reversion, unchecked by any form of selection, its extreme variability, even within the limits of the same race, ceases to be remarkable.

With respect to the beard in man, if we turn to our best guide, the Quadrumana, we find beards equally developed in both sexes of many species, but in some, either confined to the males, or more developed in them than in the females. From this fact and from the curious arrangement, as well as the bright colors of the hair about the heads of many monkeys, it is highly probable, as before explained, that the males first acquired their beards through sexual selection as an ornament, transmitting them in most cases, equally or nearly so, to their offspring of both sexes. We know from Eschricht that with mankind, the female as well as the male foetus is furnished with much hair on the face, especially round the mouth; and this indicates that we are descended from progenitors, of whom both sexes were bearded. It appears therefore at first sight probable that man has retained his beard from a very early period, whilst woman lost her beard at the same time that her body became almost completely divested of hair. Even the color of our beards seems to have been inherited from an ape-like progenitor; for when there is any difference in tint between the hair of the head and the beard, the latter is lighter colored in all monkeys and in man. In those Quadrumana in which the male has a larger beard than that of the female, it is fully developed only at maturity, just as with mankind; and it is possible that only the later stages of development have been retained by man. In opposition to this view of the retention of the beard from an early period, is the fact of its great variability in different races, and even within the same race; for this indicates reversion—long-lost characters being very apt to vary on reappearance.

Nor must we overlook the part which sexual selection may have played in later times; for we know that with savages, the men of the beardless races take infinite pains in eradicating every hair from their faces as something odious, whilst the men of the bearded races feel the greatest pride in their beards. The women, no doubt, participate in these feelings, and if so, sexual selection can hardly have failed to have effected something in the course of later times. It is also possible that the long-continued habit of eradicating the hair may have produced an inherited effect. Dr. Brown-Séquard has shown that if certain animals are operated on in a particular manner, their offspring are affected. Further evidence could be given of the inheritance of the effects of mutilations; but a fact lately ascertained by Mr. Salvin has a more direct bearing on the present question; for he has shown that the motmots, which are known habitually to bite off the barbs of the two central tail-feathers, have the barbs of these feathers naturally somewhat reduced.[1] Nevertheless with mankind, the habit of eradicating the beard and the hairs on the body would probably not have arisen until these had already become by some means reduced.

It is difficult to form any judgment as to how the hair on the head became developed to its present great length in many races. Eschricht states that in the human foetus the hair on the face during the fifth month is longer than that on the head; and this indicates that our semi-human progenitors were not furnished with long tresses, which must therefore have been a late acquisition. This is likewise indicated by the extraordinary difference in the length of the hair in the different races; in the negro the hair forms a mere curly mat; with us it is of great length, and with the American natives it not rarely reaches to the ground. Some species of Semnopithecus have their heads covered with moderately long hair, and this probably serves as an ornament and was acquired through sexual selection. The same view may perhaps be extended to mankind, for we know that long tresses are now and were formerly much admired, as may be observed in the works of almost every poet; St. Paul says, "If a woman have long hair, it is a glory to her;" and we have seen that in North America a chief was elected solely from the length of his hair.

Color of the Skin.—The best kind of evidence that in man the color of the skin has been modified through sexual selection is scanty; for in most races the sexes do not differ in this respect, and only slightly, as we have seen, in others. We know, however, from the many facts already given that the color of the skin is regarded by the men of all races as a highly important element in their beauty; so that it is a character which would be likely to have been modified through selection,

---

[1] Mr. Sproat has suggested ("Scenes and Studies of Savage Life," 1868, p. 25) this same view. Some distinguished ethnologists, amongst others M. Gosse of Geneva, believe that artificial modifications of the skull tend to be inherited.

as has occurred in innumerable instances with the lower animals. It seems at first sight a monstrous supposition that the jet-blackness of the negro should have been gained through sexual selection; but this view is supported by various analogies, and we know that negroes admire their own color. With mammals, when the sexes differ in color, the male is often black or much darker than the female; and it depends merely on the form of inheritance whether this or any other tint is transmitted to both sexes or to one alone. The resemblance to a negro in miniature of Pithecia satanas with his jet-black skin, white rolling eyeballs, and hair parted on the top of the head, is almost ludicrous.

The color of the face differs much more widely in the various kinds of monkeys than it does in the races of man; and we have some reason to believe that the red, blue, orange, almost white and black tints of their skin, even when common to both sexes, as well as the bright colors of their fur, and the ornamental tufts about the head, have all been acquired through sexual selection. As the order of development during growth generally indicates the order in which the characters of a species have been developed and modified during previous generations; and as the newly-born infants of the various races of man do not differ nearly as much in color as do the adults, although their bodies are as completely destitute of hair, we have some slight evidence that the tints of the different races were acquired at a period subsequent to the removal of the hair, which must have occurred at a very early period in the history of man.

Summary.—We may conclude that the greater size, strength, courage, pugnacity, and energy of man, in comparison with woman, were acquired during primeval times, and have subsequently been augmented, chiefly through the contests of rival males for the possession of the females. The greater intellectual vigor and power of invention in man is probably due to natural selection, combined with the inherited effects of habit, for the most able men will have succeeded best in defending and providing for themselves and for their wives and offspring. As far as the extreme intricacy of the subject permits us to judge, it appears that our male ape-like progenitors acquired their beards as an ornament to charm or excite the opposite sex, and transmitted them only to their male offspring. The females apparently first had their bodies denuded of hair, also as a sexual ornament; but they transmitted this character almost equally to both sexes. It is not improbable that the females were modified in other respects for the same purpose and by the same means; so that women have acquired sweeter voices and become more beautiful than men.

It deserves attention that with mankind the conditions were in many respects much more favorable for sexual selection, during a very early period, when man had only just attained to the rank of manhood, than during later times. For he would then, as we may safely conclude, have been guided more by his instinctive passions, and less by foresight or reason. He would have jealously guarded his wife or wives. He would not have practiced infanticide; nor valued his wives merely as useful slaves; nor have been betrothed to them during infancy. Hence we may infer that the races of men were differentiated as far as sexual selection is concerned, in chief part at a very remote epoch; and this conclusion throws light on the remarkable fact that at the most ancient period, of which we have as yet any record, the races of man had already come to differ nearly or quite as much as they do at the present day.

The views here advanced, on the part which sexual selection has played in the history of man, want scientific precision. He who does not admit this agency in the case of the lower animals will disregard all that I have written in the later chapters on man. We cannot positively say that this character, but not that, has been thus modified; it has, however, been shown that the races of man differ from each other and from their nearest allies, in certain characters which are of no service to them in their daily habits of life, and which it is extremely probable would have been modified through sexual selection. We have seen that with the lowest savages the people of each tribe admire their own characteristic qualities—the shape of the head and face, the squareness of the cheekbones, the prominence or depression of the nose, the color of the skin, the length of the hair on the head, the absence of hair on the face and body, or the presence of a great beard, and so forth. Hence these and other such points could hardly fail to be slowly and gradually exaggerated, from the more powerful and able men in each tribe, who would succeed in rearing the largest number of offspring, having selected during many generations for their wives the most strongly characterized and therefore most attractive women. For my own part I conclude that of all the causes which have led to the differences in external appearance between the races of man, and to a certain extent between man and the lower animals, sexual selection has been the most efficient.

WILLIAM ACTON

FROM

THE FUNCTIONS AND DISORDERS OF THE REPRODUCTIVE ORGANS

William Acton (1813–1875): Though a practicing Victorian surgeon, William Acton did not have a medical degree. He nonetheless wrote and published widely on the subjects of prostitution, reproductive organs, and urology. Acton was never highly regarded by his own profession, but he proclaimed himself an expert on male and female sexuality. He was the most famous proponent of the Victorian notion of female passionlessness. He believed—"happily for society"—that women, with the exception of nymphomaniacs and prostitutes, "know little of or are careless about sexual indulgences. Love of home, of children, and of domestic duties are the only passions they feel." By contrast, Acton argued strongly for the uncontrollable passions of men, and believed that denying their sexual impulses could be very detrimental to men's health. Victorian writers such as Elizabeth Blackwell and Isaac Baker Brown disputed Acton's beliefs.

NORMAL SEXUAL CONDITION IN CHILDHOOD

Any preliminary detailed analysis of the anatomy of the reproductive organs would be foreign to the purposes of the present treatise; a few words as to their relative size and appearance at different periods of life at the outset of our inquiry will suffice. In childhood the penis is naturally small, with the foreskin pointed, and not only completely covering the glans, but even extending beyond it. The attempt to uncover the glans is attended with difficulty in consequence of the existence of a natural phymosis, and similarly the process of recovering the glans owing to a natural paraphymosis, cannot be accomplished without resort to a certain degree of violence.

The mucous membrane is soft and flaccid, and (in a healthy constitution) free from the secretion called smegma by which it is covered in after life.

With sensitive children the withdrawal of the prepuce appears to promote erection, and to induce a gradual increase in the size of the penis, and such withdrawal is in all cases so far as possible to be avoided. In childhood the testes are small and flaccid, often pendent, and not sensitive to the touch. Such briefly described are the external appearance and general characteristics of the reproductive organs during childhood. We may now turn our attention to their functions. Previously to the attainment of puberty the normal condition of a healthy child is one of entire freedom from sexual impressions.

All its vital energy is employed in constructing the growing frame, in storing up external impressions, and in educating the brain to receive them. During a well-regulated childhood, and in the case of ordinary temperaments, there is no temptation to infringe this primary law of nature. The sexes, it is true, in most English homes, are allowed unrestricted companionship, and experience shows that this intimacy is in the main unattended with evil results. In the immense majority of instances, indeed, it is of great benefit. However this may be, at a very early age the pastimes of the girl and boy diverge. The boy takes to more boisterous amusements, and affects the society of boys older than himself, simply because they make rougher, or, in his opinion, manlier playfellows. The quieter games of girls are despised, and their society is to a considerable extent deserted. This apparent rudeness, often grieved over by anxious parents, may almost be regarded as a provision of nature against possible danger.

Education, of course, still further separates children as they grow into boys and girls; and the instinctive and powerful check of natural modesty is an additional safeguard. Thus it happens that with most healthy and well brought up children no sensual idea or feeling has ever entered their heads, even in the way of speculation. I believe that such children's curiosity is seldom excited on these subjects except as the result of suggestion by persons older than themselves. At any rate in healthy subjects, and especially in children brought up in the pure air and amid the simple amusements of the country, perfect freedom from, and indeed total ignorance of, any sexual attraction is the rule. The first and only feeling exhibited between the sexes in the young should be that pure fraternal and sisterly affection which it is the glory and blessing of our simple English home habits to create and foster with all their softening influences on the after life.

This state of purity and ignorant innocence in children is not in any way *unnatural*. It is true that a different rule prevails among many of the lower animals. For instance, no one can have seen young lambs gamboling together without noticing at what an early age the young rams evince the most definite sexual propensities. Precocity in them is evidently intuitive, as it cannot depend on the force of example. This contrast between children and young animals may be explained by the fact that the animal's life is much shorter than that of man, its growth is more rapid, its office in the world is lower and more material, its maturity is sooner reached, and sexual propensities are therefore naturally exhibited at a much earlier age. In still lower forms of life sexual feeling commences yet earlier. In many species of moths no sooner is the perfect insect produced than it proceeds at once to the exercise of the function of procreation, which completed, its own existence ceases.

Very different should be the case with the human being, who needs all the strength and all the nutrition he can command for the gradual development and consolidation of his more slowly maturing body and mind. The full development of the physical frame should precede reproduction. This applies to both sexes alike.

ABNORMAL SEXUAL CONDITION IN CHILDHOOD

SEXUAL PRECOCITY

It were well if the child's reproductive organs always remained in a quiescent state till puberty. This is unfortunately not the case.

Amongst the earliest disorders that we notice is sexual precocity.

In many instances, either from hereditary predisposition, bad companionship, or other evil influences, sexual feelings become developed at a very early age, and this abnormal excitement is always attended with injurious, often with the most deplorable consequences.

Slight signs are sufficient to indicate when a boy otherwise apparently healthy, and fond of playing with other boys, has this unfortunate tendency. He shows undoubted preferences. He will single out some one particular girl, and evidently derive a more than boyish pleasure from her society. His penchant does not take the ordinary form of a boy's good nature, but little attentions that are generally reserved for a later period prove that his feelings are different from the ordinary standard and sadly premature. His play with the girl is different from his play with his brothers. His kindness to her is too ardent. He follows her he knows not why. He fondles her with tenderness painfully suggestive of a vague dawning of passion. No one can find fault with him. He does nothing wrong. Parents and friends are delighted at his gentleness and politeness, and not a little amused at the traces of early flirtation. If they were wise they would rather feel profound anxiety; and he would be an unfaithful or incompetent medical adviser who did not, if an opportunity occurred, warn them that such a boy ought to be carefully watched, and removed from every influence calculated to foster his abnormal propensities.

The premature development of the sexual inclination is not merely repugnant to all we associate with the term childhood, but is also fraught with danger to dawning manhood. On the judicious treatment of a case such as has been sketched, it probably depends whether the dangerous propensity shall be so kept in check as to preserve the boy's health and innocence, or whether one more shattered constitution and wounded conscience shall be added to the victims of sexual precocity and careless training. It ought not to be forgotten that in such cases a quasi-sexual power often accompanies these premature sexual inclinations. Few, perhaps, except medical men, know how early in life a mere infant may experience erections. Frequently it may be noticed that a little child, on being taken out of bed in the morning, cannot make water at once. It would be as well if it were recognized by parents and nurses that this often depends upon a more or less complete erection.

Predisposing Causes.—What the cause of this early sexual predisposition in a young child may be, it is difficult to lay down with certainty in any given case. My own belief is, that there are sexual predisposing causes. I should specify *hereditary* predisposition as by no means the least common. It cannot be denied that as children soon after birth inherit a peculiar conformation of features or frame from the parent, so they frequently evince, even in the earlier years of childhood, mental characteristics and peculiarities that nothing but hereditary predisposition can account for. I believe that, as in body and mind, so also in the passions, the predispositions of the father are frequently inherited by the children. No man or woman can inordinately indulge their own sexual passions without at least running the risk of finding a disposition to gratify their sensual passions at an early age inherited by their offspring. In this way only can we explain the existence in generation after generation of an early and apparently almost irresistible propensity to similar tastes and feelings. No doubt vicious tendencies are frequently, perhaps most frequently *acquired*. But I firmly believe that moral as well as physical tendencies and irregularities can be transmitted to the progeny.

Exciting Causes.—There are, however, not a few directly exciting causes which can, and do frequently, not only foster this early proclivity to sexual feeling when there is hereditary predisposition, but even of themselves alone beget it.

We see in some children at a very early age an almost ungovernable disposition to touch or excite the sexual organs. This most dangerous habit is not unfrequently, I believe, produced by irritation in the rectum arising from worms. In other instances it arises from excessive irritability of the bladder. In addition to the manipulation another symptom often supervenes, viz. the constant wetting of the bed at night.

There is, besides, in many young persons, as will be mentioned hereafter, a morbid sensibility of the external organs that is excessively troublesome and often painful. This symptom may, I believe, appear very early in life, and, if not removed, lead to consequences that will be aggravated by youthful ignorance and want of self-control. It is to be wished that all medical men attached to large institutions where young boys are collected would bear this in mind, and when they have reason to suspect its existence remedy it at once. However natural the delicacy they feel in investigating such ailments, yet in this, perhaps above all other evils, prevention is better than cure.

Irritation of the glans penis arising from an unusually long prepuce or the collection of secretion under it is another exciting cause which should not be neglected. Since my attention was first called to this subject I have had abundant evidence that the influence of a long prepuce in producing sexual precocity has not been sufficiently noted. In the child the prepuce usually entirely covers the glans penis, and when, as generally happens in early life, smegma is not secreted, no ill consequences arise, but in some cases the urine lodges behind the prepuce and (especially if it becomes acrid) produces irritation which accordingly requires local treatment. A judicious mother or nurse should on observing any redness, swelling, or peculiar appearance call the attention of the surgeon to the case, as when taken in time the treatment is very simple and efficacious.

I do not recommend that the child under normal conditions should be advised, like the adult, to draw back the prepuce and employ ablution daily, but in all cases where the smegma is secreted early, daily ablutions are indispensable. As the boy grows older careful ablution of the glans and prepuce every morning will be beneficial, and if it is neglected, annoyance will be experienced, especially by those who have a long prepuce, from the collection of the secretion round the glans penis; but it should be remembered that this white secretion is natural, and not a symptom of disease. Quacks have frequently so wrought upon the fears of ignorant patients, especially those whose consciences were not clear, as to induce them to think they were laboring under some peculiar affection, whereas a little soap and water would have acted as a sufficient remedy.

A long and narrow prepuce is, in my opinion, a much more common cause of the subsequent contraction of evil habits than parents or medical men have any idea of. The collection of smegma between the glans and the prepuce is almost certain to produce irritation.

NORMAL SEXUAL CONDITIONS IN YOUTH

Youth (by which we mean that portion of a man's earthly existence during which he is *growing*—that is, in which he has not yet attained his maximum of mental and physical stature and strength) is, as regards the reproductive functions, to be divided into two periods. The line of demarcation is the occurrence of that series of phenomena which constitute what we call *puberty*. During the first of these two periods, or *childhood*, strictly so termed, the fitting condition is, as we have seen in the last chapter, absolute sexual quiescence.

In the second period, or that of youth, which we now propose to consider, quiescence wakes into all the excitement of the most animated life—a spring season, so to speak, like that so brilliantly sketched by our great poet:

"In the spring a fuller crimson comes upon the robin's breast,
  In the spring the wanton lapwing gets himself another crest,
  In the spring a livelier iris changes in the burnished dove,
  In the spring a young man's fancy lightly turns to thoughts of love."

Of the real nature of this new condition, of its temptations, of the incalculable advantages of resisting them, and of the means of doing so, it is now my purpose to speak, as plainly and concisely as possible.

Dr. Carpenter thus describes the change from childhood to youth:

"The period of youth is distinguished by that advance in the evolution of the generative apparatus in both sexes, and by that acquirement of its power of functional activity, which constitutes the state of PUBERTY. At this epoch a considerable change takes place in the bodily constitution: the sexual organs undergo a much increased development; various parts of the surface, especially the chin and the pubes, become covered with hair; the larynx enlarges, and the voice becomes lower in pitch, as well as rougher and more powerful; and new feelings and desires are awakened in the mind.

"To the use of the sexual organs for the continuance of his race MAN is prompted by a powerful instinctive desire, which he shares with the lower animals. This instinct, like the other propensities, is excited by sensations; and these may either originate in the sexual organs themselves or may be excited through the organs of special sense. Thus in man it is most powerfully aroused by impressions conveyed through the sight or touch, but in many other animals the auditory and olfactory organs communicate impressions which have an equal power, and it is not improbable that in certain *morbidly excited states of feeling* the same may be the case with ourselves."

—*Carpenter's Physiology*, 7th edition, p. 825.

With this bodily and mental change or development special functions, hitherto quiescent, begin their operations. Of these the most important in the male is the secretion of the impregnating fluid, the semen.

"From the moment," says Lallemand, "that the evolution of the generative organs commences (the testicles act), if the texture is not accidentally destroyed, they will continue to secrete up to a very advanced age. It is true that the secretion may be diminished by the absence of all excitement, direct or indirect, by the momentary feebleness of the economy, or by the action of special medicines, but it never entirely ceases from puberty up to old age." ("Les Pertes Seminales," p. 240, vol. ii.)

And now begins the trial which every healthy youth has to encounter, and from which he must come out victorious if he is to be all that he can and ought to be. The child should know nothing of this trial, and ought never to be disturbed with one sexual feeling or thought. But with puberty a very different state of things arises. A new *power* demands to be exercised, a new *want* to be satisfied. It is, I take it, of vital importance that boys and young men should know, not only the *guilt* of an illicit indulgence of their dawning passions, but also the *danger* of straining an immature power, and the solemn truth that the *want* will be an irresistible tyrant only to those who have lent it strength by yielding; that *the only true safety lies in keeping even the thoughts pure.* Nothing, I feel convinced, but a frank statement of the truth will persuade those entering upon puberty that these new feelings, powers, and delights must not be indulged.

It is very well known to medical men that the healthy secretion of semen has a direct effect upon the whole physical and mental conformation of the man. A series of phenomena attend the natural action of the testicles influencing the whole system; helping, in fact, in no small degree, to form the character itself. A function so important, which, in truth, to a great extent determines, according as it is dealt with, the happiness or misery of a life, is surely one of the last, if not the very last, that should be abused (see chapter on Semen).

But what, too often, are the facts? The youth, finding himself in possession of these sexual feelings and powers, utterly ignorant of their importance or even of their nature, except from the ribald con-

versation of the worst of his companions, and knowing absolutely
nothing of the consequences of giving way to them, fancies—as he,
with many compunctions, begins a career of depravity—that he is
obeying nature's dictates. Every fresh indulgence helps to forge the
chains of habit; and it too often happens in consequence of the morbid depression to which these errors have reduced him, that he fancies
that he is more or less ruined for this world, that he can never be
what he might have been, and that it is only by a struggle as for life
or death that he can hope for any recovery. In too many instances
there is no strength left for any such struggle, and, hopelessly and
helplessly, the victim drifts into irremediable ruin, tied and bound in
the chain of a sin with the commencement of which, ignorance had
as much to do as vice.

Not that this natural instinct is to be regarded with a Manichaean
philosophy as in itself bad. Far from it. That it is *natural* forbids such
a theory. It has its own beneficent purpose; but that purpose is not
early and sensual indulgence, but *mature and lawful love*. Let us hear
what Carpenter eloquently says on this point:

"The instinct of reproduction, when once aroused, even
though very obscurely felt, acts in man upon his mental faculties and moral feelings, and thus becomes the source, though
almost unconsciously so to the individual, of the tendency to
form that kind of attachment towards one of the opposite sex
which is known as *love*. This tendency, except in men who have
degraded themselves to the level of brutes, is not merely an
appetite or emotion, since it is the result of the combined operations of the reason, the imagination, the moral feelings, and
the physical desire. It is just in this connection of the psychical
attachment with the more corporeal instinct that the difference
between the sexual relations of man and those of the lower
animals lies. In proportion as the human being makes the temporary gratification of the mere sexual appetite his chief object,
and overlooks the happiness arising from mental and spiritual
communion, which is not only purer but more permanent, and
of which a renewal may be anticipated in another world, does
he degrade himself to a level with the brutes that perish."
—*Carpenter's Physiology*, 7th edition, p. 826.

Shakespeare makes even Iago say—

> "If the balance of our lives had not one scale of reason to poise another of sensuality, the blood and baseness of our natures would conduct us to most preposterous conclusions; but we have reason to cool our raging motions, our carnal stings, our unbitted lusts."
>
> —*Othello.*

"Nuptial love," says Lord Bacon, "maketh mankind, friendly love perfecteth it, but wanton love corrupteth and embaseth it."

Here, then, is our problem. A natural instinct, a great longing, has arisen in a boy's heart, together with the advent of the powers requisite to procure its gratification. Everything—the habits of the world, the keen appetite of youth for all that is new—the example of companions—the pride of health and strength—opportunity—all combine to urge him to give the rein to what seems a *natural* propensity. Such indulgence is, indeed, not natural, for man is not a mere animal, and the nobler parts of his nature cry out against the violation of their sanctity. Nay, more, such indulgence is *fatal*. It may be repented of. Some of its consequences may be, more or less, recovered from. But, from Solomon's time to ours, it is true that it leads to a "house of death."

The boy, however, does not know all this. He has to learn that to his immature frame every sexual indulgence is unmitigated evil. It does not occur to his inexperienced mind and heart that every illicit pleasure is a degradation, to be bitterly regretted hereafter—a link in a chain that does not need many more to be too strong to break.

"Amare et sapere vix Deo conceditur," said the ancients. It is my object, nevertheless, to point out how the two can be combined—how, in spite of all temptations, the boy can be at once loving and wise, and grow into what indeed, I think, is one of the noblest objects in the world in these our days,—a *continent* man.

CONTINENCE

In the following pages the word "continence" will be used in the sense of voluntary and entire forbearance from sexual excitement or indulgence in any form.

The abstinence must be *voluntary*, for continence must not be confounded with impotence. An impotent man is continent in a sense, but his continence, not depending on any effort of the will, is not what we are now speaking of.

Nor is the continence—which I advise, and would encourage by every means in my power—mere absence of desire arising from ignorance. That, as I shall hereafter show, I consider a dangerous condition. True continence is complete control over the passions, exercised by one who has felt their power, and who, were it not for his steady will, not only could, but would indulge them.

Again, continence must be *entire*. The fact of the indulgence being lawful or unlawful does not affect the question of continence. In this respect our definition differs from those in most dictionaries.[1]

This definition, of course, excludes the masturbator from the category of continent men, even though he may never have had connexion with a female. It can be only in a loose and inaccurate sense that an Onanist can be called continent. He is not really so. Continence consists not only in abstaining from sexual congress, but in controlling all sexual excitement. If a young man gives way to masturbation it is easy enough, as will be presently shown, for him to abstain from fornication. In fact, the one indulgence is generally incompatible with the other.

We may confidently assert that no man is entitled to the character of being continent or chaste who by any unnatural means causes expulsion of semen. On the other hand, the occasional occurrence of nocturnal emissions or wet dreams is quite compatible with, and, indeed, is to be expected as a consequence of continence, whether temporary or permanent. It is in this way that nature provides relief.

Professor Newman in his pamphlet on the relation of physiology to sexual morals has some excellent observations on this subject, which I generally coincide in, and which I prefer to quote rather than attempt to epitomize.

> "Moralists have at all times regarded strict temperance in
> food, and abstinence from strong drinks, to be of cardinal value
> in the maintenance of young men's purity. But whatever our

---

[1] The following are one or two of the definitions of the word "continence" in standard works:
"Abstinence from, or moderation in, the pleasures of physical love."—*R. Dunglison, M.D.*
"The abstaining from unlawful pleasures."—*Bailey.*
"Forbearance of lawful pleasure."—*Ash.*

care to be temperate, whatever our activity of body, it is not possible always to keep the exact balance between supply and bodily need. Every organ is liable occasionally to be over-charged, and, *in every youthful or vigorous nature*, has power to relieve itself. Considering that in man the sexual appetite is not, as in wild animals, something which comes for only a short season, and then imperatively demands gratification, but on the contrary is perennial, constant, and yet is *not* necessarily to be exercised at all, his nature cannot be harmonious and happy, unless it can right itself under smaller derangements of balance. But this is precisely what it does; and I cannot but think it of extreme importance not to allow a bugbear to be made out of *that*, which on the face of the matter is God's provision that the unmarried man shall not be harmed by perfect chastity. That it is ever other than natural, normal, and beneficial, I never heard or dreamed until I was well past the age of fifty. The Roman poet Lucretius, in a medico-philosophical discus-sion, speaks of this matter quite plainly, and treats it as *universal to mankind;* iv, 1024–1045. He imputes it to strength and youthful maturity, not to weakness; and while his description is tinged with epic extravagance, the thought of its doing any one harm evidently does not cross his mind, much less that it is an evil effect and disgraceful stain from previous vice. Now that I learn so many medical men to be unacquainted with it except as something immoderate, and, thereby, depressing and dangerous,—morbid and alarming; I have thought it a duty to make inquiries, where I could properly do so, from persons of whose true purity from early life I am thoroughly persuaded; and all that I elicit, direct or indirect, confirms me in what I have all my life believed. A clergyman reminds me that the ceremonial regulations in the books of Moses count upon it, and so does Jeremy Taylor;—dates, countries and races (says he) distant enough: he adds his belief that it is perfectly health-ful, and tends to be nearly periodical. A traveler to Jerusalem tells me that he found one of the superior monks 'unclean' for the day on account of it; and an inferior monk alluded to it as an ordinary matter. On gathering up what I know, what I have read, and what I believe on testimony, I distinctly assert, first, that this occurrence is strictly 'spontaneous,'—that it comes upon youths who not only have never practiced, but have never heard of such a thing as secret vice: that it comes on, without having been induced by any voluntary act of the person, and without any previous mental inflammation: next, that it occasionally comes upon married men, when circumstances put them for long together in the position of the unmarried; moreover, even when they become elderly, it does not wholly forsake them under such circumstances. My belief is that it is a sign of vigor. At any rate I assert most positively that it is an utter mistake to suppose that it necessarily weakens or depresses, or entails any disagreeable after-results whatever. I have never so much as once in my life had reason to think so. I have even believed that it adds to the spring of the body, and to the pride of manhood in youths. Of course there is an amount of starvation (at least I assume there is) which would supersede it; but to overdo the starvation even a little, may be an error on the wrong side.—Again, there is probably an amount of athletic practice which will take up all the supplies of full nutriment in the intensifying of muscle or of vital force, and leave no sexual superfluity. But labor so severe is stupefying to the brain and very unfavorable to high mental action. Plato is not alone in regarding athletes as unintellectual. Aristotle deprecates their system of 'overfeeding and overworking.' And after all, you will not succeed in exactly keeping the balance, whether you try by starvation or by toil; and the over careful effort will but produce either a valetudinarian, or else a religious ascetic, who is in terrible alarm lest Nature inflict upon him a momentary animal pleasure. A state of anxiety and tremor is not mentally wholesome. We must take things as they come, observing broad rules of moderation as wisely as we can, but without nervous alarm about details. The advantages of vegetarian food I have learned only late in life. I now know that I might have been wiser in my diet. With better knowledge I should have done far better as to the *quality* of food; but I do not easily believe that a more scrupulous dread of satisfying my appetite lest it cause some small sexual superfluity would have conduced either to mental or to bodily health, at any time of my life, unmarried or married."

—Loc. cit., p. 26.

Voluntary imitation or excitement of this natural relief is, in every sense of the word, incontinence. I would exclude from the category of continent men those (and they are more numerous than may be generally supposed) who actually forbear from sexual intercourse, but put no restraint upon impure thoughts or the indulgence of sexual excitement, provided intercourse does not follow. This is only physical continence: it is incomplete without mental continence also.

Such men as these, supposing the sexual excitement is followed by nocturnal emissions, as it often is, and this with great detriment to the nervous system, must not be ranked with the continents; to all intents and purposes they are ONANISTS. The subject will be further discussed in the section "On ungratified sexual excitement."

The Advantages of Continence.—If a healthy, well-disposed boy has been properly educated, by the time he arrives at the age of fourteen or sixteen he possesses a frame approaching its full vigor. His conscience is unburdened, his intellect clear, his address frank and candid, his memory good, his spirits are buoyant, his complexion is bright. Every function of the body is well performed, and no fatigue is felt after moderate exertion. The youth evinces that elasticity of body and that happy control of himself and his feelings which are indicative of the robust health and absence of care which should accompany youth. His whole time is given up to his studies and amusements, and as he feels his stature increase and his intellect enlarge, he gladly prepares for his coming struggle with the world.

If, then, the above are the advantages of continence, let us now glance at the reverse of the picture hereafter more fully considered, and notice the symptoms when a boy has been incontinent, especially in that most vicious of all ways, masturbation. In extreme cases the outward signs of debasement are only too obvious. The frame is stunted and weak, the muscles undeveloped, the eye is sunken and heavy, the complexion is sallow, pasty, or covered with spots of acne, the hands are damp and cold, and the skin moist. The boy shuns the society of others, creeps about alone, joins with repugnance in the amusements of his schoolfellows. He cannot look any one in the face, and becomes careless in dress and uncleanly in person. His intellect becomes sluggish and enfeebled, and if his evil habits are persisted in he may end in becoming a driveling idiot or a peevish valetudinarian. Such boys are to be seen in all the stages of degeneration, but what we have described is but the result towards which *they all* are tending.

The cause of the difference between these cases is very simple. The continent boy has not expended that vital fluid, semen, or exhausted his nervous energy, on the contrary, his vigor has been employed for its legitimate purpose, namely, in building up his growing frame. On the other hand, the wear and tear of the nervous system arising from the incessant excitement of sexual thoughts, the constant strain on the nervous system, and the large expenditure of semen, has exhausted the vital force of the incontinent, and has reduced the immature frame to a pitiable wreck.

Difficulty of Maintaining.—An almost infinite variety of opinion exists on this subject, between the extreme proposition on the one hand, that a young man has, or need have no sexual desire, at least to any troublesome degree, and consequently need neither take precautions, nor be warned against the danger of exciting his sexual feelings, and the equally extreme doctrine on the other hand, that the sufferings of chastity are such as to justify, or at least excuse, incontinence. My own opinion is, that where, as in the case with a very large number, a young man's education has been properly watched, and his mind has not been debased by vile practices, it is usually a comparatively easy task to be continent, and requires no great or extraordinary effort; and every year of voluntary chastity renders the task easier by the mere force of habit.

Yet it can hardly be denied that a very considerable number, even of the more or less pure, do suffer, at least temporarily, no little distress.

Lallemand has given a vivid sketch of this sexual uneasiness, which the early recollections of many of my readers may verify. "There is a constant state of orgasm and erotic preoccupation, accompanied with agitation, disquiet, and *malaise*, an indefinable derangement of all the functions. This state of distress is seen particularly in young men who have arrived at puberty, and whose innocence has been preserved from any unfortunate initiation. Their disposition becomes soured, impatient, and sad. They fall into a state of melancholy or misanthropy, sometimes become disgusted with life, and are disposed to shed tears without any cause. They seek solitude in order to dream about the great mystery which absorbs them; about those great unknown passions which cause their blood to boil. They are at the same time restless and apathetic, agitated, and drowsy.

Their head is in a state of fermentation, and nevertheless weighed down by a sort of habitual headache. A spontaneous emission or escape, which causes this state of plethora to cease, is a true and salutary crisis which for the moment re-establishes the equilibrium of the economy." (Vol. II, p. 324.)

I have quoted this passage, as containing a brilliant, though, perhaps, rather exaggerated sketch of a state of mind and body that is very common, and is the chief difficulty in the way of a youth's remaining chaste. I am, however, far from endorsing Lallemand's remark, that this distress affects those particularly "whose innocence has been preserved from any unfortunate initiations." On the contrary, it is my experience that these are just the persons who are, generally speaking, too happy and healthy to be troubled with these importunate weaknesses. The *semi-continent*, the men who indeed see the better course, and approve of it, but follow the worse—the men who, without any of the recklessness of the hardened sensualist, or any of the strength of the conscientiously pure man, endure at once the sufferings of self-denial and the remorse of self-indulgence—these are the men of whom Lallemand's words are a living description.

The facts which show the truth of this are innumerable, and apply to the youth, of whom I am now more particularly speaking, as much as to the adult. It is a matter of everyday experience to hear patients complaining that a state of continence after a certain time produces a most irritable condition of the nervous system, so that the individual is unable to settle his mind to anything:—study becomes impossible; the student cannot sit still; sedentary occupations are unbearable, and sexual ideas intrude perpetually on the patient's thoughts. When I listen to this complaint, I have little doubt of the confession that is to follow—a confession that at once explains the symptoms. Of course in such cases I am prepared to learn that the self-prescribed remedy has been most effective, that sexual intercourse has enabled the student at once to recommence his labors, the poet his verses, and the faded imagination of the painter to resume its fervor and its brilliancy; while the writer who for days has not been able to construct two phrases that he considered readable, has found himself, after relief of the seminal vessels, in a condition to dictate his best performances. In individuals constituted as these are, continence is sure to induce this state of irritability. Still, no such symptoms, however feelingly described, should ever induce a medical man even to seem to sanction his patient's continuing the fatal remedy, which is only perpetuating the disease.

In all solemn earnestness I protest against a medical man countenancing such a remedy. It is better for a youth to live a continent life. The *strictly* continent suffer little or none of this irritability; but the incontinent, as soon as seminal plethora occurs, are sure to be troubled in one or other of the modes above spoken of; while the remedy of indulgence, if effective, requires repetition as often as the inconvenience returns. If instead of gratifying his inclinations the young patient should consult a conscientious medical man, he would probably be told, and the result would soon prove the correctness of the advice given, that low diet, partial abstinence from meat and stimulants, aperient medicine (if necessary), gymnastic exercise, and self-control, will most effectually relieve the symptoms. The patient might further be advised to adopt the precautions mentioned in the chapter on Nocturnal Emissions, which will tend to prevent a repetition of the plethora.

The truth is, that most people, and especially the young, are often only too glad to find an excuse for *indulging* their animal propensities, instead of endeavoring to regulate or control them. I have not a doubt that this sexual suffering is often much exaggerated, if not invented, for this purpose. Even where it really exists (and I am free to confess that in certain individuals continence of the sexual feelings is very difficult), one of the last remedies the patient would entertain the idea of, would be, that first recommended by a conscientious professional man, viz., attention to diet—exercise—and, in fact, regimen. That there should be more available and willing testimony in favor of the remedy considered agreeable than of that involving constraint or inconvenience, is easily explicable on the supposition that the witnesses have not had experience of both systems.

If a young man wished to undergo the acutest sexual suffering, he could adopt no more certain method than to propose to be incontinent, with the avowed intention of becoming continent again, when he had "sown his wild oats." The agony of breaking off a habit which so rapidly entwines itself with every fiber of the human frame is such that it would not be too much to say to any youth commencing a career of vice—"You are going a road on which you will *never* turn back. However much you may wish it, the struggle will be too much for you. You had better stop now. It is your last chance."

There is a terrible significance in the Wise Man's words, "*None that go to her return again, neither take they hold on the paths of life.*"

How much more severe, occasional incontinence makes the necessary struggle to remain continent at all, appears from the sexual distress which widowers, or those married men to whom access to their wives is forbidden, suffer.

To show that this is not the result of my experience alone, I may quote the statement of my friend Dr. ———, who is constantly attending for serious diseases of the womb the wives of clergymen, as well as of dissenting ministers, in whose cases, for months together, marital intercourse is necessarily forbidden. He tells me that he has often been surprised at the amount of sexual suffering—the result of their compulsory celibacy—endured by the husbands of some of his patients—men in every other relation of life most determined and energetic. Indeed, it is not wonderful that it should be so, if we consider the position of such men, who for years may have indulged, with moderation, the sex-passion as we have described it, untrained to mortification in the shape of food or exercise, or marital intercourse, the secretion of perfect semen going on in obedience to the healthy course of a married man's existence. Conceive them reined up suddenly, as it were, and bidden to do battle with their instincts. Religion and morality prevent them, more than others, from having sexual intercourse with strange women; intense ignorance on the subject of the sex-passion in general, as well as misapprehension of the effects of disease of the generative organs, only aggravate their suffering: conceive all this, and it is not difficult to believe that affections of the brain may supervene.

These remarks are in no way intended as any excuse or palliation for incontinence, but as warnings to the young. These, it must be remembered, are the complaints of *incontinent* men, and I mention them here to show how much easier it is even in adult life to abstain altogether than it is to control the feelings, when they have been once excited and indulged. The real remedy for this form of sexual distress is resolute continence and the use of all the hygienic aids in our power—not the empiric receipt of present indulgence with the futile intention of curing the incontinence afterwards.

The admitted fact that continence, even at the very beginning of manhood, is frequently productive of distress, is often a struggle hard to be borne,—still harder to be completely victorious in,—is not to be at all regarded as an argument that it is an *evil*. A thoughtful writer has on this subject some admirable remarks:—"Providence has seen it necessary to make very ample provision for the preservation and utmost possible extension of all species. The aim seems to diffuse existence as widely as possible, to fill up every vacant piece of space with some sentient being, to be a vehicle of enjoyment. Hence this passion is conferred in great force. But the relation between the number of beings and the means of supporting them is only on the footing of a general law. There may be occasional discrepancy between the laws operating for the multiplication of individuals and the laws operating to supply them with the means of subsistence, and evils will be endured in consequence, even in our own highly favored species; but against all these evils and against those numberless vexations which have arisen in all ages from the attachment of the sexes, place the vast amount of happiness which is derived from this source—the center of the whole circle of the domestic affections, the sweetening principle of life, the prompter of all our most generous feelings and even of our most virtuous resolves and exertions—and every ill that can be traced to it is but as dust in the balance. And here also we must be on our guard against judging from what we see in the world at a particular era. As reason and the higher sentiments of man's nature increase in force, this passion is put under better regulation, so as to lessen many of the evils connected with it. The civilized man is more able to give it due control; his attachments are less the result of impulse; he studies more the weal of his partner and offspring. There are even some of the resentful feelings connected in early society with love, such as hatred of successful rivalry, and jealousy, which almost disappear in an advanced state of civilization. The evil springing, in our own species at least, from this passion may, therefore, be an exception mainly peculiar to a particular term of the world's progress, and which may be expected to decrease greatly in amount."

In addition to the foregoing considerations, I would venture to suggest one that should not be forgotten. Granted that continence is a *trial*, a sore trial, a bitter trial, if you will—what, I would ask, is the use or object of a trial but to *try*, to test, to elicit, strengthen and brace, whatever of sterling, whatever of valuable, there is in the thing tried? To yield at once—is this the right way to meet a trial? To lay down one's arms at the first threatening of conflict—is this a *creditable* escape from trial, to say no more? Nay, is it *safe*, when the trial is imposed by the highest possible authority?

"The first use," says the late Rev. F. Robertson, "a man makes of every power or talent given to him is a bad use. The first time a man ever uses a flail it is to the injury of his own head and of those who stand around him. The first time a child has a sharp-edged tool in his hand he cuts his finger. But this is no reason why he should not be ever taught to use a knife. The first use a man makes of his affections is to sensualize his spirit. Yet he cannot be ennobled except through those very affections. The first time a kingdom is put in possession of liberty the result is anarchy. The first time a man is put in possession of intellectual knowledge he is conscious of the approaches of skeptical feeling. But that is no proof that liberty is bad or that instruction should not be given. It is a law of our humanity that man must know both good and evil; he must know good *through* evil. There never was a principle but what triumphed through much evil; no man ever progressed to greatness and goodness but through great mistakes."

The argument in favor of the great mental, moral, and physical advantage of early continence does not want for high secular authority and countenance, as the recollection of the least learned reader will suggest in a moment. Let us be content here with the wise Greek,[1] who, to the question when men should love, answered, "A young man, not yet; an old man, not at all;" and with the still wiser Englishman,[2] who thus writes:—"You may observe that amongst all the great and worthy persons (whereof the memory remaineth, either ancient or recent) there is not one that hath been transported to the mad degree of love—which shows that great spirits and great business do keep out this weak passion. . . . By how much the more ought men to beware of this passion, which loseth not only other things, but itself. As for the other losses, the poet's relation doth well figure them:—*'That he that preferred Helena quitted the gifts of Juno and Pal-*

[1] Thales.
[2] Lord Bacon.

las:' for whosoever esteemeth too much of amorous affection, quitteth both riches and wisdom. . . . They do best who, if they cannot but admit love, yet make it keep quarter."

Aids to Continence.—Every wise man must feel that no help is to be despised in any part of the life-battle all have to fight. And in that struggle for purity, which is, at least for the young, the hardest part of it, what help to seek, and where and how to seek it, are no unimportant questions, and in a practical treatise well deserve a few words.

Religion.—Far above all other assistance must, of course, be placed the influence of religion—not the superstition of which the bitter poet speaks:

> "Humana . . . cum vita jaceret
> In terris oppressa gravi sub religione,"

but that whose chiefest beatitude is promised to the "pure in heart."

Of the direct personal influence of religion upon the individual in this respect, it is not my purpose to speak here—the very nature of that influence is, in these days, the ground of too much and too fervid controversy. It is not, however, without interest to observe the different way in which the two great western divisions of the Christian Church treat the subject of continence.

Among *modern* Protestants, I cannot help feeling that there is, both in the spoken and written teaching of their authorized ministers, a certain timorousness in dealing with the matter, which, however natural, almost gives the idea of a lack of sympathy with the arduous nature of the effort requisite to obey the commands that so urgently demand perfect purity from the consistent Christian.

It is much the same among the fathers of our Church. In those writings which are, from their antiquity—the wide assent they have commanded—the character and station of their authors—or from other causes, usually regarded as of *authority* among us, there is often a deficiency in frank and kindly discussion of the subject.

It was far from my intention, when I commenced this work, to put myself forward as a religious adviser, but I so frequently receive painful letters from young men, seeking advice how to curb the lusts of the flesh, that I was induced to inquire as to the views entertained upon the subject by the modern executive of the Church of England.

I found, on application to competent persons, that it is not deemed expedient to be very diffuse upon the observance of the seventh commandment. I was referred, indeed, by one worthy divine to the head of "Fasts and Vigils" in our Offices; but, after careful perusal, I was unable to discover much that could be of assistance to the earnest layman desirous of arming himself against the promptings of nature and imagination.

The contrast, we may remark, between the common sense and wisdom of the more ancient writers and some modern ecclesiastical views on these subjects is rather painful. All the help that one excellent clergyman can give to tempted brethren is this: "Another man is tormented by evil thoughts at night. Let him be directed to cross his arms upon his breast, and extend himself as if he were lying in his coffin. Let him endeavor to think of himself as he will be one day stretched in death. If such solemn thoughts do not drive away evil imaginations, let him rise from his bed and lie on the floor."

It is a solemn truth that the sovereignty of the will, or, in other words, the command of the man over himself and his outward circumstances, is a matter of *habit*. Every victory strengthens the victor. With one, long years of courageous self-rule have made it apparently impossible for him ever to yield. The whole force of his character, braced and multiplied by the exercise of a lifetime, drives him with unwavering energy along his chosen course of purity. The very word we have used—continence—admirably expresses the firm and watchful hold with which his trained and disciplined will grasps and guides all the circumstances and influences of his life.

Contrast with this man the feeble-willed; for him the first little concession, the first lost battle between the will and a temptation, is but the commencement of a long series of failures. Every succeeding conflict is harder because the last has been lost. Every defeat lessens the last trembling remnants of self-reliance. And at last, with the bitterest pain of all—self-contempt—gnawing at his heart, with no strength to say, "I will not"—under the tyrannous dominion of foul passions, which all the good that is left in him abhors, the man slinks and stumbles towards his grave.

But, more than this, the steady discipline of the will has a direct physical effect on the body. The young man who can command even his thoughts, will have an *easier* task in keeping himself continent than he who cannot. He who, when physical temptations assail him, can determinately apply his mind to other subjects, and employ the whole force of his will in turning away, as it were, from the danger, has a power over the body itself which will make his victory tenfold easier than his who, unable to check bodily excitement, though determined not to yield, must endure in the conflict great sexual misery.

Dr. Carter, in his "Treatise on Hysteria," makes some striking remarks on the effect of continual direction of the mind in producing emotional congestion of organs, which illustrate this view of the subject. He says: "The glands liable to emotional congestion are those which, by forming their products in larger quantity, subserve to the gratification of the excited feeling. Thus, blood is directed to the mammae by the maternal emotions, to the testes by the sexual, and to the salivary glands by the influence of appetizing odors; while in either case the sudden demand may produce an exsanguine condition of other organs, and may check some function which was being actively performed, as, for instance, the digestive."

In accordance with the same law, a steady avoidance of all impure thoughts—a turning away, so to speak, of the will from sexual subjects—will spare the young man much of the distress and temptation arising from the abnormal excitement of the reproductive system induced by the mind's dwelling much on such topics.

The essence of all this training of the will, however, lies in beginning *early*. If a boy is once fully impressed that *all* such indulgences are dirty and mean, and, with the whole force of his unimpaired energy, determines he *will* not disgrace himself by yielding, a very bright and happy future is before him.

A striking example of what resolution can do was related to me lately by a distinguished patient. "You may be somewhat surprised, Mr. Acton," said he, "by the statement I am about to make to you, that before my marriage I lived a perfectly continent life. During my university career my passions were very strong, sometimes almost uncontrollable, but I have the satisfaction of thinking that I mastered them; it was, however, by great efforts. I obliged myself to take violent physical exertion; I was the best oar of my year, and when I felt particularly strong sexual desire, I sallied out to take more exercise. I was victorious always; and I never committed fornication; you see in what robust health I am, it was exercise that alone saved me." I may mention that this gentleman took a most excellent degree, and has reached the highest point of his profession. Here then is an instance of what energy of character, indomitable perseverance, and unimpaired health will effect.

The advice given by Carpenter in the fifth edition of his work, p. 779, is as follows:—"The author would say to those of his younger readers who urge the wants of nature as an excuse for the illicit gratification of the sexual passion, 'Try the effects of close mental application to some of those ennobling pursuits to which your profession introduces you, in combination with vigorous bodily exercise, before you assert that the appetite is unrestrainable, and act upon that assertion.' Nothing tends so much to increase the desire as the continual direction of the mind towards the objects of its gratification, especially under the favoring influence of sedentary habits; whilst nothing so effectually represses it as the determinate exercise of the mental faculties upon other objects and the expenditure of nervous energy in other channels."

With reference to the vital importance of a strong, well-trained will, we may also quote the valuable testimony of Dr. Reid:—

"Let us, as psychological physicians, impress upon the minds of those predisposed to attacks of mental aberration, and other forms of nervous disease, the important truth that they have it in their power to crush, by determined, persevering, and continuous acts of volition, the floating atoms, the minute embryos, the early scintillations of insanity. Many of the diseases of the mind, in their premonitory stage, admit, under certain favorable conditions, of an easy cure, if the mind has in early life been accustomed to habits of self-control, and the patient is happily gifted with strong *volitionary power*, and brings it to bear upon the scarcely formed filaments of mental disease. We should have fewer disorders of the mind if we could acquire more power of volition, and endeavor by our energy to disperse the clouds which occasionally arise within our own horizon—if we resolutely tore the first threads of the net which gloom and ill-humor may cast around us, and made an effort to drive away the melancholy images of the imagination by incessant occupation."

It should not be forgotten that this training of the will is not without its immediate and sensible rewards. Without it, or at least without some measure of it, those faculties of the mind on the regular exercise of which our success in any pursuit, and in fact our general intellectual advancement, depend, cannot be rightly cultivated. How absolutely essential it is for the attainment of real happiness, which depends so largely upon self-approbation, has been already noticed.

Exercise and Diet.—It is not, however, sufficient to train and strengthen the mind and will; the body must be subjected to a regular and determined discipline, before the proper command can be obtained over its rebellious instincts. And this discipline, when properly carried out, will not consist in any violation of the natural rules of health, but in a strict conformity to the hygienic regulations which science has proved must be obeyed before real health and vigor can be ensured.

For instance, religious and mental discipline may be vastly assisted by partial or total abstinence from fermented drinks and exciting animal food. Experience teaches us that by merely judiciously stinting the food of man in quantity and quality, while, at the same time, the brain is kept in exercise and the body fatigued, the animal instincts may be well-nigh subjugated. I cannot, therefore, but believe that a well-directed combination of spiritual, mental, and physical training would secure, as nearly as man may hope for, a perfect result. I lay stress upon the words "judiciously" and "well-directed," because it is necessary I should guard myself against being supposed to counsel a rash or unscientific self-treatment. Much of the danger which has always attended attempts at ill-directed self-maceration,[1] by fasting and purgatives, undertaken sometimes with a view of correcting corpulency and sometimes for mortification's sake, by religious enthusiasts, will as surely wait upon unscientific training to continence. During the initiatory period, at all events, some medical superintendence is desirable to decide when the process should be commenced

---

[1] I am inclined to believe that many of the penances which ascetics in former times set themselves—such as starvation, scourging, and exposure—were the most potent means then known of restraining the animal passions, and teaching the sufferers from them to control their feelings; with the same object we may believe that many a hermit shut himself out of the world in order to escape the effect of female society. In the present day I am acquainted with individuals who in former times would have become some misdirected enthusiasts;—for human nature is little changed, although the fashion of self-chastisement has gone out. There are self-made martyrs in this nineteenth century, as there were in the sixteenth.

and how it should be graduated, what amount of pressure may be put upon each constitution, when to increase and when to relax it, what should be the nature and extent of exercise, and the quantity and quality of nutriment required to keep the system in true form and balance.

I am convinced, all other considerations apart, that were there one or two days weekly set aside by all of us for extreme moderation in diet, public health and morals would be much benefited. The writer who would rationally consider and popularize such discipline, would be entitled to our thanks as a public benefactor. At present, all healthy persons in anything like easy circumstances eat and drink too much. Our over-eating is often attended visibly by the pendulous abdomen and lethargic frame, and less obviously by depreciated mental energy, and what I may term an artificial desire for and imaginary increase of sexual power. The dining, drinking, and sexual indulgence which are practiced with unvarying regularity by too many of our young men among the middle classes who take little or no exercise, are acting as surely, though perhaps slowly, against the *mens sana in corpore sano* of the generation, as the opposite system I recommend of bodily labor and organized abstemiousness[1] would tend to its maintenance. So we come after all to the good old adage on the way to live well—"On a shilling a day, and earn it."

Healthy and Intellectual Employment and Amusement.—The passive means, namely, abstinence from exciting causes, are not, however, the only ones that must be employed in order to maintain that condition of self-restraining health which we desire to see in young men;— active hygiene is most essential. Exercise, gymnastics, regular em-

---

[1] The influence of food in modifying the process of development is seen in a very marked form in the hive-bee. If we can put confidence in the observations of apiarians we must believe that the neuters, which constitute the majority of every bee-community, are really females with the sexual organs undeveloped, the capacity for generation being restricted to the queen. If the queen should be destroyed, or removed, the bees choose two or three among the neuter eggs that have been deposited in their appropriate cells, and change those cells (by breaking down others around them) into *royal* cells, differing considerably from the rest in form, and of much larger dimensions; and the larvae when they come forth are supplied with "royal jelly," a pungent, stimulating aliment of a very different nature from the "bee-bread" which is stored up for the nourishment of the neuters. After going through its transformation, the grub thus treated comes forth a perfect queen, differing from the "neuter" into which it would otherwise have changed, not only in the development of the generative apparatus, but also in the form of the body, in the proportionate length of the wings, in the shape of the tongue, jaws, and sting; in the absence of the hollow on the thighs, in which pollen is carried, and in the absence of the power of secreting wax.

ployment, and all agencies that direct the energies of the growing frame to its increase and consolidation, and away from the indulgence of the reproductive organs, should be regularly used. I am convinced that much of the incontinence of the present day could be avoided by finding amusement, instruction, and recreation, for the young men of large towns. Every association or institution which encourages young men who desire to live virtuously to consort with one another on the principles of purity and self-denial seems to be worthy of all support and encouragement. Such bodies of young men are of the greatest use even to those who do not belong to them. They insensibly modify the tone of young men's society. They all help to render vice, at least open vice, unfashionable. This I believe has been one of the many good results arising from the praiseworthy efforts which have now for some years been made by the various Young Men's Christian Associations, to raise the tone of thought and feeling among the middle-class youth of England. Most perceptibly beneficial results, too, have been produced by the institution of reading-rooms, instruction classes, gymnasiums and places for healthy recreation, where young men may pass their leisure hours in a cheerful, agreeable way, and be not only to a great extent withdrawn from temptation, but directly brought under those influences which above all others lessen the force of that temptation. Every measure that provides healthy and rational occupation for young people—such, for instance, as the Government classes for improvement in art, and the throwing open the Kensington Museum for evening instruction—is a step in the right direction, and must tend to realize the one great object of improving the morals of the people.

Much has been written during the last few years on the national advantages of the Volunteer movement. Not the least, in my opinion, of these advantages is the direct influence it has had in promoting continence among our young men, not only by the excellent effect which drilling has had on their physique and health, but by the vigorous and interesting occupation it has afforded them for mind and body. It affords a notable instance of the effect which a well-directed movement, judiciously carried out, can have on the rising generation. Much of the dissipation and libertinage of our youth in past years has depended upon their having had literally nothing to do when their day's work was over. A pursuit which draws a man away from low society, and encourages him to spend his leisure in healthy and ennobling recreations among his equals, is most profitable to himself and his country. If the Volunteer movement had done nothing more than this, the parents of England would have had ample cause for supporting it.[1] Seeing as much as I do of the private life of young men in England, I can safely say that a healthier tone has sprung up among them of late, dependent, I believe, in great measure, on the love for athletic sports. In the course of years, I trust, it will be found to have exerted a most beneficial influence on the morals of the country.

I have now, I think, discussed the chief aids to continence. They will, I am firmly convinced, if honestly used, in most cases enable a young man to conquer in the noble endeavor to obtain and keep the mastery over his passions during the most trying period of his life. Nevertheless, I should belie my experience as a medical man if I were to represent this struggle as an easy one. It needs the whole energy of any man to succeed completely. No legitimate inducement, therefore, to the effort should be withheld. The greatest of all such inducements undoubtedly is the prospect of early marriage; and this I would urgently press on the young, that the continent man is generally the energetic man, and that to the energetic man his trial is likely to be but temporary. He may fairly look forward to the time when he may think of marriage as the happy end to very much of the temptation which in early life requires so much anxious watchfulness, and even painful effort to subdue.

Surgical aids.—In the early editions of this book I treated only of the religious, educational, and hygienic plans for enabling a young man to continue or return to a continent mode of life which were most efficacious, leaving the medical treatment to a subsequent part of the book. Now, however, I propose before going further to show what surgical means there are of assisting the youth in his struggles against the temptations of the flesh.

---

[1] The physical advantages of the Volunteer movement have, of course, struck others besides myself. In a leading article in the "Telegraph" for November, 1861, I read the following observations, which are evidently based on sound reason:—"The physical advantages of the rifle-training are also great. A man of loose life or careless habits cannot become a good shot; dissipation over-night does not give either the cool brain or the steady hand absolutely required. In fact, the 'training' and 'keeping in good condition' required for success in our public matches are, though less harsh, as absolutely needful as those required from oarsmen in the Oxford or Cambridge crews. With such a new national game, loved by young Englishmen, we need not despair of keeping up fully to the old mark the physical and moral manliness of our race."

Experience has taught me that the several remedies already considered, however beneficial in the slighter cases and in those instances where the sufferers have strong wills, are by themselves perfectly futile in a large proportion of the cases of young men who have little or no determination and perseverance. It is to this class of young men that the medical practitioner can render most important service, more especially when gymnastic remedies alone have been relied on and failed. The examination of a very large number of youths teaches me that sufferers through continence labor under a peculiar sensibility of the reproductive organs. No one who has not closely investigated this subject can have any idea of the morbid sensibility which we meet with, both externally and internally. If, therefore, we would assist the youth in maintaining continence, we must first of all palliate or remove this nervous hysterical-like sensibility which almost invariably attends such cases.

There are patients who can hardly allow the air to blow upon, or the clothes to touch their sexual organs. Such sensitive persons are afraid of using cold water, they dread the most cursory examination, and declare it would make them faint. The proposal to pass an instrument almost produces a state of catalepsy. In all these cases it is not pain, but the dread of being hurt, apparently, which produces the suffering. Once an examination is submitted to and the confidence of the patient gained, the cure progresses most rapidly. In many instances this morbid irritability is confined to the skin, others only complain when the urethra is touched, or when an instrument passes over some particular portion of the canal, yet a second introduction of the instrument produces no inconvenience. When a surgeon has to treat such abnormally nervous patients as these, he will not be surprised that previous hygienic precautions or the inculcation of moral restraints have not succeeded in preventing emissions. As soon as local remedies have dulled the morbid sensibility of the sexual organs, the greatest advantage is at once derived from the moral and hygienic remedies.

ABNORMAL CONDITION IN YOUTH

SEXUAL INTERCOURSE

The Act of Copulation.—In order to deal intelligently with cases in which sexual congress is not properly performed, it is necessary clearly to understand in what the act of copulation consists. It is thus described by Carpenter:—"When, impelled by sexual excitement, the male seeks intercourse with the female, the erectile tissue of the genital organs becomes turgid with blood, and the surface acquires a much increased sensibility. This is especially acute in the glans penis. By the friction of the glans against the rugous walls of the vagina the excitement is increased, and the impression which is thus produced at last becomes so strong that it calls forth, through the medium of the spinal cord, a reflex contraction of the muscular fibres of the vasa deferentia, and of the muscles which surround the vesiculae seminales and prostate gland. These receptacles discharge their contents into the urethra, from which they are expelled with some degree of force, and with a kind of convulsive action, by its compressor muscles. Now, although the sensations concerned in this act are ordinarily most acutely pleasurable, there appears sufficient evidence that they are by no means essential to its performance, and that the impression which is conveyed to the spinal cord *need not* give rise to a sensation in order to produce the reflex contraction of the ejaculator muscles." ("Principles of Human Physiology," 7th edition, p. 826.) The muscular contractions which produce the emissio seminis are excito-motor in their nature, being independent of the will and not capable of restraint by it when once fully excited, and being (like those of deglutition) excitable in no other way than by a particular local irritation.

As stated in the above paragraph, the sexual act is ordinarily attended with great pleasure. In fact, from the risks which animals will run to enjoy the gratification, and the recklessness with which even the wildest male will approach the tame female when in heat, it would seem that no pleasure is equal to this.[1] There is every reason to be-

---

[1] I am speaking here, it will be observed, of the pleasure experienced by the male. In the females of many animals, and especially of those low down in the scale of existence, we can scarcely believe that any gratification at all attends the act.

In fishes copulation, properly speaking, does not take place. According to Mr. Walsh, a close observer who wrote an account in the "Field" newspaper for March 7th, 1863, the mode of im-

lieve that it is the mere and simple act of emission which gives the pleasurable sensations in animals which (like many birds) have no intromittent organ. This pleasurable sensation, however, is of momentary duration; like a battery, it exhausts itself in a shock. The nervous excitement is very intense while it lasts, and, were it less momentary than it is, more mischief would probably result from repeated acts than ordinarily happens.

Parise has remarked, perhaps with some exaggeration, that "if the pleasurable moments, as well as the torments, which attend love lasted, there would be no human strength capable of supporting them, unless our actual condition were changed."

A kind of natural safeguard is provided against the nervous exhaustion consequent on the excitement of coitus, by the rapid diminution of the sensation during successive acts. Indeed, in persons who repeat coitus frequently during the same night, the pleasurable sensation will diminish so rapidly that the act at last will not be attended with any.

This pleasure, in fact, seems in its own way to be subject to the same laws which apply to our other gratifications. As Carpenter says—"Feelings of pleasure or pain are connected with particular sensations, which cannot (for the most part, at least) be explained upon any other principle than that of the necessary association of those feelings by an original law of our nature with the sensation in question. As a general rule, it may be stated that the *violent* excitement of

---

pregnation is as follows:—"The female fish does not first deposit her spawn, and then leave it to be impregnated by the male; the male cares nothing for the spawn, except to eat it; his desire is for the female, for the possession of whom he will fight as long as he is able. The spawning process is carried on in this manner:—The female works away at the ridd, and after she has made a kind of trough she lies in it quite still; the male—who, during the time she is working, is carrying on a constant war—comes up, enters the trough, and lies side by side with the female; they then fall over on their sides, and with a tremulous motion the spawn and milt are exuded at the same instant. The male then drops astern. After a short time the female again throws herself on her side, and fans up the gravel, advancing the trough a little, and covering up the deposited spawn. The operation is repeated till both fish are exhausted. A great quantity of spawn is of course wasted, being eaten by trout and other fish, which are always waiting about for the purpose. The exhaustion of the males is greater than that of the females; they die in numbers; the females do not die. You may pick up a great many exhausted and dead males, but never a female."

In some animals the act must, we would think, be an unmitigated distress and annoyance to the female. The female frog, for instance, is not only encumbered with an abdomen distended with ova, but is obliged to carry about her husband on her back as long as he may see fit, as he is provided by nature at this period with an enlarged thumb, which enables him to keep his hold, so that the female is unable to shake him off.

any sensation is disagreeable, even when the same sensation in a moderate degree may be a source of extreme pleasure."

By this merciful provision nature herself dictates that excesses must not be committed. The frequent complaint heard from persons who have committed excesses, that they experience no more pleasure in the act, is the best evidence we can have that nature's laws have been infringed.

Duration of the Act.—It is, indeed, a wise provision that in the human being the act should last but a short time—some few minutes.

In animals the greatest differences in this particular take place.

Thus I read in the "Description of the Preparations of the College of Surgeons," that "the coitus in the kangaroo, and probably in other marsupials, is of long duration, and the scrotum during that act disappears, and seems to be partially inverted during the forcible retraction of the testes against the marsupial bones."—No. 2477, *Physiological Catalogue, by Owen.*

The act of copulation, as I can testify, in the moth of the silkworm is very prolonged. The male is the smaller and darker of the two, and as soon as he leaves the grub state he is ready for the act. He then vibrates his wings with a very singular humming noise, and goes round and round the female. The tails are then approximated, copulation takes place, and lasts for days. As soon as the sexes separate, the same process is repeated, and sexual congress again occurs. It would almost appear as if the short life of these insects was passed in copulation. The female moths died first in all the cases I witnessed, but the males, although surviving the females, were dull and could hardly move, being apparently thoroughly exhausted by their reproductive labors.

In the chapter on erection we have noticed the prolonged copulation of the dog. In some other classes of animals it takes place with wonderful celerity. Among deer, for instance, it was at one time stated that coitus had never been observed even by the oldest keepers. Professor Owen mentioned that it may be witnessed in Richmond Park, somewhat in the following way:—The buck will be seen to scrape hollows two or three feet deep in certain portions of the park; to these places he leads the does. One by one, they place themselves in these hollows; the buck drives away all other bucks from the neighborhood, then, with a rush, mounts the doe; in an instant the act is accomplished, and the female retires to be replaced by another. Professor Owen says he cannot explain why these hollows should be made in the ground, as there is nothing in the conformation of the doe to require that she should be placed on a level lower than that which the buck leaps from. However, though the act itself is instantaneous, the premonitory excitement is of long duration. It is possible, therefore, that erection lasts but for an instant, and hence the convenience of this preparation and position.

Mr. Thompson, the late superintendent at the Zoological Gardens, told me that he has seen copulation take place in the stags both in the wild state and in confinement. He thinks that a peculiar place is not *necessary* for the act. He agrees that it is effected in a few moments, and that in the case of the giraffe, also, no peculiar position is necessary.

The Effect of the Act.—The immediate effect of the act on the male deserves some few remarks. Even in the healthiest and strongest person a feeling of fatigue immediately follows.

This nervous orgasm is very powerfully exhibited in some animals. The buck rabbit, for instance, after each sexual act, falls on his side, the whites of his eyes turn up, and his hind legs are spasmodically agitated. The cause of this, and the corresponding phenomena in other animals, is the nervous shock which particularly affects the spinal cord.

The way in which this shock affects a healthy man is, generally, to make him languid and drowsy for a time.

This temporary depression has not escaped the observation of the ancients, who have remarked—

"Læta venire Venus tristis abire solet;"

and again—

"Post coitum omne animal triste, nisi gallus qui cantat."

So serious, indeed, is the paroxysm of the nervous system produced by the sexual spasm, that its immediate effect is not always unattended with danger, and men with weak hearts have died in the act. Every now and then we learn that men are found dead on the night of their wedding, and it is not very uncommon to hear of inquests being held on men discovered in houses of ill-fame, without any marks of ill-usage or poison. The cause has been, doubtless, the sudden nervous shock overpowering a feeble or diseased frame.

However exceptional these cases are, they are warnings, and should serve to show that an act which *may* destroy the weak should not be tampered with even by the strong.

Lallemand well describes the test which every married man should apply in his own case:—"When connection is followed by a joyous feeling, a *bien être général*, as well as fresh vigor; when the head feels lighter, the body more elastic and ready for work; when a greater disposition to exercise or intellectual labor arises, and the genital organs evince an increase of vigor and activity, we may infer that an imperious want has been satisfied within the limits necessary for health. The happy influence which all the organs experience is similar to that which follows the accomplishment of every function necessary to the economy."

How serious—how *vital* an act, so to speak, that of copulation is, appears from the marked changes which accompany its performance in some animals. It is a well-accredited fact that in the rutting season buck venison is strong, lean, and ill-flavored. At this time, we are told, the flesh becomes soft and flabby, the hair looks "unkind;" and in birds, the feathers, after the season of breeding, are in a ruffled state, and droop. The horns of stags fall off, and the blood is occupied in supplying the consequent demand for new osseous matter.

It is before the spawning season has passed that we prefer the herring, and it is only while it is filled with roe that we care to eat the mackerel. A spent salmon is not fit food for man; and, at this period, as all fishermen are aware, the vivid colors of the trout disappear; and the fish retires exhausted and impoverished, until the vital forces are regained.

Repetition of the Act.—Whilst one individual will suffer for days after a single attempt, or even from an involuntary emission, another will not evince the least sign of depression, although the act be repeated several times in succession or on several consecutive nights. Still, as a general rule, the act is and ought to be repeated but rarely. In newly married people, of course, sexual intercourse takes place more frequently, and hence it happens that conception often fails during the first few months of wedlock, depending probably upon the fact that the semen of the male contains but few perfect spermatozoa:

in such cases it is only when the ardor of first love has abated, and the spermatozoa have been allowed the time requisite for their full development, that the female becomes impregnated.

If the married female conceives every second year, we usually notice that during the nine months following conception she experiences no great sexual excitement. The consequence is that sexual desire in the male is somewhat diminished, and the act of coition takes place but rarely. Again, while women are suckling there is usually such a demand made on the vital force by the organs secreting milk that sexual desire is almost annihilated.[1] Now, as experience teaches us that a reciprocity of desire is, to a great extent, necessary to excite the male, we must not be surprised if we learn that excesses in fertile married life are comparatively rare, and that sensual feelings in the man become gradually sobered down.

It is a curious fact that man and a few domesticated animals are alone liable to suffer from the effects of sexual excesses. In a state of nature wild female animals will not allow the approach of the male except when in a state of rut, and this occurs at long intervals and only at certain seasons of the year. The human female probably would not differ much in this respect from the wild animal, had she not been civilized, for as I shall have occasion again and again to remark, she would not for her own gratification allow sexual congress except at certain periods. The courtesan who makes a livelihood by her person may be *toujours pres*, but not so the pregnant wife or nursing mother. Love for her husband and a wish to gratify his passion, and in some women the knowledge that they would be deserted for courtesans if they did not waive their own inclinations may induce the indifferent, the passionless, to admit the embraces of their husbands.

---

[1] We are apt to believe that in the human female it is almost impossible for gestation and lactation to go on simultaneously. In the mare, however, this occurs. In large breeding establishments the mare is usually put to the stallion, and will "show to the horse" nine days after a foal is dropped. The object of this of course is that in eleven months she shall again give birth to another foal. This is the surest way to obtain foals, although the produce of a mare after being a year barren is generally stronger and presumably better than on her becoming with foal while suckling. In fact, if left a twelve month barren, mares, I am informed by competent men, are stinted with great difficulty.

   The late Mr. Blenkiron, a well-known breeder of race-horses at Middle Park, kindly looked over this note, and he told me that, although this happens, mares often require some little management "to show to a horse, although in season," and it is necessary to put the twitch on the nose to distract their attention, otherwise their affection for the foal induces them "not to show to the horse, although in season."

These are truths about which much ignorance and consequently much false reasoning prevails. No portion of my book has more surprised unmarried men than such statements as these. Married men, however, generally confirm my opinion, and not a few have acknowledged that had wives been but judicious and consulted more the feelings of their husbands, the Divorce Court would not have been so often appealed to, nor would women have had cause to complain of there being so many unfaithful husbands.

Besides this kind of natural protection against excesses, arising from the periodical unwillingness of the human female to permit congress, we find that there is not in men, particularly in the intellectual and civilized man, any need for or *natural* impulse towards that excessive periodical indulgence which we notice in the brute creation. The human male is naturally prepared to copulate at all times of the year; he is not, therefore, instinctively required to repeat the act so many times within a short period, as some domesticated animals are, for the purpose of propagating the species. The ram has been supposed to repeat the act from fifty to eighty times[1] in the course of one night. The stallion[2] is, or rather ought to be, always limited to a certain number of mares, but as he takes his mounts during a limited time (two or three months), the act is necessarily repeated very often, and at very short intervals.

Of course, these enormous copulative powers are not only *not*

---

[1] This statement has been doubted. It is founded on the hypothesis, perhaps somewhat loose, that the chest and abdomen of a ram having been covered with "ruddle" over night, and the haunches of fifty ewes found smeared with the same composition in the morning, the animal had to such a numerical extent exercised his generative functions. This may or may not be a *sequitur*; but no manner of doubt exists that the sexual power of the animal is, in fact, as well as proverbially very considerable; but let it be recollected that it is exercised only for a very short time during the twelve months.

[2] The late Mr. Grey, who had the management of a large breeding establishment at Theobalds, told me that the celebrated stallion "Teddington," who was then serving mares at his farm, was limited by his owner to forty-five mares during the season, which lasts from February to July, but as it is desirable that mares should foal early in the year, the repeated acts of connection were included in a comparatively short period. In addition to this, the same mare is repeatedly (about every nine days) put to the horse, to secure impregnation. It appears, nevertheless, that these stallions do not suffer, and Mr. Grey was of opinion that this number, forty-five, is not too much. In reply to my inquiries, he said that nothing but oats and hay are given to these horses; beans are considered to heat them. He seemed not to think that a horse can cover too *much*, but admits that he may too rapidly. He did not allow any horse in his establishment to mount more than twice a day. Two trials are generally advisable, as the first leap is often a failure. Country-travelling stallions are said to have stimulants given them, and to have as many as two hundred mounts in the season.

examples, but positive *contrasts* to what should obtain in the human being. As man has no real rutting season (which in animals appears to be a kind of periodic puberty), there is no occasion, and therefore no provision, for the sudden or excessive employment of his reproductive organs, and consequently any such excesses will be fraught with much danger. The brute, moreover, is deficient in the intellectual qualities of man: propagation of his species appears to be about the most important of the objects of his existence. Man is formed for higher purposes than this. To devote the whole energy of his nature to sensual indulgence is literally to degrade himself to the level of a brute, and to impair or totally destroy those intellectual and moral capacities which distinguish him from the inferior creation.

Marital Duties.—As I have advised continence, absolute and entire, for the young and the unmarried, so not the less urgently would I impress on the married the duty, for their own sakes, of *moderation* in sexual indulgence.

None, perhaps, but medical men can know at all (and they can know but a fraction of) the misery and suffering caused by ill-regulated desires and extravagant indulgences among married people.

Antiquity was sensible of the expediency of regulating to some extent these indulgences. Many ordinances existed among ancient nations for the purpose, of which I will give a few examples.

The following is a freely translated extract from the "Uxor Hebraica" of John Selden, lib. iii, cap. 6 (in his works, ed. 1646, vol. ii, pp. 717–720):

> "They would have the conjugal debt paid regularly by the husband in proportion to the energy unused in his avocation. According to the Misna, a man was allowed one or two weeks' leave of absence on the score of a religious vow of abstinence. Law students were exempt. A weekly debt was forced upon artificers, but a daily one upon vigorous young husbands having no occupation. Donkey-drivers (employed in transport of merchandise, &c.) were liable once a week; camel-drivers (a calling entailing much labor and traveling) once in thirty days; sailors once (at any time) in six months. This is according to the Rabbi Eliezer."

Solon required three payments a month, without reference to the husband's avocations.

Mottray states in his "Travels," vol. i, p. 250, that the Turkish law obliges husbands to cohabit with their wives once a week, and that if they neglect to do so, the wife can lodge a complaint before a magistrate.

My own opinion is that, *taking hard-worked intellectual married men residing in London as the type*, sexual congress had better not take place more frequently than once in seven or ten days; and when my opinion is asked by patients whose natural desires are strong, I advise those wishing to control their passions to indulge in intercourse twice on the same night. I have noticed that in many persons a single intercourse does not effectually empty the vasa deferentia, and that within the next twenty-four hours strong sexual feelings again arise; whereas, if sexual intercourse is repeated on the same night, the patient is able to so restrain his feelings that ten days or a fortnight may elapse without the recurrence of desire.

The reader will remark that I specially desire to confine my remarks to *hard-worked, intellectual married men residing in London*, and every year's experience teaches me that I have done well in thus limiting my remarks to the denizens of large cities. No one, perhaps, more than myself is aware that strong muscular countrymen, who have no occupation or mental drain on their systems, may and do follow out a very different course, without any apparent detriment to the system. On the other hand, I could point to the case of many a married man suffering from derangement of health solely, or at all events mainly, attributable to unsuspected sexual excesses, the best proof of which is that the health becomes restored as soon as the excesses are left off.

No one can deny that an enormous expenditure of semen can take place in men as well as in animals, but I believe medical men themselves have only recently become aware of the amount of ill-health and debility which follows the lavish waste of the seminal fluid in those who, so to speak, cannot afford it. In my own experience I have met with many persons who, as they look back to their past career, regret that ignorance of nature's laws induced them to overstep the bounds of prudence, and now attribute many of their ailments to sexual excesses continued for a long period in ignorance that they were excesses at all.[1]

It should not be forgotten that excess, even among married people, should be guarded against from higher motives than mere prudence. On this view of the subject I will quote from Bishop Jeremy Taylor's "Rule and Exercises of Holy Living;" in the chapter entitled "Rules for Married Persons, or Matrimonial Chastity," he says:

> "In their permissions and license, they must be sure to observe the order of nature and the ends of God. *He is an ill husband that uses his wife as a man treats a harlot*, having no other end but pleasure. Concerning which our best rule is, that although in this, as in eating and drinking, there is an appetite to be satisfied, which cannot be done without pleasing that desire, yet since that desire and satisfaction was intended by nature for other ends, they should never be separated from those ends, but always be joined with all or one of these ends, *with a desire of children, or to avoid fornication, or to lighten and ease the cares and sadnesses of household affairs, or to endear each other*; but never with a purpose, either in act or desire, to separate the sensuality from these ends which hallow it.
>
> "Married persons must keep such modesty and decency of treating each other that they never force themselves into high and violent lusts with arts and misbecoming devices; always remembering that those mixtures are most innocent which are *most simple* and *most natural, most orderly* and *most safe*. It is the duty of matrimonial chastity to be restrained and temperate in the use of their lawful pleasures; concerning which, although no universal rule can antecedently be given to all persons, any more than to all bodies one proportion of meat and drink, yet married persons are to estimate the degree of their license according to the following proportions.—1. That it be moderate, so as to consist with health. 2. That it be so ordered as not to be too expensive of time, that precious opportunity of working out our salvation. 3. That, when duty is demanded, it be always paid (so far as in our powers and elections) according to the foregoing measures. 4. That it be with a temperate affection,

---

[1] See further observations in chapter on Marital Excesses.

without violent transporting desires or too sensual applications. Concerning which a man is to make judgment by proportion to other actions and the severities of his religion, and the sentences of sober and wise persons, always remembering that marriage is a provision for supply of the natural necessities of the body, not for the artificial and procured appetites of the mind. And it is a sad truth that many married persons, thinking that the floodgates of liberty are set wide open, without measures or restraints (so they sail in the channel), have felt the final rewards of intemperance and lust by their unlawful using of lawful permissions. Only let each of them be temperate, and both of them be modest. Socrates was wont to say that those women to whom nature hath not been indulgent in good features and colors should make it up themselves with excellent manners, and those who were beautiful and comely should be careful that so fair a body be not polluted with unhandsome usages. To which Plutarch adds, that a wife, if she be unhandsome, should consider how extremely ugly she should be if she wanted modesty; but if she be handsome, let her think how gracious that beauty would be if she superadds chastity." (P. 70, Bell and Daldy edition, 1857.)

MARITAL EXCESSES

It is a common notion among the public, and even among professional men, that the word *excess* chiefly applies to *illicit* sexual connection. Of course, whether extravagant in degree or not, all such connection is, from one point of view, an *excess*. But any warning against sexual dangers would be very incomplete if it did not extend to the excesses too often committed by married persons in ignorance of their ill-effects. Too frequent emission of the life-giving fluid, and too frequent sexual excitement of the nervous system, are, as we have seen, in themselves most destructive. The result is the same within the marriage bond as without it. The married man who thinks that, because he is a married man, he can commit no excess, however often the act of sexual congress is repeated, will suffer as certainly and as seriously as the unmarried debauchee who acts on the same principle in his indulgences—perhaps more certainly, from his very ignorance, and from his not taking those precautions and following those rules which a career of vice is apt to teach the sensualist. Many a man has, until his marriage, lived a most continent life;—so has his wife. As soon as they are wedded, intercourse is indulged in night after night; neither party having any idea that these repeated sexual acts are excesses, which the system of neither can with impunity bear, and which to the delicate man, at least, is occasionally absolute ruin. The practice is continued till health is impaired, sometimes permanently; and when a patient is at last obliged to seek medical advice, his usual surgeon may have no idea or suspicion of the excess, and treat the symptom without recommending the removal of the cause, namely, the sexual excess; hence it is that the patient experiences no relief for the indigestion, lowness of spirits, or general debility from which he may be suffering. If, however, the patient comes under the care of a medical man in the habit of treating such cases, the invalid is thunderstruck at learning that his sufferings arise from excesses unwittingly committed. Married people often appear to think that connection may be repeated just as regularly and almost as often as their meals. Till they are told of the danger, the idea never enters their heads that they have been guilty of great and almost criminal excess; nor is this to be wondered at, since the possibility of such a cause of disease is seldom hinted at.

Some years ago a young man called on me, complaining that he was unequal to sexual congress, and was suffering from spermatorrhoea, the result, he said, of self-abuse. He was cauterized, and I lost sight of him for some time, and when he returned he came complaining that he was scarcely able to move alone. His mind had become enfeebled, there was great pain in the back, and he wished me to repeat the operation.

On cross-examining the patient, I found that after the previous cauterization he had recovered his powers, and, having subsequently married, had been in the habit of indulging in connection (ever since I had seen him, two years previously) three times a week, without any idea that he was committing an excess, or that his present weakness could depend upon this cause. The above is far from being an isolated instance of men who, having been reduced by former excesses, still imagine themselves equal to any excitement, and when their powers are recruited, to any expenditure of vital force. Some go so far as to believe that indulgence may increase these powers, just as gymnastic exercises augment the force of the muscles. This is a popular error, and requires correction. Such patients should be told that the shock on the system, each time connection is indulged in, is very powerful, and that the expenditure of seminal fluid must be particularly injurious to organs previously debilitated. It is by this and similar excesses that premature old age and debility of the generative organs is brought on.

A few months later I again saw this young man, and all his symptoms had improved under moderated indulgence, care, and tonics.

In 1856, a gentleman, twenty-three years of age, who had been married two years, came to me in great alarm, complaining that he was nervous, and unable to manage his affairs. There was pain in his back, the least exertion caused him to perspire, and he had a most careworn countenance. I may further mention that he had been highly scrofulous as a boy. I learnt that he had married a young wife, and fearing that he might be considered a Joseph, as he had never known woman beforehand (although he acknowledged to having been guilty of evil practices at school), he unconsciously fell into excess, and attempted connection nightly; latterly, erection had been deficient, emission was attended with difficulty, and he felt himself daily less able to discharge what he thought were his family duties. Having read my book, he came to me for relief, and was extremely surprised at finding that I considered he had committed excesses, believing that after marriage frequent intercourse could not be so termed. This history was given with such a *naïf* air, that I was obliged to yield implicit credence to it. I desired him to put a check on his sexual feelings, and as a remedial measure ordered him phosphorus.

In December, 1861, a stout, florid man, about forty-five years of age, was sent to me by a distinguished provincial practitioner, in consequence of his sexual powers failing him, and one of his testes being smaller than the other. On cross-examination I found that he had been married some years, and had a family. Connection had been indulged in very freely, when, about four years ago, a feeling of nervousness insensibly came over him, and about the same time his sexual powers gradually became impaired. The real object, he avowed, which he had in coming to me was to obtain some stimulus to increase his sexual powers, rather than to gain relief for the nervousness and debility under which he was laboring. Indeed, at his own request, the efforts of the country practitioner had been made in the former direction. Instead of giving remedies to excite, I told him that his convalescence must depend upon moderate indulgence, and allowing the system time to rally, and treated him accordingly.

The lengths to which some married people carry excesses is perfectly astonishing. I lately saw a married medical man who told me that for the previous fourteen years, he believed, he had *never* allowed a night to pass without having had connection, and it was only lately, on reading my book, that he had attributed his present ailments to marital excesses. The contrast between such a case as this, where an individual for fourteen years has resisted this drain on the system, and that of a man who is, as many are, prostrated for twenty-four hours by one nocturnal emission, is most striking. All experience, however, shows that, whatever may be the condition of the nervous system, as regards sexual indulgences, excesses will sooner or later tell upon any frame, and can never be indulged in with impunity. I believe general debility and impaired health dependent upon too frequent sexual relations to be much more common than is generally supposed, and that they are hardly yet sufficiently appreciated by the profession as very fruitful causes of ill health.

I will give one more instance. A medical man called on me, saying he found himself suffering from spermatorrhoea. There were general debility, inaptitude to work, and disinclination for sexual intercourse; in fact, he thought he was losing his senses, and the sight of one eye was affected. The only way in which he lost semen was, as he thought, by slight occasional oozing from the penis. I asked him at once if he had ever committed excesses. As a boy, he acknowledged having abused himself, but he married seven years previously to his visit to me, being then a hearty, healthy man, and it was only lately that he had been complaining. In answer to my further inquiry, he stated that since his marriage he had had connection two or three times a week, and often more than once a night. This one fact, I was obliged to tell him, sufficiently accounted for all his troubles. The symptoms he complained of were similar to those we find in boys who abuse themselves. It is true that it may take years to impair the health of some exceptionally strong men, just as it may be a long time before some boys are prejudicially influenced, but the ill effects of excesses are sooner or later sure to follow.

Since my attention has been particularly called to this class of ailments, I feel confident that many of the forms of indigestion, general ill-health, hypochondriasis, &c., so often met with in adults, depend upon sexual excesses. The directors of hydropathic establishments must probably hold some such opinions, or they would not have thought it expedient to separate married patients when they are undergoing the water treatment. That this cause of illness is not more widely acknowledged and acted on, arises from the natural delicacy which medical men must feel in putting such questions to their patients as are necessary to elicit the facts.

No invariable law can be laid down in a case where so much must depend upon temperament, age, climate, and other circumstances, as well as the health and strength of both parties. I maintain that in highly civilized communities the continuance of a high degree of bodily and mental vigor is inconsistent with more than a *very moderate* indulgence in sexual intercourse. The still higher principle also holds good that man was not created only to indulge his sexual appetites, and that he should subordinate them to his other duties.

It is not the body alone which suffers from excesses committed in married life. Experience every day convinces me that much of the languor of mind, confusion of ideas, and inability to control the thoughts of which some married men complain, arises from this cause. These ill effects are noticed not unfrequently in patients who have married late in life, and still more often in persons who have married a second time after having been widowers for some years.

CELIBACY

The term "celibacy" should mean continence enforced on one who is of a fit age to marry. Continence in mere boys and very young men is not what we are now speaking of. After what has preceded I shall take it for granted that every rational person must be an advocate for celibacy, or rather, the strictest continence, in the very young, and ready to admit that with a view to the full development of their being they should not only physically abstain, but so exercise their wills as not to allow their thoughts to dwell on sensual matters.

I believe I have already mentioned the fact that in children, precocious and strong sexual desires are often accompanied by and produce a dull intellect, and in the adult it is similarly found that the inordinate exercise of the sexual organs frequently annihilates the intellectual faculties. It is an undoubted fact that we meet with a large proportion of unmarried men among the intellectual, and some of the ablest works have been written by bachelors. Newton and Pitt were single, Kant disliked women. "They do best," says Bacon, "who, if they cannot but admit love, yet make it keep quarter, and sever it wholly from their serious affairs and actions of life; for if it check once with business, it troubleth men's fortunes and maketh men that they can no ways be true to their own ends."

It was doubtless from such considerations as these that our ancestors ordained that college fellows at the universities should remain single. Similar reasons probably had their influence in inducing the church of Rome to prescribe that their priests should take vows of celibacy.

Whether or not the Roman Catholic priest continues celibate may not much interest the English public;[1] but whether college fellows at the universities should be allowed to marry, has occupied a good deal of attention during the last few years.

As to that chaste form of continence, celibacy, which is practiced by a certain number of both sexes under the dominion of ideas which are of the highest order, it is undisputed that this *voluntary paralysis of the reproductive organs* protects the individual from the greater part of the affections that I have described as mainly occasioned by inordinate and too early exercise of the generative organs.

In former editions of this work I asserted that in the adult the intellectual qualities are usually in an inverse ratio to the sexual appetite.

It has been pointed out to me that there are so many exceptions to this rule, that I have thought it necessary to modify the language in which I have expressed my views. I maintain that debauchery weakens the intellect and debases the mental powers, and I reassert my opinion that if a man observes strict continence in thought as well as deed, and is gifted with ordinary intelligence, he is more likely to distinguish himself in liberal pursuits than one who lives incontinently, whether in the way of fornication or by committing marital excesses. The strictest continence, therefore, in the unmarried, and

[1] Bergeret says, "As physician during many years to religious societies I have never seen serious affections of the organs of generation in these communities."

"Continent celibacy, however, produces on the health other consequences not less severe, particularly in women; here the annihilation of the grand functions of maternity causes its victim to become phthisical."

very moderate sexual indulgence in the married state, best befit any one engaged in serious studies. In making this statement, however, I am bound to admit that in practice we meet with a large number of young men of more than average abilities, but of a delicate constitution, who cannot remain continent without becoming subject to frequent nocturnal emissions. When this is the case, the sufferer may be intellectually in a worse plight than if he were married, and so occasionally indulged in sexual intercourse. In these exceptional instances it is not true that celibacy is the state best adapted to intellectual excellence. Of this I have had satisfactory evidence year by year. Numbers of men studying at the universities come to me complaining that, although living a continent life, they have become so troubled by emissions that they are unable to pursue for any length of time hard or continuous intellectual work; their memories fail them, and their health becomes impaired. Under appropriate treatment the constitution rallies, and the intellectual powers are restored. From these and other cases that come under the care of the medical practitioner, it appears that celibacy in the adult is not unattended with danger to exceptional temperaments. These dangers, however, it should never be forgotten, very seldom attend perfect continence. It will be generally found that they are merely the penalty of past indulgences. Robust, energetic men are seldom troubled in this way —at least without some fault of their own. In all such cases incontinence is not the remedy that should be recommended, but gymnastic exercise, appropriate diet, and such measures as improve the health. It is, as we have seen, the almost universal rule that all men, old and young, who have led a continent life, so long as they continue to give themselves up to study, and take proper exercise, will not be troubled with strong sexual desires. Nevertheless, when any period of temporary idleness suspends the celibate's regular work, the sexual feeling will often reappear with redoubled force, and then real distress and often illness may ensue. Self-control is followed by nocturnal emissions, which may so increase in frequency as seriously to impair the health, while the evil results—due as I maintain to the inordinate loss of the vital fluid, semen—are attributed to previous hard work. The patient is supposed to labor under indigestion, heart disease, or general debility, and is ineffectually treated for them, whereas the medical man, instead of treating symptoms, should at once proceed resolutely to check the emissions—the cause of the ailment.

It has been my duty to investigate the causes of several instances of clerical scandal, and I have reason for believing that the seeds of a vicious life may have been sown in days when a man, prevented from marriage either by lack of means or by holding a celibate fellowship or by any similar cause, and being in a state of idleness with no incentive to exertion, has been led away by his passions to indulge in a course of illicit intercourse, which he might have escaped if, like others, he could have married.[1]

Admitting, then, as I do that celibacy is attended with many drawbacks and temptations, and much sexual and mental suffering, I still consider that it is the necessary condition of the young, while in the adult, although it is in many instances attended with some inconveniences, that these may be obviated, or at all events sensibly relieved, by due medical supervision. Unmarried men who intend to lead a celibate life must not believe that they can do so if they indiscriminately indulge in the pleasures of the table; for them abstemious diet, and regular and almost exhausting exercise under proper medical supervision, are absolutely essential, and so assisted, they may with impunity to themselves, and with advantage to society, continue to lead a celibate life.

EARLY BETROTHALS—LONG ENGAGEMENTS

In a work entitled "A Fraternal Address to Young Men," issued by the Young Men's Christian Association, early engagement is recommended. The author says, p. 52:—"Let the affections be engaged, and the prospect of marriage occupy the mind. If such betrothal be truthful and preserved in fidelity many advantages beyond those already hinted at would be enjoyed."

This opinion has been entertained by many excellent men; but if we examine it from a medical point of view, it is very doubtful, to say no more, whether it is desirable for any youth, who has his way to make in the world, to attach himself to a girl early in life, however purely and faithfully. If an adult is in a position to marry, by all means let him do so. If his sexual desires are strong, the power of the will

---

[1] Bergeret thus speaks of celibacy:—"Is celibacy a sure refuge from all chances of disease? No! Celibacy leading to illegitimate unions, to debauchery, and the libertinage of bachelors, presents more inconveniences than that which exists among married people." (See "Annales d'Hygiène," tom. xx, iv, p. 34.)

deficient, and his intellectual faculties not great, early marriage will keep him out of much mischief and temptation. All medical experience, however, proves that for any one, especially a young and susceptible man, to enter into a long engagement without any immediate hope of fulfilling it, is physically an almost unmitigated evil. It is bad for any one to be tormented with sexual ideas and ungratified desires year after year. The frequent correspondence and interviews cause a morbid dwelling upon thoughts which it would be well to banish altogether from the mind; and I have reason to know that this condition of almost constant excitement has often caused not only dangerously frequent and long-continued nocturnal emissions, but most painful affections of the testes. These results sometimes follow the progress of ordinary courtships to an alarming extent. The danger and distress may be much more serious when the marriage is postponed for years.

I am aware that to the more romantic of my readers these warnings may be very distasteful. Their idea of love is that it is a feeling too pure and spiritual to be defiled with any earthly alloy. I confess that I doubt whether any but the inexperienced really entertain this notion. During the first passionate delight of an attachment, no doubt, the lower and more mundane feelings are ignored. But they are present, nevertheless; and according to my professional experience, are tolerably certain to be aroused in every case, sooner or later. Of course, where the affection felt is true and loyal, they may be corrected and kept within the strictest bounds of the most respectful tenderness; to do this, however, in the case of a protracted engagement is a far harder task than the ardent and poetical lover allows himself at first to think.

The suffering caused by the repression of continually excited feelings that cannot be gratified, is often very great.

I am very far from wishing to degrade love to the level of mere animal passion; on the contrary, it should be a true and deep union of the whole nature, every part taking in this, as in all other matters, its own place. To ignore the bodily and secular aspect of it, however, would be as false and unwise, though not so degrading, as to forget the mental and spiritual.

It is, indeed, more than false and unwise, it is dangerous. Experience too often proves that what has commenced as a pure and most refined attachment may end very differently, if not most carefully guided. And this guidance, as I have said, may involve much troublesome and almost dangerous distress.

Continence from *all* sexual excitement in thought and deed is my advice to *all* young men; and even the adult, who is not in a position to marry, had better divert his thoughts from sexual matters as much as possible. It is wiser for him to devote himself altogether to his profession, instead of having to divide his attentions between a *fiancée* and his success in life. When the latter is attained, it will be time to think of the former. He will then be in a better position to select his partner for life.

Socially speaking, too, these long or early engagements often turn out badly. Hope deferred not only makes the heart sick, but the temper sour. Differences that the closer bond of marriage would have healed at once, or never allowed to arise, become permanent sources of disagreement, and very often the parties have to regret a youth that has been rendered less useful and less happy by an engagement which has at last to be broken off, after much suffering, to the mutual relief of both.

PATRICK GEDDES AND
J. ARTHUR THOMSON

FROM

THE EVOLUTION OF SEX

Patrick Geddes (1854–1932): Patrick Geddes, who once wrote "The child is not only the father to the man, the child is the man," described his own childhood in Scotland as practically ideal despite the austerity of his religious parents. He developed an early interest in nature, biology, and civic affairs. Geddes studied under Thomas Huxley at the Royal School of Mines in London and was soon established as a successful biologist in London and Paris. He traveled everywhere, from Mexico to Naples to India. Despite ill health and near blindness, Geddes taught at Edinburgh University, where one of his students was J. Arthur Thomson, with whom he would later collaborate on The Evolution of Sex. *Geddes's interests were varied—botany, zoology, economics, civic planning—and he was active in all these areas. Yet in science he never lived up to his early promise of becoming the "Scottish Darwin." Nevertheless, Geddes did leave an important legacy: in his concept of the organic community and in his* Evolution of Sex, *which is said to have influenced the cabinet minister of South Australia to introduce an equal rights act in the 1890s, giving suffrage to women and setting a precedent that England and the United States would follow. Geddes married twice and raised three children with his first wife, Anna Morton, a musician who died in India after thirty-one years of marriage.*

J. Arthur Thomson (1860–1931): J. Arthur Thomson was the son of a Scottish clergyman. Studying to follow in his father's footsteps, he found himself in one of Patrick Geddes's zoology classes at Edinburgh University. This experience led to a difficult struggle over whether to continue his work in theology or follow his new interest, science. He began collaborating with Geddes during his student years as a translator and eventually made the decision to abandon his dream of the ministry in favor of a scientific career. He wrote to Patrick Geddes in 1886 that upon discovering science, "I was born again in hope. . . . all things became a second time new in the light of scientific analysis." Thomson went on to have a successful career in zoology and biology.

CHAPTER I

THE SEXES AND SEXUAL SELECTION

That all higher animals are represented by distinct male and female forms is one of the most patent facts of observation, striking enough in many a beast and bird to catch any eye, and familiarly expressed in not a few popular names which contrast the two sexes. In lower animals, the contrast, and indeed the separateness, of the sexes often disappears; yet even naturalists have sometimes mistaken for different species what were afterwards recognized to be but the male and female of a single form.

§ 1. *Primary and Secondary Characters.*—When we pass from this commonplace of observation and experience to inquire more precisely into the differences between the sexes, we speedily recognize that these are of very different degrees. In some cases no marked differences whatever are recognizable; thus a male star-fish or sea-urchin looks exactly like the female, and a careful examination of the essential reproductive organs is requisite to determine whether these respectively produce male elements or eggs. In other cases, for instance in most reptiles, no external differences are at all striking, but the aspect of the internal organs, both essential and auxiliary to reproduction, at once settles the question. In a great number of cases, again, the sexes resemble one another closely, but each has certain minor structural features at once decisive as to its respective maleness or femaleness. Thus in the males there are frequently prominent organs used in sexual union, while the peculiar functions of the females are indicated in the special egg-laying or young-feeding organs. All such characters, directly associated with the essential functions of the sexes, are included under the title of *primary* sexual characters.

Of less real importance, though often much more striking, are the numerous distinctions in size, color, skin, skeleton, and the like, which often signalize either sex. These are termed *secondary* sexual characters; for though they will be shown in some cases at least to be truly part and parcel with the male or female constitution, they are only of secondary importance in the reproductive process. The beard of man and the mane of the lion, the antlers of stags and the tusks of elephants, the gorgeous plumage of the peacock or of the bird of paradise, are familiar examples of secondary sexual characters in males. Nor are females lacking in special characteristics, which serve as indices of their true nature. Large size is one of the commonest of these; while in some few cases the excellencies of color, and other adornments, are possessed by the females rather than by their mates.

The whole subject of secondary sexual characters has found its most extensive treatment in Darwin's "Descent of Man," and to that work, therefore, the more so as its limits exceed those of the present volume, the reader must be assumed to make reference. All that can be here attempted is an illustration, by representative cases, of the main differences between the sexes; from which we shall pass to Darwin's interpretation, and, after a fresh survey, to a re-statement from another point of view.

§ 2. *Illustrations from Darwin.*—Among invertebrates, prominent secondary sexual characters are rarely exhibited outside the great division of jointed-footed animals or arthropods. There, however, among crustaceans and spiders, but especially among insects, beautiful illustrations abound. Thus the great claws of crabs are frequently much larger in the males; and male spiders often differ from their fiercely coy mates, in smaller size, brighter colors, and sometimes in the power of producing rasping sounds. Among insects, the males are frequently distinguished by brighter colors attractively displayed, by weapons utilized in disposing of their rivals, and by the exclusive possession of the power of noisy love-calling. Thus, as the Greek observed, the cicadas "live happy, having voiceless wives." Not a few male butterflies are preeminently more brilliant than the females; and many male beetles fight savagely for the possession of their mates.

Passing to backboned animals, we find that among fishes the males are frequently distinguished by bright colors and ornamental appendages, as well as by structural adaptations for combat. Thus the "gemmeous dragonet" (*Callionymus lyra*) is flushed with gorgeous color, in great contrast to the "sordid" female, and is further adorned by a graceful elongation of the dorsal fin. In many cases, as in the sea-scorpion (*Cottus scorpius*), or in the stickleback (*Gasterosteus*), it is only at the reproductive period that the males are thus transformed, literally putting on a wedding-garment. Every one knows, on the other hand, the hooked lower jaw of the male salmon, which comes to be of use in the furious charges between rivals; and this is but one illustration of many structures utilized in the battle for mates. In regard to amphibians, it is enough to recall the notched crests and lurid coloring of our male newts, and the indefatigable serenading powers of male frogs and toads, to which the females are but weakly responsive. Among reptiles, differences of this sort are comparatively rare, but male snakes have often more strongly-pronounced tints, and the scent-glands become more active during the breeding season. In this, as in many other cases, love has its noisy prayer replaced by the silent appeal of fragrant incense. Among lizards, the males are often more brightly decorated, the splendor of their colors being frequently exaggerated at pairing time. They may be further distinguished by crests and wattle-like pouches; while horns, probably used in fighting, are borne by some male chameleons.

It is among birds, however, that the organic apparatus of courtship is most elaborate. The males very generally excel in brighter colors and ornaments. Beautiful plumes, elongated feathery tresses, brightly-colored combs and wattles, top-knots and curious markings, occur with marvelous richness of variety. These are frequently displayed by their possessors before the eyes of their desired mates, with what seem to us like emotions of love and vanity. Or it may be to the subtler charms of music that the wooers mainly trust. During the breeding season, the males are jealously excited and pugnacious, while some have special weapons for dealing directly with their rivals. The differences between the magnificent male birds of paradise and their soberly colored mates, between the peacock with his hundred eyes and the plain peahen, between the musical powers of the male and female songsters, are very familiar facts. Or again, the combs and "gills" of cocks, the "wattles" of turkey-cocks, the immense top-knot of the male umbrella-bird (*Cephalopterus itus*), the throat-pouch of the bustard—illustrate another series of secondary sexual characters. The spurs of cocks and allied birds are the most familiar illustrations of weapons used by the males in fighting with rivals. As in other animals, it is important to notice that male birds often acquire their special secondary characters, such as color, markings, and special forms of feathers, only as they approach sexual maturity, and sometimes retain them in all their glory only during the breeding season.

Among mammals, which stand in so many ways in marked contrast to birds, the law of battle much more than the power of charming decides the problem of courtship. Thus most of the striking secondary characters of male mammals are weapons. Yet there are crests and tufts of hair, and other acknowledgments of the beauty test, while the incense of odoriferous glands is a very frequent means of sexual attraction. The colors too of the males are often more sharply contrasted, and there are minor differences, in voice and the like, which cannot be ignored. Of weapons, the larger canine teeth of many male animals, such as boars; the special tusks of, for instance, the elephant and narwhal; the antlers of stags, all but exclusively restricted to the combative sex; the horns of antelopes, goats, etc.—which are usually much stronger in the males—are well-known illustrations. The manes of male lions, bisons, and baboons; the beards of certain goats; the crests along the backs of some antelopes; the dewlaps of bulls—illustrate another set of secondary characters. The odoriferous glands of many mammals are more developed in the males, and become specially functional during the breeding season. This is well illustrated in the case of goats, deer, shrew-mice, elephants. The differences in color are slight compared with those seen between the sexes in birds, but in not a few orders the distinction is marked enough, males being, in the great majority of cases, the more strongly and brilliantly colored. Among monkeys the difference in color in the bare regions, and the subtler decorations in the arrangement of the hair on the face, are often very conspicuous.

§ 3. *Darwin's Explanation—Sexual Selection.*—Darwin started from the occurrence of such variations, in structure and habit, as might be useful either for attraction between the sexes or in the di-

rect contests of rival males. The possessors of these variations succeeded better than their neighbors in the art of courtship; the factors
which constituted success were transmitted to the offspring; and,
gradually, the variations were established and enhanced as secondary sexual characters of the species. The process by which the possessors of the fortunate excellencies of beauty and strength outbid or
overcome their less endowed competitors, he termed "sexual selection." It is only fair, however, to state Mr. Darwin's case by direct
quotation.

Sexual selection "depends on the advantage which certain individuals have over others of the same sex and species solely in respect
of reproduction." . . . In cases where "the males have acquired their
present structure, not from being better fitted to survive in the struggle for existence, but from having gained an advantage over other
males, and from having transmitted this advantage to their male offspring alone, sexual selection must have come into action." . . . "A
slight degree of variability, leading to some advantage, however slight,
in reiterated deadly contests, would suffice for the work of sexual
selection." . . . So too, on the other hand, the females "have, by a
long selection of the more attractive males, added to their beauty or
other attractive qualities." . . . "If any man can in a short time give
elegant carriage and beauty to his bantams, according to his standard
of beauty, I can see no reason to doubt that female birds, by selecting
during thousands of generations the most melodious or beautiful
males, according to their standard of beauty, might produce a marked
effect." . . . "To sum up on the means through which, as far as we
can judge, sexual selection has led to the development of secondary
sexual characters. It has been shown that the largest number of vigorous offspring will be reared from the pairing of the strongest and
best-armed males, victorious in contests over other males, with the
most vigorous and best-nourished females, which are the first to
breed in the spring. If such females select the more attractive, and at
the same time vigorous males, they will rear a larger number of offspring than the retarded females, which must pair with the less vigorous and less attractive males. So it will be if the more vigorous
males select the more attractive, and at the same time healthy and
vigorous females; and this will especially hold good if the male defends the female, and aids in providing food for the young. The ad-

vantage thus gained by the more vigorous pairs in rearing a larger number of offspring, has apparently sufficed to render sexual selection efficient." Another sentence from Darwin's first statement of his position must, however, be added. "I would not wish," he says in the "Origin of Species," "to attribute all such sexual differences to this agency; for we see peculiarities arising and becoming attached to the male sex in our domestic animals, which we cannot believe to be either useful to the males in battle or attractive to the females."

§ 4. *Criticisms of Darwin's Explanation.*—The above explanation may be summed up in a single sentence—a congenital variation, advantageous to its possessor (usually a male) in courtship and reproduction, becomes established and perfected by the success it entails. Sexual selection is thus only a special case of the more general process of natural selection, with this difference, that the female for the most part takes the place of the general environment in the picking and choosing which is believed to work out the perfection of the species.

The more serious objections which have been hitherto urged against this hypothesis, apart altogether from criticism of special cases, are the following:—(*a*) Alfred Russel Wallace and others would explain the facts on the more general theory of natural selection, allowing comparatively little import to the alleged sexual selection exercised by the female. (*b*) Some, who allow great importance to both natural and sexual selection, are not satisfied with leaving variation a mere postulate. The position occupied by Brooks will be sketched below. (*c*) Different from either of the above is the position occupied by St. George Mivart and others, who attach comparatively little importance to either natural or sexual selection, but seek in terms of definite variation, constitutional tendencies, laws of growth —for the idea is very variously expressed—to find the primary and fundamental interpretation of sexual dimorphism.

(*a*) *Wallace's Objection.*—It is convenient to begin with Wallace's early criticism, which precedes that of Brooks in chronological order. This is the more helpful in clearing the ground, since the two theories of Wallace and Darwin are strikingly and, at first sight, irreconcilably opposed. According to Darwin, the gayness of male birds is due to selection on the part of the females; according to Wallace, the plainness of female birds is due to natural selection, which has eliminated those which persisted to the death in being gay. He points out that conspicuousness during incubation would be dangerous and fatal; the more conspicuous have, he thinks, been picked off their nests by hawks, foxes, and the like, and hence only the sober-colored females now remain. Darwin starts from inconspicuous forms, and derives gorgeous males by sexual selection; Wallace starts from conspicuous forms, and derives the sober females by natural selection; the former trusts to the preservation of beauty, the latter to its extinction. In 1773, the Hon. Daines Barrington, a naturalist still remembered as the correspondent of Gilbert White, suggested that singing-birds were small, and hen-birds mute for safety's sake. This suggestion Wallace has repeated and elaborated in reference especially to birds and insects. The female butterfly, exposed to danger during egg-laying, is frequently dull and inconspicuous compared with her mate. The original brightness has been forfeited by the sex as a ransom for life. Female birds in open nests are similarly, in many cases, colored like their surroundings; while in those birds where the nests are domed or covered, the plumage is gay in both sexes.

But in his book on "Darwinism" Wallace goes much further in his destructive criticism of Darwin's sexual selection. The phenomena of male ornament are discussed, and summed up as being "due to the general laws of growth and development," and such that it is "unnecessary to call to our aid so hypothetical a cause as the cumulative action of female preference." Or again, "if ornament is the natural product and direct outcome of superabundant health and vigor, then no other mode of selection is needed to account for the presence of such ornament." This mode of criticism, however, belongs to our third category.

(b) Brooks has called attention to the sexual differences in lizards, where the females do not incubate; or in fishes, where the females are even less exposed to danger than the males; or in domesticated birds, where, though all danger is removed, the males are still the more conspicuous and diversified sex. "The fact too that many structures, which are not at all conspicuous, are confined, like gay plumage, to male birds, also indicates the existence of an explanation more fundamental than the one proposed by Wallace, and the latter explanation gives no reason why the females of allied species should often be exactly alike when the males are very different." To the explanation which Brooks proposes we must therefore pass.

According to Darwin, Brooks says, the greater modification of the males is due to their struggling with rivals, and to their selection by the females, but "I do not believe that this goes to the root of the matter." The study of domesticated pigeons, for instance, shows that "something within the animal determines that the male should lead and the female follow in the evolution of new breeds." The same is true in other domesticated animals, where, from the nature of the circumstances, it is inadmissible to explain this with Darwin, by supposing that the male is more exposed than the female to the action of selection, whether natural or sexual. Darwin concludes, indeed, that the male is more variable than the female, but he gives no satisfactory reason why female variations should be less apt than male variations to become hereditary, or, in other words, why the right of entail is so much restricted to the male sex. Darwin merely attributes this to the greater eagerness of the males, which "in almost all animals have stronger passions than the females." The theory which Brooks maintains, is bound up with an hypothesis of heredity differing considerably from that held by Darwin. He supposes that the cells of the body give off gemmules, chiefly during change of function or of environment, and that "the male reproductive cell has gradually acquired, as its especial and distinctive function, a peculiar power to gather and store up these gemmules." The female reproductive cells keep up the general constancy of the species, the male cells transmit variations. "A division of physiological labor has arisen during the evolution of life, and the functions of the reproductive elements have become specialized in different directions." "The male cell became adapted for storing up gemmules" (the results of variations in the body), "and at the same time gradually lost its unnecessary and useless power to transmit hereditary characteristics." "We thus look to the cells of the male body for the origin of most of the variations through which the species has attained to its present organization." The males are the more variable, but more than that, their variations are much more likely to be transmitted. "We are thus able to understand the great difference in the males of allied species, the difference between the adult male and the female or young, and the great diversity and variability of secondary male characters; and we should expect to find, what actually is the case, that among the higher animals, when the sexes have long been separated, the males are more variable than the females." The contrast between Darwin and Brooks may now be summed up again in a sentence. Darwin says, the males are more diversified and richer in secondary sexual characters, chiefly because of the sexual selection exercised alike in courtship and in battle. Brooks admits sexual selection, but believes that the males are naturally or constitutionally more variable than the females, and that it is the peculiar function of the male elements to transmit variations, as opposed to the constant tradition of structure kept up by the egg-cells or ova. In other words, the females may choose, yet the males lead; nay more, they must lead, for male variations have by hypothesis most likelihood of being transmitted.

Full consideration of this hypothesis would involve much discussion of the problems of inheritance, but the general conclusion of the naturally greater variability of the males, will be stated in a different light towards the close of the following chapter. It will there be shown that the "something within the animal," which determines the preponderance of male variability, may be stated in simpler terms than are involved in Brooks's theory. Moreover, the greater variability of the males, which seems quite plain when we contrast, for instance, ruffs and reeves, requires to be proved for each case. Karl Pearson has disproved it for man.

Somewhat similar to Wallace's *later* position is that (c) occupied by St. George Mivart, who also looks for some deep constitutional reason for sexual dimorphism. The entire theory of sexual selection appears to him an unverified hypothesis, only acquiring plausibility when supported by numerous subsidiary suppositions. He submits a number of detailed criticisms; but his chief contention is, that the beauty of males, and other secondary sexual characters, are not the indirect results of a long process of external selection, but the direct expressions of the internal differences of a progressively varying internal constitution, *i.e.*, of tendencies inherent in the individual.

Mivart's position and the vague suggestions of Mantegazza and others are of importance as indication of progress towards a fundamental re-statement. As we have seen, an obvious objection to the theory of sexual selection is that, while it may in part account for the persistence and progress of secondary characters after they attained a certain degree of development, it does not account for their preservation when weak or inconspicuous. In short, the theory may account for the perfecting, but not for the origin of the characters. It may be enough to account for the length and the trimmings of the living garment, but what we wish to know is the secret of the loom. Darwin's account of the evolution of the eyes on the feathers of the Argus pheasant is indeed ingenious and interesting; but, whatever its probability, it is more important to ask what the predominant brightness of males means as a general fact in physiology. It is of interest, then, to notice the hints thrown out by Mantegazza, Wallace, and others, directly associating decorativeness with superfluous reproductive material, and the putting on of wedding-robes with the general excitement of the sexually mature organism. From this record of the discussion, it is time however to turn to a more constructive mode of treatment.

In passing, however, it should be noted that the fact of preferential or selective mating can be proved not only by observation, as the Peckhams have done in the case of spiders, but more conclusively by statistical enquiry, by investigating "whether the type and variability of the mated and unmated members of one or other sex are the same." Apart from the particular problem of secondary sexual characters, it is of the utmost importance whether the mating is selective or indiscriminate. For if natural selection is at work its effect will be checked by indiscriminate mating, and aided by preferential or, to use the wider term, selective mating.

CHAPTER II.

THE SEXES, AND CRITICISM OF SEXUAL SELECTION.

§ 1. *Sex-Differences.*—To gain a firmer and broader foundation on which to base a theory of the differences between the sexes, it is necessary to take another review of the facts of the case. Instead of considering the differences as they are expressed in the successive classes of animals, it will be more convenient to arrange them for themselves, according as they affect habit, size, length of life, and the like. The review must again be merely representative, without any attempt at completeness.

§ 2. *General Habit.*—Let us begin with an extreme yet well-known case. The female cochineal insect, laden with carmine, which some have interpreted as a reserve-product, spends much of its life like a mere quiescent gall on the cactus plant. The male, on the other hand, in his adult state is agile, restless, and short-lived. Now this is no mere curiosity of the entomologist, but in reality a vivid emblem of what is an average truth throughout the world of animals—the preponderating sensitivity of the females, the predominant activity of the males. These coccus insects are the martyrs of their respective sexes. Take another illustration, again somewhat extreme. There is a troublesome threadworm (*Heterodera schachtii*) infesting the turnip plant, which parallels in more ways than one the contrast of the coccus insects. The adult male is agile, and like many another threadworm; the adult female, however, is quiescent, and bloated like a drawn-out lemon. It may be asked, however, is not this merely the natural nemesis of parasitism? The life-history answers this objection. The two sexes are at first alike—agile, and resembling most threadworms; they become parasitic, and lose both activity and nematode form; but the interesting fact is further, that the male recovers himself, while the female remains a victim. In other insect and worm types the same story, in less accented characters, may be distinctly read. In many crustaceans, again, the females only are parasitic; and while this is in part explained by their habit of seeking shelter for egg-laying purposes, it also expresses the constitutional bias of the sex. The insect order of bee parasites (Strepsiptera) is remarkable for the completely passive and even larval character of the blind parasitic females, while the adult males are free, winged, and short-lived. Throughout the class of insects there are numerous illustrations of the excellence of the males over the females, alike in muscular power and sensory acuteness. The diverse series of efforts by which the males of so many different animals, from cicadas to birds, sustain the love-chorus, affords another set of illustrations of preeminent masculine activity.

Without multiplying instances, a review of the animal kingdom, or a perusal of Darwin's pages, will amply confirm the conclusion that on an average the females incline to passivity, the males to activity. In higher animals, it is true that the contrast shows rather in many little ways than in any one striking difference of habit, but even in the human species the contrast is recognized. Every one will admit that strenuous spasmodic bursts of activity characterize men, especially in youth, and among the less civilized races; while patient continuance, with less violent expenditure of energy, is as generally associated with the work of women.

For completeness of argument, two other facts, which will afterwards claim full discussion, may here be simply mentioned. (*a*) At the very threshold of sex-difference, we find that a little active cell or spore, unable to develop of itself, unites in fatigue with a larger more quiescent individual. Here, at the very first, is the contrast between male and female. (*b*) The same antithesis is seen, when we contrast, as we shall afterwards do in detail, the actively motile, minute, male element of most animals and many plants, with the larger passively quiescent female-cell or ovum.

It is possible that the reader may urge as a difficulty against the above contrast the exceedingly familiar case of the male bees or "drones." It must be frankly allowed that exceptions do indeed occur, though usually in conditions which afford a key to the abnormality. Thus it will be allowed that the "drones" are in a peculiar position as male members of a very complex society, in which what is practically a third sex is represented by the great body of "workers." They are no more fair examples of the natural average of males, than the hard-driven wives of the lazy Kaffir are of the normal functions of women. Nor is the exception even here a real one, for the drone, although passive as compared with the unsexed workers, is active when compared with the extraordinarily passive queen.

To the above contrast of general habit, two other items may be added, on which accurate observation is still unfortunately very restricted. In some cases the body temperature, which is an index to the pitch of the life, is distinctly lower in the females, as has been noted in cases so widely separate as the human species, insects, and plants. In many cases, furthermore, the longevity of the females is much greater. Such a fact as that women pay lower insurance premiums than do men, is often popularly accounted for by their greater immunity from accident; but the greater normal longevity on which the actuary calculates, has, as we begin to see, a far deeper and constitutional explanation.

§ 3. *Size.*—Among the higher animals, there are curious alternations in the preponderance of one sex over another in size. Thus among mammals and birds the males are in most cases the larger; the same is true of lizards; but in snakes the females preponderate. In fishes, the males are on an average smaller, sometimes very markedly so, even to the extent of not being half as large as their mates. Below the line, among backboneless animals, there is much greater constancy of predominance in favor of the females. Thus among insects, the more active males are generally smaller, and often very markedly; of spiders the same is true, and the males being often very diminutive are forced to task their agility to the utmost in making advances to their unamiable mates. So again, crustacean males are often smaller than the females; and in many parasitic species, what have been well called "pigmy" males illustrate the contrast in an almost ludicrous degree.

Two cases from aberrant worm types exhibit very vividly this same antithesis of size. Among the common rotifers, the males are almost always very different from the females, and much smaller. Sometimes they seem to have dwindled out of existence altogether, for only the females are known (*Philodina, Rotifer, Callidina, Adineta*). In *Polyarthra platyptera* the male is "hardly to be distinguished from a *Vorticella* which has become detached from its stalk." In *Hydatina senta* the male is about a third the size of the female, has no alimentary canal, and has only two or three days of adult life. In the great majority the males are "little more than perambulating bags of spermatozoa," though in a few cases, like *Rhinops vitrea*, degeneration seems hardly to have begun (Rousselet, 1897). Even when present, they are not indispensable, for parthenogenesis is very general.

In a remarkable marine worm, *Bonellia*, the male remains like a remote ancestor of the female. It lives parasitically on or within the latter, and is microscopic in size, measuring in fact only about one hundredth part of the length of its host and mate. Somewhat similar to the case of *Bonellia* is that of a viviparous coccus insect (*Lecanium hesperidum*), where the males are very degenerate, small, blind, and wingless. In spite of this condition, perhaps indeed because of it, they are very male, for even the larvae, while still within the mother, have been shown to contain fully-developed spermatozoa. In a little "bear animalcule" or Tardigrade, *Macrobiotus macronyx*, the males are about half the size of the females and decidedly more active. A particularly interesting case of sexual dimorphism in molluscs has been described by Professor E. G. Conklin. In *Crepidula plana*, which occurs in shells tenanted by hermit-crabs (*Eupagurus bernhardus*), the female is about fifteen times larger than the male, and the latter retains throughout life the power of locomotion possessed by the females in their young stages only. The females occurring along with the little hermit-crab, *Eupagurus longicarpus*, are always dwarfed, having a body volume only one-thirteenth of the more typical form. The cells of the dwarfs are of the normal size, but there are fewer of them, and the eggs are also much less numerous. But this dwarfing is a mere "modification," and not inherited; it probably depends upon pressure or upon differences of nutrition and oxygenation. That is to say, the dwarfs are not a race, but are continually recruited from the young of the giants. It is interesting, therefore, to note that environmental influences may modify the female till in size it resembles the normally dwarfish male; and that the small size of the male implies, as in the case of the dwarfs, not smaller cells, but a smaller number of cells. In both dwarfs and males, the process of cell-division has been inhibited.

Dr. T. W. Fulton, Naturalist to the Scottish Fishery Board, has made valuable statistical observations on the size and numerical proportions of male and female fishes. (1) The females are usually considerably more numerous than the males, and never less numerous except in the angler and the catfish. The proportion of females to males among flat-fishes ranges from about 1:1 in the flounder, to about 12:1 in the long rough dab. Among "round" fishes the same proportion varies from about 3:2 in the cod, to 9:2 in the common gurnard. (2) The female is longer and larger among all the flat-fishes, sometimes by as much as 30 per cent. In cod, haddock, angler, and catfish, the males are larger, while in the whiting the females are slightly larger, and in the common gurnard decidedly so.

One must not indeed base an argument on extreme cases, but there is no doubt that up to the level of amphibians at least the females are generally the larger.

Apparent exceptions occur, it is true, among the higher animals. In birds and mammals the males are usually rather larger than the females. This difference consists especially in larger bones and muscles. The apparent exception is in part the natural result of the increased stress of external activities which are thrown upon the shoulders of the males when their mates are incapacitated by incubation or pregnancy. Furthermore, we must recognize the strengthening influence of the combats between males, and the effect produced on the accumulative constitution of the females by the increased maternal sacrifice characteristic of the highest animals.

§ 4. *Other Characters.*—While it is easy to point to the general physiological import of large size and the reverse, physiology is not yet far enough advanced to afford firm foothold in dealing with the details of secondary sexual characters. It is only possible to point out the path which will eventually lead us to their complete rationale. The point of view is simple enough. The agility of males is not merely an adaptation to enable that sex to exercise its functions with relation to the other, but is a natural characteristic of the constitutional activity of maleness; and the small size of many male fishes is not an advantage at all, but simply again the result of the contrast between the more vegetative growth of the female and the costly activity of the male. So, brilliancy of color, exuberance of hair and feathers, activity of scent-glands, and even the development of weapons, cannot be satisfactorily explained by sexual selection alone, for this is merely a secondary factor. In origin and continued development they are outcrops of a male as opposed to a female constitution. To sum up the position in a paradox, all secondary sexual characters are at bottom primary, and are expressions of the same general habit of body (or to use the medical term, *diathesis*), as that which results in the production of male elements in the one case, or female elements in the other. This theory of the origin and primary meaning of those variations which culminate in marked sexual dimorphism is obviously similar to that adopted by Wallace in his book on "Darwinism."

Three well-known facts must be recalled to the reader's mind at this point; and firstly, that in a great number of cases the secondary sexual characters make their appearance step by step with sexual maturity itself. When the animal—be it a bird or insect—becomes emphatically masculine, then it is that these minor outcrops are exhibited. Thus the male bird of paradise, eventually so resplendent, is usually in its youth comparatively dull and female-like in its coloring and plumage. Very often, too, whether in the wedding-robe of male fishes or in the scent-glands of mammals, the character rises and wanes in the same rhythm as that of the reproductive periods. It is impossible not to regard at least many of the secondary sexual characters as part and parcel of the sexual diathesis—as expressions for the most part of exuberant maleness.

Secondly, when the reproductive organs are removed by castration, the secondary sexual characters are often much modified. Thus, as Darwin notes, stags never renew their antlers after castration, though normally, of course, they renew them each breeding season. The reindeer, where the horns occur on the females as well, is an interesting exception to the rule, for after castration the male still renews the growth. This however merely indicates that the originally sexual characters have become organized into the general life of the body. In sheep, antelopes, oxen, &c., castration modifies or reduces the horns; and the same is true of odoriferous glands. The parasitic crustacean *Sacculina* has been shown by Delage to effect a partial castration of the crabs to which it fixes itself, and the same has been observed by Giard in other cases. In two such cases an approximation to the female form of appendage has been observed. Rörig (1899) has shown that a diseased state of the ovaries in deer is correlated with a development of antlers, that atrophy of the testes is always followed by some peculiarity in the antler-growth, that castration of a young male always inhibits the development of antlers, and so on. Sellheim (1898, 1899) finds that in many animals of both sexes castration is followed by a prolongation of the period of bone-growth. In the case of young cocks the effects of castration are very variable, sometimes increasing, sometimes decreasing the secondary sex characters. One result is clear, however, that the whole body is affected; the larynx is intermediate in size between that of cock and hen, the syrinx is weakly developed and the capons seldom crow or do so abnormally, the brain and heart are light in weight, fat accumulates in the subcutaneous and subserous connective tissue, and the skeleton shows many abnormalities. The experiments of J. Th. Oudemans (1898) on castrating caterpillars—a difficult operation—led him to the conclusion, in marked contrast to the above, that there was little result either on the external appearance or on the habits of the adults.

Thirdly, it should also be noted that in aged females, which have ceased to be functional in reproduction, the minor peculiarities of their sex often disappear, and they become liker males, both in structure and habits—witness the familiar case of "crowing hens."

From the presupposition, then, of the intimate connection between the sexuality and the secondary characters (which is indeed everywhere allowed), it is possible to advance a step further. Thus in regard to color, that the male is usually brighter than the female is an acknowledged fact. But pigments of many kinds are physiologically regarded as of the nature of waste products. Such for instance is the guanin, so abundant on the skin of fishes and some other animals. Abundance of such pigments, and richness of variety in related series, point to preeminent activity of chemical processes in the animals which possess them. Technically expressed, abundant pigments are expressions of intense metabolism. But predominant activity has been already seen to be characteristic of the male sex; these bright colors, then, are often natural to maleness. In a literal sense animals put on beauty for ashes, and the males more so because they are males, and not primarily for any other reason whatever. We are well aware that, in spite of the researches of Krukenberg, Sorby, MacMunn, Newbigin, and others, our knowledge of the physiology of pigments is still very scanty. Yet in many cases, alike among plants and animals, pigments are expressions of disruptive processes, and are of the nature of waste products; and this general fact is at present sufficient for our contention, that bright coloring or rich pigmenting is more characteristic of the male than of the female constitution.

In the same way, the skin eruptions of male fishes at the spawning season seem more pathological than decorative, and may be directly connected with the sexual excitement. One instance of the way in which the reproductive maturity is known to effect a by no means obviously related result may be given. Every field naturalist knows that the male stickleback builds a nest among the weeds, and that he weaves the material together by mucous threads secreted from the kidneys. The little animal is also known to have strong passions; it is polygamous in relation to its mates, and most pugnacious in relation to its rivals. Professor Möbius has shown that the male reproductive organs (or testes) become very large at the breeding season, and that they press in an abnormal way upon the kidneys. This encroachment produces a pathological condition in the kidneys, and the result is the formation of a mucous secretion, somewhat similar to what occurs in renal disease in higher forms. To free itself from the irritant pressure of this secretion, the male rubs itself against external objects, most conveniently upon its nest. Thus the curious weaving instinct does not demand or find rationale in the cumulative action of natural selection upon an inexplicable variation, but is traced back to a pathological and mechanical origin in the emphatic maleness of the organism. The line of variation being thus given, it is of course conceivable that natural selection may have accelerated it.

So too, though again the physiological details are scanty, the superabundant growth of hair and feathers may be interpreted, in some measure through getting rid of waste products, for we shall see later how local katabolism favors cell multiplication. Combs, wattles, and skin excrescences point to a predominance of circulation in the skin of the feverish males, whose temperatures are known in some cases to be decidedly higher than those of the females. Even skeletal weapons like antlers may be similarly interpreted; while the exaggerated activity of the scent-glands is another expedient for excreting waste.

In regard to horns, feathers, and the like, in association with vigorous circulation, two sentences from Rolph may be quoted:— "The exceedingly abundant circulation, which periodically occurs in the at first soft frontal protuberances of stags, admits and conditions the colossal development of horn and delicate ensheathing velvet. . . . In the same way, the rich flow of blood in the feather papillae conditions the immense growth of the feathers, . . . and the same is true of hairs, spines, and teeth."

Professor J. Kennel gives expression in an interesting essay to an entirely different interpretation of such structures as antlers. It may be that they, like the horns of Ruminants, were originally possessed by both sexes, and that they have been lost by the females whose reproductive sacrifice leaves, as it were, less to spare for such expensive structures as antlers are. So it may be that the female deer have ceased to develop antlers except where the conditions of life rendered their retention indispensable, namely, in the reindeer. In other words, this may be one of the many cases in which the female is nearer not to the ancestral but to the youthful type.

Some of the even subtler differences between the sexes are of interest in illustrating the general antithesis. Thus in the love-lights of the Italian glow insect (*Luciola*), the color is said to be identical in the two sexes, and the intensity is much the same. That of the female, however, who is in other respects rather male-like in her amatory emotions, is more restricted. It is interesting further to notice that the rhythm of the light in the male is more rapid and the flashes are briefer, while that of the female is longer and the flashes more distant and tremulous.

§ 5. *Sexual Selection: Its Limit as an Explanation.*—We are now in a better position to criticize Mr. Darwin's theory. On his view, males are stronger, handsomer, or more emotional, because ancestral forms happened to become so in a slight degree. In other words, the reward of breeding-success gradually perpetuated and perfected a casual advantage. According to the present view, males are stronger, handsomer, and more emotional, simply because they are males—*i.e.*, of more active physiological habit than their mates. In phraseology which will presently become more intelligible and concrete, the males tend to live at a loss, are relatively more metabolic. The females, on the other hand, tend to live at a profit, are relatively more *anabolic*—constructive processes predominating in their life, whence indeed the capacity of bearing offspring.

No one can dispute that the nutritive, vegetative, or self-regarding processes within the plant or animal are opposed to the reproductive, multiplying, or species-regarding processes, as income to expenditure, or as building up to breaking down. But within the ordinary nutritive or vegetative functions of the body, there is necessarily a continuous antithesis between two sets of processes—constructive and destructive metabolism. The contrast between these two processes is seen throughout nature, whether in the alternating phases of cell life, or of activity and repose, or in the great antithesis between growth and reproduction; and it is this same contrast which we recognize as the fundamental difference between male and female.

Darwin notes how there are frequent gradations in the amount of difference between the sexes. Sometimes the sexes are alike dull, where we should have to suppose the æsthetic perception must somehow have been lost or inhibited; sometimes the females are dull and the males splendid—for Darwin, an example of the result of sexual æsthetic perception, this of an exquisitely subtle kind, however, and without proportionate cerebral enlargement. In a third set of cases, both sexes are splendid, which would suggest logically that the male in turn had acquired a taste for splendor. But such cases, which usually need more or less cumbrous additional hypothesis of inheritance and so on to explain them, are intelligible enough if we regard them as a relative increase of katabolism in the life-ratio throughout a series of species. The third set may be supposed to be relatively more katabolic than the first, while the second set are midway; although, it may be freely granted, a knowledge of the habits, size, etc., of the particular species, would be necessary to verify the legitimacy of this interpretation in each case.*

---

* For a discussion of the progressive development of coloring and markings, whether in butterflies or mammals, the reader may be referred to the works of Professor Eimer, especially to his work on Lepidoptera. Reference should also be made to Weismann's "Studies in the Theory of Descent," for a discussion of the markings of caterpillars and butterflies.

DR. B. TARNOWSKY

FROM

THE SEXUAL INSTINCT AND ITS MORBID MANIFESTATIONS

FROM THE DOUBLE STANDPOINT

OF JURISPRUDENCE AND

PSYCHIATRY

Benjamin Tarnowsky (ca. 1839–1899): A Russian physician who taught at the Imperial Academy of medicine in St. Petersburg. During the course of his research, he was heavily influenced by Richard von Krafft-Ebing, who wrote an epigraph for The Sexual Instinct and Its Morbid Manifestations. *Tarnowsky practiced medicine for twenty-five years before he wrote his study, often treating diseases of the genital organs. He wrote* The Sexual Instinct *with a dual intended audience of "physicians and jurists" in order to differentiate for both groups the difference "between vice and disease," or between individuals for whom pederasty and other sexual deviations are a result of an inherited disease or "proved depravity of character." He continued to conduct scientific studies and update his findings throughout his career. His work was translated into several languages, and he claimed that physicians throughout Europe confirmed his conclusions.*

PREFACE TO THE ENGLISH EDITION

Medicine undertakes to save the honor of mankind before the Court of Morality, and individuals from judges and their fellow-men. The duty and right of medical science in these studies belong to it by reason of the high aim of all human inquiry after truth.

(DR.) KRAFFT-EBING.

In the present work I sketch in broad outline those facts and observations which inspired me with the idea of making enquiry into the causes of sexual perversion—and this not merely under the influence of depravity and licentious excess; preferably, in fact I may say chiefly, I examine these causes as connected with a morbid condition of the organism, whether congenital or acquired.

Above all I make it my business to throw all the light possible on the part played by heredity and by the phenomena of arrested development, as well as by the various morbid causes conditioning the etiology of sexual perversions, and to differentiate these with the very utmost clearness from proved depravity of character—conscious and premeditated vice.

My Treatise on Sexual Perversion appeared in the first instance in Russian in 1885. A large number of Works have followed suit since in different countries, and I have enjoyed the very great satisfaction of noting that my conclusions have been in the main confirmed by all my learned fellow-workers in other parts of Europe.

Carrying my investigations further into this subject, one equally delicate and important, I have since brought together a very considerable number of fresh observations, all of which support the views originally expressed in the present work. But, as previously to last year the whole of my time was consecrated to teaching my Classes at the Academy of Medicine, leisure has hitherto failed me to draw up a fair and proper statement of my observations. From another point of view, it may be that, considering their special subject, they are still too recent to be published at once.

Meantime I am bound to state that this fresh evidence has not in any way modified my convictions on the question of sexual aberrations. I may add that the further experience of these last few years makes me insist with even greater confidence than before on the practical conclusions with regard to examination by medico-legal experts which I had previously drawn, and which are laid down in this book.

I would beg my excellent translators, Messrs. W. C. Costello, Ph.D., and A. R. Allinson, M.A., as also Mr. Charles Carrington, my Publisher, to accept my very sincere thanks for their kindness in undertaking the English Translation. I owe it to them that I am in a position to bring my book under the notice of my English colleagues, as well as that of English Jurists—Physicians and Jurists being the two classes I had particularly in view when I wrote my book.

Professor Benjamin Tarnowsky
St. Petersburg,
March 7, 1898.

INTRODUCTION

Five years ago I was called upon to give my opinion as an expert in a case of pederasty.

On looking through my observations on this subject, and comparing them with the corresponding chapters of the most widely known manuals of forensic medicine, I was struck with the want of agreement between the assertion of official science on the one hand and clinical facts on the other. Each fresh technical examination taught me more clearly to recognize not only how insufficient was the knowledge contained in the manuals dealing with perversity of genesic activity, but also the incorrectness of many of the guiding principles of examination into the actual circumstance. Later studies on this matter by Krafft-Ebing, Lombroso, Charcot, Magnan and other alienists have rendered it quite impossible to adhere to former views, and yet further confirm my conviction of the truth of the conclusions I have deduced from clinical observation.

At present the difference of opinion between the medical jurist and the clinical physician has become so broad, that it appears to be highly necessary, in order to explain these contradictions, to indicate the foundations on which approximately correct answers to medico-forensic questions may be based, and to prepare the way for wider, more united and more fruitful study of the subject.

The medical jurist sees depravity, oversatiated lust, inveterate vice, wickedness, and so on, where the clinical observer recognizes with certainty the symptoms of a morbid condition with its typical evolution and result. Where the former would punish vice, the latter enters a plea for the necessity of methodical therapeutics. On the other hand, there is a whole series of acts, which are relatively but lightly punished by the law, in which the medical jurist sees only impropriety, caprice or play carried too far, recognizing all the time the moral responsibility of the culprit, whereas the clinical observer discerns therein the outset of a grave malady, the beginning of an incurable psychical disturbance, requiring careful watching and treatment. Lastly, the clinical doctor discovers real depravity and complete moral decay in cases, where the medical jurist is more often inclined to suppose the wrong-doer a victim of violence or of fraud.

It is certainly not difficult to understand, why, in any question as to perversity of the genesic activity, the observations and conclusions of the clinical physician must take precedence in the discovery of the truth. The medical jurist has exclusively to do with incriminated persons, who first of all seek to escape punishment and therefore mostly deny quite obvious facts. Even in the rare cases of frank admission of culpability the accused sees no reason for describing the intimate causes and motives of his actions. The physician appears naturally in his eyes more as an accuser than as a defender; and when, having made up his mind to undergo the sentence, he confesses the facts, he has no object to gain in making an avowal, one generally fraught with ill consequences to himself, of his perverted sexual instincts and the impulses that drive him to gratify his genesic sense in abnormal ways. It is but seldom that the medical jurist can obtain the diaries of such individuals, their correspondence or other interesting documents, such as are for instance to be found in the classical treatises of Caspar and of Tardieu. But such diaries and autobiographies show very prominently the usual fault of all productions of the kind, viz., the wish to excite interest, to exhibit their good aspects only. In this way the description becomes exaggerated, untrue and utterly deceptive. The clinical physician on the contrary has not to examine incriminated persons. The sufferer comes to him spontaneously to seek for advice. He hopes for assistance from the physician and in all sincerity confides his ailments to him, even in their slightest details. There is no room here for premeditated fraud or conscious unveracity. The physician is therefore in a position to distinguish the initial symptoms of an anomaly or of a malady, to follow its development and observe its progress during a number of years. By such means he obtains a complete, consistent and decisive view of the disease.

The representatives of two specialties are the most frequently consulted by such patients: physicians devoted to the treatment of mental diseases and specialists for diseases of the genital organs. To the first the applicants are mostly persons with well-defined symptoms, in whom there also exists concurrent perversity of the genesic instinct, not to mention other derangements of the nervous system. The disturbance of the genesic activity is here only an accessory symptom among the series of the other more serious cerebral phenomena which trouble the patient. The specialists for mental diseases have besides opportunities for observing in their asylums the ultimate form of those maladies, which at their inception are manifested in perversity of the genesic action and terminate in complete madness.

Specialists for diseases of the genital organs are resorted to by such as find themselves suffering from any manifestations of organic anomaly, however slight, from arrested development or from the premonitory signs of incipient disease—when a diminution of the sexual power comes into prominence above all other symptoms, or finally when syphilitic infection makes an avowal inevitable of some perversity of the genesic sense of one sort or another.

Amongst those consulting the specialist of this class are: The Young Man who after attaining the age of manhood becomes aware of complete impotency where women are concerned, and is obscurely conscious of abnormal sexual promptings within; the Old Man, whose sexual activity has long ago disappeared, but who suddenly feels a new sensual impulse, an exaggerated wantonness and morbid stimulation of desire; the Husband, who idolizes his wife and from time to time gives way to the irrepressible sexual impulse, but who feels impelled to accomplish the conjugal act in some quite unusual and to his own consciousness disgusting manner; the Voluptuary, who has become aware of a diminution of his genesic power and does not know whether it is to be attributed to a quantitative or a qualitative alteration of function. All these haste first of all to the specialist in maladies of the genital organs for advice. Again it is to him the habitual pederast makes his involuntary confession, who has accidentally become inoculated with syphilis, and the boy who has recently been seduced and finds himself attacked by some trouble of the anus or rectum. The avowal of their failing is usually a source of great moral mortification to patients. It is often made in writing, with precautions of mystery and secrecy; and then a frank confession can only be expected, if the physician avoids meeting it with reproof, but holds himself ready to give his assistance.

I may further remark in this place, that nearly all pederasts, of whatever rank, are more or less known to each other, at least in large towns, and that they generally go for advice to the same physician, whose task of obtaining open and frank confessions with regard to such abnormal genesic facts is much facilitated by the fact.

In the course of my 25 years of medical practice, I have had more particularly to do with various phases of disease affecting the genital organs. And as I carefully noted all my observations I was able to make a large collection of facts bearing upon morbid manifestations of the genesic sense.

The actual criminal and the undoubted madman are two extremes, between which is found a host of unrecognized sufferers, and vicious subjects burdened with an abnormal function of the genesic action; of these two classes the latter will furnish the greater part of the material for the following investigation.

I trust that observations, not emanating from the prosecuting bench, nor from the registers of lunatic asylums, observations taken on persons belonging to society in general, who have not been bereft of their legal status, and who may be held to be sane, may supply new data for a proper differentiation between vice and disease, between congenital defect and moral lapse.

My intention has been to make my treatment of the subject intelligible not only to the physician, but also to the jurist. Therefore the exposition may be somewhat lengthened, because of the necessity of digressions in order to make it as generally comprehensible as possible. I am convinced that it can only be by an exact enquiry into so-called offenses against public morals, and a methodical exposition of the facts as compared with the usual legal procedure, that will enable jurists, thoroughly initiated into the actual state of science relating to the morbid manifestations of the genesic sense, to come to a proper conclusion.

GENERAL CONSIDERATIONS

The genesic instinct presents itself in the human being previous to the development of sexual maturity, and in a healthy organism finds expression in an impulse towards persons of the opposite sex, an impulse which soon changes into a voluntary desire for the accomplishment of the sexual act which, as it becomes more developed, may attain to the degree of a continual sexual want.

Among anomalies of the genesic functions perversity of the genesic instinct shows itself most distinctly in a morbid inclination towards persons of the same sex. Among men, who form more exclusively the subject of the present research, this form of sexual perversity is designated by the comprehensive expression of "Pederasty."[1] Bestiality and Sodomy are, as we shall see further on, no more than variations of the above-mentioned abnormal genesic impulse.

The pederastic manifestations constitute the more definite and better studied group of sexual aberrations, as they are more often the subject of judicial investigation; and for this reason the most prominent place is given in the present work to Pederasty in the widest sense of the expression.

But this vice must not be isolated in this study, without considering also its connection with the other forms and kinds of perversion of sexual activity, which we shall therefore also touch upon, as much as may be necessary for the elucidation of the subject.

As Pederasty is developed under the influence of very different causes, it must, as all other aberrations of the genesic sense, be distributed from the clinical and etiological points of view into several groups and kinds, differing considerably one from another.

The morbid manifestations of sexual activity separate first of all into two great groups, according as they develop in such subjects as are from their birth disposed to such aberrations and to nervous disorders of all sorts, or on the other hand, show themselves in persons, relatively healthy, and who are not under the influence of hereditary infirmity.

In the *first group* the disorder of the genesic functions is to be

---

[1] Formed of two Greek words, παιδὸ`ς εδαστη-Q, i.e.: *pueri amator*; better known to the Romans under the denomination of "Grecian Love."

referred to a psychopathic or neuropathic constitution; whereas in the second group we have to do with individuals, who from their birth have always enjoyed a properly constituted and normally acting nervous system.

The morbid symptoms again resulting from hereditary infirmity also show themselves under different forms.

In some cases they present themselves with the very first awakening of the genesic instinct, and in their development remain refractory to the influence of education or example, attain their greatest intensity in the period of sexual maturity and manhood, and subsist during the rest of the lifetime, with periodical diminution or increase.

These aberrations are in their nature constant and invariable, special to the particular organism, in precisely the same way as other innate peculiarities of character feeling or morality are special to the same individual.

The said disturbances constitute the first kind of hereditary infirmity, which we will denominate in general *innate Perversion of the sexual instinct*; and in this group we shall class *innate Pederasty*.

To the second division of the same group belong such modifications of the genesic activity as now and then show themselves *nolens volens* in the form of morbid attacks, which are separated by intervals, during which the sexual functions are performed in a normal manner.

The denomination *periodical Perversion of the genesic sense* in general, and *periodical Pederasty* in particular, appears to me best to represent the morbid disturbances in question, because they are in perfect analogy with the so-called periodical psychoses (mental disturbances), those higher manifestations of psychical degeneracy—a degeneracy manifesting itself in occasional outbursts of mental disturbance, while there are long intervals between the attacks during which the mental powers exhibit a relatively normal activity.

In a third class of genesic disturbances I reckon those disorders which show themselves in the well-known morbid manifestations known under the general name of Epilepsy.

During the mental disturbance incidental to this malady, there may be exhibited a sort of psychical epilepsy, in the form of an epileptic pederasty.

I regard as paroxysmal phenomena analogous to hysteria and mania those morbid manifestations of the genesic sense that are observed in the so-called erotomania and satyriasis. The description of the last named forms the termination of the group of sexual perturbations founded on hereditary infirmity.

The *second group* includes all those aberrations of the genesic activity that may be the result of education or example, or come spontaneously from personal impulse, as the expression of vicious propensity, or of willful depravity.

The expression: *"Acquired Perversion" of the sexual functions and acquired Pederasty* answers best in our opinion to the class included in the above group.

This group also contains sundry subdivisions consisting of such perturbations of the sexual functions as are the symptom of a developing disease of the nervous centers, or of the entire organism—a disease that attacks subjects who from their birth have had a healthy, well-constituted brain.

Among these are to be reckoned the sexual perversions peculiar to the decrepitude of old age—*Senile Pederasty*; and again the sexual aberrations observed during the initial period of paralytic idiocy—*Paralytic Pederasty*.

Every student of nature knows that the division into groups and species based on any particular symptom is purely conventional and artificial, and serves only to facilitate research without being grounded on any immovable, unchangeable organic foundation. The same holds good with the grouping proposed by me. It must needs undergo modifications as life goes on; the various kinds and types little by little dissolve into each other, becoming mutually complicated one with the other, acquire new, fresh shades of coloring and form, according to the composite forms of genesic aberration, which will be described as a separate group.

I have further analyzed the objective symptoms, which enable one to form an opinion on the pederastic perversion of the sexual activity, and which must needs constitute the basis of any special medico-judicial investigation.

Finally, I have endeavored to determine the data which may serve to establish a differential diagnosis of the different groups and classes of sexual aberrations.

We shall begin by describing the forms of sexual aberrations most frequently encountered.

GROUP A. PERVERSION OF THE GENESIC INSTINCT BASED ON HEREDITARY INFIRMITY

I. CONGENITAL CONTRARY-SEXUAL FEELING
(CONGENITAL PEDERASTY)

Just as children may be born with abnormally constituted extremities, trunk, head or other members, a congenital tendency may in like manner appear towards perverse modes of manifestation of the genesic instinct.

As in a physical cripple the whole organism may be more or less normally developed, apart from the particular abnormality, so in a moral abortion the psychical constitution may be more or less normal, with the exception of the particular perversion present. The irregular or faulty development of the nervous centers may present a particular character, by reason of which a functional disturbance caused thereby may be limited to any particular domain, that for instance of sexual activity.

But the faulty development of certain nervous centers is not without influence on the development of the others. It is generally possible to recognize in an abortion, notwithstanding the more or less regular constitution of the non-affected parts of the body, a number of slight deviations and irregularities which, if not apparent on a superficial view, are nevertheless discovered by careful examination. In the same way where there is congenital disturbance in limited nervous centers, it has a certain influence upon the whole of the nervous system, which shows itself in certain hardly perceptible irregularities. In order therefore to obtain a general view of the anomaly in question with all the irregularities connected with it, it is necessary to follow up its general development from its very first manifestations.

The child born with congenital sexual perversion grows up and develops to all appearance quite regularly in every way. The genesic sense alone generally awakens unusually early and, as the period of sexual maturity approaches, a whole series of abnormal morbid manifestations show themselves. The first of these symptoms is an expression of shame, not before girls or women, but in presence of grown-up men. For instance, the boy is more ashamed to undress himself before a strange man than before a woman. On the other hand he prefers the company and caresses of men to those of women. He feels a great attachment to a man, follows him about incessantly, obeys him without a murmur, is charmed with him—in one word, he "adores" a man, either a brave, generous and clever man or one with strongly developed muscles, whilst he remains quite indifferent towards women. At length he attains puberty; in the night he often has violent erections with emission of semen. The pollutions are accompanied by dreams, at first indetermined, easily forgotten; but they each time become more distinct, decided and often astonish the youth himself by their strange nature. They are not female caresses nor meetings with women that appear to him in his dreams, but the pressure of the hand, the kiss of well-built, handsome grown-up men. The final erection ending with seminal emission is not provoked in dream by a female form in seductive attitudes and movements, but by the embracing, caresses and kisses of men.

Not only does the representation of womanly form give rise to no sexual excitation, but it paralyzes all voluptuous feeling when such exists already. Among normally constituted men the heat of sexual erethism rapidly disappears at the sight of grown-up men. On the contrary this same erethism is quenched at once in the congenital pederast in the presence of women. The sight of a naked young woman leaves him indifferent, whereas that of a naked man will awaken in him feelings of lust.

From books and conversation with his comrades he discovers that something quite unusual and abnormal is taking place within him. But the strangeness to him of the phenomenon itself, the difficulty of giving it a distinct form, and his ever increasing shyness when in company with men, cause the youth to dissimulate his misfortune. Sometimes, incited thereto by companions of his age, he ventures to share the couch of some girl and to accomplish the act of manhood, but each time the effort fails and is not seldom followed by a hysterical fit.

Just as a normally constituted and sexually developed man, try as he may, cannot feel any lustful desire for another man, so it is equally impossible for the congenital pederast to accomplish coition with a woman. Such fruitless endeavors serve only to still more discourage the young man and finally inspire him with a disgust for women. He now seeks the companionship of men, pays court to them, falls in love with them and in the meantime seeks for satisfaction in onanism.

In consequence of the congenital morbid erethism, the so-called excitable weakness of the nervous system, the feelings of lubricity become soon intensified to their utmost, and often find in the simple physical contact with the beloved person the determination of an *emissio seminis*. The love of such subjects is extraordinarily violent, morbidly passionate, absorbs all their moral and sensitive faculties, and is at first purely Platonic, it is only later on that the sexual feeling and its consequent genesic impulse finds satisfaction in mutual masturbation or in onanistic excitation of the adored person. Finally, when the latter consents to it, or because he wishes to satisfy his lust otherwise, the act of sodomy is consummated, in which the morbidly disposed participator always plays the part of the passive pederast.

Concurrently with the exaggeration of sexual perversion just described, other peculiarities of the sick organism begin to show themselves. The youth is impelled to give himself a feminine appearance, likes to wear female attire, to have his hair curled, to walk about with exposed neck, and tightened waist, to scent, powder and rouge the face, to paint the eyebrows, etc. In this way is developed a type of womanish-looking men, disgusting to those of their own sex and looked upon with contempt by women, and whom it is easy to recognize by their appearance. They are generally of middle-sized or slight build, with broad hips and narrow shoulders, affecting a feminine walk and a peculiar swinging gait; with perfumed locks, eccentric dress, bracelets on their wrists, they seek by every means, laughing, talking and gesticulation, to draw the attention of men to themselves. The unhappy creature cannot realize, particularly if there is a relatively weak development of his understanding, that he is so much the more repugnant to normally constituted men the more he seeks to imitate a woman. At once fantastical, even to hysteria, envious, cowardly, mean, revengeful and spiteful, he combines in himself all the faults of the woman, without any of her qualities, and possesses none of the attractive traits of the manly character. He is therefore despicable alike to men and women.

Many such sufferers willingly acknowledge their abnormal condition which they endeavor to explain to themselves. "I have a female soul in a man's body," wrote K. H. Ulrichs, who has written quite a series of treatises, which, although very interesting as the detailed confessions of a psychopathic subject, are at the same without order and too long drawn out, as is the case with most of the same class of works.

It often happens that such patients feel depressed in mind by the knowledge of their infirmity and of their inability to fight against it. In this connection, a letter, kindly communicated to us by Professor J. Mierzejewsky, is of great interest. It is to the following effect: ". . . To speak frankly, I am even here, far away, exposed to temptations, against which I am defenseless, and I do not really know what it means; malady, or the power of youthful impressions, or want of will, against which I have been fighting in vain for more than four years—or an unlucky nature, a fatal destiny, or else an instinct that death only can cure?! That is why I at times brood on the thought of some rapid and painless poison, for in truth this instinct is in contradiction with my judgment. . . ."

A few months before his marriage with a charming girl, a patient of mine wrote to me as follows: "I am a slave to my fatal passion, I cannot abandon vice and I am not able to love Fräulein X . . . , although I feel that it is only with her that I could be happy. In her absence, I love her understanding, her soul, her visage even; but when I see her, I feel that I should not be in a condition to become her husband. . . . It would be the greatest of misfortunes. Up to the present I have never been able to have intercourse with women— with her it will be the same thing. . . . There remains for me nothing but death, if your help proves to be powerless . . ."

Sometimes the patient, perpetually tortured by jealousy of women because of their success with men, feels despair on account of his mostly unsuccessful loves, often repulsed with contempt, in a fit of melancholy takes his own life or, sinking deeper and deeper, he confines himself to the narrow circle of a few fellow-sufferers, and terminates his existence in a half stupid condition. Otherwise he may become the victim of one form or another of acute mania, if his miserable existence is not previously put an end to by some other accidental malady. The type here described combines in it the principal characteristics of the congenital pederast as most frequently met with.

However, there are others again who, in their efforts to ape the fair sex, adopt more eccentric forms. So, for instance, Taylor in this connection has written a most important observation, embodying his description of the celebrated English actress and adventuress Elisa Edwards who, after her death, was discovered to have been a man in disguise. From his earliest youth he felt an inclination for men, from the age of 14 wore female clothing, went on the stage, had many amorous adventures, lived as a Mistress, and used to fasten up his genitals, which were quite normally developed, to his body by a special bandage, so as not to be recognized.

Notwithstanding the clear, explicit expression of the inclination to copy the female sex in the above case, the sexual perversity implied differs really in no respect from that exhibited by the previously described type of the born passive pederast, or so-called "Cynede."

But besides such cases as this, there exist other intermediate forms occurring under circumstances to be presently defined,—morbid aberrations now more, now less, strongly marked, which form a gradual transition to obvious forms of hereditary mental derangement.

In the weaker defined manifestations the boy or youth exhibits only his predisposition to occupy himself with feminine work—He likes to knit, to sew, to make doll's clothes; otherwise he distinguishes himself by his peculiar preference for feminine manners, he strives to be graceful and coquettish in his demeanor, imitates the tone and voice of a woman, etc., and is awkward and out of his element and blushes when in conversation with men. On the contrary, he is quite free from embarrassment in the company of young girls, is glad to take the woman's part in dancing, always choosing for cavalier a vigorous, stalwart manly dancer, becoming quite enlivened and merry, when he has found a man to his taste, or else growing confused and troubled at his sight and running away like a timid little girl.

Another occupies all his leisure time before the looking glass; combs his hair, puts on curl-papers, paints his face, adorns his person, studying in the most serious fashion what is becoming to him and what is not. He has a wonderful remembrance of the most complicated female toilettes, and is able to describe them in all their details; in this matter he exhibits a quite delicate taste, but shows himself absolutely wanting in taste when he adopts male attire. He either sports a too violently colored necktie, or he exposes his neck so low that it appears extravagantly exaggerated, even for a woman; or else he has his hair curled in long locks, and covers his fingers with rings and puts bracelets upon his wrists.

In other less decided forms, the sexual instinct is more frequently and particularly determined by the surrounding circumstances. When the parents or the instructors of such morbid subjects fail to comprehend the signification of the above described manifestations, give them only a frivolous consideration, and even for fun encourage such feminine instincts, the inevitable result is that the morbidly disposed youth generally becomes an onanist, not feeling attracted towards the female sex, from which he more and more estranges himself, and finally on favorable occasion becomes a pederast, although, at first, he still possessed the power of sexual intercourse with women.

The more intense the morbid manifestation, the longer has the subject been addicted to masturbation, and the sooner has he become a pederast, and the sooner also does he lose the possibility of normal coition.

Yet more fatal in its effects upon subjects that way disposed is the companionship of similar morbidly affected comrades, in a still more advanced pathological condition, as often occurs in schools. By the example of elder comrades the boy early becomes a pederast and consequently at the advent of puberty his morbidly diminished desire for the female sex is still more accentuated.

Under more favorable circumstances the case has a more satisfactory culmination.

When the boy has been repressed in time, and laughed at on the first feminine imitations, he involuntarily begins to pull himself together. If he is then carefully kept away from female society, occupied as much as possible with athletic exercises, always severely reproved and punished for the slightest appearance of coquetry, graceful manner, extravagant delicacy and in general for every external feminine manifestation, by such strictly conducted education the youth attains to the normal state of puberty.

The morbidly diminished sexual inclination towards the female sex that is congenitally present, and the weakened and perverted genesic instinct—the consequence of bad surroundings and education—cause the youth in this initial period of his life to be more indifferent to sexual enjoyment than are his comrades of the same age. It frequently happens that, when he has come to manhood, after violent erethism or repeated pollutions, his first attempts at sexual intercourse with women are abortive; or that, notwithstanding their successful accomplishment, he has not found therein the same enjoyment a normally constituted being would.

However, if he perseveres in having regular intercourse, particularly with one and the same person, the genesic perversion gradually dies out, and finally the youth who from his birth was disposed to perversion of sexual instinct, grows up to be a man endowed with normal genital functions, and fit to fulfill the duties of the head of a family.

Another variety of these morbid manifestations consists in those cases, in which the touching of the hind quarters determines a sexual erethism, the gratification of which is not perverse and can happen normally. Sometimes the boy notices in quite early youth, that slight strokes on his naked posteriors caused him an agreeable sensation. He then voluntarily seeks, in play, in joke, or even as a punishment to get a few strokes. When this particular predisposition is not taken notice of, the strokes, especially those of the birch, awaken erotic excitement in the boy. Later on he fustigates himself, when he is alone, and the erethism culminates in onanism. When the period of manhood arrives, if the vicious habit, of seeking excitation in flagellation, that is to say by strokes with a birch on the posteriors, has become deep-rooted, the patient is only then able to have intercourse with women, after having been flogged previously, which for ever deprives him of the possibility of family life, and necessarily reduces him to the extremity of having recourse to masturbation or to the exclusive frequentation of prostitutes, women who sell their favors. Under such conditions the vicious propensity is still further developed. Strokes alone, even when followed by blood, are not sufficient for the patient; he requires a certain amount of violence to be exercised upon him. He must be undressed brutally, or his wrists are to be tied together, he must be fastened down to a bench, etc., during which he makes a pretense of resistance, shouts and swears. It is only by such means and flogging with birch rods that he succeeds in obtaining that degree of sexual excitation which ends in *emissio seminis*. In this morbid period he seldom goes as far as actual coition, more frequently the semen is expended even without erection—At last the patient loses altogether the faculty of performing the genesic function in a normal manner, and gradually is developed in him the predisposition to graver forms of nervous and mental disease.

It goes without saying that, when the morbid propensity is discovered early, and abnormal excitement by touching of the posteriors is carefully avoided, the period of puberty is thereby retarded as much as possible, and the efforts to overcome the congenital infirmity become more easy and more successful.

Besides the weak congenital forms, which indicate a more or less slight disposition to pederasty, there are other more violent forms, happily less common, which show a gradual transition to complete madness. Many of these subjects find their first feelings of lust excited by the sight of a naked man, particularly of his posteriors or the *orificium ani*. Dr. Albert mentions for instance cases, in which certain schoolmasters whipped their pupils without any cause, the sight of the naked buttocks of the children producing in them a state of sensual excitement which they then satisfied by masturbation.

When such subjects give themselves up early to masturbation, they seek to excite themselves by touching or rubbing against the posteriors of men, on which occasions there is often an emission of semen. They have also nocturnal pollutions accompanied by dream pictures in which naked men with strongly developed hind quarters play the principal part. Such subjects are born active pederasts; they are always indifferent to women, have no feminine propensities, but generally exhibit, besides their sexual perversion, other morbid symptoms as well, indicating a greater or less degree of degeneracy. Some display from infancy an inclination to objectless thievery; others are subject to epileptic fits, with temporary loss of consciousness; others again are afflicted with intellectual dullness, are soon fatigued by any mental labor, are slow to understand things, have a poor memory, and so forth.

On proceeding one step further in psychical degeneracy, we come to subjects who have an exclusive taste for old men. Many born pederasts feel attracted only by men with gray beards. For them neither youth, nor elegance of bodily form, nor beauty, whether in woman or in man, is of any importance; their sexual instinct can only be excited by the aspect of a gray beard, sometimes indeed by the ugliest face, rendered repulsive by deformity.

Another degree of this congenital perversion is manifested by individuals in whom the sexual excitement is produced by the aspect of lifeless objects which have no connection whatever with the sexual act. Cases are known, in which the sight of a nightcap on the head of a man, or of a woman, has caused this erethism with emission of semen. The view of a naked woman or man left the subject indifferent, but the remembrance of a nightcap, particularly if on the head of an old shriveled-up woman, or the touch of a nightcap, caused immediate erection and even emission.

Another unhappy patient had from early youth been in the habit of directing his attention to the nails in the shoes of women. The contemplation of such shoe nails procured him particular pleasure; during the night he would get up, secretly seek out such shoes, count the nails and, lying afterwards in his bed, would give himself up to all sorts of fantastic ideas, in which the benailed shoes led him to erection and precocious onanism. Later on the mere sight of a cobbler hammering nails into the soles of the patient's own boots was sufficient to cause him to emit semen without erection.

In a third case the first sexual erethism was caused by the sight of a white apron hung out to dry in the sun. He took the apron down, hung it before him, and commenced masturbating. From that moment the sight of a white apron always caused him erethism. It was, however, indifferent whether the apron was worn by a man or by a woman, or whether it hung on a clothesline, the sight of the apron invariably awakened in him the irrepressible wish to seize it and masturbate himself with it.

After he had been several times punished for stealing aprons, he entered a monastery, where he sought of his own accord to conquer his flesh by fasting and prayer, but he was not able to become master of his passion, and the remembrance of white aprons was sufficient to make him fall back into his vice.

Another experienced violent lust, terminating in spasmodic erection, when his genitals came into contact with fur, which occurred by accident, when he happened one night to cover himself with a fur rug. From that time—from the age of twelve—he was given to masturbation. The sight of the body of a man or of that of a woman, even during copulation, would not excite him in the least, but to touch a hairy little dog, which he sometimes took into his bed, always caused him erection, ending in emission: this was sometimes followed by a hysterical attack, accompanied by convulsions, sobbing, etc. His nocturnal pollutions were accompanied by dreams, in which neither men nor women played a part; he used to dream, that he was stretched naked upon a soft fur, that every point of his body pressed amorously to it, and this sensation led to erection and pollution. As he grew older, and became aware of his morbid condition, he was at times in actual despair and was often on the point of committing suicide.

He was very soon fatigued by mental work, and failed in his examinations at the University; his memory became much impaired; it always seemed to him as if his comrades regarded him in a peculiar manner and despised him. It was this last that troubled him most. He used to enquire, if it were possible to recognize his condition by the expression of his eyes? if there existed no means, by the absorption of remedies, to dissimulate his situation from *"them"*? He would cry, and sob, suffered terribly, praying to be saved from himself. "Should I find out that 'they' guess what is going on within me, I would most certainly kill myself."—These were his parting words at our last interview. Evidently the mania of being persecuted was already developing itself in him. As I was subsequently informed, he was a few months later placed in a lunatic asylum.

This patient exhibited degeneracy to a high degree. His genitals were irregularly developed, and in the bony structure of his body there were distinctly marked malformations. But similarly, in all previously cited cases, there had always been observed, besides a high degree of perversion of the sexual instinct, other manifestations as well, which indicated an abnormal development of the nervous system caused by degeneracy. Symptoms were always present of a morbid, or degenerate constitution of the nervous system.

The nightcap patient had at times hallucinations; he was inclined to melancholy and had repeatedly manifested the intention of poisoning himself. The patient whose erethism was excited by the sight of shoe nails had also fits of hysteria, of hypochondria, and was subject to hallucinations, and so forth. The amateur of white aprons was from his youth inclined to theft and had but a shallow understanding; he was later on subject to fits of melancholy with ideas of suicide. There were at the same time physical symptoms of degeneracy: the skull was irregularly formed and modified in a characteristic manner.

Dr. Krauss mentions a similar observation, where stealing was not for a criminal object, but served merely to satisfy a perverted sexual instinct. This observation is borrowed from Eulenberg and concerns a subject 45 years of age, of a hasty, spiteful character. "Often there came over him he knew not what; his head would then become heavy, hot and as if ready to burst; he could neither think nor work, and felt forced to run about like a dog. In such moments he felt an irresistible impulse to steal women's wash linen, wherever he could find any. He was never troubled by the fear of being caught; besides, he never stole other things or money. He used to put the linen on him, sometimes in the daytime, but more often at night he would lie in bed with them on. Putting them on and wearing them excited voluptuous feelings in him, and his semen was emitted involuntarily.

". . . He never sold or gave away a single one of the stolen articles, but preserved them all in cupboards and trunks, even in his mattress and in other hiding places. When he was arrested he wore several articles of female clothing and had a woman's shift next to his body. In his lodging were found above all in particular women's drawers and chemises, also corsets, bodices, stockings, handkerchiefs, in all 300 articles." In any case he never stole the linen of young women or girls with whom he was acquainted; he never knew to whom the linen belonged that he stole. His sexual instinct tended solely towards the female sex. Every other genesic aberration appears to have been absent: onanism, pederasty, lasciviousness in company with young lads. But the sexual desire for women, for natural sexual satisfaction, was also absent. He further admits, that for a long time past he has had no connection with women, but asserts himself to have been formerly able to accomplish copulation. Some years ago he was engaged to be married, but the match was broken off by the parents of the bride, which had greatly distressed him.

In connection with this an observation by Diez may be added, relating to a boy who felt an irresistible impulse to wear female clothing, which on each occasion was followed by emission of semen.

A very well studied example from the etiological point of view of congenital perversion of the sexual instinct is one lately furnished by Professor Lombroso, who relates the following case of a lad of 20 years of age who had a hereditary psychopathic tendency from his ancestors in the ascending line; his grandfather died insane, his mother suffered from sick headaches, he has a sister who is hysterical, a brother of his stutters, and one of his cousins is half an idiot.

With such predispositions already, the patient had also hurt his head in childhood, and it pained him for a long time afterwards; he had also from youth up been subject to intercostal pains and pains in the hips. From his third or fourth year he had likewise been subject to erections and violent sexual excitation at the sight of white objects, for instance even white walls, but particularly of linen hanging out to dry. The touch or the sound of the crumpling of linen would awaken lustful sensations in him. Ever since his ninth or tenth year he had masturbated himself at the sight of white starched linen. Though he possessed well-developed faculties and the desire to learn, he left school at nine years of age, stole money from his parents, several times set their house on fire, was repeatedly taken up for fighting in the streets and for carrying weapons, and was finally condemned to death for murder.

It is easy to understand how the further degrees of degeneracy, besides distinctly determined psychical and physical abnormities, may also present still more degraded forms of sexual perversion, for instance the impulse to martyrize his victims, to wound them, to see their blood flow, or the desire to violate little children. At the same time the lust finds complete satiety only in murdering, or disfiguring the victim, in swallowing morsels of the victim's flesh, or in accomplishing the genesic act upon the corpse.

S. WEIR MITCHELL

FROM

FAT AND BLOOD

AN ESSAY ON THE TREATMENT OF CERTAIN FORMS OF NEURASTHENIA AND HYSTERIA

Silas Weir Mitchell (1829–1914): Born in Philadelphia, the son of a medical professor, Silas Weir Mitchell was enormously prolific as a writer and a doctor. Maintaining a practice in Philadelphia until his death, Mitchell wrote novels, short stories, scholarly articles, and books on a variety of topics.

During the American Civil War Mitchell worked at the Turner's Lane Hospital and treated many patients with neurological disorders. His experience there led him to publish the important study Gunshot Wounds and Other Injuries of the Nerves *(1864). Like Freud and Breuer, he was interested in hysteria and discussed its treatment in* Lectures on the Diseases of the Nervous System—Especially in Women *(1881) and* Clinical Lessons on Nervous Diseases *(1897). Mitchell became famous for his "Rest Cure" and came to agree with the popular conception of himself as a genius. The Rest Cure is explained for the general reader in* Fat and Blood. *Now in disrepute, the Rest Cure required a combination of rest, massage, and avoidance of stress in order to restore neurotic women to "normal" life. Sigmund Freud and other neurologists and psychologists were influenced by this idea. Charcot was said to admire him greatly. Like Freud, Mitchell argued strongly for the interrelationship between the mental and physical components of human beings. Before one can address mental ailments, he believed, the body must first be rested.*

Mitchell married twice and was survived by his second wife and two sons. Always considered vain, Mitchell became angry and more opinionated late in life. He died of influenza during the winter of 1914.

CHAPTER I.

INTRODUCTORY.

For some years I have been using with success, in private and in hospital practice, certain methods of renewing the vitality of feeble people by a combination of entire rest and excessive feeding, made possible by passive exercise obtained through the steady use of massage and electricity.

The cases thus treated have been chiefly women of a class well known to every physician,—nervous women, who, as a rule, are thin and lack blood. Most of them have been such as had passed through many hands and been treated in turn for gastric, spinal, or uterine troubles, but who remained at the end as at the beginning, invalids, unable to attend to the duties of life, and sources alike of discomfort to themselves and anxiety to others.

In 1875 I published in "Séguin's Series of American Clinical Lectures," Vol. I., No. iv., a brief sketch of this treatment, under the heading of "Rest in the Treatment of Nervous Disease," but the scope afforded me was too brief for the details on a knowledge of which depends success in the use of rest. I have been often since reminded of this by the many letters I have received asking for explanations of the minutiae of treatment; and this must be my apology for bringing into these pages a great many particulars which are no doubt well enough known to the more accomplished physician.

In the preface to the second edition I said that as yet there had been hardly time for a competent verdict on the methods I had described. Since making this statement, many of our profession in America have published cases of the use of my treatment. It has also been thoroughly discussed by the medical section of the British Medical Association, and warmly endorsed by William Playfair, of London, Ross of Manchester, Coghill, and others; while a translation of my book into French by Dr. Oscar Jennings, with an introduction by Professor Ball, and a reproduction in German, with a preface by Professor von Leyden, have placed it satisfactorily before the profession in France and Germany.

As regards the question of originality I did not and do not now much concern myself. This alone I care to know, that by the method in question cases are cured which once were not; and as to the novelty of the matter it would be needless to say more, were it not that the charge of lack of that quality is sometimes taken as an imputation on a man's good faith.

But to sustain so grave an implication the author must have somewhere laid claim to originality and said in what respect he considered himself to have done a totally new thing. The following passage from the first edition of this book explains what was my own position:

"I do not wish," I wrote, "to be thought of as putting forth anything very remarkable or original in my treatment by rest, systematic feeding, and passive exercise. All of these have been used by physicians; but, as a rule, one or more are used without the others, and the plan which I have found so valuable, of combining these means, does not seem to be generally understood. As it involves some novelty, and as I do not find it described elsewhere, I shall, I think, be doing a service to my profession by relating my experience."

The following quotation from Dr. William Playfair's essay says all that I would care to add:

"The claims of Dr. Weir Mitchell to originality in the introduction of this system of treatment, which I have recently heard contested in more than one quarter, it is not my province to defend. I feel bound, however, to say that, having carefully studied what has been written on the subject, I can nowhere find anything in the least approaching to the regular, systematic, and thorough attack on the disease here discussed.

"Certain parts of the treatment have been separately advised, and more or less successfully practiced, as, for example, massage and electricity, without isolation; or isolation and judicious moral management alone. It is, in fact, the old story with regard to all new things: there is no discovery, from the steam-engine down to chloroform, which cannot be shown to have been partially foreseen, and yet the claims of Watt and Simpson to originality remain practically uncontested. And so, if I may be permitted to compare small things with great, will it be with this. The whole matter was admirably summed up by Dr. Ross, of Manchester, in his remarks in the discussion I introduced at the meeting of the British Medical Association at Worcester, which I conceive to express the precise state of the case:

'Although Dr. Mitchell's treatment was not new in the sense that its separate recommendations were made for the first time, it was new in the sense that these recommendations were for the first time combined so as to form a complete scheme of treatment.' "

As regards the acceptance of this method of treatment I have today no complaint to make. It runs, indeed, the risk of being employed in cases which do not need it and by persons who are not competent, and of being thus in a measure brought into disrepute. As concerns one of its essentials—massage—this is especially to be feared. It is a remedy with capacity to hurt as well as to help, and should never be used without the advice of a physician, nor persistently kept up without medical observation of its temporary and more permanent effects.

CHAPTER IV.

SECLUSION.

It is rare to find any of the class of patients I have described so free from the influence of their habitual surroundings as to make it easy to treat them in their own homes. It is needful to disentangle them from the meshes of old habits and to remove them from contact with those who have been the willing slaves of their caprices. I have often made the effort to treat them where they have lived and to isolate them there, but I have rarely done so without promising myself that I would not again complicate my treatment by any such embarrassments. Once separate the patient from the moral and physical surroundings which have become part of her life of sickness, and you will have made a change which will be in itself beneficial and will enormously aid in the treatment which is to follow. Of course this step is not essential in such cases as are merely anemic, feeble, and thin, owing to distinct causes, like the exhaustion of overwork, blood losses, dyspepsia, low fevers, or nursing. There are but too many women who have broken down under such causes and failed to climb again to the level of health, despite all that could be done for them; and when such persons are free from emotional excitement or hysterical complications there is no reason why the seclusion needful to secure them repose of mind should not be pleasantly modified in accordance with the dictates of common sense. Very often a little experimentation as to what they will profitably bear in the way of visits and the like will inform us, as their treatment progresses, how far such indulgence is of use or free from hurtful influences. Cases of extreme neurasthenia in men accompanied with nutritive failures require as to this matter cautious handling, because, for some reason, the ennui of rest and seclusion is far better borne by women than by the other sex.

Even in cases whose moral aspects do not at once suggest an imperative need for seclusion it is well to remember, as regards neurasthenic people, that the treatment involves for a time daily visits of some length from the masseur, the doctor, and possibly an electrician, and that to add to these even a single friendly visitor is often too much to be readily borne; but I am now speaking chiefly of the large and troublesome class of thin-blooded emotional women, for whom a state of weak health has become a long and, almost I might say, a cherished habit. For them there is often no success possible until we have broken up the whole daily drama of the sick room, with its little selfishness and its craving for sympathy and indulgence. Nor should we hesitate to insist upon this change, for not only shall we then act in the true interests of the patient, but we shall also confer on those near to her an inestimable benefit. An hysterical girl is, as Wendell Holmes has said in his decisive phrase, a vampire who sucks the blood of the healthy people about her; and I may add that pretty surely where there is one hysterical girl there will be soon or late two sick women. If circumstances oblige us to treat such a person in her own home, let us at least change her room, and also have it well understood how far we are to control her surroundings and to govern as to visitors and the company of her own family. Do as we may, we shall always lessen thus our chances of success, but we shall certainly not altogether destroy them.

I should add here a few words of caution as to the time of year best fitted for treatment. In the summer seclusion is often undesirable when the patient is well enough to gain help by change of air; moreover, at this season massage is less agreeable than in winter, and, as a rule, I find it harder to feed and to fatten persons at rest during our summer heats. That this rule is not without exception has been shown by Drs. Goodell and Sinkler, both of whom have attained some remarkable successes in midsummer.

One of the questions of most importance in the carrying out of this treatment is the choice of a nurse. Just as it is desirable to change the home of the patient, her diet, her atmosphere, so also is it well, for the mere alterative value of such change, to surround her with strangers and to put aside any nurse with whom she may have grown familiar. As I have sometimes succeeded in treating invalids in their own homes, so have I occasionally been able to carry through cases nursed by a mother, or sister, or friend of exceptional firmness; but to attempt this is to be heavily handicapped, and the position should never be accepted if it be possible to make other arrangements. Any firm, intelligent woman of tact, a stranger to the patient, is better than the old style of nurse, now, happily, disappearing. The nurse for these cases ought to be a young, active, quick-witted woman, capable of firmly but gently controlling her patient. She ought to be intelligent, able to interest her patient, to read aloud, and to write letters. The more of these cases she has seen and nursed, the easier becomes the task of the doctor. Young, I have said she ought to be, but youthful would be a better word. If, as she grows older, the nurse loses the strenuous enthusiasm with which she made her first entrance into her work, scarcely any amount of conscientious devotion or experience will ever replace it; but there are fortunate people who seem never to grow old in this sense. It is always to be borne in mind that most of these patients are oversensitive, refined, and educated women, for whom the clumsiness, or want of neatness, or bad manners, or immodesty of a nurse may be a sore and steadily increasing trial. To be more or less isolated for two months in a room, with one constant attendant, however good, is hard enough for any one to endure; and certain quite small faults or defects in a nurse may make her a serious impediment to the treatment, because no mere technical training will dispense in the nurse any more than in the physician with those finer natural qualifications which make their training available. Overharshness is in some ways worse than overeasiness, because it makes less pleasant the relation between nurse and patient, and the latter should regard the former as her "next friend." Let the nurse, therefore, place upon the doctor the burden of decision in disputed matters; his position will not be injured with the patient by strict enforcement of the letter of the law, while the nurse's may be. But one nurse will suit one patient and not another: so that I never hesitate to change my nurse if she does not fit the case, and to change if necessary more than once.

The degree of seclusion should be prescribed from the first, and it is far better to find that the original rules may be profitably relaxed than to be obliged to draw the lines more strictly when the patient has at first been indulged. For instance, it is well to forbid the receipt of any letters from home, unless anxious relatives insist that the patient must have home news. In that case the letters should be mere bulletins, should contain nothing, no matter how trifling, that might annoy a too sensitive person, and, most important of all, should come to the nurse and by her be read to the patient.

CHAPTER V.

REST.

I have said more than once in the early chapters of this little volume that the treatment I wished to advise as of use in a certain range of cases was made up of rest, massage, electricity, and overfeeding. I said that the use of large amounts of food while at rest, more or less entire, was made possible by the practice of kneading the muscles and by moving them with currents able to effect this end. I desire now to discuss in turn the modes in which I employ rest, massage, and electricity, and, as I have promised, I shall take pains to give, in regard to these three subjects, the fullest details, because success in the treatment depends, I am sure, on the care with which we look after a number of things each in itself apparently of slight moment.

I have no doubt that many doctors have seen fit at times to put their patients at rest for great or small lengths of time, but the person who of all others within my knowledge used this means most, and used it so as to obtain the best results, was the late Professor Samuel Jackson. He was in the habit of making his patients remain in bed for many weeks at a time, and, if I recall his cases well, he used this treatment in just the class of disorders among women which have given me the best results. What these are I have been at some pains to define, and I have now only to show why in such people rest is of service, and what I mean by rest, and how I apply it.

In No. IV. of Dr. Séguin's series of American Clinical Lectures, I was at some pains to point out the value of repose in neuralgias, and especially sciatica, in myelitis, and in the early stages of locomotor ataxia, and I have since then had the pleasure of seeing these views very fully accepted. I shall now confine myself chiefly to its use in the various forms of weakness which exist with thin blood and wasting, with or without distinct lesions of the stomach, womb, or other organs.

Whether we shall ask a patient to walk or to take rest is a question which turns up for answer almost every day in practice. Most often we incline to insist on exercise, and are led to do so from a belief that many people walk too little, and that to move about a good deal every day is well for everybody. I think we are as often wrong as right. A good brisk daily walk is for well folks a tonic, breaks down old tissues, and creates a wholesome demand for food. The same is true for some sick people. The habit of horse exercise or a long walk every day is needed to cure or to aid in the cure of disordered stomach and costive bowels, but if all exertion gives rise only to increase of trouble, to extreme sense of fatigue, to nausea, to headache, what shall we do? And suppose that tonics do not help to make exertion easy, and that the great tonic of change of air fails us, shall we still persist? And here lies the trouble: there are women who mimic fatigue, who indulge themselves in rest on the least pretense, who have no symptoms so truly honest that we need care to regard them. These are they who spoil their own nervous systems as they spoil their children, when they have them, by yielding to the least desire and teaching them to dwell on little pains. For such people there is no help but to insist on self-control and on daily use of the limbs. They must be told to exert themselves, and made to do so if that can be. If they are young, this is easy enough. If they have grown to middle life, and created habits of self-indulgence, the struggle is often useless. But few, however, among these women are free from some defect of blood or tissue, either original or acquired as a result of years of indolence and attention to aches and ailments which should never have had given to them more than a passing thought, and which certainly should not have been made an excuse for the sofa or the bed.

Sometimes the question is easy to settle. If you find a woman who is in good condition as to color and flesh, and who is always able to do what it pleases her to do, and who is tired by what does not please her, that is a woman to order out of bed and to control with a firm and steady will. That is a woman who is to be made to walk, with no regard to her complaints, and to be made to persist until exertion ceases to give rise to the mimicry of fatigue. In such cases the man who can insure belief in his opinions and obedience to his decrees secures very often most brilliant and sometimes easy success; and it is in such cases that women who are in all other ways capable doctors fail, because they do not obtain the needed control over those of their own sex. I have been struck with this a number of times, but I have also seen that to be too long and too habitually in the hands of one physician, even the wisest, is for some cases of hysteria the main difficulty in the way of a cure,—it is so easy to disobey the familiar friendly attendant, so hard to do this where the physician is a stranger. But we all know well enough the personal value of certain doctors for certain cases. Mere hygienic advice will win a victory in the hands of one man and obtain no good results in those of another, for we are, after all, artists who all use the same means to an end but fail or succeed according to our method of using them. There are still other cases in which mischievous tendencies to repose, to endless tire, to hysterical symptoms, and to emotional displays have grown out of defects of nutrition so distinct that no man ought to think for these persons of mere exertion as a sole means of cure. The time comes for that, but it should not come until entire rest has been used, with other means, to fit them for making use of their muscles. Nothing upsets these cases like over-exertion, and the attempt to make them walk usually ends in some mischievous emotional display, and in creating a new reason for thinking that they cannot walk. As to the two sets of cases just sketched, no one need hesitate; the one must walk, the other should not until we have bettered her nutritive state. She may be able to drag herself about, but no good will be done by making her do so. But between these two classes, and allied by certain symptoms to both, lie the larger number of such cases, giving us every kind of real and imagined symptom, and dreadfully well fitted to puzzle the most competent physician. As a rule, no harm is done by rest, even in such people as give us doubts about whether it is or is not well for them to exert themselves. There are plenty of these women who are just well enough to make it likely that if they had motive enough for exertion to cause them to forget themselves they would find it useful. In the doubt I am rather given to insisting on rest, but the rest I like for them is not at all their notion of rest. To lie abed half the day, and sew a little and read a little, and be interesting as invalids and excite sympathy, is all very well, but when they are bidden to stay in bed a month, and neither to read, write, nor sew, and to have one nurse,—who is not a relative,—then repose becomes for some women a rather bitter medicine, and they are glad enough to accept the order to rise and go about when the doctor issues a mandate which has become pleasantly welcome and eagerly looked for. I do not think it easy to make a mistake in this matter unless the woman takes with morbid delight to the system of enforced rest, and unless the doctor is a person of feeble will. I have never met myself with any serious trouble about getting out of bed any woman for whom I thought rest needful, but it has happened to others, and the man who resolves to send any nervous woman to bed must be quite sure that she will obey him when the time comes for her to get up.

I have, of course, made use of every grade of rest for my patients, from repose on a lounge for some hours a day up to entire rest in bed. In milder forms of neurasthenic disease, in cases of slight general depression not properly to be called melancholias, in the lesser grades of pure brain-tire, or where this is combined with some physical debility, I often order a "modified" or "partial rest." A detailed schedule of the day is ordered for such patients, with as much minuteness of care as for those undergoing "full rest" in bed. Here the patient's or the household's usual hours may be consulted, a definite amount of time allotted to duties, business, and exercise, and certain hours left blank, to be filled, within limits, at the patient's discretion or that of the nurse.

So many nervous people are worried with indecision, with inability to make up their minds to the simplest actions, that to have the responsibility of choice taken away greatly lessens their burdens. It lessens, too, the burdens which may be placed upon them by outside action if they can refuse this or that because they are under orders as to hours.

The following is a skeleton form of such a schedule. The hours, the food, the occupations suggested in each one will vary according to the sex, age, position, desires, intelligence, and opportunities of the patient.

7:30 A.M. Cocoa, coffee, hot milk, beef extract, or hot water. Bath (temperature stated). Rough rub with towel or flesh-brush: bathing and rubbing may be done by attendant. Lie down a few minutes after finishing.

8:30 A.M. Breakfast in bed. (Detail as to diet. Tonic, aperient, malt extract as ordered.) May read letters, paper, etc., if eyes are good.

10–11 A.M. Massage, if required, is usually ordered one hour after breakfast; or Swedish movements are given at that time. An hour's rest follows massage. Less rest is needed after the movements. (Milk or broth after massage.)

12 P.M. Rise and dress slowly. If gymnastics or massage are not ordered, may rise earlier. May see visitors, attend to household affairs, or walk out.

1:30 P.M. Luncheon. (Malt, tonic, etc., ordered.) In invalids this should be the chief meal of the day. Rest, lying down, not in bed, for an hour after.

3 P.M. Drive (use streetcars or walk) one to two and a half hours. (Milk or soup on return.)

7 P.M. Supper. (Malt, tonic, etc., ordered; detail of diet.)

Bed at 10 P.M. Hot milk or other food at bedtime.

This schedule is modified for convalescent patients after rest-treatment by orders as to use of the eyes: letter writing is usually forbidden, walking distinctly directed or forbidden, as the case may require. It may be changed by putting the exercise, massage, or gymnastics in the afternoon, for example, and leaving the morning, as soon as the rest after breakfast is finished, for business. Men needing partial rest may thus find time to attend to their affairs.

If massage is not ordered, there is nothing in this routine which costs money, and I have found it apply usefully in the case of hospital and dispensary patients.

In carrying out my general plan of treatment in extreme cases it is my habit to ask the patient to remain in bed from six weeks to two months. At first, and in some cases for four or five weeks, I do not permit the patient to sit up, or to sew or write or read, or to use the hands in any active way except to clean the teeth. Where at first the most absolute rest is desirable, as in cases of heart disease, or where there is a floating kidney, I arrange to have the bowels and water passed while lying down, and the patient is lifted on to a lounge for an hour in the morning and again at bedtime, and then lifted back again into the newly made bed. In most cases of weakness, treated by rest, I insist on the patient being fed by the nurse, and, when well enough to sit up in bed, I order that the meats shall be cut up, so as to make it easier for the patient to feed herself.

In many cases I allow the patient to sit up in order to obey the calls of nature, but I am always careful to have the bowels kept reasonably free from costiveness, knowing well how such a state and the efforts it gives rise to enfeeble a sick person.

The daily sponging bath is to be given by the nurse, and should be rapidly and skillfully done. It may follow the first food of the day, the early milk, or cocoa, or coffee, or, if preferred, may be used before noon, or at bedtime, which is found in some cases to be best and to promote sleep.

For some reason, the act of bathing, or even the being bathed, is mysteriously fatiguing to certain invalids, and if so I have the general sponging done for a time but thrice a week.

Most of these patients suffer from use of the eyes, and this makes it needful to prohibit reading and writing, and to have all correspondence carried on through the nurse. But many neurasthenic people also suffer from being read to, or, in other words, from any prolonged effort at attention. In these cases it will be found that if the nurse will read the morning paper, and as she does so relate such news as may be of interest, the patient will bear it very well, and will by degrees come to endure the hearing of such reading as is already more or less familiar.

Usually, after a fortnight I permit the patient to be read to,— one to three hours a day,—but I am daily amazed to see how kindly nervous and anemic women take to this absolute rest, and how little they complain of its monotony. In fact, the use of massage and the battery, with the frequent comings of the nurse with food, and the doctor's visits, seem so to fill up the day as to make the treatment less tiresome than might be supposed. And, besides this, the sense of comfort which is apt to come about the fifth or sixth day,—the feeling of ease, and the ready capacity to digest food, and the growing hope of final cure, fed as it is by present relief,—all conspire to make most patients contented and tractable.

The intelligent and watchful physician must, of course, know how far to enforce and when to relax these rules. When it is needful, as it sometimes is, to prolong the state of rest to two or three months, the patient may need at the close occupation of some kind, and especially such as, while it does not tax the eyes, gives the hands something to do, the patient being, we suppose, by this time able to sit up in bed during a part of the day.

The moral uses of enforced rest are readily estimated. From a restless life of irregular hours, and probably endless drugging, from hurtful sympathy and over-zealous care, the patient passes to an atmosphere of quiet, to order and control, to the system and care of a thorough nurse, to an absence of drugs, and to simple diet. The result is always at first, whatever it may be afterwards, a sense of relief, and a remarkable and often a quite abrupt disappearance of many of the nervous symptoms with which we are all of us only too sadly familiar.

All the moral uses of rest and isolation and change of habits are not obtained by merely insisting on the physical conditions needed to effect these ends. If the physician has the force of character required to secure the confidence and respect of his patients, he has also much more in his power, and should have the tact to seize the proper occasions to direct the thoughts of his patients to the lapse from duties to others, and to the selfishness which a life of invalidism is apt to bring about. Such moral medication belongs to the higher sphere of the doctor's duties, and, if he means to cure his patient permanently, he cannot afford to neglect them. Above all, let him be careful that the masseuse and the nurse do not talk of the patient's ills, and let him by degrees teach the sick person how very essential it is to speak of her aches and pains to no one but himself.

I have often asked myself why rest is of value in the cases of which I am now speaking, and I have already alluded briefly to some of the modes in which it is of use.

Let us take first the simpler cases. We meet now and then with feeble people who are dyspeptic, and who find that exercise after a meal, or indeed much exercise on any day, is sure to cause loss of power or lessened power to digest food. The same thing is seen in an extreme degree in the well-known experiment of causing a dog to run violently after eating, in which case digestion is entirely suspended. Whether these results be due to the calling off of blood from the gastric organs to the muscles, or whether the nervous system is, for some reason, unable to evolve at the same time the force needed for a double purpose, is not quite clear, but the fact is undoubted, and finds added illustrations in many of the class of exhausted women. It is plain that this trouble exists in some of them. It is likely that it is present in a larger number. The use of rest in these people admits of no question. If we are to give them the means in blood and flesh of carrying on the work of life, it must be done with the aid of the stomach, and we must humor that organ until it is able to act in a more healthy manner under ordinary conditions. It may be wise to add that occasional cases of nervousness or of nervous disturbance of digestion are seen in which the patient assimilates food better if permitted to move about directly after a meal; and I recall one instance of very persistent gastric catarrh where the uncomfortable symptoms following meals only began to disappear when as an experiment the patient was ordered to take a quiet half-hour's stroll after each meal, instead of the rest usually ordered.

I am often asked how I can expect by such a system to rest the organs of mind. No act of will can force them to be at rest. To this I should answer that it is not the mere half-automatic intellectuation which is harmful in men or women subject to states of feebleness or neurasthenia, and that the systematic vigorous use of mind on distinct problems is within some form of control. It is thought with the friction of worry which injures, and unless we can secure an absence of this, it is vain to hope for help by the method I am describing. The man harassed by business anxieties, the woman with morbidly-developed or ungoverned maternal instincts, will only illustrate the causes of failure. Perhaps in all dubious cases Dr. Playfair's rule is not a bad one, to consider, and to let the patient consider, this mode of treatment as a hopeful experiment, which may have to be abandoned, and which is valueless without the cordial and submissive assistance of the patient.

The muscular system in many of such patients—I mean in ever-weary, thin, and thin-blooded persons—is doing its work with constant difficulty. As a result, fatigue comes early, is extreme, and lasts long. The demand for nutritive aid is ahead of the supply, or else the supply is incompetent as to quality, and before the tissues are re-builded a new demand is made, so that the materials of disintegration accumulate, and do this the more easily because the eliminative organs share in the general defects. And these are some of the reasons why anemic people are always tired; but, besides this, all real sensations are magnified by women whose nervous systems have become sensitive owing to a life of attention to their ailments, and so at last it becomes hard to separate the true from the false, and we are thus led to be too skeptical as to the presence of real causes of annoyance. Certain it is that rest, under proper conditions, is found by such sufferers to be a great relief; but rest alone will not answer, and it is needful, as I shall show, to bring to our help certain other means, in order to secure all the good which repose may be made to insure.

In dealing with this, as with every other medical means, it is well to recall that in our attempts to help we may sometimes do harm, and we must make sure that in causing the largest share of good we do the least possible evil.

The one goes with the other, as shadow with light, and to no therapeutic measure does this apply more surely than to the use of rest.

Let us take the simplest case,—that which arises daily in the treatment of joint troubles or broken bones. We put the limb in splints, and thus, for a time, check its power to move. The bone knits, or the joint gets well; but the muscles waste, the skin dries, the nails may for a time cease to grow, nutrition is brought down, as an arithmetician would say, to its lowest terms, and when the bone or joint is well we have a limb which is in a state of disease. As concerns broken bones, the evil may be slight and easy of relief, if the surgeon will but remember that when joints are put at rest too long they soon fall a prey to a form of arthritis, which is the more apt to be severe the older the patient is, and may be easily avoided by frequent motion of the joints, which, to be healthful, exact a certain share of daily movement. If, indeed, with perfect stillness of the fragments we could have the full life of a limb in action, I suspect that the cure of the break might be far more rapid.

What is true of the part is true of the whole. When we put the entire body at rest we create certain evils while doing some share of good, and it is therefore our part to use such means as shall, in every case, lessen and limit the ills we cannot wholly avoid. How to reach these ends I shall by and by state, but for a brief space I should like to dwell on some of the bad results which come of our efforts to reach through rest in bed all the good which it can give us, and to these points I ask the most thoughtful attention, because upon the care with which we meet and provide for them depends the value which we will get out of this most potent means of treatment.

When we put patients in bed and forbid them to rise or to make use of their muscles, we at once lessen appetite, weaken digestion in many cases, constipate the bowels, and enfeeble circulation.

When we put the muscles at absolute rest we create certain difficulties, because the normal acts of repeated movement insure a certain rate of nutrition which brings blood to the active parts, and without which the currents flow more largely around than through the muscles. The lessened blood supply is a result of diminished functional movement, and we need to create a constant demand in the inactive parts. But, besides this, every active muscle is practically a throbbing heart, squeezing its vessels empty while in motion, and relaxing, so as to allow them to fill up anew. Thus, both for itself and in its relations to the areolar spaces and to the rest of the body, its activity is functionally of service. Then, also, the vessels, unaided by changes of posture and by motion, lose tone, and the distant local circuits, for all of these reasons, cease to receive their normal supply, so that defects of nutrition occur, and, with these, defects of temperature.

I was struck with the extent to which these evils may go, in the case of Mrs. P. aet. 52, who was brought to me from New Jersey, having been in bed fifteen years. I soon knew that she was free of grave disease, and had stayed in bed at first because there was some lack of power and much pain on rising, and at last because she had the firm belief that she could not walk. After a week's massage I made her get up. I had won her full trust, and she obeyed, or tried to obey me, like a child. But she would faint and grow deadly pale, even if seated a short time. The heartbeats rose from sixty to one hundred and thirty, and grew feeble; the breath came fast, and she had to lie down at once. Her skin was dry, sallow, and bloodless, her muscles flabby; and when, at last, after a fortnight more, I set her on her feet again, she had to endure for a time the most dreadful vertigo and alarming palpitations of the heart, while her feet, in a few minutes of feeble walking, would swell so as to present the most strange appearance. By and by all this went away, and in a month she could walk, sit up, sew, read, and, in a word, live like others. She went home a well-cured woman.

Let us think, then, when we put a person in bed, that we are lessening the heartbeats some twenty a minute, nearly a third; that we are causing the tardy blood to linger in the by-ways of the blood-round, for it has its byways; that rest in bed binds the bowels, and tends to destroy the desire to eat; and that muscles at rest too long get to be unhealthy and shrunken in substance. Bear these ills in mind, and be ready to meet them, and we shall have answered the hard question of how to help by rest without hurt to the patient.

When I first made use of this treatment I allowed my patients to get up too suddenly, and in some cases I thus brought on relapses and a return of the feeling of painful fatigue. I also saw in some of these cases what I still see at times under like circumstances—a rapid loss of flesh.

I now begin by permitting the patient to sit up in bed, then to feed herself, and next to sit up out of bed a few minutes at bedtime. In a week, she is desired to sit up fifteen minutes twice a day, and this is gradually increased until, at the end of six to twelve weeks, she rests on the bed only three to five hours daily. Even after she moves about and goes out, I insist for two months on absolute repose at least two or three hours daily, and this must be understood to mean seclusion as well as bodily quiet, free from the intrusion of household cares, visitors, or any form of emotion or excitement, pleasurable or otherwise. In cases of long-standing it may be desirable to continue this period of isolation and to order as well an hour's lying down after each meal for many months, in some such methodical way as is suggested in the schedule.

The use of a hammock is found by some people to be a very agreeable change from the bed during a part of the day.

The physician who discharges his patient when she rises from her bed after her two or three months' treatment, or who neglects to consider the moral and mental needs and aspects of each case, will find that many will relapse. Even when the patient has left the direct care of the doctor and returned to home and its avocations she will find help and comfort in the knowledge that she can apply to him if necessary, and it is well to hold some sort of relation by occasional visits or correspondence, however brief, for six months or a year after treatment has been completed.

CHAPTER VII.

ELECTRICITY.

Electricity is the second means which I have made use of for the purpose of exercising muscles in persons at rest. It has also an additional value, of which I shall presently speak.

In order to exercise the muscles best and with the least amount of pain and annoyance, we make use of an induction current, with interruptions as slow as one in every two to five seconds, a rate readily obtained in properly-constructed batteries.[1] This plan is sure to give painless exercise, but it is less rapid and less complete as to the quality of the exercise caused than the movements evolved by very rapid interruptions. These, in the hands of a clever operator who knows his anatomy well, are therefore, on the whole, more satisfactory, but they require some experience to manage them so as not to shock and disgust the patient by inflicting needless pain. The poles, covered with absorbent cotton well wetted with salt water, which may be readily changed, so as not to use the same material more than once, are placed on each muscle in turn, and kept about four inches apart. They are moved fast enough to allow of the muscles being well contracted, which is easily managed, and with sufficient speed, if the assistant be thoroughly acquainted with the points of Ziemssen. The smaller electrode should cover the motorpoint and the larger be used upon an indifferent area. After the legs are treated, the muscles of the belly and back and loins are gone over systematically, and finally those of the chest and arms. The face and neck are neglected. About forty minutes to an hour are needed; but at first a less time is employed. The general result is to exercise in turn all the external muscles.[2]

No such obvious and visible results are seen as we observe after massage, but the thermal changes are much more constant and remarkable, and show at least that we are not dealing with an agent which merely amuses the patient or acts alone through some mysterious influence on the mental status.

A half-hour's treatment of the muscles commonly gives rise to a marked elevation of temperature, which fades away within an hour or two. This effect is, like that from massage, most notable in persons liable to fever from some organic trouble, and it varies as to its degree in individuals who have no such disease.

The first case, Miss B., aet. 20, is an example of tubercular disease of the apex of the right lung. She had a morning temperature of 98½° to 99½°, and an evening temperature of 100° to 102°.

Mrs. R., aet. 40, the next case, was merely a rather anemic, feeble,

---

[1] Most induction batteries are without any arrangement for making infrequent breaks in the current.
[2] In the extreme constipation of certain hysterical women, good may be done by placing one conductor in the rectum and moving the other over the abdomen so as to cause full movement of the muscles. This means must at first be employed cautiously, and the amount of electricity carefully increased. It is doubtful if any movement of the intestinal muscle fibers is thus caused, but that it is a useful method of stimulation in obstinate cases may be taken as proved.

and thin woman, who for years had not been able to endure any prolonged effort. She got well under the general treatment, gaining thirteen pounds on a weight of ninety-eight pounds, her height being five feet and one inch. The facts as to rise of temperature are most remarkable, and, I need not say, were carefully observed.

The third case, Miss M., aet. 33, was that of a pallid woman, the daughter of a well-known physician in the South. She suffered for six years with "nervous exhaustion," headaches, pain in the back, intense depression of spirits, nausea, and repeated attacks of hysteria. She slept only under anodynes, and used stimulants freely. Under the use of rest and the adjuvant treatment described, Miss M. made a thorough recovery, and was restored to useful active life.

Mrs. P., aet. 38, was a rather nervous woman, easily tired, but not anemic and not very thin. She improved greatly under the treatment.

Miss R., aet. 27, was a fair case of hysterical conditions; overuse of chloral and bromides; anorexia and loss of flesh and color.

I have given these full details because I have not seen elsewhere any statement of the rather remarkable phenomena which they exemplify. It may be that a part at least of the thermal change is due to the muscular action, although this seems hardly competent to account for any large share in the alteration of temperature, and we must look further to explain it fully. No mental excitement can be called upon as a cause, since it continues after the patient is perfectly accustomed to the process. I should add, also, that in most cases the subject of the experiment was kept in ignorance of the fact that a rise of the thermometer was to be expected. Is it not possible that the current even of an induction battery has the power so to stimulate the tissues as to cause an increase in the ordinary rate of disintegrative change? Perhaps a careful study of the secretions might lend force to this suggestion. That the muscular action produced by the battery is not essential to the increase of bodily heat is shown by the next set of facts to which I desire to call attention.

Some years ago, Messrs. Beard and Rockwell stated that when an induced current is used for fifteen to thirty minutes daily, one pole on the neck and one on either foot, or alternately on both, the persistent use of this form of treatment is decidedly tonic in its influence. I believe that in this opinion they were perfectly correct, and I am now able to show that, when thus employed, the induced current causes also a decided rise of temperature in many people, which proves at least that it is in some way an active agent, capable of positively influencing the nutritive changes of the body.

The rise of temperature thus caused is less constant, as well as less marked, than that occasioned by the muscle treatment. I do not think it necessary to give the tables in full. They show in the best cases rises of one-fifth to four-fifths of a degree F., and were taken with the utmost care to exclude all possible causes of error.

The mode of treatment is as follows: At the close of the muscle-electrization one pole is placed on the nape of the neck and one on a foot for fifteen minutes. Then the foot pole is shifted to the other foot and left for the same length of time.

The primary current is used, as being less painful, and the interruptions are made as rapid as possible, while the cylinder or control wires are adjusted so as to give a current which is not uncomfortable.

It is desirable to have electricity used by a practiced hand, but of late I have found that intelligent nurses may suffice, and this, of course, materially lessens the cost. In very timid or nervous people, or those who at some time have been severely "shocked" by the application of electricity in the hands of charlatans, it is common to find the patient greatly dreading a return to its use. In this case, if the battery be started and the poles moved about on the surface as usual, but without any connection being made, one of two things will happen,—either the patient will naturally find it very mild, and will submit fearlessly to a gentle and increasing treatment, or else her apprehensions will so dominate her as to cause her to complain of the effects as exciting or tiring her, or as spoiling her sleep. A few words of kindly explanation will suffice to show her how much expectation has to do with the apparent results, and she will be found, if the matter be managed with tact, to have learned a lesson of wide usefulness throughout her treatment.

However, there are occasional, though very rare, cases in which it is impossible to use faradism at all by reason of the insomnia and nervousness which result even after very careful and gentle application of the current. On the other hand, some patients find the effect of the electric application so soothing as to promote sleep, and will ask to have it repeated or regularly given in the evening.

J. J. ATKINSON

FROM

<u>PRIMAL LAW</u>

James Jasper Atkinson (1839–1899): Born to Scottish parents in India, James Jasper Atkinson moved to the French colony of New Caledonia at a young age. He was fascinated by the laws and customs of the colonized people and devoted his life to observing and analyzing them. He began his research while still unaware of the considerable anthropological work already in existence during his lifetime. Later, however, he joined the Anthropological Institute and turned his attention to the writings of anthropologists John McLennan, John Avebury, and others.

Atkinson was primarily interested in "primitive" families. His Primal Law concludes that sexual jealousy was the primary motive for the evolution of marriage and small families. Atkinson died in New Caledonia in 1899.

CHAPTER I

MAN IN THE BRUTAL STAGE

Mr. Darwin on the primitive relations of the sexes.—Primitive man monogamous or polygamous.—His jealousy.—Expulsion of young males.—The author's inferences as to the evolution of Primal Law.—A customary Rule of Conduct evolved.—Traces surviving in savage life.—The customs of Avoidance.—Custom of Exogamy arose in the animal stage.—Brother and Sister Avoidance.—The author's own observation of this custom in New Caledonia.—Strangeness of such a custom among houseless nomads in Australia.—Rapid decay under European influences.

"Man, as I have attempted to show, is certainly descended from some Apelike Creature. We may, indeed, conclude, from what we know of the jealousy of all Male Quadrupeds, armed as many of them are with special weapons for battling with their rivals, that promiscuous intercourse in a state of Nature is extremely improbable. Therefore, looking far enough back in the Stream of Time, and judging from the Social habits of Man as he now exists, the most probable view is that he aboriginally lived in small communities, each with a single wife, or, if powerful, with several, whom he jealously guarded against all other Men. Or he may not have been a social animal[1] and yet have lived with several wives like the Gorilla—for all the natives agree that but one adult male is seen in a band; when the young male grows up, a contest takes place for the mastery, and the strongest, by killing or driving out the others, establishes himself as head of the Community.

"Younger males, being thus expelled and wandering about, would, when at last successful in finding a partner, prevent too close interbreeding within the limits of the same family."

Mr. Darwin, in the foregoing sentences, affirms the improbability of Promiscuity in the Sexual Relations of Man during the Animal Stage, and, incidentally, the Unity of the Human Race in its origin. Both theories are contested. The following thesis, however, on the Genesis of Primal Law in Human Marriage, treats of a *conjectural* series of events in the Ascent of Man, events which involve a state of the intersexual relationships amidst our primitive ancestors identical with that portrayed in the *Descent of Man*. My essay includes further, as regards the continued evolution of society, the development of a theory, based on my "Primal Law," which, if correct, would seem also to confirm Mr. Darwin's ideas as to Unity of Origin.

I am content, for my part, to hope that my hypothesis, however novel some of its conclusions, is in its general tenor in accord with the views of so great a naturalist as Mr. Darwin. His exposition of the probable relations, within the family group, of the male and female prototypes of mankind, and more especially of the antagonistic attitude, *inter se*, of the older and younger males, is indeed literally prophetic of the Primal Law, whose existence I surmise. This law is

[1] Mr. Atkinson's theory is based on the idea that our supposed anthropoid ancestor was eminently unsocial.—Andrew Lang

the inevitable corollary of Mr. Darwin's statement, if Man was ever to emerge from the Brute. My theory, in fact, viewed as to its genesis, is simply evolved from a consideration of the potential results of the attitude of such creatures as our ancestors then were, when subjected to the effects of those changes of environment, which alone, to my deeming, could have fixed modifications towards the human type. Mr. Darwin's premises, indeed, as to the Early Social economy of our Race in the animal stage, inevitably entail, if progress was to be made, the evolution of law in regulation of Marriage relationship, having regard to the fierce sexual jealousy of the males, on the one hand, and on the other to the patent truth that in the peaceful aggregation of our ancestors alone lay the germ of Society.

This would above all be the case if, reasoning by analogy, we provisionally accept, as the probable nearest approach to man's direct ancestors, the actual Anthropoids. These, such as the Gorilla, are undoubtedly amongst the most unsocial of animals as regards the attitude of the adult males *inter se*. From the very difficulty of the problem of the congregation of such creatures in friendly unison within the group, we may infer that, in its solution, there will be found the key to the whole question of the Ascent from Brute to Man. In that ascent, Habit, the parent of Law, must have been conquered, and modified into the direction of novel Custom, a shock to the older economy of life. Again, the new rule of conduct, necessarily inchoate (considering the presumed feeble intellectuality of the creatures concerned, animals more or less brutish) must yet be of facile interpretation to its subjects, though, as befits *Homo alalus*, it must have been quite mute in operation. The new Rule of Conduct would not be expressed in terms of speech, a function, *ex hypothesi*, not yet evolved. The rule, as it was to my mind, I here propose to attempt to unfold as the "Primal Law"; hoping to show that therein lay the beginning of law and order, and that, whilst itself arising in a natural manner, in its incidental creation of a first standard of a possible right and wrong, it laid, so to speak, one of the foundations of that moral sense, which has seemed to place so wide a space between man and other creatures.

The prior existence of this law, in the semi-brutish stage of our physical and ethical evolution, might have been deductively evolved, even if no traces of it had remained to our day. It will be, however, my endeavor to point out that evidence of its existence (abundant as it appears to me) is to be found in certain obscure customs which are common to most actual savage races. The customs of so-called "avoidance" between near relations will have the principal interest for us, although primitive marriage and inheritance will be found of corroborative value. Survivals and myths can be shown to point to the undeniable occurrence of this "Primal Law" in the earlier life-history of the non-civilized peoples. The myths, however, may be merely early guesses about the unknown past of the race.

Amongst marriage customs that which has given rise to most discussion as regards its origin is "Exogamy" or marriage outside the family group, or outside the limit of the totem name. My general argument, as will be seen, places me in antagonism with all theories yet advanced on the subject. But Mr. Lang, in *Custom and Myth*, 1884 (p. 258), hazards, as his own impression, a conception of this matter which I will note—namely, that "Exogamy may be connected with some early idea of which we have lost touch," and he adds, "If we only knew the origin of the prohibition to marry within the *family*[1] all would be plain sailing." However utterly beyond human ken, in these our latter days, any truthful image of so remote a past may seem to be, it is yet precisely this hypothetic early idea which I hope to be able to expose. If I am correct, we shall find that it was connected with the sexual relations of primitive man, *whilst in the animal stage*, and especially with the mutual marital rights of the males within a group. Such idea in travail, hastened and sharpened by needs of environment, created issues which necessarily gave birth to a "Primal Law" prohibitory of marriage between certain members of a family or local group, and thus, in natural sequence, led to *forced* connubial union *beyond* its circle the family, or local group—that is, led to Exogamy. But if such was in reality the original order of succession in the growth of custom, it becomes evident that Exogamy as a *habit* (not as an expressed law) must have been of primordial evolution. Thus (in contradistinction to generally received opinion and to Mr. McLennan's theory in particular) Exogamy must have been a cause rather than an effect in relation to its ordinary concomitants, i.e., Female Infanticide as a custom, Polyandry as a fixed institution, and Totemism as connected with exogamous groups, within which mar-

[1] I ought to have said "within the community, whether local or of recognized kindred, indicated by the totem name."—A. L.

riage was forbidden. As thus my new hypothesis finds itself in opposition to those of recognized authorities, it is evident that it will require to account for all the facts if it is to hold its ground.

However convinced the author may be by the array of seemingly confirmatory details in favor of his hypothesis, it is possible that from their paucity they may yet to others seem to constitute but a feeble line of defensive proof. But if the theory shall prove in itself to have merit, this defect (arising, as I believe, from lack of general anthropological knowledge on my part, for I dwell "far from books") will quickly be remedied, for a hundred other details in favor of my view will be at once perceived by more experienced students. Should my hypothesis really furnish the clue to the problem of the prohibition to marry within the family name, or totem name, all the rest will doubtless become "plain sailing" in competent hands.

In any case before my conjecture is definitely laid aside as erroneous, it may, let us hope, be considered desirable to await fuller evidence as to the extent of the operation, in actual savage life, of that particular custom of "Avoidance" which I consider, in its inception, and as the earliest law, to have been a "vera causa" of widest operation in primitive social evolution. "Avoidance" is, however, today, a mere faint image of a remote past, and its genetic significance has utterly faded from among even those people who yet, with strange conservatism, still blindly yield an everyday obedience to it, in form at least. Belonging to a class of savage habits presenting features so extraordinary, "Avoidance between brother and sister" has ever been a puzzle to inquirers. This Avoidance is only the most obscure of all the numerous cases of the strange habit, but it is also that which, up to the present, seems least to have attracted the notice of anthropologists. In this class of custom, the Avoidance of which most frequent mention has been made in literature, is avoidance between mother-in-law and son-in-law, whereas that between brother and sister is to my knowledge but rarely mentioned. And yet, as far as my own experience goes (and it extends over more than a quarter of a century among primitive peoples in the South Seas), Avoidance of brother and sister is not only as common as, but infinitely more strict and severe in action than, the Avoidance of "Mothers-in-law." It is indeed probable that the very severity of observance has led to its being so little noticed. For by the action of this law, a brother and a sister, after childhood, are kept so far apart from one another, that only those who have actually lived long amidst natives can be expected to have had a chance of being aware of the restraints to intercourse between them. Even then it would be from some such casual occurrence as the accidental recontre of the two, placing them thus in sudden and unavoidable proximity to each other, which would lead to an observation, by an European, of their extraordinary attitude and behavior under such circumstances.

My own attention was primarily only drawn to this matter by noting the grave scandal and excitement caused in a native community by the momentary isolation, in a canoe, of a brother and sister. The affair became so very serious for the brother that he disappeared from the tribe for over a year. Indeed, the rigorous severity of this particular law in daily action is almost incredible. In New Caledonia, for instance, all intercourse between a brother and sister by speech or sign is absolutely prohibited from a very early age. Whilst the girl will remain in the paternal home, the boy, at the age of seven or eight (when not, as is usual, adopted by the maternal uncle), only comes there for his meals, partaken again solely with the other males. He dwells until married in the large general bachelors' hut, set apart for youths in all villages. Even after marriage, if brother and sister have to communicate with each other on family matters, such communication must be made through the intermediary of a third person, nor can the sister enter the brother's hut even after his marriage, despite the presence of her sister-in-law therein. If the two should unexpectedly meet in some narrow path, the girl will throw herself face downwards into the nearest bush, whilst the boy will pass without turning his head, and as if unaware of her presence.

They cannot mention each other's names, and if the sister's name is mentioned publicly before the brother, he will show much embarrassment, and if it is repeated he will retire precipitately. She can eat nothing he has carried or cooked. Whilst, then, such propinquity as is implied in the mutual habitation of the same hut by these two would be scandalously impossible, it is not uncommon to find a mother-in-law and son-in-law, whilst in Avoidance, living under the same roof. It is obvious that in the latter case each detail of "Avoidance" in act or speech would be easily remarked by Europeans, whereas no chance of such observation between the adult brother and sister could possibly arise, they being kept, as we see, so utterly apart. It is to be noted, however, that the seemingly instinctive natural affection between two so nearly related is not quenched by these strange restraints. They remain interested in each other's welfare, and in cases of sickness, for instance, keep themselves informed of each other's condition through third persons. So great, however, is the depth in action (on these lines) of the feeling of avoidance in this matter, that I am convinced that the infanticide of twins, which only takes place in New Caledonia when the children are of different sexes, arises from the idea of a too close propinquity in the womb. Further evidence as to the very widespread existence of this custom in the South Seas I will leave to a later stage, only noting here that I have been astonished to find, in answer to inquiries, that it is well recognized amongst the aborigines of Australia.

[Mr. Atkinson has left a blank space for an expected communication from the late Mr. Curr. On "Avoidance" in Australia, between brother and sister, Messrs. Spencer and Gillen write: "A curious custom exists with regard to the mutual behavior of elder and younger sisters and their brothers. A man may speak freely to his elder sisters in blood, but those who are tribal *Ungaraitcha* must only be spoken to at a considerable distance. To younger sisters, blood and tribal, he may not speak, or, at least, only at such a distance that the features are indistinguishable. . . . We cannot discover any explanation of this restriction in regard to the younger sister; it can hardly be supposed that it has anything to do with the dread of anything like incest, else why is there not as strong a restriction in the case of the elder sisters?"]

Now the occurrence of this particular habit amidst a race of nomad hunters, forced by the exigencies of the chase to wander about in isolated groups, composed for the most part of single families, and where the separation of the sexes cannot possibly be arranged, as with the hut and village dwelling Caledonians, is a most remarkable fact. When we take into consideration the disturbing effects of such an avoidance in the internal economy of such a family circle, the significance of the circumstance is great as regards our general argument. It becomes, indeed, evident that the fundamental cause of the custom involving this daily and hourly dislocation of domestic life, must lie very deep in savage society. If, however, our theory as to the idea which dominated the inception of this strange habit shall turn out to be correct, then it will be seen that no surprise need be felt, if the genesis of this rule should prove to be in the animal stage, that traces of the superstructure should exist to our day. Now that attention will perhaps be more closely drawn to this, till recently the least observed of the cases of Avoidance, I feel sure that proof of its existence will be found in abundance in the present or past of all primitive peoples.[1] In view of its unexpectedly wide dissemination in Australia, hope may be felt that research will find it as a working factor in many peoples where its presence has been least expected, and not only in Australasia. It is possible that a stricter examination of the inner life of lower races in Africa and Asia will allow a perfectly legitimate inference that they are still under the influence of its effect, although the custom itself may be no longer in actual force. It is also possible, as I have said, that Survivals and Myths may point conclusively to its having had its day amongst the highest nations, with whom all traditions of it have been lost before the dawn of history. [Rather the reverse is the case; see the marriage of Zeus and Hera, brother and sister, and of the Incas, &c.—A. L.]

In many cases philological evidence based on the derivation of the root syllable of the word "sister," a word which in the tongues of peoples still obedient to this law is from a root implying "Avoidance," may afford affirmative proof, as circumstantial as unexpected, that this custom was once as universal as my theory would require.[2] If difficulty is felt in the acceptation of an hypothesis of such wide significance, simply based on an obscure lower custom so little noted in anthropological literature as to permit doubts of its existence, I can only repeat that a cognizance of the traits of this particular habit of avoidance and its effect as a factor in savage life demands such conditions of residence and chances of observation, as can fall to the lot of few. I may add that it is one of the very first customs to disappear after contact with whites, especially missionaries, being, as it is, in such extreme divergence with the economy of the European family, in regard to the mutual attitude of brother and sister.

It is more than a quarter of a century since the author had his attention first drawn to the practice. The evolution of the idea of its possible identity with the Primal Law has led to a continued and close observation; he is thus able to certify as to its rapid disappearance.

---

[1] Mr. Atkinson's forecast was correct. Brother and sister avoidance is very widely diffused.—A. L.
[2] The author does not give examples of words for "sister" implying avoidance. But we elsewhere show that in Lifu (Melanesia) the word for "sister" means "not to be touched."—A. L.

Brother and sister avoidance was at that time, thirty years ago, quite universal in New Caledonia; now in many places it is unknown, even as a tradition, among the younger aborigines. In view of the probability of a similar oblivion among other peoples, the immediate collection of evidence is urgent, and further delay seems dangerous and even culpable.

Thus, however much to the present advantage of the theory as regards the custom it would have been to cull larger proofs from that vast field of literature only to be procured in older lands, it has seemed desirable to make this thesis public without further delay. As we have said, if the theory is correct, wider students will bring forward cogent facts in further proof from existing knowledge, whilst continued research should afford evidence so complete of the widespread existence of the custom in the present and past of the human race, as to render my speculation as to its origin less seemingly illegitimate.[1]

---

[1] Other speculations have now been advanced, especially by Mr. Crawley.—A. L.

HAVELOCK ELLIS

FROM

STUDIES IN THE PSYCHOLOGY OF SEX: SEXUAL INVERSION

Henry Havelock Ellis (1859–1939): Born in Croydon, England, Havelock Ellis was a teacher in Australia by the age of nineteen. He soon developed an interest in medicine and trained to become a physician in London. During his training as a medical assistant, he attended a number of women in labor. Though Ellis received his medical degree in 1889, he never practiced. Instead he turned to writing and editing for English journals on literary and social subjects. Later he published numerous books on subjects that varied from The Soul of Spain *(1908) to* A Study of British Genius *(1904) to* The World of Dreams *(1911).*

Despite his varying interests, Ellis's fame derives from his work on sexuality. He was married for twenty-five years to Edith Lees Ellis, believed to be a lesbian. Despite this fact, his marriage was emotionally satisfying, as was his extramarital relationship with Francoise Delisle. Both relationships led him to emphasize the interrelation of love and sex. Expanding on the work begun by Krafft-Ebing, and influenced by the Breuer-Freud studies on hysteria, Ellis's contributions to the field of sexuality were enormous. His was the first distinguished scientific book on homosexuality (Sexual Inversion, *1897). His own work the subject of a vicious trial, Ellis crusaded vigorously against sex-censorship. He also researched masturbation. (Sigmund Freud described auto-eroticism as "the happy term invented by Havelock Ellis.") Like Freud, Ellis formulated many psychological theories about sex and eroticism, which he described in the seven-volume* Studies in the Psychology of Sex *(1897–1928). He believed that male sexuality was essentially aggressive and sadistic and that female sexuality was passive and masochistic. Ellis died in Suffolk in 1939.*

CHAPTER V.

THE NATURE OF SEXUAL INVERSION.

Analysis of Histories—Race—Heredity—General Health—
First Appearance of Homosexual Impulse—Sexual Precocity
and Hyperesthesia—Suggestion and Other Exciting Causes of
Inversion—Masturbation—Attitude Toward Women—Erotic
Dreams—Methods of Sexual Relationship—Pseudo-sexual
Attraction—Physical Sexual Abnormalities—Artistic and Other
Aptitudes—Moral Attitude of the Invert.

Before stating briefly my own conclusions as to the nature of sexual
inversion, I propose to analyze the facts brought out in the histories which I have been able to study.[1]

Race.—All my cases, 49 in number, are British and American.
Ancestry, from the point of view of race, was not made a matter of
special investigation. It appears, however, that at least 29 are English
or mainly English; at least 5 are Scotch or of Scotch extraction; 1 is
Irish and 2 others largely Irish; 4 have German fathers or mothers;
another is of German descent on both sides, while another is of remote German extraction; 2 are partly French. Except the presence of
the German element, there is nothing remarkable in this ancestry. I
am inclined to think that the presence of the German element is not
accidental. Apart from the fact that the study of inversion has been
mainly carried on in Germany, we may bear in mind the fact, well
brought out in Raffalovich's interesting discussion of "German
friendship," that there is a marked tendency for German friendship
to assume a sexually emotional warmth.

Heredity.—It is always difficult to deal securely with the significance of heredity, or even to establish a definite basis of facts. I have
by no means escaped this difficulty, for in most cases I have not even
had an opportunity of cross-examining the subjects whose histories I
have obtained. Still, the facts, so far as they emerge, have some interest. I possess some record of heredity in 41 of my cases. Of these,
not less than 14 assert that they have reason to believe that other

---

[1] The following analysis is based on somewhat fuller versions of my histories than it was necessary
to publish in the preceding chapters, as well as on various other histories which I was unable to
publish at all. Numerous apparent discrepancies may thus be explained.

cases of inversion have occurred in their families, and, while in some it is only a strong suspicion, in others there is no doubt whatever.[1] In one case there is reason to suspect inversion on both sides. Eighteen, so far as can be ascertained, belong to reasonably healthy families; minute investigation would probably reduce the number of these, and it is noteworthy that even in some of the healthy families there was only one child born of the parents' marriage. In 17 cases there is more or less frequency of morbidity or abnormality—eccentricity, alcoholism, neurasthenia, or nervous disease—in one or both sides, in addition to inversion or apart from it. In some of these cases the inverted offspring is the outcome of the union of a very healthy with a thoroughly morbid stock; in some others there is a minor degree of abnormality on both sides.

I do not attach great importance to these results. I am fairly certain that thorough investigation would very considerably enlarge the proportion of cases with morbid heredity. At the same time this enlargement would be chiefly obtained by bringing minor abnormalities to the front, and it would then have to be shown how far the families of average or normal persons are free from such abnormalities. The apologist of sexual inversion asks: What family is free from neuropathic taint? At present it is difficult to answer this question precisely. I believe that a fairly large proportion of families are free from such taint, but it seems probable that the families to which the inverted belong do not usually present such profound signs of nervous degeneration as we were formerly led to suppose. What we vaguely call "eccentricity" is common among them; insanity is much rarer.

General Health.—It is possible to speak with more certainty of the health of the individual than of that of his family. Of the 49 cases, 31—or about two-thirds—may be said to enjoy good, and sometimes even very good, health, though occasionally there is some slight qualification to be made. In 14 cases the health is delicate, or at best only fair; in these cases there is sometimes a tendency to consumption, and often marked neurasthenia and a more or less unbalanced temperament. Three cases (Nos. II, III, XXXV) are morbid to a consid-

---

[1] This hereditary character of inversion is a fact of great significance, and, as it occurs in cases with which I am well acquainted, I can have no doubt concerning the existence of the tendency. The influence of suggestion may often be entirely excluded, especially when the persons are of different sex. Both Krafft-Ebing and Moll have noted a similar tendency; see, *e.g.*, Moll, *Konträre Sexualempfindung*, 1899, p. 364.

erable degree; the remaining case (XXX) has had insane delusions which required treatment in an asylum. At least 13, who are included among those as having either good or fair health, may be described as of extremely nervous temperament, and in most cases they so describe themselves; a certain proportion of these—at least 7—combine great physical and, especially, mental energy with this nervousness; all these are doubtless of neurotic temperament. Only 2 or 3 of the cases can be said to be conspicuously lacking in energy. On the whole, therefore, a very large proportion of these inverted individuals are passing through life in an unimpaired state of health, which enables them to do at least their fair share of work in the world; in a very considerable proportion of my cases that work is of high intellectual value. Only in 4 cases, it will be seen, or at most 5, can the general health be said to be distinctly bad.

This result may, perhaps, seem surprising. It must, however, be remembered that my cases do not, on the whole, represent the class which alone the physician is usually able to bring forward: *i.e.*, the sexual inverts who are suffering from a more or less severe degree of complete nervous breakdown.

First Appearance of Homosexual Instinct.—Out of 43 cases, in 4 the instinct veered round to the same sex in adult age; in 3 of these there had been a love-disappointment with a woman; no other cause than this can be assigned for the transition; but it is noteworthy that in at least 2 of these cases the sexual instinct is undeveloped or morbidly weak, while the third individual is of somewhat weak *physique*, and the fourth has long been in delicate health. In another case (No. XXXV), also somewhat morbid, the development was rather more complicated.

In 39 cases the abnormal instinct began in early life, without previous attraction to the opposite sex. In 17 of these it dates from about puberty, usually beginning at school. In 24 cases the tendency began before puberty: *i.e.*, in 16 between the ages of 5 and 11, usually between 7 and 9, while in the other 8 the instinct began to manifest itself as early as the subject can remember. It must not be supposed that, in these numerous cases of the early appearance of homosexuality, the manifestations were of a specifically physical character, although erections are noted in a few cases. For the most part sexual manifestations at this early age, whether homosexual or heterosexual, are purely psychic. Their general character may be judged from 3 cases—two in men, the other in a woman (XIII, XXV, XLII)—in which I have stated the evolution of the instinct in some detail.[1]

Sexual Precocity and Hyperesthesia.—It is a fact of considerable interest and significance that in so large a number of my cases there was distinct precocity of the sexual emotions, both on the physical and psychic sides. There can be little doubt that, as many previous observers have found, inversion tends strongly to be associated with sexual precocity. I think it may further be said that sexual precocity tends to encourage the inverted habit where it exists. Why this should be so is obvious, if we believe—as there is some reason for believing—that at an early age the sexual instinct is comparatively undifferentiated in its manifestations. The precocious accentuation of the sexual impulse leads to definite crystallization of the emotions at a premature stage. It must be added that precocious sexual energy is likely to remain feeble, and that a feeble sexual energy adapts itself more easily to homosexual relationships, in which there is no definite act to be accomplished, than to normal relationships. It is difficult to say how many of my cases exhibit sexual weakness. In 3 or 4 it is evident, and it may be suspected in many others, especially in those who are, and often describe themselves as, "sensitive" or "nervous." In some cases there is marked hyperesthesia, or irritable weakness. Hyperesthesia simulates strength, and, while there can be little doubt that some sexual inverts do possess unusual sexual energy, in others it is but apparent; the frequent repetition of seminal emissions, for example, may be the result of weakness as well as of strength.[2] It must be added that this irritability of the sexual centers is, in a considerable proportion of inverts, associated with marked emotional tendencies to affection and self-sacrifice. In the extravagance of his affection and

[1] In this connection I may quote an observation by Mr. Raffalovich: "It is natural that the invert should very clearly recall the precocity of his inclinations. In the existence of every invert a moment arrives when he discovers the enigma of his homosexual tastes. He then classes all his recollections, and to justify himself in his own eyes he remembers that he has been what he is from his earliest childhood. Homosexuality has colored all his young life; he has thought over it, dreamed over it, reflected over it—very often in perfect innocence. When he was quite small he imagined that he had been carried off by brigands, by savages; at five or six he dreamed of the warmth of their chests and of their naked arms. He dreamed that he was their slave and he loved his slavery and his masters. He has had not the least thought that is crudely sexual, but he has discovered his sentimental vocation."

[2] A certain association between sexual weakness and homosexuality may be seen in the homosexual tendencies of old men, who no longer possess the power of effecting normal coitus.

devotion, as has been frequently observed, the male invert frequently resembles the normal woman.

Suggestion and Other Exciting Causes of Inversion.—In 13 of my cases—*i.e.*, in about a quarter—there is reason to believe that some event, or special environment, in early life had more or less influence in turning the sexual instinct into homosexual channels, or in calling out a latent inversion. In 3 cases a disappointment in normal love seems to have produced a profound nervous and emotional shock, acting, as we seem bound to admit, on a predisposed organism, and developing a fairly permanent tendency to inversion. In 5 cases there was seduction by an older person, but in at least 1 or 2 of these there was already a well-marked predisposition. In 5 other cases, example, usually at school, may probably be regarded as having exerted some influence. It is noteworthy that in very few of my cases can we trace the influence of any definite "suggestion," as asserted by Schrenck-Notzing, who believes that, in the causation of sexual inversion (as undoubtedly in the causation of erotic fetichism), we must give the first place to "accidental factors of education and external influence." He records the case of a little boy who innocently gazed in curiosity at the penis of his father who was urinating, and had his ears boxed, whence arose a train of thought and feeling which resulted in complete sexual inversion. In the very detailed history of Case XXVI we have a parallel incident, and here we see clearly that the homosexual tendency already existed. I do not question the occurrence of such incidents, but I refuse to accept them as supplying the causation of inversion, and in so doing I am supported by all the evidence I am able to obtain. I am in agreement with a correspondent who wrote:—

> "Considering that all boys are exposed to the same order of suggestions (sight of a man's naked organs, sleeping with a man, being handled by a man), and that only a few of them become sexually perverted, I think it reasonable to conclude that those few were previously constituted to receive the suggestion. In fact, suggestion seems to play exactly the same part in the normal and abnormal awakening of sex."

I would go so far as to assert that for normal boys and girls the developed sexual organs of the adult man or woman—from their size, hairiness, and the mystery which envelops them—nearly always exert a certain fascination, whether of attraction or horror.[1] But this has no connection with homosexuality, and scarcely with sexuality at all. Thus, in one case known to me, a boy of six or seven took pleasure in caressing the organs of another boy, twice his own age, who remained passive and indifferent; yet this child grew up without ever manifesting any homosexual instinct. The seed of suggestion can only develop when it falls on a suitable soil. If it is to act on a fairly normal nature the perverted suggestion must be very powerful or iterated, and even then its influence will probably only be temporary, disappearing in the presence of the normal stimulus.[2]

I have, therefore, but little to say of the influence of suggestion, which has sometimes been exalted to a position of the first importance in books on sexual inversion. This is not because I underestimate the great part played by suggestion in many fields of normal and abnormal life. It is because I have been able to find but few decided traces of it in sexual inversion. In many cases, doubtless, there may be some slight elements of suggestion in developing the inversion, though they cannot be traced.[3] Their importance seems usually questionable even when they are discovered. Take Schrenck-Notzing's case of the little

[1] Leppmann mentions the case (certainly extreme and abnormal) of a little girl of 8 who spent the night hidden on the roof, merely in order to be able to observe in the morning the sexual organs of an adult male cousin (*Bulletin de l'Union Internationale de Droit Pénal*, 1896, p. 118).

[2] I may add that I see no fundamental irreconcilability between the point of view here adopted and the facts brought forward (and wrongly interpreted) by Schrenck-Notzing. In his *Beiträg zur Aetiologie der Conträrer Sexualempfindung* (Vienna, 1895), this writer states: "The neuropathic disposition is congenital, as is the tendency to precocious appearance of the appetites, the lack of psychic resistance, and the tendency to imperative associations; but that heredity can extend to the object of the appetite, and influence the contents of these characters, is not shown. Psychological experiences are against it, and the possibility, which I have shown, of changing these impulses by experiment and so removing their danger to the character of the individual." It need not be asserted that "heredity extends to the object of the appetite," but simply that heredity culminates in an organism which is sexually best satisfied by that object. It is also a mistake to suppose that congenital characters cannot be, in some cases, largely modified by such patient and laborious processes as those carried on by Schrenck-Notzing. In the same pamphlet this writer refers to moral insanity and idiocy as supporting his point of view. It is curious that both these congenital manifestations had independently occurred to me as arguments against his position. The experiences of Elmira Reformatory and Bicêtre show that both the morally insane and the idiotic can be greatly improved by appropriate treatment. Schrenck-Notzing seems to be unduly biased by his interest in hypnotism and suggestion.

[3] I fully admit, as all investigators must, the difficulty of tracing the influence of early suggestions, especially in dealing with persons who are unaccustomed to self-analysis. Sometimes it happens, especially in regard to erotic fetichism, that, while direct questioning fails to reach any early formative suggestion, such influence is casually elicited on a subsequent occasion.

boy whose ears were boxed for what his father considered improper curiosity. I find it difficult to realize that a mighty suggestion can thereby be generated unless a strong emotion exists for it to unite with; in that case the seed falls on prepared soil. Is the wide prevalence of normal sexuality due to the fact that so many little boys have had their ears boxed for taking naughty liberties with women? If so, I am quite prepared to accept Schrenck-Notzing's explanation as a complete account of the matter. I know of one case, indeed, in which an element of what may fairly be called suggestion can be detected. It is that of a physician who had always been on very friendly terms with men, but had sexual relations exclusively with women, finding fair satisfaction, until the confessions of an inverted patient one day came to him as a revelation; thereafter he adopted inverted practices and ceased to find any attraction in women. But even in this case, as I understand the matter, suggestion merely served to reveal his own nature to the man. For a physician to adopt the perverted habits which the visit of a chance patient suggests to him can scarcely be a phenomenon of pure suggestion. We have no reason to suppose that this physician practiced every perversion he heard of from patients; he adopted that which fitted his own nature.[1]

I may here quote three American cases (not previously published), for which I am indebted to the kindness of Prof. G. Frank Lydston, of Chicago. They seem to me to illustrate the only kind of suggestion which does play a common part in the evolution of inversion. I give them in Dr. Lydston's words:—

> Case I.—A man, 45 years of age, attracted by the allusion to my essay on "Social Perversion" contained in the English translation of Krafft-Ebing's *Psychopathia Sexualis*, consulted me regarding the possible cure of his condition. This individual was a finely educated, very intelligent man, who was an excellent linguist, had considerable musical ability, and was in the employ of a firm whose business was such as to demand on the part of its employees considerable legal acumen, clerical ability, and knowledge of real-estate transactions. This man stated that

[1] "If an invert acquires, under the influence of external conditions," Féré has lately written (*L'Instinct Sexuel*, p. 238), "it is because he was born with an aptitude for such acquisition: an aptitude lacking in those who have been subjected to the same conditions without making the same acquisitions."

at the age of puberty, without any knowledge of perversity of
sexual feeling, he was thrown intimately in contact with males
of more advanced years, who took various means to excite his
sexual passions, the result being that perverted sexual practices
were developed, which were continued for a number of years.
He thereafter noticed an aversion to women. At the solicita-
tions of his family he finally married, without any very intelligent idea as to what, if anything, might be expected of him
in the marital relation. Absolute impotence—indeed, repugnance for association with his wife—was the lamentable sequence. A divorce was in contemplation when, fortunately for
all parties concerned, the wife suddenly died. Being a man of
more than ordinary intelligence, this individual, prior to seeking my aid, had sought vainly for some remedy for his unfortunate condition. He stated that he believed that there was an
element of heredity in his case, his father having been a dip-
somaniac and one brother having died insane. He nevertheless
stated it to be his opinion that, notwithstanding the hereditary
taint, he would have been perfectly normal from a sexual standpoint had it not been for acquired impressions at or about the
period of puberty. This man presented a typically neurotic type
of *physique*, complained of being intensely nervous, was prematurely gray, of only fair stature, and had an uncontrollable
nystagmus, which, he said, had existed for some fifteen years.
As might be expected, treatment in this case was of no avail. I
began the use of hypnotic suggestion at the hands of an expert
professional hypnotist. The patient, being called out of the
State, finally gave up treatment, and I have no means of knowing what his present condition is.

Case II.—A lady patient of mine who happened to be an
actress, and consequently a woman of the world, brought to
me for an opinion some correspondence which had passed between her younger brother and a man living in another State,
with whom he was on quite intimate terms. In one of these
letters various flying trips to Chicago for the purpose of meeting the lad, who, by the way, was only seventeen years of age,
were alluded to. It transpired also, as evidenced by the letters,
that on several occasions the young lad had been taken on trips
in Pullman cars by his friend, who was a prominent railroad

official. The character of the correspondence was such as the average healthy man would address to a woman with whom he was enamored. It seemed that the author of the correspondence had applied to his boy affinity the name Cinderella, and the protestations of passionate affection that were made toward Cinderella certainly would have satisfied the most exacting woman. The young lad subsequently made a confession to me, and I put myself in correspondence with his male friend, with the result that he called upon me and I obtained a full history of the case. The method of indulgence in this case was the usual one of oral masturbation, in which the lad was the passive party. I was unable to obtain any definite data regarding the family history of the elder individual in this case, but understand that there was a taint of insanity in his family. He himself was a robust, fine-looking man, above middle age, who was well educated and very intelligent, as he necessarily must have been, because of the prominent position he held with an important railway company. I will state, as a matter of interest, that the lad in this case, who is now twenty-three years of age, has recently consulted me for *impotentia coëundi*, manifesting a frigidity for women, and, from the young man's statements, I am convinced that he is well on the road to confirmed sexual perversion.

An interesting point in this connection is that the young man's sister, the actress already alluded to, has recently had an attack of acute mania.

I have had other unpublished cases that might be of interest, but these two are somewhat classical, and typify to a greater or less degree the majority of other cases. I will, however, mention one other case, occurring in a woman.

Case III.—A married woman, 40 years of age. Has been deserted by her husband because of her perverted sexuality. Neurotic history on both sides of the family, and several cases of insanity on mother's side. In this case affinity for the same sex and perverted desire for the opposite sex existed, a combination by no means infrequent. Hypnotic suggestion tried, but without success. Cause was evidently suggestion and example on the part of another female pervert with whom she associated before marriage. Marriage was late, at age of 35.

In all these cases there was an element of what may be called suggestion, but it was really much more than this; it was probably in each case active seduction by an elder person of a predisposed younger person. It will be observed that in each case there was, at the least, an organic neurotic basis for suggestion and seduction to work on. I cannot regard these cases as entitled to modify the attitude I have here taken up.

Masturbation.—Moreau believed that masturbation was a cause of sexual inversion, and Krafft-Ebing looks upon it as leading to all sorts of sexual perversions; Dr. Conolly Norman is of the same opinion. Moll emphatically denies that masturbation can be the cause of inversion, though admitting that it may serve to strengthen it when already existing. I have myself made special inquiries on this point, and am of the same opinion. That masturbation, especially at an early age, may enfeeble the sexual activities, and so predispose them to inversion, I certainly believe. But beyond this there is little in the history of my male cases to lead me to attach importance to masturbation as a cause of inversion. It is true that 25 out of 30 admit that they have practiced masturbation,—at all events, occasionally or at some period in their lives,—and it is probable that this proportion is larger than that found among normal people. Even if so, however, it is not difficult to account for, bearing in mind the fact that the homosexual person has not the same opportunities as has the heterosexual person to gratify his instincts, and that masturbation may sometimes legitimately appear to him as the lesser of two evils.[1] Not only has masturbation been practiced at no period in at least 5 of the cases (for concerning several I have no information), but in several others it was never practiced until long after the homosexual instinct had appeared, and then only occasionally. In 5 it was only practiced at puberty; in 5, however, it began before the age of puberty; 9 left off before about the age of twenty. Unfortunately, as yet, we have little definite evidence as to the prevalence and extent of masturbation among normal individuals.

---

[1] One of my subjects writes: "Inverts are, I think, naturally more liable to indulge in self-gratification than normal people, partly because of the perpetual suppression and disappointment of their desires, and also because of the fact that they actually possess in themselves the desired form of the male. This idea is a little difficult of explanation, but you can readily imagine to what frenzies of self-abuse a normal man would be impelled supposing that he included in his own the form of the female."

Among the women masturbation is found in at least 3 cases out of 5. In one case there was no masturbation until comparatively late in life, and then only at rare intervals and under exceptional circumstances. In another case, some years after the homosexual attraction had been experienced, it was practiced, though not in excess, from the age of puberty for about four years, and then abandoned; during these years the physical sexual feelings were more imperative than they were afterward felt to be. In a third case masturbation was learned spontaneously soon after puberty, and practiced in excess before the manifestations of inversion became definite. In all these cases the subjects are emphatic in asserting that this practice neither led to, nor was caused by, the homosexual attraction, which they regard as a much higher feeling, and it must be added that the occasional practice of masturbation is very far from rare among fairly normal women.[1]

While this is so, I am certainly inclined to believe that an early and somewhat excessive indulgence in masturbation, though not an adequate cause, is a favoring condition for the development of inversion, and that this is especially so in women. The sexual precocity indicated by early and excessive masturbation doubtless reveals an organism already predisposed to homosexuality. But, apart from this, when masturbation arises spontaneously at an early age on a purely physical basis it seems to tend to produce a divorce between the physical and the psychic aspects of sexual love. The sexual manifestations are all diverted into this material direction, and the child is ignorant that such phenomena are normally allied to love; then when a more spiritual attraction, probably to a person of the same sex, appears with adolescent development, this divorce is perpetuated. Instead of the physical and psychic feelings appearing together when the age for sexual attraction comes, the physical feelings are prematurely twisted from their natural end, and it becomes abnormally easy for a person of the same sex to step in and take the place rightfully belonging to a person of the opposite sex. This has certainly seemed to me the course of events in some cases I have observed.

Attitude Toward the Opposite Sex.—In 8 cases (of whom 2 are

---

[1] I do not here enter upon the consideration of the normal prevalence and significance of masturbation and allied phenomena, as I have dealt with this subject in the study of "Auto-erotism," in volume ii of these *Studies*.

married and others purposing to marry) there is sexual attraction to both sexes, a condition usually called psychosexual hermaphroditism. In such cases, although there is pleasure and satisfaction in relationships with both sexes, there is usually a greater degree of satisfaction in connection with one sex. Most of my psychosexual hermaphrodites prefer their own sex. It is curiously rare to find a person, whether man or woman, who by choice exercises relationships with both sexes and prefers the opposite sex. This would seem to indicate that psychosexual hermaphrodites are really simple inverts.

In any case psychosexual hermaphroditism merges imperceptibly into simple inversion. In 12 of 35 cases of simple inversion in men there has been connection with women, in some instances only once or twice, in others during several years, but it was always with an effort or from a sense of duty and anxiety to be normal; they never experienced any real pleasure in the act, or sense of satisfaction after it. Two of these cases are married, but in both cases marital relationships entirely ceased after a few years. Three other cases were attracted to women when younger, but are not now; another once felt sexually attracted to a boyish woman, but never made any attempt to obtain any relationships with her; 1 or 2 others, again, have tried to have connection with women, but failed. The largest proportion of my cases have never had any sexual intimacy with the opposite sex, but experience what, in the case of the male invert, is sometimes called *horror feminae*. But, while woman as an object of sexual desire is disgusting to them, and it is usually difficult for a genuine invert to have connection with a woman except by setting up images of his own sex, for the most part they are capable of genuine friendships, irrespective of sex.

It is, perhaps, not difficult to account for the horror—much stronger than that normally felt toward a person of the same sex—with which the invert often regards the sexual organs of persons of the opposite sex. It cannot be said that the sexual organs of either sex under the influence of sexual excitement are esthetically pleasing; they only become emotionally desirable through the parallel excitement of the beholder. When the absence of parallel excitement is accompanied in the beholder by the sense of unfamiliarity, all the conditions are present for the production of intense *horror feminae* or *horror masculis*, as the case may be.

Erotic Dreams.—Our dreams follow, as a general rule, the same impulses that stir our waking psychic life. The normal man in sexual vigor dreams of loving a woman, the inverted man dreams of loving a man, the inverted woman of loving a woman. There are a few exceptions,[1] and these are generally explicable by the subject's past or present experiences. In one case that I have brought forward the evolution and varying character of the erotic dreams is recorded in some detail; in this case they began in a rudimentary form at the early age of eight; in two other cases dreams of more or less sexual character began still earlier. Of my cases, only 3 state that there are no erotic dreams, while 23 acknowledge that the dreams are concerned more or less with persons of the same sex. Of these, at least 14 assert or imply that their dreams are exclusively of the same sex. Two (XVII and XVIII), though apparently inverted congenitally, have had erotic dreams of women, in the case of XVII more frequently than of men; these two exceptions have no apparent explanation. Another appears to have sexual dreams of a nightmare character in which women appear. In another case there were always at first dreams of women, but this subject had sometimes had connection with prostitutes, and is not absolutely indifferent to women. In the cases of distinct psychosexual hermaphroditism there is no unanimity: one dreams of his own sex, another dreams of both sexes, one usually dreams of the opposite sex, and one man, while dreaming of both, dislikes those dreams in which women figure.

It may be added that, as Moll has pointed out, the vividness with which the inverted instinct usually displays itself in dreams has some value in diagnosis when we are not quite sure how far the inverted tendency is radical. There is usually less unwillingness to confess to a perverted dream than to a perverted action.

Physical Abnormalities.—The circumstances under which my cases were investigated usually rendered information under this head difficult to obtain. In one case the penis is very large, while in two others it is distinctly undeveloped, and the testicles small and flabby. It seems probable that both these deviations are fairly frequent, especially in the direction of incomplete development.

Perhaps the most interesting physical abnormality observed in my cases is the fairly well-marked gynecomasty in Case XXX. In this

[1] Näcke and Colin Scott independently refer to cases in which normal subjects are liable to inverted dreams, and Féré mentions a case in which the inversion appeared to be limited to dreams.

case the breasts swelled and became red; a similar condition of gynecomasty has been observed in connection with inversion by Moll, Laurent, and Wey.

My observations on women are too few to permit of any assured result, but I am distinctly of opinion that undeveloped sexual organs are frequent among inverted women. Putting together 9 cases by various observers (including 2 original observations) in which attention was paid to the sexual parts, only 4 were normal; the other 5 were all, more or less, undeveloped. In one of the women there is an unusual growth of hair on the legs.[1]

A tendency to defect of anatomical sexual development is known to be correlated with a general tendency to what is termed infantilism, and also to feminism and masculism. I am much impressed by the frequency with which the signs of infantilism in the general bodily structure occur in inverts.[2]

It seems to me, on a review of all the facts that have come under my observation, that while there is no necessary connection between infantilism, feminism, and masculinism, physical and psychic, on the one hand, and sexual inversion on the other, yet that there is a distinct tendency for the signs of the former group of abnormalities to occur with unusual frequency in inverts, and while I am not in a position to bring forward a sufficient body of evidence in support of this opinion, I have little doubt that it will be forthcoming in the future.[3]

---

[1] Unusual growth of hair on the body seems frequently to occur in both sexes in association with either abnormal sexual impulses or in excessively strong normal impulse. A woman physician in the United States, who knows many inverts of her own sex, tells me that she has observed this growth of hair on the legs. In two cases, also, she has observed supernumerary teeth, and she finds facial asymmetry very common.

[2] For an enumeration and study of these signs see an able and well-illustrated series of papers (which do not touch on the present question) by H. Meige, "L'Infantilisme, le Féminisme, et les Hermaphrodites Antiques," L'Anthropologie, 1895. In the Post-graduate (edited by Dr. Dana, New York), for January, 1896, there are also photographs of two men (four views of face and body of each) who earned their living, one as a lady's maid, the other as a female cook; these photographs are well worth study, though unaccompanied by histories.

[3] It is curious to find a medico-legal record of this connection long before inversion was recognized. In June, 1833 (see, for example, Annual Register under this date), a man died who had lived as a kept woman under the name of Eliza Edwards. He was very effeminate in appearance, with beautiful hair, in ringlets two feet long, and a cracked voice; he played female parts in the theater "in the first line of tragedy," and "appeared as a most lady-like woman." The coroner's jury "strongly recommended to the proper authorities that some means may be adopted in the disposal of the body which will mark the ignominy of the crime."

Krafft-Ebing (Psychopathia Sexualis, eighth edition, p. 263) tells of an inverted physician (a man of masculine development and tastes) who had had sexual relations with 600 more or less

If we are justified in believing that there is a tendency for inverted persons to be somewhat arrested in development, approaching the child type, we may connect this fact with the marked sexual precocity of inverts, for precocity is commonly accompanied by rapid arrest of development.

A correspondent, who is himself an invert, furnishes the following notes of cases he is well acquainted with; I quote them here, as they illustrate the anomalies commonly found:—

1. A., male, eldest child of typically neurotic family. Three children in all: 2 male and 1 female. The other 2 are somewhat eccentric, unsocial, and sexually frigid, 1 in a marked degree. The curious point about this case is that A., the only one of the family possessed of mental ability and social qualifications, should be inverted. Parents' marriage was very ill assorted and inharmonious, the father being of great stature and the mother abnormally small and of highly nervous temperament, both of feeble health. Ancestry unfortunate, especially on mother's side.

2. B., male, invert, younger of 2 sons, no other children, has extremely feminine disposition and appearance, of considerable personal attraction, has great musical talent. Penis very small and marked breast-development.

3. C., male, invert, younger of 2 sons; no other children. Interval of six years between first and second son. Parents' marriage one of great affection, but degenerate ancestry on mother's side. Cancer and scrofula in family.

4. D., male, invert, second child of 6; remainder girls. Of humble social position. Considerable depravity evinced by all the members of this family, with the exception of D., who alone proved steady, honest, and industrious.

5. E., male, invert, second son of family of 3, the youngest child being a girl, still-born. Of extreme neurotic temperament

---

inverted men. He observed no tendency to sexual malformation among them, but very frequently an approximation to a feminine form of body, as well as insufficient hair, delicate complexion, and high voice. Well-developed breasts were not rare, and some 10 per cent showed a taste for feminine occupations.

fostered by upbringing. Effeminate in build and disposition; musically gifted.

6. F., male, invert, second child of family of 5. Eldest child a girl, died in youth. After F. a boy G., a girl H., and another girl still-born. Parents badly matched, mother of considerable mental and physical strength, father last representative of moribund stock, the result of intermarriage. Children all resembling father in appearance and mother in disposition. Drink-tendency in both boys, to which F.'s death at the age of 30 was mainly due. G. committed suicide some years later. The girl H. married into a family with worse ancestry than her own. Has two children:—

7. I. and J., boy and girl, both inverted as far as I am able to judge. The boy was born with some deformity of the feet and ankles; is of effeminate tastes and appearance. Boy resembles mother, and girl, who is of great physical development, resembles father.

The same correspondent adds:—

"I have noticed little abnormal with regard to the genital formation of inverts. There are, however, frequent abnormalities of proportion in their figures, the hands and feet being noticeably smaller and more shapely, the waist more marked, the body softer and less muscular. Almost invariably there is either cranial malformation or the head approaches the feminine in type and shape."

Artistic and Other Aptitudes.—An examination of my cases reveals the interesting fact that 32, or 68 per cent., possess artistic aptitude in varying degree. Galton found, from the investigation of nearly 1000 persons, that the average showing artistic tastes in England is only about 30 per cent. It must also be said that my figures are probably below the truth, as no special point was made of investigating the matter, and also that in many of my cases the artistic aptitudes are of high order.

With regard to the special avocations of my cases, it must, of course, be said that no occupation furnishes a safeguard against inversion. There are, however, certain occupations to which inverts are specially attracted. Acting is certainly one of the chief of these. Three of my cases belong to the dramatic profession, and others have marked dramatic ability. Art, again, in its various forms, and music, exercise much attraction. In my experience, however, literature is the avocation to which inverts seem to feel chiefly called, and that, moreover, in which they may find the highest degree of success and reputation. At least half a dozen of my cases are successful men of letters. They especially cultivate those regions of *belles-lettres* which lie on the border-land between prose and verse. Though they do not usually attain much eminence in poetry, they are often very accomplished writers of verse. They may be attracted to history, but do not usually attempt tasks of great magnitude, involving much patient labor. Science seems to have singularly little attraction for them, and, in England at all events, I do not know, and have not even heard of, any invert who has attained any degree of eminence in this field. Among doctors, indeed, inversion seems to be fairly liable to occur; 4 of my cases are doctors.[1]

The tendency to dramatic aptitude among sexual inverts has attracted the attention of previous investigators in this field. Thus, Moll refers to the frequency of artistic, and especially dramatic, talent among inverts, and remarks that the cause is doubtful. After pointing out that the lie which they have to be perpetually living renders inverts always actors, he goes on to say:—

> Apart from this, it seems to me that the capacity and the inclination to conceive situations and to represent them in a masterly manner corresponds to an abnormal predisposition of the nervous system, just as does sexual inversion; so that both phenomena are due to the same source.

I am in agreement with this statement; the congenitally inverted may, I believe, be looked upon as a class of individuals exhibiting nervous

[1] Moll's experience in Germany is very similar to mine. He mentions the prevalence of inversion among literary men. He also remarks that, of all avocations, the highest proportion of inverts is found among male actors and music-hall artists who take women's parts. Jäger (in an unpublished chapter of his *Entdeckung der Seele*, printed in *Jahrbüch für Sexuelle Zwischenstufen*, B. 2, p. 108) mentions the frequency of homosexuality among barbers and waiters. I have been told that among London hair-dressers homosexuality is so prevalent that there is even a special attitude which the client may adopt in the chair to make known that he is an invert. In Chicago, also, Dr. Kiernan informs me, inversion is specially prevalent among barbers. Moll refers to its frequency among waitresses. I have no information regarding London waitresses, but I have received the history of a homosexual waitress from Sydney, New South Wales.

characters which, to some extent, approximate them to persons of artistic genius. The dramatic and artistic aptitudes of inverts are, therefore, partly due to the circumstances of the invert's life, which render him necessarily an actor,—and in some few cases lead him into a love of deception comparable with that of a hysterical woman,—and partly, it is probable, to a congenital nervous predisposition allied to the predisposition to dramatic aptitude.

One of my correspondents has long been interested in the frequency of inversion among actors and actresses. He knew an inverted actor who told him he adopted the profession because it would enable him to indulge his proclivity; but, on the whole, he regards this tendency as due to "hitherto unconsidered imaginative flexibilities and curiosities in the individual. The actor, *ex hypothesi*, is one who works himself by sympathy (intellectual and emotional) into states of psychological being that are not his own. He learns to comprehend—nay, to live himself into—relations which were originally alien to his nature. The capacity for doing this—what makes a born actor— implies a faculty for extending his artistically acquired experience into life. In the process of his trade, therefore, he becomes at all points sensitive to human emotions, and, sexuality being the most intellectually undetermined of the appetites after hunger, the actor might discover in himself a sort of sexual indifference, out of which a sexual aberration could easily arise. A man devoid of this imaginative flexibility could not be a successful actor. The man who possesses it would be exposed to divagations of the sexual instinct under esthetical or merely wanton influences. Something of the same kind is applicable to musicians and artists, in whom sexual inversion prevails beyond the average. They are conditioned by their esthetical faculty, and encouraged by the circumstances of their life to feel and express the whole gamut of emotional experience. Thus they get an environment which (unless they are sharply otherwise differentiated) leads easily to experiments in passion. All this joins on to what you call the 'variational diathesis' of men of genius. But I should seek the explanation of the phenomenon less in the original sexual constitution than in the exercise of sympathetic, assimilative emotional qualities, powerfully stimulated and acted on by the conditions of the individual's life. The artist, the singer, the actor, the painter, are more exposed to the influences out of which sexual differentiation in an abnormal direction may arise. Some persons are certainly made abnormal by nature, others, of this sympathetic artistic temperament, may become so through their sympathies plus their conditions of life." It is possible there may be some element of truth in this view, which my correspondent regarded as purely hypothetical.

In this connection I may, perhaps, mention a moral quality which is very often associated with dramatic aptitude, and also with minor degrees of nervous degeneration, and that is vanity and the love of applause. While among a considerable section of inverts it is not more marked than among the non-inverted, if not, indeed, less marked, among another section it is found in an exaggerated degree. In Case XXXVIII vanity and delight in admiration, both as regards personal qualities and artistic productions, reach an almost morbid extent. And the quotations from letters written by various others of my subjects show a curious complacency in the description of their personal physical characters, markedly absent in other cases.

The most marked pre-occupation with personal beauty which I have seen recorded of an invert occurs in the history of himself written by a young Italian of good family, and sent by him to M. Zola in the hope—itself a sign of vanity—that the distinguished novelist would make it the subject of one of his works. The history is reproduced in the *Archives d'Anthropologie Criminelle* (1894) and in Dr. Laupts's *Perversion et Perversité Sexuelles* (1896). I quote the following passage: "At the age of 18 I was, with few differences, what I am now (at 23). I am rather below the medium height (1.65 meters), well proportioned, slender, but not lean. My torso is superb; a sculptor could find nothing against it, and would not find it very different from that of Antinoüs. My back is very arched (*cambré*), perhaps too much so; and my hips are very developed; my pelvis is broad, like a woman's; my knees slightly approximate; my feet are small; my hands superb; the fingers curved back and with glistening nails, rosy and polished, cut squarely like those of ancient statues. My neck is long and round, the nape charmingly adorned with downy hairs. My head is charming, and at 18 was more so. The oval of it is perfect, and strikes all by its infantine form. At 23 I am to be taken for 17 at most. My complexion is white and rosy, deepening at the faintest emotion. The forehead is not beautiful; it recedes slightly and is hollow at the temples, but, fortunately, it is half-covered by long hair, of a dark blonde, which curls naturally. The head is perfect in form, because of the curly hair, but on examination there is an enormous protuberance at the occiput. My eyes are oval, of a gray blue, with dark chestnut eyelashes and thick, arched eyebrows. My eyes are very liquid, but with dark circles, and bistered; and they are subject to slight temporary inflammation. My mouth is fairly large, with thick red lips, the lower pendent; they tell me I have the Austrian mouth. My teeth are dazzling, though three are decayed and stopped; fortunately, they cannot be seen. My ears are small and with very colored lobes. My chin is very fat, and at 18 it was smooth and velvety as a woman's; at present there is a slight beard, always shaved. Two beauty spots, black and velvety, on my left cheek, contrast with my blue eyes. My nose is thin and straight, with delicate nostrils and a slight, almost insensible curve. My voice is gentle, and people always regret that I have not learned to sing." This description is noteworthy as a detailed portrait of a sexual invert of a certain type; the whole history is interesting and instructive.

Certain peculiarities in taste as regards costume have rightly or wrongly been attributed to inverts,—apart from the tendency of a certain group to adopt feminine habits,—and may here be mentioned. Tardieu many years ago referred to the taste for keeping the neck uncovered. This peculiarity may certainly be observed among a considerable proportion of inverts, especially the more artistic among them. The cause does not appear to be precisely vanity so much as that physical consciousness which is so curiously marked in inverts, and induces the more feminine among them to cultivate feminine grace of form, and the more masculine to emphasize the masculine athletic habit.

It has also been remarked that inverts exhibit a preference for green garments. In Rome *cinaedi* were for this reason called *galbanati*. Chevalier remarks that some years ago a band of pederasts at Paris wore green cravats as a badge. This decided preference for green is well marked in several of my cases of both sexes, and in some at least the preference certainly arose spontaneously. Green (as Jastrow and others have shown) is very rarely the favorite color of adults of the Anglo-Saxon race, though some inquirers have found it to be more commonly a preferred color among children, especially girls.

The frequent inability of male inverts to whistle was first pointed out by Ulrichs. Many of my cases confess to this inability, while some of the women inverts can whistle admirably. Although this inability of male inverts is only found among a minority, I am quite satisfied that it is well marked among a considerable minority. One of my correspondents, M. N., writes to me: "With regard to the general inability of inverts to whistle (I am not able to do so myself), their fondness for green (my favorite color), their feminine calligraphy, skill at female occupations, etc., these all seem to me but indications of the one principle. To go still farther and include trivial things, few inverts even smoke in the same manner and with the same enjoyment as a man, they have seldom the male facility at games, cannot throw at a mark with precision, or even spit!"

Nearly all these peculiarities indicate a minor degree of nervous disturbance and lead to modification, as my correspondent points out, in a feminine direction. It is scarcely necessary to add that they by no means necessarily imply inversion. Shelley, for instance, was unable to whistle, though he never gave an indication of inversion, but he was a person of somewhat abnormal and feminine organization, and he illustrates the tendency of these apparently very insignificant functional anomalies to be correlated with other and more important psychic anomalies.

Moral Attitude of the Invert.—There is some interest in tracing the invert's own attitude toward his anomaly, and his estimate of its morality. As my cases are not patients seeking to be cured of their perversion, this attitude cannot be taken for granted. I have noted the moral attitude in 41 cases. In 3 the subjects loathe themselves, and have fought in vain against their perversion. Seven or 8 are doubtful, and have little to say in justification of their condition, which they regard as perhaps morbid. The remainder, a large majority (including all the women) are, on the other hand, emphatic in their assertion that their moral position is precisely the same as that of the normally constituted individual; 1 or 2 even regard inverted love as nobler than ordinary sexual love; several add the proviso that there should be consent and understanding on both sides, and no attempt at seduction. The chief regret of 1 or 2 is the double life they are obliged to lead. It is noteworthy that even when the condition is regarded as morbid, and even when a life of chastity has, on this account, been deliberately chosen, it is very rare to find an invert expressing any wish to change his sexual ideals. The male invert cannot find, and has no desire to find, any sexual charm in a woman, for he finds all possible charms united in a man. And a woman invert writes: "I cannot conceive a sadder fate than to be a woman—an average woman reduced to the necessity of loving a man!"

It will be seen that my conclusions under this head are in striking contrast to those of Westphal, who believed that every invert regarded himself as morbid, and probably show a much higher proportion of self-approving inverts than any previous series. This is due partly to the way in which the cases were obtained, and partly to the fact that they may be said, on the whole, to represent the intellectual aristocracy of inversion, including a large number of individuals who, often not without severe struggles, have found consolation in the example of the Greeks, or elsewhere, and have succeeded in attaining a *modus vivendi* with the moral world, as they have come to conceive it.

CHAPTER VI.

THE THEORY OF SEXUAL INVERSION.

What is Sexual Inversion?—Causes of Diverging Views—The Theory of Suggestion Unworkable—Importance of the Congenital Element in Inversion—The Theory of the Female Soul—Embryonic Hermaphroditism as a Key to Inversion—Inversion as a Variation or "Sport"—Comparison with Color-blindness, Color-hearing, and Similar Abnormalities—What Is an Abnormality?—Not Necessarily a Disease—Relation of Inversion to Degeneration—Exciting Causes of Inversion—Seldom Operative in the Absence of Predisposition.

The analysis of these cases leads directly up to a question of the first importance: What is sexual inversion? Is it, as many would have us believe, an abominable acquired vice, to be stamped out by the prison? or is it, as a few assert, a beneficial variety of human emotion which should be tolerated or even fostered? Is it a diseased condition which qualifies its subject for the lunatic asylum? or is it a natural monstrosity, a human "sport," the manifestations of which must be regulated when they become antisocial? There is probably an element of truth in more than one of these views. I am prepared to admit that very widely divergent views of sexual inversion are largely justified by the position and attitude of the investigator. It is natural that the police-official should find that his cases are largely mere examples of disgusting vice and crime. It is natural that the asylum superintendent should find that we are chiefly dealing with a form of insanity. It is equally natural that the sexual invert himself should find that he and his inverted friends are not so very unlike ordinary persons. We have to recognize the influence of professional and personal bias and the influence of environment, one investigator basing his conclusions on one class of cases, another on a quite different class of cases. Naturally, I have largely founded my own conclusions on my own cases. I believe, however, that my cases and my attitude toward them justify me in doing this with some confidence. I am not in the position of one who is pleading *pro domo*, nor of the police-official, nor even of the physician, for these persons have not come to me for treatment. I approach the matter as a psychologist who has ascertained certain definite facts, and who is founding his conclusions on those facts.

The first point which impresses me is that we must regard sexual inversion as largely a congenital phenomenon, or, to speak more accurately, as a phenomenon which is based on congenital conditions. This, I think, lies at the root of the right comprehension of the matter. There are at the present day two streams of tendency in the views regarding sexual inversion: one seeking to enlarge the sphere of the acquired (represented by Binet,—who, however, recognizes predisposition,—Schrenck-Notzing, and others), the other seeking to enlarge the sphere of the congenital (represented by Krafft-Ebing, Moll, Féré, and others). There is, as usually happens, truth in both these views. But inasmuch as those who represent the acquired view often emphatically deny any congenital element, I think we are specially called upon to emphasize this congenital element. The view that sexual inversion is entirely explained by the influence of early association, or of "suggestion," is an attractive one, and at first sight it seems to be supported by what we know of erotic fetichism, by which a woman's hair, or foot, or even clothing, becomes the focus of a man's sexual aspirations. But it must be remembered that what we see in erotic fetichism is merely the exaggeration of a normal impulse; every lover is to some extent excited by his mistress's hair, or foot, or clothing. Even here, therefore, there is really what may fairly be regarded as a congenital element; and, moreover, there is reason to believe that the erotic fetichist usually displays the further congenital element of hereditary neurosis. Therefore, the analogy with erotic fetichism does not bring much help to those who argue that inversion is purely acquired. It must also be pointed out that the argument for acquired or suggested inversion logically involves the assertion that normal sexuality is also acquired or suggested. If a man becomes attracted to his own sex simply because the fact or the image of such attraction is brought before him, then we are bound to believe that a man becomes attracted to the opposite sex only because the fact or the image of such attraction is brought before him. This theory is wholly unworkable. In nearly every country of the world men associate with men, and women with women; if association and suggestion were the only influential causes, then inversion, instead of being the exception, ought to be the rule throughout the human species, if not, indeed, throughout the whole zoölogical series. We should, moreover, have to admit that the most fundamental human instinct is so constituted as to be equally well adapted for sterility as for that propagation of the race which, as a matter of fact, we find dominant throughout the whole of life. We must, therefore, put aside entirely the notion that the direction of the sexual impulse is merely a suggested phenomenon; such a notion is entirely opposed to observation and experience, and will with difficulty fit into a rational biological scheme.

The rational way of regarding the normal sexual impulse is as an inborn organic impulse, developing about the time of puberty.[1] At

---

[1] It is denied by some (Meynert, Näcke, etc.) that there is any sexual *instinct* at all. I may as well, therefore, explain in what sense I use the word. I mean an inherited aptitude the performance of

this period suggestion and association may come in to play a part in defining the object of the emotion; the soil is now ready, but the variety of seeds likely to thrive in it is limited. That there is a greater indefiniteness in the aim of the sexual impulse at this period we may well believe. This is shown not only by occasional tentative signs of sexual emotion directed toward the same sex, but by the usually vague and non-sexual character of the normal passion at puberty. But the channel of sexual emotion is not thereby turned into an utterly abnormal path. Whenever this permanently happens we are, I think, bound to believe—and we have many grounds for believing—that we are dealing with an organism which from the beginning is abnormal. The same seed of suggestion is sown in various soils; in the many it dies out, in the few it flourishes. The cause can only be a difference in the soil.

If, then, we must postulate a congenital abnormality in order to account satisfactorily for at least a large proportion of sexual inverts, wherein does that abnormality consist? Ulrichs explained the matter by saying that in sexual inverts a male body coexists with a female soul: *anima muliebris in corpore virili inclusa*. Even writers with some pretension to scientific precision, like Magnan and Gley, have adopted this phrase in a modified form, considering that in inversion a female brain is combined with a male body or male glands. This is, however, not an explanation. It merely crystallizes into an epigram the superficial impression of the matter. As an explanation it is to a scientific psychologist unthinkable. We only know soul as manifested through body; and, although if we say that a person seems to have the body of a man and the feelings of a woman we are saying what

---

which normally demands for its full satisfaction the presence of a person of the opposite sex. It might be asserted that there is no such thing as an instinct for food, that it is all imitation, etc. In a sense this is true, but the automatic basis remains. A chicken from an incubator needs no hen to teach it to eat. It seems to discover eating and drinking, as it were, by chance, at first eating awkwardly and eating everything, until it learns what will best satisfy its organic mechanism. There is no instinct for food, it may be, but there is an instinct which is only satisfied by food. It is the same with the "sexual instinct." The tentative and omnivorous habits of the newly hatched chicken may be compared to the uncertainty of the sexual instinct at puberty, while the sexual pervert is like a chicken that should carry on into adult age an appetite for worsted and paper. It may be added here that the question of the hereditary nature of the sexual instinct has been exhaustively discussed and decisively affirmed by Moll in his *Untersuchungen über die Libido Sexualis*, 1898. Moll (*Konträre Sexualempfindung*, p. 413) attaches much importance to the inheritance of the normal aptitudes for sexual reaction in an abnormally weak degree as a factor in the development of sexual perversions.

is often true enough, it is quite another matter to assert dogmatically that a female soul, or even a female brain, is expressing itself through a male body. That is simply unintelligible. I say nothing of the fact that in male inverts the feminine psychic tendencies may be little if at all marked, so that there is no "feminine soul" in the question; nor of the further important fact that in a very large proportion of cases the body itself presents secondary sexual characters that are distinctly modified.

We can probably grasp the nature of the abnormality better if we reflect on the development of the sexes and on the latent organic bisexuality in each sex. At an early stage of development the sexes are indistinguishable, and throughout life the traces of this early community of sex remain. The hen fowl retains in a rudimentary form the spurs which are so large and formidable in her lord, and sometimes she develops a capacity to crow, or puts on male plumage. Among mammals the male possesses useless nipples, which occasionally even develop into breasts, and the female possesses a clitoris, which is merely a rudimentary penis, and may also develop. The sexually inverted person does not usually possess any gross exaggeration of these signs of community with the opposite sex. But, as we have seen, there are a considerable number of more subtle approximations to the opposite sex in inverted persons, both on the physical and the psychic side. Putting the matter in a purely speculative shape, it may be said that at conception the organism is provided with about 50 per cent of male germs and about 50 per cent of female germs, and that, as development proceeds, either the male or the female germs assume the upper hand, killing out those of the other sex, until in the maturely developed individual only a few aborted germs of the opposite sex are left. In the homosexual person, however, and in the psychosexual hermaphrodite, we may imagine that the process has not proceeded normally, on account of some peculiarity in the number or character of either the original male germs or female germs, or both, the result being that we have a person who is organically twisted into a shape that is more fitted for the exercise of the inverted than of the normal sexual impulse, or else equally fitted for both.[1]

---

[1] I do not present this view as more than a picture which helps us to realize the actual phenomena which we witness in homosexuality, although I may add that so able a teratologist as Dr. J. W. Ballantyne considers that "it seems a very possible theory."

The idea that sexual inversion is a variation, perhaps due to imperfect sexual differentiation, or reversion of type, seems to have had its origin in the speculations of Ulrichs. From the medical side it appears to have been first set forth (in America) by Kiernan (*American Lancet*, 1884, and *Medical Standard*, November and December, 1888), and Lydston (*Philadelphia Medical and Surgical Reporter*, September, 1889, and *Addresses and Essays*, 1892). Kiernan writes (in further maintaining his position in a paper on "Responsibility in Sexual Perversion," read before the Chicago Medical Society in 1892): "The original bisexuality of the ancestors of the race, shown in the rudimentary female organs of the male, could not fail to occasion functional, if not organic, reversions, when mental or physical manifestations were interfered with by disease or congenital defect. It seems certain that a femininely functionating brain can occupy a male body, and *vice versâ*. Males may be born with female genitals and *vice versâ*. The lowest animals are bisexual, and the various types of hermaphroditism are more or less complete reversions to the ancestral type. That the femininely functionating brain alone should be developed at times, with its psychical consequences, is to be expected." And Lydston (*Addresses and Essays*, p. 246) remarks: "Just as we may have variations of physical form and of mental attributes, in general, so we may have variations and perversions of that intangible entity, sexual affinity"; and (p. 46) he refers to failure of development and imperfect differentiation of generative centers, comparable to conditions like hypospadias and epispadias. Dr. G. de Letamendi, Dean of the Faculty of Medicine of Madrid, in a paper read before the International Medical Congress at Rome in 1894, set forth a principle of panhermaphroditism—a hermaphroditic bipolarity—which involves the existence of latent female germs in the male, latent male germs in the female, which latent germs may strive for, and sometimes obtain, the mastery. In Germany a patient of Krafft-Ebing has worked out the same idea, connecting inversion with fetal bisexuality (eighth edition *Psychopathia Sexualis*, p. 227). Krafft-Ebing himself simply asserts that, whether congenital or acquired, there must be *Belastung*; inversion is a "degenerative phenomenon," a functional sign of degeneration (Krafft-Ebing, "Zur Erklärung der conträren Sexualempfindung," *Jahrbuch für Psychiatrie*, 1894). In the later editions of *Psychopathia Sexualis*, however, Krafft-Ebing has gone farther, adopting an explanation on the lines of an original bisexuality (English translation of tenth edition, pp. 336–7). In much the same language as I have used (though independently) he argues that there has been a struggle in the centers, homosexuality resulting when the center antagonistic to that represented by the sexual gland conquers, and psychosexual hermaphroditism resulting when both centers are too weak to obtain victory, in either case such disturbance being a manifestation of degeneration. Moll, while accepting the explanation on embryological lines as "a happy thought" (*Konträre Sexualempfindung*, p. 411), points out, very truly, that the phenomena are too complicated to be entirely explained in this way.

Thus in sexual inversion we have what may fairly be called a "sport," or variation, one of those organic aberrations which we see throughout living nature, in plants and in animals.

It is not here asserted, as I would carefully point out, that an inverted sexual instinct, or organ for such instinct, is developed in early embryonic life; such a notion is rightly rejected as absurd. What we may reasonably regard as formed at an early stage of development is strictly a predisposition; that is to say, such a modification of the organism that it becomes more adapted than the normal or average organism to experience sexual attraction to the same sex. The sexual invert may thus be roughly compared to the congenital idiot, to the instinctive criminal, to the man of genius, who are all not strictly concordant with the usual biological variation (because this is of a less subtle character), but who become somewhat more intelligible to us if we bear in mind their affinity to variations. A correspondent compares inversion to color-blindness; and such a comparison is reasonable. Just as the ordinary color-blind person is congenitally insensitive to those red-green rays which are precisely the most impressive to the normal eye, and gives an extended value to the other colors, —finding that blood is the same color as grass, and a florid complexion blue as the sky,—so the invert fails to see emotional values patent to normal persons, transferring those values to emotional associations which, for the rest of the world, are utterly distinct. Or we may compare inversion to such a phenomenon as color-hearing, in which there is not so much defect, as an abnormality of nervous tracks producing new and involuntary combinations.[1] Just as the color-hearer instinctively associates colors with sounds, like the young Japanese lady who remarked when listening to singing, "That boy's voice is red!" so the invert has his sexual sensations brought into relationship with objects that are normally without sexual appeal. And inversion, like color-hearing, is found more commonly in young subjects, tending to become less marked, or to die out, after puberty. Color-hearing, while an abnormal phenomenon, it must be added, cannot be called a diseased condition, and it is probably much less frequently associated with other abnormal or degenerative stigmata than is inversion; there is often a congenital element, shown by the tendency to hereditary transmission, while the associations are developed in very early life, and are too regular to be the simple result of suggestion.

All these organic variations, which I have here mentioned to illustrate sexual inversion, are abnormalities. It is important that we should have a clear idea as to what an abnormality is. Many people imagine that what is abnormal is necessarily diseased. That is not the case, unless we give the word disease an inconveniently and illegitimately wide extension. It is both inconvenient and inexact to speak of color-blindness, criminality, and genius as diseases in the same sense as we speak of scarlet fever or tuberculosis or general paralysis as diseases. Every congenital abnormality is doubtless due to a peculiarity in the sperm or oval elements or in their mingling, or to some disturbance in their early development. But the same may doubtless be said of the normal dissimilarities between brothers and sisters. It is quite true that any of these aberrations may be due to antenatal disease, but to call them abnormal does not beg that question. If it is thought that any authority is needed to support this view, we can scarcely find a weightier than that of Virchow, who has repeatedly insisted on the right use of the word "anomaly," and who teaches that, though an anomaly may constitute a predisposition to disease, the study of anomalies—pathology, as he would call it, ter-

---

[1] Since this chapter was first published (in the *Centralblatt für Nervenheilkunde*, February, 1896), Féré has also compared congenital inversion to color-blindness and similar anomalies (Féré, "La Descendance d'un Inverti," *Revue Générale de Clinique et Thérapeutique*, 1896), while Ribot has referred to the analogy with color-hearing (*Psychology of the Emotions*, Part II, Chapter VII).

atology as we may perhaps prefer to call it—is not the study of disease, which he would term nosology; the study of the abnormal is perfectly distinct from the study of the morbid.[1] Virchow considers that the region of the abnormal is the region of pathology, and that the study of disease must be regarded distinctly as nosology. Whether we adopt this terminology, or whether we consider the study of the abnormal as part of teratology, is a secondary matter, not affecting the right understanding of the term "anomaly" and its due differentiation from the term "disease."

A word may be said as to the connection between sexual inversion and degeneration. In France especially, since the days of Morel, the stigmata of degeneration are much spoken of. Sexual inversion is frequently regarded as one of them: *i.e.*, as an episodic *syndrome* of a hereditary disease, taking its place beside other psychic stigmata, such as kleptomania and pyromania. Krafft-Ebing also so regards inversion. Strictly speaking, the invert is degenerate; he has fallen away from the genus. So is a color-blind person. But Morel's conception of degenerescence has unfortunately been coarsened and vulgarized.[2] As it now stands, we gain little or no information by being told that a person is a "degenerate." When we find a complexus of well-marked abnormalities, we are fairly justified in asserting that we have to deal with a condition of degeneration. Inversion is frequently found in such a condition. I have, indeed, already tried to suggest

[1] Thus at the Innsbruck meeting of the German Anthropological Society, in 1894, Virchow thus expressed himself: "I am of opinion that a transformation, a metaplasia, a change from one species into another,—whether in individual animals or plants, or individuals or their tissues,—cannot take place without anomaly, for, if no anomaly appears, this new departure is impossible. *The physiological norm hitherto subsisting is changed*, and we cannot well call that anything else but an anomaly. But in old days an anomaly was called παθοϛ, and in this sense every departure from the norm is for me a pathological event. If we have ascertained such a pathological event, we are further led to investigate what *pathos* was the special cause of it. . . . This cause may be, for example, an external force, or a chemical substance, or a physical agent, producing in the normal condition of the body a change, an anomaly (παθοϛ). This can become hereditary under some circumstances, and then become the foundation for certain small hereditary characters which are propagated in a family; in themselves they belong to pathology, even although they produce no injury. For I must remark that pathological does not mean harmful; it does not indicate disease; disease in Greek is νόσος, and it is nosology that is concerned with disease. The pathological under some circumstances can be advantageous" (*Correspondenz-blatt von Deutsch Gesellschaft für Anthropologie*, 1894). Putting aside the question of terminology, these remarks are of interest when we are attempting to find the wider bearings of such an anomaly as sexual inversion.

[2] It is this fact which has caused the Italians to be shy of using the word "degeneration"; thus, Marro, in his great work, *I Caratteri dei Delinquenti*, has made a notable attempt to analyze the phenomena lumped together as degenerate into three groups: atypical, atavistic, and morbid.

that a condition of diffused minor abnormality may be regarded as the basis of congenital inversion. In other words, inversion is bound up with a modification of the secondary sexual characters.[1] But little is gained by calling these modifications "stigmata of degeneration," a term which threatens to disappear from scientific terminology, to become a mere term of literary and journalistic abuse. So much may be said concerning a conception or a phrase of which far too much has been made in popular literature. At the best it remains vague and little fitted for scientific use.[2]

Sexual inversion, therefore, remains a congenital abnormality, to be classed with the other congenital abnormalities which have psychic concomitants. At the very least such congenital abnormality usually exists as a predisposition to inversion. It is probable that many persons go through the world with a congenital predisposition to inversion which always remain latent and unroused; in others the instinct is so strong that it forces its own way in spite of all obstacles; in others, again, the predisposition is weaker, and a powerful exciting cause plays the predominant part.

We are thus led to the consideration of the causes that excite the latent predisposition. A great variety of causes has been held to excite to sexual inversion. It is only necessary to mention those which I have found influential. The most important of these is undoubtedly our school-system, with its segregation of boys and girls apart from each other during the important periods of puberty and adolescence. Many congenital inverts have not been to school at all, and many who have been pass through school-life without forming any passionate or sex-

---

[1] Kurella goes so far as to regard the invert as a transitional form between the complete man, or the complete woman, and the genuine sexual hermaphrodite (preface to the German edition of Laurent's *Les Bisexués*, 1896; and *Centralblatt für Nervenheilkunde*, May, 1896). This view is supported by what we see in animals (see pp. 2 *et seq.*), but scarcely accounts for all the facts in the human subject. Moll (*Konträre Sexualempfindung*, p. 411) would regard some cases of inversion as the development of contrary secondary sexual characters, but is not inclined to extend this explanation widely. Krafft-Ebing (*Psychopathia Sexualis*, English translation, pp. 336–7, 1899), while denying the possibility of "a feminine brain in a masculine body," thinks we can admit "a feminine psychosexual center in a masculine brain." At the same time he points out that "hermaphroditism and sexual inversion stand in no relation to each other."

[2] The inverted impulse is sometimes (as by Näcke) considered an obsession, developing on a neurasthenic or neurotic basis. That there is an analogy and, indeed, a distinct relationship between obsessions and sexual perversions I fully believe, but obsessions are so vague, capricious, and ill understood, that I am not inclined to press the analogy very far. We cannot explain the little known by the less known. I would rather explain obsessions by reference to the sexual impulse, than the sexual impulse by reference to obsessions.

ual relationship; but there remains a large number who date the development of homosexuality from the influences and examples of school-life. The impressions received at the time are not less potent because they are often purely sentimental and without any obvious sensual admixture. Whether they are sufficiently potent to generate permanent inversion alone may be doubtful, but, if it is true that in early life the sexual instincts are less definitely determined than when adolescence is complete, it is conceivable, though unproved, that a very strong impression, acting even on a normal organism, may cause arrest of sexual development on the psychic side. It is a question I am not in a position to settle.

Another important exciting cause of inversion is seduction. By this I mean the initiation of the young boy or girl by some older and more experienced person in whom inversion is already developed, and who is seeking the gratification of the abnormal instinct. This appears to be a not uncommon incident in the early history of sexual inverts. That such seduction—sometimes an abrupt and inconsiderate act of mere sexual gratification—could by itself produce a taste for homosexuality is highly improbable; in individuals not already predisposed it is far more likely to produce disgust, as it did in the case of the youthful Rousseau. "He only can be seduced," as Moll puts it, "who is capable of being seduced." No doubt it frequently happens in these, as so often in more normal "seductions," that the victim has offered a voluntary or involuntary invitation.

Another exciting cause of inversion, to which little importance is usually attached, but which I find to have some weight, is disappointment in normal love. It happens that a man in whom the homosexual instinct is yet only latent, or at all events held in a state of repression, tries to form a relationship with a woman. This relationship may be ardent on one or both sides, but—often, doubtless, from the latent homosexuality of the lover—it comes to nothing. Such love-disappointments, in a more or less acute form, occur at some time or another to nearly everyone. But in these persons the disappointment with one woman constitutes motive strong enough to disgust the lover with the whole sex and to turn his attention toward his own sex. It is evident that the instinct which can thus be turned round can scarcely be strong, and it seems probable that in some of these cases the episode of normal love simply serves to bring home to the invert the fact that he is not made for normal love. In other cases, it seems,—especially those that are somewhat feeble-minded and un-balanced,—a love-disappointment really does poison the normal instinct, and a more or less impotent love for women becomes an equally impotent love for men. The prevalence of homosexuality among prostitutes must certainly be, to a large extent, explained by a similar and better-founded disgust with normal sexuality.

These three influences, therefore,—example at school, seduction, disappointment in normal love,—all of them drawing the subject away from the opposite sex and concentrating him on his own sex, are powerful exciting causes of inversion; but they mostly require a favorable organic predisposition to act on, while there are a large number of cases in which no exciting cause at all can be found, but in which, from earliest childhood, the subject's interest seems to be turned on his own sex, and continues to be so turned throughout life.

At this point I conclude the analysis of the psychology of sexual inversion as it presents itself to me. I have sought only to bring out the more salient points, neglecting minor points, neglecting also those groups of inverts who may be regarded as of secondary importance. The average invert, moving in ordinary society, so far as my evidence extends, is most usually a person of average general health, though very frequently with hereditary relationships that are markedly neurotic. He is usually the subject of a congenital predisposing abnormality, or complexus of minor abnormalities, making it difficult or impossible for him to feel sexual attraction to the opposite sex, and easy to feel sexual attraction to his own sex. This abnormality either appears spontaneously from the first, by development or arrest of development, or it is called into activity by some accidental circumstance.

MARIE JENNEY HOWE

FROM

AN ANTI-SUFFRAGE MONOLOGUE

Marie Jenney Howe (1871–1934): A well-known speaker and organizer, Marie Jenney Howe was born in Syracuse, New York, and studied ministry at Meadville Theological School in Pennsylvania, where she received her Bachelor of Divinity. After graduation she was a Unitarian minister in Des Moines, Iowa. After her marriage to Frederic C. Howe, she became active in the women's movement, campaigning for equal rights and suffrage. Howe was an admirer of George Sand, the nineteenth-century French writer, and authored a biography of Sand entitled George Sand: The Search for Love *and edited* The Intimate Journal of George Sand. *Howe's description of Sand's struggles might have reflected her own frustrations at being a woman ahead of her time: "When [Sand's] emotions upset her life, she got rid of them in writing, and these outpourings testify how much inner rebellion the tremendous personality which was George Sand had to contend with, in order to do a man's work in the world."*

Please do not think of me as old-fashioned. I pride myself on being a modern up-to-date woman. I believe in all kinds of broad-mindedness, only I do not believe in woman suffrage because to do that would be to deny my sex.

Woman suffrage is the reform against nature. Look at these ladies sitting on the platform. Observe their physical inability, their mental disability, their spiritual instability and general debility! Could they walk up to the ballot box, mark a ballot, and drop it in? Obviously not. Let us grant for the sake of argument that they could mark a ballot. But could they drop it in? Ah, no. All nature is against it. The laws of man cry out against it. The voice of God cries out against it—and so do I.

Enfranchisement is what makes man man. Disfranchisement is what makes woman woman. If women were enfranchised every man would be just like every woman and every woman would be just like every man. There would be no difference between them. And don't you think this would rob life of just a little of its poetry and romance?

Man must remain man. Woman must remain woman. If man goes over and tries to be like woman, if woman goes over and tries to be like man, it will become so very confusing and so difficult to explain to our children. Let us take a practical example. If a woman puts on a man's coat and trousers, takes a man's cane and hat and cigar, and goes out on the street, what will happen to her? She will be arrested and thrown into jail. Then why not stay at home?

I know you begin to see how strongly I *feel* on this subject, but I have some reasons as well. These reasons are based on logic. Of course I am not logical. I am a creature of impulse, instinct, and intuition—and I glory in it. But I know that these reasons are based on logic because I have culled them from the men whom it is my privilege to know.

My first argument against suffrage is that the women would not use it if they had it. You couldn't drive them to the polls. My second argument is, if the women were enfranchised they would neglect their homes, desert their families, and spend all their time at the polls. You may tell me that the polls are only open once a year. But I know women. They are creatures of habit. If you let them go to the polls once a year, they will hang round the polls all the rest of the time.

I have arranged these arguments in couplets. They go together in such a way that if you don't like one you can take the other. This is my second anti-suffrage couplet. If the women were enfranchised they would vote exactly as their husbands do and only double the existing vote. Do you like that argument? If not, take this one. If the women were enfranchised they would vote against their own husbands, thus creating dissension, family quarrels, and divorce.

My third anti-suffrage couplet is—women are angels. Many men call me an angel and I have a strong instinct which tells me it is true; that is why I am anti, because "I want to be an angel and with the angels stand." And if you don't like that argument take this one.

Women are depraved. They would introduce into politics a vicious element which would ruin our national life.

Fourth anti-suffrage couplet: women cannot understand politics. Therefore there would be no use in giving women political power, because they would not know what to do with it. On the other hand, if the women were enfranchised, they would mount rapidly into power, take all the offices from all the men, and soon we would have women governors of all our states and dozens of women acting as President of the United States.

Fifth anti-suffrage couplet: women cannot band together. They are incapable of organization. No two women can even be friends. Women are cats. On the other hand, if women were enfranchised, we would have all the women banded together on one side and all the men banded together on the other side, and there would follow a sex war which might end in bloody revolution.

Just one more of my little couplets: the ballot is greatly overestimated. It has never done anything for anybody. Lots of men tell me this. And the corresponding argument is—the ballot is what makes man man. It is what gives him all his dignity and all of his superiority to women. Therefore if we allow women to share this privilege, how could a woman look up to her own husband? Why, there would be nothing to look up to.

I have talked to many woman suffragists and I find them very unreasonable. I say to them: "Here I am, convince me." I ask for proof. Then they proceed to tell me of Australia and Colorado and other places where women have passed excellent laws to improve the condition of working women and children. But I say, "What of it?" These are facts. I don't care about facts. I ask for proof.

Then they quote the eight million women of the United States who are now supporting themselves, and the twenty-five thousand married women in the City of New York who are self-supporting. But I say again, what of it? These are statistics. I don't believe in statistics. Facts and statistics are things which no truly womanly woman would ever use.

I wish to prove anti-suffrage in a womanly way—that is, by personal example. This is my method of persuasion. Once I saw a woman driving a horse, and the horse ran away with her. Isn't that just like a woman? Once I read in the newspapers about a woman whose house caught on fire, and she threw the children out of the window and carried the pillows downstairs. Does that show political acumen, or does it not? Besides, look at the hats that women wear! And have you ever known a successful woman governor of a state? Or have you ever known a really truly successful woman president of the United States? Well, if they could they would, wouldn't they? Then, if they haven't, doesn't that show they couldn't? As for the militant suffragettes, they are all hyenas in petticoats. Now do you want to be a hyena and wear petticoats?

Now, I think I have proved anti-suffrage; and I have done it in a womanly way—that is, without stooping to the use of a single fact or argument or a single statistic.

I am the prophet of a new idea. No one has ever thought of it or heard of it before. I well remember when this great idea first came to me. It waked me in the middle of the night with a shock that gave me a headache. This is it: woman's place is in the home. Is it not beautiful as it is new, new as it is true? Take this idea away with you. You will find it very helpful in your daily lives. You may not grasp it just at first, but you will gradually grow into understanding of it.

I know the suffragists reply that all our activities have been taken out of the home. The baking, the washing, the weaving, the spinning are all long since taken out of the home. But I say, all the more reason that something should stay in the home. Let it be woman. Besides, think of the great modern invention, the telephone. That has been put into the home. Let woman stay at home and answer the telephone.

We antis have so much imagination! Sometimes it seems to us that we can hear the little babies in the slums crying to us. We can see the children in factories and mines reaching out their little hands to us, and the working women in the sweated industries, the under-paid, underfed women, reaching out their arms to us—all, all crying as with one voice, "Save us, save us, from Woman Suffrage." Well may they make this appeal to us, for who knows what woman suffrage might not do for such as these. It might even alter the conditions under which they live.

We antis do not believe that any conditions should be altered. We want everything to remain just as it is. All is for the best. Whatever is, is right. If misery is in the world, God has put it there; let it remain. If this misery presses harder on some women than others, it is because they need discipline. Now, I have always been comfortable and well cared for. But then I never needed discipline. Of course I am only a weak, ignorant woman. But there is one thing I do understand from the ground up, and that is the divine intention toward woman. I *know* that the divine intention toward woman is, let her remain at home.

The great trouble with the suffragists is this; they interfere too much. They are always interfering. Let me take a practical example.

There is in the City of New York a Nurses' Settlement, where sixty trained nurses go forth to care for sick babies and give them pure milk. Last summer only two or three babies died in this slum district around the Nurses' Settlement, whereas formerly hundreds of babies have died there every summer. Now what are these women doing? Interfering, interfering with the death rate! And what is their motive in so doing? They seek notoriety. They want to be noticed. They are trying to show off. And if sixty women who merely believe in suffrage behave in this way, what may we expect when all women are enfranchised?

What ought these women to do with their lives? Each one ought to be devoting herself to the comfort of some man. You may say, they are not married. But I answer, let them try a little harder and they might find some kind of a man to devote themselves to. What does the Bible say on this subject? It says, "Seek and ye shall find." Besides, when I look around me at the men, I feel that God never meant us women to be too particular.

Let me speak one word to my sister women who are here today. Women, we don't need to vote in order to get our own way. Don't misunderstand me. Of course I want you to get your own way. That's what we're here for. But do it indirectly. If you want a thing, tease. If that doesn't work, nag. If that doesn't do, cry—crying always brings them around. Get what you want. Pound pillows. Make a scene. Make home a hell on earth, but do it in a womanly way. That is so much more dignified and refined than walking up to a ballot box and dropping in a piece of paper. Can't you see that?

Let us consider for a moment the effect of woman's enfranchisement on man. I think some one ought to consider the men. What makes husbands faithful and loving? The ballot, and the monopoly of that privilege. If women vote, what will become of men? They will all slink off drunk and disorderly. We antis understand men. If women were enfranchised, men would revert to their natural instincts such as regicide, matricide, patricide, and race-suicide. Do you believe in race-suicide or do you not? Then, isn't it our duty to refrain from a thing that would lure men to destruction?

It comes down to this. Some one must wash the dishes. Now, would you expect man, man made in the image of God, to roll up his sleeves and wash the dishes? Why, it would be blasphemy. I know that I am but a rib and so I wash the dishes. Or I hire another rib to do it for me, which amounts to the same thing.

Let us consider the argument from the standpoint of religion. The Bible says, "Let the women keep silent in the churches." Paul says, "Let them keep their hats on for fear of the angels." My minister says, "Wives, obey your husbands." And my husband says that woman suffrage would rob the rose of its fragrance and the peach of its bloom. I think that is so sweet.

Besides, did George Washington ever say, "Votes for women?" No. Did the Emperor Kaiser Wilhelm ever say, "Votes for women?" No. Did Elijah, Elisha, Micah, Hezekiah, Obadiah, and Jeremiah ever say, "Votes for women?" No. Then that settles it.

I don't want to be misunderstood in my reference to woman's inability to vote. Of course she could get herself to the polls and lift a piece of paper. I don't doubt that. What I refer to is the pressure on the brain, the effect of this mental strain on woman's delicate nervous organization and on her highly wrought sensitive nature. Have you ever pictured to yourself Election Day with women voting? Can you imagine how women, having undergone this terrible ordeal, with their delicate systems all upset, will come out of the voting booths and be led away by policemen, and put into ambulances, while they are fainting and weeping, half laughing, half crying, and having fits upon the public highway? Don't you think that if a woman is going to have a fit, it is far better for her to have it in the privacy of her own home?

And how shall I picture to you the terrors of the day after election? Divorce and death will rage unchecked, crime and contagious disease will stalk unbridled through the land. Oh, friends, on this subject I feel—I feel, so strongly that I can—not think!

ELIZA BURT GAMBLE

FROM

THE SEXES IN SCIENCE AND HISTORY

AN INQUIRY INTO THE DOGMA OF WOMAN'S INFERIORITY TO MAN

Eliza Burt Gamble (1841–1920): Eliza Burt Gamble's The Sexes in Science and History: An Inquiry into the Dogma of Woman's Inferiority to Man, *published in 1916, is a revised version of an earlier work,* The Evolution of Woman *(1893). A naturalist, Gamble began an investigation into human development in 1885. During her studies, she read Darwin's* The Descent of Man *and was greatly influenced by its theories, although disturbed to find that Darwin and other scientists "seemed inclined to ignore certain facts . . . which tend to prove the superiority of the female organism."*

Gamble believed the basis for women's perceived inferiority stemmed from a theological prejudice, and she hoped to use scientific data and evidence to disprove these beliefs. Claiming the highest respect for Darwin, she nonetheless believed that he was as susceptible to such prejudices as anyone, and Gamble used his own theories of evolution to conclude that females are not only equal but superior to males.

PREFACE TO FIRST EDITION

After a somewhat careful study of written history, and after an investigation extending over several years of all the accessible facts relative to extant tribes representing the various stages of human development, I had reached the conclusion, as early as the year 1882, that the female organism is in no wise inferior to that of the male. For some time, however, I was unable to find any detailed proof that could consistently be employed to substantiate the correctness of this hypothesis.

In the year 1885, with no special object in view other than a desire for information, I began a systematized investigation of the facts which at that time had been established by naturalists relative to the development of mankind from lower orders of life. It was not, however, until the year 1886, after a careful reading of *The Descent of Man*, by Mr. Darwin, that I first became impressed with the belief that the theory of evolution, as enunciated by scientists, furnishes much evidence going to show that the female among all the orders of life, man included, represents a higher stage of development than the male. Although at the time indicated, the belief that man has descended from lower orders in the scale of being had been accepted by the leading minds both in Europe and America, for reasons which have not been explained, scientists, generally, seemed inclined to ignore certain facts connected with this theory which tend to prove the superiority of the female organism.

Scarcely considering at the outset whether my task would eventually take the form of a magazine article, or whether it would be extended to the dimensions of a book, I set myself to work to show that some of the conclusions of the savants regarding the subject of sex-development are not in accord with their premises.

While writing the first part of this volume, and while reasoning on the facts established by scientists in connection with the observations which have been made in these later years relative to the growth of human society and the development of human institutions, it seemed clear to me that the history of life on the earth presents an unbroken chain of evidence going to prove the importance of the female; and, so struck was I by the manner in which the facts of science and those of history harmonize, that I decided to embrace within my work some of the results of my former research. I therefore set about the task of tracing, in a brief manner, the growth of the primary characters observed in the two diverging sex-columns, according to the facts and principles enunciated in the theory of natural development.

It is not perhaps singular, during an age dominated by theological dogmatism, and in which no definite knowledge relative to the development of life on the earth had been gained, that man should have regarded himself as an infinitely superior being. Neither is it remarkable that woman, who was supposed to have appeared later on the scene of action than did her male mate, and who owed her existence to a surgical operation performed upon him, should have been regarded simply as an appendage, a creature brought forth in response to the requirements of the masculine nature.

The above doctrines when enunciated by theologians need cause little surprise, but with the dawn of a scientific age it might have been expected that the prejudices resulting from those doctrines might disappear. When, however, we turn to the most advanced scientific writings of the present century, we find that the prejudices which throughout thousands of years have been gathering strength are by no means eradicated, and any discussion of the sex question is still rare in which the effects of these prejudices may not be traced. Even Mr. Darwin, notwithstanding his great breadth of mental vision and the important work which he accomplished in the direction of original inquiry, whenever he had occasion to touch on the mental capacities of women, or more particularly on the relative capacities of the sexes, manifested the same spirit which characterizes the efforts of an earlier age; and throughout his entire investigation of the human species, his ability to ignore certain facts which he himself adduced, and which all along the line of development tend to prove the superiority of the female, is truly remarkable.

We usually judge of a man's fitness to assume the rôle of an original investigator in any branch of human knowledge, by noting his powers of observation and generalization, and by observing his capacity to perceive connections between closely related facts; also, by tracing the various processes by which he arrives at his conclusions. The ability, however, to collect facts, and the power to generalize and draw conclusions from them, avail little, when brought into direct opposition to deeply rooted prejudices.

The indications are strong that the time has at length arrived when the current opinions concerning sex capacity and endowment demand a revision, and when nothing short of scientific deductions, untainted by the prejudices and dogmatic assumptions of the past, will be accepted.

As has been stated, the object of this volume is to set forth the principal data brought forward by naturalists bearing on the subject of the origin and development of the two lines of sexual demarcation, and by means of the facts observed by explorers among peoples in the various stages of development, to trace, so far as possible, the effect of such differentiation upon the individual, and upon the subsequent growth of human society.

CHAPTER V

THE SUPREMACY OF THE MALE

An unprejudiced review of the facts relative to the differentiation of the two sexes, as set forth by naturalists, reveals not only the primary principles involved in human progress, but shows also the source whence these principles originated. These facts serve also to explain that "mental superiority" of man over woman observed by Mr. Darwin and others in the present stage of human growth.

Notwithstanding the superior degree of development which, according to the facts elaborated by scientists, must belong to the female in all the orders of life below mankind, Mr. Darwin would have us believe that so soon as the human species appeared on the earth the processes which for untold ages had been in operation were reversed, and that through courage and perseverance, or patience, qualities which were the result of extreme selfishness, or which were acquired while in pursuit of animal gratification, man finally became superior to woman. The following furnishes an example of Mr. Darwin's reasoning upon this subject. He says:

> The chief distinction in the intellectual powers of the two sexes is shown by man's attaining to a higher eminence, in whatever he takes up, than can woman—whether requiring deep thought, reason, or imagination, or merely the use of the senses and the hands. If two lists were made of the most eminent men and women in poetry, painting, sculpture, music (inclusive both of composition and performance), history, and philosophy, with half-a-dozen names under each subject, the two lists would not bear comparison. . . .
>
> Now, when two men are put into competition, or a man with a woman, both possessed of every mental quality in equal

perfection, save that one has higher energy, perseverance, and courage, the latter will generally become more eminent in every pursuit, and will gain the ascendancy. He may be said to possess genius—for genius has been declared by a great authority to be patience; and patience, in this sense, means unflinching, undaunted perseverance.

Doubtless, for the purpose of strengthening his position, Mr. Darwin quotes the following from John Stuart Mill: "The things in which man most excels woman are those which require most plodding and long hammering at single thoughts." And in summing up the processes by which man has finally gained the ascendancy over woman he concludes:

> Thus man has ultimately become superior to woman. It is, indeed, fortunate that the law of the equal transmission of characters to both sexes prevails with mammals; otherwise it is probable that man would have become as superior in mental endowment to woman, as the peacock is in ornamental plumage to the peahen.

Notwithstanding this conclusion of Mr. Darwin, in view of the facts elaborated by himself, we cannot help thinking that it is indeed fortunate that the law of the equal transmission of characters to both sexes prevails with mammals, otherwise it is probable that man would never have had any higher ambition than the gratification of his animal instincts, and would never have risen above those conditions in which he struggled desperately for the possession of the female. All the facts which have been observed relative to the acquirement of the social instincts and the moral sense prove them to have originated in the female constitution, and as progress is not possible without these characters, it is not difficult to determine within which of the sexes the progressive principle first arose. Even courage, perseverance, and energy, characters which are denominated as thoroughly masculine, since they are the result of Sexual Selection, have been and still are largely dependent on the will or choice of the female.

In his zeal to prove the superiority of man over woman, and while emphasizing energy, perseverance, and courage as factors in development, Mr. Darwin seems to have overlooked the importance of the distinctive characters belonging to the female organism, viz., perception and intuition, combined with greater powers of endurance, the first two of which, under the low conditions occasioned by the supremacy of the animal instincts, have thus far had little opportunity to manifest themselves. A fairer statement relative to the capacities of the two sexes and their ability to succeed might have been set forth as follows:

When a man and a woman are put in competition, both possessed of every mental quality in equal perfection, save that one has higher energy, more patience, and a somewhat greater degree of physical courage, while the other has superior powers of intuition, finer and more rapid perceptions, and a greater degree of endurance (the result of an organism freer from imperfections), the chances of the latter for gaining the ascendancy will doubtless be equal to those of the former as soon as the animal conditions of life are outgrown, and the characters peculiar to the female constitution are allowed expression. Mr. Darwin's quotation from J. Stuart Mill, that the things in which man excels woman are those which require most plodding and long hammering at single thoughts, is evidently true, and corresponds with the fundamental premises in the theory of development as set forth by all naturalists. The female organism is not a plodding machine, neither is the telephone nor the telegraph, yet these latter devices accomplish the work formerly done by the stagecoach much more rapidly, and in a manner better suited to civilized conditions. So soon as women are freed from the unnatural restrictions placed upon them through the temporary predominance of the animal instincts in man, their greater powers of endurance, together with a keener insight and an organism comparatively free from imperfections, will doubtless give them a decided advantage in the struggle for existence. While patience is doubtless a virtue, and while during the past ages of human experience it has been of incalculable value to man, it will not, under higher conditions, be required in competing for the prizes of life.

Woman's rapid perceptions, and her intuitions which in many instances amount almost to second sight, indicate undeveloped genius, and partake largely of the nature of deductive reasoning; it is reasonable to suppose therefore that as soon as she is free, and has for a few generations enjoyed the advantages of more natural methods of education and training, and those better suited to the female constitution, she will be able to trace the various processes of induction by which she reaches her conclusions. She will then be able to reason inductively up to her deductive conceptions.

The worthlessness of Mr. Darwin's comparison between men and women in performing the various activities of life is already clearly apparent. Although less than half a century has elapsed since *The Descent of Man* was written women are already successfully competing with men in nearly all the walks of life both high and low, and this too notwithstanding the fact that these occupations have heretofore been regarded as belonging exclusively to men. We have seen that Mr. Darwin mentions music as a vocation in which man's superiority over woman is manifested, yet already in the United States, there is not one male musician who would be willing to match his skill against that of any one of the four best woman performers.

It is a well understood fact that neither individuals nor classes which upon every hand have been thwarted and restrained, either by unjust and oppressive laws, or by the tyranny of custom, prejudice, or physical force, have ever made any considerable progress in the actual acquirement of knowledge or in the arts of life. Mr. Darwin's capacity for collecting and formulating facts seems not to have materially aided him in discerning the close connection existing at this stage of human progress between the masculinized conditions of human society and the necessary opportunities to succeed in the higher walks of life; in fact, he seems to have forgotten that all the avenues to success have for thousands of years been controlled and wholly manipulated by men, while the activities of women have been distorted and repressed in order that the "necessities" of the male nature might be provided for. Besides, it seems never to have occurred to him that as man has still not outgrown the animal in his nature, and as the intellectual and moral age is only just beginning to dawn, the time is not yet ripe for the direct expression of the more refined instincts and ideas peculiar to the female organism, and, as thus far, only that advancement has been made which is compatible with the supremacy of the lower instincts, woman's time has not yet come.

Although women are still in possession of their natural inheritance, a finer and more complex organism comparatively free from imperfections, and although, as a result of this inheritance, their intuitions are still quicker, their perceptions keener, and their endurance greater, the drain on their physical energies, caused by the abnormal development of the reproductive energies in the opposite sex, has, during the ages of man's dominion over her, been sufficient to preclude the idea of success in competing with men for the prizes of life. Although an era of progress has begun, ages will doubtless be required to eradicate abuses which are the result of constitutional defects, and especially so as the prejudices and feelings of mankind are for the most part in harmony with such abuses.

If we examine the subject of female apparel, at the present time, we shall observe how difficult it is to uproot long-established prejudices which are deeply rooted in sensuality and superstition; and this is true notwithstanding the fact that such prejudices may involve the comfort and even the health of half the people, and seriously affect the welfare of unborn generations. An examination of the influences which have determined the course of modern fashions in woman's clothing will show the truth of this observation.

Of all the senses which have been developed, that of sight is undoubtedly the most refined, and when in the human species it is cultivated to a degree which enables its possessor to appreciate the beautiful in Nature and in Art, we are perhaps justified in designating it as the intellectual sense. In point of refinement, the sense of hearing comes next in order, yet among creatures as low in the scale of being as birds, we find that females not only appreciate the beautiful, but that they are charmed by pleasing and harmonious sounds, and that if males would win their favor it must be accomplished by appeals through these senses to the higher qualities developed within them.

Although the female of the human species, like the female among the lower orders of life, is capable of appreciating fine coloring, and to a considerable extent the beautiful in form, the style of dress adopted by women is not an expression of their natural ideas of taste and harmony. On the contrary, it is to Sexual Selection that we must look for an explanation of the incongruities and absurdities presented by the so-called female fashions of the past and present. The processes of Sexual Selection, which, so long as the female was the controlling agency in courtship, worked on the male, have in these later ages been reversed. For the reason that the female of the human species has so long been under subjection to the male, the styles of female dress and adornment which have been adopted, and which are still in vogue, are largely the result of masculine taste. Woman's business in life has been to marry, or, at least, it has been necessary for her, in order to gain her support, to win the favor of the opposite sex. She must, therefore, by her charms, captivate the male.

With the progress of civilization and since women as economic and sexual slaves have become dependent upon men for their support, no male biped has been too stupid, too ugly, or too vicious to take to himself a mate and perpetuate his imperfections. This unchecked freedom of the male to multiply his defects is responsible for present conditions.

As for thousands of years women have been dependent on men not only for food and clothing but for the luxuries of life as well, it is not singular that in the struggle for life to which they have been subjected they should have adopted the styles of dress which would be likely to secure to them the greatest amount of success. When we remember that the present ideas of becomingness or propriety in woman's apparel are the result of ages of sensuality and servitude, it is not remarkable that they are difficult to uproot, and especially so as many of the most pernicious and health-destroying styles involve questions of female decorum as understood by a sensualized age.

Mr. Darwin calls attention to the fact that women "all over the world" adorn themselves with the gay feathers of male birds. Since the beautiful plumage of male birds has been produced according to female standards of taste, and since it is wholly the result of innate female ideas of harmony in color and design, it is not perhaps remarkable that women, recognizing the original female standards of beauty, should desire to utilize those effects which have been obtained at so great an expenditure of vital force to the opposite sex, especially as men are pleased with such display, and, as under present conditions of male supremacy, the female of the human species is obliged to captivate the male in order to secure her support.

Ever since the dominion of man over woman began a strict censorship over her dress has been maintained. Although in very recent times women are beginning to exercise a slight degree of independence in the matter of clothes, still, because of existing prejudices and customs they have not yet been able to adopt a style of dress which admits of the free and unrestricted use of the body and limbs. It is believed that woman, the natural tempter of man, if left to her own sinful devices, would again as of old attempt to destroy that inherent purity of heart and cleanliness of life which characterize the male constitution. Woman's ankles and throat seem to be the most formidable foes against which innocent man has to contend, so the concealment of these offending members is deemed absolutely necessary for his protection and safety. Ecclesiastics, a class whose duty it has ever been to regulate and control the movements of women, seem to think that the ankles and throats of women were intended not for the use and convenience of their possessors but as snares to entrap holy men.

It would thus appear that the present fashions for female apparel have a deeper significance than we have been in the habit of ascribing to them. We are still living under conditions peculiar to a sensual age, and have not yet outgrown the requirements which condemn women to a style of dress which hinders the free movements of the body and which checks all the activities of life. In one way the woman of the present time may be said to resemble the male Argus pheasant, whose decorations, although they serve to please his mate, greatly hinder his power of motion and the free use of his body and limbs.

When we consider that apparel is but one, and a minor one, of the strictures under which women have labored during the later era of human existence and when we consider all the ignoble and degrading uses to which womanhood has been subjected, the wonder is not that women have failed in the past to distinguish themselves in the various fields of intellectual labor in which men have achieved a limited degree of success, but that they have had sufficient energy and courage left to enable them even to attempt anything so far outside the boundary of their prescribed "sphere," or that they have been able to transmit to their male offspring those powers through which they have gained their present stage of progress.

With regard to Mr. Darwin's comparison of the intellectual powers of the two sexes, and his assertion that man attains to a higher eminence in whatever he takes up than woman—that, for instance, he surpasses her in the production of poetry, music, philosophy, etc., the facts at hand suggest that if within mankind no higher motives and tastes had been developed than those derived

from selfishness and passion, there would never have arisen a desire
for poetry, music, philosophy, or science, or, in fact, for any of the
achievements which have been the result of the more exalted activities
of the human intellect. However, because of the subjection of the
higher faculties developed in mankind, the poetry, music, and painting of the past betray their sensuous origin and plainly reveal the
stage of advancement which has been reached, while history, philosophy, and even science, judging from Mr. Darwin's methods, have
not yet wholly emerged from the murky atmosphere of a sensuous
age.

It will be well for us to remember that the doctrine of the Survival of the Fittest does not imply that the best endowed, physically
or otherwise, have always succeeded in the struggle for existence. By
the term Survival of the Fittest we are to understand a natural law
by means of which those best able to overcome the unfavorable conditions of their environment survive and are able to propagate their
successful qualities. We must bear in mind that neither the growth
of the individual nor that of society has proceeded in an unbroken
or uninterrupted line; on the contrary, during a certain portion of
human existence on the earth, the forces which tend toward degeneration have been stronger than those which lie along the line of true
development.

We are assured that the principles of construction and destruction are mutually employed in the reproductive processes, that continuous death means continuous life,—the katabolic or disruptive
tendencies of the male being necessary to the anabolic or constructive habits of the female. As it is in reproduction, so has it been
through the entire course of development. Side by side, all along the
line, these two tendencies have been in operation; the grinding, rend-
ing, and devouring processes which we denominate Natural Selection,
alongside those which unite, assimilate, and protect. As a result of
the separation of the sexes there have been developed on the one side
extreme egoism, or the desire for selfish gratification; on the other,
altruism, or a desire for the welfare of others outside of self. Hence,
throughout the later ages of human existence, since the egoistic principles have gained the ascendancy, may be observed the unequal
struggle for liberty and justice, against tyranny, and the oppressors of
the masses of the human race. From present appearances it would

seem that the disruptive or devouring forces have always been in the ascendancy. The philosophy of history, however, teaches the contrary. With a broader view of the origin and development of the human race, and the unexpected light which within the last few years has been thrown upon prehistoric society and the grandeur of past achievement, a close student of the past is able to discern a faint glimmering of a more natural age of human existence, and is able to observe in the present intense struggles for freedom and equality, an attempt to return to the earlier and more natural principles of justice and liberty, and so to advance to a stage of society in which selfishness, sensuality, and superstition no longer reign supreme.

The status of women always furnishes an index to the true condition of society, one or two superficial writers to the contrary notwithstanding. For this phenomenon there is a scientific reason, namely: society advances just in proportion as women are able to convey to their offspring the progressive tendencies transmissible only through the female organism. It is plain, therefore, that mankind will never advance to a higher plane of thinking and living until the restrictions upon the liberties of women have been entirely removed, and until within every department of human activity, their natural instincts, and the methods of thought peculiar to them be allowed free expression. The following is from Mr. Buckle's lecture on "The Influence of Women on the Progress of Knowledge":

> I believe and I hope before we separate to convince you, that so far from women exercising little or no influence over the progress of knowledge, they are capable of exercising, and have actually exercised an enormous influence; that this influence, is, in fact, so great that it is hardly possible to assign limits to it; and that great as it is, it may with advantage be still further increased. I hope, moreover, to convince you that this influence has been exhibited not merely from time to time in rare, sudden, and transitory ebullitions, but that it acts by virtue of certain laws inherent in human nature; and that, although it works as an undercurrent below the surface, and is therefore invisible to hasty observers, it has already produced the most important results, and has affected the shape, the character, and the amount of our knowledge.

Through the processes involved in the differentiation of sex and the consequent division of functions, it has been possible during the past six thousand or seven thousand years (a mere tithe of the time spent by mankind upon the earth) for women to become enslaved, or subjected to the lower impulses of the male nature. Through the capture of women for wives, through the exigencies of warfare, the individual ownership of land, and the various changes incident to a certain stage of human existence, the finer sensibilities which characterize women have been overshadowed, and the higher forces which originated within them and which are transmitted in the female line, have been temporarily subdued by the great sexual ardor inherent in the opposite sex; it is not, therefore, singular that the degree of progress attained should appear to be wholly the result of male activity and acumen. Yet, notwithstanding the degradation to which women in the position assigned them by physical force have been obliged to submit, their capacity for improvement has suffered less from the influences and circumstances of their environment than has that of men. As the higher faculties are transmitted through women equally to both sexes, in the impoverishment of their inheritance on the female side, men have suffered equally with women, while, through their male progenitors, they have inherited appetites and habits (the result of a ruder and less developed structure) which weaken and degrade the entire constitution.

Doubtless, so soon as women have gained sufficient strength to enable them to maintain their independence, and after the higher faculties rather than the animal propensities rule supreme, men, through the imperfections in their organism, and the appetites acquired through these imperfections, will, for a considerable length of time, find themselves weighted in the struggle for supremacy, and this, too, by the very characters which under lower conditions are now believed to have determined their success.

It is not unlikely, however, that through Sexual Selection the characters or qualities unfavorable to the higher development of man will in time be eliminated. The mother is the natural guardian and protector of offspring; therefore, so soon as women are free they will doubtless select for husbands only those men who, by their mental, moral, and physical endowments are fitted to become the fathers of their children. Only those women will become mothers who hope to secure to their offspring immunity from the giant evils with which society is afflicted. In this way, and this way only, may these evils be eradicated.

Under purer conditions of life, when by the higher powers developed in the race the animal propensities have become somewhat subdued by man, we may reasonably hope that the "struggle for existence," which is still so relentlessly waged, will cease, that man will no longer struggle with man for place or power, and that the bounties of earth will no longer be hoarded by the few, while the many are suffering for the necessities of life; for are we not all members of one family, and dependent for all that we have on the same beneficent parent—Nature?

Although the two principles, the constructive and destructive, are closely allied, the higher faculties have been acquired only through the former—the highest degree of progress is possible only through union or cooperation, or, through the uniting and binding force, maternal love, from which has been developed, first, sympathy among related groups, and later an interest which is capable of extending itself not only to all members of the human race, but to every sentient creature. There is, therefore, little wonder that for thousands of years of human existence, the female principle was worshiped over the entire habitable globe as the source of all light and life—the Creator and Preserver of the Universe.

We are only on the threshold of civilization. Mankind may as yet have no just conception of their possibilities, but so soon as, through the agencies now in operation for the advancement of the race, the "necessities" of the male nature no longer demand and secure the subjection of women and the consequent drain on the very fountain whence spring the higher faculties, a great and unexpected impetus will be given to progress.

The fact that a majority of women have not yet gained that freedom of action necessary to the absolute control of their own persons, nor acquired a sufficient degree of independence to enable them to adopt a course of action in their daily life which they know to be right, shows the extent to which selfishness, twin brother to sensuality, has clouded the conscience and warped the judgment in all matters pertaining to human justice. So closely has women's environment been guarded that in addition to all the restrictions placed upon their liberties, a majority of them are still dependent for food and clothing on pleasing the men, who still hold the purse-strings. Yet Mr. Darwin, the apostle of original scientific investigation, concludes:

"If men are capable of decided prominence over women in many subjects, the average mental powers in men must be above those of women."

MARIE STOPES

FROM

MARRIED LOVE

A NEW CONTRIBUTION TO THE
SOLUTION OF SEX DIFFICULTIES

Marie Stopes (1880–1958): Born in Edinburgh, Marie Stopes obtained her Ph.D. in Munich in 1904. After teaching for two years at Manchester University, Stopes traveled to Japan on a scientific expedition. In 1911 she married a Canadian botanist, Reginald Ruggles Gates, but the marriage was annulled five years later on the grounds of nonconsummation.

The dissolution of her marriage led her to read widely on the subject of sexuality, and her research inspired her to write Married Love, *which details an ideal marriage. Stopes explained that marriage and sexual pleasure should be shared equally between husband and wife. Unlike Margaret Sanger, who saw the availability of birth control as an attack on poverty, Stopes saw it as a means of increasing women's sexual pleasure by removing the fear of conception. Although the book might be considered moderate by today's standards since it only mentioned controversial subjects like birth control in passing, Stopes had a difficult time finding a publisher willing to back the project. Margaret Sanger was very impressed with the manuscript and offered to help Stopes find an American publisher, but the book was eventually backed by Humphrey Verdon Roe, a supporter of female emancipation and accessible birth control. Roe and Stopes married in 1918 soon after the publication of* Married Love, *and Stopes retained the name Dr. Marie Stopes throughout her career.*

Married Love *was a success and it was followed by* Wise Parenthood *(1918) and* Letter to Working Mothers *(1919). Stopes became increasingly concerned with the need for available birth control and the problems of the working class. In 1921 she founded the Society for Constructive Birth Control and Racial Progress. That same year Marie Stopes and Humphrey Roe opened the first birth-control clinic in England, the* Mother's Clinic, *which still operates in London today.*

CHAPTER II

THE BROKEN JOY

What shall be done to quiet the heart-cry of the world? How answer the
dumb appeal for help we so often divine below eyes that laugh?—Æ in "The
Hero in Man."

Dreaming of happiness, feeling that at last they have each found
the one who will give eternal understanding and tenderness, the
young man and maiden marry.[1]

At first, in the time generally called the honeymoon, the unaccustomed freedom and the sweetness of the relation often does bring
real happiness. How long does it last? Too often a far shorter time
than is generally acknowledged.

In the first joy of their union it is hidden from the two young
people that they know little or nothing about the fundamental laws
of each other's being. Much of the sex-attraction (not only among
human beings, but even throughout the whole world of living creatures) depends upon the differences between the two that pair; and
probably taking them all unawares, those very differences which drew
them together now begin to work their undoing.

But so long as the first illusion that each understands the other
is supported by the thrilling delight of ever-fresh discoveries, the sensations lived through are so rapid and so joyous that the lovers do
not realize that there is no firm foundation of real mutual knowledge
beneath their feet. While even the happiest pair may know of divergencies about religion, politics, social custom, and opinions on
things in general, these, with goodwill, patience, and intelligence on
either side, can be ultimately adjusted, because in all such things there
is a common meeting ground for the two. Human beings, while differing widely about every conceivable subject in such human rela-

[1] In this, and in most of the generalizations found in this book, I am speaking of things as they are
in Great Britain. While, to a considerable extent, the same is true of America and the Scandinavian
countries, it must be remembered all through that I am speaking of the British, and primarily of
our educated classes.

tions, have at least *thought* about them, threshed them out, and discussed them openly for generations.

But about the much more fundamental and vital problems of sex, there is a lack of knowledge so abysmal and so universal that its mists and shadowy darkness have affected even the few who lead us, and who are prosecuting research in these subjects. And the two young people begin to suffer from fundamental divergencies, before perhaps they realize that such exist, and with little prospect of ever gaining a rational explanation of them.

Nearly all those whose own happiness seems to be dimmed or broken count themselves exceptions, and comfort themselves with the thought of some of their friends, who, they feel sure, have attained the happiness which they themselves have missed.

It is generally supposed that happy people, like happy nations, have no history—they are silent about their own affairs. Those who talk about their marriages are generally those who have missed the happiness they expected. True as this may be in general, it is not permanently and profoundly true, and there are people who are reckoned, and still reckon themselves, happy, but who yet unawares reveal the secret disappointment which clouds their inward peace.

Leaving out of account *"femmes incomprises"* and all the innumerable neurotic, super-sensitive, and slightly abnormal people, it still remains an astonishing and tragic fact that *so* large a proportion of marriages lose their early bloom and are to some extent unhappy.

For years many men and women have confided to me the secrets of their lives; and of all the innumerable marriages of which the inner circumstances are known to me, there are tragically few which approach even humanly attainable joy.

Many of those considered by the world, by the relatives, *even by the loved and loving partner*, to be perfectly happy marriages, are secretly shadowed to the more sensitive of the pair.

Where the bride is, as are so many of our educated girls, composed of virgin sweetness shut in ignorance, the man is often the first to create "the rift within the lute"; but his suffering begins almost simultaneously with hers. The surface freedom of our women has not materially altered, cannot materially alter, the pristine purity of a girl of our northern race. She generally has neither the theoretical knowledge nor the spontaneous physical development which might give the capacity even to imagine the basic facts of physical marriage, and her bridegroom may shock her without knowing that he was doing so. Then, unconscious of the nature, and even perhaps of the existence, of his fault, he is bewildered and pained by her inarticulate pain.

Yet I think, nevertheless, it is true that in the early days of marriage the young man is often even more sensitive, more romantic, more easily pained about all ordinary things, and he enters marriage hoping for an even higher degree of spiritual and bodily unity than does the girl or the woman. But the man is more quickly blunted, more swiftly rendered cynical and is readier to look upon happiness as a Utopian dream than is his mate.

On the other hand, the woman is slower to realize disappointment, and more often by the sex-life of marriage is of the two the more *profoundly* wounded, with a slow corrosive wound that eats into her very being and warps all her life.

Perfect happiness is a unity composed of a myriad essences; and this one supreme thing is exposed to the attacks of countless destructive factors.

Were I to touch upon all the possible sources of marital disappointment and unhappiness, this book would expand into a dozen bulky volumes. As I am addressing those who I assume have read, or can read, other books written upon various ramifications of the subject, I will not discuss the themes which have been handled by many writers, nor deal with abnormalities which fill so large a part of most books on sex.

In the last few years there has been such an awakening to the realization of the corrosive horror of all aspects of prostitution that there is no need to labor the point that no marriage can be happy where the husband has, in buying another body, sold his own health with his honor, and is tainted with disease. Surely today every thoughtful young person realizes that such disease may wreck not only the man and infect his wife with horrors unimaginable, but that it may destroy the health and even the very existence of his unborn children.

Nor is it necessary, in speaking to well-meaning, optimistic young couples, to enlarge upon the obvious dangers of drunkenness, self-indulgence, and the cruder forms of selfishness.

It is with the subtler infringements of the fundamental laws we have to deal. And the prime tragedy is that, as a rule, the two young people are both unaware of the existence of such decrees. Yet here, as elsewhere in nature, the lawbreaker is punished whether he is aware of the existence of the law he breaks or not.

In the state of ignorance which so largely predominates today, the first sign that things are amiss between the two who thought they were entering paradise together, is generally a sense of loneliness, a feeling that the one who was expected to have all in common is outside some experience, some subtle delight, and fails to understand the needs of the loved one. Trivialities are often the first indicators of something which takes its roots unseen in the profoundest depths. The girl may sob for hours over something so trifling that she cannot even put into words its nature, while the young man, thinking that he had set out with his soul's beloved upon an adventure into celestial distances, may find himself apparently up against a barrier in her which appears as incomprehensible as it is frivolous.

Then, so strange is the mystical interrelation between our bodies, our minds, and our souls, that for crimes committed in ignorance of the dual functions of the married pair, and the laws which harmonize them, the punishments are reaped on planes quite diverse, till new and ever new misunderstandings appear to spring spontaneously from the soil of their mutual contact. Gradually or swiftly each heart begins to hide a sense of boundless isolation. It may be urged that this statement is too sweeping. It is, however, based on innumerable actual lives. I have heard from women whose marriages are looked upon by all as the happiest possible expressions of human felicity, the details of secret pain of which they have allowed their husbands no inkling. Many men will know how they have hidden from their beloved wives a sense of dull disappointment, perhaps at her coldness in the marital embrace, or from the sense that there is in her something elusive which always evades their grasp.

This profound sense of misunderstanding finds readier expression in the cruder and more ordinary natures. The disappointment of the married is expressed not only in innumerable books and plays, but even in comic papers and all our daily gossip.

Now that so many "movements" are abroad, folk on all sides are emboldened to express the opinion that it is marriage itself which is at fault. Many think that merely by loosening the bonds, and making it possible to start afresh with someone else, their lives would be made harmonious and happy. But often such reformers forget that he or she who knows nothing of the way to make marriage great and beautiful with one partner, is not likely to succeed with another. Only by a reverent study of the Art of Love can the beauty of its expression be realized in linked lives.

And even when once learnt, the Art of Love takes time to practice. As Ellen Key says, "Love requires peace, love will dream; it cannot live upon the remnants of our time and our personality."

There is no doubt that Love loses, in the haste and bustle of the modern turmoil, not only its charm and graces, but some of its vital essence. The evil results of the haste which so infests and poisons us are often felt much more by the woman than by the man. The over-stimulation of city life tends to "speed up" the man's reactions, but to retard hers. To make matters worse, even for those who have leisure to spend on lovemaking, the opportunities for peaceful, romantic dalliance are less today in a city with its tubes and cinema shows than in woods and gardens where the pulling of rosemary or lavender may be the sweet excuse for the slow and profound mutual rousing of passion. Now physical passion, so swiftly stimulated in man, tends to override all else, and the untutored man seeks but one thing—the accomplishment of desire. The woman, for it is in her nature so to do, forgives the crudeness, but sooner or later her love revolts, probably in secret, and then for ever after, though she may command an outward tenderness, she has nothing within but scorn and loathing for the act which should have been a perpetually recurring entrancement.

So many people are now born and bred in artificial and false surroundings, that even the elementary fact that the acts of love should be *joyous* is unknown to them. A distinguished American doctor made this amazing statement: "I do not believe mutual pleasure in the sexual act has any particular bearing on the happiness of life." This is, perhaps, an extreme case, yet so many distinguished medical men, gynecologists and physiologists, are either in ignorance or error regarding some of the profoundest facts of human sex-life, that it is not surprising that ordinary young couples, however hopeful, should break and destroy the joy that might have been their lifelong crown.

CHAPTER V

MUTUAL ADJUSTMENT

Love worketh no ill to his neighbor.—ST. PAUL.

In the average man of our race desire knows no season beyond the slight slackening of the Winter months and the heightening of Spring. Some men have observed in themselves a faintly marked monthly, some quite a definite fortnightly, rhythm; but in the majority of men desire, even if held in stern check, is merely slumbering. It is always present, ever ready to wake at the lightest call, and often so spontaneously insistent as to require perpetual conscious repression.

It would go ill with the men of our race had women retained the wild animals' infrequent seasonal rhythm, and with it her inviolable rights in her own body save at the mating season. Woman, too, has acquired a much more frequent rhythm; but, as it does not equal man's, he has tended to ignore and override it, coercing her at all times and seasons, either by force, or by the even more compelling power of "divine" authority and social tradition.

If man's desire is perpetual and woman's intermittent; if man's desire naturally wells up every day or every few days, and woman's only every fortnight or every month, it may appear at first sight impossible for the unwarped needs of both natures simultaneously to be satisfied in a paired union of two only.

The sense that a satisfactory mutual adjustment is not within the realms of possibility has, indeed, obsessed our race for centuries. The result has been that the supposed need of one of the partners has tended to become paramount, and we have established the social traditions of a husband's "rights" and wifely "duty." As one man quite frankly said to me: "As things are it is impossible for both sexes to get what they want. One *must* be sacrificed. And it is better for society that it should be the woman."

Nevertheless, the men who consciously sacrifice the women are in a minority. Most men act in ignorance. Our code, however, has blindly sacrificed not only the woman, but with her the happiness of the majority of men, who, in total ignorance of its meaning and results, have grown up thinking that women should submit to regularly frequent, or even nightly, intercourse. For the sake of a few moments of physical pleasure they lose realms of ever-expanding joy and tenderness; and while men and women may not realize the existence of an untrodden paradise, they both suffer, if only half consciously, from being shut out from it.

Before making some suggestions which may help married people to find not only a *via media* of mutual endurance, but a *via perfecta* of mutual joy, it is necessary to consider a few points about the actual nature of man's "desire." In the innumerable books addressed to the young which I have read, I have not found one which gives certain points regarding the meaning of the male sex-phenomena which must be grasped before it is possible to give rational guidance to intelligent young men. The general ground plan of our physiology is told to us in youth because it, so obviously, is right for us to know it accurately and in a clean scientific way, rather than to be perpetually perplexed by fantastic imaginings. But the physiology of our most profoundly disturbing functions is ignored—in my opinion, criminally ignored. To describe the essentials, simple, direct and scientific language is necessary, though it may surprise those who are accustomed only to the hazy vagueness which has led to so much misapprehension of the truth. Every mating man and woman should know the following: The sex-organs of a man consist not only of the tissues which give rise to the living, moving, ciliated cells, the *sperms*, and of the penis through which they pass and by means of which they are directed into the proper place for their deposition, the woman's vagina. The woman's vaginal canal, which has an external opening covered by double lips, is generally of such a size as to allow entry of the erect penis. At the inner end of the vagina lies the smaller opening, even more important, of the neck of the womb. The sperm must penetrate this smaller opening to effect conception, though sex union is completed in the vagina save in special circumstances. In both men and women associated with the primary and essential structures there are other tissues and glands which have numerous subsidiary but yet very important parts to play; some of which influence almost every organ in the body. Man's penis, when inactive, is soft, small, and drooping. But when stimulated (and I use this word in its scientific sense), either by physical touch which acts through the nerves and muscles directly, or indirectly through messages from the brain, it increases greatly in size, and becomes stiff, turgid, and erect. Many men imagine that the

turgid condition of an erection is due to the local accumulation of
sperms, and that these can only be naturally got rid of by an ejaculation. This is entirely wrong. The enlargement of the penis is not
at all due to the presence of actual sperm, but is due to the effects of
the nervous reaction on the blood-vessels, leading to the filling, principally of the *veins*, and much less of the arteries. As the blood enters
but does not leave the penis, the venous cavities in it fill up with
venous blood until the whole is rigid. When rigid this organ is able
to penetrate the female entrance, and there the further stimulation
of contact calls out the sperms from their storehouses, the seminal
vesicles, and they pass down the channel (the urethra) and are expelled. If this is clear, it will be realized that the stiffening and erection does not *necessarily* call for relief in the ejaculation of sperm. If
the veins can empty themselves, as they naturally do when the nervous excitement which restricted them locally passes, the erection will
subside without any loss of sperms, by the mere passing back of the
locally excessive blood into the ordinary circulatory system. This can
happen quite naturally and healthily when the nerves are soothed,
either physically or as a result of a sense of mental peace and exaltation. When, on the other hand, the local excitement culminates in
the calling up and expulsion of the sperms, after it has once started
the ejaculation becomes quite involuntary and the sperms and the
secretions associated with them pass out of the system and are entirely
lost.

Of what does this loss consist? It is estimated that there are somewhere between two and five hundred million sperms in a single average ejaculation. Each single one of these (in healthy men) is capable
of fertilizing a woman's egg-cell and giving rise to a new human
being. (Thus by a single ejaculation one man might fertilize nearly
all the marriageable women in the world!) Each single one of those
minute sperms carries countless hereditary traits, and each consists
very largely of nuclear plasm—the most highly specialized and richest
substance in our bodies. The analysis of the chemical nature of the
ejaculated fluid reveals among other things a remarkably high per-
centage of calcium and phosphoric acid—both precious substances in
our organization.

It is therefore the greatest mistake to imagine that the semen is
something to be got rid of *frequently*—all the vital energy and nerve-
force involved in its ejaculation and the precious chemical substances

which go to its composition can be better utilized by being transformed into other creative work on most days of the month. And so mystic and wonderful are the chemical transformations going on in our bodies that the brain can often set this alchemy in motion, particularly if the brain is helped by *knowledge*. A strong will can often calm the nerves which regulate the blood-supply, and order the distended veins of the penis to retract and subside without wasting the semen in an ejaculation.

But while it is good that a man should be able to do this often, it is not good to try to do it always. The very restraint which adds to a man's strength up to a point, taxes his strength when carried beyond it. It is my belief that just sufficient restraint to carry him through the ebb-tides of his wife's sex-rhythm is usually the right amount to give the best strength, vigor, and joy to a man if both are normal people. If the wife has, as I think the majority of healthy, well-fed young women will be found to have, a fortnightly consciousness or unconscious *potentiality* of desire, then the two should find a perfect mutual adjustment in having fortnightly unions; for this need not be confined to only a single union on such occasion. Many men, who can well practice restraint for twelve or fourteen days, will find that one union only will not then thoroughly satisfy them; and if they have the good fortune to have healthy wives, they will find that the latter, too, have the desire for several unions in the course of a day or two. If the wave-crests are studied, it will be seen that they spread over two or three days and show several small minor crests. This is what happens when a woman is thoroughly well and vital; her desire recurs during a day or two, sometimes even every few hours if it does not, and sometimes even when it does, receive satisfaction.

Expressed in general terms (which, of course, will not fit everybody) my view may be formulated thus: The mutually best regulation of intercourse in marriage is to have three or four days of repeated unions, followed by about ten days without any unions at all, unless some strong external stimulus has stirred a mutual desire.

I have been interested to discover that the people known to me who have accidentally fixed upon this arrangement of their lives are *happy*: and it should be noted that it fits in with the charts I give which represent the normal, spontaneous feeling of so many women.

There are many women, however, who do not feel, or who may not at first recognize, a second, but have only one time of natural pleasure in sex in each moon-month. Many men of strong will and temperate lives will be able so to control themselves that they can adjust themselves to this more restrained sex-life, as do some with whom I am acquainted. On the other hand, there will be many who find this period too long to live through without using a larger amount of energy in restraining their impulse than is justifiable. It seems to me never justifiable to spend so much energy and willpower on restraining natural impulses, that valuable work and intellectual power and poise are made to suffer. If, then, a strongly sexed husband, who finds it a real loss to his powers of work to endure through twenty-six days of abstinence, should find himself married to a wife whose vitality is so low that she can only take pleasure in physical union once in her moon-month (in some it will be before, in some a little time after, her menstrual flow), he should note carefully the time she is spontaneously happy in their union, and then at any cost restrain himself through the days immediately following, and about a fortnight after her time of desire he should set himself ardently to woo her. Unless she is actually out of health he is more likely then than at any other time to succeed not only in winning her compliance, but also in giving her the proper feeling and attaining mutual ecstasy.

The husband who so restrains himself, even if it is hard to do it, will generally find that he is a thousandfold repaid not only by the increasing health and happiness of his wife, and the much intenser pleasure he gains from their mutual intercourse, but also by his own added vitality and sense of self-command. A fortnight is not too long for a healthy man to restrain himself with advantage.

Sir Thomas Clouston says ("Before I Wed," 1913): "Nature has so arranged matters that the more constantly control is exercised the more easy and effective it becomes. It becomes a habit. The less control is exercised the greater tendency there is for a desire to become a *craving* of an uncontrollable kind, which is itself of the nature of disease, and means death sooner or later." This conclusion is not only the result of the intellectual and moral experience of our race, but is supported by physiological experiments.

While a knowledge of the fundamental laws of our being should in the main regulate our lives, so complex are we, so sensitive to a myriad impressions, that clockwork regularity can never rule us.

Even where the woman is strongly sexed, with a well-marked recurrence of desire, which is generally satisfied by fortnightly unions, it may not infrequently happen that, in between these periods, there may be additional special occasions when there springs up a mutual longing to unite. These will generally depend on some event in the lovers' lives which stirs their emotions; some memory of past passion, such as an anniversary of their wedding; or perhaps will be due to a novel, poem, or picture which moves them deeply. If the man she loves plays the part of tender wooer, even at times when her passion would not spontaneously arise, a woman can generally be stirred so fundamentally as to give a passionate return. But at the times of her ebb tides the stimulus will have to be stronger than at the high tides, and it will then generally be found that the appeal must be made even more through her emotional and spiritual nature and less through the physical than usual.

The supreme law for husbands is: Remember that each act of union must be tenderly wooed for and won, and that no union should ever take place unless the woman also desires it and is made physically ready for it.

While in most marriages the husband has to restrain himself to meet the wife's less frequently recurrent rhythm, there are, on the other hand, marriages in which the husband is so under-sexed that he cannot have ordinary union save at very infrequent intervals without a serious effect on his health. If such a man is married to a woman who has inherited an unusually strong and over-frequent desire, he may suffer by union with her, or may cause her suffering by refusing to unite. But the variations in the sex-needs and the sex-ideas of different healthy people are immense, far greater than can be suggested in this book.

Ellis states that the Queen of Aragon ordained that six times a day was the proper rule in legitimate marriage! So abnormally sexed a woman would today probably succeed in killing by exhaustion a succession of husbands, for the man who could match such a desire is rare, though perhaps less exceptional than such a woman.

Though the timing and the frequency of union are the points about which questions are oftenest asked by the ignorant and well-meaning, and are most misunderstood, yet there are other fundamental facts concerning coitus about which even medical men seem surprisingly ignorant. Regarding these, a simple statement of the physiological facts is essential.

An impersonal and scientific knowledge of the structure of our bodies is the surest safeguard against prurient curiosity and lascivious gloating. This knowledge at the back of the minds of the lovers, though not perhaps remembered as such, may also spare the unintentioned cruelty of behavior which so readily injures one whose lover is ignorant.

What actually happens in an act of union should be known. After the preliminaries have mutually aroused the pair, the stimulated penis, enlarged and stiffened, is pressed into the woman's vagina. Ordinarily when a woman is not stimulated, the entrance to this canal, as well as the exterior lips of soft tissue surrounding it, are drier and rather crinkled, and the vaginal opening is smaller than the man's distended penis. But when the woman is what is physiologically called tumescent (that is, when she is ready for union and has been profoundly stirred) local parts are flushed by the internal blood-supply and to some extent are turgid like those of the man, while a secretion of mucus lubricates the opening of the vagina. The walls of the vaginal canal, being ridged with very extensible muscles, readily stretch to receive and fit the enlarged organ of the man. In an ardent woman the vaginal orifice may even spontaneously contract and relax. (So powerful is the influence of thought upon our bodily structure that in some people all these physical results may be brought about by the thought of the loved one, by the enjoyment of tender words and kisses, and the beautiful subtleties of wooing.) It can therefore be readily imagined that when the man tries to enter a woman whom he has *not* wooed to the point of stimulating her natural physical reactions of preparation, he is endeavoring to force his entry through a dry-walled opening too small for it. He may thus cause the woman actual pain, apart from the mental revolt and loathing she is likely to feel for a man who so regardlessly uses her. On the other hand, in the tumescent woman the opening, already naturally prepared, is lubricated by mucus, and all the nerves and muscles are ready to react and easily accept the man's entering organ. This account is of the meeting of two after the woman has been already married. The first union of a virgin girl differs, of course, from all others, for on that occasion the hymen is broken. One would think that every girl who was about to be married would be told of this necessary rupturing of the membrane and the temporary pain it would cause her; but even still large numbers of girls are allowed to marry in complete and cruel ignorance. What is even more surprising is the corresponding ignorance, not only of many men, but of men married some time, concerning this feature of a virgin woman's structure. It should be known that as a rule if complete penetration by the man is effected on a single occasion or hastily after marriage, quite considerable resistance may be offered by the membrane and pain experienced by the woman. Tender and loving husbands increasingly consider this, and to reduce or eliminate it approach their brides gradually, exercising self-restraint over several days at least, thus rupturing the membrane little by little. Brides should be prepared for a slightly painful initiation, and should be taught that it is transient and that their part is not to shrink from it and thus to unnerve a sensitive bridegroom, but to assist in every way by self-control coupled with self-yielding. Once the barrier is broken down, union is easy and delightful. Women differ considerably, however, in the strength of the membrane; in some the membrane is so delicate it ruptures easily in one night, others have so firm a structure that after several attempts the man finds penetration absolutely impossible. This sometimes leads to great disappointment, the man thinking himself lacking in virility, but without reason, for I know of several women who had to have a slight slit in the membrane (of course done by a medical practitioner) after several weeks of marriage, as their tissues were unusually resistant.

It should be realized that a man does not woo and win a woman once for all when he marries her: *he must woo her before every separate act of coitus*, for each act corresponds to a marriage as other creatures know it. Wild animals are not so foolish as man; a wild animal does not unite with his female without the wooing characteristic of his race, whether by stirring her by a display of his strength in fighting another male, or by exhibiting his beautiful feathers or song. And we must not forget that the wild animals are assisted by nature; they generally only woo just at the season when the female is beginning to feel natural desire. But man, who wants his mate all out of season as well as in it, has a double duty to perform, and must himself rouse, charm, and stimulate her to the local readiness which would have been to some extent naturally prepared for him had he waited till her own desire welled up. But here it is necessary to repeat what cannot be too vividly realized: woman's love is stirred *primarily* through her heart and mind, and the perfect lover need not lag awaiting her bodily and spontaneous help, but can rouse and raise it to follow their soaring minds.

To render a woman ready before uniting with her is not only the merest act of humanity to save her pain, but is of value from the man's point of view, for (unless he is one of those relatively few abnormal and diseased variants who delight only in rape) the man gains an immense increase of sensation from the mutuality thus attained, and the health of both the man and the woman is most beneficially affected.

Assuming now that the two are in the closest mental and spiritual, as well as sensory, harmony: in what position should the act be consummated? Men and women, looking into each other's eyes, kissing tenderly on the mouth, with their arms round each other, meet face to face. And that position is symbolic of the coming together of the two who meet gladly.

It seems incredible that today educated men should be found who—apparently on theological grounds—refuse to countenance any other position. Yet one wife told me that she was crushed and nearly suffocated by her husband, so that it took her hours to recover after each union, but that "on principle" he refused to attempt any other position than the one he chose to consider normal, although he was ignorant of so obvious a requirement as that he should support his weight on his elbows. Mutual well-being should be the guide for each pair.

A rigidity of mental as well as physical capacity seems to characterize some excellent and well-meaning people, and among those whose marriages fail to reach that height of perfection in a physical sense which they intellectually desire are those who are either entirely ignorant that sex-union may be accomplished in many various positions, or those who consider any other position but the most usual one to be wrong.

Yet, curiously enough, it sometimes comes to light that a pair do not even know the usual position, and in my own experience several couples who have failed to have children, or have failed to obtain the complete delight of union, have revealed that the woman did not know that it is not only her arms which should embrace her lover. Consequently, entry was to him both difficult and sometimes impossible.

In addition to this, that spontaneous movement which comes so naturally to those who are highly stirred, needs in far too many of our moderns to be encouraged and cultivated. A pair should, impelled by the great wave of feeling within them, be as pliable as the seaplants moved by the rushing tides, and they should discover for themselves which of the innumerable possible positions of equilibrium results in the greatest mutual satisfaction. In this matter, as in so many others of the more intimate phases of sex-life, there should not harden a routine, but the body should become at the service of intense feeling a keen and pliable instrument.

It is perhaps not generally realized how great are the variations of size, shape, and position of the sex-parts in different individuals, yet they differ more even than the features of the face and hands. It happens, therefore, that the position which suits most people is unsatisfactory for others. Some, for instance, can only benefit by union when both are lying on their sides. Though medically this is generally considered unfavorable for or prohibitive of conception, yet I know women who have had several children and whose husbands always used this position. Many a man who fails to rouse full sex-feeling in his wife during union and who finds her crushed and weary after it, would gain immensely himself and give to her both health and happiness were he to lie on his side by her and, as though carrying her in his arms, to embrace her thus. In this matter every couple should find out for themselves which of the many possible positions best suits them *both*.

When the two have met and united, the usual and normal result is that, after a longer or shorter interval, the man's mental and physical stimulation reaches a climax in sensory intoxication and in the ejaculation of semen. Where the two are perfectly adjusted, the woman simultaneously reaches the crisis of nervous and muscular reactions very similar to his. This mutual orgasm is extremely important, but in many cases the man's climax comes so swiftly that the woman's reactions are not nearly ready, and she is left without it. Though in some instances the woman may have one or more crises before the man achieves his, it is, perhaps, hardly an exaggeration to say that 70 or 80 per cent of our married women (in the middle classes) are deprived of the full orgasm through the excessive speed of the husband's reactions, or through some maladjustment of the relative shapes and positions of the organs. So deep-seated, so profound are woman's complex sex-instincts as well as her organs, that in rousing them the man is rousing her whole body and soul. And this takes time. More time, indeed, than the average, uninstructed husband gives to it. Yet woman has at the surface a small vestigial organ called the clitoris, which corresponds morphologically to the man's penis, and which, like it, is extremely sensitive to touch-sensations. This little crest, which lies anteriorly between the inner lips round the vagina, enlarges when the woman is really tumescent, and by the stimulation of movement it is intensely roused and transmits this stimulus to every nerve in her body. But even after a woman's dormant sex-feeling is aroused and all the complex reactions of her being have been set in motion, it may even take as much as from ten to twenty minutes of actual physical union to consummate her feeling, while two or three minutes often completes the union for a man who is ignorant of the need to control his reactions so that both may experience the added benefit of a mutual crisis to love. There are some organic features which, being slightly abnormal, need special medical treatment, but the hastiness of most healthy men is largely due to mental ignorance alone, and can be conquered by a persistent and consciously exerted will.

A number of well-meaning people demand from men absolute "continence" save for procreation only. They overlook the innumerable physiological reactions concerned in the act, as well as the subtle spiritual alchemy of it, and propound the view that "the opposition to continence, save for procreation only, has but one argument to put forward, and that is appetite selfishness." ("The Way of God in Marriage.")

I maintain, however, that it should be realized that the complete act of union is a triple consummation. It symbolizes, and at the same time actually enhances, the spiritual union; there are a myriad subtleties of soul-structures which are compounded in this alchemy. At the same time the act gives the most intense physical pleasure and benefit which the body can experience, and it is a *mutual*, not a selfish, pleasure and profit, more calculated than anything else to draw out an unspeakable tenderness and understanding in both partakers of this sacrament; while, thirdly, it is the act which gives rise to a new life by rendering possible the fusion of one of the innumerable male sperms with the female egg-cell.

It should never be forgotten that without the discipline of self-control there is no lasting delight in erotic feeling. The fullest delight, even in a purely physical sense, can be attained only by those who curb and direct their natural impulses.

Dr. Saleeby's words are appropriate in this connection (Introduction to Forel's "Sexual Ethics," 1908): "Professor Forel speaks of subduing the sexual instinct. I would rather speak of transmuting it. The direct method of attack is often futile, always necessitous of effort, but it is possible for us to transmute our sex-energy into higher forms in our individual lives, thus justifying the evolutionary and physiological contention that it is the source of the higher activities of man, of moral indignation, and of the 'restless energy' which has changed the surface of the earth."

Forel says ("The Sexual Question," 1908): "Before engaging in a lifelong union, a man and woman ought to explain to each other their sexual feelings so as to avoid deception and incompatibility later on." This would be admirable advice were it possible for a virgin girl to know much about the reactions and effects upon her mind and body of the act of coitus, but she does not. She may take it as an absolute rule, however, that unless the touch of the man's hand on hers, and the contact of his lips, are sweet and delicious to her, the man can never be a true husband. Both before and after marriage a delicate and noble frankness about their feelings and desires is due from each to each of the two who are to be welded into one by life together. Actually it often takes several years for eager and intelligent couples fully to probe themselves and to discover the extent and meaning of the immensely profound physiological and spiritual results of marriage. Yet it is true that an early frankness would save much misery when, as happens not infrequently, one or other of the pair marry with the secret determination to have no children.

So various are we all as individuals, so complex all the reactions and interactions of sex-relations, that no hard-and-fast rule can be laid down. Each couple, after marriage, must study themselves, and the lover and the beloved must do what best serves them both and gives them the highest degree of mutual joy and power. There are, however, some laws which should be inviolable. Their details can be gathered from the preceding pages, and they are summed up in the words: "Love worketh no ill to the beloved."

MARGARET SANGER

FROM

WOMAN AND THE NEW RACE

Margaret Sanger (1883–1966): A nurse on the Lower East Side of New York City, Margaret Sanger quickly became aware of the need for birth control for poor families. A witness to infant and mother deaths and dangerous illegal abortions, Sanger connected these problems with women's inability to control their reproductive lives.

She became a speaker and writer for Socialist groups and wrote an article on venereal disease for The Call, *which was censored by the government. Finding little scientific and medical information on birth control in the United States, Sanger visited Europe in 1913, where she learned about the diaphragm and spoke with followers of Malthus. After returning to the United States, she was arrested for the publication of her pamphlet,* Family Limitations, *and fled to England to avoid prosecution, but only after arranging for the distribution of 100,000 illegal copies of the pamphlet. While in England Sanger met and worked with Marie Stopes and Havelock Ellis. After her return to New York, and the death of her daughter, the charges against Sanger were dropped, but she was later arrested and jailed for opening a birth-control clinic in Brooklyn.*

Sanger founded or served with numerous groups and organizations connected with birth control and the prevention of sexually transmitted diseases. Among others, she founded the National Birth Control League (now Planned Parenthood) in 1915, organized an International Birth Control Conference in 1925, and edited and published the journal Birth Control Review. *She continued to face legal difficulties; her clinic was raided in 1929 and five employees were arrested. Throughout her life she toured globally, lecturing and writing constantly. By the time of her death in 1966, the movement had become a respectable one with support from many physicians and even presidents Truman and Eisenhower. She once commented on her fierce dedication: "For me, it has not been difficult, never was, to decide upon my one great truth . . . children must be brought into this strange little planet of ours by choice, not by chance."*

CHAPTER IX

CONTINENCE—IS IT PRACTICABLE OR DESIRABLE?

Thousands of well-intentioned people who agree that there are times and conditions under which it is woman's highest duty to avoid having children advocate continence as the one permissible means of birth control. Few of these people agree with one another, however, as to what continence is. Some have in mind absolute continence. Others urge continence for periods varying from a few weeks to many years. Still others are thinking of Karezza, or male continence, as it is sometimes called.

The majority of physicians and sex psychologists hold that the practice of absolute continence is, for the greater part of the human race, an absurdity. Were such continence to be practiced, there is no doubt that it would be a most effective check upon the birth rate. It is seldom practiced, however, and when adhered to under compulsion the usual result is injury to the nervous system and to the general health. Among healthy persons, this method is practicable only with those who have a degree of mentally controlled development as yet neither often experienced nor even imagined by the mass of humanity.

Absolute continence was the ideal of the early Christian church for all of its communicants, as shall be seen in another chapter. We shall also see how the church abandoned this standard and now confines the doctrine of celibacy to the unmarried, to the priesthood and the nuns.

Celibacy has been practiced in all ages by a few artists, propagandists and revolutionists in order that their minds may be single to the work which has claimed their lives and all the forces of their beings may be bent in one direction. Sometimes, too, such persons have remained celibate to avoid the burden of caring for a family.

The Rev. Dr. Thomas Robert Malthus, who in 1798 issued the first of those works which exemplified what is called the Malthusian doctrine, also advocated celibacy or absolute continence until middle age. Malthus propounded the now widely recognized principle that population tends to increase faster than the food supply and that unlimited reproduction brings poverty and many other evils upon a nation. His theological training naturally inclined him to favor continence—not so much from its practicability, perhaps, as because he believed that it was the only possible method.

We would be ignoring a vital truth if we failed to recognize the fact that there are individuals who through absorption in religious zeal, consecration to a cause or devotion to creative work are able to live for years or for a lifetime a celibate existence. It is doubtless true that the number of those who are thus able to transmute their sex forces into other creative forms is increasing. It is not with these, however, that we are concerned. Rather it is with the mass of humanity, who practice continence under some sort of compulsion.

What is the result of forcing continence upon those who are not fitted or do not desire to practice it? The majority opinion of medical science and the evidence of statistics are united on this point. Enforced continence is injurious—often highly so.

"Physiology," writes Dr. J. Rutgers in *Rassenverbesserung*, "teaches that every function gains in power and efficiency through a certain degree of control, but that the too extended suppression of a desire gives rise to pathological disturbances and in time cripples the function. Especially in the case of women may the damage entailed by too long continued sexual abstinence bring about deep disturbances."

All this, be it understood, refers to persons of mature age. For young men and women under certain ages, statistics and the preponderance of medical opinion agree that continence is highly advisable, in many cases seemingly altogether necessary to future happiness. The famous Dr. Bertillon, of France, inventor of the Bertillon system of measurements for the human body, has made, perhaps, the most exhaustive of all studies in this direction. He demonstrates a large mortality for the boy who marries before his twentieth year. When single, the mortality of French youths averages only 14 per thousand; among married youths it rises to 100 per thousand. Which shows that it is six or eight times more perilous for a youth to be incontinent than continent up to that age. Dr. Bertillon's conclusions are that men should marry between their twenty-fifth and thirtieth years, and that women should marry when they have passed twenty. With the single exception of young men and women below the ages noted, Dr. Bertillon's statistics tell a very different story. And where it relates to celibates, it is a shocking one.

"Dr. Bertillon shows that in France, Belgium and Holland married men live considerably longer than single ones," writes Dr. Charles R. Drysdale, in summing up the matter in "The Population Question," "and are much less subject to becoming insane, criminal or vicious." From the same studies we learn that the conjugal state is also more favorable to the health of the woman over twenty years of age, in the three countries covered.

An analysis of criminal records showed that more than twice as many unmarried men and women had been held for crimes of all kinds than married persons. Rates based upon 10,000 cases of insanity among men and women in the same countries showed 3.95 per thousand for male celibates against 2.17 for married men. For single women the rate was 3.4 against but 1.9 for married women. Insanity was reduced one-half among women by marriage.

More startling still is the evidence of the mortality statistics. Bertillon found that the death rates of bachelors and widowers averaged from nearly two to nearly three times as high as those of married men of the same ages. Dr. Mayer, in his *Rapports Conjugaux*, showed that the death rates among the celibate religious orders studied were nearly twice as high as those of the laity.

Can anyone knowing the facts ask that we recommend continence as a birth-control measure?

Virtually all of the dangers to health involved in absolute continence are involved also in the practice of continence broken only when it is desired to bring a child into the world. In the opinion of some medical authorities, it is even worse, because of the almost constant excitation of unsatisfied sex desire by the presence of the mate. People who think that they believe in this sort of family limitation have much to say about "self-control." Usually they will admit that to abstain from all but a single act of sexual intercourse each year is an indication of high powers of self-restraint. Yet that one act, performed only once a year, might be sufficient to "keep a woman with one child in her womb and another at her breast" during her entire childbearing period. That would mean from eighteen to twenty-four children for each mother, provided she survived so many births and lactations. Contraceptives are quite as necessary to these "self-controlled" ones who do not desire children every year as to those who lead normal, happy love lives.

From the necessity of contraceptives and from the dangers of this limited continence certain persons are, of course, relieved. They are the ones whose mental and spiritual development is so high as to make this practice natural to them. These individuals are so exceedingly rare, however, that they need not be discussed here. Moreover, they are capable of solving their own problems.

Few who advocate the doctrine of absolute continence live up to it strictly. I met one woman who assured me that she had observed it faithfully in the thirteen years since her youngest child was born. She had such a loathing for sexual union, however, that it was doubtless the easiest and best thing for her to do.

Loathing, disgust or indifference to the sex relationship nearly always lies behind the advocacy to continence except for the conscious purpose of creating children. In other words, while one in ten thousand persons may find full play for a diverted and transmuted sex force in other creative functions, the rest avoid the sex union from repression. These are two widely different situations—one may make for racial progress and the happiness of the few individuals capable of it; the other poisons the race at its fountain and brings nothing but the discontent, unhappiness and misery which follow enforced continence. For all that, an increasing number of persons, mostly women, are advocating continence within marriage.

Sexual union is nearly always spoken of by such persons as something in itself repugnant, disgusting, low and lustful. Consciously or unconsciously, they look upon it as a hardship, to be endured only, to bring "God's image and likeness" into the world. Their very attitude precludes any great probability that their progeny will possess an abundance of such qualities.

Much of the responsibility for this feeling upon the part of many thousands of women must be laid to two thousand years of Christian teaching that all sex expression is unclean. Part of it, too, must be laid to the dominant male's habit of violating the love rights of his mate.

The habit referred to grows out of the assumed and legalized right of the husband to have sexual satisfaction at any time he desires, regardless of the woman's repugnance for it. The law of the state upholds him in this regard. A husband need not support his wife if she refuses to comply with his sexual demands.

Of the two groups of women who regard physical union either with disgust and loathing, or with indifference, the former are the less numerous. Nevertheless, there are many thousands of them. I have listened to their stories often, both as a nurse in obstetrical cases and as a propagandist for birth control. An almost universal cause of their attitude is a sad lack of understanding of the great beauties of the normal, idealistic love act. Neither do they understand the uplifting power of such unions for both men and women. Ignorance of life, ignorance of all but the sheer reproductive function of mating, and especially a wrong training, are most largely responsible for this tragic state of affairs. When this ignorance extends to the man in such a degree as to permit him to have the all too frequent coarse and brutal attitude toward sex matters, the tragedy is only deepened.

Truly the church and those "moralists" who have been insisting upon keeping sex matters in the dark have a huge list of concealed crimes to answer for. The right kind of a book, a series of clear, scientific lectures, or a common-sense talk with either the man or woman will often do away with most of the repugnance to physical union. When the repugnance is gone, the way is open to that uplift-ment through sex idealism which is the birthright of all women and men.

When I have had the confidence of women indifferent to physical union, I have found the fault usually lay with the husband. His idea of marriage is too often that of providing a home for a female who would in turn provide for his physical needs, including sexual satis-faction. Such a husband usually excludes such satisfaction from the category of the wife's needs, physical or spiritual.

This man is not concerned with his wife's sex urge, save as it responds to his own at times of his choosing. Man's code has taught woman to be quite ashamed of such desires. Usually she speaks of indifference without regret; often proudly. She seems to regard her-self as more chaste and highly endowed in purity than other women who confess to feeling physical attraction toward their husbands. She also secretly considers herself far superior to the husband who makes no concealment of his desire toward her. Nevertheless, because of this desire upon the husband's part, she goes on "pretending" to mutual interest in the relationship.

Only the truth, plainly spoken, can help these people. The woman is condemned to physical, mental and spiritual misery by the ignorance which society has fixed upon her. She has her choice between an enforced continence, with its health-wrecking consequences and its constant aggravation of domestic discord, and the sort of prostitution legalized by the marriage ceremony. The man may choose between enforced continence and its effects, or he may resort to an unmarried relationship or to prostitution. Neither of these people— the one schooled directly or indirectly by the church and the other trained in the sex ethics of the gutter—can hope to lift the other to the regenerating influences of a pure, clean, happy love life. As long as we leave sex education to the gutter and houses of prostitution, we shall have millions of just such miserable marriage failures.

Such continence as is involved in dependence upon the so-called "safe period" for family limitation will harm no one. The difficulty here is that the method is not practical. It simply does not work. The woman who employs this method finds herself in the same predicament as the one who believes that she is not in danger of pregnancy when she does not respond passionately to her husband. That this woman is more likely to conceive than the emotional one is a well-known fact. The woman who refuses to use contraceptives, but who rejects sex expression except for a few days in the month, is likely to learn too soon the fallacy of her theory as a birth-control method.

For a long time the "safe period" was suggested by physicians. It was also the one method of birth control countenanced by the ecclesiastics. Women are learning from experience and specialists are discovering by investigation that the "safe period" is anything but safe for all women. Some women are never free from the possibility of conception from puberty to the menopause. Others seemingly have "safe periods" for a time, only to become pregnant when they have begun to feel secure in their theory. Here again, continence must give way, as a method of birth control, to contraceptives.

In the same category as the "safe period," as a method of birth control, must be placed so-called "male continence." The same practice is also variously known as "Karezza," "Sedular Absorption" and "Zugassent's Discovery." Those who regard it as a method of family limitation are likely to find themselves disappointed.

As a form of continence, however, if it can be called continence, it is asserted to bring none of the long course of evils which too often follow the practice of lifelong abstinence, or abstinence broken only when a child is desired. Its devotees testify that they avoid ill effects and achieve the highest possible results. These results are due, probably, to two factors.

First, those who practice Karezza are usually of a high mental and spiritual development and are, therefore, capable of an exalted degree of self-control without actual repression. Second, they have the benefit of that magnetic interchange between man and woman which makes for physical, mental and spiritual well-being. This stimulation becomes destructive irritation in ordinary forms of continence.

The Oneida Community, a religious group comprising about 130 men and 150 women, which occupied a part of an old Indian reservation in the state of New York, were the chief exponents of "male continence." The practice was a religious requirement with them and they laid great stress upon three different functions which they attributed to the sexual organs. They held that these functions were urinary, reproductive and amative, each separate and distinct in its use from the others. Cases are cited in which both men and women are said to have preserved their youth and their sexual powers to a ripe old age, and to have prolonged their honeymoons throughout married life. The theory, however, interesting as it may be when considered as "continence," is not to be relied upon as a method of birth control.

Summing it all up, then, continence may meet the needs of a few natures, but it does not meet the needs of the masses. To enforce continence upon those whose natures do not demand it is an injustice, the cruelty and the danger of which has been underestimated rather than exaggerated. It matters not whether this wrong is committed by the church, through some outworn dogma; by the state, through the laws prohibiting contraceptives, or by society, through the conditions which prevent marriage when young men and women reach the age at which they have need of marriage.

The world has been governed too long by repression. The more fundamental the force that is repressed, the more destructive its action. The disastrous effects of repressing the sex force are written plainly in the health rates, the mortality statistics, the records of crime and the entry books of the hospitals for the insane. Yet this is not all the tale, for there are still the little understood hosts of sexually abnormal people and the monotonous misery of millions who do not die early nor end violently, but who are, nevertheless, devoid of the joys of a natural love life.

As a means of birth control, continence is as impracticable for most people as it is undesirable. Celibate women doubtless have their place in the regeneration of the world, but it is not they, after all, who will, through experience and understanding recreate it. It is mainly through fullness of expression and experience in life that the mass of women, having attained freedom, will accomplish this unparalleled task.

The need of women's lives is not repression, but the greatest possible expression and fulfillment of their desires upon the highest possible plane. They cannot reach higher planes through ignorance and compulsion. They can attain them only through knowledge and the cultivation of a higher, happier attitude toward sex. Sex life must be stripped of its fear. This is one of the great functions of contraceptives. That which is enshrouded in fear becomes morbid. That which is morbid cannot be really beautiful.

A true understanding of every phase of the love life, and such an understanding alone, can reveal it in its purity—in its power of upliftment. Force and fear have failed from the beginning of time. Their fruits are wrecks and wretchedness. Knowledge and freedom to choose or reject the sexual embrace, according as it is lovely or unlovely, and these alone, can solve the problem. These alone make possible between man and woman that indissoluble tie and mutual passion, and common understanding, in which lies the hope of a higher race.

CHAPTER XIV

WOMAN AND THE NEW MORALITY

Upon the shoulders of the woman conscious of her freedom rests the responsibility of creating a new sex morality. The vital difference between a morality thus created by women and the so-called morality of today is that the new standard will be based upon knowledge and freedom while the old is founded upon ignorance and submission.

What part will birth control play in bringing forth this new standard? What effect will its practice have upon woman's moral development? Will it lift her to heights that she has not yet achieved, and if so, how? Why is the question of morality always raised by the objector to birth control? All these questions must be answered if we are to get a true picture of the relation of the feminine spirit to morals. They can best be answered by considering, first, the source of our present standard of sex morals and the reasons why those standards are what they are; and, second, the source and probable nature of the new morality.

We get most of our notions of sex morality from the Christian church—more particularly from the oldest existing Christian church, known as the Roman Catholic. The church has generally defined the "immoral woman" as one who mates out of wedlock. Virtually, it lets it go at that. In its practical workings, there is nothing in the church code of morals to protect the woman, either from unwilling submission to the wishes of her husband, from undesired pregnancy, or from any other of the outrages only too familiar to many married women. Nothing is said about the crime of bringing an unwanted child into the world, where often it cannot be adequately cared for and is, therefore, condemned to a life of misery. The church's one point of insistence is upon the right of itself to legalize marriage and to compel the woman to submit to whatever such marriage may bring. It is true that there are remedies of divorce in the case of the state, but the church has adhered strictly to the principle that marriage, once consummated, is indissoluble. Thus, in its operation, the church's code of sex morals has nothing to do with the basic sex rights of the woman, but enforces, rather, the assumed property rights of the man to the body and the services of his wife. They are man-made codes; their vital factor, as they apply to woman, is submission to the man.

Closely associated with and underlying the principle of submission has been the doctrine that the sex life is in itself unclean. It follows, therefore, that all knowledge of the sex physiology or sex functions is also unclean and taboo. Upon this teaching has been founded woman's subjection by the church and, largely through the influence of the church, her subjection by the state to the needs of the man.

Let us see how these principles have affected the development of the present moral codes and some of their shifting standards. When we have finished this analysis, we shall know why objectors to birth control raise the "morality" question.

The church has sought to keep women ignorant upon the plea of keeping them "pure." To this end it has used the state as its moral policeman. Men have largely broken the grip of the ecclesiastics upon masculine education. The ban upon geology and astronomy, because they refute the biblical version of the creation of the world, are no longer effective. Medicine, biology and the doctrine of evolution have won their way to recognition in spite of the united opposition of the clerics. So, too, has the right of woman to go unveiled, to be educated and to speak from public platforms, been asserted in spite of the condemnations of the church, which denounced them as destructive of feminine purity. Only in sex matters has it succeeded in keeping the bugaboo alive.

It clings to this last stronghold of ignorance, knowing that woman free from sexual domination would produce a race spiritually free and strong enough to break the last of the bonds of intellectual darkness.

It is within the marriage bonds, rather than outside them, that the greatest immorality of men has been perpetrated. Church and state, through their canons and their laws, have encouraged this immorality. It is here that the woman who is to win her way to the new morality will meet the most difficult part of her task of moral house cleaning.

In the days when the church was striving for supremacy, when it needed single-minded preachers, proselyters and teachers, it fastened upon its people the idea that all sexual union, in marriage or out of it, is sinful. That idea colors the doctrines of the Church of Rome and many other Christian denominations to this hour. "Marriage, even for the sake of children was a carnal indulgence" in earlier times, as Principal Donaldson points out in "The Position of Women Among the Early Christians." It was held that the child was "conceived in sin," and that as the result of the sex act, an unclean spirit had possession of it. This spirit can be removed only by baptism, and the Roman Catholic baptismal service even yet contains these words: "Go out of him, thou unclean spirit, and give place unto the Holy Spirit, the Paraclete."

In the *Intellectual Development of Europe*, John William Draper, speaking of the teaching of celibacy among the Early Fathers, says:

"The sinfulness of the marriage relation and the preëminent value of chastity followed from their principles. If it was objected to such practices that by their universal adoption the human species would soon be extinguished and no man would remain to offer praises to God, these zealots, remembering the temptations from which they had escaped, with truth replied that there would always be sinners enough in the world to avoid that disaster, and that out of their evil work, good would be brought. Saint Jerome offers us the pregnant reflection that though it may be marriage that fills the earth, it is virginity that replenishes heaven."

The early church taught that there were enough children on earth. It needed missionaries more than it needed babies, and impressed upon its followers the idea that the birth wails of the infant were a protest against being born into so sordid a world.

Thus are we presented with one of the enormous inconsistencies of the church in sex matters. The teachings of the "Early Fathers" were in effect the advocacy of an attempt to enforce birth control through absolute continence, while later it reverted, as it reverts today, to the Mosaic injunction to "be fruitful and multiply."

The very force of the sex urge in humanity compelled the church to abandon the teaching of celibacy for its general membership. Paul, who preferred to see Christians unmarried rather than married, had recognized the power of this force. In the seventh chapter of the First Epistle to the Corinthians (according to the Douay translation of the Vulgate, which is accepted by the Church of Rome), he said:

"8—But I say unto you the unmarried and the widows; it is good if they continue even as I.

"9—But if they do not contain themselves, let them marry, for it is better to marry than to be burnt."

When the church became a political power rather than a strictly religious institution, it needed a high birth rate to provide laymen to support its increasingly expensive organization. It then began to exploit the sex force for its own interest. It reversed its position in regard to children. It encouraged marriage under its own control and exhorted women to bear as many children as possible. The world was just as sordid and the birth wails of the infants were just as piteous, but the needs of the hierarchy had changed. So it modified the standard of sex morality to suit its own requirements—marriage now became a sacrament.

Shrewd in changing its general policy from celibacy to marriage, the church was equally shrewd in perpetuating the doctrine of woman's subjection for its own interest. That doctrine was emphatically stated in the Third Chapter of the First Epistle of Peter and the Fifth Chapter of Paul's Epistle to the Ephesians. In the Douay version of the latter, we find this:

"22—Let women be subject to their husbands as to the Lord.

"23—Because the husband is the head of the wife; as Christ is the head of the Church.

"24—Therefore, as the Church is subject to Christ, so let the wives be to their husbands in all things."

These doctrines, together with the teaching that sex life is of itself unclean, formed the basis of morality as fixed by the Roman church.

Nor does the King James version of the Bible, generally used by Protestant churches to-day, differ greatly in these particulars from the accepted Roman Catholic version, as a comparison will show.

If Christianity turned the clock of general progress back a thousand years, it turned back the clock two thousand years for woman. Its greatest outrage upon her was to forbid her to control the function of motherhood under any circumstances, thus limiting her life's work to bringing forth and rearing children. Coincident with this, the churchmen deprived her of her place in and before the courts, in the schools, in literature, art and society. They shut from her heart and her mind the knowledge of her love life and her reproductive functions. They chained her to the position into which they had thrust her, so that it is only after centuries of effort that she is even beginning to regain what was wrested from her.

"Christianity had no favorable effect upon women," says Donaldson, "but tended to lower their character and contract the range of their activity. At the time when Christianity dawned upon the world, women had attained great freedom, power and influence in the Roman empire. Tradition was in favor of restriction, but by a concurrence of circumstances, women had been liberated from the enslaving fetters of the old legal forms. They enjoyed freedom of intercourse in society. They walked in the public thoroughfares with veils that did not hide their faces. They dined in the company of men. They studied literature and philosophy. They took part in political movements. They were allowed to defend their own law cases if they liked, and they helped their husbands in the government of provinces and the writing of books."

And again: "One would have imagined that Christianity would have favored the extension of women's freedom. In a very short time women are seen only in two capacities—as martyrs and deaconesses (or nuns). Now what the early Christians did was to strike the male out of the definition of man, and human being out of the definition of woman. Man was a human being made to serve the highest and noblest purposes; woman was a female, made to serve only one."

Thus the position attained by women of Greece and Rome through the exercise of family limitation, and in a considerable degree of voluntary motherhood, was swept away by the rising tide of Christianity. It would seem that this pernicious result was premeditated, and that from the very early days of Christianity, there were among the hierarchy those who recognized the creative power of the feminine spirit, the force of which they sought to turn to their own uses. Certain it is that the hierarchy created about the whole love life of woman an atmosphere of degradation.

Fear and shame have stood as grim guardians against the gate of knowledge and constructive idealism. The sex life of women has been clouded in darkness, restrictive, repressive and morbid. Women have not had the opportunity to know themselves, nor have they been permitted to give play to their inner natures, that they might create a morality practical, idealistic and high for their own needs.

On the other hand, church and state have forbidden women to leave their legal mates, or to refuse to submit to the marital embrace, no matter how filthy, drunken, diseased or otherwise repulsive the man might be—no matter how much of a crime it might be to bring to birth a child by him.

Woman was and is condemned to a system under which the lawful rapes exceed the unlawful ones a million to one. She has had nothing to say as to whether she shall have strength sufficient to give a child a fair physical and mental start in life; she has had as little to do with determining whether her own body shall be wrecked by excessive childbearing. She has been adjured not to complain of the burden of caring for children she has not wanted. Only the married woman who has been constantly loved by the most understanding and considerate of husbands has escaped these horrors. Besides the wrongs done to women in marriage, those involved in promiscuity, infidelities and rapes become inconsequential in nature and in number.

Out of woman's inner nature, in rebellion against these conditions, is rising the new morality. Let it be realized that this creation of new sex ideals is a challenge to the church. Being a challenge to the church, it is also, in less degree, a challenge to the state. The woman who takes a fearless stand for the incoming sex ideals must expect to be assailed by reactionaries of every kind. Imperialists and exploiters will fight hardest in the open, but the ecclesiastic will fight longest in the dark. He understands the situation best of all; he best knows what reaction he has to fear from the morals of women who have attained liberty. For, be it repeated, the church has always known and feared the spiritual potentialities of woman's freedom.

And in this lies the answer to the question why the opponent of birth control raises the moral issue. Sex morals for women have been one-sided; they have been purely negative, inhibitory and repressive. They have been fixed by agencies which have sought to keep women enslaved; which have been determined, even as they are now, to use woman solely as an asset to the church, the state and the man. Any means of freedom which will enable women to live and think for themselves first will be attacked as immoral by these selfish agencies.

What effect will the practice of birth control have upon woman's moral development? As we have seen in other chapters, it will break her bonds. It will free her to understand the cravings and soul needs of herself and other women. It will enable her to develop her love nature separate from and independent of her maternal nature.

It goes without saying that the woman whose children are desired and are of such number that she can not only give them adequate care but keep herself mentally and spiritually alive, as well as physically fit, can discharge her duties to her children much better than the overworked, broken and querulous mother of a large, unwanted family.

Thus the way is open to her for a twofold development; first, through her own full rounded life, and next, through her loving, unstrained, full-hearted relationship with her offspring. The bloom of mother love will have an opportunity to infuse itself into her soul and make her, indeed, the fond, affectionate guardian of her offspring that sentiment now pictures her but hard facts deny her the privilege of being. She will preserve also her love life with her mate in its ripening perfection. She will want children with a deeper passion, and will love them with a far greater love.

In spite of the age-long teaching that sex life in itself is unclean, the world has been moving to a realization that a great love between a man and woman is a holy thing, freighted with great possibilities for spiritual growth. The fear of unwanted children removed, the assurance that she will have a sufficient amount of time in which to develop her love life to its greatest beauty, with its comradeship in many fields—these will lift woman by the very soaring quality of her innermost self to spiritual heights that few have attained. Then the coming of eagerly desired children will but enrich life in all its avenues, rather than enslave and impoverish it as do unwanted ones today.

What healthier grounds for the growth of sound morals could possibly exist than the ample spiritual life of the woman just depicted? Free to follow the feminine spirit, which dwells in the sanctuary of her nature, she will, in her daily life, give expression to that high idealism which is the fruit of that spirit when it is unhampered and unviolated. The love for her mate will flower in beauty of deeds that are pure because they are the natural expression of her physical, mental and spiritual being. The love for desired children will come to blossom in a spirituality that is high because it is free to reach the heights.

The moral force of woman's nature will be unchained—and of its own dynamic power will uplift her to a plane unimagined by those holding fast to the old standards of church morality. Love is the greatest force of the universe; freed of its bonds of submission and unwanted progeny, it will formulate and compel of its own nature observance to standards of purity far beyond the highest conception of the average moralist. The feminine spirit, animated by joyous, triumphant love, will make its own high tenets of morality. Free womanhood, out of the depths of its rich experiences, will observe and comply with the inner demands of its being. The manner in which it learns to do this best may be said to be the moral law of woman's being. So, in whatever words the new morality may ultimately be expressed, we can at least be sure that it will meet certain needs.

First of all, it will meet the physical and psychic requirements of the woman herself, for she cannot adequately perform the feminine functions until these are met. Second, it will meet the needs of the child to be conceived in a love which is eager to bring forth a new life, to be brought into a home where love and harmony prevail, a home in which proper preparation has been made for its coming.

This situation implies in turn a number of conditions. Foremost among them is woman's knowledge of her sexual nature, both in its physiology and its spiritual significance. She must not only know her own body, its care and its needs, but she must know the power of the sex force, its use, its abuse, as well as how to direct it for the benefit of the race. Thus she can transmit to her children an equipment that will enable them to break the bonds that have held humanity enslaved for ages.

To achieve this she must have a knowledge of birth control. She must also assert and maintain her right to refuse the marital embrace except when urged by her inner nature.

The truth makes free. Viewed in its true aspect, the very beauty and wonder of the creative impulse will make evident its essential purity. We will then instinctively idealize and keep holy that physical-spiritual expression which is the foundation of all human life, and in that conception of sex will the race be exalted.

What can we expect of offspring that are the result of "accidents"—who are brought into being undesired and in fear? What can we hope for from a morality that surrounds each physical union, for the woman, with an atmosphere of submission and shame? What can we say for a morality that leaves the husband at liberty to communicate to his wife a venereal disease?

Subversion of the sex urge to ulterior purposes has dragged it to the level of the gutter. Recognition of its true nature and purpose must lift the race to spiritual freedom. Out of our growing knowledge we are evolving new and saner ideas of life in general. Out of our increasing sex knowledge we shall evolve new ideals of sex. These ideals will spring from the innermost needs of women. They will serve these needs and express them. They will be the foundation of a moral code that will tend to make fruitful the impulse which is the source, the soul and the crowning glory of our sexual natures.

When women have raised the standards of sex ideals and purged the human mind of its unclean conception of sex, the fountain of the race will have been cleansed. Mothers will bring forth, in purity and in joy, a race that is morally and spiritually free.

STELLA BROWNE

FROM
STUDIES IN
FEMININE INVERSION

Stella Browne (1882–1955): Stella Browne was a socialist and feminist who fought for women's contraceptive and abortion rights. She was a member of the Communist Party and later the Labour Party. Browne was acquainted with Havelock Ellis, and his ideas on sexuality influenced her work. Beginning in 1914 and throughout the twenties, she belonged to the Malthusian League, which educated workers about contraception. Later she helped to found the Abortion Law Reform Association in 1936.

I must apologize for what I feel to be a misleading title chosen for reasons of brevity and economy of effort in the framing of notices; for, what I have to put before you today are only very fragmentary data, and suggestions of a peculiarly obscure subject. They have, however, this validity; that they are the result of close and careful observation, conducted so far as I am consciously aware, without any prejudice, though they would probably be much more illuminating had they been recorded by an observer who was herself entirely or predominantly homosexual. I hope that the endless omissions will be to some extent supplied by comment and criticism, from our members, in the course of debate.

My material would have been both less limited and much more definite and intimate had I been able to include cases which have been told me in confidence. Those, of course, I have omitted.

The cases which I will now briefly describe to you are all well-known to me; they are all innate, and very pronounced and deeply rooted, not episodical. At the same time though I am sure there has been, in some of them at least, no definite and conscious physical expression, they are absolutely distinguishable from affectionate friendship. They have all of them in varying degrees, the element of passion: and here I should like to quote a definition of passion by Desmond McCarthy, which seems to me very apt and very true:

> It differs from lust in the intensity with which the personality of the object is apprehended, and in being also an excitement of the whole being, and, therefore, not satisfied so simply: from other kinds of love, in that it is intensely sexual and not accompanied, necessarily, by any contemplation of the object as good, or any strong desire for his or her welfare apart from the satisfaction of itself.

Now for my cases, and then a few comments and conclusions.

Case A. Member of a small family, but numerous cousins on both sides. The mother's family is nervous, with a decided streak of eccentricity of varying kinds, and some of its members much above the average in intelligence. The father's family much more commonplace, but robust. She is of small-boned frame, but childish rather than feminine in appearance, the liberating and illuminating effect of some definite and direct physical sex-expression, have had, and still have, a disastrous effect on a nature which has much inherent force and many fine qualities. Her whole outlook on life is subtly distorted and dislocated, moral values are confused and a false standard of values is set up. The hardening and narrowing effect of her way of life is shown in a tremendous array of prejudices on every conceivable topic: caste prejudices, race prejudices, down to prejudices founded on the slightest eccentricity of dress or unconventionality of behavior; also in an immense intolerance of normal passion, even in its most legally sanctioned and certificated forms. As to unlegalized sex-relationships, they are of course considered the very depth alike of depravity and of crass folly. And all the while, her life revolves round a deep and ardent sex-passion, frustrated and exasperated through functional repression, but entirely justified in her own opinion as pure family affection and duty! Though the orthodox and conventional point of view she takes on sex-questions, generally, would logically condemn just *that* form of sex-passion, as peculiarly reprehensible.

Case B. Also the member of a small family though with numerous cousins, paternal and maternal. Family of marked ability—on both sides, especially the mother's. Of very graceful and attractive appearance, entirely feminine, beautiful eyes and classical features, but indifferent to her looks and abnormally lacking in vanity, self-confidence and animal vitality generally, though no one is quicker to appreciate any beauty or charm in other women. I think she is a pronounced psychic invert whose intuitive faculties and bent towards mysticism have never been cultivated. Keen instinctive delicacy and emotional depth, enthusiastically devoted and generous to friends; much personal pride (though no vanity) and reserve. Too amenable to group suggestions and the influences of tradition. Artistic and musical tastes and a faculty for literary criticism which has lain fallow for want of systematic exercise. Rather fond of animals and devoted to children, especially to young relatives and the children of friends. Has done good philanthropic work for children, but is essentially interested in *persons* rather than in theories, or institutions. Is a devout Christian and I think gets much support and comfort from her religious beliefs. A distaste, even positive disgust, for the physical side of sex, which is tending more and more to manifest itself in conventional moral attitudes and judgments. General social attitude towards men less definitely *hostile* than that of Case A, but absolutely aloof. Devoted to women friends and relatives, yet has had no full and satisfying expression of this devotion. This inhibition of a whole infinitely important set of feelings and activities has weakened her naturally very sound judgment, and also had a bad permanent effect on her bodily health.

Case C. The sixth, and second youngest of a large and very able and vigorous family. Tall, and of the typical Diana build; long limbs, broad shoulders, slight bust, narrow hips. Decidedly athletic. Voice agreeable in tone and quite deep, can whistle well. Extremely energetic and capable, any amount of initiative and enthusiasm, never afraid to assume responsibility; very dominating and managing, something of a tyrant in practice, though an extreme democrat in theory, and most intolerant towards different emotional temperaments. Scientific training; interested in politics and public affairs; logical and rationalistic bent of mind. Emotionally reserved, intense, jealous and monopolistic. Will always try to express all emotion in terms of reason and moral theory, and is thus capable of much mental dishonesty, while making a fetish of complete and meticulous truthfulness. An agnostic and quite militant and aggressive. The episode in her life which I observed fairly closely was a long and intimate friendship with a young girl—ten years her junior—of a very attractive and vivacious type, who roused the interest of both men and women keenly. Cleverness and physical charm in girls appealed to her, but she instinctively resented any independent divergent views or standard of values. For years she practically formed this girl's mental life, and they spent their holidays together. When the girl fell in love with and impulsively married a very masculine and brilliantly gifted man, who has since won great distinction in his special profession, C's agony of rage and desolation was terrible and pitiable, though here again, she tried to hide the real nature of her loss by misgivings as to the young man's "type of ethical theory"—her own phrase! I cannot for a moment believe that she was ignorant of her own sex nature, and I hope she has by now found free and full personal realization with some beloved woman—though, unless the beloved woman is exceptionally understanding or exceptionally docile, it will be a stormy relationship. She is a very strong personality, and a born ruler. Her attitude towards men was one of perfectly unembarrassed and equal comradeship.

Case D. Is on a less evolved plane than the three aforementioned, being conspicuously lacking in refinement of feeling and, to some extent, of habit. But is well above the average in vigor, energy and efficiency. A decided turn for carpentry, mechanics and executive manual work. Not tall; slim, boyish figure; very hard, strong muscles, singularly impassive face, with big magnetic eyes. The dominating tendency is very strong here, and is not held in leash by a high standard of either delicacy or principle. Is professionally associated with children and young girls, and shows her innate homosexual tendency by excess of petting and spoiling, and intense jealousy of any other person's contact with, or interest in the children. I do not definitely know if there is any physical expression of her feelings, beyond the kissing and embracing which is normal, and even, in some cases conventional, between women or between women and children. But the *emotional tone* is quite unmistakable; will rave for hours over some "lovely kiddy," and injure the children's own best interests, as well as the working of the establishment, by unreasonable and unfair indulgence.

Her sexual idiosyncrasy in the post which she occupies is extremely harmful, and together with her jealous and domineering nature, leads to a general atmosphere of slackness and intrigue, and the children under her care, of course, take advantage of it. As she has had medical training, I cannot suppose she is ignorant on the subject of her own sex nature. Member of a large family, mostly brothers.

Case E. This was a case which at one time was fairly well-known to me, and is very well marked. Two assistant mistresses at a girl's boarding-school were completely inseparable. They took all their walks together, and spent all their time when they were "off duty" and not walking, in one another's rooms—they occupied adjoining rooms.

One of them was a slim, graceful, restless, neurotic girl with a distinct consumptive tendency; quick in perception and easy in manner, but it seemed to me then, and it seems still, decidedly superficial and shallow. The other partner was an invert of the most pronounced physical type. Her tall, stiff, rather heavily muscular figure, her voice, and her chubby, fresh-colored face, which was curiously eighteenth-century in outline and expression, were so like those of a very young and very well-groomed youth, that all the staff of the school nicknamed her "Boy," though I do not believe any of them clearly realized what this epithet—and her intimacy with a woman of such strongly contrasted type, implied. "Boy" was extremely self-conscious and curiously inarticulate; she had musical tastes and played rather well—not in the colorless and amateurish style of the musical hack. I think music was an outlet for her. She was also fond of taking long walks, and of driving, and of dogs and horses. Beyond these matters I don't think I ever heard her express an opinion about anything. The intimacy with her restless, tricky adored one ran its course, unhindered either by circumstances, or by unconscious public opinion. There was some idealism in the relationship, at least on "Boy's" side.

There was no community of intellectual interests—or rather there was community in the mutual absence of intellectual interests. I lost sight of them completely, but heard later that the friend had taken a post in South Africa, and "Boy" was planning to join her there, but I do not know whether this plan materialized.

I have omitted from consideration that episodical homosexuality on the part of women who are normally much more attracted to men, of which every experienced observer must know instances.

I have also left out of consideration here, various instances known to me of passionate but unconscious inversion in girls whose sex life is just beginning. All of these are important, and may throw helpful light not only on the problem inversion, but on the sexual impulse of women generally.

There exists no document in modern English literature comparable in authenticity or artistic merit, as a study of the female homosexual or bisexual temperaments, with the hauntingly beautiful verse of Renee Vivien (Pauline Tarn) or the vivid autobiographical novels of Colette Willy (Gabrielle Gautheir Villars).

I know of two modern English novels in which the subject is touched on with a good deal of subtlety, and in both cases in association with school life. *Regiment of Women* by Clemence Dane—a brilliant piece of psychology, and a novel by an Australian writer, cruder and shorter, but unmistakably powerful, *The Getting of Wisdom* by Henry Handel Richardson. There is frank and brilliant description of the feminine intermediate and homosexual temperaments in *I, Mary MacLane* (New York, Stokes & Co).

I would draw your attention to one quality which two of my cases have in common, and to a very marked degree: the maternal instinct. Two of the most intensely maternal women I know are cases A and B, both congenital inverts.

A friend has suggested to me that in such cases in the future, the resources of developed chemistry and biology will be made use of, in artificial fertilization. And I now see in reading Dr. Marie Stopes's interesting Essay "Married Love," that she makes a similar suggestion, though not with reference to inversion.

This problem of feminine inversion is very pressing and immediate, taking into consideration the fact that in the near future, for at least a generation, the circumstances of women's lives and work will tend, even more than at present, to favor the frigid, and next to the frigid, the inverted types. Even at present, the social and affectional side of the invert's nature has often fuller opportunity of satisfaction than the heterosexual woman's, but often at the cost of adequate and definite physical expression. And how decisive for vigor, sanity and serenity of body and mind, for efficiency, for happiness, for the mastery of life, and the understanding of one's fellow creatures—just this definite physical expression is! The lack of it, "normal" and "abnormal," is at the root of most of what is most trivial and unsatisfactory in women's intellectual output, as well as of their besetting vice of cruelty. How can anyone be finely or greatly creative, if one's supreme moral law is a negation! Not to *live*, not to *do*, not even to try to understand.

In the cases which I have called A and B, sexual experience along the lines of their own psychic idiosyncrasy would have revealed to them definitely where they stood, and as both are well above the average in intelligence, would have been a key to many mysteries of human conduct which are now judged with dainty shrinking from incomprehensible folly and perversity.

I am sure that much of the towering spiritual arrogance which is found, e.g., in many high places in the Suffrage movement, and among the unco guid generally, is really unconscious inversion.

I think it is perhaps not wholly uncalled for, to underline very strongly my opinion that the homosexual impulse *is not in any way superior* to the normal; it has a fully equal right to existence and expression, it is no worse, no lower; *but no better*.

By all means let the invert—let all of us—have as many and varied "channels of sublimation" as possible; and far more than are at present available. But, to be honest, are we not too inclined to make "sublimation" an excuse for refusing to tackle fundamentals? The tragedy of the repressed invert is apt to be not only one of emotional frustration, but complete dislocation of mental values.

Moreover, our present social arrangements, founded as they are on the repression and degradation of the normal erotic impulse, artificially stimulate inversion and have thus forfeited all right to condemn it. There is a huge, persistent, indirect pressure on women of strong passions and fine brains to find an emotional outlet with other women. A woman who is unwilling to accept either marriage—under present laws—or prostitution, and at the same time refuses to limit her sexual life to autoerotic manifestations, will find she has to struggle against the whole social order for what is nevertheless her most precious personal right. The right sort of woman faces the struggle and counts the cost well worth while; but it is impossible to avoid seeing that she risks the most painful experiences, and spends an incalculable amount of time and energy on things that should be matters of course. Under these conditions, some women who *are not innately or predominantly homosexual* do form more or less explicitly erotic relations with other women, yet these are makeshifts and essentially substitutes, which cannot replace the vital contact, mental and bodily, with congenial men.

No one who has observed the repressed inverted impulse flaring into sex antagonism, or masked as the devotion of daughter or cousin or the solicitude of teacher or nurse, or perverted into the cheap, malignant cant of conventional moral indignation, can deny its force. Let us recognize this force, as frankly as we recognize and reverence the love between men and women. When Paris was devouring and disputing over Willy and Colette Willy's wonderful Claudine stories, another gifted woman writer, who had also touched on the subject of inversion, defended not only the artistic conception and treatment of the stories (they need no defense, and remain one of the joys and achievements of modern French writing), but also their ethical content: Mme. Rachilde wrote *"une amoureuse d'amour n'est pas une vicicuse."*

After all: every strong passion, every deep affection, has its own endless possibilities, of pain, change, loss, incompatibility, satiety, jealousy, incompleteness: why add wholly extraneous difficulties and burdens? Harmony may be incompatible with freedom; we do not yet know, for few of us know either. But both truth and the most essential human dignity are incompatible with things as they are.

SIGMUND FREUD

FROM

NEW INTRODUCTORY
LECTURES ON
PSYCHO-ANALYSIS

Sigmund Freud (1856–1939): Sigmund Freud was born in Freiberg, Moravia, but his family moved to Vienna when he was three. He was educated in modern and classical languages and later studied medicine at the University of Vienna. While a practitioner and biological researcher in neuropathology, Freud began to use cocaine in 1884 and published several articles on the use of the drug as a stimulant, an analgesic, and an aid in morphine withdrawal.

After studying in Paris with neurologist J. M. Charcot, Freud married Martha Bernays in 1886, with whom he had six children. The years following his marriage were spent in neurological practice, extensive writing, and time with his family. He became involved in hypnosis as a cure for hysteria and worked with Josef Breuer on the publication of Studies in Hysteria *(1895). Their collaborative efforts broke down when Breuer refused to join Freud in his more radical psychoanalytical research, particularly his emphasis on sexuality as a supreme motivating force. Increasingly, Freud's career grew more focused in this area. His doctrine of the unconscious, which affirms the significance of the psychological events that occur outside of conscious awareness, remains enormously influential. To Freud, dreams, slips of the tongue, and fantasies were not trivial, as many had believed, but important clues to the human psychological makeup. His major publications include* The Interpretation of Dreams *(1900),* Three Essays on the Theory of Sexuality *(1905),* The Ego and the Id *(1923),* Totem and Taboo *(1913), and* Civilization and Its Discontents *(1927).*

From 1936 to 1937, Freud was offered foreign asylum from the Nazis but chose to remain in Vienna out of identification with other Jews unable to leave.

Following the Nazi occupation of Austria, he left for England in 1938. He died in London while in exile.

LECTURE XXXIII: FEMININITY[1]

Ladies and Gentlemen,—All the while I am preparing to talk to you I am struggling with an internal difficulty. I feel uncertain, so to speak, of the extent of my license. It is true that in the course of fifteen years of work psychoanalysis has changed and grown richer; but, in spite of that, an introduction to psycho-analysis might have been left without alteration or supplement. It is constantly in my mind that these lectures are without a *raison d'être*. For analysts I am saying too little and nothing at all that is new; but for you I am saying too much and saying things which you are not equipped to understand and which are not in your province. I have looked around for excuses and I have tried to justify each separate lecture on different grounds. The first one, on the theory of dreams, was supposed to put you back again at one blow into the analytic atmosphere and to show you how durable our views have turned out to be. I was led on to the second one, which followed the paths from dreams to what is called occultism, by the opportunity of speaking my mind without constraint on a department of work in which prejudiced expectations are fighting today against passionate resistances, and I could hope that your judgment, educated to tolerance on the example of psycho-analysis, would not refuse to accompany me on the excursion. The third lecture, on the dissection of the personality, certainly made the hardest demands upon you with its unfamiliar subject matter; but it was impossible for me to keep this first beginning of an ego-psychology back from you, and if we had possessed it fifteen years ago I should have had to mention it to you then. My last lecture, finally, which you were probably able to follow only by great exertions, brought forward necessary corrections—fresh attempts at solving the most important conundrums; and my introduction would have been leading

[1] [This lecture is mainly based on two earlier papers: "Some Psychical Consequences of the Anatomical Distinction between the Sexes" (1925*j*) and "Female Sexuality" (1931*b*). The last section, however, dealing with women in adult life, contains new material. Freud returned to the subject once again in Chapter VII of the posthumous *Outline of Psycho-Analysis* (1940*a* [1938]).]

you astray if I had been silent about them. As you see, when one starts making excuses it turns out in the end that it was all inevitable, all the work of destiny. I submit to it, and I beg you to do the same.

Today's lecture, too, should have no place in an introduction; but it may serve to give you an example of a detailed piece of analytic work, and I can say two things to recommend it. It brings forward nothing but observed facts, almost without any speculative additions, and it deals with a subject which has a claim on your interest second almost to no other. Throughout history people have knocked their heads against the riddle of the nature of femininity—

> Häupter in Hieroglyphenmützen,
> Häupter in Turban und schwarzem Barett,
> Perückenhäupter und tausend andre
> Arme, schwitzende Menschenhäupter. . . .[1]

Nor will *you* have escaped worrying over this problem—those of you who are men; to those of you who are women this will not apply—you are yourselves the problem. When you meet a human being, the first distinction you make is "male or female?" and you are accustomed to make the distinction with unhesitating certainty. Anatomical science shares your certainty at one point and not much further. The male sexual product, the spermatozoon, and its vehicle are male; the ovum and the organism that harbors it are female. In both sexes organs have been formed which serve exclusively for the sexual functions; they were probably developed from the same [innate] disposition into two different forms. Besides this, in both sexes the other organs, the bodily shapes and tissues, show the influence of the individual's sex, but this is inconstant and its amount variable; these are what are known as the secondary sexual characters. Science next tells you something that runs counter to your expectations and is probably calculated to confuse your feelings. It draws your attention to the fact that portions of the male sexual apparatus

---

[1] Heads in hieroglyphic bonnets,
 Heads in turbans and black birettas,
 Heads in wigs and thousand other
 Wretched, sweating heads of humans. . . .

(Heine, *Nordsee* [Second Cycle, VII, "Fragen"].)

also appear in women's bodies, though in an atrophied state, and vice versa in the alternative case. It regards their occurrence as indications of *bisexuality*,[1] as though an individual is not a man or a woman but always both—merely a certain amount more the one than the other. You will then be asked to make yourselves familiar with the idea that the proportion in which masculine and feminine are mixed in an individual is subject to quite considerable fluctuations. Since, however, apart from the very rarest cases, only one kind of sexual product—ova or semen—is nevertheless present in one person, you are bound to have doubts as to the decisive significance of those elements and must conclude that what constitutes masculinity or femininity is an unknown characteristic which anatomy cannot lay hold of.

Can psychology do so perhaps? We are accustomed to employ "masculine" and "feminine" as mental qualities as well, and have in the same way transferred the notion of bisexuality to mental life. Thus we speak of a person, whether male or female, as behaving in a masculine way in one connection and in a feminine way in another. But you will soon perceive that this is only giving way to anatomy or to convention. You cannot give the concepts of "masculine" and "feminine" *any* new connotation. The distinction is not a psychological one; when you say "masculine," you usually mean "active," and when you say "feminine," you usually mean "passive." Now it is true that a relation of the kind exists. The male sex cell is actively mobile and searches out the female one, and the latter, the ovum, is immobile and waits passively. This behavior of the elementary sexual organisms is indeed a model for the conduct of sexual individuals during intercourse. The male pursues the female for the purpose of sexual union, seizes hold of her and penetrates into her. But by this you have precisely reduced the characteristic of masculinity to the factor of aggressiveness so far as psychology is concerned. You may well doubt whether you have gained any real advantage from this when you reflect that in some classes of animals the females are the stronger and more aggressive and the male is active only in the single act of sexual union. This is so, for instance, with the spiders. Even the functions

[1] [Bisexuality was discussed by Freud in the first edition of his *Three Essays on the Theory of Sexuality* (1905*d*), *Standard Ed.*, **7**, 141-4. The passage includes a long footnote to which he made additions in later issues of the work.]

of rearing and caring for the young, which strike us as feminine *par excellence*, are not invariably attached to the female sex in animals. In quite high species we find that the sexes share the task of caring for the young between them or even that the male alone devotes himself to it. Even in the sphere of human sexual life you soon see how inadequate it is to make masculine behavior coincide with activity and feminine with passivity. A mother is active in every sense towards her child; the act of lactation itself may equally be described as the mother suckling the baby or as her being sucked by it. The further you go from the narrow sexual sphere the more obvious will the "error of superimposition"[1] become. Women can display great activity in various directions, men are not able to live in company with their own kind unless they develop a large amount of passive adaptability. If you now tell me that these facts go to prove precisely that both men and women are bisexual in the psychological sense, I shall conclude that you have decided in your own minds to make "active" coincide with "masculine" and "passive" with "feminine." But I advise you against it. It seems to me to serve no useful purpose and adds nothing to our knowledge.[2]

One might consider characterizing femininity psychologically as giving preference to passive aims. This is not, of course, the same thing as passivity; to achieve a passive aim may call for a large amount of activity. It is perhaps the case that in a woman, on the basis of her share in the sexual function, a preference for passive behavior and passive aims is carried over into her life to a greater or lesser extent, in proportion to the limits, restricted or far reaching, within which her sexual life thus serves as a model. But we must beware in this of underestimating the influence of social customs, which similarly force women into passive situations. All this is still far from being cleared up. There is one particularly constant relation between femininity and instinctual life which we do not want to overlook. The suppression of women's aggressiveness which is prescribed for them constitutionally and imposed on them socially favors the development of powerful

[1] [I.e., mistaking two different things for a single one. The term was explained in *Introductory Lectures*, XX, *Standard Ed.*, **16**, 304.]
[2] [The difficulty of finding a psychological meaning for "masculine" and "feminine" was discussed in a long footnote added in 1915 to the *Three Essays* (1905*d*), *Standard Ed.*, **7**, 219–20, and again at the beginning of a still longer footnote at the end of Chapter IV of *Civilization and Its Discontents* (1930*a*), ibid., **21**, 105–6.]

masochistic impulses, which succeed, as we know, in binding eroti-
cally the destructive trends which have been diverted inwards. Thus
masochism, as people say, is truly feminine. But if, as happens so
often, you meet with masochism in men, what is left to you but to
say that these men exhibit very plain feminine traits?

And now you are already prepared to hear that psychology too
is unable to solve the riddle of femininity. The explanation must no
doubt come from elsewhere, and cannot come till we have learnt how
in general the differentiation of living organisms into two sexes came
about. We know nothing about it, yet the existence of two sexes is a
most striking characteristic of organic life which distinguishes it
sharply from inanimate nature. However, we find enough to study in
those human individuals who, through the possession of female genitals, are characterized as manifestly or predominantly feminine. In
conformity with its peculiar nature, psycho-analysis does not try to
describe what a woman is—that would be a task it could scarcely
perform—but sets about enquiring how she comes into being, how
a woman develops out of a child with a bisexual disposition. In recent
times we have begun to learn a little about this, thanks to the circumstance that several of our excellent women colleagues in analysis
have begun to work at the question. The discussion of this has gained
special attractiveness from the distinction between the sexes. For the
ladies, whenever some comparison seemed to turn out unfavorable to
their sex, were able to utter a suspicion that we, the male analysts,
had been unable to overcome certain deeply rooted prejudices against
what was feminine, and that this was being paid for in the partiality
of our researches. We, on the other hand, standing on the ground of
bisexuality, had no difficulty in avoiding impoliteness. We had only
to say: "This doesn't apply to *you*. You're the exception; on this point
you're more masculine than feminine."

We approach the investigation of the sexual development of women
with two expectations. The first is that here once more the constitution will not adapt itself to its function without a struggle. The
second is that the decisive turning points will already have been prepared for or completed before puberty. Both expectations are
promptly confirmed. Furthermore, a comparison with what happens
with boys tells us that the development of a little girl into a normal
woman is more difficult and more complicated, since it includes two

extra tasks, to which there is nothing corresponding in the development of a man. Let us follow the parallel lines from their beginning. Undoubtedly the material is different to start with in boys and girls: it did not need psycho-analysis to establish that. The difference in the structure of the genitals is accompanied by other bodily differences which are too well known to call for mention. Differences emerge too in the instinctual disposition which give a glimpse of the later nature of women. A little girl is as a rule less aggressive, defiant and self-sufficient; she seems to have a greater need for being shown affection and on that account to be more dependent and pliant. It is probably only as a result of this pliancy that she can be taught more easily and quicker to control her excretions: urine and feces are the first gifts that children make to those who look after them, and controlling them is the first concession to which the instinctual life of children can be induced. One gets an impression, too, that little girls are more intelligent and livelier than boys of the same age; they go out more to meet the external world and at the same time form stronger object cathexes. I cannot say whether this lead in development has been confirmed by exact observations, but in any case there is no question that girls cannot be described as intellectually backward. These sexual differences are not, however, of great consequence: they can be outweighed by individual variations. For our immediate purposes they can be disregarded.

Both sexes seem to pass through the early phases of libidinal development in the same manner. It might have been expected that in girls there would already have been some lag in aggressiveness in the sadistic anal phase, but such is not the case. Analysis of children's play has shown our women analysts that the aggressive impulses of little girls leave nothing to be desired in the way of abundance and violence. With their entry into the phallic phase the differences between the sexes are completely eclipsed by their agreements. We are now obliged to recognize that the little girl is a little man. In boys, as we know, this phase is marked by the fact that they have learnt how to derive pleasurable sensations from their small penis and connect its excited state with their ideas of sexual intercourse. Little girls do the same thing with their still smaller clitoris. It seems that with them all their masturbatory acts are carried out on this penis-equivalent, and that the truly feminine vagina is still undiscovered by both sexes. It is true that there are a few isolated reports of early vaginal sensations as well, but it could not be easy to distinguish these from sensations in the anus or vestibulum; in any case they cannot play a great part. We are entitled to keep to our view that in the phallic phase of girls the clitoris is the leading erotogenic zone. But it is not, of course, going to remain so. With the change to femininity the clitoris should wholly or in part hand over its sensitivity, and at the same time its importance, to the vagina. This would be one of the two tasks which a woman has to perform in the course of her development, whereas the more fortunate man has only to continue at the time of his sexual maturity the activity that he has previously carried out at the period of the early efflorescence of his sexuality.

We shall return to the part played by the clitoris; let us now turn to the second task with which a girl's development is burdened. A boy's mother is the first object of his love, and she remains so too during the formation of his Oedipus complex and, in essence, all through his life. For a girl too her first object must be her mother (and the figures of wet nurses and foster mothers that merge into her). The first object-cathexes occur in attachment to the satisfaction of the major and simple vital needs, and the circumstances of the care of children are the same for both sexes. But in the Oedipus situation the girl's father has become her love object, and we expect that in the normal course of development she will find her way from this paternal object to her final choice of an object. In the course of time, therefore, a girl has to change her erotogenic zone and her object— both of which a boy retains. The question then arises of how this happens: in particular, how does a girl pass from her mother to an attachment to her father? or, in other words, how does she pass from her masculine phase to the feminine one to which she is biologically destined?

It would be a solution of ideal simplicity if we could suppose that from a particular age onwards the elementary influence of the mutual attraction between the sexes makes itself felt and impels the small woman towards men, while the same law allows the boy to continue with his mother. We might suppose in addition that in this the children are following the pointer given them by the sexual preference of their parents. But we are not going to find things so easy; we scarcely know whether we are to believe seriously in the power of which poets talk so much and with such enthusiasm but which cannot be further dissected analytically. We have found an answer of quite another sort by means of laborious investigations, the material for which at least was easy to arrive at. For you must know that the number of women who remain till a late age tenderly dependent on a paternal object, or indeed on their real father, is very great. We have established some surprising facts about these women with an intense attachment of long duration to their father. We knew, of course, that there had been a preliminary stage of attachment to the mother, but we did not know that it could be so rich in content and so long lasting, and could leave behind so many opportunities for fixations and dispositions. During this time the girl's father is only a troublesome rival; in some cases the attachment to her mother lasts beyond the fourth year of life. Almost everything that we find later in her relation to her father was already present in this earlier attachment and has been transferred subsequently on to her father. In short, we get an impression that we cannot understand women unless we appreciate this phase of their pre-Oedipus attachment to their mother.

We shall be glad, then, to know the nature of the girl's libidinal relations to her mother. The answer is that they are of very many different kinds. Since they persist through all three phases of infantile sexuality, they also take on the characteristics of the different phases and express themselves by oral, sadistic anal and phallic wishes. These wishes represent active as well as passive impulses; if we relate them to the differentiation of the sexes which is to appear later—though we should avoid doing so as far as possible—we may call them masculine and feminine. Besides this, they are completely ambivalent, both affectionate and of a hostile and aggressive nature. The latter often only come to light after being changed into anxiety ideas. It is not always easy to point to a formulation of these early sexual wishes; what is most clearly expressed is a wish to get the mother with child and the corresponding wish to bear her a child—both belonging to the phallic period and sufficiently surprising, but established beyond doubt by analytic observation. The attractiveness of these investigations lies in the surprising detailed findings which they bring us. Thus, for instance, we discover the fear of being murdered or poisoned, which may later form the core of a paranoic illness, already present in this pre-Oedipus period, in relation to the mother. Or another case: you will recall an interesting episode in the history of analytic research which caused me many distressing hours. In the period in which the main interest was directed to discovering infantile sexual traumas, almost all my women patients told me that they had been seduced by their father. I was driven to recognize in the end that these reports were untrue and so came to understand that hysterical symptoms are derived from fantasies and not from real occurrences. It was only later that I was able to recognize in this fantasy of being seduced by the father the expression of the typical Oedipus complex in women. And now we find the fantasy of seduction once more in the pre-Oedipus prehistory of girls; but the seducer is regularly the mother. Here, however, the fantasy touches the ground of reality, for it was really the mother who by her activities over the child's bodily hygiene inevitably stimulated, and perhaps even roused for the first time, pleasurable sensations in her genitals.[1]

I have no doubt you are ready to suspect that this portrayal of the abundance and strength of a little girl's sexual relations with her mother is very much overdrawn. After all, one has opportunities of seeing little girls and notices nothing of the sort. But the objection is not to the point. Enough can be seen in the children if one knows how to look. And besides, you should consider how little of its sexual wishes a child can bring to pre-conscious expression or communicate at all. Accordingly we are only within our rights if we study the residues and consequences of this emotional world in retrospect, in people in whom these processes of development had attained a specially clear and even excessive degree of expansion. Pathology has always done us the service of making discernible by isolation and exaggeration conditions which would remain concealed in a normal state. And

---

[1] [In his early discussions of the aetiology of hysteria Freud often mentioned seduction by adults as among its commonest causes (see, for instance, the second paper on the neuropsychoses of defense (1896b), Standard Ed., 3, 164, and "The Aetiology of Hysteria" (1896c), ibid., 208). But nowhere in these early publications did he specifically inculpate the girl's father. Indeed, in some additional footnotes written in 1924 for the Gesammelte Schriften reprint of Studies on Hysteria, he admitted to having on two occasions suppressed the fact of the father's responsibility (see Standard Ed., 2, 134 n, and 170 n.). He made this quite clear, however, in the letter to Fliess of September 21, 1897 (Freud, 1950a, Letter 69), in which he first expressed his skepticism about these stories told by his patients. His first published admission of his mistake was given several years later in a hint in the second of the Three Essays (1905d), Standard Ed., 7, 190, but a much fuller account of the position followed in his contribution on the aetiology of the neuroses to a volume by Löwenfeld (1906a), ibid., 7, 274–5. Later on he gave two accounts of the effects that this discovery of his mistake had on his own mind—in his "History of the Psycho-Analytic Movement" (1914d), ibid., 14, 17–18 and in his Autobiographical Study (1925d), ibid., 20, 33–5. The further discovery which is described in the present paragraph of the text had already been indicated in the paper on "Female Sexuality" (1931b), ibid., 21, 238.]

since our investigations have been carried out on people who were by no means seriously abnormal, I think we should regard their outcome as deserving belief.

We will now turn our interest on to the single question of what it is that brings this powerful attachment of the girl to her mother to an end. This, as we know, is its usual fate: it is destined to make room for an attachment to her father. Here we come upon a fact which is a pointer to our further advance. This step in development does not involve only a simple change of object. The turning away from the mother is accompanied by hostility; the attachment to the mother ends in hate. A hate of that kind may become very striking and last all through life; it may be carefully overcompensated later on; as a rule one part of it is overcome while another part persists. Events of later years naturally influence this greatly. We will restrict ourselves, however, to studying it at the time at which the girl turns to her father and to enquiring into the motives for it. We are then given a long list of accusations and grievances against the mother which are supposed to justify the child's hostile feelings; they are of varying validity which we shall not fail to examine. A number of them are obvious rationalizations and the true sources of enmity remain to be found. I hope you will be interested if on this occasion I take you through all the details of a psycho-analytic investigation.

The reproach against the mother which goes back furthest is that she gave the child too little milk—which is construed against her as lack of love. Now there is some justification for this reproach in our families. Mothers often have insufficient nourishment to give their children and are content to suckle them for a few months, for half or three-quarters of a year. Among primitive peoples children are fed at their mother's breast for two or three years. The figure of the wet nurse who suckles the child is as a rule merged into the mother; when this has not happened, the reproach is turned into another one—that the nurse, who fed the child so willingly, was sent away by the mother too early. But whatever the true state of affairs may have been, it is impossible that the child's reproach can be justified as often as it is met with. It seems, rather, that the child's avidity for its earliest nourishment is altogether insatiable, that it never gets over the pain of losing its mother's breast. I should not be surprised if the analysis of a primitive child, who could still suck at its mother's breast when it was already able to run about and talk, were to bring the same reproach to light. The fear of being poisoned is also probably connected with the withdrawal of the breast. Poison is nourishment that makes one ill. Perhaps children trace back their early illnesses too to this frustration. A fair amount of intellectual education is a prerequisite for believing in chance; primitive people and uneducated ones, and no doubt children as well, are able to assign a ground for everything that happens. Perhaps originally it was a reason on animistic lines. Even today in some strata of our population no one can die without having been killed by someone else—preferably by the doctor. And the regular reaction of a neurotic to the death of someone closely connected with him is to put the blame on himself for having caused the death.

The next accusation against the child's mother flares up when the next baby appears in the nursery. If possible the connection with oral frustration is preserved: the mother could not or would not give the child any more milk because she needed the nourishment for the new arrival. In cases in which the two children are so close in age that lactation is prejudiced by the second pregnancy, this reproach acquires a real basis, and it is a remarkable fact that a child, even with an age difference of only 11 months, is not too young to take notice of what is happening. But what the child grudges the unwanted intruder and rival is not only the suckling but all the other signs of maternal care. It feels that it has been dethroned, despoiled, prejudiced in its rights; it casts a jealous hatred upon the new baby and develops a grievance against the faithless mother which often finds expression in a disagreeable change in its behavior. It becomes "naughty," perhaps, irritable and disobedient and goes back on the advances it has made towards controlling its excretions. All of this has been very long familiar and is accepted as self-evident; but we rarely form a correct idea of the strength of these jealous impulses, of the tenacity with which they persist and of the magnitude of their influence on later development. Especially as this jealousy is constantly receiving fresh nourishment in the later years of childhood and the whole shock is repeated with the birth of each new brother or sister. Nor does it make much difference if the child happens to remain the mother's preferred favorite. A child's demands for love are immoderate, they make exclusive claims and tolerate no sharing.

An abundant source of a child's hostility to its mother is provided by its multifarious sexual wishes, which alter according to the phase of the libido and which cannot for the most part be satisfied. The strongest of these frustrations occur at the phallic period, if the mother forbids pleasurable activity with the genitals—often with severe threats and every sign of displeasure—activity to which, after all, she herself had introduced the child. One would think these were reasons enough to account for a girl's turning away from her mother. One would judge, if so, that the estrangement follows inevitably from the nature of children's sexuality, from the immoderate character of their demand for love and the impossibility of fulfilling their sexual wishes. It might be thought indeed that this first love-relation of the child's is doomed to dissolution for the very reason that it is the first, for these early object-cathexes are regularly ambivalent to a high degree. A powerful tendency to aggressiveness is always present beside a powerful love, and the more passionately a child loves its object, the more sensitive does it become to disappointments and frustrations from that object; and in the end the love must succumb to the accumulated hostility. Or the idea that there is an original ambivalence such as this in erotic cathexes may be rejected, and it may be pointed out that it is the special nature of the mother-child relation that leads, with equal inevitability, to the destruction of the child's love; for even the mildest upbringing cannot avoid using compulsion and introducing restrictions, and any such intervention in the child's liberty must provoke as a reaction an inclination to rebelliousness and aggressiveness. A discussion of these possibilities might, I think, be most interesting; but an objection suddenly emerges which forces our interest in another direction. All these factors—the slights, the disappointments in love, the jealousy, the seduction followed by prohibition—are, after all, also in operation in the relation of a *boy* to his mother and are yet unable to alienate him from the maternal object. Unless we can find something that is specific for girls and is not present or not in the same way present in boys, we shall not have explained the termination of the attachment of girls to their mother.

I believe we have found this specific factor, and indeed where we expected to find it, even though in a surprising form. Where we expected to find it, I say, for it lies in the castration complex. After all, the anatomical distinction [between the sexes] must express itself in psychical consequences. It was, however, a surprise to learn from analyses that girls hold their mother responsible for their lack of a penis and do not forgive her for their being thus put at a disadvantage.

As you hear, then, we ascribe a castration complex to women as well. And for good reasons, though its content cannot be the same as with boys. In the latter the castration complex arises after they have learnt from the sight of the female genitals that the organ which they value so highly need not necessarily accompany the body. At this the boy recalls to mind the threats he brought on himself by his doings with that organ, he begins to give credence to them and falls under the influence of fear of castration, which will be the most powerful motive force in his subsequent development. The castration complex of girls is also started by the sight of the genitals of the other sex. They at once notice the difference and, it must be admitted, its significance too. They feel seriously wronged, often declare that they want to "have something like it too," and fall a victim to "envy for the penis," which will leave ineradicable traces on their development and the formation of their character and which will not be surmounted in even the most favorable cases without a severe expenditure of psychical energy. The girl's recognition of the fact of her being without a penis does not by any means imply that she submits to the fact easily. On the contrary, she continues to hold on for a long time to the wish to get something like it herself and she believes in that possibility for improbably long years; and analysis can show that, at a period when knowledge of reality has long since rejected the fulfillment of the wish as unattainable, it persists in the unconscious and retains a considerable cathexis of energy. The wish to get the longed-for penis eventually in spite of everything may contribute to the motives that drive a mature woman to analysis, and what she may reasonably expect from analysis—a capacity, for instance, to carry on an intellectual profession—may often be recognized as a sublimated modification of this repressed wish.

One cannot very well doubt the importance of envy for the penis. You may take it as an instance of male injustice if I assert that envy and jealousy play an even greater part in the mental life of women than of men. It is not that I think these characteristics are absent in men or that I think they have no other roots in women than envy for the penis; but I am inclined to attribute their greater amount in women to this latter influence. Some analysts, however, have shown an inclination to depreciate the importance of this first installment of penis envy in the phallic phase. They are of opinion that what we find of this attitude in women is in the main a secondary structure

which has come about on the occasion of later conflicts by regression
to this early infantile impulse. This, however, is a general problem of
depth psychology. In many pathological—or even unusual—instinctual attitudes (for instance, in all sexual perversions) the question
arises of how much of their strength is to be attributed to early infantile fixations and how much to the influence of later experiences
and developments. In such cases it is almost always a matter of com-
plemental series such as we put forward in our discussion of the aetiology of the neuroses. Both factors play a part in varying amounts
in the causation; a less on the one side is balanced by a more on the
other. The infantile factor sets the pattern in all cases but does not
always determine the issue, though it often does. Precisely in the case
of penis envy I should argue decidedly in favor of the preponderance
of the infantile factor.

The discovery that she is castrated is a turning point in a girl's
growth. Three possible lines of development start from it: one leads
to sexual inhibition or to neurosis, the second to change of character
in the sense of a masculinity complex, the third, finally, to normal
femininity. We have learnt a fair amount, though not everything,
about all three.

The essential content of the first is as follows: the little girl has
hitherto lived in a masculine way, has been able to get pleasure by
the excitation of her clitoris and has brought this activity into relation
with her sexual wishes directed towards her mother, which are often
active ones; now, owing to the influence of her penis-envy, she loses
her enjoyment in her phallic sexuality. Her self-love is mortified by
the comparison with the boy's far superior equipment and in consequence she renounces her masturbatory satisfaction from her clitoris,
repudiates her love for her mother and at the same time not infrequently represses a good part of her sexual trends in general. No
doubt her turning away from her mother does not occur all at once,
for to begin with the girl regards her castration as an individual misfortune, and only gradually extends it to other females and finally to
her mother as well. Her love was directed to her *phallic* mother; with
the discovery that her mother is castrated it becomes possible to drop
her as an object, so that the motives for hostility, which have long
been accumulating, gain the upper hand. This means, therefore, that
as a result of the discovery of women's lack of a penis they are debased
in value for girls just as they are for boys and later perhaps for men.

You all know the immense aetiological importance attributed by our neurotic patients to their masturbation. They make it responsible for all their troubles and we have the greatest difficulty in persuading them that they are mistaken. In fact, however, we ought to admit to them that they are right, for masturbation is the executive agent of infantile sexuality, from the faulty development of which they are indeed suffering. But what neurotics mostly blame is the masturbation of the period of puberty; they have mostly forgotten that of early infancy, which is what is really in question. I wish I might have an opportunity some time of explaining to you at length how important all the factual details of early masturbation become for the individual's subsequent neurosis or character: whether or not it was discovered, how the parents struggled against it or permitted it, or whether he succeeded in suppressing it himself. All of this leaves permanent traces on his development. But I am on the whole glad that I need not do this. It would be a hard and tedious task and at the end of it you would put me in an embarrassing situation by quite certainly asking me to give you some practical advice as to how a parent or educator should deal with the masturbation of small children.[1] From the development of girls, which is what my present lecture is concerned with, I can give you the example of a child herself trying to get free from masturbating. She does not always succeed in this. If envy for the penis has provoked a powerful impulse against clitoridal masturbation but this nevertheless refuses to give way, a violent struggle for liberation ensues in which the girl, as it were, herself takes over the role of her deposed mother and gives expression to her entire dissatisfaction with her inferior clitoris in her efforts against obtaining satisfaction from it. Many years later, when her masturbatory activity has long since been suppressed, an interest still persists which we must interpret as a defense against a temptation that is still dreaded. It manifests inself in the emergence of sympathy for those to whom similar difficulties are attributed, it plays a part as a motive in contracting a marriage and, indeed, it may determine the choice of a husband or lover. Disposing of early infantile masturbation is truly no easy or indifferent business.

---

[1] [Freud's fullest discussion of masturbation was in his contribution to a symposium on the subject in the Vienna Psycho-Analytical Society (1912f), *Standard Ed.*, **12**, 241 ff., where a number of other references are given.]

Along with the abandonment of clitoridal masturbation a certain amount of activity is renounced. Passivity now has the upper hand, and the girl's turning to her father is accomplished principally with the help of passive instinctual impulses. You can see that a wave of development like this, which clears the phallic activity out of the way, smooths the ground for femininity. If too much is not lost in the course of it through repression, this femininity may turn out to be normal. The wish with which the girl turns to her father is no doubt originally the wish for the penis which her mother has refused her and which she now expects from her father. The feminine situation is only established, however, if the wish for a penis is replaced by one for a baby, if, that is, a baby takes the place of a penis in accordance with an ancient symbolic equivalence. It has not escaped us that the girl has wished for a baby earlier, in the undisturbed phallic phase: that, of course, was the meaning of her playing with dolls. But that play was not in fact an expression of her femininity; it served as an identification with her mother with the intention of substituting activity for passivity. *She* was playing the part of her mother and the doll was herself: now she could do with the baby everything that her mother used to do with her. Not until the emergence of the wish for a penis does the doll-baby become a baby from the girl's father, and thereafter the aim of the most powerful feminine wish. Her happiness is great if later on this wish for a baby finds fulfillment in reality, and quite especially so if the baby is a little boy who brings the longed-for penis with him. Often enough in her combined picture of "a baby from her father" the emphasis is laid on the baby and her father left unstressed. In this way the uncient masculine wish for the possession of a penis is still faintly visible through the femininity now achieved. But perhaps we ought rather to recognize this wish for a penis as being *par excellence* a feminine one.

With the transference of the wish for a penis-baby on to her father, the girl has entered the situation of the Oedipus complex. Her hostility to her mother, which did not need to be freshly created, is now greatly intensified, for she becomes the girl's rival, who receives from her father everything that she desires from him. For a long time the girl's Oedipus complex concealed her pre-Oedipus attachment to her mother from our view, though it is nevertheless so important and leaves such lasting fixations behind it. For girls the Oedipus situation is the outcome of a long and difficult development; it is a kind of preliminary solution, a position of rest which is not soon abandoned, especially as the beginning of the latency period is not far distant. And we are now struck by a difference between the two sexes, which is probably momentous, in regard to the relation of the Oedipus complex to the castration complex. In a boy the Oedipus complex, in which he desires his mother and would like to get rid of his father as being a rival, develops naturally from the phase of his phallic sexuality. The threat of castration compels him, however, to give up that attitude. Under the impression of the danger of losing his penis, the Oedipus complex is abandoned, repressed and, in the most normal cases, entirely destroyed, and a severe super-ego is set up as its heir. What happens with a girl is almost the opposite. The castration complex prepares for the Oedipus complex instead of destroying it; the girl is driven out of her attachment to her mother through the influence of her envy for the penis and she enters the Oedipus situation as though into a haven of refuge. In the absence of fear of castration the chief motive is lacking which leads boys to surmount the Oedipus complex. Girls remain in it for an indeterminate length of time; they demolish it late and, even so, incompletely. In these circumstances the formation of the super-ego must suffer; it cannot attain the strength and independence which give it its cultural significance, and feminists are not pleased when we point out to them the effects of this factor upon the average feminine character.

To go back a little. We mentioned as the second possible reaction to the discovery of female castration the development of a powerful masculinity complex. By this we mean that the girl refuses, as it were, to recognize the unwelcome fact and, defiantly rebellious, even exaggerates her previous masculinity, clings to her clitoridal activity and takes refuge in an identification with her phallic mother or her father. What can it be that decides in favor of this outcome? We can only suppose that it is a constitutional factor, a greater amount of activity, such as is ordinarily characteristic of a male. However that may be, the essence of this process is that at this point in development the wave of passivity is avoided which opens the way to the turn towards femininity. The extreme achievement of such a masculinity complex would appear to be the influencing of the choice of an object in the sense of manifest homosexuality. Analytic experience teaches us, to be sure, that female homosexuality is seldom or never a direct continuation of infantile masculinity. Even for a girl of this kind it seems

necessary that she should take her father as an object for some time
and enter the Oedipus situation. But afterwards, as a result of her
inevitable disappointments from her father, she is driven to regress
into her early masculinity complex. The significance of these disappointments must not be exaggerated; a girl who is destined to become
feminine is not spared them, though they do not have the same effect.
The predominance of the constitutional factor seems indisputable;
but the two phases in the development of female homosexuality are
well mirrored in the practices of homosexuals, who play the parts of
mother and baby with each other as often and as clearly as those of
husband and wife.

What I have been telling you here may be described as the prehistory
of women. It is a product of the very last few years and may have
been of interest to you as an example of detailed analytic work. Since
its subject is woman, I will venture on this occasion to mention by
name a few of the women who have made valuable contributions to
this investigation. Dr. Ruth Mack Brunswick [1928] was the first to
describe a case of neurosis which went back to a fixation in the pre-
Oedipus stage and had never reached the Oedipus situation at all.
The case took the form of jealous paranoia and proved accessible to
therapy. Dr. Jeanne Lampl-de Groot [1927] has established the incredible phallic activity of girls towards their mother by some assured
observations, and Dr. Helene Deutsch [1932] has shown that the
erotic actions of homosexual women reproduce the relations between
mother and baby.

It is not my intention to pursue the further behavior of femininity
through puberty to the period of maturity. Our knowledge, moreover, would be insufficient for the purpose. But I will bring a few
features together in what follows. Taking its prehistory as a starting
point, I will only emphasize here that the development of femininity
remains exposed to disturbance by the residual phenomena of the
early masculine period. Regressions to the fixations of the pre-
Oedipus phases very frequently occur; in the course of some women's
lives there is a repeated alternation between periods in which masculinity or femininity gains the upper hand. Some portion of what
we men call "the enigma of women" may perhaps be derived from
this expression of bisexuality in women's lives. But another question
seems to have become ripe for judgment in the course of these re-

searches. We have called the motive force of sexual life "the libido." Sexual life is dominated by the polarity of masculine–feminine; thus the notion suggests itself of considering the relation of the libido to this antithesis. It would not be surprising if it were to turn out that each sexuality had its own special libido appropriated to it, so that one sort of libido would pursue the aims of a masculine sexual life and another sort those of a feminine one. But nothing of the kind is true. There is only one libido, which serves both the masculine and the feminine sexual functions. To it itself we cannot assign any sex; if, following the conventional equation of activity and masculinity, we are inclined to describe it as masculine, we must not forget that it also covers trends with a passive aim. Nevertheless the juxtaposition "feminine libido" is without any justification. Furthermore, it is our impression that more constraint has been applied to the libido when it is pressed into the service of the feminine function, and that—to speak teleologically—Nature takes less careful account of its [that function's] demands than in the case of masculinity. And the reason for this may lie—thinking once again teleologically—in the fact that the accomplishment of the aim of biology has been entrusted to the aggressiveness of men and has been made to some extent independent of women's consent.

The sexual frigidity of women, the frequency of which appears to confirm this disregard, is a phenomenon that is still insufficiently understood. Sometimes it is psychogenic and in that case accessible to influence; but in other cases it suggests the hypothesis of its being constitutionally determined and even of there being a contributory anatomical factor.

I have promised to tell you of a few more psychical peculiarities of mature femininity, as we come across them in analytic observation. We do not lay claim to more than an average validity for these assertions; nor is it always easy to distinguish what should be ascribed to the influence of the sexual function and what to social breeding. Thus, we attribute a larger amount of narcissism to femininity, which also affects women's choice of object, so that to be loved is a stronger need for them than to love. The effect of penis-envy has a share, further, in the physical vanity of women, since they are bound to value their charms more highly as a late compensation for their original sexual inferiority. Shame, which is considered to be a feminine characteristic *par excellence* but is far more a matter of convention than might be supposed, has as its purpose, we believe, concealment of genital deficiency. We are not forgetting that at a later time shame takes on other functions. It seems that women have made few contributions to the discoveries and inventions in the history of civilization; there is, however, one technique which they may have invented—that of plaiting and weaving. If that is so, we should be tempted to guess the unconscious motive for the achievement. Nature herself would seem to have given the model which this achievement imitates by causing the growth at maturity of the pubic hair that conceals the genitals. The step that remained to be taken lay in making the threads adhere to one another, while on the body they stick into the skin and are only matted together. If you reject this idea as fantastic and regard my belief in the influence of lack of a penis on the configuration of femininity as an *idée fixe*, I am of course defenseless.

The determinants of women's choice of an object are often made unrecognizable by social conditions. Where the choice is able to show itself freely, it is often made in accordance with the narcissistic ideal of the man whom the girl had wished to become. If the girl has remained in her attachment to her father—that is, in the Oedipus complex—her choice is made according to the paternal type. Since, when she turned from her mother to her father, the hostility of her ambivalent relation remained with her mother, a choice of this kind should guarantee a happy marriage. But very often the outcome is of a kind that presents a general threat to such a settlement of the conflict due to ambivalence. The hostility that has been left behind follows in the train of the positive attachment and spreads over on to the new object. The woman's husband, who to begin with inherited from her father, becomes after a time her mother's heir as well. So it may easily happen that the second half of a woman's life may be filled by the struggle against her husband, just as the shorter first half was filled by her rebellion against her mother. When this reaction has been lived through, a second marriage may easily turn out very much more satisfying.[1] Another alteration in a woman's nature, for which lovers are unprepared, may occur in a marriage after the first child is born. Under the influence of a woman's becoming a mother

---

[1] [This had already been remarked upon earlier, in "The Taboo of Virginity" (1918a), *Standard Ed.*, **11**, 206.]

herself, an identification with her own mother may be revived, against which she had striven up till the time of her marriage, and this may attract all the available libido to itself, so that the compulsion to repeat reproduces an unhappy marriage between her parents. The difference in a mother's reaction to the birth of a son or a daughter shows that the old factor of lack of a penis has even now not lost its strength. A mother is only brought unlimited satisfaction by her relation to a son; this is altogether the most perfect, the most free from ambivalence of all human relationships.[1] A mother can transfer to her son the ambition which she has been obliged to suppress in herself, and she can expect from him the satisfaction of all that has been left over in her of her masculinity complex. Even a marriage is not made secure until the wife has succeeded in making her husband her child as well and in acting as a mother to him.

A woman's identification with her mother allows us to distinguish two strata: the pre-Oedipus one which rests on her affectionate attachment to her mother and takes her as a model, and the later one from the Oedipus complex which seeks to get rid of her mother and take her place with her father. We are no doubt justified in saying that much of both of them is left over for the future and that neither of them is adequately surmounted in the course of development. But the phase of the affectionate pre-Oedipus attachment is the decisive one for a woman's future: during it preparations are made for the acquisition of the characteristics with which she will later fulfill her role in the sexual function and perform her invaluable social tasks. It is in this identification too that she acquires her attractiveness to a man, whose Oedipus attachment to his mother it kindles into passion. How often it happens, however, that it is only his son who obtains what he himself aspired to! One gets an impression that a man's love and a woman's are a phase apart psychologically.

The fact that women must be regarded as having little sense of justice is no doubt related to the predominance of envy in their mental life; for the demand for justice is a modification of envy and lays down the condition subject to which one can put envy aside. We also regard women as weaker in their social interests and as having less

[1] [This point seems to have been made by Freud first in the *Introductory Lectures*, XIII, *Standard Ed.*, **15**, 206. He repeated it in a footnote to Chapter VI of *Group Psychology* (1921c), *Standard Ed.*, **18**, 101 n., and in *Civilization and its Discontents* (1930a), ibid., **21**, 113. That exceptions may occur is shown by the example above, p. 66.]

capacity for sublimating their instincts than men. The former is no doubt derived from the dissocial quality which unquestionably characterizes all sexual relations. Lovers find sufficiency in each other, and families too resist inclusion in more comprehensive associations. The aptitude for sublimation is subject to the greatest individual variations. On the other hand I cannot help mentioning an impression that we are constantly receiving during analytic practice. A man of about thirty strikes us as a youthful, somewhat unformed individual, whom we expect to make powerful use of the possibilities for development opened up to him by analysis. A woman of the same age, however, oftens frightens us by her psychical rigidity and unchangeability. Her libido has taken up final positions and seems incapable of exchanging them for others. There are no paths open to further development; it is as though the whole process had already run its course and remains thenceforward insusceptible to influence—as though, indeed, the difficult development to femininity had exhausted the possibilities of the person concerned. As therapists we lament this state of things, even if we succeed in putting an end to our patient's ailment by doing away with her neurotic conflict.

That is all I had to say to you about femininity. It is certainly incomplete and fragmentary and does not always sound friendly. But do not forget that I have only been describing women in so far as their nature is determined by their sexual function. It is true that that influence extends very far; but we do not overlook the fact that an individual woman may be a human being in other respects as well. If you want to know more about femininity, enquire from your own experiences of life, or turn to the poets, or wait until science can give you deeper and more coherent information.

Ⓟ PLUME

MERIDIAN

ESSAY COLLECTIONS

☐ **CONCEIVED WITH MALICE** *Literature as Revenge in the Lives and Works of Virginia and Leonard Woolf, D.H. Lawrence, Djuna Barnes, and Henry Miller.* **by Louise De Salvo.** Full of enticing literary gossip, the author vividly describes how these great literary figures each perceived an attack on the self—and struck back through their art, creating lasting monuments to their deepest hurts and darkest obsessions. "Delicious, intelligent, irresistible, one of the darker pleasures."—Carole Maso, author of *The American Woman in the Chinese Hat* (273234—$13.95)

☐ **WRITING THE SOUTHWEST by David King Dunaway.** The common thread that links such writers as Edward Abbey, Tony Hillerman, Joy Harjo, Barbara Kingsolver, and Terry McMillan is an understanding of the interplay between humans and the earth. This compelling collection offers outstanding selections of contemporary southwestern literature along with a biographical profile, a bibliography, and an original interview with each of the 14 authors included. (273943—$12.95)

☐ **DESIRE AND IMAGINATION** *Classic Essays in Sexuality.* **Edited by Regina Barreca, Ph.D.** While the 19th century has come to be thought of as an age of prudery and restraint, there was at that time a veritable explosion of research, study, and writing done on provocative subjects like female desire, erotic stimuli, homosexuality, and masturbation. These twenty rarely seen essays from writers like Martineau, Krafft-Ebing, Darwin Ellis, Sanger, and Freud illuminate the way in which we choose even today to define what is "normal" behavior and what is regarded with suspicion. (011507—$13.95)

☐ **MASSACRE OF THE DREAMERS** *Essays on Xicanisma.* **by Ana Castillo.** In this provocative collection of essays, award-winning poet, novelist, scholar, and activist/curandera Ana Castillo becomes a voice for Mexic Amerindian women silenced for hundreds of years by the dual censorship of being female and brown-skinned. She explores all aspects of their collective identity and aims to inform, raise consciousness, and incite Chicanas—and all caring people—to change mainstream society from one of exclusion to inclusion. "Castillo goes after our hearts and minds, not territory or power."—*Village Voice* (274249—$11.95)

Prices slightly higher in Canada.

Visa and Mastercard holders can order Plume, Meridian, and Dutton books by calling
1-800-253-6476.
They are also available at your local bookstore. Allow 4-6 weeks for delivery.
This offer is subject to change without notice.

℗ **PLUME**   ⓜ **MERIDIAN**   (0452)

UNIQUE COLLECTIONS

☐ **NEW AMERICAN SHORT STORIES** *The Writers Select Their Own Favorites* **edited by Gloria Norris.** This unique anthology brings together twenty of today's most distinguished practitioners of the short story, including Alice Adams, T. Coraghessan Boyle, John Updike and many others—each of whom has selected a favorite from his or her recent work. It is a rich panorama of the best in contemporary fiction.   (258790—$9.95)

☐ **THE MERIDIAN ANTHOLOGY OF RESTORATION AND EIGHTEENTH-CENTURY PLAYS BY WOMEN. Edited by Katharine M. Rogers.** The women represented in this groundbreaking anthology—the only collection of Restoration and eighteenth-century plays devoted exclusively to women—had but one thing in common: the desire to ignore convention and write for the stage. These women legitimized the profession for their sex.
(011108—$14.95)

☐ **THE MERIDIAN ANTHOLOGY OF EARLY WOMEN WRITERS** *British Literary Women From Aphra Behn to Maria Edgeworth 1660–1800* **edited by Katharine M. Rogers and William McCarthy.** Here are nineteen stunning pre-nineteenth-century female literary talents never before collected in a single volume. Their stories bring to light the rich heritage of early literary creativity among women.   (008484—$14.95)

Prices slightly higher in Canada.

Visa and Mastercard holders can order Plume, Meridian, and Dutton books by calling
1-800-253-6476.
They are also available at your local bookstore. Allow 4-6 weeks for delivery.
This offer is subject to change without notice.

Ⓟ **PLUME**

LITERARY ESSENTIALS

☐ **THE ESSENTIAL DR. JEKYLL & MR. HYDE** *The Definitive Annotated Edition of Robert Louis Stevenson's Classic Novel.* **Leonard Wolf, Editor.** This is the complete text of Robert Louis Stevenson's classic tale, fully annotated with thousands of fascinating facts and legends . . . everything you wanted to know about literature's most famous split personality. Also included here are dozens of illustrations, a three-dimensional representation of the Jekyll house, and stunning new Jekyll & Hyde artwork. (269695—$14.95)

☐ **THE ESSENTIAL DRACULA edited by Leonard Wolf.** This complete, restored text of Bram Stoker's original novel is fully annotated with thousands of fascinating facts and legends about Dracula, Transylvania, and vampires . . . everything you ever wanted to know about literature's most infamous Count. (269431—$15.00)

☐ **THE ESSENTIAL FRANKENSTEIN** *The Definitive Annotated Edition of Mary Shelley's Classic Novel.* **Leonard Wolf, Editor.** The complete original text of Mary Shelley's classic 1816 novel, fully annotated with thousands of fascinating facts and legends . . . everything you ever wanted to know about literature's most famous Creature. (269687—$15.00)

☐ **THE ROQUELAURE READER** *A Companion to Anne Rice's Erotica.* **by Katherine Ramsland. Written in cooperation with Anne Rice.** In this book the author describes not only *The Sleeping Beauty* trilogy, the erotic novels Anne Rice wrote under the name A.N. Roquelaure, but two other erotic novels Anne Rice wrote as Anne Rampling. The author places this body of erotica within the context of Anne Rice's life, thought, and work, profiles key characters, and details the special features of each novel, provides wonderful trivia quizzes for Roquelaure readers, and includes two chapters cut from the novel *Exit to Eden.* (275105—$12.95)

Prices slightly higher in Canada.

Visa and Mastercard holders can order Plume, Meridian, and Dutton books by calling
1-800-253-6476.
They are available at your local bookstore. Allow 4-6 weeks for delivery.
This offer is subject to change without notice.

Ⓟ **PLUME**

THE FINEST IN SHORT FICTION

(0452)

☐ **HAUNTED** *Tales of the Grotesque.* **by Joyce Carol Oates.** This collection of sixteen tales-ranging from classic ghost stories to portrayals of chilling psychological terror—raises the genre to the level of fine literature. It is complex, multilayered, and gripping fiction that is very scary indeed. (273749—$10.95)

☐ **PLAYBOY STORIES** *The Best of Forty Years of Short Fiction.* **Edited by Alice K. Turner.** The very best short story from each of *Playboy's* forty years—with a special bonus from 1971, when tales by Nobel Prize winner Gabriel Garcia Marquez and Vladimir Nobokov demanded to be included—are gathered in this superlative anthology. The result is an enthralling array and rich variety of literary genius, by such names as Joyce Carol Oates. Nadine Gordimer, Isaac Bashevis Singer, James Jones and many more. (271177—$13.95)

☐ **RHYTHM AND REVOLT** *Tales of the Antilles.* **Edited by Marcela Breton.** The tropical world of the Antilles is an extraordinary diversity of race, language, and history. This rich and vibrant multiplicity comes brilliantly alive in the 25 short stories that make up this unique and essential anthology. Reaching all the way back to the 1920s, and featuring the most talented Caribbean authors at work today, this collection includes stories from Juan Bosch, Lydia Cabrera, Guillermo Cabrera Infante, René Depestre, Samuel Selvon, and Ana Lydia Vega, among many other superb writers. (271789—$12.95)

☐ **BODIES OF WATER by Michelle Cliff.** These short stories tell of oppression and liberation, prejudice and compassion, and are colored by the vivid imagery and emotive, spare language of this remarkable author. Many of the characters and incidents within these stories are linked, connecting images of water and travel, yet catalogs a separate incident from the layered geography and history of America. "Passions seethe below the surface . . . lean, controlled, full of meticulous images."—*San Diego Tribune* (273757—$9.95)

☐ **THE COLLECTED STORIES by Reynolds Price.** Marked by grace and intensity, and often filled with autobiographical detail, the author's exquisitely crafted stories impart a deep understanding of the joy, agony, and, above all, the goodness of life. "Eminently worth reading."—*San Francisco Chronicle* (272181—$12.95)

Prices slightly higher in Canada.

Visa and Mastercard holders can order Plume, Meridian, and Dutton books by calling
1-800-253-6476.
They are also available at your local bookstore. Allow 4-6 weeks for delivery.
This offer is subject to change without notice.